T0398056

"This handbook sheds long overdue light on the status quo of major heritage languages mostly outside the U.S. It succeeds in presenting an important case to language educators, namely that they belong to a community and the more opportunities for dialogue that are created, such as this book, the better heritage education will be. This book also fulfills an important task—to indirectly argue that program development and teaching of heritage languages is an international field of research and policy making. This book is insightful not only for language educators but also for administrators, government officials and community leaders in both the U.S. and beyond."

Gabriela Nik. Ilieva, New York University, USA

The Routledge Handbook of Heritage Language Education

The Routledge Handbook of Heritage Language Education provides the rapidly growing and globalizing field of heritage language (HL) education with a cohesive overview of HL programs and practices relating to language maintenance and development, setting the stage for future work in the field. Driving this effort is the belief that if research and pedagogical advances in the HL field are to have the greatest impact, HL programs need to become firmly rooted in educational systems. Against a background of cultural and linguistic diversity that characterizes the twenty-first century, the volume outlines key issues in the design and implementation of HL programs across a range of educational sectors, institutional settings, sociolinguistic conditions, and geographical locations, specifically: North and Latin America, Europe, Israel, Australia, New Zealand, Japan, and Cambodia. All levels of schooling are included as the teaching of the following languages are discussed: Albanian, Arabic, Armenian (Eastern and Western), Bengali, Brazilian Portuguese, Chinese, Czech, French, Hindi-Urdu, Japanese, Khmer, Korean, Pasifika languages, Persian, Russian, Spanish, Turkish, Vietnamese, and Yiddish. These discussions contribute to the development and establishment of HL instructional paradigms through the experiences of "actors on the ground" as they respond to local conditions, instantiate current research and pedagogical findings, and seek solutions that are workable from an organizational standpoint. *The Routledge Handbook of Heritage Language Education* is an ideal resource for researchers and graduate students interested in heritage language education at home or abroad.

Olga E. Kagan is Professor in the Department of Slavic, East European and Eurasian Languages and Cultures at the University of California, Los Angeles (UCLA), Director of the National Heritage Language Resource Center, and Co-editor of the *Heritage Language Journal*.

Maria M. Carreira is Professor of Spanish at California State University, Long Beach. She is also Co-director of the National Heritage Language Resource Center, Chair of the SAT Spanish Committee, and Associate Editor of *Hispania*.

Claire Hitchins Chik is Associate Director of the Title VI National Heritage Language Resource Center (NHLRC). She has also edited articles for the NHLRC's journal, the *Heritage Language Journal*, and guest-edited a volume: *Special Issue on Advancing HL Speakers' Skills*.

Routledge Handbooks in Linguistics

Routledge Handbooks in Linguistics provide overviews of a whole subject area or sub-discipline in linguistics and survey the state of the discipline including emerging and cutting-edge areas. Edited by leading scholars, these volumes include contributions from key academics from around the world and are essential reading for both advanced undergraduate and postgraduate students.

Further titles in this series can be found online at www.routledge.com/series/RHIL.

The Routledge Handbook of Heritage Language Education

From Innovation to Program Building

Edited by Olga E. Kagan, Maria M. Carreira, and Claire Hitchins Chik

Routledge
Taylor & Francis Group

NEW YORK AND LONDON

First published 2017
by Routledge
711 Third Avenue, New York, NY 10017

and by Routledge
2 Park Square, Milton Park, Abingdon, Oxon, OX14 4RN

Routledge is an imprint of the Taylor & Francis Group, an informa business

© 2017 Taylor & Francis

The right of Olga E. Kagan, Maria M. Carreira, and Claire Hitchins Chik to be identified as the authors of the editorial material, and of the authors for their individual chapters, has been asserted in accordance with sections 77 and 78 of the Copyright, Designs and Patents Act 1988.

Library of Congress Cataloging-in-Publication Data
Names: Kagan, Olga, editor. | Carreira, Maria, editor. | Chik, Claire Hitchins, 1960– editor.
Title: The Routledge handbook of heritage language education :
    from innovation to program building / edited by Olga E. Kagan,
    Maria M. Carreira, Claire Hitchins Chik.
Description: New York, NY ; Milton Park, Abingdon, Oxon :
    Routledge, [2017] | Series: Routledge Handbooks in Linguistics
Identifiers: LCCN 2016036569 | ISBN 9781138845787 (hardback) |
    ISBN 9781317541530 (web pdf) | ISBN 9781317541523 (epub) |
    ISBN 9781317541516 (mobipocket/kindle)
Subjects: LCSH: Native language—Study and teaching—Handbooks, manuals,
    etc. | Linguistic minorities—Education—Handbooks, manuals, etc. |
    Education, Bilingual—Handbooks, manuals, etc. | Language and culture—
    Handbooks, manuals, etc.
Classification: LCC P53.5 .R68 2017 | DDC 418.0071—dc23
LC record available at https://lccn.loc.gov/2016036569

ISBN: 978-1-138-84578-7 (hbk)
ISBN: 978-1-315-72797-4 (ebk)

Typeset in Bembo
by Apex CoVantage, LLC

Contents

Contents

Contents

Contributors

Jim Anderson is Senior Lecturer in Languages in Education in the Department of Educational Studies at Goldsmiths, University of London. His work focuses on theories and methods of second language learning and bilingualism, including Content and Language Integrated Learning (CLIL); multilingualism and new literacies; and language policy. He is Co-editor with Vicky Macleroy of *Multilingual Digital Storytelling: Engaging creatively and critically with literacy* (2016).

Mojgan Mokhatebi Ardakani has expertise in research and academic teaching in the Department of Educational Studies, Macquarie University, Australia. Her research interests include formal and informal heritage/community language education, sociocultural theory of language learning, and the role of motivation and identity in language learning.

Saeid Atoofi works as an Assistant Professor in the Department of Linguistics at the University of Chile. With wide educational and research training in psychology, applied linguistics, linguistic anthropology, and semiotics, he has two main research interests: (1) the study of Second Language Acquisition from a semiotic perspective and (2) the role of discourse strategies in learning.

Netta Avineri is TESOL/TFL Visiting Professor at the Middlebury Institute of International Studies (MIIS) at Monterey, California, where she teaches Linguistics, Education, Intercultural Competence, and International Education Management courses. She serves as the MIIS Intercultural Competence Committee Chair and co-founded the campus-wide Intercultural Digital Storytelling Project. Her research interests include language and social justice, interculturality, heritage language socialization, service-learning, and language-teacher education. She has a forthcoming book focused on research methods for language teaching, serves as Associate Editor for the *Heritage Language Journal*, and is a recipient of the Russ Campbell Young Scholars Award in Heritage Language Education.

Ava Becker-Zayas is a PhD candidate in the Department of Language and Literacy Education at the University of British Columbia. Her doctoral research examines the heritage language socialization of third-generation Chilean-Canadian children, with a focus on identity construction and the negotiation of social memory.

Shereen Bhalla is a Research Associate at the Center for Applied Linguistics where she works on research projects and serves as the moderator of the Language Policy Research Network (LPReN). Her research focuses on heritage and community language learning, language policy, and Indian English, among other areas of interest.

Dana Scott Bourgerie is Professor of Chinese and Chair of the Department of Asian and Near Eastern Languages at Brigham Young University, with research interests in Chinese dialect studies, sociolinguistics, and language acquisition. He was founding director of BYU's National Chinese Flagship Center (2002–2013) and has served a number of other professional roles, including president of the Chinese Language Teachers Association, *The Journal of the Chinese Language Teachers Association-US* board member, Fulbright Scholar at the Chinese University of Hong Kong, and visiting professor at Paññāsāstra University of Cambodia.

Jelena Brazauskienė is Associate Professor at Vilnius University, Lithuania. Her research interests include modern Russian language, applied linguistics, sociolinguistics, and lexicography, topics that she also lectures on at Vilnius University. She is an author of several papers on linguistics and has written textbooks and teacher reference books for teaching Russian as a foreign language.

Maria M. Carreira is Co-director of the National Heritage Language Resource Center at UCLA and Professor of Spanish at California State University, Long Beach, USA. Her research focuses on heritage language pedagogy and the education of Latino children. Her most recent book publication is *Voces: Latino Students on Life in the United States* (2014), co-authored with Thomas Beeman.

Claire Hitchins Chik is Associate Director of the Title VI National Heritage Language Resource Center (NHLRC). In this role she works to promote research on heritage language speakers and the development of pedagogical approaches that meet both the linguistic and affective needs of this population. She has also edited articles for the NHLRC's journal, the *Heritage Language Journal*, and guest-edited a volume, *Special Issue on Advancing HL Speakers' Skills* (2013, Vol. 10, 2).

Meral Dollnick was born in Turkey and studied German Linguistics and Literature and Education at the Freie Universität, Berlin, writing her doctoral dissertation on an empirical longitudinal study of Turkish and German written texts of primary-school children in Berlin. She has worked for many years as Academic Advisor on curricula and materials for bilingual and German second language teaching for the Berlin Ministry of Education. Concurrently, she has worked as a research assistant in several projects on Turkish/German bilingualism and is currently Vice President of the Berlin Institute for Multilingualism in the Immigrant Society.

Masako O. Douglas is a Professor of Japanese at California State University, Long Beach. Her research interests include Japanese Heritage Language (JHL) curriculum design and pedagogy. She is an editorial board member of the *Heritage Language Journal* and a board member of the Mother Tongue, Heritage Language, and Bilingual Education Association (Japan). She also serves as Chair of the JHL Special Interest Group of the American Association of Teachers of Japanese.

Patricia (Patsy) A. Duff is Professor of Language and Literacy Education at the University of British Columbia. Her research, publications, and teaching address second, foreign, and heritage language education and use internationally as well as in Canada; language socialization and development in multilingual contexts across the lifespan; and research methods in applied linguistics.

Guus Extra is Emeritus Professor of Language and Minorities at Tilburg University, the Netherlands. His research interests have focused on language use, maintenance, and loss of immigrant minority groups, and on multilingualism and education, both at the national and European levels.

A major publication, provided in a range of languages, is *Language Rich Europe: Trends in Policies and Practices for Multilingualism in Europe* (2012), co-edited with Kutlay Yagmur.

Robert J. Fouser is a Senior Lecturer of Korean Language and Literature at the Ohio State University. He founded the Korean Language Program at Kagoshima University in Japan and taught Korean language teacher development courses at Seoul National University. In 2012, he was awarded a citation from the Ministry of Culture, Sports, and Tourism in South Korea for his contribution to Korean language education. His research interests are Korean language education, language education policy in Japan and South Korea, and second language acquisition from sociolinguistic perspectives.

Juliana Gomes is a PhD candidate in the Department of Didactics and Educative Organization at the Universitat de Barcelona, Spain, specializing in Language Teaching. Her research interests include bilingualism, language acquisition, identity, bilingual literacy, teaching strategies, and curriculum and teacher training for heritage languages.

Annette Herkenrath, who completed her doctorate in general linguistics at Hamburg University and is currently affiliated with Justus Liebig University, Giessen, specializes in Turkish linguistics and multilingualism, combining discourse-analytical, sociolinguistic, and morphosyntactic approaches to monolingual and bilingual spoken Turkish. She has worked on child bilingualism (Hamburg), autobiographical narratives (Dortmund), and impersonal constructions (Uppsala); taught multilingualism and structural aspects of Turkish (Hamburg, Uppsala, Koblenz, Giessen); and published on topics such as *wh-* constructions, clause combining, discourse particles, receptive multilingualism, language contact, corpus-linguistic methods, and written Kurmanji.

Fabrice Jaumont holds a PhD in International Education from New York University. His research interests include comparative and international education, education development, educational diplomacy and philanthropy, heritage language and bilingual education, and community development. He is the author of *Unequal Partners: American Foundations and Higher Education Development in Africa* (2016). His upcoming book, *The Bilingual Revolution* (2017), features the development of dual-language programs in public schools in New York. He currently serves as Program Officer for the FACE Foundation in New York and as Education Attaché for the Embassy of France to the United States.

Olga E. Kagan is Undergraduate Advisor and Professor in the UCLA Department of Slavic, East European and Eurasian Languages and Cultures and is in charge of the department's language programs. She is Director of the UCLA Center for World Languages and the National Heritage Language Resource Center (a Title VI Center). She has published textbooks of Russian, both as a foreign and heritage language, and her main research interest is the teaching of heritage languages. In 2015 she received the MLA Award for Distinguished Service to the Profession.

Shushan Karapetian is a Postdoctoral Fellow in the department of Near Eastern Languages and Cultures at UCLA. Her dissertation, *"How Do I Teach My Kids My Broken Armenian?": A Study of Eastern Armenian Heritage Language Speakers in Los Angeles*, won the Society for Armenian Studies Distinguished Dissertation Award for 2011–2014. Her research interests focus on heritage languages and speakers, particularly on the case of Armenian heritage speakers in the Los Angeles community, about which she has presented and lectured widely. She is currently serving on multiple committees in the Los Angeles Armenian community aimed at reforming Armenian language instruction and promoting the use of the Armenian language.

Benoît Le Dévédec is an International Education Consultant specializing in the development of cultural and educational organizations. He holds an Agrégation d'anglais from the French Ministry of Education and a Master's in French linguistics from Université de Rennes 2. He worked as a secondary-school teacher in France and the United Kingdom, as Education Attaché in Belgium, and as Manager of the French Heritage Language Program in New York.

Alejandro Lee is Associate Professor of Spanish and Contemporary Spanish American Literature at Central Washington University, in Ellensburg, Washington. His areas of research and teaching interests include heritage language studies, the Chinese diaspora in Latin America, and Hispanic paremiology. He collaborates regularly with the National Heritage Language Resource Center at UCLA.

Duanduan Li is Associate Professor of Chinese Applied Linguistics in the Department of Asian Studies at the University of British Columbia. Her research interests concern the teaching and learning of Chinese as both a heritage and non-heritage language, the design of appropriate curriculum and materials for postsecondary Chinese instruction, and pragmatic language socialization in both English and Chinese.

Ala Lichačiova is a Professor at Vilnius University, Lithuania. Her research interests are language in social contexts, communicative culture, and Russian language in the mass media, all of which are also the focus of her teaching at the university. She is an editorial board member of the journal *Slavistica Vilnensis* (Vilnius University). She has published a textbook on Russian phonetics, a comparative study of Russian communicative culture, and papers on language and identity and attitudes toward the Russian language in Lithuania.

Yongcan Liu is a Lecturer at the Faculty of Education, University of Cambridge. His research interests lie in community/heritage language education, multilingualism in education, and Vygotsky's sociocultural theory of mind. He has recently been involved in a series of linked projects on the schooling experience of Eastern European migrant children with English as an additional language and is a co-investigator of an Arts and Humanities Research Council project on multilingualism. He currently serves as series editor of Routledge Chinese Language Pedagogy, overseeing its research monograph and teacher professional development series.

Sunil Loona is a psychologist and works as Senior Advisor at the National Centre for Multicultural Education in Norway. He is Editor of one of the Centre's two websites, morsmal.no. He is also a member of the Board of Directors at the Norwegian Centre against Racism, an independent foundation working to combat racism and discrimination in Norway.

Marta McCabe is a Research Scientist at Charles University, Prague, English as a Foreign Language Instructor at Durham Technical Community College, North Carolina, and President of the Czech and Slovak School of North Carolina. She studies transnational migration and heritage language education in Czech and Slovak communities, and has published in the *International Journal of the Sociology of Language* and contributed a chapter to *Immigration and Education in North Carolina: The Challenges and Responses in a New Gateway State* (in press).

Gabriela Meier is a Lecturer in Language Education at the Graduate School of Education, University of Exeter, UK. Besides her teaching, she supervises doctoral projects and has published research in the field of bilingual and multilingual approaches to education, for instance on two-way immersion education in Berlin and London, and she co-authored a book entitled *The Multilingual Turn in Languages Education: Opportunities and Challenges* (2014).

Robyn Moloney is a Senior Lecturer in the Department of Educational Studies, Macquarie University, Australia. She teaches undergraduate student teachers in the methodology areas of Languages and English as a Second Language, and supervises doctoral projects in language education and teacher development. Her research interests include heritage language learners, pedagogy, and intercultural teacher education.

Francisco Naranjo Escobar has a Bachelor's Degree in Linguistics Applied to Translation and worked for the Universidad de Santiago, Chile, upon graduation. He is currently a graduate student in the Master of Applied Linguistics program at the University of Melbourne, Australia, where his research interests include Program Evaluation, Teaching of Heritage Languages, and Curriculum Design. Francisco speaks Spanish, English, and Japanese, and also works with Portuguese as a research language.

Finex Ndhlovu is senior lecturer in Applied Linguistics at the University of New England, Australia. His research interests sit at the cutting edge of contemporary linguistic and sociocultural theories around language, identity, and sociality in relation to transnational African diaspora communities. His most recent major publications are *Becoming an African Diaspora in Australia: Language, Culture, Identity* (2014) and *Hegemony and Language Policies in Southern Africa: Identity, Integration, Development* (2015).

Helle Lykke Nielsen is Associate Professor at the University of Southern Denmark. Her research interests focus on Arabic as a foreign language, Arabic in the Scandinavian linguistic landscape, and Arab immigration to Denmark.

Shobna Nijhawan is Associate Professor of Hindi at the Department of Languages, Literatures and Linguistics, York University, Toronto. She is the author of *Women and Girls in the Hindi Public Sphere* (2012), Editor of *Nationalism in the Vernacular: Hindi, Urdu, and the Literature of Indian Freedom* (2010), and has published articles on pedagogies surrounding less commonly taught languages and cultures as well as technology-enhanced learning. Her most recent publications are on transnational feminist movements centered in South Asia (*Journal of Women's History*) and the emergence of the Hindi public sphere in colonial Lucknow.

Kaya Oriyama is Lecturer in the Japanese Programme, School of Languages and Cultures, Victoria University of Wellington, New Zealand. Her research interests are in applied linguistics and sociolinguistics, particularly bilingualism and multilingualism, biliteracy and multilingual literacy, identity, heritage language acquisition and maintenance, heritage language education, language policy, and second language acquisition of Japanese.

Carol W. Pfaff, PhD in Linguistics, UCLA 1973, has specialized in language development in multilingual settings. She taught in Linguistics Departments in California and Texas, and was Professor of Linguistics at the John F. Kennedy Institute for North American Studies at the Freie Universität,

Berlin (1977–2009). She has been Principal Investigator of research projects on Turkish/German bilingual children and adolescents in Berlin and has also investigated language policies in Germany. Starting in 2016/17, she will be Senior Professor at the Department of German and Linguistics, focusing on aspects of multilingualism, at the Humboldt Universität zu Berlin.

Meilutė Ramonienė is Professor and Head of the Department of Lithuanian Studies at Vilnius University, Lithuania. Her research interests include applied linguistics, sociolinguistics, and onomastics, which she also lectures on at Vilnius University. She is the author of several textbooks and teacher reference books for teaching Lithuanian as a second language. Her published output also includes papers on language use and language attitudes, language and identity, and bilingualism and multilingualism in Lithuania.

Alegría Ribadeneira is head of the Foreign Languages Program and Associate Professor of Spanish at Colorado State University–Pueblo, a Hispanic-serving institution. She actively researches and presents on issues of instruction, assessment, and program development that take into account the unique needs of heritage language learners in mixed classrooms. She is involved in heritage language teaching advocacy through the American Council of Foreign Language Teaching and the National Heritage Language Resource Center.

Jane F. Ross is President of the French Heritage Language Program, part of the FACE Foundation. A graduate of Swarthmore College, she has had an extensive career as an educator and educational consultant, and is currently pursuing a PhD in International Education at New York University. Her research focuses on the role of French schools in the United States.

Birgit Schumacher has worked as a teacher in Germany and France, above all in French-German bilingual and intercultural schools. She co-authored textbooks for German and French, published by Nathan and Cornelsen, as well as articles about Staatliche Europa-Schule Berlin (SESB). Currently, she acts as Coordinator of SESB primary streams and as Inspector for 14 schools in the European Schools system in seven countries.

Mila Schwartz is Professor of Language and Education and Head of the Language Program (MA) at Oranim Academic College of Education, and a Research Fellow at the Institute of Information Processing and Decision Making, University of Haifa. Her research interests include studying language policy and models of early bilingual education; language, cognitive, and sociocultural development of early sequential bilinguals; family language policy; and bilingual teachers' pedagogical development. She has managed many research projects, published over 50 empirical papers in peer-reviewed scientific journals, and edited two books.

Corinne A. Seals is a Lecturer of Applied Linguistics at Victoria University of Wellington in New Zealand, Academic Advisor to the Community Languages Association of New Zealand, and an editor of the *Journal of Home Language Research*. Her research interests include heritage language acquisition and maintenance, language policy, language and identity, and linguistic landscapes.

Ana Souza is a Senior Lecturer in TESOL and Applied Linguistics at Oxford Brookes University, England. Her research interests include bilingualism, language and identity, language choices, Brazilian migration, language planning (in families and migrant churches), complementary schools, the teaching of Portuguese as a heritage language, and the training of language teachers. Her work has been published in edited books, such as *Português como Língua de Herança* *em Londres: recortes em casa, na igreja e na escola* (2016), and academic journals, such as *Children &* *Society, Current Issues in Language Planning, International Journal of Multilingualism, Language Issues,* and *Women's Studies International Forum*.

Raymonde Sneddon was a teacher in East London specializing in working with bilingual pupils, their families, and their communities. As a teacher, a teacher educator, a researcher, and a community activist, she has been involved in the study, evaluation, and development of complementary schools in London. She also has a major research interest in the development of biliteracy in young children and is the author of *Bilingual Books—Biliterate Children* (2009) and Co-editor of *Children's Literature in Multilingual Classrooms—from Multiliteracy to Multimodality* (2015). She is currently a Visiting Research Fellow in the Cass School of Education at the University of East London.

Robert M. Uriu is an Associate Professor of Political Science at the University of California, Irvine, where he specializes in International Relations and the political economy of East Asia. During the last seven years he has also served as Chair of the Board of Trustees of Orange Coast Gakuen.

Anna Verschik is Professor of General Linguistics at Tallinn University, Estonia. Her scholarly interests include language contacts, Baltic and post-Soviet sociolinguistics, and Yiddish in the Baltic countries, including Yiddish as a heritage language and Lithuanian-Yiddish bilingualism. She has published on contact-induced language change (the current impact of Estonian on Russian), code-switching, and post-Yiddish ethnolects. She has edited special issues of journals on language contacts in the post-Soviet space and Estonian sociolinguistics and co-edited a volume on family language policy with Mila Schwartz.

Mats Wennerholm has been Project Leader at the Swedish National Agency for Education since 2001. His work focuses on national school improvement measures for the quality education of migrant children. He has also worked with national projects concerning mother tongue education and mother tongue guidance, education in Nordic languages, and language education for national minorities, especially Roma.

Terrence G. Wiley is President of the Center for Applied Linguistics in Washington, DC, Professor Emeritus at Arizona State University, and Special Graduate Professor at the University of Maryland, College Park. He specializes in educational language policy and heritage and community language education, among other areas of applied linguistics. He is Co-editor of the *Handbook on Heritage, Community, and Native American Language Education in the United States: Research, Policy and Practice* (2014) and was founding Co-editor of the *Journal of Language, Identity, and Education* and the *International Multilingual Research Journal*.

Louisa Willoughby is a Lecturer in Linguistics at Monash University, Australia. Her research focuses on the intersecting areas of language and identity, heritage language maintenance, and language policy in health and education. Much of her work has focused on migrant languages, but more recently she has explored how these issues apply to sign language users.

Wayne E. Wright is Professor and the Barbara I. Cook Chair of Literacy and Language in the College of Education at Purdue University. He is Co-editor of the *Journal of Language, Identity, and Education*, Editor of the *Journal of Southeast Asian American Education and Advancement*, Co-editor of the Bilingual Education and Bilingualism book series published by Multilingual Matters,

Co-editor of the *Handbook of Bilingual and Multilingual Education* (2015), and author of *Foundations of Teaching English Language Learners: Research, Theory, Policy, and Practice* (2nd ed., 2015).

André Zampaulo earned his PhD in Hispanic Linguistics from the Ohio State University and currently works at California State University, Fullerton, as an Assistant Professor of Spanish and Portuguese Linguistics. His main research interests include Spanish and Portuguese phonetics and phonology, dialectology, and historical Romance linguistics.

Illustrations

Figures

Tables

Introduction

Claire Hitchins Chik, Maria M. Carreira, and Olga E. Kagan

Large-scale immigration and unprecedented mobility in the twentieth and early twenty-first centuries are radically changing the global linguistic landscape. As a result, populations speaking languages other than dominant societal ones has become a widespread phenomenon in many regions of the world. Against this background of cultural and linguistic diversity, the chapters in this volume shed light on the teaching of non-dominant languages across a wide range of geographical sites: North and Latin America, Europe, Israel, Australia, New Zealand, Japan, and Cambodia. All levels of schooling are included as the following languages are discussed: Albanian, Arabic, Armenian (Eastern and Western), Bengali, Brazilian Portuguese, Chinese, Czech, French, Hindi-Urdu, Japanese, Khmer, Korean, Pasifika languages, Persian, Russian, Spanish, Turkish, Vietnamese, and Yiddish. Within the confines of a single volume, only a fraction of geographical areas and languages can be covered, and our hope is that future volumes and research will make up for those we have not been able to include.

Non-dominant societal languages go by a number of terms in the research literature, including heritage, community, or immigrant languages, or as mother tongues. In this volume, the term "heritage language" (HL) is most frequently used, and while the term is also commonly used in connection with indigenous languages, in this collection we focus solely on immigrant languages. Immigrant communities and their languages emanate from points of origin outside the host country, typically a country in which the HL is the national language, but also from diasporic communities resident in numerous countries, as is the case with Western Armenian and Yiddish. Indigenous languages, which trace a long history in the place where they are spoken today (Hinton, 2001), face different challenges that deserve a deeper and separate study, hence their exclusion from this volume.

The Place of This Volume in the Field of Heritage Language Research

The field of HL education is still relatively new. In terms of research, the last decade can aptly be characterized as one of vigorous innovation, as attested by a proliferation in publications, professional meetings, and professional development projects (Van Deusen-Scholl, 2014). Much of this work has had as its objective the presentation and dissemination of recent findings in both basic research and pedagogy. Innovation in the area of pedagogy has included the development of HL-specific methodologies, instructional materials, and assessment tools, along with advances in the area of teacher training. While the need for further exploration in these areas continues, there is also a need to direct our attention to the next phase of development in the field, namely the establishment, and eventual institutionalization, of HL instructional paradigms that respond to, and instantiate, current research and pedagogical findings and that are workable from an organizational standpoint. A central goal of this volume is therefore to document the state of institutionalization of HL education by taking stock of HL programs and practices relating to HL maintenance and development in numerous educational settings.

The task we set is not to present models that other programs could follow (although we hope some readers will find applicable designs), but rather to take a look at the diversity of approaches and outcomes and to highlight "profiles of struggling and exemplary programs to illuminate effective practices" (Beaudrie, 2012, p. 215). In addition, we hope that this volume will break new ground by building bridges between educators of all countries dealing with HL teaching. Driving this effort is the belief that in order for HL programs to become firmly rooted in an educational system, they need to become institutionalized.

Research indicates that maintenance of the HL is best achieved through linguistic exposure both in informal contexts, particularly the home environment, as well as formal educational contexts. Focusing on the latter context, the chapters in this volume speak to the need for teaching and curricular paradigms for this population of learners to become assimilated into educational initiatives. As growing numbers of HL learners (HLLs) seek to expand their exposure through formal instruction, language departments and teachers trained in foreign language methodologies have struggled to serve their needs. The authors in this volume all share a belief in the importance of providing appropriate language education to these children and of preserving and building on their home-based bilingualism. Their contributions outline key issues in the design and implementation of HL programs that are consonant with these goals and that are grounded in the research and best practices of the field of HL education.

Organization of the Volume

The chapters in this volume are organized into seven parts. Focusing on demographics, Part I, *A Landscape of Heritage/Community Languages: Demographic Surveys*, documents the changing and growing presence of HL-speaking populations in many regions of the world. In contrast to other parts of the volume, this section does not present specific programs or sites but, rather, provides an overview of the linguistic landscape of different parts of the world with a view towards setting the stage for the discussion of specific sites and programs that appear in the other parts of the volume.

The five chapters composing this section are as follows: Extra looks at the complex linguistic landscape of Europe comparing, in particular, the supporting societal structures and policies that apply to the teaching and maintenance of regional minority languages and immigrant languages. Ndhlovu and Willoughby provide an overview of Australia's changing demographics and consider implications for HL education. Wiley and Bhalla's discussion of U.S. demographics compares languages taught in schools to the presence of HLs in this country. Zampaulo offers a historical overview of immigrant communities and languages in Latin America. Finally, Duff and Becker-Zayas consider Canadian language policies and practices that bear on HL teaching against the backdrop of different immigration waves.

Part II, *Community Initiatives: After-School Programs*, documents five community-run programs. Uriu and Douglas analyze the process of moving from a curriculum suited to students who will return to Japan to one that is designed with HLLs residing permanently in the U.S. in mind. Sneddon describes strategies used by Albanian and Bengali communities in East London to address two common problems faced by community-run schools: lack of resources, including facilities, and difficulty finding trained teachers. Souza and Gomes discuss the introduction of HL-specific pedagogical innovations in two Brazilian Portuguese community schools, one in London and the other in Barcelona, and evaluate to what extent these innovations have been assimilated into the structures of both schools. McCabe examines the ways in which a group of community schools teaching Czech in the U.S. and Europe have grown from informal gatherings of parents into complex educational organizations, detailing strategies used to address the different needs of Czech-speaking communities across these areas. Mokhatebi Ardakani and Moloney discuss the ways in which HL maintenance is fostered in the home, arguing that formal instruction in all settings should capitalize on the language resources acquired in the family in order to build on these and connect with HLLs' lives.

Part III, *Community Initiatives: All-Day Pre-, Primary, and Secondary Schools*, discusses full-time programs organized by local communities. Karapetian presents a variety of issues facing the Armenian community in Los Angeles, among them two languages (Western and Eastern Armenian) spoken within the community and different approaches to teaching these languages. Bourgerie explores four long-established Chinese schools in Cambodia, focusing on the changes that have taken place since the 1990s, including the introduction of Mandarin as the medium of instruction rather than the home dialects of the students. Atoofi and Naranjo Escobar give an account of well-established Japanese schools in Chile that educate children in accordance with the Japanese national curriculum, even though the students are often Spanish dominant. Schwartz explains the rationale for establishing Russian-Hebrew kindergartens in Israel that originally used the children's home language, Russian, until the age of three, but with changing demographics started introducing Hebrew earlier.

Three chapters in Part IV, *Language Minority Communities and the Public School System: Opportunities and Challenges*, focus on American public high schools and one on schools in the UK. Kagan describes a study of language offerings in public high schools in Los Angeles in an attempt to understand whether schools are responsive to the demographics of communities in their neighborhoods. Chik and Wright examine Vietnamese and Khmer programs in public schools in the Los Angeles area, focusing on the ways in which these programs are supported at the organizational and classroom levels as they strive to meet the needs of their HL populations. Jaumont, Dévédec, and Ross describe an innovative program for French-speaking immigrants (mainly from Haiti and West Africa) that has been organized in partnership with several New York public schools. In the final paper in this section, Anderson describes an art-based HL pedagogy and multilingual digital storytelling project that is accompanied by the creation of professional development materials for teachers that can support these innovations going forward.

The five chapters in Part V, *Maintenance of Heritage/Community Languages in Public Schools: The Impact of Government Policy and Sociopolitical Change*, examine factors that are external to local contexts as they impinge on HL programs. Focusing on Australia, Oriyama discusses the ways in which enrollment criteria in high-stakes Higher School Certificate courses for four Asian languages resulted in only unrealistically high-level courses being available to many HL students, discouraging them from studying their HLs, and how a grassroots movement by the Japanese community eventually reformed Australian policy on heritage language education. Ramonienė, Lichačiova, and Brazauskienė analyze the change in status of the Russian language in Lithuania following the restoration of the Republic of Lithuania in 1990, noting the precipitous fall in numbers of students enrolled in full-time public schools using Russian as the medium of instruction, but also noting the stabilization of these numbers over time. Seals depicts the wide range of efforts and strategies, at both the national and local levels, that are currently going into Pasifika HL education in New Zealand, including early childhood, primary, secondary, and after-school programs. Loona and Wennerholm focus on HL education in the public school systems in Norway and Sweden, noting that in Sweden language maintenance has been stressed in contrast to Norway's policy of transitional bilingualism, but that even in the more favorable Swedish environment, implicit ideologies present in "hidden curricula" undermine the validity and thus appeal of HL programs. Meier and Schumacher examine documents dating from 1986 to 2012 relating to a two-way immersion (TWI) program in Berlin, tracing the process from its introduction to its official acceptance into the mainstream school system, i.e., its institutionalization.

Part VI, *Heritage/Community Languages in Higher Education*, examines the opportunities for HL maintenance encountered by postsecondary students. Informed by a national survey of foreign language programs conducted by the National Heritage Language Resource Center, Carreira examines the state of HL teaching and program and curriculum design in postsecondary institutions in the United States. Nielsen's analysis of three Arabic university programs in Denmark speaks to the negative impact that clashes between top-down language policies and bottom-up educational choices can have on HL programs, even well-designed, successful, and longstanding ones. Ribadeneira and Lee offer a detailed analysis of the process of adoption, implementation, and institutionalization of innovative pedagogical approaches and courses for Spanish HL speakers at two U.S. universities that serve sizable Hispanic populations. The programs represent two different, but effective, approaches to serving the needs of their HLL populations. Nijhawan's chapter describes how the implementation and institutionalization of the Hindi-Urdu heritage stream at York University in Canada is embedded both in this university's larger efforts of internationalization, as well as in a departmental approach to HL pedagogy that is inclusive of a wide range of home languages and cultures and that instantiates a learner-centered approach.

Part VII, *Heritage/Community Language Maintenance from a Lifespan Perspective: Formal and Informal Contexts*, explores the maintenance of HLs across multiple levels of schooling and in daily contexts outside of formal instruction. Duff, Liu, and Li review the literature on Chinese as a heritage language (CHL) in Anglophone countries, reporting on the ways in which a changing geopolitical context and technologically connected Chinese diaspora influence the nature and extent of CHL in the home, community schools, public schools, and postsecondary programs. Pfaff, Dollnick, and Herkenrath report on the opportunities for the maintenance and development of Turkish in Germany across all levels of schooling, concluding that while not all students with Turkish HL backgrounds can access such programs, Turkish is gradually becoming recognized as part of multilingual Europe. Fouser looks at Korean as an HL in the context of Japan, arguing that recent changes in discourse on Korea and Koreans in Japan, including the widespread appeal of Korean pop culture, have moved Korean from a fringe subject to a popular choice. Avineri and Verschik examine the maintenance of Yiddish in the U.S. and Lithuania through the efforts of four programs, describing the challenges they face in terms of limited resources as well as the lack of a geographical heartland in which Yiddish is spoken, but pointing out that these challenges can create opportunities for innovation and inventiveness.

The Framework of Institutionalization

We have asked the authors contributing to this volume to frame their discussion of key issues in the design and implementation of HL programs in view of the concept of institutionalization put forward by Ekholm and Trier (1987) and elaborated by other authors in Miles, Ekholm, and Vandenberghe (1987). This common framework provides both a tool for comparing programs across institutional levels and countries, as well as a formal means for gauging the state of institutionalization in the field of HL teaching.

At its most basic, Ekholm and Trier (1987) define institutionalization as "a process through which an organization assimilates an innovation into its structure" (p. 13). In the educational context, the term "institutionalization" can span a wide range of contexts, from individual classrooms to an entire school or school district, all the way to the national level, including policy making.

Notwithstanding these differences, six indicators of institutionalization can prove useful from the point of view of understanding the state of institutionalization of HL teaching:

1. Acceptance by relevant participants who see the innovation as valuable and as legitimately belonging;
2. Widespread use of the innovation throughout the organization, district, or geographical site;
3. Firm expectation that use of the practice and/or product will continue;
4. The innovation is stable and routinized and is no longer seen as "novel";
5. Continuation does not depend on the actions or motivations of specific individuals but on the culture or structure of the organization or on procedures that have been put in place to support the innovation; and
6. Time, space, personnel, funding, and other resources are routinely allocated.

(Adapted from Ekholm & Trier, 1987, p. 17; Eiseman, Fleming, & Roody, 1990, pp. 12–13; Miles & Louis, 1987, p. 26)

Lessons Learned

The extent to which the particular HL programs described in this volume, and more generally, the field of HL teaching, meet the six indicators of institutionalization and reflect other aspects of the institutionalization framework remains an open question. This is not surprising, given the wide range of conditions and contexts in which HLs are situated. Despite these differences, the chapters in this volume converge on a number of factors and conditions that bear on issues of institutionalization. The list below is not an exhaustive compilation of those factors and conditions, but rather represents some of the most salient issues identified by our contributors, as well as our own observations.

1. Teachers, administrators, and parents looking to establish or grow an HL program can use an approach that builds on a wide variety of models or strategies, from programs in mainstream schools to those run by local HL communities; from programs that are closely aligned with foreign entities to independent, locally run programs; and from programs with strict academic standards to those that take a more general approach to cultural and linguistic maintenance.
2. Even within a given type of HL program, level of education, or language, innovations are not one-size-fits-all, but ideally respond to the unique needs and resources of each context. Experimentation and bottom-up problem solving can help identify the unique needs and strengths of each context and craft responsive solutions.
3. A common feature of many successful and sustainable programs is that they are able to weave together a variety of networks (e.g., HL community organizations, local and foreign ministries of education, educational institutions, etc.) to support local and supra-local goals. This makes it possible to simultaneously respond to local needs and leverage international connections and resources.
4. Successful innovation is rooted in effective HL pedagogy, which draws on learning opportunities in the home and community. Ideally, in the school context, HL learning opportunities are not confined to HL classes but are embedded throughout the curriculum and extracurricular school activities.
5. Successful integration of HL pedagogy relies on defining clear incentives for students, language programs, and schools, as well as on codifying HL policies and procedures and including them in institutional documents.

6. The professional development of both faculty and administrators is key to the successful implementation and maintenance of HL programs, and more generally, the institutionalization of the field. A collaborative and reflective model of professional development that emphasizes social processing of knowledge can help teachers, parents, and administrators identify and respond to changing institutional needs.
7. Language ideology and politics, both at the societal level and within schools, play an important role in both facilitating and hindering the process of institutionalization.
8. The adoption, implementation, and institutionalization of HL practices into a curriculum or program is a long, labor-intensive, and fluid process that requires constant advocacy, research, professional development, focused work, negotiations, and collaboration.

Closing Thoughts

Altogether, the chapters in this volume provide a broad outline of the current state of HL education across many regions of the world and set the stage for future work in this area. Beyond practical and theoretical takeaways, the programs described in this volume also serve as a testimony to the astonishing energy, dedication, and creativity that go into offering HL instruction. When Agnes He (2010) calls the heritage language "the language of the heart," she cuts to the core of the vitality of these programs, many of which are only possible because of the efforts of parents and teachers volunteering in heritage language schools, starting programs in educational institutions, or advocating for policies that promote HL development at the level of local or national government, in many cases under unfavorable conditions. This book is dedicated to those individuals.

Acknowledgments

Several people deserve thanks for helping prepare this volume. Susan Bauckus copyedited the Reference sections for most of the chapters, including entries in multiple languages. Arturo Diaz, Heleana Melendez, and Armani Ronaldo Rosiles helped with copyediting and technical issues. Also invaluable was the organizational support we received from Kathryn Paul. The volume is as rich as it is because of our contributors, and we would like to thank them for their willingness to answer numerous questions and make many revisions. We would also like to thank Kathrene Binag and Rebecca Novack at Routledge for all their help and encouragement.

We wish to gratefully acknowledge the help from the volume reviewers:

Tanja Anstatt, Saeid Atoofi, Elisa Duder, Erika Gilson, Linda Godson, Kimberly Helmer, Gabriela Nik. Ilieva, Orlando Kelm, Soohee Kim, Susan Kresin, Kimi Kondo-Brown, Manel Lacorte, Oksana Laleko, Jinsook Lee, Gerda Lobo, David Lopez, Anna Mikhailova, Robert Moser, Alan Paul, Joy Kreeft Peyton, Leon Potter, Michael Putnam, Angela Scarino, Sarah Shin, Joseph Salmons, Alla Smyslova, Nelleke van Deusen-Scholl, Polina Vinogradova.

References

Beaudrie, S. (2012). Research on university-level Spanish heritage language programs in the United States: The current state of affairs. In S. M. Beaudrie & M. A. Fairclough (Eds.), *Spanish as a heritage language in the United States: The state of the field* (pp. 203–222). Washington, DC: Georgetown University Press.

Eiseman, J. W., Fleming, D. S., & Roody, D. S. (1990). *Making sure it sticks: The school improvement leader's role in institutionalizing change*. Andover, MA: The Regional Laboratory. Retrieved from http://files.eric.ed.gov/fulltext/ED326965.pdf

Ekholm, M., & Trier, U. P. (1987). The concept of institutionalization: Some remarks. In M. B. Miles, M. Ekholm, & R. Vandenberghe (Eds.), *Lasting school improvement: Exploring the process of institutionalization* (pp. 13–21). Leuven, Belgium: Acco.

He, A. W. (2010). The heart of heritage: Sociocultural dimensions of heritage language learning. *Annual Review of Applied Linguistics, 30,* 66–82.

Hinton, L. (2001). Language revitalization: An overview. In L. Hinton & K. Hale (Eds.), *The green book of language revitalization in practice* (pp. 3–18). London, UK: Academic Press.

Miles, M. B., Ekholm, M., & Vandenberghe, R. (1987). *Lasting school improvement: Exploring the process of institutionalization.* Leuven, Belgium: Acco.

Miles, M. B., & Louis, K. S. (1987). Research on institutionalization: A reflective review. In M. B. Miles, M. Ekholm, & R. Vandenberghe (Eds.), *Lasting school improvement: Exploring the process of institutionalization* (pp. 25–44). Leuven, Belgium: Acco.

Van Deusen-Scholl, N. (2014). Research on heritage language issues. In T. G. Wiley, J. K. Peyton, D. Christian, S.C.K. Moore, & N. Liu (Eds.), *Handbook of heritage, community, and Native American languages in the United States: Research, policy, and educational practice* (pp. 76–84). New York, NY: Routledge.

Part I
A Landscape of Heritage/ Community Languages
Demographic Surveys

The Constellation of Languages in Europe

Comparative Perspectives on Regional Minority and Immigrant Minority Languages

Guus Extra

1 Semantics of the Targeted Field

Linguistic diversity has always been conceived as a constituent characteristic of European identity (Arzoz, 2008). Both the European Commission (established in Brussels, Belgium) and the Council of Europe (established in Strasbourg, France) have published many policy documents in which language diversity is cherished as a key element of the multicultural identity of Europe. This language diversity is considered to be a prerequisite rather than an obstacle for a united European space in which all citizens are equal, but not the same, and enjoy equal rights (Council of Europe, 2000). However, as will be shown in this chapter, some languages play a more important role in the European public and political discourse on "celebrating linguistic diversity," the motto of the European Year of Languages (Coss, 2001). The constellation of languages in Europe actually functions as a descending hierarchy (Extra & Gorter, 2008; Nic Craith, 2006) with the following ranking of categories:

- English as *lingua franca* for transnational communication;
- national or official state languages of European countries;
- regional minority (RM) languages across Europe;
- immigrant minority (IM) languages across Europe.

In the official EU discourse, RM languages are referred to as *regional or minority* languages and IM languages as *migrant* languages. Whereas the national languages of the EU with English increasingly on top are celebrated most at the EU level, RM languages are celebrated less and IM languages least. IM languages are only marginally covered by EU language promotion programs and, so far, are mainly considered in the context of provisions for learning the national languages of the migrants' countries of residence.

There is a great need for educational policies in Europe that take new realities of multilingualism into account. Processes of internationalization and globalization have brought European nation-states to the world, but they have also brought the world to European nation-states. This bipolar pattern of change has led to both convergence and divergence of multilingualism across Europe. On the one hand, English is increasingly on the rise as *lingua franca* for transnational communication across the borders of European nation-states (Jenkins, 2010), at the cost of all other official state languages of Europe, in particular French and German. The upward mobility of English is clearly visible in recent European Commission reports such as *Special Eurobarometer 386* (European Commission, 2012) and *Key Data on Teaching Languages at School in Europe* (Eurostat, 2012). In spite of many objections to the hegemony of English (Phillipson, 2003), this process of convergence is enhanced by the extension of the EU to Eastern Europe. Within the borders of European nation-states, however, there is an increasing divergence of languages at home (often referred to in Europe as "mother tongues"; Extra, 2010) due to large-scale processes of global migration.

Even at the level of (co-)official state languages, Europe's identity is to a great extent determined by cultural and linguistic diversity (Haarmann, 1995). Table 1.1 serves to illustrate this diversity in terms of EU (candidate) Member States with their estimated populations (ranked in decreasing order) and corresponding (co-)official state languages.

As Table 1.1 makes clear, there are large differences in population size among EU Member States. German, French, English, Italian, Spanish, and Polish belong, in this order, to the six most widely spoken official state languages in the present EU, whereas Turkish would come second to German in an enlarged EU. Table 1.1 also shows the close connection between nation-state references and official state language references. In 27 out of 30 cases, distinct languages are the clearest feature distinguishing one nation-state from its neighbors (Barbour, 2000), the only exceptions (and for different reasons) being Belgium, Austria, and Cyprus. This match between nation-state references and official state language references obscures the existence of other categories of languages spoken across European nation-states (Haberland, 1991; Nic Craith, 2006). While many of these languages are indigenous minority languages with a regional territorial base, many others originate abroad and lack such a base. We will refer to these languages as regional minority (RM) languages and immigrant minority (IM) languages, respectively (Extra & Gorter, 2001), in this way expressing both their shared main property and their major constituent difference. As all of these RM and IM languages are spoken by different language communities and not at statewide levels, it may seem logical to refer to them as "community languages," a term commonly used in the UK, thus contrasting them with the official languages of nation-states. However, this term would lead to confusion because it is also used to refer to the EU's official state languages. In that sense, the designation "community languages" is occupied territory, at least in the EU jargon. A final argument in favor of using the term "immigrant" languages is its use on the *Ethnologue: Languages of the World* website (Lewis, Simons, & Fennig, 2016), a valuable and widely used standard resource of cross-national information on this topic.

A number of other issues need to be kept in mind as well. First of all, in spite of their status as minority languages, RM and IM languages in some EU Member States have larger numbers of speakers than many of the official state languages mentioned in Table 1.1. Moreover, RM and IM languages in one EU nation-state may be official state languages in another nation-state. Examples of the former result from language border crossing in adjacent nation-states, such as Finnish in Sweden or Swedish in Finland. Examples of the latter result from processes of migration, in particular from Southern to Northern Europe, such as Portuguese, Spanish, Italian, or Greek. It should also be kept in mind that many, if not most, IM languages in particular European nation-states originate from countries outside Europe. It is the context of migration and minorization that makes our proposed distinction between RM and IM languages ambiguous; however, we see no good alternative. In our opinion, the proposed distinction will lead at least to awareness raising

Table 1.1 Overview of 30 EU (Candidate) Member States with Estimated Populations and (Co-)Official State Languages

Nr	Member States	Population (in millions)	(Co-)official State Language(s)
1	Germany	81.2	German
2	France	66.4	French
3	United Kingdom	64.9	English
4	Italy	60.8	Italian
5	Spain	46.4	Spanish
6	Poland	38.0	Polish
7	Romania	19.9	Romanian
8	The Netherlands	16.9	Dutch (Nederlands)
9	Belgium	11.3	Dutch, French, German
10	Greece	10.8	Greek
11	Czech Republic	10.5	Czech
12	Portugal	10.4	Portuguese
13	Hungary	9.8	Hungarian
14	Sweden	9.7	Swedish
15	Austria	8.6	Austrian-German
16	Bulgaria	7.2	Bulgarian
17	Denmark	5.7	Danish
18	Finland	5.5	Finnish, Swedish
19	Slovakia	5.4	Slovak
20	Ireland	4.6	Irish, English
21	Croatia	4.2	Croatian
22	Lithuania	2.9	Lithuanian
23	Slovenia	2.1	Slovenian
24	Latvia	2.0	Latvian
25	Estonia	1.3	Estonian
26	Cyprus	0.8	Greek, Turkish
27	Luxembourg	0.6	Luxemburgish, French, German
28	Malta	0.4	Maltese, English
	Candidate Member States	*Population (in millions)*	*Official State Language*
29	Turkey	78.7	Turkish
30	Macedonia	2.1	Macedonian

Note: The June 2016 "Brexit" outcomes of the EU Referendum in the UK will lead to a complex and lengthy disentanglement of the EU and UK, the political and sociolinguistic effects of which could not be foreseen at the time of writing.

Source: "EuroStat Newsrelease 124: EU population estimates at 1 January 2015" by EuroStat (2015).

and may ultimately lead to an inclusive approach in the European conceptualization of minority languages (Extra & Gorter, 2008; Extra & Yağmur, 2012).

2 The Role of Language in Identifying Diversity of Population Groups

Collecting reliable and comparable information about the diversity of population groups in EU countries is no easy task. More interesting than numbers or estimates of the size of particular groups, however, are the criteria used for determining such numbers or estimates. It is common EU practice to present data on RM groups on the basis of home language use and/or ethnicity while data on IM groups is based on nationality and/or country of birth. However, convergence between these criteria for the two groups emerges over time in terms of home language and ethnicity, because of strong intergenerational erosion in the utility of nationality or birth-country statistics for IM groups (Barni & Extra, 2008).

Comparative population figures for EU Member States are available from the EU's Statistical Office of the EU in Luxembourg (EuroStat). Over the last decades, an overall decrease in the indigenous population has been observed in most EU countries; at the same time, there has been an increase in the IM figures. For a variety of reasons, however, reliable and comparable demographic information on IM groups in EU countries is difficult to obtain. Seemingly simple questions like *How many Turkish residents live in Germany compared to France?* cannot easily be answered. For some groups or countries, no updated information is available or no such data has ever been collected. Moreover, official statistics reflect only IM groups with legal resident status. Most importantly, however, the most widely used criteria for IM status—nationality and/or country of birth—have become less valid over time because of an increasing trend towards naturalization and births within the countries of immigration. In addition, most residents from former colonies already have the nationality of their country of immigration.

Another source of disparity is the different data collection systems being used, resulting in different types of databases, which are difficult to compare (Poulain, 2008). The following three types of data collection may take place in various combinations:

- nationwide census data, collected at fixed intervals from 5–10 years (in 23 out of 28 EU countries);
- regularly (monthly or yearly) updated administrative register data at the municipal and national level (e.g., in Scandinavian countries and the Netherlands);
- small- or large-scale statistical survey data among particular subsets of population groups, collected at regular intervals (e.g., in France or in Italy, or on Frisian in the Netherlands).

Against this background, four criteria for defining and identifying population diversity are listed in Table 1.2 in terms of their major advantages and disadvantages.

Table 1.2 reveals that there is no simple way to solve identification issues. Moreover, inspection of the criteria for diversity of population groups is as important as the figures themselves. From a European perspective, a predictable top-down development can be seen over time in the utility and utilization of different types of criteria, progressing from nationality and birth-country criteria in first and second generations to ethnic self-categorization and home language in future generations. The latter two criteria are generally considered complementary criteria and need not coincide, as languages may be conceived to variable degrees as core values of ethnocultural identity in contexts of migration and minorization. In addition, the top-down development over time, progressing from the first two to the last two criteria, will lead to convergence in the criteria for identifying RM and IM groups. Another point to note is that multiplicity is a common

Table 1.2 Criteria for the Definition and Identification of Population Diversity (P/F/M = Person/Father/ Mother)

Criterion	Advantages	Disadvantages
Nationality (NAT) (P/F/M)	• objective • relatively easy to establish	• (intergenerational) erosion through naturalization or double NAT • NAT not always indicative of ethnicity/ identity • some (e.g., ex-colonial) groups have NAT of immigration country
Birth country (BC) (P/F/M)	• objective • relatively easy to establish	• intergenerational erosion through births in immigration country • BC not always indicative of ethnicity/ identity • invariable/deterministic: does not take into account dynamics in society (in contrast to all other criteria)
Self-categorization (SC)	• touches the heart of the matter • emancipatory: SC takes into account person's own conception of ethnicity/identity	• subjective by definition: also determined by the language/ethnicity of interviewer and by the spirit of the times • multiple SC possible • historically charged, especially by World War II experiences
Home language (HL)	• HL is significant criterion of ethnicity in communication processes • HL data are prerequisite for government policy in areas such as public information or education	• complex criterion: who speaks what language to whom and when? • language is not always a core value of ethnicity/identity • useless in one-person households

Source: Reprinted with permission from "Multilingual Europe: Facts and policies," by G. Extra and D. Gorter (2008). Copyright 2008 by Mouton de Gruyter.

property for three out of four of the criteria mentioned in Table 1.2: it holds for nationality, ethnicity, and home language, but not for birth country. It should finally be mentioned that the home language question offers more perceptual transparency and societal utility (e.g., in educational and media policies) than the ethnicity question.

In 23 out of 28 EU countries, nationwide censuses are held, but at variable intervals. Scandinavian countries and the Netherlands rely on yearly updated administrative (municipal) registers in combination with periodic sample surveys. Questions on ethnicity and language feature in the censuses of 13 and 17 EU countries, respectively (Extra & Gorter, 2008, pp. 18–21). There is, however, wide variation in the operationalization of questions about language, which makes cross-national comparison of the data difficult. The three most commonly asked questions on language use relate to mother tongue (11 countries), (other) language(s) spoken (frequently) (6 countries), and language(s) (most frequently) spoken at home (5 countries). While the mother tongue question is most widely used in Europe, this question has been criticized for its lack of empirical validity in English-dominant countries outside Europe, in particular in Australia, Canada, and the U.S. (Extra & Gorter, 2008, pp. 21–24). In these countries, the most widely asked language question in the census refers to language(s) spoken at home—next to or instead of English. Therefore, while the focus in these non-European English-dominant countries is on immigrant languages, the focus in EU countries—if non-national languages are considered at all—is on RM languages. For the first time in its history, the UK introduced a LOTE (Languages Other Than English) question into its 2011 census, taking an inclusive perspective on both RM and IM languages.

At present, far less empirical data on IM languages are available across European nation-states than in English-dominant countries. As a result, language policies in this domain in continental Europe are commonly developed in the absence of even the most basic empirical evidence on language diversity.

3 Regional Minority Languages and Immigrant Minority Languages across Europe

RM and IM languages have many more issues in common than is usually thought (Extra & Gorter, 2008, p. 9). These commonalities include their distribution, their domestic and public vitality, the determinants of language maintenance versus language shift towards majority languages, the relationship between language, ethnicity, and identity, and the status of minority languages in schools, in particular in the compulsory stages of primary and secondary education.

In Europe, both RM and IM languages can be considered dominated languages as opposed to dominant national languages. The dominant status of the latter becomes visible in such domains as government, education, the media, and public services and spaces. The argument for promoting the status of RM and IM languages in any of these domains is commonly based on responsiveness to people's cultural rights or cultural demands (May, 2011). It holds for both RM and IM languages that language transmission may occur in two major domains: the home and the school. RM or IM language speakers often experience a mismatch between the language of the home and that of the school. Whether parents in such contexts continue to transmit their heritage language to their children is strongly dependent on the degree to which these parents, or the minority group to which they belong, conceive of this language as a core value of cultural identity (Smolicz, 1980, 1992).

Many RM languages did not become designated as minority languages until the eighteenth and nineteenth centuries when, during the processes of state formation in Europe, they found themselves excluded from the state level, in particular from general education. Furthermore, RM languages did not become official languages in most of the states that were then established (see Table 1.1). Centralizing tendencies and an ideology of *one language—one state* have threatened the continued existence of RM languages. The same ideology threatens the continued existence of IM languages, both in the home and the school. For most RM languages across Europe, some kind of educational provisions have been established in an attempt to reverse ongoing language shift (Fishman, 2001). Only in the last few decades have some RM languages become relatively well protected in legal terms, as well as through affirmative educational programs, both at the Member State level and at the level of the EU at large. Educational programs are offered much less commonly for most IM languages, which are more vulnerable in the context of a *one language— one state* ideology, as will be outlined below.

Some countries keep fairly accurate figures on RM languages as a result of a language question that has been included in the census several times; in other cases, we only have rough estimates by insiders of the language group (usually language activists who want to boost the figures) or by outsiders (e.g., state officials who want to downplay the number of speakers).

While there have always been speakers of IM languages in Europe, these languages have only recently emerged as minority languages spoken on a wide scale. Typological differences between IM languages across EU nation-states exist in terms of the status of IM languages as EU or non-EU languages, or as languages of former colonies. Taken from the latter perspective, for example, Indian languages are prominent in the United Kingdom, as are Maghrebi Arabic languages in France, Congolese languages in Belgium, and Surinamese languages in the Netherlands. Turkish and Arabic are good examples of "non-European" languages that are spoken and learned by millions of first- and second-generation IM groups in Europe.

Most studies in Europe have focused on a spectrum of IM languages at the level of one particular multilingual city (Eversley et al., 2010), one particular nation-state (Alladina & Edwards, 1991), or one particular IM language at the European level (Obdeijn & De Ruiter, 1998 on Arabic in Europe, or Jørgensen, 2003 on Turkish in Europe). A number of studies, however, have taken both a cross-national and a cross-linguistic perspective on the status and use of IM languages in Europe (Extra & Gorter, 2008; Extra & Yağmur, 2004). The Multilingual Cities project, coordinated by Extra and Yağmur (2004), has delivered a wealth of data: evidence on both the distribution and vitality of IM languages was collected by means of home language surveys among multicultural school populations, gathering data from the homes of more than 160,000 primary-school children in six European cities on a European north-south axis from Göteborg, Hamburg, The Hague, Brussels, Lyon, to Madrid.

Apart from similarities in conceptual issues surrounding RM and IM languages across Europe, some major differences arise as well. The first major difference relates to their spatial distribution, both at the European and at the national level. At the European level, RM languages have a stronger appearance than IM languages in Central and Eastern Europe, whereas the reverse picture emerges for most Western European countries (Extra & Yağmur, 2012). At the national level, RM languages tend to be more prominent phenomena in rural areas, whereas IM languages tend to concentrate in urban areas. The first phenomenon can be demonstrated with the latest 2011 UK census data on Welsh, which shows the highest concentrations of Welsh speakers in the least populated areas of Wales and the lowest concentrations in southeastern areas, which are more urban and densely populated.

Over time and across all industrialized Western European countries, a decrease can be observed in the size of RM populations and an increase in IM populations. Similarly inverse trends appear in a decrease in the vitality of RM languages and in an increase and diversification of IM languages across Europe.

Large-scale data collection mechanisms across European countries, if available at all, tend to focus on RM languages, while data collection for IM languages is just beginning to emerge in some countries. In the EU, the UK is a front-runner in this regard with its 2011 Census LOTE question that is inclusive and not limited to RM languages. Unfortunately, however, the UK question asks about an informant's main language rather than about the repertoire of language(s) used at home. A question about the informant's main language is ambiguous because of its lack of domain specification, which will predictably lead to an underestimation of language diversity and will complicate cross-continental comparisons of LOTE outcomes (Extra, 2010, p. 119). The top 10 LOTEs in the 2011 UK Census are, in ranked order: Polish, Punjabi, Urdu, Bengali, Gujarati, Yoruba, Arabic, French, Chinese, and Portuguese (7 non-EU and 3 EU languages). For the two other largest EU countries, Germany and France (see Table 1.1), no nationwide IM language data collection mechanisms are available. Major IM languages in Germany are Turkish, Kurdish, Russian, Arabic (with recent refugees from Syria increasing their number), Greek, Dutch, Igbo, Polish, Italian, Serbian, and Croatian (6 non-EU and 5 EU languages). In France, major IM languages are (Maghrebi) Arabic, Spanish, Italian, Portuguese, and English (1 non-EU and 4 EU languages).

A final major difference between RM and IM languages across Europe relates to the status of support structures. Support structures for RM languages, in particular in education, tend to be organized in a top-down manner, at the level of both regional and European authorities. An example is the Council of Europe's European Charter for Regional or Minority Languages, which came into operation in March 1998 (Council of Europe, 2014). The Charter is aimed at the protection and the promotion of "the historical regional or minority languages of Europe," and functions as an instrument for the comparison of legal measures and facilities of Member States for language promotion (López, Ruiz Vieytez, & Libarona, 2012; Nic Craith, 2003). However, the Charter does not define the concepts of "regional" and "minority" languages, and it explicitly excludes IM languages. States are free in their choice of which RM languages to include, and the degree of protection is not prescribed; thus, a state can choose more or less stringent policies. The result is a wide variety of provisions across EU Member States (Grin, 2003).

Top-down support structures for IM languages, both at the European and at the national levels, are much weaker than for RM languages, and support tends to be bottom-up from parents at the local or national level. Although IM languages are often conceived of and transmitted as core values by IM language groups, they are much less protected than RM languages by affirmative action and legal measures in, for example, education. In fact, the learning and certainly the teaching of IM languages are often seen by majority language speakers and by policy makers as obstacles to integration and as a threat to national identity. A rarely addressed paradox in the European versus national public and political discourse on language diversity becomes visible:

*   linguistic diversity at the European level is commonly conceived of as an inherent property of European identity and a prerequisite for integration, accompanied by devices as "celebrating linguistic diversity" or "diversity within unity"; and
*   linguistic diversity at the national level, in particular with respect to IM languages, is often conceived of as a threat to national identity and an obstacle for integration.

A clash of paradigms emerges in those areas where RM languages and IM languages appear in strong co-occurrence. Good examples of such areas in Spain are Barcelona and Catalonia at large with a co-occurrence of Spanish, Catalan, and a range IM languages (Carrasco, 2008, p. 28). The Language Rich Europe project (Extra & Yağmur, 2012) offers a detailed comparative analysis of the current status of RM and IM languages and language policies in 25 European countries and regions.

4 Concluding Remarks

It is remarkable that the teaching of RM languages is generally advocated as a matter of course for reasons of fairness, social cohesion, group identity, or economic benefit, while such arguments are rarely made in favor of teaching IM languages. The 1977 guideline of the Council of European Communities on education for "migrant" children (Directive 77/486, dated 25 July 1977) has become completely outdated nowadays. It needs to be put in a new and increasingly multicultural context and be extended to pupils originating from non-EU countries who form the large part of IM children at European primary schools. Besides, most of the so-called migrants in EU countries have taken up citizenship of the countries in which they live, and in many cases belong to second- or third-generation groups. Against this background, there is a growing need for overarching human rights, including language rights, for all Europeans, irrespective of their ethnic, cultural, religious, or language background. For similar inclusive approaches to IM and RM language rights we refer to Nic Craith (2006) and May (2011).

The heads of state and government of all EU Member States gathered in March 2002 in Barcelona and called upon the European Commission to take further action to promote plurilingualism across Europe, in particular by promoting the learning and teaching of at least two additional languages from a very early age (Nikolov & Curtain, 2000). A more recent initiative, supported by the Council of Europe and coordinated by the European Centre for Modern Languages in Graz, Austria, has been the Valeur project 2004–2007 (McPake et al., 2007). Its ambitions were to bring together information on educational provisions for non-national languages in more than 20 European countries, focus on the outcomes of these provisions for students by the time they have left school, identify good practices and draw conclusions about how provisions can be developed, promote a greater awareness of the issues involved, and create a network for developing new initiatives.

Also the European Commission's thinking has developed in this area, and Section 4.1 of the EC's well-known 2008 Communication is entitled *Valuing all languages* (European Commission, 2008). In particular, advocating that all EU citizens learn three languages, appealing for language learning to begin early, and suggesting that a wide range of languages be offered to allow children to choose family languages based on the principle of personal adoption, open the door to the above-mentioned inclusive approach. Although this may sound paradoxical (Phillipson, 2003), an inclusive approach can also be advanced by accepting the role of English as *lingua franca* for transnational communication across Europe, apart from the national language of schooling and a language of personal adoption.

The above-mentioned principles are aimed at reconciling bottom-up and top-down pleas in Europe for plurilingualism, and are inspired by large-scale and enduring experiences with the learning and teaching of English (as an L1 or L2) and one Language Other Than English for all children implemented in the State of Victoria, Australia (Extra & Yağmur, 2004, pp. 99–105). The Victorian School of Languages in Melbourne has led to an internationally recognized breakthrough in the conceptualization of plurilingual policies in terms of making this provision feasible and mandatory for all children (including a minority of L1 English-speaking children) and offering a broad spectrum of LOTEs (in 2015, more than 50 languages were offered in primary and secondary education). This agency has provided government support for realizing a Language Other Than English vision derived from multicultural policy perspectives.

Adopting the above-mentioned principles would recognize plurilingualism in an increasingly multicultural environment as an asset for all youngsters and for society at large. The EU, the Council of Europe, and UNESCO could function as leading transnational agencies in promoting such concepts. The UNESCO *Universal Declaration of Cultural Diversity* (Appadurai & Winkin, 2002) is very much in line with the views expressed here, in particular in its plea to encourage linguistic diversity, to respect the mother tongue at all levels of education, and to foster the learning of more than one language from a very early age.

References

Alladina, S., & Edwards, V. (Eds.). (1991). *Multilingualism in the British Isles* (Volume 1: The older mother tongues and Europe; Volume 2: Africa, the Middle East and Asia). London, UK, and New York, NY: Longman.

Appadurai, A., & Winkin, Y. (2002). *UNESCO Universal Declaration on Cultural Diversity.* Paris, France. Retrieved from http://unesdoc.unesco.org/images/0012/001271/127162e.pdf

Arzoz, X. (Ed.). (2008). *Respecting linguistic diversity in the European Union.* Amsterdam, Netherlands: John Benjamins.

Barbour, S. (2000). Nationalism, language, Europe. In S. Barbour & C. Carmichael (Eds.), *Language and nationalism in Europe* (pp. 1–17). Oxford, UK: Oxford University Press.

Barni, M., & Extra, G. (Eds.). (2008). *Mapping linguistic diversity in multicultural contexts*. Berlin, Germany: Mouton de Gruyter.

Carrasco, S. (2008). Barcelona and Catalonia: A multilingual reality between an old paradox and a new opportunity. In C. Kenner & T. Hickey (Eds.), *Multilingual Europe: Diversity and learning* (pp. 28–32). London, UK: Trentham Books.

Coss, S. (2001). The European year of languages. Retrieved from http://aiic.net/p/354

Council of Europe. (2000). *Linguistic diversity for democratic citizenship in Europe: Towards a framework for language education policies*. Proceedings of the Council of Europe: Innsbruck, Austria, 10–12 May 1999. Education Committee, Council for Cultural Co-operation, Strasbourg, France.

Council of Europe. (2014). European charter for regional or minority languages ("About the Charter"). Retrieved from http://www.coe.int/t/dg4/education/minlang/aboutcharter/default_en.asp

Directive 77/486. (1977). Directive 77/486 of the Council of the European Communities on the schooling of children of migrant workers. *Official Journal of the European Communities*, Appendix 3, 32–33. Brussels, Belgium: Council of the European Communities.

European Commission. (2008). *Multilingualism: An asset for Europe and a shared commitment*. Communication from the Commission to the European Parliament, the Council, the European Economic and Social Committee, and the Committee of the Regions, Brussels, Belgium.

European Commission. (2012). Europeans and their languages [Special Eurobarometer 386 report]. Brussels, Belgium. Retrieved from http://ec.europa.eu/public_opinion/archives/ebs/ebs_386_en.pdf

EuroStat. (2012). *Key data on teaching languages at school in Europe*. Brussels, Belgium: Education, Audiovisual and Culture Executive Agency. Retrieved from http://ec.europa.eu/languages/policy/strategic-framework/documents/key-data-2012_en.pdf

EuroStat. (2015). EuroStat Newsrelease 124: EU population estimates at 1 January 2015. Retrieved from http://ec.europa.eu/eurostat/documents/2995521/6903510/3-10072015-AP-EN.pdf/d2bfb01f-6ac5-4775-8a7e-7b104c1146d0

Eversley, J., Mehmedbegović, D., Sanderson, A., Tinsley, T., Von Ahn, M., & Wiggins, R. D. (2010). *Language capital: Mapping the languages of London's schoolchildren*. London, UK: CILT National Centre for Languages.

Extra, G. (2010). Mapping linguistic diversity in multicultural contexts: Demolinguistic perspectives. In J. Fishman & O. García (Eds.), *Handbook of language and ethnic identity* (pp. 107–122). Oxford, UK: Oxford University Press.

Extra, G., & Gorter, D. (Eds.). (2001). *The other languages of Europe: Demographic, sociolinguistic and educational perspectives*. Clevedon, UK: Multilingual Matters.

Extra, G., & Gorter, D. (Eds.). (2008). *Multilingual Europe: Facts and policies*. Berlin, Germany: Mouton de Gruyter.

Extra, G., & Yağmur, K. (Eds.). (2004). *Urban multilingualism in Europe: Immigrant minority languages at home and school*. Clevedon, UK: Multilingual Matters.

Extra, G., & Yağmur, K. (Eds.). (2012). *Language rich Europe: Trends in policies and practices for multilingualism in Europe*. Cambridge, UK: British Council/Cambridge University Press.

Fishman, J. (2001). *Can threatened languages be saved? Reversing language shift, revisited: A 21st century perspective*. Clevedon, UK: Multilingual Matters.

Grin, F. (2003). *Language policy evaluation and the European Charter for regional or minority languages*. Hampshire, UK: Palgrave Macmillan.

Haarmann, H. (1995). *Europäische Identität und Sprachenvielfalt*. Tübingen: Max Niemeyer.

Haberland, H. (1991). Reflections about minority languages in the European Community. In F. Coulmas (Ed.), *A language policy for the European community: Prospects and quandaries* (pp. 179–213). Berlin, Germany: Mouton de Gruyter.

Jenkins, J. (2010). *English as lingua franca: Attitude and identity*. Oxford, UK: Oxford University Press.

Jørgensen, J. N. (Ed.). (2003). *Turkish speakers in North Western Europe*. Clevedon, UK: Multilingual Matters.

Lewis, M., Simons, G., & Fennig, C. (Eds.). (2016). *Ethnologue: Languages of the world* (19th ed.). Dallas, TX: SIL International. Retrieved from http://www.ethnologue.com

López, A., Ruiz Vieytez, E., & Libarona, I. (Eds.). (2012). *Shaping language rights: Commentary on the ECRML*. Strasbourg, France: Council of Europe.

May, S. (2011). *Language and minority rights: Ethnicity, nationalism and the politics of language* (2nd ed.). Oxford, UK: Routledge.

McPake, J., Tinsley, P., Broeder, P., Mijares, L., Latomaa, S., & Martyniuk, W. (2007). *Valuing all languages in Europe*. Graz, Austria: European Centre for Modern Languages.

Nic Craith, M. (2003). Facilitating or generating linguistic diversity: The European Charter for regional or minority languages. In G. Hogan-Brun & S. Wolff (Eds.), *Minority languages in Europe: Frameworks, status, prospects* (pp. 56–72). Hampshire, UK: Palgrave Macmillan.

Nic Craith, M. (2006). *Europe and the politics of language: Citizens, migrants and outsiders*. Hampshire, UK: Palgrave Macmillan.

Nikolov, M., & Curtain, H. (Eds.). (2000). *An early start: Young learners and modern languages in Europe and beyond*. Strasbourg, France: Council of Europe.

Obdeijn, H., & De Ruiter, J. J. (Eds.). (1998). *Le Maroc au coeur de l'Europe: L'enseignement de la langue et culture d'origine (ELCO) aux éleves marocains dans cinq pays européens*. Tilburg, Netherlands: Tilburg University Press, Syntax Datura.

Phillipson, R. (2003). *English-only Europe? Challenging language policy*. London, UK: Routledge.

Poulain, M. (2008). European migration statistics: Definitions, data and challenges. In M. Barni and G. Extra (Eds.), *Mapping linguistic diversity in multicultural contexts* (pp. 43–66). Berlin, Germany: Mouton de Gruyter.

Smolicz, J. (1980). Language as a core value of culture. *Journal of Applied Linguistics, 11*, 1–13.

Smolicz, J. (1992). Minority languages as core values of ethnic cultures: A study of maintenance and erosion of Polish, Welsh, and Chinese languages in Australia. In W. Fase, K. Jaspaert, & S. Kroon (Eds.), *Maintenance and loss of minority languages* (pp. 277–305). Amsterdam, Netherlands: Benjamins.

2

Migration, Heritage Languages, and Changing Demographics in Australia

Finex Ndhlovu and Louisa Willoughby

1 Introduction

Australia has always been multilingual, with over 250 indigenous languages spoken at the time of White Settlement in 1788 (Clyne, 1991, p. 6). But multilingualism has sat uneasily alongside the "monolingual mindset" (Clyne, 2005) that the British colonists brought with them and it has been a point of policy dispute, linked to fears of social fragmentation, throughout the history of modern Australia. We see this uneasiness most clearly in the passage of the Immigration Restriction Act of 1901 (Commonwealth of Australia, 1902), more commonly known as the White Australia Policy,[1] which included a language proficiency instrument aimed at excluding people whose linguistic, cultural, political, and racial identities were considered undesirable.

Drawing on census data, past and present trends in migration, and attitudes towards immigrant heritage languages (HLs) in Australia, this chapter looks at issues and challenges for widespread use and maintenance of HLs in immigrant communities between the mid-1900s and the present. Indigenous languages will not be a focus of the chapter.

We discuss several aspects of the HL situation in Australia with an eye on implications for current and future HL education. The next section provides a brief historical overview of Australia's language-in-migration policy and early developments in HL policy. In the third section the discussion turns to demographic information drawn from the 2011 census and analyzes internal variations within and across immigrant communities as well as patterns of HL maintenance and use across generations. The key questions addressed in this section are: What can we learn about the HL situation from census data on home language(s)? What do census data hide and reveal about issues of HL diversity? The fourth section, focusing on new waves of migrants from multilingual backgrounds, follows; in this section, we look at the language profiles and language practices of African migrants to illustrate how their complex language use patterns both confirm and challenge traditional and bureaucratic approaches to documenting HLs. The last paragraph of this section draws attention to the politics of Mandarin Chinese and the enormous difficulties in equitably assessing HL learners of Mandarin in Australia. The fifth section concludes by showing linkages between the history of Australian immigration and current HL policy developments. In the concluding section we also provide some reflections on implications for a more progressive, dynamic, and versatile HL education policy for Australia and other comparable international contexts.

2 Heritage Languages in Australian Immigration Policy—Historical Overview

The current situation and the broader societal attitudes towards HLs in Australia have to be understood within the historical context of the country's immigration policies that date back to the early 1900s. The evolution of Australia's language-in-migration policies has always been intricately entwined with hegemonic monolingual thinking as well as fears of the perceived threats of multilingualism and cultural diversity. Three distinct phases can be identified in the history of Australian immigration policies, namely, (a) the period of outright exclusion of unwanted cultural and racial groups (1901–57); (b) the period of assimilation (1958–72); and (c) the period of assimilation–tolerance that is often misconstrued as integration (1972 to the present) (Ndhlovu, 2014, p. 37).

Starting from the formative years of a federal political system in the early 1900s, Australia's migration policies have betrayed a consistent use and/or abuse of language tests for the purpose of including "superior" racial groups and excluding the "problematic" and non-desired "other" races. From 1901 up to the late 1970s, language-based exclusion was actuated through Section 3(a) of the Immigration Restriction Act, which required all prospective immigrants from non-European countries to pass a dictation test in a European language selected by the immigration officer, with Asian racial groups being the main targets of this legislation. As McNamara and Roever have noted:

> Care was taken to ascertain which languages the person in question did know, and then the test was given in a language that the person did *not* know; the person would fail the test and then be excluded on that basis.
>
> *(2006, p. 160, emphasis in original)*

The rigor and effort exerted in establishing the linguistic identities of prospective immigrants was applied for the wrong reason altogether. Rather than using this knowledge to recognize and value HLs by ensuring that the person was tested in the language he/she knew best, the knowledge was used against that person.

At the end of World War II, Australia embarked on a mass immigration policy under the slogan *populate or perish*. While the preference for British migrants remained, the desire to attract over two million migrants over the next 20 years, and the growing refugee crisis in Europe, saw Australia first open its immigration channels to displaced persons in Northern and Western Europe before extending opportunities to residents of Italy, Greece, the Balkan countries, Lebanon, and Turkey by the end of the 1960s (Martin, 1978, pp. 30–31). Under these conditions, the White Australia Policy was no longer tenable and the dictation test was finally abandoned in 1958 (Tavan, 2005). Well into the 1970s, however, there remained a heavy emphasis on the assimilation of new migrants, including a strong expectation that they would learn English and speak it in their homes as soon as possible. From the mid-1970s, the increasing political voice of migrant groups, combined with concerns that social disadvantage was becoming entrenched in certain migrant populations, saw a more explicitly multiculturalist discourse taken up by both major political parties. Language services were a key component of this changing outlook, with the federal government funding ESL classes in schools (1971), establishing the Telephone Interpreting Service (1972) and migrant language broadcasters (Special Broadcasting Services radio and television, 1978), and developing a national policy on languages (1984) that fostered the teaching of migrant languages (alongside traditional foreign languages, such as French) in Australian schools (see Ozolins, 1993, for a comprehensive review of developments in Australian language policy). This was also a time when Australia began to see significant migration from Asia, beginning in 1975 with refugees from Vietnam and continuing apace in the 1980s and 1990s with skilled migration from China and other Southeast Asian nations.

This period of explicitly multiculturalist policy was to prove quite brief, however, with policy from the 1990s placing an increasing emphasis on the need for strong English proficiency (see Clyne, 2005). We see this focus on English in education with the Australian Language and Literacy Policy of 1991, which included little of the rhetoric on the importance of HL education of previous policies, instead focusing on the need to build strong written English skills for HL speakers (Department of Employment, Education and Training & Dawkins, 1991). In terms of immigration policy, the ghost of the dictation test can be seen in various tests reintroduced for migrants, including the Australian Assessment of Communicative English Skills Test (1992), the Australian History and Values Test (2007), and the Special Test of English Proficiency (1994) (McNamara & Shohamy, 2008; Ndhlovu, 2008). Under the Citizenship Test introduced in 2007, permanent residents who wish to take out Australian citizenship must successfully complete a citizenship test in English before submitting an application (Department of Immigration and Border Protection, n.d.). However, although the current citizenship test does have traces of a narrow, subjective, monolingual, and monocultural view of Australia because it does not pay attention to the HLs of intending immigrants, it is not quite as exclusive as the dictation test, as it does not, for example, deliberately prevent refugees from passing the test.

This shift in language policy has been mirrored by a shift in Australian immigration policy since the mid-1980s, most notably including a major reallocation of places within annual immigration quotas towards skilled immigration at the expense of the family reunion and humanitarian visa streams. Since the early 2000s, border protection has also been a major political issue, in spite of the numbers of asylum seekers arriving by boat rarely exceeding 20,000 per annum (Parliament of Australia, 2013). The point of greater significance here is that Australian attitudes towards HLs have to be looked at through the prism of identity politics, power configuration, and dynamics of the global economy, particularly in relation to neighboring Asian countries.

3 Languages in the 2011 Census

This section draws on customized data from the 2011 Australian Census of Population and Housing (Australian Bureau of Statistics, 2012b), which was extracted by the second author using the TableBuilder Pro application (Australian Bureau of Statistics, 2012a). Language data from the census comes from answers to the questions "Does the person speak a language other than English [LOTE] at home? (if more than one language other than English write the one that is spoken most often)" and "How well does the person speak English?" with the options of answering *very well, well, not well, not at all* (Australian Bureau of Statistics, 2009). As Kipp, Clyne, and Pauwels (1995, p. 26) have noted, the census data on languages spoken at home may undercount the total number of LOTE speakers, as it will not capture those who do not use a community language at home but make regular use of it in other social situations such as visiting extended family. The option to list one language only is also problematic in an increasingly diverse and multilingual society, and one that may particularly affect speakers of African languages. Some readers might also challenge the decision to code Filipino and Tagalog, or the different Chinese varieties, as separate languages,[2] and the figures given subsequently in this chapter would change significantly if different coding decisions were made in respect to these languages. For all these reasons we urge some caution in interpreting the figures that follow and in the following section will complement this statistical data with a discussion based on our own qualitative research with multilingual HL speakers.

At the time of the 2011 census, the Australian population was slightly over 21.5 million. Of these, 3.9 million, or 18%, reported speaking a LOTE at home. As Table 2.1 shows, the census records 39 languages spoken by more than 20,000 Australians, including 8 spoken by more than

Table 2.1 Languages Spoken by More Than 20,000 Australians

Language	# of speakers
Mandarin	336,409
Italian	299,833
Arabic	287,176
Cantonese	263,674
Greek	252,217
Vietnamese	233,388
Spanish	117,497
Hindi	111,352
Tagalog	81,455
German	80,370
Korean	79,785
Punjabi	71,230
Macedonian	68,847
Croatian	61,546
Turkish	59,623
French	57,739
Indonesian	55,869
Filipino	55,403
Serbian	55,115
Polish	50,693
Tamil	50,150
Sinhalese	48,193
Russian	44,059
Japanese	43,690
Dutch	37,248
Urdu	36,836
Thai	36,680
Samoan	36,575
Bengali	35,645
Afrikaans	35,031
Persian (excluding Dari)	34,561
Maltese	34,395
Gujarati	34,211
Portuguese	33,352
Khmer	29,518
Nepali	27,154
Malayalam	25,111
Chinese, so described	23,798
Assyrian Neo-Aramaic	21,479
Hungarian	20,881
Dari	20,180

Source: Compiled from "Languages Spoken at Home" by sex for Australia as place of residence [Data tables]. Selected population characteristics. *Australian Census of Population and Housing, 2011*. Copyright 2011 by Australian Bureau of Statistics. (Australian Bureau of Statistics, 2012b).

100,000 people. These languages represent a range of Australian immigration vintages from the earliest postwar migrant communities (e.g., German, Dutch) up to languages spoken in current top immigration source countries (e.g., Hindi, Mandarin).

Australia is a highly urbanized country, with just two cities—Sydney and Melbourne—accounting for 57% of the total population and 71% of the country's LOTE speakers. These and other major cities vary in the concentration of LOTE speakers: for example, Arabic is much more widely spoken in Sydney (2.7% of the population) than in Melbourne (1.3%), while the reverse can be said for Greek (2.2% in Melbourne, 1.3% in Sydney); and Italian remains much stronger in Melbourne and Adelaide (2.3% and 2.1%) than in any of the other state capital cities (Karidakis & Arunachalam, 2016, p. 14). While Mandarin and Cantonese are two of the most widely spoken LOTEs in all state capitals, their speakers make up a much higher proportion of the total population in Melbourne and Sydney.

For the most part LOTE-speaking communities in Australia show relative gender balance. However, there are more female than male speakers in the following languages: Filipino/Tagalog (59%), Japanese (60%), and Thai (66%). This reflects a noted trend for women from these cultures to marry exogamously and move to Australia in much larger numbers than men (Walker & Heard, 2015). The opposite trend is seen in a number of languages from the Indian subcontinent, with the number of women speakers being particularly unbalanced, as indicated in the following percentages: Hazaranghi (36%), Punjabi (41%), Nepali (43%), and Urdu (44%). Exogamy has been widely noted as a cause of language shift in the second generation (Clyne, 1991), as it reduces the chances that the HL will be the primary or only language of parent-child interaction, and may pose a risk to the continued maintenance of these languages with imbalanced speaker bases.

Communities have highly varied immigration histories, with factors such as the migration vintage and pathway (e.g., as refugees or through the skilled migration scheme) and average length of residence in Australia profoundly influencing the linguistic profile of the community. In Table 2.2 we present information on three variables that we see as most relevant for the future of HL education for the 21 languages that recorded more than 50,000 speakers in the 2011 census. These are the proportion of speakers that are born in Australia, claim to speak English not well or not at all, and are under the age of 20.

The proportion of people in a community who do not speak English well can be an important incentive for language maintenance, as they form a group of interlocutors with whom others must use the HL in order to communicate. In particular, low parental English proficiency can be a motivation for HL maintenance in the second generation (e.g., Clyne, 1991). In Table 2.2 we see that Korean, Vietnamese, Cantonese, and Mandarin all have a comparatively high proportion of speakers who report low English skills. By contrast, communities where most people report strong command of English either have a long history of settlement in Australia (e.g., German, French) or come from societies where English is widely spoken alongside local languages (e.g., Hindi, Tamil, Filipino).

In the general population 26% of people are under the age of 20. Most of the communities in Table 2.2 show a slightly lower proportion of young people—standouts are Arabic (32%), Vietnamese (29%), and Turkish (27%) for the highest proportion and Italian (8%), Polish (11%), and German (14%) for the lowest. These figures point to the changing future of HL education in Australia, with demand for well-established European languages receding as their populations age. When we compare the proportion of speakers under 20 with that of speakers born in Australia, we can also note a variety of trends in language maintenance across generations. Loosely, we can classify languages into several groups. On the one hand we have languages such as Italian and Greek, which have a large proportion of second- (or even third- or fourth-)generation

Table 2.2 Selected Population Characteristics: Languages Spoken by More Than 50,000 Australians

Language	Born in Australia		Speaks English not well/not at all		Aged under 20	
	n	*%*	*n*	*%*	*n*	*%*
Mandarin	42,981	13	78,340	23	68,113	20
Italian	129,042	43	42,405	14	22,764	8
Arabic	119,090	41	46,032	16	91,576	32
Cantonese	58,381	22	64,695	25	52,316	20
Greek	137,199	54	41,510	16	40,070	16
Vietnamese	72,633	31	75,791	32	67,056	29
Spanish	29,331	25	14,473	12	20,676	18
Hindi	15,294	14	5,713	5	23,379	21
Tagalog	6,176	8	2940	4	14,768	18
German	17,839	22	2,538	3	11,191	14
Korean	11,072	14	25,921	32	20,346	26
Punjabi	8,870	12	6,037	8	12,300	17
Macedonian	28,654	42	11,450	17	11,629	17
Croatian	21,721	35	8,071	13	7,413	12
Turkish	26,013	44	11,912	20	16,240	27
French	14,165	25	2,689	5	11,102	19
Indonesian	9,570	17	4,986	9	13,311	24
Filipino	3,511	6	1,846	3	10,095	18
Serbian	14,717	27	9,856	18	10,640	19
Polish	11,577	23	5,566	11	5,453	11
Tamil	6,546	13	3,967	8	11,387	23

Source: Compiled from "Languages spoken at home" by age, place of birth, English proficiency, and Australia as place of residence [Data tables]. *Australian Census of Population and Housing, 2011*. Copyright 2011 by Australian Bureau of Statistics. (Australian Bureau of Statistics, 2012c).

speakers but relatively few young people. While these languages have been well maintained to date, they are likely to see fewer enrollments in HL classes in coming years. These stand in contrast to languages such as Turkish, Arabic, and Vietnamese, which have a large number of Australian-born speakers and those under 20 who may be interested in attending HL classes. Languages such as Filipino, Tamil, and Mandarin form a third group with relatively few second-generation speakers as yet, but relatively youthful populations. Children from these communities may be interested in attending more advanced HL classes that target those who have had some formal schooling in the HL. In the coming years we will also likely see growth in the number of second-generation speakers of these languages, who may be interested in attending HL classes pitched at a lower level.

In addition to the relatively large linguistic communities discussed so far, it is important to note the growing prominence of languages of our Pacific neighbors in Australia. Limited economic opportunities and the threat of climate change have seen mass migration from many Pacific islands, to the point where a number of languages now have a speaker base in Australia and mainland New Zealand that is almost as large as those in the ancestral homeland. These languages include Samoan, which had over 36,000 speakers in Australia in 2011, Tongan (16,000), and Cook Island Maori (4,600, with an additional 10,000 speakers of New Zealand Maori (see Starks, Gibson, and Bell (2015) for speaker numbers in New Zealand). Current numbers of speakers of Nuie, Tokelauen, and Tuvaluan in Australia are under 1,000 but can be expected to increase as climate change makes these islands uninhabitable and their entire populations are resettled.[3] The Royal Society of New Zealand (2013) emphasizes the role New Zealand should play in supporting the maintenance of these languages as an important question for language policy, and it is an area where Australia arguably needs to play a role if maintenance is to be successful.

4 Current Trends—Multilingual Practices of New Waves of Migrants

As globalization increases the ease with which people, goods, and ideas can spread around the world, the idea that migrants orient to a single host or heritage society and language is arguably too simplistic. As Duarte and Gogolin (2013, p. 4) note, the canonical immigrants, who move permanently once in their life from country X to country Y, is now joined in increasing numbers by those who have much more complex back and forward flows, such as temporary migration due to work or fleeing conflict, third country resettlement, or transnationals who maintain strong ongoing connections to their country of origin that may or may not lead to return migration in the future. Recent studies in regional and metropolitan Australia (Ndhlovu, 2013, 2014, 2015b; Willoughby, 2014) show that new waves of immigrants and diasporas have complex linguistic repertoires and cultural profiles that surpass current explanatory frames of multiculturalism and multilingualism paradigms.

African migrants with refugee backgrounds, in particular, are reported as having complex language profiles reflecting their convoluted migration journeys that took them through several countries as asylum seekers (Ndhlovu, 2013, 2014). All refugee background African migrants who participated in these studies indicated they each had different levels of knowledge of at least five languages, ranging from full proficiency to incomplete knowledge of unrelated language varieties. African immigrants and diaspora communities in regional and metropolitan Australia report using six language categories in ways that sidestep bureaucratic conceptual logics such as the census data presented in section 2 above. First are varieties of English, mainly African Englishes and Australian English, which are used across a range of domains including in employment and social networking processes with non-African background communities in Australia. The second category consists of African cross-border languages such as Swahili, Kriol, Arabic, and Amharic that are spoken across the national borders of more than two African countries. These were found to be important means of facilitating social networking and community building by people originally from the same regions in Africa. For example, Kriol and its variants is a common language for people from the West African nations of Liberia, Sierra Leone, Ghana, Nigeria, Gambia, and Cameroon. Similarly, Swahili is a common language for most people from Kenya, Tanzania, Uganda, Burundi, South Sudan, and Democratic Republic of Congo (DRC). A third category of languages is that of small ethnic languages spoken mainly at the family level where they function as a means for the intergenerational transmission of close-knit family ties and cultural practices. The fourth category is that of languages acquired along the refugee journey, in first, second, or third countries providing asylum. For instance, some people who migrated as refugees from the central African countries of DRC, Rwanda, and Burundi were found to be proficient in the Shona and Chinyanja languages of Zimbabwe and Zambia, respectively. African migrants from these central African countries acquired Shona and Chinyanja along their refugee journeys, which included several years as asylum seekers in Zambia and Zimbabwe prior to their permanent resettlement in Australia. These complex language profiles that are tied to migration histories and journeys are not captured in current bureaucratic language documentation practices that record HLs on the basis of nationality or country of origin/birth.

Similar issues arise around the relationship many immigrants have to Mandarin Chinese. As noted in section 2, Australia is home to thousands of speakers of Chinese varieties other than Mandarin, yet for political reasons only Mandarin is taught through the school system. The Chinese state has worked hard to promote the idea of Mandarin as a unifying language across the Chinese diaspora in recent years (Archer, Francis, & Mau, 2010), and this, together with the perceived utility of Mandarin as a world language, has seen Mandarin become very popular with families who have a Chinese background but who do not speak this language (and may not speak any Chinese variety) at home (Willoughby, 2014). Mandarin has also been heavily promoted to Australian students of all backgrounds as a modern foreign language, with the result that the constituency for high school Mandarin classes ranges from recent arrivals who have had most of their education in Mandarin (and want to maintain their skills and/or get an easy mark) through to heritage learners with varied degrees of proficiency, and finally to complete novices. Needless to say, this complex situation creates enormous difficulties in equitably assessing these students and demonstrates the need to offer Mandarin at varied proficiency levels with relatively strict criteria for who may enter lower level classes (for more on this issue see Elder, 2000; Scarino, 2012; Willoughby, 2014). Clearly, HL education in Australia is challenging not only because of the diverse relationships a student may have to the different languages in the repertoire, but also the varying skill levels we may see within a language group.

5 Conclusion

Global conditions of complex and unprecedented migration-driven diversity prompt the need for a reexamination and reflection on the theoretical toolkit needed for analyzing and understanding the phenomena of HLs. Traditional analytical categories such as "speech community," "ethnic group," "national language," "home language," and "mother tongue" are now very difficult to pin down in any meaningful way; and the often assumed relations between ethnicity, citizenship, residence, origin, legal status, religion, and language are no longer as straightforward as previously thought (Jørgensen & Juffermans, 2011). Migrant identities are now largely tied to shared migration histories and other cultural and social experiences that cut across the ethnic and speech community divide. While ethnicity and affiliation to specific speech communities or national language groups may still remain, they are no longer the sole prime markers of HL affiliations in predominantly immigrant societies where diasporas construct and (re)negotiate their identities on the basis of shared migration histories and other life experiences. This essentially means the current framing of multilingualism and language diversity in relation to HLs in Australia is fraught with many blind spots and unpromising associations. For example, the current bureaucratic counting of multiple standard languages equates to what could be termed "multiple monolingualisms" (Ndhlovu, 2014, p. 9), which does not necessarily translate into meaningful recognition of the multiple ways in which people with diverse migration histories and itineraries both conceptualize and use languages. What is being missed by such a view of multilingualism is that the issue is not so much about the "number" of such "objects" that are accommodated in HL education policies. Rather, the important point is how such entities are conceptualized and used in fluid and crisscrossing ways that eschew any easy generalization. This is particularly evidenced by the HL practices and profiles of new waves of migrants in Australia.

We therefore conclude that HLs and the associated notions of monolingualism and multilingualism need to be reconceptualized in order to accurately capture and describe the actual language practices of real people in everyday life where the linguistic identities of groups and individuals are not put into boxes of nationality or country of origin. As Blommaert, Leppänen, Pahta, Virkkula, and Räisänen (2012) advise us, we need to start from a strong awareness that the phenomenology of language in society has changed, has become more complex and less predictable than we thought it was. We have the advantage over earlier generations of being able to draw on a far more sophisticated battery of sociolinguistic insights and understandings (p. 18).

In line with these ideas of Blommaert et al. (2012), we suggest diversification of conceptual imaginings of HLs by drawing on what Ndhlovu (2015a) calls "ignored lingualism," a term that refers to those conceptualizations of language and linguistic usages that are currently not being recognized in the discourse and praxis of HL policy in linguistically and culturally diverse settings. For example, non-standard language varieties such as Kriol and Pidgin English spoken by people from the West African countries of Sierra Leone, Liberia, Nigeria, Ghana, and Cameroon are currently not recognized in Australian HL policy. Language varieties such as these defy nation-state-centric census ideologies of language and constitute a form of ignored lingualism because they do not sit well within the monolingual habitus of mainstream HL policy settings. Instead of seeing HLs as compartmentalized and countable objects that are tied to specific nation-states and national identities, we suggest they be seen as resources that can be employed strategically and socially in the form of fluid and transient language practices that cross the traditional boundaries of speech community and nationality.

Notes

1 The White Australia Policy legalized racism, discrimination, and the exclusion of non-white people from immigrating to Australia in favor of those of Anglo-Saxon heritage. The policy was crafted at the same time that Australia became a federation, composed of six formally disunited colonies, in 1901. Although this policy was gradually abolished beginning in the late 1950s and replaced with multiculturalism, its remnants continue to inform current debates and conversations on Australian national identity.
2 The 2011 census codes languages following the Australian Standard Classification of Languages (ASCL), Second Edition, Revision 1 (Australian Bureau of Statistics, 2011).
3 The resettlement plan for these islands is to move the population to New Zealand; however, Australia and New Zealand have a common migration zone allowing free movement of people between the two countries. The weak New Zealand economy means that over 600,000 New Zealand citizens currently live in Australia, many of whom are from Pasifika backgrounds (Australian government, n.d.).

References

Archer, L., Francis, B., & Mau, A. (2010). The culture project: Diasporic negotiations of ethnicity, identity and culture among teachers, pupils and parents in Chinese language schools. *Oxford Review of Education*, *36*(4), 407–426.

Australian Bureau of Statistics. (2009). *Information paper: Census of population and housing, nature and content, Australia 2011* (No. Cat. No. 2008.0). Canberra: Australian Bureau of Statistics.

Australian Bureau of Statistics. (2011). *Census dictionary, 2011.* Australian Standard Classification of Languages [ASCL]. Retrieved from http://www.abs.gov.au/ausstats/abs@.nsf/Lookup/2901.0Chapter6102011

Australian Bureau of Statistics. (2012a). TableBuilder Pro [Application for Australian 2011 Census data]. Retrieved from http://www.abs.gov.au/websitedbs/censushome.nsf/home/tablebuilder

Australian Bureau of Statistics. (2012b). Languages spoken at home by sex for Australia as a place of residence [Data tables]. *Australian Census of Population and Housing, 2011.* Retrieved from http://www.abs.gov.au/websitedbs/censushome.nsf/home/data

Australian Bureau of Statistics. (2012c). Languages spoken at home by age, place of birth, English proficiency, and Australia as a place of residence [Data tables]. *Australian Census of Population and Housing, 2011.* Retrieved from http://www.abs.gov.au/websitedbs/censushome.nsf/home/data

Australian Government. (n.d.). Department of immigration and border protection: Fact sheet—New Zealanders in Australia [Web page]. Retrieved from https://www.border.gov.au/about/corporate/information/fact-sheets/17nz

Blommaert, J., Leppänen, S., Pahta, P., Virkkula, T., & Räisänen, T. (Eds.). (2012). *Dangerous multilingualism: Northern perspectives on order, purity and normality.* London, UK: Palgrave Macmillan.

Clyne, M. (1991). *Community languages: The Australian experience.* Cambridge, UK: Cambridge University Press.

Clyne, M. (2005). *Australia's language potential.* Sydney, Australia: UNSW Press.

Commonwealth of Australia. (1902). *Commonwealth parliamentary debates: Session 1901–1902* (Vol. 3, 7 August, 1901, pp. 3500–3501). The Government of the Commonwealth of Australia.

Department of Employment, Education and Training, & Dawkins, J. (1991). *Australia's language: The Australian language and literacy policy: Companion volume to the policy information paper, August 1991.* Canberra, Australia: Australian Government Publishing Service.

Department of Immigration and Border Protection. (n.d.). Citizenship test. In *Citizenship pathways and processes.* Australian Government. Retrieved from https://www.border.gov.au/Trav/Citi/pathways-processes

Duarte, J., & Gogolin, I. (2013). Introduction: Linguistic superdiversity in educational institutions. In J. Duarte & I. Gogolin (Eds.), *Linguistic superdiversity in urban areas: Research approaches* (pp. 1–24). Amsterdam, Netherlands: John Benjamins Publishing.

Elder, C. (2000). Outing the native speaker: The problem of diverse learner backgrounds in "foreign" language classrooms—an Australian case study. *Language, Culture and Curriculum, 13*(1), 86–108.

Jørgensen, N., & Juffermans, K. (2011). Superdiversity. *NOW research network: A toolkit for transnational communication in Europe.* Retrieved from http://orbilu.uni.lu/handle/10993/6656

Karidakis, M., & Arunachalam, D. (2016). Shift in the use of migrant community languages in Australia. *Journal of Multilingual and Multicultural Development, 37*(1), 1–22.

Kipp, S., Clyne, M., & Pauwels, A. (1995). *Immigration and Australia's language resources.* Canberra: Australian Government Publishing Service.

Martin, J. (1978). *The migrant presence.* Sydney, Australia: George Allen & Unwin.

McNamara, T., & Roever, C. (2006). *Language testing: The social dimension.* Malden, UK: Blackwell Publishing.

McNamara, T., & Shohamy, E. (2008). Language tests and human rights. *International Journal of Applied Linguistics, 18*(1), 89–95.

Ndhlovu, F. (2008). A critical discourse analysis of the language question in Australia's immigration policies: 1901–1957. *ACRAWSA E-Journal, 4*(2), 1–14.

Ndhlovu, F. (2013). Language nesting, superdiversity and African diasporas in regional Australia. *Australian Journal of Linguistics, 33*(4), 426–448.

Ndhlovu, F. (2014). *Becoming an African diaspora in Australia: Language, culture, identity.* London, UK: Palgrave Macmillan.

Ndhlovu, F. (2015a). *Hegemony and language policies in Southern Africa: Identity, integration, development.* Newcastle upon Tyne, UK: Cambridge Scholars Publishers.

Ndhlovu, F. (2015b). Marginality and linguistic cartographies of African denizens as spheres of possibility in regional Australia. *Australasian Review of African Studies, 36*(1), 7–28.

Ozolins, U. (1993). *The politics of language in Australia.* Cambridge, UK: Cambridge University Press.

Parliament of Australia. (2013). Boat arrivals since 1976 by calendar year [Appendix A of Boat arrivals in Australia since 1976]. Retrieved from http://www.aph.gov.au/About_Parliament/Parliamentary_Departments/Parliamentary_Library/pubs/rp/rp1314/BoatArrivals#_Toc347230718

Royal Society of New Zealand. (2013). Languages in Aotearoa New Zealand. Retrieved from http://www.royalsociety.org.nz/media/Languages-in-Aotearoa-New-Zealand.pdf

Scarino, A. (2012). A rationale for acknowledging the diversity of learner achievements in learning particular languages in school education in Australia. *Australian Review of Applied Linguistics, 35*(3), 231–250.

Starks, D., Gibson, A., & Bell, A. (2015). Pasifika Englishes in New Zealand. In J. Williams, E. W. Schnei-
der, P. Trudgill, & D. Schreier (Eds.), *Further studies in the lesser-known varieties of English* (pp. 288–304).
Cambridge, UK: Cambridge University Press.

Tavan, G. (2005). *The long slow death of white Australia.* Melbourne, Australia: Scribe Publications.

Walker, L., & Heard, G. (2015). Interethnic partnering: Patterns by birthplace, ancestry and indigenous status.
In G. Heard & A. Dharmalingam (Eds.), *Family formation in 21st century Australia* (pp. 53–75). Dordrecht,
Netherlands: Dordrecht Springer.

Willoughby, L. (2014). Meeting the challenges of heritage language education: Lessons from one school
community. *Current Issues in Language Planning, 15*(3), 265–281.

3

The Demographics of Heritage and Community Languages in the United States

Terrence G. Wiley and Shereen Bhalla

In an attempt to document the linguistic profile of the United States (U.S.), this chapter addresses the linguistic demographic diversity of the country based on current and historical U.S. Census data, while noting the strengths and limitations of such data. It also references data from several major national surveys of foreign language (FL) education in an attempt to assess whether the country's efforts to promote education in languages other than English are improving or declining over time, and the extent to which educational programs are tapping into the vast pool of multilingualism within U.S. families. The chapter notes that the failure to adequately appreciate and tap into the nation's internal diversity represents a missed opportunity to build on its linguistic resources. In discussions regarding language diversity in the U.S., diversity is often presumed to be a problem or even a threat to linguistic unity and the hegemony of English (Wiley, 2004, 2005). Meanwhile, others decry what is perceived to be a FL learning crisis in this country, where the percentage of those learning FLs has declined. On closer analysis, language diversity within the country's population is often depicted as menacing, whereas the learning of FLs, initially by monolingual speakers of English, is seen to be a positive individual achievement (Wiley, 2007b). The chapter concludes by revisiting guidelines (Spolsky, 2011) for a national language policy that would recognize and build on the country's language diversity.

1 Sources of Language Diversity for the United States

The sources of linguistic diversity in the form of heritage and community languages[1] in the U.S. and its various territories are complex. Prior to the arrival of Spanish, English, Dutch, French, and Russian colonizers in the lands now under its domain, what eventually became the U.S. and its territories were inhabited by indigenous native peoples, who spoke a vast array of Native American and Pacific island languages, many of which remain today. Historically, Spanish is an old colonial language, but it became "native" to groups who were later conquered or annexed by the U.S. Despite having this fundamental relationship to the nation, it is now often considered an "immigrant" language, spoken by those from countries that have never been or are not currently under U.S. jurisdiction. Additional languages, such as Tagalog, Ilocano, and other languages of the Philippines are also difficult to classify. They are currently considered immigrant languages, although the Philippines came under American rule from 1898 through 1946. English itself is problematic in that it was an old colonial language that was also a major immigrant language, and is now considered a common language. Although the U.S. does not have an official language, English functions in that capacity for a majority of states, although Hawaii and New Mexico have co-official languages, Hawaiian and Spanish, respectively.

The sources of language diversity in the U.S. result from several phenomena rooted in American history: (1) immigration, both voluntary, as in the case of most European and recent immigrants, and involuntary, as in the case of enslaved Africans, (2) expansion through conquest or annexation, and (3) social transmission, both informal through family and community efforts, as well as through formal instruction. The policy disposition of the federal government and its constituent states toward language diversity has been somewhat mixed, ranging from active promotion to restriction. By the time of the first U.S. Census in 1790, over 60% of the European population identified as being "English" and another 18% identified as "Scotch," "Scotch Irish," or "Irish." Some knowledge of Celtic languages along with English can be assumed among these immigrants. Those indicating "German," "French," "Dutch," "Swedish," or "unassigned" accounted for about 21% (Parrillo, 2009, p. 67). Language data were not collected at that time; thus ethnic identification serves as a rough indicator of language background.

Among the large African-origin population, native languages had been repressed even as English literacy was restricted. Prior to the establishment of the U.S. as a republic, Southern colonies imposed the first restrictive language policies under the auspices of "slave codes" designed to regulate the language and literacy practices of enslaved Africans and those coming into contact with them. Slave codes prohibited the use of native African languages while also imposing "compulsorily ignorance laws," which prevented African Americans from becoming literate in English (Weinberg, 1995). Despite these repressive measures, there is evidence of the influence of African languages as well as literacy in Arabic among some of the enslaved (Lepore, 2002).

Native Americans were treated differently. Despite motivations to teach English to Native Americans during the colonial period, missionaries found it necessary to use Indian languages to communicate with this population (Gray, 1999). Gradually, a number of tribes developed some degree of bilingualism after contact with French, Spanish, and English colonizers. As recently as the nineteenth century some tribes, such as the Cherokee, had achieved a relatively high degree of native language literacy through their own school systems and presses (Weinberg, 1995). This came to an abrupt end with the imposition of compulsory English-only boarding schools from the 1880s through the 1930s. The boarding school movement resulted in rapid native language loss. In the early nineteenth century in Hawaii, native language literacy had been promoted by missionaries, resulting in nearly universal adult literacy in a short period. By the end of the century, however, Western diseases and subsequent education restrictions on the Hawaiian language resulted in the decimation of both the population and Hawaiian literacy (Beckman & Heck, 1998; Wilson, 2014). Overall, restrictive policies greatly disrupted the intergenerational transmission of languages among Native Americans and Pacific island peoples who had been incorporated into the U.S. and its territories.

European immigrants generally fared differently. German immigrants, for example, began coming to North American in the 1680s; thus, German settlements were widespread long before the establishment of the modern German State in 1871. Well into the nineteenth and

Table 3.1 Sources of Language Diversity throughout U.S. History and Mode of Incorporation/Transmission

Immigration Voluntary or Involuntary	Territorial Expansion Conquest or Annexation	Social Transmission Informally and Formally
■ Voluntary and involuntary (in the case of the enslaved) colonization and immigration to 1776 ■ Immigration from western Europe before and after the Civil War ■ Restricted Chinese immigration starting in 1882 followed by restrictions against other Asians ■ Continued Western European immigration, with increased Eastern European immigration through World War I (1914–1918) ■ Immigration quotas favoring Western Europeans from 1923 through 1965 ■ More equitable immigration policies following 1965 ■ Refugee integration	■ 13 British Colonies to 1776 ■ In 1779 the U.S. became a new nation that included territories as far west as the Mississippi ■ Subsequent westward expansion included the Louisiana Purchased in 1803, Florida ceded by Spain in 1821 ■ Texas Annexation (1845) ■ Mexican Cession of the southwest (1848) ■ Gadsden Purchase (1853) ■ Alaska purchased (1867) ■ Hawaii Annexation (1898) ■ Philippines (1901–1946) and Puerto Rico (1901) ■ Various Pacific Island Territories (1945)	■ Intergenerational transmission through the family and extended family networks ■ Language maintenance through social networks ■ Community-based language instruction ■ Formal language education, in public or private programs ■ Self-directed education ■ Transnational existences

twentieth centuries, German language education and bilingual education were prevalent in the U.S. (Luebke, 1980; Toth, 1990; Wiley, 1998). In the decades immediately following the American Civil War (1861–1865), German immigration rapidly increased, soon to be eclipsed by immigration from Eastern and Southern Europe by the 1890s and leading up to World War I (1914–1918). World War I, coupled with increasing anti-immigrant sentiment, unleashed widespread xenophobia and gave impetus to the Americanization movement (1915–1925), which promoted English while restricting instruction in FLs. Nevertheless, German and other European languages remained prevalent until late in the twentieth century (see Table 3.2). It was not until the 1970 U.S. Census that Spanish surpassed German as the second-most-spoken language in the U.S.

Largely as a result of changes in ethnically restrictive immigration policies after 1965, along with changes in international migration patterns, immigration from Mexico and Central America increased greatly along with immigration from Asian countries, from which it had previously long been restricted. Refugees from Cuba, Southeast Asia, and more recently a wide array of countries have added to the current linguistic diversity of the country. Despite the liberalization of immigration policies, the dominance of ideologies and educational policies emphasizing English results in rapid language shift to English and the failure to retain heritage and community languages (Arias & Faltis, 2012; McField, 2014; Moore, 2014; Wiley, Lee, & Rumberger, 2009).

Table 3.2 Mother Tongue of the Foreign-Born Population: 1910–1970

Language	All races		White			
	1970*	1960*	1940*	1930	1920	1910
Total	9,619,302	9,738,155	11,109,620	13,983,405	13,712,754	13,345,545
Mother tongue data available	9,523,155	9,360,179	10,861,120	13,941,172	13,705,588	13,229,273
English	1,697,825	1,937,184	(NA)	(NA)	(NA)	(NA)
Spanish (³)	1,696,240	813,429	428,360	743,286	556,111	258,131
German	1,201,535	1,332,399	1,589,040	2,188,006	2,267,128	2,759,032
Italian	1,025,994	1,277,585	1,561,100	1,808,289	1,624,998	1,365,110
Yiddish (²)	438,116	503,605	924,440	1,222,658	1,091,820	1,051,767
Polish	419,912	581,936	801,680	965,899	1,077,392	943,781
French	410,580	330,220	359,520	523,297	466,956	528,842
Uralic languages	199,543	266,286	338,300	378,196	423,986	349,180
Greek	193,745	180,781	165,220	189,066	174,658	118,379
Chinese	190,260	89,609	(NA)	(NA)	(NA)	(NA)
Hungarian	161,253	213,118	241,220	250,393	290,419	229,094
Tagalog	152,498	73,500	(NA)	(NA)	(NA)	(NA)
Russian (⁴)	149,277	276,834	356,940	315,721	392,049	57,926
Portuguese	140,299	91,592	83,780	110,197	105,895	72,649
Swedish	131,408	225,607	423,200	615,465	643,203	683,218
Dutch	127,834	130,482	102,700	133,142	136,540	126,045
Japanese	118,090	95,027	(NA)	(NA)	(NA)	(NA)
Ukrainian	96,635	106,974	35,540	68,485	55,672	25,131
Lithuanian	95,188	99,043	122,660	165,053	(NA)	(NA)
Norwegian	94,365	152,687	232,820	345,522	362,199	402,587
Serbo-Croatian (⁵)	83,064	86,957	70,600	109,923	125,844	105,669
Slovak	82,561	125,000	171,580	240,196	274,948	166,474
Arabic	73,657	49,908	50,940	67,830	57,557	32,868
Czech	70,703	91,711	159,640	201,138	234,564	228,738
Danish	58,218	85,421	122,180	178,944	187,162	183,844
Celtic (¹)	45,459	42,765	(NA)	(NA)	(NA)	(NA)
Armenian	38,323	37,270	40,000	51,741	37,647	23,938
Finnish	38,290	53,168	97,080	124,994	132,543	119,948
Hebrew (²)	36,112	38,346	(NA)	(NA)	(NA)	(NA)
Korean	34,748	8,550	(NA)	(NA)	(NA)	(NA)
Romanian	26,055	38,019	43,120	56,964	62,336	42,277

Language	All races		White			
	1970*	1960*	1940*	1930	1920	1910
Hindi	22,017	3,493	(NA)	(NA)	(NA)	(NA)
Flemish	20,801	30,254	31,900	42,263	45,696	25,780
Slovene	19,178	32,108	75,560	77,671	80,437	123,631
Turkish	16,646	14,063	(NA)	10,457	6,627	4,709
Persian	15,986	6,936	(NA)	(NA)	(NA)	(NA)
Asian and Pacific island languages n.e.c.	13,102	14,534	(NA)	(NA)	(NA)	(NA)
Thai (Laotian)	11,695	1,666	(NA)	(NA)	(NA)	(NA)
Albanian	7,528	7,297	(NA)	7,586	5,515	2,312
Indonesian languages	6,915	7,273	(NA)	(NA)	(NA)	(NA)
African languages	6,605	982	(NA)	(NA)	(NA)	(NA)
Native American languages	5,809	2,463	(NA)	(NA)	(NA)	(NA)
Polynesian languages	4,956	1,372	(NA)	(NA)	(NA)	(NA)
Basque	2,169	1,580	(NA)	(NA)	(NA)	(NA)
Caucasian	421	192	(NA)	(NA)	(NA)	(NA)
Bulgarian	(NA)	(NA)	(NA)	12,128	12,853	18,341
Lettish	(NA)	(NA)	(NA)	7,590	(NA)	(NA)
Other languages	325,074	360,019	389,240	446,026	481,543	382,048
Mother tongue n.e.c.	189,170	8,113	63,880	3,352	1,228	646
Mother tongue data not available	96,147	377,976	248,500	42,233	7,166	116,272

Note: *Indicates sample data; (NA) Not available; n.e.c. Not elsewhere classified.
  For 1970, includes 10,031 cases of Breton (which appears to be an unrealistically large number), and 10,208 cases of Other Balto-Slavonic languages. In 1960, the 535 cases of Breton were included with French. For 1960, includes 49,610 cases of Other Balto-Slavonic languages.
[1]For 1970, assumes that all individuals with Celtic mother tongue are White.
[2]For 1910–1940, Hebrew is included with Yiddish.
[3]For White in 1960, the published estimate (794,714) includes Basque. The estimate here assumes that all individuals with Basque mother tongue (1,580) are White.
[4]For 1920, probably includes a "considerable proportion" of individuals of Yiddish mother tongue erroneously reported as of Russian mother tongue. See sources in text.
[5]For White in 1960, the published estimate (87,997) includes Dalmatian. The estimate here assumes that all individuals with Dalmatian mother tongue (1,137) are White.

Source: Adapted from "Historical Census Statistics on the Foreign-Born Population of the United States: 1850 to 2000," by C. Gibson and K. Jung (2006), U.S. Census Bureau Working Paper Number POP-WP081.

2 Data Sources for Demographic Analyses of the Diversity in the U.S. National Population

The primary source of data for language diversity has come from the decennial censuses held by the U.S. Census Bureau, which was first conducted in 1790. The 2000 Census was the last one to include questions on place of birth and language. Those questions are now asked in the American Community Survey (ACS), which is also directed by the U.S. Census Bureau. ACS is an ongoing survey that samples three million households per year to estimate demographic indicators between the censuses. ACS's Question 14 asks informants whether they speak a language other than English at home; if so, they are asked to name that language, and also to say how well they speak English (very well, well, not well, not at all) (U.S. Census Bureau, 2016).

Table 3.3 Languages Other Than English Most Commonly Spoken in the Home

Languages other than English most commonly spoken in the home, 2006–2010	Languages other than English most commonly spoken in the home, 2008–2012
1 Spanish	1 Spanish
2 Chinese	2 Chinese
3 French	3 Hindi
4 Hindi	4 French
5 Vietnamese	5 Vietnamese
6 German	6 German
7 Korean	7 Arabic
8 Arabic	8 Korean
9 Filipino/Tagalog	9 Filipino/Tagalog
10 Russian	10 Russian

Source: Created from American Community Survey data using the Integrated Public Use Microdata Series (Ruggles et al., 2010).

3 School-Based Data for Foreign Language Instruction

In assessing the role of formal education in promoting heritage and community languages in the U.S., one of the foremost challenges results from the manner in which questions about languages are framed. Languages other than English are typically categorized as "foreign" or "modern" and more recently "world" languages. Occasionally, data are being tracked for programs in, for example, "Spanish for native speakers," or "Vietnamese literacy for native speakers," where "native" for the most part refers to heritage students, but comprehensive data regarding the number or percentage of heritage learners are lacking. Even in the case of FL instruction, large-scale data, particularly up-to-date comprehensive data, are difficult to find.

For K–12 school data, the two most important sources come from periodic surveys conducted by the Center for Applied Linguistics (CAL) and the American Council on the Teaching of Foreign Languages (ACTFL). CAL conducted three nationally representative surveys in 1987, 1997, and 2008 of K–12 public and private school programs to determine which languages are being taught and what percentage of schools is offering them at the elementary, middle, and secondary levels (Rhodes & Pufahl, 2010; Ruggles et al., 2010). These surveys have focused primarily on programmatic practices that help to ascertain national trends across time (comparing 1987, 1997,

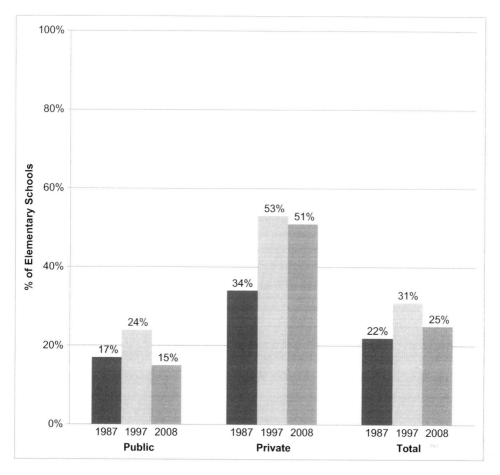

Figure 3.1   U.S. Elementary Schools Teaching Foreign Languages (Public, Private, Total) (1987, 1997, 2008)

Source: Reprinted with permission from "Foreign Languages Offered by Elementary Schools with Foreign Language Programs" by I. Pufahl and N. C. Rhodes, 2011, *Foreign Language Annals, 44*(2), p. 261. Copyright 2011 by Foreign Language Annals.

and 2008) and have been particularly useful in documenting increases or declines in the percent of programs offering various languages. By focusing on FL instruction, these surveys have not provided data on instruction specifically targeting heritage-community education programs (Fee, Rhodes, & Wiley, 2014).

In Figure 3.1, the decline in offerings of FL instruction between 1997 and 2008 is evident. In 1997, approximately 31% of elementary schools taught FLs compared with 25% in 2008. This results in a statistically significant decrease of 6% in FL instruction. However, Figure 3.1 also shows that a reverse trend occurred between 1987 and 1997, when the percentage of elementary schools offering FLs jumped from 22% to 31%, resulting in an almost 10% increase before the 6% decline between 1997 and 2008.

Similar to the decline in elementary school language instruction, middle and high schools also saw a drop in schools offering FL instruction between 1997 and 2008, from 86% to 79%

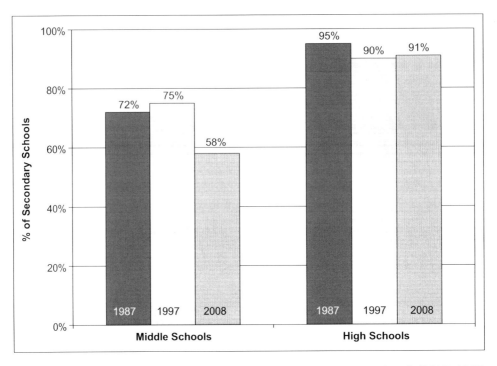

Figure 3.2 U.S. Middle and High Schools Teaching Foreign Languages (Total) (1987, 1997, 2008)

Source: Reprinted with permission from "Foreign Languages Offered by Elementary Schools with Foreign Language Programs" by I. Pufahl and N. C. Rhodes, 2011, *Foreign Language Annals, 44*(2), p. 262. Copyright 2011 by Foreign Language Annals.

(see Figure 3.2). One reason for this decline is the decrease of language instruction at the middle school level from 1997, when 75% of middle schools offered language instruction, to 2008, when the percentage decreased to 58%. However, both private and public high schools maintained FL instruction in the same range, with a slight decrease from 95% in 1987 to 91% in 2008.

When examining FL programs in primary and secondary schools, Spanish was the most commonly taught language and increased in the number of offerings from 1997 to 2008. In 2008, 88% of the elementary schools with language programs taught Spanish, compared to 79% in 1997 (Figure 3.3). From 1997 to 2008, Spanish was offered by 93% of secondary schools with language programs. In 1997, 19% of all public elementary schools in the U.S. taught Spanish; in 2008, only 12% did. Similarly, in 1997, 62% of all U.S. middle schools taught Spanish; in 2008, only 55% did. On the other hand, in 1997, 41% of all private elementary schools nationwide offered Spanish, while in 2008, 46% did (Fee et al., 2014, pp. 10–11).

In terms of other languages, both French and German were offered in fewer schools between 1997 and 2008. Latin and Japanese were also less frequently offered at secondary schools in 2008 compared to 1997. In addition, in spite of Chinese being the second-most-spoken language other than English in the U.S., the total number of schools offering Chinese is relatively small, 3%–4%.

Turning to the national survey conducted by ACTFL (American Council on the Teaching of Foreign Languages [ACTFL], 2010), important data on K–12 language instruction from this

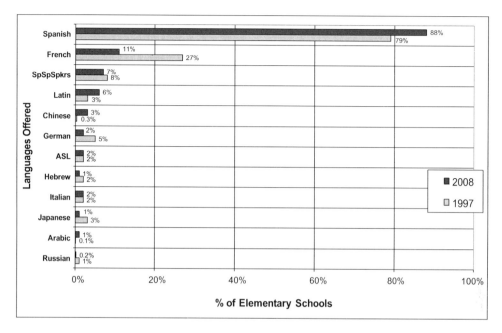

Figure 3.3 Foreign Languages Offered by Elementary Schools with Foreign Language Programs

Note: "SpSpSpkrs" stands for "Spanish for Spanish speakers."

Source: Reprinted with permission from "Foreign Languages Offered by Elementary Schools with Foreign Language Programs" by I. Pufahl and N. C. Rhodes, 2011, *Foreign Language Annals, 44*(2), p. 264. Copyright 2011 by Foreign Language Annals.

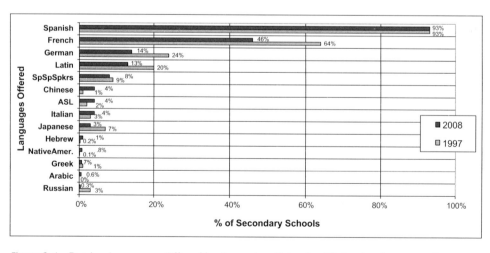

Figure 3.4 Foreign Languages Offered by Secondary Schools with Foreign Language Programs

Note: "SpSpSpkrs" stands for "Spanish for Spanish speakers."

Source: Reprinted with permission from "Foreign Languages Offered by Elementary Schools with Foreign Language Programs" by I. Pufahl and N. C. Rhodes, 2011, *Foreign Language Annals, 44*(2), p. 265. Copyright 2011 by Foreign Language Annals.

source adds to our understanding of the topic. Whereas the CAL surveys have focused on program data, ACTFL focuses on FL enrollment data collected from the various states. Thus, looking at the CAL and ACTFL surveys provides useful information regarding both programs and enrollments. The strength of the ACTFL survey is that it attempts to provide comprehensive national data by language and state; however, it is dependent on how well the various states collect and report such data. For this reason, ACTFL was not able to provide data for all 50 states; only 34 reported. Additionally, ACTFL has, thus far, collected data without disaggregating enrollments for students who may be heritage or community language learners, given that few programs make this distinction.

In an attempt to begin addressing this issue, Fee et al. (2014) compared the ACTFL K–12 FL enrollment data for selected states against ACS census data reporting on the number of potential heritage learners living in households where languages other than English are being spoken. This comparison provides a crude indicator regarding how many potential heritage-community language (HL-CL) learners might be enrolled in FL courses. However, we can assume that many students enrolled in such classes are not HL-CL learners, but are true FL learners. Thus, where we see a much higher number of potential HL-CL learners in comparison to the actual number of learners, we can assume that there is a significant lack of participation by potential HL-CL learners. These numbers correspond to Fee, Rhodes, and Wiley's (2014) findings, and are reflected in the updated ACS-ACTFL comparisons for selected states shown in Figure 3.6.

4 Student Enrollment in Foreign Language Classroom

In addition to the decline in the number of FL programs in primary and secondary schools, enrollment in these classes also declined. According to Fee et al. (2014), in 2008 an estimated 4.2 million out of 27.5 million elementary school students (15%) in the U.S. were enrolled in FL classes. From 1997 to 2008, the number of public elementary school students enrolled in language classes declined from 2.5 million to 2.2 million, while the number of private elementary school students enrolled in language classes increased from 1.5 million to almost 2 million (Fee et al., 2014).

At the secondary school level, an estimated 10.5 million students out of 25.7 million (41%) were enrolled in language classes in 2008, a decrease from nearly 12 million (52%) in 1997. Of the students participating in language classes in 2008, about 2.3 million attended middle or junior high schools, 6.7 million attended high schools, and 1.5 million attended combined junior/senior high schools (Fee et al., 2014).

Figure 3.5 compares languages other than English spoken in the home. Spanish remains dominant in the homes of school-aged children in the U.S. overall. However, over two million 5–18-year-olds live in homes where languages other than Spanish are spoken. The nine other languages listed in Figure 3.5 (Chinese, Hindi, French, Vietnamese, German, Arabic, Korean, Filipino/Tagalog, and Russian) are very rarely offered for heritage language (HL) study in primary or secondary schools (Fee et al., 2014).

In comparing the list of the top 10 languages spoken in homes in the U.S. against the most commonly taught FLs in U.S. schools, it becomes clear that there is a disconnect between FL education and HL skills. The ACTFL (2012) survey examined K–12 student FL enrollment and found a significant discrepancy between the languages of HL-speaking students and FL enrollment. The 10 most commonly spoken languages in homes by 5–18-years-olds based on 2007 through 2011 ACS data compared against the top FLs studied in K–12 schools based on the ACTFL 2007–2008 student enrollment study are shown in Figure 3.6.

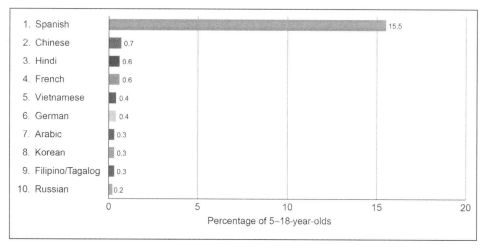

Figure 3.5 Languages Most Commonly Spoken in the Home in the U.S., 5–18-Year-Olds (2008–2012) without Subgroups

Source: Created from American Community Survey data using the Integrated Public Use Microdata Series (Ruggles et al., 2010).

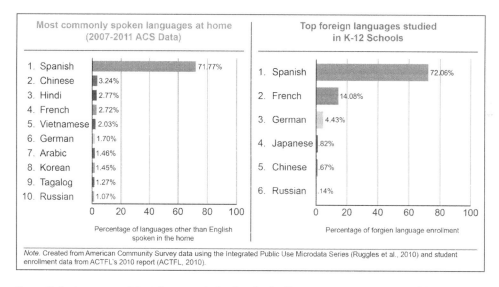

Figure 3.6 Languages Most Commonly Spoken in the Home among 5–18-Year-Olds (American Community Survey, ACS Data) versus Foreign Languages Studied in K–12 Schools (2007–2008) (ACTFL Student Enrollment Data).

Source: Created from American Community Survey data using the Integrated Public Use Microdata Series (Ruggles et al., 2010) and student enrollment data from ACTFL's 2010 report (ACTFL, 2010).

Figure 3.6 demonstrates how little FL enrollment reflects HL communities and HL speakers in U.S. schools. While Spanish ranks number one on both lists, most Spanish FL courses are not designed for Spanish heritage speakers. As shown in Figures 3.3 and 3.4 above, CAL's 2008 national survey found that only 7% of elementary schools and 8% of secondary schools with FL programs offered Spanish for Spanish Speakers courses (Rhodes & Pufahl, 2010). The data presented in Figures 3.2, 3.3, 3.4, and 3.5 indicate that FL education has not responded to the demographic changes occurring within immigrant and HL-speaking communities in the United States (see Kagan, this volume, for a discussion of this phenomenon in Los Angeles). Despite having moved up to the third and seventh spots, respectively, as the most commonly spoken languages in homes with 5–18-year-olds, Hindi and Arabic are noticeably missing from FL enrollment data in the United States. Furthermore, Vietnamese, Korean, and Tagalog are not commonly found in FL offerings either. These languages represent missed opportunities to encourage and promote the language development of heritage speakers.

5 Trends in Higher Education

Since 1958, the Modern Language Association (MLA) has conducted and analyzed data to determine which languages have seen significant increases or decreases in U.S. higher education. In 2009, as part of this series, the MLA published a report of a survey that examined enrollments in languages other than English in higher education institutions (Modern Language Association [MLA], 2010). The MLA's 2010 report analyzes survey data collected in fall 2009 of undergraduate- and graduate-level enrollments in courses offered in languages other than English. Findings from the 2009 survey represent almost 99.9% of all higher educational intuitions in the United States (MLA, 2010).

The report found that enrollment ratios for the top 10 most studied languages stayed unchanged from the MLA's previous report based on survey data collected in 2006. Spanish continues to be the most studied language on college campuses with a 5.1% increase in enrollment since 2006 (MLA, 2010). Additionally, Spanish, French, German, and American Sign Language (ASL) remain the most studied languages among undergraduate and graduate students, despite a slow pace in enrollment gains. Arabic saw an increase of 46.3% from 2006 to 2009, jumping from the 10th most studied language in 2006 to the 8th in 2009. Italian, Japanese, and Chinese were the 5th, 6th, and 7th most studied languages, with Latin and Russian completing the list of the top 10 enrollments (MLA, 2010).

6 Conclusion: The Need for a Comprehensive Policy That Embraces the Multilingual Reality of the United States

Recent concerns about the "foreign language education crisis" based on some of the dismal statistics on FL education in the U.S. are not new (Wiley, 2007a, 2007b). The late U.S. Senator Paul Simon, for example, drew attention to this in his book, *The Tongue-Tied American: Confronting the Foreign Language Crisis*, first published in 1980. Senator Simon focused on three major areas where he felt the United States was weakened by the lack of foreign-language abilities: national security, diplomacy, and international business. Decades later, his themes still resonate in public policy debates, with increased focus on defense and national security concerns, as the testimony of a recent federal panel indicate:

> Currently, only 74 percent of the State Department's "language-designated" positions are filled with adequately qualified personnel while only 28% of language jobs at the Defense

Department are "filled with personnel at the required foreign-language proficiency level," remarked Laura Junor, a deputy assistant secretary of defense, in her statement. . . . Without a fully capable team working on the nation's most pressing international conflicts and diplomacy issues, national security is compromised. The prospects of the next generation filling the gaps are dire. As Eduardo Ochoa, the Education Department's assistant secretary of post-secondary education reported, only 30 percent of high school students and eight percent of post-secondary students are enrolled in a foreign language course. As for less-commonly taught critical languages, less than one percent of post-secondary students are enrolled in courses.

(Editorial, Language Magazine*)*

In attempting to identify the cause of the U.S.'s failure to promote foreign language education, Simon (1980) lamented the influence of the early twentieth century Americanization movement, with its emphasis on English only and anti-foreign-language stance, which still held sway in popular discourse and ideologies about learning languages in the U.S. In fact, the 1980s saw a resurgence of anti-immigrant sentiment in the form of the English-Only movement that targeted "foreign" immigrant languages (Wiley, 2004). Today, we can add to that movement's lingering influence perceptions regarding the rise of English, an international language, which have resulted in complacency for some that knowing English is sufficient given its much-hyped role in the global economy and, particularly, in global higher education. It is clear today, as it was to Simon decades ago, that the fundamental reasons for the lack of policies and programs relate to a failure to value and nurture the linguistic resources within the population of the multilingual U.S. This is not a demographic problem but a failure to provide a guiding strategy that could "bring together the issues of foreign, heritage, and immigrant languages and start to build a unified policy that will include heritage languages . . . and the traditional values of learning other languages and cultures" (Spolsky, 2011, p. 5).

Spolsky (2011) has outlined a number of principles that could help to guide such an effort: "The first is the development of policies to ensure that there is no linguistic discrimination— that languages and speakers of specific languages are not ignored in the provision of civic services" (p. 5). These are essentially "protective rights"—that is, protections from discrimination (Wiley, 2007b). Next, there is a need to ensure that there are "adequate programs for teaching English to all, native-born or immigrant, old or young" (Spolsky, 2011, p. 5). This would require "the development of respect both for multilingual capacity, the cognitive advantages of which have been shown (Bialystok, 2001; Spolsky, 2011), and for diverse individual languages" (p. 5). Spolsky contends that this would require "a multi-branched language capacity program that

- strengthens and integrates a variety of language education programs;
- connects heritage programs with advanced training programs;
- builds on heritage and immersion and overseas-experience approaches to constantly replenish a cadre of efficient multilingual citizens capable of professional work using their multilingual skills; and
- provides rich and satisfying language instruction that leads to a multilingual population with knowledge of and respect for other languages and cultures" (p. 5).

A national policy with such a broad, comprehensive scope would help to recognize and build on the significant language diversity within the United States while helping to better link the country's citizens with a multilingual world.

Note

1 "Heritage language" tends to be the widely accepted expression in the U.S. when referring to speakers or learners of ancestral or family and community languages in addition to English, the dominant language. The HL label, however, is not always preferred or accepted in all contexts, particularly outside the U.S., or even inside the U.S. by some Native American language speakers (see Wiley, 2014 for elaboration on the definition and utility of the construct). Thus, our preference is to use "heritage and community" languages to be more inclusive for those who prefer not to use or identify with the HL label.

References

American Council on the Teaching of Foreign Languages (ACTFL). (2010). *Foreign language enrollments in K–12 public schools: Are students prepared for a global society?* Alexandria, VA: Author.

Arias, M. B., & Faltis, C. (2012). *Implementing educational language policy in Arizona: Legal, historical and current practices in SEI.* Bristol, UK: Multilingual Matters.

Bialystok, E. (2001). *Bilingualism in development: Language, literacy, and cognition.* Cambridge, UK: Press Syndicate of the University of Cambridge.

Beckman, M. K. P., & Heck, R. H. (1998). *Culture and education in Hawaii: The silencing of native voices.* Mahwah, NJ: Lawrence Erlbaum.

Editorial: Feds Face Foreign Language Crisis. [Editorial]. (n.d.). Language magazine. Retrieved from http://languagemagazine.com/?page_id=4182

Fee, M., Rhodes, N. C., & Wiley, T. G. (2014). Demographic realities, challenges, and opportunities. In T. G. Wiley, J. K. Peyton, D. Christian, S. K. Moore, & N. Liu (Eds.), *Handbook on heritage, community, and Native American language education in the United States: Research, policy and practice* (pp. 6–18). London, UK: Routledge.

Gibson, C., & Jung, K. (2006). *Historical census statistics on the foreign-born population of the United States: 1850 to 2000: U.S. Census Bureau working paper number POP-WP081.* Washington, DC: U.S. Census Bureau. Retrieved from http://www.census.gov/library/working-papers/2006/demo/POP-twps0081.html

Gray, E. G. (1999). *New world Babel: Languages and nations in early America.* Princeton, NJ: Princeton University Press.

Lepore, J. (2002). *A is for American: Letters and other characters in the newly United States.* New York, NY: Vintage.

Luebke, F. C. (1980). Legal restrictions on foreign languages in the Great Plains states, 1917–1923. In P. Schach (Ed.), *Languages in conflict: Linguistic acculturation on the great plains* (pp. 1–19). Lincoln, NE: University of Nebraska Press.

McField, G. P. (Ed.). (2014). *The miseducation of English learners: A tale of three states and lessons to be learned.* Charlotte, NC: Information Age Publishing.

Modern Language Association (MLA). (2010). Enrollments in languages other than English in United States institutions of higher education, Fall 2009. Retrieved from http://www.mla.org/pdf/2009_enrollment_survey.pdf

Moore, S. C. K. (2014). *Language policy processes and consequences: Arizona case studies.* Bristol, UK: Multilingual Matters.

Parrillo, V. N. (2009). *Diversity in America* (3rd ed.). Los Angeles, CA: Pine Forge Press.

Pufahl, I., & Rhodes, N. C. (2011). Foreign language instruction in U.S. schools: Results of a national survey of elementary and secondary schools. *Foreign Language Annals, 44*(2), 258–288.

Rhodes, N. C., & Pufahl, I. (2010). *Foreign language teaching in U.S. schools: Results of a national survey.* Washington, DC: Center for Applied Linguistics.

Ruggles, S., Alexander, J. T., Genadek, K., Goeken, R., Schroeder, M. B., & Sobek, M. (2010). *Integrated public use microdata series: Version 5.0 [Machine-readable database].* Minneapolis, MN: University of Minnesota.

Simon, P. (1980). *The tongue-tied American: Confronting the foreign language crisis.* New York, NY: Continuum.

Spolsky, B. (2011). *Does the United States need a language policy?* Washington, DC: Center for Applied Linguistics. Retrieved from http://www.cal.org/resource-center/briefs-digests/digests/%28offset%29/15

Toth, C. (1990). *German-English bilingual schools in America: The Cincinnati tradition in historical context.* New York, NY: Peter Lang.

U.S. Census Bureau. (2016). *Why we ask: Language spoken at home, American Community Survey (ACS).* Washington, DC: Author. Retrieved from http://www2.census.gov/programs-surveys/acs/about/qbyqfact/2016/Language.pdf

Weinberg, M. (1995). *A chance to learn: A history of race and education in the United States.* Long Beach, CA: California State University Press.

Wiley, T. G. (1998). The imposition of World War I era English-only policies and the fate of German in North America. In T. Ricento & B. Burnaby (Eds.), *Language and politics in the United States and Canada: Myths and realities* (pp. 211–242). Mahwah, NJ: Lawrence Erlbaum Associates.

Wiley, T. G. (2004). Language policy and English-only. In E. Finegan & J. R. Rickford (Eds.), *Language in the USA: Perspectives for the twenty-first century* (pp. 319–338). Cambridge, UK: Cambridge University Press.

Wiley, T. G. (2005). *Literacy and language diversity in the United States* (2nd ed.). Washington, DC and McHenry, IL: Center for Applied Linguistics & Delta Systems.

Wiley, T. G. (2007a). The foreign language "crisis" in the U.S.: Are heritage and community languages the remedy? *Critical Inquiry in Language Studies, 4*(2–3), 179–205.

Wiley, T. G. (2007b). Heritage and community languages in the national language debate. *Modern Language Journal, 91*(2), 252–255.

Wiley, T. G. (2014). The problem of defining heritage and community languages and their speakers: On the utility and limitations of definitional constructs. In T. G. Wiley, J. K. Peyton, D. Christian, S. K. Moore, & N. Liu (Eds.), *Handbook on heritage, community, and Native American language education in the United States: Research, policy and practice* (pp. 19–26). London, UK: Routledge.

Wiley, T. G., Lee, J. S., & Rumberger, R. W. (2009). *The education of language minority immigrants in the United States.* Bristol, UK: Multilingual Matters.

Wilson, W. H. (2014). Hawaiian: A Native American language official for a state. In T. G. Wiley, J. K. Peyton, D. Christian, S. K. Moore, & N. Liu (Eds.), *Handbook on heritage, community, and Native American language education in the United States: Research, policy and practice* (pp. 219–228). London, UK: Routledge.

4

Demographics and Heritage Languages in Latin America

An Overview

André Zampaulo

1 Introduction

For more than five hundred years, Latin America has hosted and incorporated a substantial number of diverse immigrant communities from around the world. From its colonial period under the rule of Spain, Portugal, and other European countries, to its fast-paced integration with the globalized world in current times, this region has represented a beacon for immigrants who left their native countries in search of new opportunities and, thus, have helped form local identities, both in the past and in the present. Many scholars have centered their efforts on understanding the historical immigration trends and the mosaic of motivations for immigrant waves to Latin American countries. However, much still remains to be explored and unveiled, particularly with regard to the patterns of heritage language (HL) maintenance and the shifts within the immigrant communities that have established themselves in the new world.

This chapter presents an overview of the most prominent immigration patterns in Latin America, especially those during the nineteenth and twentieth centuries, as well as the current status of immigrant languages vis-à-vis the dominant societal languages in the region, namely Spanish and Portuguese. In particular, special attention is drawn to demographic information about different generations of immigrant communities and how their languages are manifested today as a mark of their heritage. Due to the region's extensive territory, this chapter focuses on the demographics and languages of immigrant communities within a select group of countries, namely, Mexico in North America and Peru, Argentina, and Brazil in South America. While every effort is made to provide the reader with a thorough overview of both historical and present-day issues pertaining to the languages of immigrant communities in each of those countries, the defining presence and impact of certain immigrant groups invariably receives more consideration than others. Such is the case of Western European immigrants, particularly Italians and Germans in Brazil and Argentina, and Asian immigrants, primarily the large Japanese communities in Brazil and in Peru. As will be argued, these and other immigrant groups have contributed to shaping Latin American social and linguistic identity while still retaining traits of their descent and, in some cases, promoting their heritage through the use of language and the expression of cultural norms. As an overview, the content of this chapter aims to represent a reference and a springboard for further exploration of issues on demographics and HLs in Latin

America, while contributing to the increasing body of research on this topic in conjunction with other regions rich in immigrant communities and HLs, such as the United States and Canada. The many indigenous communities of Latin America, while contributing to the variety of HLs in the region, will not be the focus of this chapter.

This chapter is organized as follows. The next section details the main immigrant waves to Latin America during the second half of the nineteenth century through the first three decades of the twentieth century, a post-independence period during which the identity of most Latin American countries was being shaped and in which immigrants from Europe and Asia played a remarkable role. Subsequently, this chapter presents a snapshot of what has happened since those massive immigrant waves to the region, particularly with regard to the consequences of their assimilation into the local culture and the maintenance of their language (or lack thereof) by subsequent generations. Concluding remarks are offered in the final section of the chapter, along with possible issues to be explored by further research.

2 Immigration Patterns to Latin America

In simplistic terms, Latin America represents an intercontinental region comprised of countries from North, Central, and South America, where Romance languages predominate, namely, Spanish, Portuguese, French, and their creole varieties. A total of 20 republics are traditionally considered to be part of this region: Mexico in North America; six out of the seven countries in Central America (Belize being the only exception, since English is its official language); Cuba, the Dominican Republic, and Haiti in the Caribbean; and 10 republics of South America (all but Guyana, Suriname, and French Guiana). However, geographical location and linguistic heritage are not the only factors that set this region apart. Despite their many differences in size, climate, population, and social development, Latin American countries—particularly those that formed part of the Spanish and Portuguese empires—share a similar colonial past, which is crucial to understanding not only the process of their independence (mostly during the first half of the nineteenth century) but also their patterns of economic and social development and the shaping of their overall identity.

Since the inception of its colonization process by European explorers at the end of the fifteenth century, Latin America has represented a land of new opportunities for immigrants from all over the world, who have contributed decisively to the history of the region. Throughout the colonial period, the Spanish and the Portuguese composed the vast majority of immigrants to the region. Although it is difficult to determine the exact number of immigrants during this period, researchers argue that European immigrants did not arrive in great numbers at first. Marcílio (1984), for example, points out that by the mid-1500s there were approximately three to four thousand Europeans in Brazil. By the end of the seventeenth century, however, Europeans already represented one third of Brazil's 300,000 inhabitants. Although most of these were of Portuguese descent, foreigners from other parts of the world were also found, e.g., immigrants who had fled from religious persecution; French, Dutch, and English explorers; and, of course, a large number of slaves who had been brought from Africa. In the Spanish-speaking colonies, by contrast, the population featured mainly Spaniards, indigenous peoples, and African slaves, since the Spanish crown enforced tighter immigration rules both for Spaniards and nationals of other countries (Sánchez-Albornoz, 1984). Not until the mid-nineteenth century, after the independence of most Latin American countries, did immigrants begin to arrive in massive numbers, particularly from other parts of Europe, due to political and economic factors.

After lifting most of their immigration restrictions from colonial times, the newly independent countries in Latin America now welcomed new waves of immigrants, particularly from

Europe. As Sánchez-Albornoz (1986) points out, for example, Swiss and German immigrants established their colonies in southern Brazil and Chile, where they "prospered and preserved their language" (p. 126). In some cases, foreigners constituted a majority of the population, as was the case in Uruguay where, in 1868, almost three-fourths of the nation's population was of foreign origin (cf. also Oddone, 1986). In fact, from the 1870s to the 1930s, Latin America, and more prominently Argentina and Brazil, received a large number of immigrants, particularly from Western Europe. The main cause for their exodus was economic in nature, as Latin America offered a favorable environment, especially in agriculture. With the abolition of slavery and the region's need for workers in the fields, coupled with the availability of manpower in Europe and the willingness to emigrate in response to political and economic crises, immigrants sought promising opportunities to build a better life in the New World. As for Asian immigrants, Chinese nationals also participated in this wave, constituting almost 2% of the Peruvian population in 1876 and 3% of the Cuban population a year later (cf. de la Riva, 1966).

In general, however, it is difficult to establish the exact number of immigrants to Latin America between the late nineteenth and the early twentieth centuries, since there is no agreement between the official records of the immigrants' countries of origin and that of their final destination. Additionally, many immigrants did not settle permanently in one place, while others arrived illegally. Nevertheless, it is estimated that between six and eight million immigrants arrived in Brazil, Argentina, Uruguay, and Chile between 1881 and 1930 (Sánchez-Albornoz, 1986), making these countries, together with Cuba, the main immigration destinations during this period. On the other hand, Mexico, despite having the second largest population in Latin America, received only roughly 30,000 immigrants during the first three decades of the twentieth century, mainly because of the political instability resulting from the revolution it went through at that time.

Among the nationalities that composed the immigration waves and contributed the most to Latin America were Italians, Spaniards, Portuguese, Germans, Slavs, Middle-Easterners, and the Japanese. Italians, however, formed the largest immigrant group of all, representing about half the immigrant population by the end of the nineteenth century. In Brazil, for example, Italians represented 36% of the four million immigrants admitted to the country, most of whom settled in the state of São Paulo. Spaniards came in third in Brazil, after the Portuguese, constituting about half a million immigrants. Approximately 300,000 Germans arrived between 1824 and the 1940s, especially in southern Brazil, where they established most of their colonies. Following World War I, in the early twentieth century, immigrants from Poland, Russia, and the former Austro-Hungarian Empire also joined the immigration wave from Europe, alongside Syrians and Lebanese nationals, although these groups never reached the large numbers that Western Europeans did.

From outside of Europe, however, came another important immigrant group—the Japanese—who initially arrived in Brazil at the beginning of the twentieth century to work on coffee farms, but soon moved to the cities, especially São Paulo, where they established the largest Japanese community outside Japan. Researchers estimate that about 70,000 Japanese immigrants arrived in Brazil during the first three decades of the twentieth century, ranking first among immigrant groups by 1934 (Sánchez-Albornoz, 1986; cf. also Tsuchida, 1978). In addition to Brazil, the Japanese also founded important communities in Mexico and Peru. From 1890 to 1978, a total of seven waves of Japanese immigration had arrived in Mexico, totaling about 10,000 immigrants, whose main destinations were Sonora, Coahuila, Baja California, and Mexico City (Mishima, 1982). As is the case in many current Japanese communities abroad, private schools were established so that children of Japanese descent could not only learn their parents' and grandparents' language, but also keep in touch with their heritage culture. Peru was the second most preferred destination for Japanese immigrants in South America, after Brazil. Today Peru's Japanese community (i.e., immigrants and their descendants) is estimated to be around 90,000 members (Córdoba Toro, 2014). The impact of their community on Peruvian culture is felt particularly in sports, literature, and politics. In fact, a descendant of Japanese immigration, former president Alberto Fujimori, governed the country from 1990 to 2000.

Finally, in Central America, neither the Japanese nor the Europeans arrived in massive numbers. Instead, 145,000 Jamaicans, Central America's largest group of immigrants, arrived in the region to participate in the construction of railways, harvest fruit for American companies, and help build the Panama Canal at the beginning of the twentieth century. As a result, English may still be heard in some areas of the Atlantic coast, particularly in Costa Rica (cf. Aguilar-Sánchez, 2005).

With regard to the assimilation of the newly arrived immigrants into the culture and language of their new countries, one could argue that those groups who came in massive numbers went through a very quick assimilatory process, despite occasional tensions and conflicts. As Gallo (1986) points out, European immigration had a profound impact on the local lifestyle, especially in Argentina and southern Brazil, where foreign-born Europeans (especially those from Southern Europe) were never a significant minority vis-à-vis the local-born population of immigrant descent, and in many cases outnumbered this latter population. Additionally, because the two biggest immigrant groups—Italians and Spaniards—displayed similar cultural, religious, and linguistic habits to already-established populations, a rapid assimilation process ensued. Moreover, such fast assimilation, along with government policies, helped give rise to societies where the dominant languages, Spanish and Portuguese, left little to no room for the HLs of other immigrant groups to thrive. Consequently, these languages now survive mainly in the form of occasional idioms or words that are part of the local speech community, but are not spoken natively by later descendants. One possible exception to this pattern was German immigration to southern Brazil and Argentina, since Germans tended to form tighter communities and not assimilate as easily and quickly as Italians, Spaniards, and Portuguese. Fausto (1986) argues that Germans constituted a "distinct cultural community" (p. 783) in southern Brazil in the late 1930s. However, for political reasons that resulted from Brazil's siding with the allies during World War II, the maintenance of German language and cultural heritage was viewed as problematic.

The significant impact that immigration had on Latin America's cultural and linguistic environment from 1870 to 1930 contrasts sharply with the immigration patterns during the second half of the twentieth century, particularly because of the profound consequences of the great economic depression of the 1930s and World War II. One of these consequences was the restriction on incoming immigrants that was enforced by many countries, as immigrants were seen as a threat to local citizens in the already scarce job market—a similar position taken by some of today's anti-immigration groups in the United States and Western Europe. Thus, immigration to Latin America has proceeded at considerably lower levels since 1950, with a few notable exceptions, such as the nearly 40,000 South Koreans who immigrated to the region (particularly to Brazil, Paraguay, Argentina, and Bolivia) in the 1960s and 1970s, mostly as a result of the socioeconomic instability in their home country after the Korean War (Buechler, 2004). Moreover, immigration has been less well documented since then (Merrick, 1994), in part because immigrant children were registered as citizens of the receiving countries and as speakers of the language of the receiving country, i.e., their dominant language in most cases, which has made it difficult to generate reliable statistical records on the number of speakers of other languages in the region (cf. Bolognini & Payer, 2005). All of these factors have contributed to the lack of substantive research on the interaction between heritage and dominant languages in Latin America, if one compares it to the vitality of the field in other parts of the world, such as in the United States and Canada. The following section discusses the available information on and presents a snapshot of the current status of HLs in the areas of Latin America where most immigrants arrived over a century or more ago.

3 Demographics and Heritage Languages

As previously mentioned, the history of Latin America, particularly during the late decades of the nineteenth and the early decades of the twentieth century, is marked by substantial waves of immigrants from around the world, who have contributed decisively to the economic development of the countries that received them, and in some cases have altered cultural norms and language patterns in the region. Despite their rich immigration history, however, virtually all Latin American countries are still largely dominated by either Portuguese (Brazil) or Spanish (all of Hispanic America). Thus, the objectives of this section are twofold: (i) to provide a current picture of the languages of the most prominent immigrant groups in the history of the region that are of neither Portuguese nor Spanish descent, namely Italian and German in Brazil and Argentina and Japanese both in Brazil and in Peru; and (ii) to identify areas of possible further inquiry so as to motivate future research in the field of HL education in these regions.

4 German in Brazil and Argentina

In the 1930s, the number of German immigrants and their descendants in Brazil was estimated at 1.2 million, most of whom lived in small colonies in the south. They preserved their dialects by establishing private schools for their children in addition to printing and distributing local newspapers in German (Mailer, 2003). In the town of Blumenau, in the southern state of Santa Catarina, for example, German was the most widely spoken language among the majority of its citizens from 1850 to 1940 (Fossile, 2010). However, due to the devastating effects of World War II—with Brazil joining the United States and the allies—and the *Campanha de Nacionalização do Ensino* [Campaign for the Nationalization of Teaching] during President Vargas' *Estado Novo* [New State] (1937–1945), the teaching and speaking of the German language, as well as any language except for Portuguese, were practically brought to a halt (Seyferth, 1997). This period of *silenciamento linguístico* [linguistic silencing], as historians and linguists commonly label it (cf. Bolognini & Payer, 2005), had a profound negative impact on the transmission of German and other languages in the country. An entire generation ceased speaking German and, thus, their children were not given a chance to acquire it at home or at school. Consequently, the vast majority of German-descendant Brazilians nowadays are native speakers of Portuguese, with a few words or expressions in German occasionally surfacing in their speech. Those who learn and speak German do so as any other foreign language, that is, by studying it either in language schools or abroad in German-speaking countries. The outlook for the maintenance of German as an HL is further complicated because only a few universities in southern Brazil offer a major in German, mainly due to the general public's lack of interest in this language.

A similar snapshot may be taken of the current status of German in Argentina, with a few marginal differences. Currently about half a million Argentinians are of German descent. About 300,000 Argentinians are estimated to have spoken a dialect of German natively at home in the years following World War II (cf. Bein, 2012). Today, however, that number has dropped to 200,000, 0.5% of Argentina's population of 40 million. Although most speakers who were born before 1960 still have a good command of the language, the reality is that for subsequent generations, German in Argentina, like in Brazil, has primarily become a foreign language that students learn mostly in language schools or abroad. This is the case even in the 21 German-Argentinian private schools, where a total of roughly 20,000 students take German almost exclusively as a foreign language (Bein, 2012).

5 Italian in Brazil and Argentina

Italian can still be heard in a few mainly rural communities in southern and southeastern Brazil (cf. Caira, 2009). In general terms, however, the maintenance of Italian in Brazil has followed a path similar to German and other immigrant languages. The policies of "nationalization" during the Vargas regime, including the government's campaign to promote Portuguese as the national language, had a devastating effect on the teaching and learning of Italian from one generation to the next during the twentieth century. Because Italians constituted the main immigrant group in Brazil's recent history, it is quite common for one to hear certain words or idioms from Italian that have survived in the speech of those communities. However, as in Brazil, the maintenance of Italian in Argentina has not been robust. In 2004, only 15,500 students took Italian as a regular subject in public elementary and middle schools, while 62,000 did so in private schools (Patat, 2004). Bein (2012) argues that the cultural and linguistic assimilation experienced by Argentina's Italian community was such that, at the national level, Italian has lost its vitality as an HL and those who learn it do so as a foreign language.

In fact, the Argentinian population today is overwhelmingly made up of monolingual Spanish speakers, despite the country's rich history of immigration. Many factors have contributed to this linguistic homogeneity (cf. Fontanella de Weinberg, 1979), but one of the key factors has been government policies that enforced the teaching and learning of Spanish in public schools. Bein (2012) cites Common Education Law #1420 of 1884 in particular, which established universal schooling for children. Under this law many children of immigrants went to public schools and were the first in their families to acquire a formal education. As a result, Spanish became the first written language found in these families, since immigrant parents were often illiterate and only spoke their dialectal variety of Italian. The lack of linguistic unity and the many dialectal differences within the Italian community, which many times were unintelligible to one another, along with Italian's linguistic proximity to Spanish, were also important factors in the rapid process of cultural and linguistic assimilation of Italians into Argentinian society. Additionally, their settlement in urban zones, particularly in the cities of Buenos Aires, Córdoba, and Rosario, heavily disfavored their concentration in enclosed communities, and thus promoted their immersion and constant contact with local Spanish speakers. Finally, Italian never enjoyed the international prestige that other European languages such as French or English did throughout the immigration period of the nineteenth and twentieth centuries. This lack of prestige may have been another reason for the lack of interest in preserving Italian as an HL.

6 Japanese in Brazil and Peru

Of all the most important immigrant languages in Brazil, Japanese is perhaps the only one that might enjoy the status of an HL in that it is still spoken in a few homes, although the variety spoken is now influenced by Brazilian Portuguese. In fact, it is called *koronia-go* [colony's language], since it is mainly used within the community of Japanese descendants in Brazil. According to the *Centro de Estudos Nipo-Brasileiros* [Center for Japanese-Brazilian Studies] (n.d.), nearly 1.3 million Japanese descendants, representing all generations, live in Brazil today, but only 0.23% actually speaks Japanese natively or as an HL (cf. Doi, 2004). Of this number, first-generation speakers (*issei*) represent 12.51%; second-generation speakers (*nissei*) account for 30.85%; third-generation speakers (*sansei*) make up 41.33%; and fourth-generation speakers (*yonsei*) represent 12.95%

(Bolognini & Payer, 2005). Similar to that of Italian and German, most speakers of Japanese descent are now native speakers of Portuguese and only a few Japanese words and expressions occasionally appear in their speech, such as those related to food (e.g., *sushi*, *tempura*), sports (*judo*), or entertainment (*karaoke*).

In Peru, it is estimated that nearly 35,000 people spoke Japanese toward the end of the twentieth century (Morimoto, 1991). As with the Japanese community in Mexico, a few private, bilingual Japanese-Spanish schools were created in Peru to meet the demands of the local Japanese community after World War II. However, nowadays teaching mostly conforms to the Peruvian government's guidelines, and the student population includes Japanese and non-Japanese descendants, with schools jointly administered by both Peruvian and Japanese principals (Lausent-Herrera, 1991). Because the quality of education in Japanese schools is usually higher than that of Peruvian public schools, the former are sought after even by members from outside the community (cf. Shintani, 2007). Explanations include the positive assessment of traditional values taught in the Japanese educational system and also the accomplishments of the Japanese community in the economic life of Peru. The Japanese, however, still maintain a tighter community than other immigrant groups, which historically has not contributed to a rapid assimilation process.

As for the current status of Japanese as an HL in Peru, Niland (2012) argues that very few speakers actually claim it as their native tongue, and those people are mostly 60-plus years old from the first generation *issei* and the second generation *nissei*, representing 17% and 9% of the Japanese community, respectively. Younger speakers, who tend to display at least some knowledge of Japanese, study it as a foreign language, either in Peru or in Japan, and thus do not learn it at home anymore. In fact, Niland (2012) finds that many families of Japanese descent do not use their HL at home at all, while others only incorporate a few culture-specific words into their speech. The importance and prestige of English has also contributed to the decline in the learning and usage of Japanese in Peru, because English enjoys more prestige in the workplace, both domestically and overseas. Therefore, one may infer that the value of Japanese as an HL in Peru has declined with the rise of English and with the power of Spanish as the dominant societal language.

7 Concluding Remarks

This chapter has presented an overview of the main historical immigration patterns in Latin America and a snapshot of the current status of the immigrant languages that were brought to the region from the end of the nineteenth through the beginning of the twentieth centuries. Despite having received massive waves of immigrants, particularly from Western Europe, but also from other countries such as Japan, Latin American countries are by and large dominated by speakers of Spanish or Portuguese, i.e., the languages of the respective countries that ruled them until their independence in the nineteenth century. As previously discussed, linguistic, social, and political factors all contributed to the assimilation of immigrant groups to the region, which resulted in the decline of the preservation and transmission of their languages vis-à-vis the dominant societal languages.

Further research will shed light on the future status of immigrant languages in Latin America as this region becomes more interconnected with the world and receives new groups of immigrants in the twenty-first century. Although massive immigration waves such as those observed a century or more ago are unlikely for the foreseeable future, HL scholars will find a promising area of study in Latin America in the decades to come.

Further Reading

Bethell, L. (Ed.). (1986/1994). *The Cambridge history of Latin America* (Vols. 2–8). Cambridge UK: Cambridge University Press.

Bletz, M. E. (2010). *Immigration and acculturation in Brazil and Argentina: 1890–1929.* New York, NY: Palgrave Macmillan.

Cho, J. J. (2000). *Asians in Latin America: A partially annotated bibliography of select countries and people.* Stanford, CA: Center for Latin American Studies, Stanford University.

Cintra, J. T. (1971). *La migración japonesa en Brasil (1908–1958)* [Japanese migration in Brazil (1908–1958)]. Mexico City, Mexico: El Colegio de México.

De Decca, E. S. (1993). Immigrants in Brazil: Tension and cultural identity. In *Ibero-American heritage curriculum: Latinos in the making of the United States of America, yesterday, today and tomorrow* (pp. 895–910). Albany, NY: New York State Education Department.

Fontanella de Weinberg, M. B. (1978). Algunos aspectos de la asimilación lingüística de la población inmigratoria en la Argentina [Some aspects of linguistic assimilation of the immigrant population in Argentina]. *International Journal of the Sociology of Language, 18,* 5–36.

Fukunaga, P. M. (1983). *The Brazilian experience: The Japanese immigrants during the period of the Vargas regime and the immediate aftermath, 1930–1946* (Doctoral dissertation). University of California, Santa Barbara, CA. ProQuest Dissertations and Theses Global, # 8410107.

Hall, M. M. (1969). *The origins of mass immigration to Brazil, 1871–1914* (Doctoral dissertation). Columbia University, New York, NY.

Sakuda, A. (1999). *El futuro era el Perú: 100 años o más de inmigración japonesa* [The future was Peru: 100 years or more of Japanese immigration]. Lima, Peru: ESICOS.

References

Aguilar-Sánchez, J. (2005). English in Costa Rica. *World Englishes, 24*(2), 161–172.

Bein, R. (2012). *La política lingüística respecto de las lenguas extranjeras en la Argentina a partir de 1993* [Linguistic policy on foreign languages in Argentina since 1993] (Unpublished doctoral dissertation). University of Vienna, Austria.

Bolognini, C. Z., & Payer, M. O. (2005). Línguas de imigrantes [The languages of immigrants]. *Ciência e Cultura [Science and Culture], 57*(2), 42–46.

Buechler, S. (2004). Sweating it in the Brazilian garment industry: Korean and Bolivian immigrants and global economic forces in São Paulo. *Latin American Perspectives, 31*(3), 99–119.

Caira, R. (2009). *O italiano falado em Curitiba por um grupo de falantes nativos que vive no Brasil há cerca de cinquenta anos* [The Italian spoken in Curitiba by a group of native speakers living in Brazil for approximately fifty years] (Unpublished master's thesis). University of São Paulo, Brazil.

Centro de Estudos Nipo-Brasileiros [Center for Japanese-Brazilian Studies]. (n.d.). [Web site]. Retrieved from http://www.cenb.org.br/

Córdoba Toro, J. (2014). Los japoneses en el Perú: Inmigración iberoamericana nº 4 [The Japanese in Peru: Ibero-American Immigration, No. 4]. *Iberoamérica Social.* Retrieved from http://iberoamericasocial. com/los-japoneses-en-el-peru-inmigracion-iberoamericana-no4/

de la Riva, J. P. (1966). Demografía de los culíes chinos en Cuba [The demography of Chinese coolies in Cuba] (1853–1874). *Revista de la Biblioteca Nacional José Martí [Journal of the José Martí National Library], 57,* 3–32.

Doi, E. T. (2004). Japonês [Japanese]. In *Enciclopédia das línguas no Brasil [Encyclopedia of languages in Brazil].* Instituto de Estudos da Linguagem, Campinas State University, Brazil. Retrieved from http://www. labeurb.unicamp.br/elb2/pages/noticias/lerNoticia.lab?categoria=6&id=221

Fausto, B. (1986). Brazil: The social and political structure of the First Republic, 1889–1930. In L. Bethell (Ed.), *The Cambridge history of Latin America* (Vol. 5, pp. 779–830). Cambridge, UK: Cambridge University Press.

Fontanella de Weinberg, M. B. (1979). *La asimilación lingüística de los inmigrantes. Mantenimiento y cambio de lengua en el sudoeste argentino* [The linguistic assimilation of immigrants: Language maintenance and change in Southwestern Argentina]. Bahía Blanca, Argentina: Universidad Nacional del Sur.

Fossile, D. K. (2010). O ensino da língua alemã no sul do Brasil [German language teaching in Southern Brazil]. *Profiscientia, 5,* 43–60.

Gallo, E. (1986). Argentina: Society and politics, 1880–1916. In L. Bethell (Ed.), *The Cambridge history of Latin America* (Vol. 5, pp. 359–391). Cambridge, UK: Cambridge University Press.

Lausent-Herrera, I. (1991). *Pasado y presente de la comunidad japonesa en el Perú* [*The past and present of the Japanese community in Peru*]. Lima, Peru: IEP Ediciones.

Mailer, V. C. de O. (2003). *O alemão em Blumenau: uma questão de identidade e cidadania* [*German in Blumenau: An issue of identity and citizenship*] (Unpublished master's thesis). Federal University of Santa Catarina, Brazil.

Marcílio, M. L. (1984). The population of colonial Brazil. In L. Bethell (Ed.), *The Cambridge history of Latin America* (Vol. 2, pp. 37–66). Cambridge: Cambridge University Press.

Merrick, T. (1994). The population of Latin America, 1930–1990. In L. Bethell (Ed.), *The Cambridge history of Latin America* (Vol. 6 (part 1), pp. 3–61). Cambridge, UK: Cambridge University Press.

Mishima, M. E. O. (1982). *Siete migraciones japonesas en México: 1890–1978* [*Seven Japanese migrations in Mexico: 1890–1978*]. Mexico, DF: El Colegio de México.

Morimoto, A. (1991). *Población de origen japonés en el Perú: Perfil actual* [*Peru's population of Japanese origin: Current profile*]. Lima, Peru: Ausonia.

Niland, L. (2012). Japoñolés: El uso del japonés, español e inglés en la comunidad peruano japonesa [Japoñolés: The use of Japanese, Spanish and English in the Peruvian Japanese community]. *Fulbright Grantee Projects*. Retrieved from http://digitalcommons.linfield.edu/fulbright/1/

Oddone, J. A. (1986). The formation of modern Uruguay, c. 1870–1930. In L. Bethell (Ed.), *The Cambridge history of Latin America* (Vol. 5, pp. 453–474). Cambridge, UK: Cambridge University Press.

Patat, A. (2004). *L'italiano in Argentina* [*Italian in Argentina*]. Perugia, Italy: Guerra Edizioni, Università per Stranieri di Siena.

Sánchez-Albornoz, N. (1984). The population of colonial Latin America. In L. Bethell (Ed.), *The Cambridge history of Latin America* (Vol. 2, pp. 3–36). Cambridge, UK: Cambridge University Press.

Sánchez-Albornoz, N. (1986). The population of Latin America, 1850–1930. In L. Bethell (Ed.), *The Cambridge history of Latin America* (Vol. 4, pp. 121–152). Cambridge, UK: Cambridge University Press.

Seyferth, G. (1997). A assimilação dos imigrantes como questão nacional [Immigrant assimilation as a national issue]. *Mana: Estudos de antropologia social* [*Mana: Studies in social anthropology*], *3*(1), 95–131.

Shintani, R. (2007). The Nikkei community of Peru: Settlement and development. *Ritsumeikan Studies in Language and Culture*, *18*(3), 79–94.

Tsuchida, N. (1978). *The Japanese in Brazil, 1908–1941* (Unpublished doctoral dissertation). University of California, Los Angeles, CA.

5

Demographics and Heritage Languages in Canada

Policies, Patterns, and Prospects

Patricia A. Duff and Ava Becker-Zayas

1 Introduction

Linguistic diversity in Canada, as elsewhere, is closely connected with its political, social, and educational history, policies, and initiatives—as well as events leading to the migration of those seeking better or safer lives. Successive waves of immigration to Canada have comprised newcomers whose languages have facilitated communication within their Canadian ethnolinguistic groups and beyond, and have contributed not only to Canada's ethnic vitality and identity (Jedwab, 2014) but also to the society's functioning as a whole.

In this chapter, we describe the historical and contemporary context of multilingualism in Canada with a particular focus on the construction, status, and maintenance of heritage languages (HLs). We begin by summarizing immigration trends and policies since the early twentieth century, and then draw on national census data from the past 30 years to discuss patterns of language shift, both in terms of self-reported official-language and HL use, and in terms of the changing linguistic composition of Canada according to countries or regions of origin.

To focus our discussion, we profile the demographics of Canada's three largest cities (Toronto, Montreal, and Vancouver), which have been major hubs of immigration, (re)settlement, and commerce. We then discuss how language policies at various levels (federal, provincial, district, and family) have influenced the role and vitality of different HLs, education in these languages, and attitudes toward them held by minority-language speakers and the wider Canadian society. Throughout, we consider additional issues of relevance to an overview of HLs in the Canadian context, such as: the commodification of HLs (in theory and in practice); debates surrounding the moral and financial responsibility of Canadians to support their own HLs; the identities and agency of community members in relation to the maintenance of their heritage (and other) languages; and the emergent topic of race and HL maintenance (e.g., Shin, 2010).

2 Issues and Policy Contexts: Indigenous and Heritage Languages in Canadian Society and Education

Canada distinguishes between its *official* languages, English and French, and its *non-official* languages, i.e., *heritage* languages, such as Spanish and Punjabi, and *indigenous* languages, such as Cree and Inuktitut. The distinction stems primarily from each language's history or provenance, and also from federal and provincial language education funding and policy (Burnaby, 2008; Duff & Li, 2009).[1] Policies of official bilingualism and multiculturalism enacted in the 1970s privileging English and French have projected a somewhat ambiguous message to newcomers: that cultural diversity is welcomed, but proficiency in English or French is valued, supported, and expected (Duff, 2008). Considerable funding is therefore dedicated to English or French education, particularly for second-language learners of these languages (i.e., Anglophones learning French and Francophones learning English, and some support for newcomers learning either language).[2]

Indigenous and HL education share many of the same challenges in attempts to "institutionalize" them, particularly in small communities with relatively few speakers of those languages, either locally or internationally. These challenges in both indigenous and immigrant contexts often include having too few fluent, trained teachers or elders, inadequate teaching materials, insufficient duration and intensity of instruction, and insufficient opportunities to use the language outside of classrooms. Furthermore, the social power and cachet of global languages such as English pose intense competition.

Given that immigrant languages are normally spoken by entire societies in sending countries (often with established mass media resources available in those languages), it might appear that supporting heritage languages would be less challenging than sustaining indigenous languages. Nevertheless, language shift data reveal otherwise. Within just a generation or two, HL-background speakers in Canada tend to shift to the use of one of the official languages in their homes and daily lives (Duff, 2007; Jedwab, 2014). Commonly reported HL maintenance challenges include peer, societal, and self-imposed assimilation pressures, especially for school-aged children; the perceived stigma of using a non-official language, especially in public, and even within the HL community when not proficient in the HL; the dearth of suitable educational resources, media, teachers, and curriculum; and finally, a lack of institutional recognition of the value of HL knowledge or mastery, which undermines children's and youth's attempts to use the HL outside of the home. Furthermore, an increase in linguistically mixed families also contributes to a shift toward the shared language, typically one of the two official languages. This latter factor, according to Jedwab (2014), is very significant in intergenerational language transmission: the children of two parents who actively use the same non-official language are much more likely to speak that language as their mother tongue than those whose parents have another pattern of communication (see the "mixed-union" discussion below). All of these factors, then, can contribute to diminished motivation for youth and families to engage with their HL in a sustainable way.

Against this backdrop of social and linguistic diversity, language education policies have been developed to support the learning of Canada's languages both formally and informally, through public and private means. Unfortunately, the types and levels of support, particularly for HLs, have been subject to political and economic vicissitudes, with government support seemingly strongest from the mid-1970s to the early 1990s as new federal policies were being implemented. More recently, however, HL maintenance and education have aroused suspicion and even hostility by those who question why public funding and support should be expended for minority languages rather than majority ones, with the exception of French in Anglophone Canada for Francophone minorities (see also Burnaby, 2008, Duff, 2008; Ricento & Cervatiuc, 2010). Many ethnolinguistic communities have therefore established community schools, cultural or religious centers, and personal social networks to nurture linguistic and cultural connections and competencies for themselves and their children. In addition, many families develop their own rules for home language use, although the language of the dominant community is often spoken regardless (e.g., Guardado, 2009).

3 Settlement Patterns

Immigration Trends and Policies

Despite its longstanding reputation for welcoming both volitional and reluctant migrants, Canada's immigration policies have always been influenced by political, economic, and at times even racist motivations (e.g., Yu, 2009). According to some sources, Canada's acceptance of asylum seekers did not really begin until after World War II (Abella & Molnar, 2006). From the late 1960s through the early 1990s, economic changes in Canada and humanitarian crises in other parts of the world brought about a great change in Canadian immigration trends and policies. To begin with, until the late 1960s, immigration in Canada originated primarily in Europe and the United States. However, in the 1970s, immigration policies were put into place to welcome the tens of thousands of refugees fleeing political turmoil in regions such as Latin America and Southeast Asia. In the 1980s, Canada experienced an economic recession, which prompted policies to facilitate business- or investor-class migration. This initiative was very successful and saw a rise in populations from certain parts of Asia, for example. In addition, while family reunification has been an integral part of Canadian identity and immigration policy since the early twentieth century, beginning in the 1970s it has been the subject of significant debate and scrutiny. The Harper government's (2006–2015) immigration reforms emphasized economic outcomes (Neborak, 2013), effectively prioritizing the acceptance of people who are presumed to integrate successfully and quickly into the labor market. By contrast, Canada's recently elected prime minister, Justin Trudeau, promotes immigration policies more aligned with those advanced by his father's government four decades ago[3] (e.g., The Immigration Act of 1976, which included two immigration classes dedicated to families, one to refugees, and one to "independent" immigrants). Nevertheless, immigration will undoubtedly continue to be a subject of controversy and change as Canada struggles to meet the challenges of an increasingly diverse and immigration-dependent nation (Statistics Canada, 2013b).

Census Data: Affordances and Constraints

Because the data for this section of the chapter are drawn from the Canadian Census conducted in 1981, 1991, and 2001 as well as the National Household Survey (NHS) in 2011 (e.g., Statistics Canada, 2013a, 2013b), it is worth briefly addressing some of the advantages and limitations of using census data as a means of creating a demographic profile of the country and discussing changes over time. Largely for political reasons, the long-form version of the Canadian Census was discontinued in 2011, and households instead completed a short form. On the short form people do not tend to specify a language other than English or French as their mother tongue (Statistics Canada, 2013b), whereas on the long form, they reported other (non-official) language use in a more complete manner. Both the Canadian Census and the NHS surveyed samples of the Canadian population, in both cities and rural areas, but the number and kinds of questions they asked differed. We have therefore needed to combine information from the regular census (1981, 1991, and 2001) and then from the NHS (2011) in order to offer the observations in following sections.

General National Trends Regarding Recent Immigration, Ethnic Origins, and HLs in Canada

Canada has the world's second-highest foreign-born population (after Australia), ahead of the U.S., Germany, and the UK (Statistics Canada, 2013b). According to the most recent census,

Table 5.1 Canada's Top 10 Non-official Languages ("Mother Tongues"), in Descending Order

	1971	2011
1	German	Punjabi
2	Italian	Chinese (nonspecific)
3	Ukrainian	Spanish
4	Dutch	Italian
5	Polish	German
6	Greek	Cantonese
7	Chinese (nonspecific)	Tagalog
8	Portuguese	Arabic
9	Magyar/Hungarian	Mandarin
10	Yiddish, Croatian/Serbian	Portuguese

Source: Adapted from Canadian Census data from 1971 and 2011 (Statistics Canada, n.d.).

conducted in 2011, the 10 non-official languages ("mother tongues") in Canada with the largest numbers of speakers were as follows, in descending order (see Table 5.1): Punjabi, Chinese (language or dialect not specified), Spanish, Italian, German, Cantonese, Tagalog, Arabic, Mandarin, and Portuguese. If the Chinese (unspecified), Cantonese, and Mandarin numbers are combined, this cluster constitutes the largest group of languages spoken in the country after English and French, and more than double the number of Punjabi speakers. These languages reflect immigration trends from the Asian countries of India and what we will refer to as Greater China, primarily China, Hong Kong, and Taiwan. Of those whose mother tongue is either Punjabi or Mandarin, more than 80% are reported to speak these languages at home the majority of the time (Statistics Canada, n.d.). European languages include those that have speakers from earlier generations, namely Italian, German, and Portuguese, as well as Spanish, whose speakers are mostly newer arrivals. In addition, Tagalog and Arabic have become salient, widely spoken mother tongues in Canada, whose numbers are increasing markedly with each successive survey.

The set of languages reported for 2011 (see Table 5.1) stands in marked contrast with comparable data for the top 10 most spoken non-official languages from the 1971 census (see Duff, 2008, for other comparisons) in which European languages (other than English and French) were much more significant and sizable. In fact, in the 1971 set, the only language (group) with origins outside Europe was Chinese, in comparison to the 2011 data, which included six non-European languages. Note that Spanish (in marked contrast to the U.S.) was not ranked among the top 10 most widely spoken languages in 1971, but increased immigration from the Caribbean, Mexico, and Central and South America since 1971 has resulted in Spanish becoming the third most spoken non-official language in 2011.

Toronto, Vancouver, Montreal: 1981–2011

For reasons of space, in this section we give a general overview of the most recent three decades of census-reported language use and ethnic origins in Canada's three largest metropolitan areas in terms of population and immigration levels: Toronto, Vancouver, and Montreal. Each city also represents a different province: Ontario, British Columbia (BC), and Quebec, respectively. Ontario and Quebec, in eastern Canada, constitute the historical "center" of the country in terms of settlement/colonization, population size, and political power (although with different ethnolinguistic/colonial populations); BC, in the far west, was settled later.

In general, as noted earlier, over the past 40 years major urban centers in Canada have witnessed a gradual shift away from European immigration. Since the end of the twentieth century, the majority of newcomers to Canada have come from Asia, as well as from countries in which Arabic and Spanish are spoken. The population's increasing diversity has been accompanied by a shift in census response categories, which accounts for some of the variability and confusion in the tables below. These data come from the place of birth/ethnic origin and home languages/non-official languages sections of the National Census conducted by Statistics Canada (n.d.).[4] *National* linguistic self-report census data (whether framed as "mother tongue" or "home language") is a bit easier to interpret than *municipal* household data collected by the NHS (Statistics Canada, 2011). For the latter, the questionnaire prompt or description is surprisingly vague and, indeed, perplexing for applied linguists: "languages, other than English or French, in which the respondent *can conduct a conversation*" (Statistics Canada, 2013a, emphasis added). The data generated, however, do seem to correspond to broader immigration and demographic trends and we will interpret these as mostly referring to HLs or languages spoken at home (as they are also described in some government reports of Census or NHS data). With that caveat in mind, we consider some general historical trends and differences among our three major immigrant-receiving metropolitan areas, often using the umbrella terms "census" and "census-respondents" to refer to data from the Census and the NHS.

Toronto

Immigration and Languages

Toronto, in the central-eastern province of Ontario, is considered a "major immigration gateway" to Canada, according to Statistics Canada, since 30%–40% of new immigrants in the last decade have settled in the Toronto region and roughly half of the population (46%) is now foreign-born (Statistics Canada, 2006, n.d.). Until the 1980s, the largest number of new immigrants settling in Toronto came from continental Europe, the UK, Asia, and the Americas. Since that time, the city has experienced a decrease in immigration from Europe, particularly from Italy and Portugal, and a sharp increase in immigration from Asia, namely the People's Republic of China (hereafter "China"), India, and more recently, the Philippines. Toronto has also become home to a large community of residents from the Caribbean as well as Central and South America.

Since 1991, as shown in Table 5.2, Chinese languages (combined, but with the largest proportion indicating Cantonese specifically) have held the top position in the ranking of non-official languages spoken by Torontonians (as "mother tongue" or as "language spoken"), but it was only in 2011 that other Asian languages, namely Punjabi, Urdu, and Tamil from South Asia and Tagalog from Southeast Asia, filled four of the top five other positions (Statistics Canada, 2012).[5] This ranking roughly corresponds to the settlement data for the city from the 2011 census, which reports India, China, and the Philippines as the top three countries of origin represented by Toronto residents. While the change in the top first languages (mother tongues) was quite minimal between 1991 and 2001, it was much more substantial in the first decade of the twenty-first century with this wholesale shift from European languages (Italian, Portuguese, Spanish, and Polish, respectively) to Asian languages. (Unfortunately, 1971 and 1981 census data did not specify which non-official languages were spoken, but in 1981 a third of census respondents reported speaking a home language other than English [Statistics Canada, n.d.].)

Patricia A. Duff and Ava Becker-Zayas

Table 5.2 Non-official Languages Spoken by Census Respondents in Toronto (1991–2011; top five only)

	1991 "Mother tongue"	2001 "Mother tongue"	2011 "Non-official language spoken"
1	Chinese	Chinese	Chinese
2	Italian	Italian	Punjabi
3	Portuguese	Portuguese	Urdu
4	Spanish	Punjabi	Tamil
5	Polish	Spanish	Tagalog

Source: Adapted from Canadian Census data on Toronto from 1991, 2001, 2011 (Statistics Canada, n.d.; see endnote 5 regarding "Chinese").

Vancouver

Immigration and Languages

Similar to Toronto, Vancouver's primary immigrant groups in the 1980s were from Europe, Asia, and the Americas, but the order was somewhat inverted, given Vancouver's location in British Columbia, on the Pacific Rim. Unlike other parts of the country, therefore, newcomers to Vancouver have immigrated in larger numbers from East Asia (Greater China, in particular), over an extended period.[6] The 1990s and 2000s saw slight fluctuations in Asian and (mostly Anglo-) European immigration, with both nonetheless being among the largest source of immigrants in Vancouver. While China currently is the top sending country, other 2011 data indicate that immigration from other Asian countries and special administrative regions is also in ascendance (e.g., India, the Philippines), replacing the earlier significant migrant groups of English, Scottish, Irish, and German. "East Indian" migrants, mainly from northern India, are also listed among the top five in 1991 and 2001 but not in 2011.

Therefore, as in Toronto, Chinese languages and Punjabi, the dominant language of the Indian (Indo-Canadian) community in Vancouver, and the single dominant language when Chinese varieties are not combined, held the top positions (besides English) as mother tongues/languages spoken by residents of Metro Vancouver in the 2011 census (see Table 5.3). But unlike Toronto,

Table 5.3 Non-official Languages Spoken by Census Respondents in Vancouver (1991–2011; top five only)

	1991 "Mother tongue"	2001 "Mother tongue"	2011 "Non-official language spoken"
1	Chinese	Chinese	Chinese
2	Punjabi	Punjabi	Punjabi
3	Vietnamese	Tagalog/ German (tie)	Tagalog
4	Spanish	Spanish	Korean
5	Tagalog/ Italian (tie)	Farsi	Farsi

Source: Adapted from Canadian Census data on Vancouver from 1991, 2001, 2011 (Statistics Canada, n.d.; see endnote 5 regarding "Chinese").

62

the top three languages spoken in Vancouver since before the 1990s have been Asian languages. Vietnamese and Korean, for example, do not appear among the top five home languages in Toronto, but they do in Vancouver. The relatively high level of immigration from English-speaking parts of the world such as the United Kingdom or United States also contributes to a rather unique "immigrant" or "newcomer" environment in the city (both Anglo and non-Anglo), with implications for how HLs are viewed and supported (or not supported) by the broader population.[7] Finally, Farsi has taken the fifth position in Vancouver rankings since 2001, making it one of the most widely spoken languages from the Middle East on Canada's west coast.

Montreal

Immigration and Languages

Likely due to its location in French-speaking Canada (in the province of Quebec, which also has somewhat different immigration quotas and policies), Montreal's immigration history and profile are quite different from Vancouver's or Toronto's. In 2011, for example, immigration from France, Italy, and prior French colonies (e.g., Morocco, Algeria, Haiti) predominated.

Like Vancouver and Toronto, Montreal is experiencing a gradual shift away from European immigrant languages, in this case Italian, Greek, and Portuguese. Although Spanish, a language of European origins, has retained its position as the second-most-spoken non-official language in the city over the past 25 years (see Table 5.4), its linguistic proximity to French and the longstanding affinities between Francophones in Quebec and Hispanophone cultures, particularly in the Americas, have contributed to its position. In 2011, Arabic surpassed Italian and Spanish as the language group with the largest apparent number of speakers in Montreal, a trend that is distinct from both Toronto and Vancouver demographics. Chinese languages also appear to be on the rise in Montreal (ranked number 5 in 1991 and 2001, and number 4 in 2011), although they are not as well represented as they are in Toronto or Vancouver. In addition, French-based creole languages such as Haitian Creole were among the top five non-official language groups in Montreal in 2011.

Census respondents, including those in our three focal cities, generally reported increased *non-official home language use* compared to previous years—but not at the expense of official languages (Statistics Canada, 2012). Canadians are increasingly reporting the use of multiple languages in the home (due, for example, to mixed-ethnic unions) as well as the use of a non-official language as the primary language in the home. There are currently more speakers of non-European HLs,

Table 5.4 Non-official Languages Spoken by Census Respondents in Montreal (1991–2011; top five only)

	1991 "Mother tongue"	2001 "Mother tongue"	2011 "Non-official language spoken"
1	Italian	Italian	Arabic
2	Spanish	Spanish	Spanish
3	Greek	Arabic	Italian
4	Portuguese	Greek	Chinese
5	Chinese	Chinese	Creoles

Note: Statistics Canada (2012) listed "Creole" in singular in 2011; the main language in the "Creoles/Creole" category is Haitian creole.

Source: Adapted from Canadian Census data on Montreal from 1991, and 2001 and the NHS from 2011 (Statistics Canada, n.d.).

particularly Asian ones, than there are of non-English/French-European languages (Statistics Canada, 2012). Thus, these languages are being maintained *and* English or French are also being spoken increasingly. Much like Duff (2007) observed nearly 10 years ago, multilingualism—regardless of settlement city—appears to be increasing in Canada, among first- and second-generation immigrants in particular.

4 Socioeconomic, Generational, and Racial Considerations in Heritage Language Retention

In general, language shift in Canada follows the three-generation model of loss Fishman (2001) proposed, although the Canadian HL literature suggests that language shift is slowed by transnational lifestyles and the investment of substantial resources by parents and communities themselves (e.g., Guardado & Becker, 2014). With previous immigration policies that sought to increase "highly skilled" immigrants and accepted fewer applicants from family-reunification and refugee categories, HL maintenance in Canada was becoming increasingly related to socioeconomic class and the perceived usefulness of HLs to facilitate international business and trade (cf. Ricento, 2005). The recent change in government promises to slow, if not reverse, the commodification of HLs and their speakers that previous immigration policies fostered (Justin Trudeau, the leader of the Liberal Party, was elected in late 2015).

The centrality of identity (ethnic, linguistic, cultural, etc.) has been consistently emphasized in qualitative research on HL maintenance (see Leeman, 2015). Given the rise of "mixed unions" in Canada, involving not just different ethnicities or languages but also the possibility of visible minority status for one partner, or two visible minority backgrounds for both partners (e.g., Korean and Japanese; Japanese and Caucasian; Statistics Canada, 2014),[8] the underexplored implications of "mixed race" identities and HL maintenance beg further inquiry. Of direct relevance to this chapter is the finding that roughly 45% of mixed-union couples shared a common mother tongue, whereas 55% did not; nearly 90% of non-mixed-union couples, in contrast, reported having the same mother tongue (Statistics Canada, 2014). Research examining mixed unions, identity, and HL maintenance, and other aspects of family dynamics, such as single-parent families (Guardado, 2002; Iqbal, 2005), adoptive families (Fogle, 2012), and "mixed" families (Shin, 2010)—that is, mixed-union parents with children—remains underrepresented in Canada and elsewhere.

5 Conclusion: Future Directions for Heritage Language Research in Canada

Canadian scholars have begun to argue more forcefully for pedagogical and policy support of societal multilingualism (also called plurilingualism) through mainstream education. One critical recommendation is that more legitimate "space" be provided for languages in school curricula, not simply in language classes, which are for the most part optional in the curriculum. Such "institutionalization" and "mainstreaming" of HL education through activities developing students' multilingual literacies, metalinguistic awareness, and identities are designed to benefit all students, not just HL learners (e.g., Cummins, 2005, 2014; Cummins & Early, 2011; Naqvi, McKeough, Thorne, & Pfitscher, 2013). Paradoxically, in some jurisdictions (e.g., British Columbia), language policy and curriculum documents have in recent years stated that language courses taught for credit at schools should be for *non-HL* students—although, in fact, many (if not most, particularly at the highest grade levels) of the students taking the courses in Punjabi, Mandarin, or Korean hail from HL backgrounds, according to their teachers and district language coordinators

(Duff, 2008). HL students are, according to such policies, precluded from building on their own linguistic backgrounds and resources. An approach based on the Common European Framework of Reference to Languages, which has gained traction in Canadian provinces in recent years (Council of Ministers of Education, 2010), would give students credit through a "language passport" or "portfolio" approach for the various kinds of linguistic expertise and experience they have and also wish to expand upon.

As a former colony of England and France, Canada's immigration and linguistic heterogeneity stand at the core of its national history and identity. Canada has never been only French- and English-speaking, nor has it been solely European, as myths firmly rooted in the national imaginary suggest (Haque, 2012). Pervasive use of the term "linguistic duality" by government agencies and organizations, including many modern language educators, to refer to Canada's linguistic landscape and identity perpetuates such misconceptions (Duff, 2008). Research (e.g., Yu, 2009) concerning vital early East-Asian, South-Asian, Pacific Islander, and other settlers and migrants in British Columbia more than a century ago, for example, belies such myths, and further evidence can be found in the tremendous linguistic diversity of Canada's indigenous peoples. But as immigration patterns change and the country's cultural and linguistic composition becomes more diverse, ideological and practical questions about how to move forward as an inclusive and cohesive society become more acute.

Finally, future research would benefit from greater granularity and specificity in census data with respect to language proficiency and retention/use of various languages. In addition, complementing such data with in-depth case studies of families and communities (e.g., Guardado, 2009) would help put a human face on some of these data and illustrate some of the richness, tensions, and nuances of daily life in multilingual contexts for minority-language speakers that simply cannot be captured through census snapshots.

Notes

1 Note that, according to Burnaby (2008), some indigenous languages are now considered "official" within particular northern regions, such as the North West Territories and Nunavut.
2 Approximately 21% of Canadians reported speaking French as their primary home language in the 2011 census (Statistics Canada, n.d.).
3 Pierre Elliott Trudeau, 1968–1979 and 1980–1984.
4 For access to the Statistics Canada tables referred to here, readers are encouraged to consult the Canadian Census Analyzer (Computing in the Humanities and Social Sciences Data Centre, n.d.), an archival website hosted by Computing in the Humanities and Social Sciences (CHASS) at the University of Toronto. The Analyzer is available to University of Toronto affiliates, and non-affiliates may access it through a subscription. The 2011 Census data are also available through Statistics Canada (n.d.).
5 Note that we are combining Chinese languages for our reporting here; Statistics Canada otherwise provides rankings with, for example, Cantonese, Chinese (not otherwise specified, or "n.o.s."), Mandarin, etc., as distinct entities, which is not always helpful in seeing which other linguistic groups are most commonly spoken in cities. If the Chinese languages are *not* collapsed or combined in this manner, Cantonese is the most widely spoken language in Toronto, followed by Punjabi, Chinese n.o.s., then Urdu, and Tagalog, and in Vancouver the top-ranked language is Punjabi, followed by Cantonese, Chinese n.o.s., Mandarin, Tagalog, and Korean. In Montreal there is no change. By collapsing the Chinese languages, we obscure some key differences in specific varieties, but also provide room for other non-Chinese languages in the top five languages shown.
6 It is worth noting that some of these geopolitical nuances are lost under umbrella terms such as "Asia" and "Chinese" in census reporting.
7 Canadian immigration policy has been explicitly racist at intervals throughout the country's history (Kelley & Trebilcock, 1998; Yu, 2009), and in the late nineteenth and early twentieth centuries especially targeted the Chinese (Taylor, 1991), who would otherwise have constituted a much larger proportion of (new) Canadians during those years.

8 The main visible minority categories, according to this survey, are Japanese, Latin American, Black, Filipino, Arab, Korean, Southeast Asian, West Asian, Chinese, and South Asian, listed in order of highest to lowest number of "mixed unions" for each ethnicity/minority group in 2011; e.g., nearly 80% of Japanese are reported to be in mixed unions, while nearly 50% of Latin Americans are.

References

Abella, I. R., & Molnar, P. (2006). Refugees. In *The Canadian Encyclopedia*. Retrieved from http://www.thecanadianencyclopedia.ca/en/article/refugees/

Burnaby, B. (2008). Language policy and education in Canada. In S. May & N. H. Hornberger (Eds.), *Language policy and political issues in education: Encyclopedia of language and education* (Vol. 1, pp. 331–341). New York, NY: Springer.

Computing in the Humanities and Social Sciences Data Centre. (n.d.). *The Canadian Census Analyzer* [*Retrieval tool for Canadian Census data*]. Toronto, Ontario, Canada: University of Toronto. Retrieved from http://dc.chass.utoronto.ca/census/index.html

Council of Ministers of Education, Canada. (2010). *Working with the Common European Framework of Reference for Languages (CEFR) in the Canadian context: Guide for policy-makers and curriculum designers*. Toronto, Ontario, Canada: Author. Retrieved from http://www.cmec.ca/docs/assessment/CEFR-canadian-context.pdf

Cummins, J. (2005). A proposal for action: Strategies for recognizing heritage language competence as a learning resource within the mainstream classroom. *Modern Language Journal, 89*, 585–592.

Cummins, J. (2014). Mainstreaming plurilingualism: Restructuring heritage language provision in schools. In P. Trifonas & T. Aravossitas (Eds.), *Rethinking heritage language education* (pp. 1–19). Cambridge, UK: Cambridge University Press.

Cummins, J., & Early, M. (Eds.). (2011). *Identity texts: The collaborative creation of power in multilingual schools*. London, UK: Trentham Books.

Duff, P. (2007). Multilingualism in Canadian schools: Myths, realities, and possibilities. *Canadian Journal for Applied Linguistics, 10*(2), 149–163.

Duff, P. (2008). Heritage language education in Canada. In D. Brinton, O. Kagan, & S. Bauckus (Eds.), *Heritage language education: A new field emerging* (pp. 71–90). New York, NY: Routledge/Taylor & Francis.

Duff, P., & Li, D. (2009). Indigenous, minority, and heritage language education in Canada: Policies, contexts, and issues. *Canadian Modern Language Review, 66*(1), 1–8.

Fishman, J. A. (2001). *Can threatened languages be saved? Reversing language shift, revisited: A 21st century perspective*. Clevedon, England: Multilingual Matters.

Fogle, L. W. (2012). *Second language socialization and learner agency: Adoptive family talk*. Bristol, UK: Multilingual Matters.

Guardado, M. (2002). Loss and maintenance of first language skills: Case studies of Hispanic families in Vancouver. *Canadian Modern Language Review/ La Revue Canadienne Des Langues Vivantes, 58*(3), 341–363.

Guardado, M. (2009). Speaking Spanish like a Boy Scout: Language socialization, resistance, and reproduction in a heritage language scout troop. *Canadian Modern Language Review/ La Revue Canadienne Des Langues Vivantes, 66*(1), 101–129.

Guardado, M., & Becker, A. (2014). Glued to the family: The role of familism in heritage language development strategies. *Journal of Language, Culture and Curriculum, 27*(2), 163–181. doi: 10.1080/07908318.2014.912658

Haque, E. (2012). *Multiculturalism within a bilingual framework: Language, race, and belonging in Canada*. Toronto, Ontario, Canada: University of Toronto Press.

Iqbal, I. (2005). Mother tongue and motherhood: Implications for French language maintenance in Canada. *Canadian Modern Language Review/ La Revue Canadienne Des Langues Vivantes, 61*, 305–323.

Jedwab, J. (2014). Canada's "other" languages: The role of non-official languages in ethnic persistence. In P. Trifonas & T. Aravossitas (Eds.), *Rethinking heritage language education* (pp. 237–253). Cambridge, UK: Cambridge University Press.

Kelley, N., & Trebilcock, M. J. (1998). *The making of the mosaic: A history of Canadian immigration policy*. Toronto, Ontario, Canada: University of Toronto Press.

Leeman, J. (2015). Heritage language education and identity in the United States. *Annual Review of Applied Linguistics, 35*, 100–119. doi: 10.1017/S0267190514000245

Naqvi, R., McKeough, A., Thorne, K., & Pfitscher, C. (2013). Dual language books as an emergent literacy resource: Culturally and linguistically responsive teaching and learning. *Journal of Early Childhood Literacy*, *13*, 501–528.

Neborak, J. (2013). Family reunification? A critical analysis of citizenship and immigration Canada's 2013 reforms to the family class [RCIS Working Paper No. 2013/8]. Toronto, Ontario, Canada: Ryerson Centre for Immigration and Settlement. Retrieved from http://www.ryerson.ca/content/dam/rcis/documents/RCIS_WP_Neborak_No_2013_8.pdf

Ricento, T. (2005). Problems with the "language-as-resource" discourse in the promotion of heritage languages in the U.S.A. *Journal of Sociolinguistics*, *9*(3), 348–368.

Ricento, T., & Cervatiuc, A. (2010). Language minority rights and educational policy in Canada. In J. E. Petrovic (Ed.), *International perspectives on bilingual education: Policy, practice, and controversy* (pp. 21–42). Charlotte, NC: Information Age Publishing.

Shin, S. (2010). What about me? I'm not like Chinese but I'm not like American: Heritage-language learning and identity of mixed-heritage adults. *Journal of Language, Identity & Education*, *9*(3), 203–219.

Statistics Canada. (2006). *Immigration in Canada: A portrait of the foreign-born population, 2006 census: Portraits of major metropolitan centres*. Catalogue no. 97-557-XIE2006001. Ottawa, Ontario, Canada: Author. Retrieved from http://www12.statcan.ca/census-recensement/2006/as-sa/97-557/p24-eng.cfm

Statistics Canada. (2011). *Aboriginal languages in Canada [Language report]: 2011 census of population: Analytical products*. Catalogue no. 98-314-x2011003. Ottawa, Ontario, Canada: Author. Retrieved from http://www12.statcan.gc.ca/census-recensement/2011/as-sa/98-314-x/98-314-x2011003_3-eng.cfm

Statistics Canada. (2012). *Linguistic characteristics of Canadians [Language report]: 2011 census of population: Analytical products*. Catalogue no. 98-314-X2011001. Ottawa, Ontario, Canada: Author. Retrieved from https://www12.statcan.gc.ca/census-recensement/2011/as-sa/98-314-x/98-314-x2011001-eng.cfm

Statistics Canada. (2013a). *Methodological document on the 2011 Census language data [Analytical document report]: 2011 census of population: 2011 census reference materials*. Catalogue no. 98-314-XWE2011051. Ottawa, Ontario, Canada: Author. Retrieved from http://www12.statcan.gc.ca/census-recensement/2011/ref/guides/98-314-x/98-314-x2011051-eng.cfm#a1

Statistics Canada. (2013b). *Immigration and ethnocultural diversity in Canada [Analytical document report]: National Household Survey, 2011*. Catalogue no. 99-010-X2011001. Ottawa, Ontario, Canada: Author. Retrieved from http://www12.statcan.gc.ca/nhs-enm/2011/as-sa/99-010-x/99-010-x2011001-eng.pdf

Statistics Canada. (2014). *Mixed unions in Canada [NHS in Brief report]: National Household Survey, 2011*. Ottawa, Ontario, Canada: Author. Retrieved from http://www12.statcan.gc.ca/nhs-enm/2011/as-sa/99-010-x/99-010-x2011003_3-eng.pdf

Statistics Canada. (n.d.). *Canadian census [data from 1981, 1991, 2001, 2011]*. Toronto, Ontario, Canada: Author. Retrieved from http://www.statcan.gc.ca/start-debut-eng.html

Taylor, K. (1991). Racism in Canadian immigration policy. *Canadian Ethnic Studies*, *23*(1), 1.

Yu, H. (2009). Global migrants and the new Pacific Canada. *International Journal*, *64*, 1011–1026.

Part II
Community Initiatives
After-School Programs

6

Crisis, Change, and Institutionalization

Adopting a New Curriculum at a Japanese Weekend School

Robert M. Uriu and Masako O. Douglas

1 Introduction

This chapter describes how the leadership of a small, independent language school, Orange Coast Gakuen (OCG), tried to fundamentally change its approach to teaching the Japanese language.[1] OCG is located in Orange County, California, roughly halfway between Los Angeles and San Diego, and was established in 1975 by Japanese immigrants, making it one of the oldest Japanese weekend schools in the region. The school holds classes for four and a half hours on Saturday mornings, and has a 39-week school year that begins in early August and ends in mid-June.

We start with a discussion of how institutional change is an inherently political process, and argue that politics can be particularly important when a school is first considering a curriculum change. While this volume focuses on the subsequent process of institutionalization, we look first at how actors who are committed to maintaining the status quo are often able to block the introduction of major change. We argue that such changes are more likely after some sort of institutional crisis in which the existing status quo is disrupted and stakeholders are forced to reassess their interests. At the same time, major change also requires that a viable alternative is available that can be implemented at a reasonable cost. It is thus not surprising that schools often find it difficult to initiate, much less institutionalize, major curriculum change.

We then discuss this process as it relates to the experience of OCG. As described in section 2, teachers and parents at the school had for years debated whether to change its traditional curriculum, but were never able to form a consensus on which alternative to adopt. It was only after a major crisis, in which the school became independent from an umbrella organization known as the System, to which it had belonged, that major change became possible. As described in section 3, leaders were able to use this opportunity to finally introduce a less traditional, more appropriate heritage language curriculum.

Implementing the new curriculum involved a number of years filled with conflict and tension for all involved, as discussed in sections 4, 5, and 6. Fortunately, we believe that we have turned a corner, and have made considerable progress toward institutionalizing the new curriculum. While we are by no means yet "out of the woods," we have now reached the stage of trying to make this curriculum change a permanent one.

2 The Politics of Initiating Curricular Change

We start by recognizing that institutionalization of a new curriculum will always involve a political process, implying that stakeholders with different levels of power and influence pursue their own interests in an organizational setting. In a typical school, shareholders such as administrators, teachers, and parents may advocate policies that they believe are best for the institution, but might also pursue more selfish motivations. As Ekholm and Trier (1987) argue, institutionalization often involves "dialectic tensions," or a constant but shifting struggle between the established "local culture" and the new "contra culture" (p. 15). The outcome of this struggle is indeterminate and may also be *independent* of the merits of the innovation in question. That is, even good ideas may be rejected as the result of actors pursuing self-serving political motives.

The Proclivity for the Status Quo

Politics can play an even more decisive role in the "pre-initiation stage," when an organization is first debating whether to even try to adopt an innovation. Organizations, and the stakeholders that compose them, often develop a preference for maintaining the status quo, and are thus inherently resistant to change—a situation political scientists describe as "institutional stasis." Proposals to introduce a fundamental curriculum change, for instance, might be opposed by current teachers who will be required to learn a new method. Another stakeholder that might be reluctant to consider a change is the school administration, which may have invested considerable resources in support of the older method of teaching, including teaching materials and equipment. Replacing or modifying these existing assets will be potentially very costly. Still others might have simply become used to the old way of doing things, especially if the old approach had been moderately successful. Put simply, making any change in a curriculum will involve costs, ranging from physical costs to the more psychic costs of adapting to something new.

In the language of this volume, any new curriculum ideas would have to replace, or displace, a curriculum that has itself already been institutionalized. Ekholm, Vandenberghe, and Miles (1987) describe this as a process of "de-institutionalization" (p. 244), in which the power of those who oppose change is somehow reduced or bypassed as a prerequisite for an innovation to be introduced. When an organization is stable and operating smoothly, the defenders of the status quo will likely have the upper hand. While change is of course not impossible, any new ideas need to be extremely compelling if they are to overcome built-in resistance to change.

The Role of Crisis

Others have noted the many factors that may affect curricular reform, including organizational complexity, the decision-making process, the degree of consensus and divisiveness, time constraints, financial pressures, issues involving staff workload and development, and student abilities and limitations (Cheung & Wong, 2011; Gruba, Moffat, Sondergaard, & Zobel, 2004). We focus here on the importance of crisis, which we understand as a period of difficulty, trouble, or instability. It is in these times that existing definitions of interests are more likely to be disrupted, questioned, and perhaps changed. The result may be what political scientists refer to as a "policy space," in which political relationships become more fluid, and actors have more room to introduce new ideas, build new coalitions, and transform existing structures.

In an educational setting, a common form of crisis is one in which most stakeholders realize that the current approach to teaching is simply not working. In the face of mounting evidence that the organization is not achieving its goals, more and more stakeholders may question current practices. The school may face pressure to change directions, either from inside stakeholders or from the school's clientele. In crises, stakeholders may see their interests as no longer served by the status quo, and political upheaval may make it more likely that an alternative will be considered. The level of crisis we have in mind here goes well beyond what Surry and Ely (2001) describe as "dissatisfaction with the status quo," which they define as an "innate feeling" that "things could be better," or a sense of "falling behind" (p. 189). But everybody, always, has some dissatisfaction or a feeling that the things could be better; our argument is that a high level of crisis is often needed in order for actors to *act*.[2]

Even if a school is actively seeking a new approach, this alone may not be enough to lead to the adoption of a new curriculum, given that major stakeholders might agree that "we have to try something new," but the question will remain, "what?" For initiation of an innovation to take place there must be an alternative available (Merton, as cited in Miles & Louis, 1987, p. 31) that not only promises to solve the current crisis, but that can also be adopted at an acceptable cost. There is no guarantee, however, that an alternative curriculum that is better than the current one will be found. Additionally, even if research indicates that a new curriculum will be a superior one, stakeholders must be confident that it will work in practice. Because the costs of change tend to be immediate and certain, whereas the benefits may be long-term and uncertain, it is perhaps not surprising that many good ideas are not even considered, much less implemented.

To conclude this section, we question models that imply a neat, organized process in which a school identifies a potential innovation, does a careful cost-benefit analysis, and then systematically implements the innovation. This sort of rational model may have the process backwards: Perhaps, in practice, organizations more often face a crisis and only *then* initiate a search for solutions.[3] While an institution in crisis should of course do its best to conduct a rational analysis of costs and benefits, our point is that the messy process of politics and crisis may itself play a major role in the decision to adopt a curriculum change in the first place.

3 Prelude to Change: OCG's Curriculum Before the Crisis

As a typical Japanese heritage language (HL) school, OCG has long grappled with a problem that has beset many other similar schools: whether to adopt traditional teaching methods used in Japan, versus adopting an approach that is more suited to Japanese children born and raised in the U.S. The dominant approach used in most Japanese language schools has been a version of Japan's national curriculum, or the approach "prescribed by the Japanese government for students in Japan" (Doerr & Lee, 2009, p. 426), henceforth referred to as *kokugo kyōiku*. This has been the case with most of the Japanese schools in Orange County. Not only was the *kokugo kyōiku* approach used by the largest Japanese school organization in the area that caters to families who plan on returning to Japan, but also variants of the approach were adopted by a number of new Japanese language schools and private tutoring schools (*juku*) that have recently entered the market, even as demand for Japanese language instruction has declined. The school System that OCG was a part of used a watered-down version of *kokugo kyōiku* instruction.

While the *kokugo kyōiku* approach may be appropriate for children who will return to Japan after a few years' stay in the U.S., it is less suitable for children born in the U.S., or who will be living here for longer than five years (Douglas, n.d.). The essential problem is that children raised in Japan are already fluent in age-appropriate interpersonal communication skills and have acquired basic grammatical and cultural knowledge before they start formal schooling. The job of the school is thus to help students acquire literary skills and academic language. In this context, a curriculum that focuses on reading and writing is effective. This approach, however, will often be counterproductive for students raised in the U.S., even those living in a predominantly

Japanese-language home environment. Many things differ, including the students' level of every-day exposure to the language, range of vocabulary, and basic cultural understandings. This implies that, because children raised here have not already developed sufficient oral and conversational skills, the rigorous academic training methods used in schools in Japan may not be effective: For many students, memorizing *kanji* lists or passages from books will be tedious and meaningless if they do not already know what most of the words mean.

For most of its history, OCG has also used a modified version of *kokugo kyōiku*, despite the fact that nearly all of our families had decided to stay permanently in the U.S., even those families in which both parents had been born and raised in Japan. In addition, over the years we have seen an increase in the number of parents born and raised in the U.S., as well as parents who are not of Japanese descent. Many at the school recognized that the traditional approach did not make sense, but effecting change was difficult to achieve. Part of the reason was that OCG had always been at least moderately successful as a school, and thus few saw the need for a dramatic change. OCG has always had some very good, caring, and hardworking teachers, and our Parent Association (PA) has always been extremely active. As a result, over the years our enrollment had held steady at around the hundred-student mark, and many of our more proficient students were able to do quite well in this environment. At the same time, a growing number of students, most of whom simply lacked the necessary language background, did less well. Many struggled, becoming less interested in what was being taught and disenchanted with studying Japanese altogether. This situation put our teachers in a bind: If they followed the traditional approach and taught at a rapid pace, many students would struggle, but if they made instruction less rigorous, the more proficient students would feel less challenged and therefore less motivated. Keeping all students engaged and motivated is always the most difficult task for any teacher, so this dilemma caused some considerable discontent among our students, parents, and teachers.

OCG's road to its curriculum change began around 2008, when a handful of our teachers received some training in the HL approach. We refer to these teachers, who later played a key role in the curriculum makeover, as our "core teachers." By a stroke of great fortune, three experts in Japanese HL instruction were located just 15 miles away, at the California State University, Long Beach. After attending numerous workshops and presentations by these professors, who later became our "Long Beach advisors," our core teachers had become convinced of the viability of the approach.

The HL approach is a sophisticated one that is strongly grounded in advanced educational theory, but at the same time also embodies basic common sense. The approach, as we have adopted it, reflects many of the principles of Content-Based Language Instruction (CBLI). All class instruction and activities are in Japanese only. The curriculum recognizes that students learn more when they are interested in what they are studying, and when they perceive that what they are learning is relevant to them. Instruction thus integrates learning of language and content that is built around topics students are familiar within their own lives. Teachers use the study of a certain topic as a vehicle for teaching vocabulary, *kanji*, and grammar, as well as culture, critical thinking, and collaborative skills. By keeping the students engaged and focused on content, students will be more motivated and acquire their language skills in a very natural way. The approach also recognizes that students learn more when they are having fun. It is thus highly interactive, with an emphasis on positive interactions between teacher and student, small group activities, class discussions, and hands-on activities ranging from class cooking projects to school-wide cultural events. The curriculum is also structured to achieve recognized goals and age-appropriate standards, so it is thus not any less challenging than the traditional approach. But it is certainly more enjoyable, making it more likely that students will continue with their studies in the future, in college and hopefully beyond, i.e., creating "lifelong learners" of Japanese.

Around this time the OCG core teachers pushed through an important structural reform, which was to divide our classes into two separate tracks. One was labeled the Japanese as a Heritage Language (JHL) track, for students with a relatively strong background in the Japanese language (with one or both native parents, but most importantly the requirement that Japanese be predominantly spoken at home). The second track was for students with less background, where Japanese is not the primary language in the home environment. We labeled this the Japanese as a Foreign Language (JFL) track, but it should be noted that for the majority of these students Japanese was not truly a "foreign" language. In some cases, at least one parent was from Japan, and so some Japanese was usually spoken at home. In addition, these students often have a certain amount of cultural knowledge, such as familiarity with Japanese festivals, food, and so on.[4] This change helped solve the problem of how best to organize classes in which students' levels of language proficiency ranged so widely. Previously we had divided classes strictly by grade, with 11 classes covering children from kindergarten age through 12th grade. The HL approach advocates a multi-level approach, in which more than one grade is combined into one class. This approach allows teachers to observe and assess a student's development over time, while students are more comfortable in that they are able to study under the same teacher for more than a single year.

Over time, our core teachers also introduced elements of the HL approach into their classroom practices. In the process, they found that far more effective learning outcomes resulted, and became convinced that this curriculum would be our best choice, given the makeup of our families and students. Implementing this major change, however, met with considerable resistance. Many of our other teachers were wedded to *kokugo kyōiku* as the only way to teach Japanese, and further had no interest in learning any new approach. The strongest opponents of change were a handful of very vocal parents who were convinced that only the *kokugo kyōiku* approach was acceptable. Many of these parents reasoned that this approach had been effective in their own cases, so must be suitable for their children, and that anything that deviated from the approach used in Japan must be somehow less advanced, or somehow not as "authentic." Others felt that their children only learned when they were heavily challenged and forced to work extremely hard. These parents thus fit the stereotype described by Doerr and Lee (2009), in that they argued that the *kokugo kyōiku* approach was "the legitimate one and everything else is not" (p. 427).

At the same time, many parents on the opposite side of the spectrum had come to realize that the *kokugo kyōiku* approach was not effective for their children, but these parents did not have a good idea of what alternative approach would be better. Still another group of our parents had much lower expectations regarding language proficiency, and seemed to be more interested in having their children exposed to Japanese culture. These parents were the most strongly opposed to *kokugo kyōiku*, but also had little idea about what method would be more effective.

With our teachers, parents, and administrators pulling in different directions, we continued to spin our wheels, with little movement in one direction or another. Change was also not forthcoming from above, as the System to which we belonged was content with staying with the curriculum approach it had always followed, whether it was effective or not.

In sum, before the crisis of 2010, many in the school were not entirely happy with how Japanese was being taught, and many had a vague desire for change and improvement, while some supported the status quo. The main stakeholders at the school, the teachers and System administrators, did not have any consensus on what sort of changes would work. Without a crisis to impel us toward taking action, plus an attractive alternative that people could get behind, our school would almost certainly not have initiated any change. More likely, opposing factions would have canceled each other out, and would have blocked any effort toward reform. At most, we would have dabbled in piecemeal, incremental experimentation rather than true curriculum reform.

4 Initiating Organizational and Curricular Change: The Crisis of 2010

Many factors contributed to our decision to become an independent school. What we perceived as the System's lack of interest in curriculum reform was one factor in this decision. Equally important was what we perceived to be interference in OCG's longstanding autonomy. Even while we were a part of the System, OCG traditionally enjoyed a great deal of autonomy, including the hiring of teachers and many decisions related to the structure of our classes. The OCG parents thus reacted very strongly when the System attempted to demote or remove our core teachers, which we saw as petty and unjustified. At the same time, we were also concerned about the System's overall financial stability. For all of these reasons, the leadership of our PA was concerned enough to lobby OCG's board to take action. The board initially reacted cautiously, but after a half year of sometimes tense town hall meetings, negotiations with the System administrators, and a great deal of wrangling and debate, the board became convinced that reconciliation with the System was no longer possible. In June of 2010, the school held a secret ballot vote of its parents, who overwhelmingly voted to become an independent school.

In that summer before what would be our first school year, the board was given a unique chance to initiate a total remake of the school. This began as a top-down process, with a small number of people in decision-making positions. However, the board made a concerted effort to be as inclusive as possible and to consult as widely as it could. To do this it created a Steering Committee, which included our core teachers and the leadership of our PA. This committee sought to bring in as many opinions as possible, including parents, teachers, alumni, and other school supporters. After months of seemingly endless meetings, the board was able to come to some crucial decisions.

One important early decision was to reconfigure our governance structure so that all stakeholders would have a more effective voice in running the school. This was done by including representatives of the teachers and parents as formal members of the board. This is not a typical arrangement for a board, but we were determined to avoid the typical problem of board members becoming out of touch and not making decisions that serve the interests of everyone in the school. By giving the teachers and parents a more formal voice in the governance process, the goal was to increase their level of "buy-in" to whatever decisions were finally made. Even if one group was not entirely happy with a given decision, at least their representative would have been a part of the process, and would have been able to stand up for their interests. While this perhaps made our early discussions more time-consuming and sometimes difficult, the process also gave our eventual decisions more legitimacy and support.

Another change we made was to limit the extent of power that any one person could wield. We thus decided not to create the position of school principal. Rather, the board itself would act as a decision-making and governing body. And because the leadership of the teachers and the parents were both included as formal members of the board, in effect it was all of the stakeholders at the school who collectively ran OCG. Related to this, one of our unspoken norms was that operational authority should be delegated to the teachers and parents wherever possible, with the board only reserving final responsibility for approving such things as hiring decisions, budgets, and the like. And finally, to ensure that the school's leadership would always be accountable to our parents, we established that board members and PA leaders were to be elected directly by current parents, and subject to recall if necessary. This gave parents the final say over selecting their leadership, but it also built in incentives for leaders to stay in close contact with our current parents and to be actively involved with how the school was operating in practice.

It should be noted here that our inclusive board reflected what Ekholm and Trier (1987) refer to as the need for "collective ownership" (p. 15) if an innovation is to succeed. Of course, no one on the board knew anything about such theoretical issues; we were instead motivated by democratic principles of representation and accountability and, perhaps, a Japanese cultural proclivity for consensus building. Also relevant were the extensive and inclusive discussions that occurred prior to the introduction of the changes to the board, which expanded those that participated and contributed from a few to a broadly representative community. In this way, to use Ekholm and Trier's words, the innovations became "owned" (p. 15) by many. In hindsight, all these steps greatly aided the later process of institutionalization.

The decision to adopt the new curriculum was in a sense a more fundamental change than the organizational one involved in restructuring the board. However, it was arrived at without as much controversy as might be expected, given our years of debate and stasis. The driving force here was our core teachers, who made a compelling case to the board in terms of the philosophy and potential of the approach. The board members were very receptive to these ideas; they had for years grappled with our curriculum problems, and had come to the conclusion that the traditional approach was not suitable for our student population. It therefore only took a handful of meetings between some of the board members and the Long Beach professors to convince us of the wisdom of revamping the curriculum. Not only was their teaching philosophy a compelling one, it would make us an innovative school and, if successful, would give us a more distinctive identity. The decision to adopt the new curriculum was made without a lot of contentious debate.

OCG's Post-Independence Prospects

Looking back, the school's outlook in that first summer as an independent school was bleak. First, as mentioned, we were operating in a very competitive environment, so dissatisfied parents could easily join another school. Second, our former System decided to open a new branch not too far away from us, which siphoned off a substantial group of our former parents. Some of these parents preferred to remain loyal to the System, while others lacked confidence that OCG's new leadership would be able to successfully operate a school (which was understandable, as none of us had actually run a school before). Finally, some of our parents preferred the more traditional approach to teaching. As a result, in those ulcer-inducing weeks following our decision to go independent, OCG lost a third of its students and more than half of its teachers. Not only was the school reduced to its smallest size in recent history—59 students and four teachers—no one knew if our enrollments would recover or continue in a straight-line, downward trend.

In hindsight, and knowing that the school has not only survived but today seems to be thriving, we can perhaps see silver-lining advantages in some of these developments. The most important was that we were able to start over with a blank slate. First, many potential opponents of the new curriculum, both among teachers and parents, had already "voted with their feet" by switching to one of our rival schools. Because of this, we were able to bypass the normal political process, which involves what Ekholm and Trier (1987) describe as careful negotiations with the "local culture" (p. 15), or powerful vested interests, and the need to convince each group of the necessity for change.

Second, the abrupt nature of our crisis meant that we were given the opportunity to do a complete makeover of the curriculum. Rather than trying to introduce a new curriculum in a piecemeal fashion over a long period, it was perhaps better to introduce it in one fell swoop. This corresponds to what Eiseman, Fleming, and Roody (1990) call "Going for Broke," or choosing a wide-scale rather than incremental approach. A higher risk of failure may be present in this approach, but if successful, "then systemwide diffusion and institutionalization will be more easily achieved" (p. 34).

Of course, it should be clear that we are NOT recommending our near implosion as a model for others to follow! Obviously, the crisis we experienced was far more extreme than any school would consciously strive for—few schools would see losing so many of its students and teachers as an acceptable price to introduce a new curriculum. Far better would be the normal, sometimes arduous task of convincing stakeholders to embrace change. While we stand by our argument that *some* sort of crisis is often needed to shake up the status quo, the crisis hopefully will not be as extreme as ours.

In the end, perhaps our biggest advantage lay in the quality of our OCG parents, who over the years had developed a sense of connection to the school and to each other. Our PA had always been very active, and this included involving all families in putting on cultural events, fundraising, and numerous other activities to help the school. In the process, many had developed friendships and even a degree of loyalty to each other, to our teachers, and to the school. Viewed in a different perspective, we should perhaps focus more on the fact that fully two-thirds of our families decided to stay with us, despite what was surely a high degree of uncertainty and skepticism about our future.

As OCG embarked on its first year, then, the school leadership had already made a strong commitment to a new curriculum that sounded very good in theory, but which we had not seen tried on a large scale elsewhere. In fact, we had actually made a much deeper commitment, as we had staked the school's viability on the success of the new curriculum. In short, in our case initiation and institutionalization were not simply abstract processes; in many ways they were synonymous with our very survival as an ongoing school.[5]

5 Implementing the New Curriculum: The Rocky First Years

We did not know it then, but declaring independence turned out to be the easy part. We faced ongoing difficulties in our first three years stemming from operating a new school while at the same time implementing a new curriculum. These goals proved to be much more difficult and costly, and involved higher levels of stress and tension, than any of us had imagined. Many tasks were involved, but the main ones in those early years included training all our teachers in the new approach, creating suitable teaching materials, and convincing our remaining parents that the new curriculum was the best for their children.

Here it is necessary to state in the strongest terms that without the guidance of our Long Beach advisors, we would not have been able to accomplish any of these early tasks. Looking back, it turns out that one of the board's most important decisions was to retain the services of these advisors in a formal way. The advisors provided a level of expertise and authority that ensured that everyone in the school would continue to move in the same direction. For instance, there were of course a number of occasions when our teachers or parents questioned some of the elements of the new curriculum. Had these questions remained unaddressed, they may very well have formed into doubts, then criticisms, and then perhaps outright opposition. But because our advisors were able to explain the thinking and philosophy behind the new curriculum, we did not have to face this situation. In our case, in addition to collective ownership and inclusive discussions that drew in members from within the organization, expertise and personnel from outside the organization also contributed to institutionalization (Ekholm et al., 1987).

Our Teachers: Overworked and Underpaid

The most important and difficult early task was to adequately train our new teachers in the curriculum, and to make sure that it was consistently used in their classes. The advisors met with our teachers every Saturday after school and also held a series of workshops to train them in new pedagogical techniques, including the design of curricular goals and objectives, multi-age and multi-level differentiated instruction, standards- and proficiency-based instruction, assessment design, scaffolding, spiraling, and many other current "best practice" teaching approaches. These training sessions were especially frequent in that first year, but have continued to this day. Behind the scenes, the advisors consulted weekly with the teachers on their upcoming lesson plans, and spent many hours suggesting changes in the details of each lesson. Every week, at least one of the advisors came to the school to observe the teachers in action, and then offered real-time tips and advice on how to improve their classes. We cannot endorse enough the argument by Ekholm et al. (1987, p. 250) that external support is an important element of institutionalization.

In practice, however, the process of training our teachers was a difficult one that resulted in considerable conflict. The first problem was that all of our teachers faced a steep learning curve early on, as the new curriculum was not easy to master. This was true even for the core teachers who had endorsed the curriculum, as they had only been exposed to its general principles. But these teachers and some of the new teachers we hired were enthusiastic about learning and improving, and were highly motivated to put in the required effort. On the other hand, some of our other teachers proved to be either unable or unwilling to embrace the new curriculum. Some were willing but found the new method too difficult to learn, or were not able to change their old ways of teaching. Still others had been trained in traditional teaching techniques and remained resistant to the new approach. These teachers tended to view the suggestions from our advisors as uncomfortable criticisms, which created a different sort of tension.

A second burden the teachers faced was that each of them had to create new class materials, sometimes from scratch. The problem here was that there were almost no existing teaching materials that fit our new approach. Most published textbooks were created in Japan and so naturally followed the *kokugo kyōiku* approach, while materials created in the U.S., which were somewhat better for us, were limited, and in any case none had explicitly adopted our methods. The board therefore decided to create our own instructional materials. Our advisors were again very helpful in this regard. For some of our classes they either wrote our early textbooks or arranged for other experts to write them. For other classes the advisors provided a curriculum guidebook that laid out the philosophy of the approach and some basic materials that could be adopted for classroom use. While these source materials were important and helpful, our teachers found that they needed to supplement them by creating additional classroom materials, including handouts, homework, and interactive and visual materials such as hands-on class activities and PowerPoint presentations. From our second year on, some of our core teachers took over the task of writing their own textbooks for their classes, an incredibly time- and effort-intensive process, which the school then published. (We are not aware of this practice in any other similar language school setting.)

Another problem was that our teachers were not only overworked but initially underpaid, at least compared to the work they were doing. The board supported our teachers by hiring teaching assistants (TAs) and assigned a group of parents to assist in creating classroom materials. We also provided technology for each classroom, including projectors, document cameras, and remote clickers. The board approved an immediate raise in pay for all teachers, which made us competitive with the average language school. We also approved "curriculum stipends" to compensate teachers for their outside-of-class work in creating new materials, and established a policy of reimbursement for all materials used in class. Finally, we instituted a bonus system, which rewarded teachers who stayed with the school with a percentage of their annual salary.

This support, however, had its limits, especially in those first years. We faced a number of constraints in this regard. First, the board decided to hold our tuition at its former level, which was already extremely low, in an attempt to give the impression of stability and continuity. Second, the board decided to separate our curriculum budget from the rest of the school budget, and then make sure that our tuition income fully covered all curriculum-related expenses, including teacher salaries and textbook and material expenses, without relying on fundraising or other sources of income. (This might seem logical, but it was not the practice of our former System.) And finally, we had no way of knowing if our enrollment numbers would recover, so we felt that we could not raise teacher salaries too quickly. All of these constraints meant that our ability to be more generous on teacher compensation was severely circumscribed. The school leadership was painfully aware that our teachers felt overburdened and underpaid. And it gave us a rather helpless feeling to see how hard the teachers were working and knowing that, although we were doing what we could, we simply did not have the budget flexibility to do more.

All of these problems contributed naturally to us losing a large number of teachers, some of them very good ones. And, as good teachers are the lifeblood of any school, our high level of teacher turnover was without a doubt our biggest early problem, not only because of emotional ties but also because when a teacher left, the efforts and costs of training went with him or her. More of a problem was that hiring and training replacement teachers was also difficult, as our entire region has been experiencing a shortage of qualified teachers. While candidates were always told that they needed to learn our approach, we continued to have the same problems as in our first year—namely, that some of our new hires turned out to be unwilling or unable to learn the curriculum.

Things came to a head at the end of our third year when four of our teachers suddenly announced that they would not be returning the following year. This development caught the school leadership by surprise because all of them had embraced the new curriculum, and were teachers we hoped to build the school around in the future. We were suddenly faced with the panic-inducing possibility of returning to square one, with only our original core teachers remaining. At a long meeting with all of the teachers the school leadership agreed to make a number of changes, including decreasing the workload and increasing compensation. As discussed in the next section, this meeting represented a turning point for us: Not only did almost all of the teachers decide to stay, but our problem of high teacher turnover began to improve.

Our Parents: Receptive but Skeptical

Another important early task was to demonstrate to our remaining parents that the new curriculum was in fact working. Parents often have difficulty judging the effectiveness of a curriculum given that learning is a slow process and not usually noticeable from week to week. The advisors were again instrumental in dispelling some of the uncertainty among our parents. They held a number of workshops in which they explained the philosophy behind the curriculum, and in subsequent years were able to present some statistical evidence of how successful the approach had been. But their biggest role was simply being the voice of authority, which included their ability to address any questions or quasi-criticisms with solid academic research. As our first years drew to a close, our parents were mostly supportive of the new approach.

Perhaps even more important was that parents could see for themselves what was going on in their child's classrooms. The most immediate change was a noticeable improvement in the attitudes of the students, who were much more engaged in the content and conduct of classroom instruction. As a result, most parents were quite enthusiastic and vocal in their support of what we were doing, and the few who were not yet fully convinced by the approach, could see that the classroom environment had improved considerably. We counted it as a victory of sorts that no one was strongly critical of the new approach.

6 Institutionalizing the Curriculum: Progress and Remaining Tasks

By the criteria in this volume, and in spite of the incredible turmoil of those early years, the school had already made enormous strides in institutionalizing the new curriculum by the end of the third year. The school's leadership had committed itself to making the curriculum a permanent one, and it was in "stable, routinized" as well as "widespread use" (Eiseman et al., 1990, p. 15) in all classrooms. The board made "routine allocations of money and resources" (Eiseman et al., 1990, p. 15) in support of the curriculum, although it wanted to do more. And yet, even if we had early on met some important criteria for institutionalization, this does not mean that we were confident our innovations would last.

In retrospect, the teachers' meeting at the end of our third year was a turning point, and by the beginning of the next school year it had become clear that the future outlook was at least stable, if not bright. As of the writing of this chapter, not only do all of our classes follow the curriculum, but our current teachers are all committed to it. While teacher turnover is still a problem, the situation is now better than before. Among our parents, almost all have come to accept our teaching approach, and presumably their decision to stay with us reflects some level of satisfaction. Perhaps the best evidence is that the school has continued to attract more students, to the point that by our fifth anniversary as an independent school we had nearly tripled in size compared to that first summer of turmoil, growing from 59 students in 2010 to 160 in 2015, while our teacher roster has increased from our original four core teachers to more than 20 educational personal, including TAs and teachers of culture-focused classes.

It is now clear that the decision to adopt the new curriculum was the right one. Worth noting is that the relative quality of any curricular innovation has to be the single most important factor in determining whether it will become successfully institutionalized. This sounds like common sense, but some writings on institutionalization seem to discuss so many factors and criteria that the focus on the inherent quality of the innovation itself is at times obscured. But the best-planned, most well-thought-out strategy for institutionalization will only work if the innovation is, in fact, a good one. Luckily for us, the approach that we adopted is indeed very compelling and attractive, and this alone accounts for much of our progress toward institutionalization.

At the same time, we also know that we have more work to do in the coming years if the curriculum is to be fully institutionalized. The remaining tasks revolve around continuing to reduce teacher turnover, cementing the curriculum in all of the classes, keeping our parents happy, and socializing future leaders into supporting the approach.

Keeping the Teachers Happy

Over the past two years our rate of teacher turnover has declined considerably. One reason is that we have increased teacher pay to the point that we are well above the average for weekend language schools. We also continue to support the teachers through material purchases, TA support, and retention bonuses, and we now also pay extra for oversized classes. However, if we truly are one of the best schools around (as we now believe we are), we need to do more to be the best in terms of our pay scale.

More importantly, the burden on our teachers has declined. First, all of our current teachers have been fully trained in the new curriculum approach, and can now focus on fine-tuning their teaching techniques. This has also allowed us to reduce the number of workshops and after-school meetings. Second, our current teachers have built up most of the materials they need for their classes, which they can use from year to year. We have also created an online system that allows our teachers to more effectively share materials and ideas with each other. Our teachers are still working hard to improve their teaching materials, but they at least no longer have to create everything from scratch.

Our next step is to make our teaching materials more concrete, organized, and as close to permanent as possible. The school has thus embarked on a "Curriculum Project," which aims to have each teacher collect all of their class materials in a more systematic way, including a full set of lesson plans, PowerPoint presentations, class activity materials, handouts, assessment materials, and the like. Having these instructional materials organized in a more or less permanent form ensures that they can be used year after year, with only minor editing. This promotes institutionalization in that the details of the curriculum are laid out, and future changes will likely be mostly incremental.

A second goal is to create a system in which we have a cadre of qualified and trained teachers who are ready and able to step in to teach whenever needed. We have made progress toward this goal in two ways. First, as teacher turnover has declined, we have been able to be more selective in whom we hire. We can now make learning and following our curriculum a more forceful requirement of being hired and can also use it as a condition for continued employment. Second, we have been working to train potential teachers by hiring them in TA-type roles, which not only gives them exposure to the approach, but also allows them to accumulate hands-on, direct experience before they are asked to handle their own classroom. We also have a "mentor" system, in which experienced teachers are assigned to guide and train our newcomers, and potential teachers are also asked to participate in all of our workshops and study groups. These practices allow us to better judge which teachers will be able to teach most effectively, and in which class environment. Teacher turnover cannot be avoided, but with materials, training, and support available, a new teacher can step into the role more easily.

Keeping Our Parents Happy

Another task ahead for us is to continue to keep parents content and supportive of the approach. As our current parent complaints seem to be limited to "normal" issues, such as classroom discipline or a specific teacher, rather than focused on the curriculum itself, this is perhaps a sign that we have indeed made great progress toward institutionalization. Also, a great many of our new parents have chosen the school precisely because they were attracted by our curriculum approach. As our student count has increased, the school is no longer as desperate to keep each and every one of them as we were in those first years. We now realize that if a family strongly prefers a more traditional approach to teaching they (and we) will perhaps be better off if they join a different school. This perspective has made us more confident in focusing on making *our* curriculum stronger and more effective.

One interesting change over time is that most of our parents, the vast majority of whom have joined us over the past five years, now no longer have any recollection of what our old system was like. For these parents, being told that students are now more engaged in learning—while certainly true—does not carry much weight. We need to keep our parents satisfied with the progress their children are making *now*. This is to some extent made easier because for most of our parents, our way of teaching is the only way they know. Even for those parents who have been taught in Japan, and so know what a traditional approach would look like, ours is the only program in which they have seen their *children* being taught. And a growing number of our younger parents have no experience with Japanese language instruction of *any* kind. Thus, for most of them, our way of teaching is the only one they know or can even imagine—perhaps the very definition of an institutionalized curriculum.

Making the Curriculum "Independent of Persons"

Among the last tasks remaining for us is to make the curriculum so entrenched that it will remain in place even if many of our current teachers and parent leaders were to leave the school. As Eiseman et al. (1990) argue, an important stage in institutionalization occurs when the innovation can survive even after the people who initiated the change leave—what they refer to as an innovation having "person independence" (p. 15). We may be at the point where the curriculum would still remain intact if we were to lose *some* of our current teachers, but this might not be the case if we were to again see a major exodus. As discussed above, cementing a permanent set of curriculum materials will strengthen our ability to withstand future teacher turnover, the goal being to ensure that any new teacher will easily be able to step in and continue teaching our curriculum.

Similarly, the board and PA will need to keep socializing new leaders to support the current approach and way of doing things. The board has seen some turnover over the years, but all of our new members are committed to the curriculum. So far, it seems that potential future leaders of our PA are also supportive of the current curriculum. The strength and commitment of our parents to the school and to each other have always been the school's greatest asset, and this appears to remain as strong as ever.

However, it is also important to recognize that we are not yet "independent of persons" when it comes to our curriculum advisors. Even though their direct role and the level of their involvement have decreased compared to the early years, we still depend on them in many ways. While our commitment to the broad approach is not likely to change, the approach itself is a dynamic one that is constantly being updated and improved. Thus, we will need to retain their expertise if we are to keep up with the most current best practices. In addition, we rely on the advisors to continue to train our new teachers, the constant process of helping our current teachers improve, and finally their role in educating our parents about the benefits of the approach. Their authoritative voice continues to be important in keeping us all moving in a common direction. We will need them to continue to play some sort of role for the foreseeable future.

7 Conclusion: Changing the OCG Identity

Many levels of institutionalization have been discussed in this chapter. But there is a deeper, and perhaps final, level of institutionalization that has not—what political scientists would call an "ideational" level, where actors come to redefine their very "identity" in ways that incorporate a new understanding of their interests and values. This may be what Ekholm and Trier (1987) mean when they speak of a new curriculum becoming a "constituent element of the institution" (p. 14). At that point, stakeholders no longer think of the new curriculum as new or innovative. Rather, they simply think in terms of "this is how we do things," or even more basically, "this is who we are." We will consider our new curriculum fully institutionalized when we achieve this final and deepest level of institutionalization. Although most of our teachers and parents are supportive, there is still a constant need to educate and socialize them with regard to our approach.

It is still the case that the continued institutionalization of this curriculum is tied to our school's survival. We are increasingly confident that we will survive, and hopefully continue to thrive. At the same time, we are also fully aware that there is a great deal of work that remains to be done before we can fully stabilize the school and ensure the continued use of the curriculum. We are all committed to the hard work ahead. But perhaps we should also think back to where we were when we started out, and to appreciate how far we have come, and just how remarkable it is that we have been able to reach our current point.

Notes

1 This paper is based on the authors' participant observation and involvement in the process of curricular change, one as a political scientist who was a school administrator during the period discussed, the other as a specialist in heritage language education who served as one of the school's curriculum advisors. The authors thank Claire Hitchins Chik, our anonymous reviewer, and the OCG Board of Directors for their useful comments and suggestions.
2 As our reviewer points out, change can also be introduced by more positive developments, such as the sudden availability of external funds. This point is well taken, but in our experience with educational institutions, more negative forms of crises are far more common.
3 As one example, see Eiseman et al. (1990). Surry and Ely (2001, p. 185) refer to the standard model of adoption of an innovation as starting with acquiring "knowledge" of a new education technology, then proceeding in an orderly fashion from there. We suggest that reality is usually much messier than these models.
   The political process, of course, continues even after the initial adoption of a new curriculum. Stakeholders may still be wedded to the traditional approach, and may work to undermine the new curriculum. These activities may range from such things as denigrating the new approach, to blocking needed funding, to lobbying decision makers to revert to the old system. The politics of resistance have the potential to derail very promising new educational ideas.
4 According to a survey of the home environment of families at the school, the majority of our families were bilingual, often consisting of mothers who are native speakers of Japanese and fathers who are native speakers of English (Douglas, Kataoka, & Chinen, 2013).
5 It is worth noting here that these concerns for survival may pertain more to independent, private schools. That is, public schools, schools that are part of a larger school system, or that are affiliated with another organization such as a church, may be much more stable. In those cases, even if an innovation were to fail, the school itself would likely remain viable. We did not have that luxury.

References

Cheung, A. C. K., & Wong, P. M. (2011). Factors affecting the implementation of curriculum reform in Hong Kong. *International Journal of Educational Management, 26*(1), 39–54.

Doerr, N., & Lee, K. (2009). Contesting heritage: Language, legitimacy, and schooling at a weekend Japanese language school in the United States. *Language and Education, 23*(5), 425–441.

Douglas, M. (n.d.). Japanese. *Teaching heritage languages: Start teaching: Lesson 10*. Retrieved from http://startalk.nhlrc.ucla.edu/default_startalk.aspx

Douglas, M., Kataoka, H., & Chinen, K. (2013). Development of Japanese as a heritage language in the Los Angeles conurbation. *Heritage Language Journal, 10*(2), 43–63.

Eiseman, J. W., Fleming, D. S., & Roody, D. S. (1990). *Making sure it sticks: The school improvement leader's role in institutionalizing change*. Andover, MA: The Regional Laboratory.

Ekholm, M., & Trier, U. P. (1987). The concept of institutionalization: Some remarks. In M. B. Miles, M. Ekholm, & R. Vandenberghe (Eds.), *Lasting school improvement: Exploring the process of institutionalization* (pp. 13–21). Leuven, Belgium: Acco.

Ekholm, M., Vandenberghe, R., & Miles, M. B. (1987). Conclusions and implications. In M. B. Miles, M. Ekholm, & R. Vandenberghe (Eds.), *Lasting school improvement: Exploring the process of institutionalization* (pp. 243–267). Leuven, Belgium: Acco.

Gruba, P., Moffat, A., Sondergaard, H., & Zobel, J. (2004). *What drives curriculum change?* Retrieved from http://crpit.com/confpapers/CRPITV30Gruba2.pdf

Miles, M. B., & Louis, K. S. (1987). Research on institutionalization: A reflective review. In M. B. Miles, M. Ekholm, & R. Vandenberghe (Eds.), *Lasting school improvement: Exploring the process of institutionalization* (pp. 25–44). Leuven, Belgium: Acco.

Surry, D. W., & Ely, D. P. (2001). Adoption, diffusion, implementation, and institutionalization of educational innovations. Retrieved from http://www.southalabama.edu/coe/bset/surry/papers/adoption/chap.htm

7

Sustainable Approaches to Complementary Education in England

Raymonde Sneddon

1 Introduction

Immigrant communities in the UK have a long tradition of developing complementary schools, i.e., community-run programs held after regular school hours or on weekends that teach the home, or heritage, languages spoken by these communities (McLean, 1985). As newly arrived immigrants discover that their children lose the active use of the home language once they start school, and more established communities experience a loss of cultural identity, they have demonstrated great ingenuity and creativity in setting up schools for their children to address these trends.

The present chapter outlines the context in which these schools have developed: the patterns of immigration that have created the language ecology and the educational and political contexts in which they operate. Immigration trajectories, socioeconomic status, and political power impact different communities in different ways. The swings and roundabouts of government policy present different opportunities and challenges to particular communities as they seek to raise their profile in the wider community, establish legitimacy for their language, and develop sustainable structures for the language and cultural education of their children.

This chapter focuses on two well-established, innovative, and contrasting models of complementary education, both operating in the east of London, that were developed in response to the very different socioeconomic, historical, and geographical situations of the communities that set them up: a program in the Borough of Tower Hamlets developed by the Bangladeshi community and funded by the Tower Hamlets Borough Council; and the Shpresa Programme, created and supported by the Albanian refugee community in the Borough of Newham.[1] Using the concept of institutionalization developed by Miles, Ekholm, and Vandenberghe (1987), the chapter explores the ways in which the schools have developed innovative approaches and curricula, engaged partners, and built networks, and created procedures for sustainability that are replicable in different communities, while also evaluating the different vulnerabilities of the two approaches.

2 Migration and Language

London has long been a magnet for immigration. The east end of London in particular, with its employment opportunities and cheap housing, has traditionally been the point of arrival of new migrants. As migrants prosper, they move to areas deemed more desirable and make room for new communities. Prior to World War II, the majority of immigrants to London were Irish, Polish, and Russian Jews (Block, 2005; Fishman, 1997). After the war, in addition to the migrants who came as political refugees, Britain actively encouraged economic immigration, especially from Southern Europe and the New Commonwealth countries, to support reconstruction and a growing economy (Linguistic Minorities Project, 1985). The legacy of this period has resulted in a number of distinctive neighborhoods in the greater London area (and in other industrial cities in the Midlands and the north of England) becoming identified with a particular second- or third-generation community (Baker & Eversley, 2000; von Ahn, Lupton, Greenwood, & Wiggins, 2010). Within these neighborhoods, networks and services were developed that included complementary schools. By the 1980s, the most commonly taught languages were Bengali, Greek, Gujerati, Punjabi, Turkish, and Urdu.

Since the 1990s, the language ecology of the UK has changed substantially, as wars, famine, ecological catastrophes, and a global movement of labor within and beyond the European Union have brought new communities—transnationally connected and socioeconomically stratified—to settle, and greatly increase the nature and scale of diversity in the whole country (Goodson, Coaffee, & Rowlands, 2010; Vertovec, 2007). In 2008, a poll of languages spoken in London schools recorded 233 languages (Eversley et al., 2010). Substantial numbers of children in London schools now speak Albanian, Amharic, Bulgarian, Latvian, Lithuanian, and Romanian, with Polish being the most widely spoken language of all. However, as pointed out above, these children learn English quickly and start to lose the family language rapidly as schooling progresses, leading migrant parents to seek out mother tongue education after they are settled and have overcome their first priority of economic survival.

3 The Development of Complementary Schools in England

Mother tongue schools have been set up not only to ensure that children learn the family language but also to strengthened their "cultural and religious identity in the face of the threat of cultural assimilation" (Verma, Zec, & Skinner, 1994, p. 12). Such schools vary greatly in size and organization, reflecting the varying needs of communities at the micro-level and the resources available to them: A dozen pupils may meet in someone's living room, while the parents of several hundred pupils may hire the facilities of a large school after hours. Some schools are run entirely by volunteers, while others have salaried teachers. The social and economic status of communities has an impact on the kinds of organizations that they can support. The prospects for sustainability vary greatly as a result. For example, a large Arabic school in west London and a large Iranian school in north London draw their pupils from professional families who can afford to pay fees that cover the full cost of running the school. While they are generally dependent on the enthusiasm and expertise of individuals in the community when they are founded, once established, they can employ experienced staff and continue to operate as long as there is a need for them in the community.

However, a majority of schools offer their services to economically disadvantaged communities (especially new arrivals and refugees) unable to pay more than modest fees, if any at all. These depend on grant aid from a range of sources including, from the 1970s onwards, small grant schemes for local community groups offered by a number of local authorities. However, the politics of austerity and changing priorities have greatly reduced the number of authorities offering this assistance. Several charitable foundations such as the Trust for London and the Paul Hamlyn Foundation sometimes offer substantial grants, but these are always tied to the development of innovative practices and are time limited.

Some schools are isolated and operate informally; others become registered charities; some come under umbrella organizations that provide a framework that encompasses training and teaching materials. Schools have different priorities and procedures: Some teach curricula that prepare their students for English public examinations, such as the General Certificate of Secondary Education (GCSE), taken at age 16, and Advanced (A) Levels, taken at age 18, where these are available in the community language, while others are more focused around issues of culture and personal identity (Conteh, Martin, & Robertson, 2007; Lytra & Martin, 2010).

4 Multilingualism in Education and Political Discourse

The status of complementary schools is closely related to the status of the languages they teach, and there is currently a debate in the UK about the implications of the terminology used in this area. The term "heritage languages," widely used in North America (e.g., Valdés, 2005), is not common in the UK. The most widely used term is "community languages," by which is meant the languages spoken by communities originating in migration. The term was originally used in education to distinguish these languages from the modern languages (all European) taught in the mainstream school curriculum.

From the 1980s, it has also been possible to study a number of community languages in mainstream schools, and examinations (GCSE and A Levels) are currently available in 22 languages (though take-up is low and GCSE/A Level qualifications for lesser taught languages are under threat from government policy at present). However, the distinction between community languages and modern languages is now deemed to be inappropriate. For example, Mandarin and Arabic, community languages that are recognized as having significant economic importance, are now taught as modern languages in the school curriculum (Anderson, 2008), and French, the most popular modern language, is now also considered a community language given that it is widely spoken by recent migrants from Francophone Africa as well as by a substantial expatriate community from France (Sneddon, 2014).

There is profound ambivalence in public discourse in England in relation to the bilingualism and multilingualism of immigrant communities. When substantial numbers of children arrived in the 1970s, they were expected to assimilate and learn English rapidly (Bourne, 1991). Settled communities lobbied for education in their languages in mainstream schools, and a major study, *The Other Languages of England*, documented the development and prevalence of mother tongue teaching in England in both the complementary and the mainstream sectors (Linguistic Minorities Project, 1985). However, hopes of developing a policy for sustainable community language education within mainstream schools were dashed by the Swann Report into the Education of Children from Ethnic Minority Groups, which concluded that language maintenance was "best achieved within the ethnic communities themselves" (Department of Education and Science, 1985, p. 406). Although the Swann Report did not recommend the teaching of community languages in the mainstream sector, it did make recommendations to support the complementary sector, in particular through a recommendation that mainstream schools offer their premises to complementary schools and that community language teachers be included in professional training opportunities. The Inner London Education Authority (ILEA) was one of the few authorities to implement these recommendations. The ILEA (which was abolished in 1990) also supported the teaching of community languages through a Mother Tongue Inspectorate that deployed a team of 40 peripatetic teachers in mainstream schools. When a National Curriculum came into force in 1988, it was resolutely monolingual and English focused (Department of Education and Science, 1988).

In the early twenty-first century, attitudes within government to the teaching of community languages in the mainstream and complementary sectors became more positive. A report from the Department of Education noted the benefits that pupils derived from attending complementary schools (Department for Education and Skills, 2003). Financial support was offered (on a time-limited basis) to the National Resource Centre for Supplementary Education (NRC) to develop a national database of complementary schools and a Quality Framework to raise standards of management and teaching. The National Languages Strategy (Department for Education and Skills, 2002), in creating a strategy for the teaching of languages to all 7- to 11-year-olds within mainstream schools, specified that any language could be taught, subject to demand and the availability of teachers.

A project that made a significant impact on community languages and complementary schools was the Our Languages project (The National Archives, n.d.), funded by the Department for Children, Schools and Families and run by CILT, the National Centre for Languages (confusingly still called CILT from its earlier title, Centre for Information on Language Teaching), with the aim of encouraging the teaching of community languages. A particular strength of the project was the way it sought out, documented, and disseminated through its website innovative practices in language teaching and developed partnership arrangements between complementary and mainstream schools. It encouraged the development of teaching resources (Anderson, 2008) and published a Tool Kit to encourage the further development of teaching partnerships.

The increased demand for the teaching of community languages in both the mainstream and the complementary school sectors led to the development of teacher education courses in 10 universities (CILT, 2005). A survey of teacher education provision carried out by Ofsted (Office for Standards in Education, 2008), the UK's school inspection service, noted the popularity of flexible training courses, which enabled university language education departments to collaborate with both mainstream and complementary schools.

The initiatives described above were very positive in terms of promoting both the learning of a wider range of languages and the value of developing the multilingualism that was already present in the community. However, the teaching of community languages was not backed by any resources, and a new National Curriculum made as little reference to bilingualism as its predecessor (Department for Education, 2014). A coalition government elected in 2010 stated its position with respect to community languages as follows:

> The Government recognises the benefits that derive from the maintenance of ethnic minority linguistic and cultural traditions, but believes the main responsibility for maintaining mother tongue rests with the ethnic minority communities themselves. We believe that English should be the medium of instruction in schools.
>
> *(Overington, 2012, p. 5)*

While the coalition government and its successor have been active in encouraging more language teaching, they have not responded to urgent calls from the business community and the diplomatic and security services to build on the existing language skills of bilingual citizens and to widen the range of languages being taught in schools (Tinsley, 2013). With respect to community languages, at the time of writing, the pendulum has swung again to a far less positive position. In the first place, a failure to fund the Our Languages website has led to its closure. The flexible training courses for teachers have also been closed as a substantial reduction in language-student numbers allocated by the government to teacher education establishments made it impractical to run them. In addition, communities are currently challenging a proposal to reduce the number of languages for which qualifications are available at examination level (Steer, 2015). The constant changes in the policy context in which they operate add to the challenges faced by complementary schools that aim to provide high-quality, sustainable education services to their communities.

5 Sustainability and Institutionalization of Complementary Schools

Sustainability is a constant concern for complementary schools, and there are a number of reasons why they come and go. As organizations set up by communities to meet their specific language and cultural needs, they begin and end as the language ecology of their area changes. Schools may close for a number of reasons, some of which are very specific and local: For example, demand drops in the community as members move out of the area in search of better opportunities, and a new generation is less enthusiastic about learning the family language. As attendance at the schools is voluntary, children will vote with their feet if the quality of their experience declines, whether through a change of leadership, a shortage of good teachers, or a shortage of funds that restricts access to resources and good premises.

Miles et al. (1987) have used the concept of institutionalization to explore how innovative educational projects become adopted and embedded into the regular practice of educational institutions, ensuring their stability. Ekholm and Trier (1987) discuss the process of institutionalization through an evaluation of the challenges facing the adoption of new educational technology in schools. Eiseman, Fleming, and Roody (1990) recommend the use of the following six indicators of institutionalization:

1. Acceptance by relevant participants—a perception that the innovation legitimately belongs;
2. Stabilization and routinization of the innovation;
3. Widespread use of the innovation throughout the institution or organization;
4. Firm expectation that use of the practice and/or product will continue within the institution or organization;
5. Continuation does not depend upon the actions of specific individuals but upon the organizational culture, structures, or procedures; and
6. Routine allocations of time and money.

(Adapted from pp. 12–13)

Both local circumstances and volatile language policy present a challenge to the sustainability of the complementary school sector as well as the teaching of community languages in the mainstream sector. This chapter will focus on the former environment.

Whether individual complementary school projects can survive and become institutionalized in the sense of becoming embedded, sustainable, and replicable within the mainstream local environment in which they operate depends on the extent to which they can respond to and meet the identified needs of the communities they serve, as well as seize opportunities for overcoming the challenges presented by current government policy. The following two sections offer examples of two contrasting models of innovative complementary schools working to develop sustainability in the east of London: the first from an established second- and third-generation community originating from Bangladesh, and the second from a recently migrated community of ethnic Albanians, most of whom arrived in Britain as refugees.

The author has a long history of involvement in the complementary school sector, both on the operational side, as a founding trustee of the Resource Unit for Supplementary and Mother

Tongue Schools (the forerunner of the present National Resource Centre for Supplementary Education), as founder of a complementary school, and as a researcher. She was approached by Shpresa for a formal evaluation of their complementary school program, which led to several studies from 2008 to 2013. The Tower Hamlets model of local authority-funded support was well known to the author through her involvement in an advisory capacity, through the joint development of teacher education opportunities, and extended interviews with key personnel in the local authority.

6 Bengali in Tower Hamlets

As mentioned in the introductory section, the east end of London has hosted many communities, both of refugees and economic migrants. The majority of the Bangladeshi community in the UK settled in the London Borough of Tower Hamlets, close to the City of London, taking advantage of the availability of skilled and semi-skilled employment opportunities. A majority of this community originate from the district of Sylhet in Bangladesh. While they speak Sylheti, a dialect of Bengali, they are educated in standard Bengali (Sneddon & Martin, 2012).

While the Bangladeshi community in Tower Hamlets is generally economically disadvantaged, the density of the community puts them in a unique position in the UK: 54% of all schoolchildren in Tower Hamlets are of Bangladeshi heritage. Another distinctive factor is their substantial community and political engagement. In addition to developing the usual commercial, social, and religious facilities, the community engages strongly with the democratic process and, for the last few years, councillors of Bangladeshi heritage have been in a majority on the Tower Hamlets Borough Council. This has enabled them to ensure that the local education authority has funded the mother tongue education that their constituents requested in both the mainstream and the complementary sectors.

Early in the Bengali settlement of Tower Hamlets, community organizations set up classes to teach Bengali to their children, using their own premises and employing their own teachers. In the mid-1990s, the Council took the decision to coordinate the work of these classes, and the teachers became part-time Council employees. At that point a few had UK teaching qualifications, some had qualifications from Bangladesh, and some had no formal teaching qualifications. To support the latter group, the Council negotiated with Tower Hamlets College to provide an accredited course for community language teachers. In 2002, the Council worked with the University of East London to develop a Post-Graduate Certificate of Education course (the standard teaching qualification in the UK) in Bengali and sponsored candidates to enroll in it.

Individual schools in the UK have considerable autonomy over their budget and their staffing. However, Tower Hamlets Council, through its Community Language Service (CLS) (originally known as the Mother Tongue Service), has retained a central role in the organization of language teaching in the borough, both of the traditionally commonly taught foreign languages such as French and Spanish and of the languages spoken by local communities. CLS is run by a team of six municipal civil servants and is responsible for recruiting, training, deploying, supporting, and monitoring teachers in partnership with community organizations and mainstream schools. CLS currently has a strong focus on monitoring the quality of the services offered in these organizations.

At the time of writing, CLS deploys teachers in partnership with community organizations in out-of-hours classes in 90 venues across the borough. While this program was originally developed as requested by the Bangladeshi community, all substantially represented minority communities in the borough have benefited from the policy. The majority of these teachers may teach Bengali, but also taught are Arabic, Cantonese, French, Lithuanian, Mandarin, Portuguese, Somali, Spanish, Urdu, and Vietnamese (Community Language Service [CLS], n.d.). A further support for community classes is the free use of mainstream schools after hours for those that do not have their own premises.

As the teaching of a modern language became mandatory in primary schools in 2014, the CLS team took responsibility for coordinating the establishment of this provision. While individual schools are free to employ their own teachers, many choose to buy into a service from CLS; this can range from the deployment of a peripatetic teacher to a full package that also includes a specially developed curriculum, monitoring, and assessment. The package is available for Arabic, Bengali, French, and Spanish. Integrating the management of teaching the more traditional modern languages with the languages of the community greatly raises the status of the latter, and that of the complementary schools that teach them in the area. This is evident in the integrated guide produced by the CLS, which covers languages taught both in mainstream schools and out-of-hours programs. The aim is:

> To complement the work of schools in raising attainment for all pupils by developing and delivering cost effective, coherent and inclusive language services.
>
> To play a central role in partnership with schools, Third Sector organisations and wider communities to deliver the council's vision for learning and achievement.
>
> *(CLS, 2007, p. 4)*

Tower Hamlets has, for a number of years, funded the development of a Scheme of Work for mother tongue teaching that blends the cultural input that the community values with the interests of London school children and the language requirements of the English examination system. This developed into the Scheme of Work for modern languages (Arabic, Chinese, French, Somali, and Spanish; Uddin & Mitchell, 2010). Assessment protocols were created (Uddin & Mitchell, 2002) and the first of a series of teaching guides has been produced (Hannan, 2014).

In recent years CLS has developed a monitoring system for classes offered in complementary schools. Pupil progress is monitored through tests carried out in Years 2 and 6 (ages 6 and 11). The results are entered into a database and the information on individual pupils is shared with parents and the pupils' mainstream schools. As well as regular in-service training, teachers are subject to performance management and are specifically trained to conduct and moderate exams. Secondary schools are notified about primary pupils with language skills who are about to enter their schools to ensure that pupils are placed in the appropriate sets.[2]

CLS is keen to promote the value of bilingualism, community learning, and mainstream/complementary school collaborations. It continues to explore innovative ways of encouraging the teaching of a wider range of languages at examination level. In 2010, it introduced a program to encourage pupils to take language GCSEs early (between the ages of 12 and 14, instead of the usual age of 16). As part of this program, GCSE classes in Arabic, Bengali, Mandarin, and Urdu are held in several venues, both complementary and mainstream. This initiative has proved to be very popular, with over two hundred students in the program, and has resulted in a very high standard of grades achieved, with 97% of pupils obtaining grades A★ (the very highest grade) to C. As a result of this success, a similar program has been introduced for A Levels (M. A. Hannan, personal communication, April 28, 2015).

The Council is intent on celebrating the achievements of its language learners. As well as holding a high-profile award ceremony to celebrate exam successes, the Mayor of Tower Hamlets hosts a yearly International Language Day event to highlight the achievements of pupils in the borough's complementary classes. Pupils aged 3 to 17 take to the stage to perform dance, poetry, music, and drama for a large audience. A writing competition is included, and parents and mainstream schools participate in the event.

While a few local authorities in England offer support for complementary schools and celebrate their achievements, none do so on the scale of Tower Hamlets. By taking responsibility for and funding the teaching of languages, the borough ensures that children are taught in safe and suitable premises which are free of charge, and that they are taught by trained and monitored teachers. They also ensure that pupils have access to public examinations (where these exist in a particular language) as not all schools are registered for all language examinations. By providing free, well-qualified staff and a curriculum relevant to London pupils, CLS contributes to the relevance of complementary schools in pupils' lives and therefore to their sustainability. They also remove the biggest fundraising challenge and ensure continuity, as leaving teachers are promptly replaced, and supply teachers are available to cover absences.

7 Albanian in Newham

While an established Bengali community has been able, through geographical concentration, to gain some measure of local political power and to create the viable system of complementary education described above, a new community formed by asylum seekers in the UK has worked to create an alternative model of sustainable complementary education with a minimum of resources.

Ethnic Albanians arrived in the UK in substantial numbers beginning in 1992, after fleeing the war in Kosovo. Many obtained refugee status and were dispersed throughout London. As the community's most immediate needs were met, the Albanians soon discovered that their children settled well into English schools, learned the language quickly, and then started losing the language of the home. This motivated families to create social structures for family support and language and cultural maintenance (Sneddon & Martin, 2012). In 2003, a group of women who had arrived as refugees set up the Shpresa Programme (*shpresa* means "hope" in Albanian) in the east London Borough of Newham. As well as providing a range of essential services, it focused strongly on integrating children into the mainstream school system, creating classes for children to learn Albanian, and supporting families to help their children with their schooling.

The women who started Shpresa arrived in the UK with nothing. They benefited from government policies and initiatives designed to promote integration and employment for refugees and also from charitable trusts that prioritized the needs of their children (Sneddon & Martin, 2012). Through personal experience they discovered the benefits of volunteering in mainstream organizations. In this way, they mixed with the local population, learned English, and acquired knowledge and skills that led to employment opportunities.

These experiences are at the heart of the model of complementary education that Shpresa developed. The organization approached schools that were known to have numbers of Albanian-speaking children and offered them a partnership: In return for free use of school premises to run Albanian classes at weekends or after hours, they offered information on the Albanian community, advice on how to meet the children's needs, and workshops for Albanian parents on how to support their children's learning and build relationships with their teachers. Shpresa also organized English classes for parents and, among many other training opportunities, courses for classroom assistants in mainstream schools that are accredited by official exam boards and run by organizations funded by the government that provide training for the unemployed. Shpresa then deploys the assistants as volunteers in its mainstream partner schools. Many women have obtained employment through this route, and the accreditation gained has provided many with a stepping-stone to further study and qualifications. In this and other ways, Shpresa makes a point of being responsive to the local needs of the community members and the mainstream schools with which they are in partnership.

While the after-school Albanian classes are run in a number of locations in partnership with different mainstream schools, these and other activities are managed centrally by the core Shpresa staff team. Among other roles, this team provides the pedagogical training for the volunteer teachers of Albanian. The trainers were previously teachers in Albania or Kosovo and had found out about UK pedagogical practices by spending time in mainstream schools. Teaching resources and approaches gained from these experiences were imported into their lessons and training program, with volunteer teachers, in turn, implementing these ideas into their own classes. The author has noted in classroom observations how effective the Albanian teachers are at engaging the pupils in very active learning.

In addition to Albanian language classes, Shpresa provide sports, drama, and a very popular dance program. Shpresa staff and volunteers are skilled at organizing major events to showcase the talents of their students. Some volunteers run lunchtime language and dance clubs in mainstream schools to which Albanian children can bring their friends, and all of the students can participate in school performances that showcase Albanian culture.

While consultation and user participation have been key features of the Shpresa program from the beginning, a particularly significant role is played by the students themselves. Young people take responsibilities in the organization from an early age. As well as planning and organizing events, they have input into strategy, have representatives on the board, and take part in an annual Children's Congress to which they elect representatives. Children from age 10 are trained to mentor younger children, and older pupils lead groups and are trained in public speaking and chairing meetings. They are encouraged to use and develop these skills further in the wider society and to volunteer, both within and beyond Shpresa.

Impact studies have shown that the Shpresa/mainstream school partnership model works well. An early study was commissioned by the head teacher[3] of a primary school that had 84 Albanian-speaking pupils in order to evaluate the partnership between his school and Shpresa. The study highlighted the benefits to both the children's cultural confidence, their attainment in school, and the positive impact the project had on parent-teacher relationships. The head teacher commented:

> All I have got for them is praise. As a model of how things work, it's a very good model. I could convince other schools as well. All I get is really good pay-back for it, in community relations, parental relations, and during an Ofsted inspection, for example. I am more than happy. There are no disadvantages.
>
> *(as cited in Sneddon, 2009, p. 3)*

At the time of writing, Albanian classes are operating in 10 complementary schools, located in partner mainstream schools, in eight boroughs in London, providing services for five hundred children aged 5 to 18. The success of this model has led to Shpresa being invited to seminars and conferences, which has in turn led to many requests for advice and guidance from other community organizations. As a result, in 2012 Shpresa was funded for three years to develop their Albanian teaching program and to mentor activists from the African Portuguese, Bangladeshi, Eritrean, Lithuanian, Polish, Somali, Romanian, and Turkish communities to set up their own complementary schools.

Volunteer coordinators from these communities were trained in leadership skills and learned management while volunteering in the Shpresa office. They were offered guidance on all key aspects of setting up an organization: identifying local needs, consulting with potential users (both parents and children), understanding the legal framework and health and safety regulations, child protection, bookkeeping, financial management, and writing grant applications. Shpresa also made available sample documents that each community could adapt to its own requirements. As the new structures emerged, Shpresa supported the coordinators in negotiating free access to run pilot complementary classes in mainstream schools after hours with a view to developing a long-term partnership (Sneddon, 2014). When head teachers agreed to such arrangements, they usually wanted a trial period to make sure the complementary school operated effectively and did not in any way disrupt the work of their school. Volunteer assistants are part of the package.

As the Albanian classes led to rising standards of Albanian literacy among students, older students became concerned that there was no GCSE or A Level available to recognize their achievements in the language. The students had experience of campaigning for issues of concern to them, such as a recent campaign to end the detention of children in refugee centres, and decided to extend this experience to the issue of certification. Their lobbying and petitioning led to a meeting with officials at the Department of Education, who praised their initiative. However, the students were surprised to be told that such decisions were made on a commercial basis by independent examination boards. They appealed for public support from academics and journalists to help them gain access to the chief executive of the appropriate exam board, who had originally refused to meet them (Bearne, 2011). In the process, the students engaged with young people from the Somali and Eritrean communities, and they campaigned together for the establishment of GCSEs in a wide range of languages. Having brought large numbers of students from several communities into their negotiations, the Shpresa students eventually struck a deal by which they would obtain an Albanian GCSE if they raised enough funding to cover the initial development cost and guarantee a number of candidates every year (Sneddon, 2014). At the time of this writing, the students had raised three-quarters of the required funds.

8 Discussion

The question of sustainability is uppermost in the minds of complementary school organizers, especially when the community is expressing a strong demand for their services. With respect to the two models described in this chapter, the categories suggested by Eiseman et al. (1990) and listed above provide a useful starting point for exploring this issue. Both models have many positive indicators of sustainability, but at the same time, the pertinent issues in each context are very different.

The categories listed by Eiseman et al. (1990) generally apply to an innovation introduced into a school which is then expected to adapt. In the two cases described above, the innovations have originated within the communities and involve the establishment of complementary schools as well as new ways of interacting with the language ecology of their environment. The Shpresa Programme model of partnership between complementary and mainstream schools became accepted in the mainstream environment after a head teacher commissioned an evaluation study and recommended the model to colleagues. Together with the publication of papers based on the study (Sneddon, 2009), this made the model more widely known, led to invitations to Shpresa representatives to speak at both community and academic conferences, and resulted in further recognition. The innovative nature of the model was featured as an example of good practices on the website of the Our Languages project and attracted development funding from the Paul Hamlyn Foundation, known for its support of educational innovation. All Shpresa complementary schools are run in consultation with users and mainstream schools, and this model has spread through both informal and formal mentoring to other linguistic communities (as described above) as well as to Albanian schools in north and west London. There is an expectation that the Shpresa's innovative model of complementary school organization will continue, and that the building of partnerships between Albanian schools and mainstream agencies will provide stability on both the logistical level, for instance, access to classroom facilities, as well as at the level of pedagogical training and classroom practices.

Continuation, the fifth point in the framework, is a concern for all organizations set up and run by dedicated and charismatic individuals. The current founder and director of Shpresa has been supported from the beginning by two women who share her commitment. The core staff delegate roles and responsibilities effectively to ensure that there are sufficient procedures in place and administrative and leadership skills in the organization to ensure continuity when founders leave, although this remains an area of risk with respect to sustainability. The development of the mentored schools (African Portuguese, Bengali, Eritrean, Lithuanian, Polish, Romanian, Somali, and Turkish) revealed the strengths of the model as members of these communities worked together with Shpresa to establish the new schools and make their presence known in the community, but it also revealed the vulnerabilities in that several of the schools depended on direct Shpresa support to negotiate with mainstream schools for free use of premises. In addition, the Polish school struggled with a high turnover of volunteer teachers, who left as soon as they could obtain paid employment elsewhere, and the Lithuanian school is wholly dependent on basic teaching materials that parents bring, as it has no funding to operate. It is a tribute to the work of volunteers from all of the communities involved that only one of these new schools, the Portuguese, actually closed. It had become heavily reliant on its charismatic coordinator, and when she left, the network of volunteers she had trained felt unable to operate without her.

As far as Shpresa itself is concerned, a considerable part of its success can be accounted for by a strong infrastructure, good management, and sound policies and procedures (Sneddon, 2012). Staff and volunteers make use of all professional training available in their area on all aspects of running an organization that works with children. As the number of children involved in their classes increases, so do opportunities for new activities to be developed to meet young people's interests. The role of volunteers is a crucial part of the organization's success. Volunteers within the organization cascade training to newcomers. The accredited courses run for them have ensured that many volunteers are able to pursue their education and take up paid employment opportunities in the community. This success has been recognized through the Queen's Award for Volunteering, which the director of Shpresa received at Buckingham Palace.

The final point in the framework, namely routine allocations of time and money, is a complex one. While good management has ensured that the best use is made of both time and money, the main vulnerability of the organization is economic, and this has implications for time management. Although the organization relies heavily on volunteers and agreements that provide it with free teaching premises, it still needs core funding to operate. The complexity of its operation across schools and boroughs makes it necessary to have a salaried director and funding to pay some teachers and specialist trainers who may offer training (for example, in child protection) that is not freely available from other sources, and funding for teaching resources is needed. An office is also essential for administrative and training purposes. The organization is dependent on funds from various charitable trusts, all of which have different criteria for funding, with different timelines and outcome measures requiring extensive reports and evaluations. All funding is time-limited, and funders have complex and very competitive application procedures.

There are other areas of vulnerability as well: The partnership approach does not appeal to many mainstream schools that are keen to raise additional funding from renting their premises after regular school hours. The reliance on volunteers may become more difficult as a result of the very success of the Shpresa model: Volunteers gain language skills, experience, and qualifications and go in search of paid work to support their families.

With respect to the Tower Hamlets model, the sustainability issues are very different. The local Council's financial support for the teaching of community languages outside of regular school hours has been in place since the 1990s and, although it is non-statutory, is widely accepted as a legitimate mainstream service offered by the Council through the offices of the CLS, which is an integral part of the Council's Education Department. Not only is the service offered by CLS stable, but the Council continues to develop new initiatives to increase participation in a wider range of language learning in the borough. Participation is also widespread: The fact that classes in multiple languages are held in 90 locations throughout the borough ensures that the service is widely available. The service is not in any sense time-limited, and new pupils are continually enrolling in out-of-hour classes. Another strong indicator of sustainability is the fact that both staff time and funding are centrally allocated to this project from the Tower Hamlets Council budget. While the service CLS provides is not dependent on the dedication of any single individual—new staff are recruited to fill vacancies that occur from time to time with no adverse effect on the service—it is, however, dependent on the political priorities and decisions of the elected representatives in the Council.

The vulnerabilities of this project are of a very different nature from those faced by the Shpresa Programme. The risk factors are essentially political and demographic, and a number of factors could have an impact on the survival of the CLS program and the network of Bengali schools. As the local community of Bangladeshi origin moves into its third and fourth generation, CLS has already noted that the latest generation of pupils are less familiar with Bengali and are often learning it almost as a second language in a classroom setting (Hannan, 2014). It is possible that the maintenance of the family language and the development of literacy in it may become less of a priority for the community. As more prosperous Bengali families move out of the area to better housing opportunities in the suburbs (Glynn, 2006), the political influence that brought about the focus on community languages may no longer be strong enough to sustain it. At the time of writing, the greatest threat to the service is a planned and very substantial program of cuts in local authority budgets imposed by the national government to reduce the UK's budgetary deficit. Many local authorities are concerned that this may reduce their ability to fund all but essential and statutory services (Hastings, Bailey, Bramley, Gannon, & Watkins, 2015). This situation could force elected representatives to either reduce or close CLS regardless of the wishes of their constituents.

Through studying the two programs, it becomes apparent that, although their areas of vulnerability are different, they have many points in common: Both rely on good organization and strong management. Both organizations collaborate with university researchers to develop teacher education, to carry out evaluations, and to explore the benefits of multilingualism in their communities. The legitimacy of both programs is underpinned by networking. The Tower Hamlets model can be seen as very top-down from a local point of view, as CLS works in partnership with a wide range of community organizations, secondary schools, and families. By contrast, the Shpresa Programme, as a bottom-up organization, works with other complementary schools and community groups in east London to create a network that can lobby politicians and attempt to influence policy.

Both programs are, at least in theory, highly replicable. Given the financial means and the political will to prioritize resources as the Borough of Tower Hamlets does, any local authority with substantial linguistic minorities that value the maintenance of their heritage language could fund their own CLS to organize and finance the teaching of community languages. However, to re-create the political pressure would require many communities to come together in a common purpose, and this, as Shpresa knows, is a long and difficult process. While the Shpresa model can much more easily be replicated on a small local scale, it requires a very considerable investment of time and energy from volunteers as well as strong networking skills and the ability to raise funds from a range of sources.

9 Conclusion

The lessons of the last 40 years of complementary schools in the UK suggest that future trends in government policy with respect to community languages are not going to be easy to predict. Communities that are not in a position to fully finance their own language-teaching services will need to continue relying on what have traditionally been the strengths of the sector: being close and responsive to the needs of the local community and being innovative and flexible. They will need to use all of their skills, networking abilities, and pragmatism to sustain their services in a volatile policy context.

Notes

1 Local government in London is composed of two levels: an overarching entity, the Greater London Authority, and over 30 boroughs, including Tower Hamlets and Newham. These boroughs each have a locally elected council that is often referred to as the "local authority."
2 Many secondary schools in the UK stream pupils according to ability and place them into different sets. A "set" is used synonymously with a "stream."
3 The head teacher carries out functions similar to those of the school principal in the United States.

References

Anderson, J. (2008). Initial teacher education for teachers of Arabic, Mandarin Chinese, Panjabi and Urdu. In C. Kenner & T. Hickey (Eds.), *Multilingual Europe: Diversity and learning* (pp. 152–157). Stoke-on-Trent, UK: Trentham Books.

Baker, P., & Eversley, J. (Eds.). (2000). *Multilingual capital: The languages of London's schoolchildren and their relevance to economic, social and educational policies.* London, UK: Battlebridge Publications.

Bearne, S. (2011, October 14). New fronts in the battle for community languages. *TES.* Retrieved from https://www.tes.com/article.aspx?storycode=6116531

Block, D. (2005). *Multilingual identities in a global city: London stories.* Basingstoke, UK: Palgrave Macmillan.

Bourne, J. (1991). *Moving into the mainstream: LEA provision for bilingual pupils.* Windsor, UK: NFER-Nelson.

CILT, the National Centre for Languages. (2005). *Language trends 2005: Community language learning in England, Wales and Scotland.* London, UK: CILT. Retrieved from http://www.alcantaracoms.com/wp-content/uploads/2014/05/languagetrends2005-community-final-report.pdf

Community Language Service [CLS]. (2007). *Community and modern foreign languages classes [Service directory].* London, UK: Tower Hamlets Council.

Community Language Service [CLS]. (n.d.). Out of school language classes. Retrieved from http://www.towerhamlets.gov.uk/lgnl/education_and_learning/extra-curricular_activities/out_of_school_language_classes.aspx

Conteh, J., Martin, P., & Robertson, L. H. (2007). Multilingual learning stories from schools and communities in Britain: Issues and debates. In J. Conteh, P. Martin, & L. H. Robertson (Eds.), *Multilingual learning stories from schools and communities in Britain* (pp. 1–22). Stoke-on-Trent, UK: Trentham Books.

Department for Education. (2014, July 16). Statutory guidance: The national curriculum in England: English programmes of study. Retrieved from https://www.gov.uk/government/publications/national-curriculum-in-england-english-programmes-of-study/national-curriculum-in-england-english-programmes-of-study

Department of Education and Science. (1985). Education for all. *Report of the committee of enquiry into the education of ethnic minority groups (The Swann Report): Chairman, Lord Swann.* London, England: Her Majesty's Stationery Office. Retrieved from the Education in England website http://www.educationengland.org.uk/documents/swann/swann1985.html

Department of Education and Science. (1988). *The school curriculum*. London, UK: Her Majesty's Stationery Office.

Department for Education and Skills. (2002). *Languages for all: Languages for life: A strategy for England*. Annesley, UK: Department for Education and Skills. Retrieved from http://www.education.gov.uk/publications/eOrderingDownload/DfESLanguagesStrategy.pdf

Department for Education and Skills. (2003, March). Aiming high: Raising attainment for minority ethnic pupils. *Ref: DfES/0183/2003*. Retrieved from https://www.education.gov.uk/consultations/downloadableDocs/213_1.pdf

Eiseman, J. W., Fleming, D. S., & Roody, D. S. (1990). *Making sure it sticks: The school improvement leader's role in institutionalizing change*. Andover, MA: The Regional Laboratory.

Ekholm, M., & Trier, U. P. (1987). The concept of institutionalization: Some remarks. In M. B. Miles, M. Ekholm, & R. Vanderberghe (Eds.), *Lasting school improvement: Exploring the process of institutionalization* (pp. 13–21). Leuwen, Belgium: Acco.

Eversley, J., Mehmedbegovic, D., Sanderson, A., Tinsley, T., von Ahn, M., & Wiggins, R. D. (2010). *Language capital: Mapping the languages of London's schoolchildren*. London, UK: Institute of Education and CILT.

Fishman, W. (1997). Allies in the Promised Land: Reflections on the Irish and the Jews in the East End. In A. J. Kershen (Ed.), *London: The Promised Land?* (pp. 38–49). Aldershot, UK: Avebury.

Glynn, S. (2006, July). Playing the ethnic card—politics and ghettoisation in London's East End. Retrieved from http://www.geos.ed.ac.uk/homes/sglynn/Ghettoisation.pdf

Goodson, L., Coaffee, J., & Rowlands, R. (2010). Connected communities: Resilient, mutual self-help in cities of growing diversity. Retrieved from http://www.ahrc.ac.uk/documents/project-reports-and-reviews/connected-communities/resilient-mutual-self-help-in-cities-of-growing-diversity/

Hannan, M. A. (2014). *Bengali resource book 1*. London, UK: Tower Hamlets Community Languages Service.

Hastings, A., Bailey, N., Bramley, G., Gannon, M., & Watkins, D. (2015). *The cost of the cuts: The impact on local government and poorer communities*. York, UK: The Joseph Rowntree Foundation.

Linguistic Minorities Project. (1985). *The other languages of England*. London, UK: Routledge and Kegan Paul.

Lytra, V., & Martin, P. (Eds.). (2010). *Sites of multilingualism: Complementary schools in Britain today*. Stoke-on-Trent, UK: Trentham Books.

McLean, M. (1985). Private supplementary schools and the ethnic challenge of state education in Britain. In C. Brock & W. Tulasiewicz (Eds.), *Cultural identity and educational policy* (pp. 326–345). London, UK: Croom Helm.

Miles, M. B., Eckholm, M., & Vandenberghe, R. (Eds.). (1987). *School improvement: Exploring the process of institutionalization*. Leuven, Belgium: Acco.

National Archives. (n.d.). Our languages [Archived web content]. Retrieved from http://webarchive.nationalarchives.gov.uk/20101227105751/ http://www.ourlanguages.org.uk/

Office for Standards in Education. (2008). Every language matters: An evaluation of the extent and impact of initial training to teach a wider range of world languages. Retrieved from http://dera.ioe.ac.uk/8173/1/Every%20language%20matters%20(PDF%20format).pdf

Office for Standards in Education. (2009, June). Children's services and skills: Departmental report, 2008–09. Retrieved from https://www.gov.uk/government/uploads/system/uploads/attachment_data/file/238633/7597.pdf

Overington, A. (2012, February 15). A brief summary of government policy in relation to EAL learners. Retrieved from http://www.naldic.org.uk/Resources/NALDIC/Research%20and%20Information/Documents/Brief_summary_of_Government_policy_for_EAL_Learners.pdf

Sneddon, R. (2009, September). *Hope, literacy and dancing*. Paper presented at the British Educational Research Association Conference, University of Manchester, Manchester, UK.

Sneddon, R. (2012). Shpresa programme: An evaluation of the Paul Hamlyn funded project. Retrieved from http://www.shpresaprogramme.com/documents/SHPRESA%20evaluation12.pdf

Sneddon, R. (2014). Complementary schools in action: Networking for language development in East London. *Multilingua, 33*(5–6), 577–602.

Sneddon, R., & Martin, P. (2012). Alternative spaces of learning in East London: Opportunities and challenges. *Diaspora, Indigenous and Minority Education, 6*(1), 34–49.

Steer, P. (2015, May 8). Exam board chief: Unless we act soon, even GCSE French and German could face the chop. *TES Connect*. Retrieved from https://www.tes.com/news/school-news/breaking-views/exam-board-chief-unless-we-act-soon-even-gcse-french-and-german

Tinsley, T. (2013). *Languages: The state of the nation: Demand and supply of language skills in the UK*. London, UK: British Academy.

Uddin, J., & Mitchell, I. (2002). *Assessment framework for mother tongue teaching for pupils aged 5–11*. London, UK: Tower Hamlets Mother Tongue Service.

Uddin, J., & Mitchell, I. (2010). *Scheme of work for modern languages [Internal pamphlet]*. London, UK: Tower Hamlets Mother Tongue Service.

Valdés, G. (2005). Bilingualism, heritage language learners, and SLA research: Opportunities lost or seized? *The Modern Language Journal, 89*(3), 410–426.

Verma, G., Zec, P., & Skinner, G. (1994). *The ethnic crucible: Harmony and hostility in multi-ethnic schools*. London, UK: Falmer Press.

Vertovec, S. (2007). *New complexities of cohesion in Britain: Super-diversity, transnationalism and civil-integration*. Wetherby, UK: Communities and Local Government Publications.

von Ahn, M., Lupton. R, Greenwood, C., & Wiggins, D. (2010). Languages, ethnicity and education in London [DoQQS Working Paper No. 10–12]. London, UK: Institute of Education. Retrieved from http://repec.ioe.ac.uk/REPEc/pdf/qsswp1012.pdf

8

Innovations in the Teaching of Portuguese as a Heritage Language

The Case of Brazilian Complementary Schools in London and Barcelona

Ana Souza and Juliana Gomes[1]

1 Introduction

The teaching of Brazilian Portuguese as a Heritage Language (POLH, from the Portuguese *Português como Língua de Herança*) is a recent phenomenon (Mendes, 2012). This situation is due to emigration from Brazil becoming significant only in the second half of the 1980s, when the U.S. was the main destination for Brazilians venturing abroad. According to the Brazilian Institute of Geography and Statistics (Instituto Brasileiro de Geografia e Estatística [IBGE], 2011), the U.S. is still the country with the largest number of Brazilian emigrants; however, Europe has also emerged as an important destination for this population.

After Portugal, Spain has the most significant number of Brazilians, as reported by the Brazilian Ministry of International Relations (MRE, 2015). Of the Brazilians who settle in Spain, 22% have chosen to settle in Catalonia, in northeastern Spain (Solé, Cavalcanti, & Parella, 2011). According to the Instituto d'Estadística de Catalunya [Institute of Statistics of Catalonia] (2014), 9% of the Brazilians in this region are children aged 0 to 14 years old. The statistics are actually higher if the number of children with dual nationality is considered. Despite this, the number of institutions that cater to these children is limited to three, one in Madrid and two in Barcelona.[2] Two of these institutions only offer cultural activities and only one of them, located in Barcelona, includes language instruction.

The UK has the third-largest number of Brazilian immigrants in Europe (MRE, 2015), with over 6% of these emigrants having settled in England (IBGE, 2011), the highest concentration being in London. These statistics are reflected in the number of complementary schools, i.e., weekend schools run by the community, that teach Brazilian POLH in London, which increased from 1 to 13 between 1997 and 2014 (Souza & Barradas, 2014).

This chapter discusses the introduction of innovations in the teaching of POLH in relation to the organizational changes developed in two complementary schools: the one in Barcelona that includes language instruction and another in London. These schools were developed independently of each other, with the London school predating the Barcelona school. Both focus schools are presented with a description of their educational contexts as well as their procedural and organizational innovations. This description is followed by an evaluation of how far the relevant innovations have been assimilated into the structures of both schools, i.e., institutionalized. This evaluation is done within Ekholm and Trier's (1987) framework, which considers five indicators of institutionalization, some of which will be considered in this chapter. The description and the evaluation of both schools are based on questionnaires, participant observation, and in-depth interviews with their directors, teachers, and pedagogical coordinators—the latter having responsibility for overseeing both the overall pedagogical direction of the school as well as its implementation at the classroom level.

The examples used to illustrate how the two Brazilian complementary schools in Europe are dealing with innovations show that they follow six stages toward institutionalization: (1) parents feel the need to socialize their children with other families; (2) a small group of parents together socialize their own children informally; (3) other families are attracted to the idea and join the group; (4) the initial group of parents becomes the Executive Committee and the school is formally created; (5) teachers from outside the group are hired; and (6) growth leads to changes in the procedural and structural organization of the school.

We argue that both schools experience these six stages of institutionalization in a cyclical process, as shown in Figure 8.1 below. The arrival of new migrant families and the formation of new families abroad create a constant flow of members joining the schools. These members bring with them their needs, which influence the actions of the Executive Committee of the schools and the hiring of new teachers. The families, the committees, and the teachers influence the procedural and structural changes in the schools, which attract more families to join and sustain the cycle of innovations.

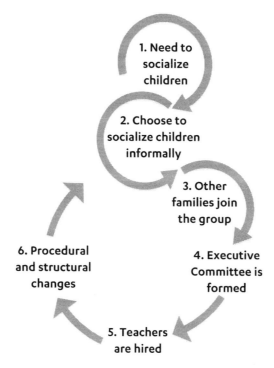

Figure 8.1   Institutionalization Stages of Brazilian Complementary Schools in London and in Barcelona

We conclude by emphasizing the importance of collaboration and of consciously engaging with change to ensure innovations are successfully implemented.

2 The Study

This chapter draws on data collected from the two focus Brazilian complementary schools between December 2014 and February 2015 in London and Barcelona.

With the purpose of exploring the innovation process followed by these schools, we interviewed some of their stakeholders. A total of three teachers, one coordinator, and six directors linked to the school in London between 1997 and 2004 were interviewed individually. The participants in Barcelona, three teachers and two directors, have links with the school that range in length from one to five years. Both sets of participants were selected due to their direct involvement with the innovations in their schools. We acknowledge, however, that this chapter discusses the perspective only of members who had a positive experience of the institutionalization process, as they are the ones who have been closely involved with the schools. Accessing the participants who had a negative experience was a challenge which we hope to overcome in future studies. Having said that, the core group of volunteers at the schools mostly agreed and supported the innovations.

The interviews were semi-structured, lasted up to two hours, and were conducted in accordance with ethical considerations. All the participants were provided with an information sheet and had the chance of asking further questions before signing an informed consent with permission for their interviews to be audio-recorded. They were guaranteed confidentiality in relation to their specific comments. Furthermore, the participants read a draft of this chapter before publication. In this way, transparency in the research process was ensured and the participants had the opportunity to weigh in on our understanding of the information they had provided.

The data provided by each participant were transcribed in Portuguese and then initially analyzed according to the categories set in the interview guide and the questionnaire used in the semi-structured interviews. Any other relevant issues raised by the participants were then added to the analysis.

3 From Innovation to Institutionalization: Theoretical Background

Institutionalization is the stage in which innovations are assimilated into the structure of a school and become part of its routine (Ekholm & Trier, 1987). Although innovation tends to be discussed as an improvement, Morrish (1976/2012) reminds us that it is in fact the introduction of something new and different, but not necessarily good nor better. Therefore, considering institutionalization to be the last stage of a school improvement process means that an innovation has been judged as having a positive impact. This is the case in the Brazilian complementary schools we discuss. School improvement, in turn, is a strategy for educational change that is rooted in practice (Creemers & Kyriakides, 2012). But what is change? Change is a move from a presently accepted state of affairs to the adoption of a new one. Miles (1967, as cited in Morrish, 1976/2012) argues that "change tends to be more spontaneous than 'innovation', which is more planned and deliberate" (p. 22). However, based on the processes experienced by the schools described in this chapter, we consider the boundaries between these phenomena ("change" and "innovation") to be blurred and, thus, use them interchangeably to discuss an aspect that tends to be the focus of educational change: the curriculum.

Kelly (1997/2009) advocates that "curriculum" should be used to describe the overall rationale for educational programs, whereas "syllabus" is limited to the planning of the content to be transmitted. These terms (curriculum and syllabus) are commonly misused, including by the schools we discuss. In examining their contexts more closely, it is clear that what they describe as curriculum is, instead, a list of topics and grammar points, which corresponds to syllabus. Nonetheless, the procedural and structural organization adopted by the Brazilian complementary schools in developing their lists of topics and grammar points are relevant in better understanding the educational changes they experienced.

For school improvement to be successful, school staff need to hold a positive attitude towards lifelong learning, adopt shared goals, have mutual respect, be supportive of each other, and not fear taking risks (Creemers & Kyriakides, 2012). The nurturing of collaboration in schools can sustain a community of learners and potentially contribute to the efficacy of the change being implemented (Antonacci & Bernhardt, 1998). In fact, Ekholm and Trier's (1987) five indicators that institutionalization is taking place relate to how people work together. They are (1) the successful negotiations in which people are involved to reach agreements on the innovations; (2) the allocation of time, material, and personnel resources for the implementation of innovations; (3) the acceptance of the innovation as being legitimate by different parties; (4) the creation of organizational procedures to avoid dependence on specific persons for the continuation of the change implemented; and (5) the acceptance of the innovation as a common practice with diminished visibility.

We adopt these indicators as the framework for evaluating how far innovations have been assimilated into the structures of the Brazilian complementary schools in London and Barcelona.

4 From Innovation to Institutionalization: An Evaluation

In evaluating the institutionalization of these schools, it seems important to mention the close relationship that the researchers have with the settings. Souza was a volunteer in the school in London between 1999 and 2004. In the first year, she volunteered as a classroom assistant. Due to her professional background, she soon got involved with pedagogical issues and volunteered as an assistant pedagogical coordinator. This role lasted for a year, during which time the innovations started to take place. In 2000, the coordinator left the school and Souza was promoted to the role. In that capacity she structured the school into groups, or levels, according to age and linguistic competence, developed a materials bank, wrote a Teachers' Handbook, and implemented new procedures for planning the annual syllabus and the individual lessons. Gomes, in turn, has worked in the school in Barcelona since 2012. She started as a teaching assistant and due to her academic and professional background with preschool children, became a class teacher of the six- to seven-year-old group in 2013. In 2015, she joined the school's Executive Committee as a secretary.

Being insiders gave us rich insights into the running of the schools and firsthand knowledge of the process of introducing the innovation. Nevertheless, we are aware of the ethical implications of our duplicate roles as participants in the improvement of the schools as well as researchers. We understand the importance of positioning ourselves in a way which allows qualitative data to be appropriately represented and have considered ways to keep a balance between being insiders and outsiders, an important issue in qualitative research (Meksenas, 2002). In addition to our reflection on our insider/outsider roles, as noted earlier, the participants had the opportunity to read and give feedback on our understanding of the information they had provided and we had observed.

The Brazilian Complementary School in London

In England, heritage languages are mainly taught in complementary schools (Lytra & Martin, 2010). These schools are created by migrant groups to preserve their linguistic and cultural heritage as a complement to the formal education offered by their host society (Keating, Solovova, & Barradas, 2013). In keeping with this tradition, Brazilian families in the UK have shown how important the Portuguese language is to their communities by organizing institutions to maintain their children's use of Portuguese (Souza, 2008). The first Brazilian complementary school on record in London offered lessons on Saturday mornings between 10 a.m. and 12 p.m. in rented rooms in a community center. The school was founded by a group of mothers in 1997, and is the focus of this study. Between then and 2004, the school faced innovations related to two organizational aspects: (1) becoming legally classified as a charity institution and (2) the implementation of procedural and structural changes regarding how pupils were grouped and how content planning was done for an entire year as well as for individual lessons. For the purpose of the discussion in this chapter, we focus mainly on the latter aspect.

Content planning was a complex multi-step process. It started with the annual meeting between the teachers, the coordinators, and the Executive Committee of the school to decide on an overall theme for the academic year. The teachers were then given a scheme of work[3] template to be completed with topics for each of their lessons. A second meeting was held between the coordinators and the teachers to bring their ideas together and consider the vocabulary items and grammar points to be explored within the topics they presented. The coordinators collected the teachers' draft schemes of work, which were then cross-referenced and revised to ensure that similar topics were covered in all four groups around the same time. The language content was also checked for its suitability to the age and the level of the different groups. The revised schemes of work were emailed to the teachers for their perusal. In a third meeting, materials and activities were suggested by the team for the different lessons. Having completed the cycle for the annual planning, the teachers were given lesson plan templates and were expected to plan their lessons for the month, i.e., four sessions, in advance and with as much detail as possible. Monthly meetings were held between the coordinators and the teachers to discuss their lesson plans, exchange further ideas on activities, and share teaching materials. This planning input was followed up by lesson observations that included a feedback session to evaluate the teachers' achievements and to support them in developing their teaching skills.

Negotiations

Careful consideration of the needs of the school and its pupils led to the adoption of a system for planning the annual program and individual lessons as well as for standardizing their lesson content. The changes emerged from a period of expansion (stage 3 of the institutionalization process, refer to Figure 8.1), which required more structural and procedural organization (stage 6). As a member of the school Executive Committee described it: "As the school developed, things were being improved in response to the demands of the parents and the experience of the different people joining us"[4] (Committee member 3). The improvements included the hiring of teachers (stage 5) to deliver lessons, instead of the informal socialization activities organized by the mothers who started the group (stages 1 and 2).

All the participants (directors, coordinators, and teachers) were consulted about the proposed changes and felt that there was space for them to make suggestions. Both informal and formal agreements were made for implementing the changes, as one of the teachers explains below:

> We were regularly consulted. There was space for us to make suggestions and participate actively. The result of our negotiations was recorded as we went along, and then it was published in a document called the Teachers' Handbook.
>
> *(Teacher 1)*

Resource Allocation

Being a registered charity, the school in London charged only a nominal fee to cover room rental and teachers' and assistants' salaries. The Executive Committee was organized by and consisted of parents who worked for free along with other volunteers (stage 4 of the institutionalization process). All the activities that took place in addition to the weekly two hours of teaching were done on a goodwill basis.

The discussions, the planning, and the implementation of the innovations were slotted into personal calendars as needed. Consequently, none of the participants could say precisely how much time was used for these activities; nevertheless, at least for some periods the time commitment was extensive. A committee member describes the situation as follows: "There was a period in which the school basically took over almost everything I did. It was part of my weekends and of my week." (Committee member 1)

Although there was no allocation of extra financial resources for these activities, the teachers felt supported. They recalled having been given articles to read on issues related to the teaching of POLH by the coordinator and being involved in the development of guidelines and materials. The account below is representative of the teachers' opinions:

> It was always like 'Let's do it together'. . . . I felt at ease to say when I was having difficulties and to ask for help. . . . It was very important because it made me feel that we were working as a team, we supported each other . . . we were given suggestions [on what to include in our lessons and on how to present them to the children]. I had the freedom to make choices and felt supported on how to better implement them.
>
> *(Teacher 3)*

Rise in Legitimacy

The teachers' high level of involvement in the negotiations (see Negotiations above) enabled them to also have a high level of familiarization with the changes, which built a sense of their legitimacy. Teachers did not need incentives or encouragement to try to implement the changes suggested. On the contrary, seeing themselves as part of the process, they were extremely motivated to experiment with the changes proposed. As one of the teachers explains below, the pedagogical meetings contributed to the incorporation of positive changes into their routines:

> The meetings were crucial in my learning of how to adapt my previous experience in Brazil to the teaching of Portuguese as a community language. . . . The meetings created a space in which we could discuss and reflect on our different perspectives. I learned a lot . . . in this process. It supported me to make decisions about the content of my lessons in relation to the themes covered and the grammar points explored.
>
> *(Teacher 2)*

These feelings were shared by the members of the Executive Committee, who saw the school activities as having a dual function: improving the overall structure and organization of the school and of the learning experience of their children by responding to the needs of the families. For instance, Committee member 2 said:

> The *Play and Sing* group, for example, was created because a member of the Committee had their second child. Then we started asking, 'Why can their older child attend lessons but

we do not offer anything to their second child?' Personal issues such as these made us very involved with the changes.

Organizational Conditions

The school started with its founders socializing their children informally in a mothers' group (stage 1 of the institutionalization process). They soon realized that there was a need to get formally organized (stage 2). However, it took a few years for the Executive Committee members to develop specific roles and a vision for the school. As the school evolved (stage 3), this led to the restructuring of the school from an informal to a more formal entity, including establishing it as a charity in 2000 (stage 4). Committee member 4 describes the process as follows:

> We started to have meetings with the new volunteers . . . and the new Committee members on how to work as a charity institution. We took a step forward in relation to formally structuring the administration of the school.

In addition, the role of pedagogical coordinators was created, which meant a change in the organizational structure of the school. This created a supportive network within the school in which the Committee members supported the coordinators, who then supported the teachers in implementing the changes. All parties involved acknowledged that both coordinators had a key role in the innovations, as illustrated below by Committee member 6:

> The changes were very centred on the pedagogical coordinators . . . All the decisions relating to teaching and teachers were left to them. We were involved in the changes proposed by them, but we fully trusted their professional knowledge and experience.

Diminishing Visibility

The indicators of acceptance of the innovations as common practices with diminished visibility overlap with the creation of organizational conditions for the innovations (stage 6). In the case of the complementary school in London, a Teachers' Handbook was produced in 2003 to compile individual documents produced in response to the needs identified in the change process. Involving the teachers and documenting this process was a way of ensuring continuity in the work being developed, as one of the coordinators explains:

> It was an attempt to develop a more coherent work plan and one which could enable continuity. . . . The turnover of the teachers is very high! So the people who joined later would need to know what to do, which direction to go, what is expected of them.
>
> *(Coordinator 1)*[5]

The changes have been adopted as standard procedure, aided by processes of ongoing documentation, an important element of which is the Teachers' Handbook. As one of the Committee members confirms: "There was definitely continuity [of the changes implemented in 2003]. All the documentation that was produced before I joined the school was kept in use." (Committee member 5)

Those interviewed overwhelmingly felt that the organizational conditions accompanying the innovations in this school meant that the changes were accepted by the majority of stakeholders and adopted as the school's routine procedures.

Brazilian Complementary School in Barcelona

The teaching of POLH in Barcelona started in 2010 (Moroni & Gomes, 2015). A school was created as an association in 2009 by a group of Brazilian parents who considered it important to transmit their language and culture to their children as they grew up in Catalonia (stage 1 in the institutionalization process). A teaching program started in 2010 with the recruitment of teachers (stage 5) for classes being held on Saturday mornings between 11:30 a.m. and 1:30 p.m. in a public Civic Centre. Since then, the number of pupils has increased fivefold (stage 2).

As in London, the increase in the number of pupils and their diverse linguistic profiles led to the implementation of changes in relation to (1) their grouping in different classes and (2) the development of teaching content. In order to allow for a parallel comparison to the school in London, only the second type of change experienced by the school in Barcelona is discussed below.

Negotiations

In Barcelona, all the interviewees agreed that the changes being implemented were responses to an increasing number of students and families engaged in the project (stage 3), which had considerably increased the administrative workload and demanded a restructuring and a division of labor that was not needed before (stage 4). One member of their Executive Committee highlighted the organic way in which these changes began to be developed: "The need to structure the school became evident and we started to do it in the way we thought to be correct." (Committee member 1)

Having said that, all the decisions concerning the school organization were proposed and discussed between parents and the Executive Committee through formal meetings in which both groups had voting rights. In regards to the weekly lessons, two meetings per year were held between parents and teachers. In other words, all the changes were discussed in a formal and collective way. This process had a positive impact on the change negotiations, as noted by one of the teachers: "These meetings give us the opportunity to listen to the parents' feedback [on their children's experiences in the school] and to provide them with relevant information about our work in the classroom." (Teacher 2)

Resource Allocation

The school in Barcelona is a registered non-profit association. It started its activities with no financial support, except for the monthly fees paid by the parents to cover the teachers' salaries and the purchase of teaching materials. Three years after its foundation, however, the school was one of the first Brazilian institutions in Europe to receive a recently created grant from the Brazilian government in support of the teaching of POLH through the *Programa de Difusão de Língua e Cultura* (Ministério das Relações Exteriores, n.d.).

As in London, the parents and the members of the Executive Committee in Barcelona cannot say precisely how much time they dedicate to the activities of the school. Nevertheless, with the aim of not overloading any of their members, the school adopted an organizational structure in 2014 (stage 4), as an Executive Committee member explains: "Due to the rapid growth [of the school], the need to delegate tasks and create proceedings became evident. So . . . we created four sub-committees: teaching issues, financial resources, educational projects, and cultural events." (Committee member 2)

This new organizational structure is an important support network for the teachers, despite the fact that it does not include a pedagogical coordinator. The sub-committee for teaching issues focuses on communication between the Executive Committee, the parents, and the teachers. It also liaises with the sub-committee for financial resources in regards to the acquisition of teaching materials and the teachers' participation in courses, workshops, and other events related to the teaching of POLH. In the words of one of the teachers, "Heritage language is a new field and a new context for us. Attending training is essential for [the development of] our work." (Teacher 1)

Rise in Legitimacy

The participants in Barcelona reported having high levels of familiarity with the change process that their school was undergoing (stage 6). This is a result, in part, of the team ethos of the school, which is highlighted by one of the teachers:

> Whenever an issue is raised, either by the parents or by the Executive Committee, we [teachers] are consulted. We know that our views are taken into account. As such, I can say that the changes are agreed in a collective way.
>
> *(Teacher 3)*

This participation in the decision-making process is highly valued, as another teacher emphasizes: "Taking part in the school's decision-making process and being able to reflect on relevant issues as a group contribute to the better acceptance of the changes suggested." (Teacher 1)

The adoption of standards for promoting pupils from one academic year to another serves by way of example of how different parties are involved in the process of making decisions in this school. The teachers decided among themselves that learning criteria should replace the age-based criterion by which students progressed to the next level. Their suggestions were then presented to the Executive Committee. Having agreed on the proposals made by the teachers, a second meeting that included the parents was organized. It was only after the three parties had become familiar with, understood, and agreed on the changes that they were implemented.

Organizational Conditions

The changes in the school in Barcelona have affected the way in which it is managed and the procedures it follows (stage 6). Focusing on the latter issue, the teachers are presently writing a document which aims to record the procedures they are developing, including the selection of themes for the academic year, the content of the individual lessons, the teaching resources, the aims of the different groups, and the assessment criteria. One of the teachers pinpoints the relevance of this document for the school:

> Writing this document has been an enriching experience. This project is enabling us to reflect as a group on which aspects of our work we would like to develop further, which new procedures could be implemented, and what could be adapted or even discarded.
>
> *(Teacher 1)*

Furthermore, there is an agreement on the need to establish standards which make the work possible without being bound to a particular person, as stated by one of the Executive Committee members: "It's important for the [future of the] school that it is able to continue its activities independently of who is running it." (Committee member 2)

Diminishing Visibility

During the period of data collection, the participants in Barcelona had a strong sense that they were experiencing changes in the way the school works. Nonetheless, as time went by some of the changes were no longer as visible as when first implemented, as the example given by one of the teachers indicates:

> We have suddenly realized that a year ago we did not know which criteria to use to split the classes. In fact, a lot of conflict was generated because of this issue. Nowadays, the way the classes are divided is an established procedure for all of us—directors, teachers and parents. We feel as if it has always been like this!
>
> *(Teacher 1)*

5 Discussion

The school in London completed the cycle of change in question in 2004, whereas the school in Barcelona was still in the process of implementing its innovations at the time of data collection. Nonetheless, both had the grouping of the students and procedural and structural organization as relevant innovations. The schools' negotiations regarding change included both informal and formal agreements through which directors, coordinators, teachers, and parents were consulted. Applying Ekholm and Trier's (1987) indicators of institutionalization, the negotiations in order to agree on these innovations are, in general terms, reported to be successful in both schools.

Innovations pertaining to the number of groups and their characteristics resulted from the growth of the Brazilian community in London and in Barcelona, as the profile of the children attending the lessons became more varied in relation to age and language competence. The new families demanded lessons for children aged less than a year to preteens. The new population of pupils included children who had been born in Europe and only spoke the local language and children who had been born in Brazil, migrated at a later age, and only spoke Portuguese. There were also children of the same age whose linguistic profile varied along a continuum between these two extremes. In Barcelona, the linguistic context is even more complex due to the fact that Catalonia has two official languages: Spanish and Catalan. Despite these complexities, the schools were responsive to the changes observed in their communities and acted to facilitate the incorporation of these changes into their services. Being responsive to change is the attitude advocated by Blenkin, Edwards, and Kelly (1992) as necessary to ensuring a positive relationship between individuals and change itself.

Both schools started their activities with very restricted allocation of resources. Ekholm and Trier (1987, p. 17) point out that the routine allocation of resources is important for institutionalization, and the schools had to face this challenge as volunteer-run organizations. Both Executive Committees are made up of volunteers, and the only initial material resources they had were the nominal fees paid by the parents to cover room rental and teachers' salaries. Consequently, they resorted to fundraising events to support their activities. The school in London became famous for its June parties, *Festas Juninas*. The school in Barcelona is known for its carnival celebrations, *Carnavais*. Both events are integral to Brazilian cultural and social celebrations. Therefore, the goals of the events helped the institutions in both their fundraising initiatives as much as they provided yet another context for the socialization of their members and the dissemination of Brazilian culture in their host countries. A better financial context, however, was presented to the school in Barcelona when it received a grant from the Brazilian government shortly after it began its program of innovation in the teaching of POLH. The school in London, by contrast, faced its institutionalization process before these grants were available. Having said that, their status as a charity in the UK allowed them to benefit from lower venue rental fees. In spite of these advantages, financial resources are still a challenge for both schools.

It is also relevant to consider these schools' situation in relation to human resources. Many of the teachers of POLH are not trained to teach in the context of complementary schools. They tend to be primary or secondary teachers from Brazil who were trained to teach monocultural learners with high monolingual competence in Portuguese. As discussed above, the learners of POLH present a great variety of competencies in both Portuguese and the language of the host country—in our case, English or Spanish and Catalan. There are also a number of teachers with a background in psychology or the arts. These teachers make significant contributions to the teaching of POLH by virtue of their areas of expertize, nevertheless there are limitations to what they can offer in terms of language teaching pedagogy, especially in the case of schools led by non-educators. The pedagogical growth of these individuals depends highly on their motivation, since the resources available to financially support their training and professional development are extremely restricted. In the case of the complementary school in London, teachers were paid to attend only one formal meeting a month during the institutionalization process. All the other consultations were done in the teachers' free time and were not financially rewarded. Moreover, formal teacher training courses started in London only in 2013 (Abrir, n.d.), and thus did not affect the group of teachers in this study. The teachers in Spain have an advantage in that one of the members of the school Executive Committee is a teacher and teacher training courses were available to them only three years after the establishment of the school. Nevertheless, both schools would benefit from more financial resources, which would naturally imply better possibilities for training their teachers both in-house and at other institutions.

It appears, however, that the limitations in the resources (i.e., material and personnel) available to these schools were not an obstacle to the involvement of teachers and directors in the process of innovation. The Executive Committee members and the teachers in both locations were highly involved and engaged, not due to financial interest but rather to their social and emotional commitment to the cause of serving the needs of their students. A teacher in Barcelona states that her "relationship with the school is not only professional" but that she is "emotionally linked to the school and its other members." Similar statements were made by the participants in London. They were aware of the limitations of the context in which they worked and were highly motivated to contribute to any possible improvement that could result from their participation. In other words, they were extremely committed to learning and contributed to the creation of an environment where collaboration and mutual support is nurtured.

Another indicator of institutionalization that Ekholm and Trier (1987) point to is the lack of dependence of an innovation on "specific persons" (p. 17). Despite the collaboration and atmosphere of mutual support, the dependence of the innovations on the figure of the coordinators in the school in London was clear, as reported in the interviews for this study. Being aware of the situation, one of the coordinators considered it important to create organizational procedures and documentation for the continuation of the changes, independent of particular coordinators and teachers. In the case of the school in Barcelona, the figure of the pedagogical coordinator does not exist. Consequently, the teachers themselves have voiced their own concerns about the organizational structure of the school, and there is less dependency on one single figure for the changes to take place. Nevertheless, the same need to document the changes is reported. As pointed out by one of the teachers in Barcelona, having a record of the changes and producing a guiding document for the school is relevant in order to "ensure that their founding aims are followed when they [the people who developed the project] are no longer part of the group." This lack of dependency on one single person, and an awareness of the disadvantages of this situation, together with the development of systems that can be passed forward to ensure continuity of instruction are signs of institutionalization in both schools (Ekholm & Trier, 1987).

In the school in London, having organizational procedures that included team meetings, deciding on pedagogical content and planning together, and developing guidelines were paramount in contributing to the acceptance of the innovation as a common practice and eventually its diminished visibility (Ekholm & Trier, 1987, p. 17). The documents produced reflected the discussions between directors and teachers and the experiences the teachers and coordinators had in working together. Instead of explaining the changes or imposing them on the teachers, the coordinators consulted with the teachers and gave them the opportunity to experiment with new ideas, to share their knowledge and experience, to work together, to be involved. This meant that shared goals were developed within a supportive environment, important ingredients for the success of any school improvement (Creemers & Kyriakides, 2012). Feeling part of the process ensured high levels of acceptance of the changes by the teachers.

The teachers in Barcelona were the ones who had the initiative to develop criteria for the different groups or levels of students. Additionally, their pedagogical project (i.e., the definition of objectives, the selection of content, and the use of diagnostic and formative assessments) is in development.[6] The teachers liaise face-to-face as well as online in order to discuss their ideas and write them up in the form of documents. Although these are the early stages of the institutionalization process in Barcelona, there are already signs that the visibility of the changes being implemented is diminishing.

6 Conclusion

The Brazilian complementary school in London and the one in Barcelona illustrate six stages of the institutionalization process (see Figure 8.1) involving changes that resulted from the collaboration among teachers and other members of the school. Collaboration is an essential characteristic of schools that nurture and sustain a community of learners (Antonacci & Bernhardt, 1998). Moreover, "the school as a learning community [is] where life-long learning takes place for all stakeholders for their own continuous growth and development . . . and mistakes become agents for further learning and improvement" (Voulalas & Sharpe, 2005, p. 191). That is, an ethos of collaboration is crucial for the successful implementation of innovations.

In the case of the school in London, the first cycle of institutionalizing their innovations took seven years. Although this length of time might appear to be too long, it has been acknowledged that changes related to group behavior have much higher levels of difficulty and thus take much longer to instantiate than other types, such as changes related to knowledge (Morrish, 1976/2012). Furthermore, instead of accelerating change, we should facilitate it (Blenkin et al., 1992). This means that differences (or similarities) in pace of change at each school should be respected.

Another challenge mentioned by the London participants was the change in the school leadership. Some of the new leaders had a different approach when relating to their staff or were not very familiar with the innovations being implemented. Yet another challenge was that the adoption of documentation that supported the innovations gave a false sense that the teachers alone could ensure the establishment of the change and its insertion into the school routine. They relied on their Teachers' Handbook and decided not to have a coordinator for a period of about six months after it was produced. It was then noticed that collegiality—i.e., continuous teacher-teacher and teachers-administrators talks about the lessons, lesson plans, selection of materials, and learning (Little, 1981, in Antonacci & Bernhardt, 1998)—was disappearing. Fortunately, the negative effects of the lack of collegiality were soon noticed by the team and a new coordinator was hired to ensure continuity of their innovations.

As pointed out by Morrish (2012), "Things never just stay as they are, they change whether they improve or decay" (p. 15). Therefore, it is important that complementary schools are aware of the stages discussed above, so that they can approach their institutionalization process in a more conscious way and ensure improvement. Additionally, although not covered in this chapter, specific linguistic and pedagogical challenges faced by the schools should be considered to ensure the design of strategies that address them adequately. After all, positive change "simply will not happen without planning and effort" (Eiseman, Fleming, & Roody, 1990, p. 24).

Notes

1 The authors thank the school teachers, coordinators and directors for their participation in the study reported in this chapter, especially the Executive Committee members Irene Costa and Priscila Diniz (1997–1999); Julia Felmanas and Luciana Buzak (1997–2002); Marina Michalski and Zélia Edwards (2000–2002), Iricê Godoi (2000–2003) and Regina Mester (2004–2009); the pedagogical coordinator Aline Belisário (1998–1999); the teachers Marjorie Gubert (1998–2003), Fabiana Fajfer (2002–2003) and Cláudio Souza (2002–2006) in London, as well as the Executive Committee members Edilaine de Aguiar and Andreia Moroni; and the teachers Bruna Hecht (2014–2015), Giselle Macedo and Michelle Soares in Barcelona.
2 This was the situation at the time this chapter was written.
3 In the UK, a scheme of work is a document in which teachers describe lesson aims, objectives, and activities; time activities; list lesson resources; and present assessments and homework.
4 All the interviews were conducted in Portuguese and translated into English by the authors.
5 The school had two coordinators between 1998 and 2004. The first one is being referred to as Coordinator 1, and the second is one of the authors (see section 4).
6 Therefore, they are not reported in this chapter yet.

References

Abrir. (n.d.). Oportunidade única: oficinas gratuitas para professores de português [Unique opportunity: Free workshops for Portuguese teachers] [Web log]. Retrieved from https://blog.abrir.org.uk/2013/06/04/oportunidade-unica-oficinas-gratuitas-para-professores-de-portugues/

Antonacci, P., & Bernhardt, R. (1998). The role of collaboration in the process of change. In R. Bernhardt, C. Hedley, G. Cattaro, & V. Svolopoulos (Eds.), *Curriculum leadership: Rethinking schools for the 21st century* (pp. 55–68). New York, NY: Hampton.

Blenkin, G., Edwards, G., & Kelly, A. (1992). *Change and the curriculum.* London, UK: Paul Chapman.

Creemers, B., & Kyriakides, L. (2012). *Improving quality in education: Dynamic approaches to school improvement.* Abingdon, UK: Routledge.

Eiseman, J. W., Fleming, D. S., & Roody, D. S. (1990). *Making sure it sticks: The school improvement leader's role in institutionalizing change.* Andover, MA: The Regional Laboratory.

Ekholm, M. R., & Trier, U. P. (1987). The concept of institutionalization: Some remarks. In M. B. Miles, M. R. Ekholm, & R. Vandenberghe (Eds.), *Lasting school improvement: Exploring the process of institutionalization* (pp. 13–21). Leuven, Belgium: Acco.

Instituto Brasileiro de Geografia e Estatística (IBGE). (2011). Censo Demográfico 2010: características da população e dos domicílios resultados do universo [Demographic census 2010: Population and household characteristics universal results]. Retrieved from http://biblioteca.ibge.gov.br/visualizacao/periodicos/93/cd_2010_caracteristicas_populacao_domicilios.pdf

Instituto d'Estadística de Catalunya [Institute of Statistics of Catalonia]. (2014). Població estrangera. Per sexe i edat quinquennal [Foreign population by sex and age, quinquennial]. Retrieved from http://www.idescat.cat/poblacioestrangera/?res=a&nac=d342&b=1&lang=es

Keating, M. C., Solovova, O., & Barradas, O. (2013). Políticas de língua, multilinguismos e migrações: para uma reflexão policêntrica sobre os valores do português no espaço europeu [Language policy, multilingualism and migration: Toward a polycentric reflection on the values of the Portuguese in Europe]. In L. P. Moita Lopes (Ed.), *O Português no Século XXI—cenário geopolítico e sociolinguístico [Portuguese in the 21st Century: A geopolitical and sociolinguistic scenario]* (pp. 219–248). São Paulo, Brazil: Parábola.

Kelly, A. V. (1997/2009). *The Curriculum: Theory and practice.* London, UK: Sage.

Lytra, V., & Martin, P. (Eds.). (2010). *Sites of multilingualism: Complementary schools in Britain today.* London, UK: Trentham.

Meksenas, P. (2002). *Pesquisa social e ação pedagógica: conceitos, métodos e práticas* [*Social research and pedagogical action: Concepts, methods and practices*]. São Paulo, Brazil: Edições Loyola.

Mendes, E. (2012). Vidas em português: perspectivas culturais e identitárias em contexto de português língua de herança [Lives in Portuguese: Cultural and identity perspectives in the context of Portuguese as a heritage language]. *Platô, 1*(2). Retrieved from http://www.youblisher.com/p/781082-Plato-Volume-1-N-2-Coloquio-da-Praia-V1-1

Ministério das Relações Exteriores (MRE). (2015, August). Brasileiros no mundo [Brazilians around the world]. Retrieved from http://www.brasileirosnomundo.itamaraty.gov.br/a-comunidade/estimativas-populacionais-das-comunidades/estimativas-populacionais-brasileiras-mundo-2014/Estimativas-RCN2014.pdf

Ministério das Relações Exteriores [Ministry of Foreign Affairs]. (n.d.). Divisão de Promoção da Língua Portuguesa [Division to promote the Portuguese language] [Web site]. Retrieved from http://dc.itamaraty.gov.br/divisao-de-promocao-da-lingua-portuguesa-dplp-1

Moroni, A., & Gomes, J. (2015). El Portugués como Lengua de herencia hoy y el trabajo de la Associação e Pais de Brasileirinhos na Catalunha [Portuguese as a heritage language today and the work of the association and parents of Brazilian speakers in Catalonia]. *Revista de Estudios Brasileños, 2*(2), 21–35. doi: 10.3232/REB.2015.V2.N2.02

Morrish, I. (1976/2012). *Aspects of educational change.* London, UK: Routledge.

Solé, C., Cavalcanti, L., & Parella, S. (2011). La inmigración brasileña en la estructura socioeconómica de España [Brazilian immigration in the socioeconomic structure of Spain]. *Observatorio Permanente de la inmigración* [*Permanent Immigration Observatory*]. Retrieved from http://extranjeros.empleo.gob.es/es/ObservatorioPermanenteInmigracion/Publicaciones/fichas/archivos/La-inmigracion-brasilena-en-la-estructura-socioeconomica-de-Espana.pdf

Souza, A. (2008). How linguistic and cultural identities are affected by migration. *Language Issues, 19*(1), 36–42.

Souza, A., & Barradas, O. (2014). Português como Língua de Herança: Políticas Linguísticas na Inglaterra [Portuguese as heritage language: Linguistic policies in England]. *Revista SIPLE, 6,* article 1. Retrieved from http://www.siple.org.br/index.php?option=com_content&view=article&id=297:portugues-como-lingua-de-heranca-politicas-linguisticas-na-inglaterra&catid=69:edicao-6&Itemid=112

Voulalas, Z. D., & Sharpe, F. G. (2005). Creating schools as learning communities: Obstacles and processes. *Journal of Educational Administration, 43*(2), 187–208.

9

Czech Heritage Language Education in Communities in the United States and Europe

Marta McCabe

1 Introduction

The Czech Republic is home to about 10.5 million people today. In addition, approximately 2.2 million people who live outside the country claim Czech heritage (Ministry of Foreign Affairs of the Czech Republic, 2011). Among this 2.2 million, only a minority actively use the Czech language. While first-generation immigrants, i.e., people born in the Czech Republic, continue to use the Czech language, subsequent generations typically experience language loss to varying degrees (Fillmore, 1991; Kouritzin, 1999). In the U.S., for instance, descendants of earlier Czech immigrants have often retained only an identification with Czech culture but not necessarily the use of the language (Dutkova-Cope, 2006; Eckert & Hannan, 2009). Since the 1990s, however, with a new wave of immigration beginning from the Czech Republic and the entire region of Central and Eastern Europe, maintenance of heritage languages (HLs) has become an important goal of many of these communities. Although much HL research in the U.S. has focused on Asian and Latin American immigrants, current research documents HL maintenance efforts in Central and Eastern European communities from Romania (Nesteruk, 2010; Petruscu, 2014), Poland (Kozminska, 2015), Turkey (Otcu, 2009), Lithuania (Tamošiūnaitė, 2013), Greece (Aravossitas, 2010), and Ukraine (Chumak-Horbatsch, 1999). Some of these language minorities have access to many well-established HL schools while other groups may lack such educational networks.

The purpose of this chapter is to describe the current state of Czech HL education in the U.S. and Europe and to examine the degree of institutionalization of the respective programs, focusing on a group of community schools that represents a new, successful, and growing initiative in Czech HL education. Drawing on Ekholm and Trier (1987), I use the term *institutionalization* to mean "a process through which an organization assimilates an innovation into its structure" (p. 13). This process can refer to innovations or changes made within an existing program or to the establishment of a new organization. To analyze the degree of institutionalization of the existing Czech HL programs, I examine the following: (1) the types, locations, and dates of establishment of the programs; (2) the educational practices, including the types of language instruction, enrichment programs, qualification of teachers, teaching materials, and numbers of participants; and (3) the financial and material resources enabling program stability. Data for this analysis were collected mainly from publicly viewable websites and Facebook pages of the Czech government and the respective HL programs. I have confirmed the data and collected additional information via personal conversations with 11 HL school directors.

This chapter is divided into five sections: the first section provides available statistics about Czech speakers living abroad; the second section describes the current state of Czech HL education in the U.S.; the third part focuses on the situation of Czech HL education in Europe, the fourth section describes the types of collaboration among the schools and between the schools and the Czech government, and the last section provides an assessment of the degree of institutionalization of the various Czech HL programs while also discussing implications of the findings.

2 Czech Language Speakers Abroad

According to Ministry of Foreign Affairs of the Czech Republic (2011), most of the 2.2 million people with Czech origins living outside the Czech Republic are found in the U.S. (1.5 million), Canada (120,000), Austria (55,000), Germany (50,000), Slovakia (47,000), the United Kingdom (30,000–40,000), Argentina (30,000), Australia (27,000), and France (20,000–30,000). Other countries with large populations of people with Czech heritage include Switzerland, Ireland, and Croatia (each between 10,000 and 20,000), and also Ukraine, Sweden, Belgium, and Italy (each between 4,000 and 6,000). These numbers constitute only rough estimates because accurate data are not available (Ministry of Foreign Affairs of the Czech Republic, 2011). It is important to note, however, that most of these people are descendants of earlier immigrants who may no longer speak or understand the Czech language. In fact, among the 1.5 million people claiming Czech ancestry in the U.S. today, only 47,385 people aged five and older are currently speaking Czech at home (U.S. Census Bureau, 2015), which equals to about 3% of all people claiming Czech heritage in the U.S.

The current population of Czech speakers abroad includes descendants of the largest wave of Czech immigration to the U.S. (1948–1914), political émigrés from the communist Czechoslovakia (1948–1989), and more substantively, the post-1989 wave of emigration. It is estimated that about 200,000 Czechs emigrated between 1989 and 2007 (ČTK, 2014; Ministry of Foreign Affairs of the Czech Republic, 2011). The typical new Czech emigrant is a young and highly educated professional seeking better career opportunities, higher income, higher living standards, and quality education abroad. Often, instead of returning home, these young people find desirable jobs abroad and settle there permanently (Ciborová, 2014; ČTK, 2014). Today, these new Czech emigrants are raising children abroad and one of their main concerns is how to help these children maintain the Czech language. Many parents have become involved in long-established Czech cultural organizations and begun reintroducing Czech language classes in these venues, while other enthusiastic parents have established new organizations with the sole purpose of providing Czech heritage language education.

Among the many Czech HL programs currently operating worldwide, at least 23 Czech HL schools are based in the U.S. and at least 45 in Europe. On both continents, at least half of the schools were conceived by dedicated parents and founded or revived relatively recently, between 2011 and 2015. In addition to the rapid increase in the number of programs, these new schools represent a qualitatively different type of Czech cultural organizations compared to the past. While in the second half of the twentieth century most traditional Czech organizations in the U.S. focused on the maintenance of the *cultural heritage*, the newly established programs aim specifically at providing education in the Czech *language*. This recent shift from a focus on cultural heritage to a genuine concern with language acquisition is promising in terms of building a more sustainable HL education.

3 Czech Heritage Language Education in the United States

The earliest wave of Czech immigration into the U.S. dates back to the sixteenth century, when seeking religious freedom was the main motivation. A more substantive wave arrived between 1848 and 1914, with an estimated 350,000 Czechs, or one-sixteenth of the Czech nation, coming to America (Ference, 1993; Hrouda, 2011). During this era, the Czech language was maintained by active use in the communities, through print, and in about 100 Czech HL schools (Vaculík, 2009, p. 283). The first Czech school opened in New York City in 1856, followed shortly by Chicago and other cities in Texas, Nebraska, and Wisconsin (Dutkova-Cope, 2006; Hrouda, 2011). Over the course of the twentieth century, however, the Czech immigration flow decreased markedly in part as a result of the U.S. Immigration Act of 1924, which suppressed immigration from Southern and Eastern Europe and prioritized immigrants from Northern and Western European countries, and in part because emigration from the former communist Czechoslovakia was restricted due to political reasons. The low influx of new Czech immigrants into the U.S. resulted in language attrition and loss in the established communities (Dutkova-Cope, 2006; Eckert & Hannan, 2009). Over time, many Czech cultural organizations retained an identification with Czech culture that did not necessarily include the use of the language (Hrouda, 2011). At present, however, the U.S. is experiencing a noticeable increase in immigration from the Czech Republic, enabled mainly by the fall of the Communist regimes in the region in 1989. The numbers of Czech speakers among the foreign-born population five years and older grew from 27,739 in 1990, to 31,051 in 2000 (Gibson & Jung, 2006). In 2011, the U.S. Census Bureau (2015) reported 47,385 Czech language speakers in the U.S.

Types and Locations of Czech Heritage Language Programs in the U.S.

The 23 Czech HL programs that operate across the U.S. today can be divided into two major categories. The first group includes schools that operate as part of older and well-established Czech cultural organizations (about 14 programs). Some of these organizations have been offering Czech language classes for over 100 years, while others have resumed or added language instruction only recently. These programs are concentrated mainly in the traditional destinations of Czech immigration, such as in Texas, Minnesota, Illinois, and the Northeast. The schools in the second group (about nine programs) were generally founded only recently, between the years 2012 and 2015, and they operate as independent non-profit organizations. They operate mainly on the West Coast and in other new and non-traditional immigrant destinations, such as Georgia or North Carolina. Figure 9.1 illustrates the locations of both types of programs.

In addition to their location and length of operation, other important differences exist between these two categories of HL programs. First, the newly established independent schools generally have the legal status of a non-profit organization and thus enjoy greater freedom in decision-making about staffing, tuition, fundraising, collaboration, publicity, etc. On the other hand, schools operating within a larger heritage organization must collaborate with the directors and officers of the larger institution. However, being part of an established organization often brings important benefits, such as additional funding or access to a cost-free facility. Second, traditional ethnic institutions are usually focused on organizing multiple cultural events throughout the year and the provision of Czech language classes is only one of their many objectives. On the other hand, all of the newly established programs have been founded with the single purpose of providing Czech HL education. Finally, all newly established HL programs are mainly focused on children while many of the traditional cultural organizations focus primarily on adults, and thus may offer language classes only for adults (refer to Figure 9.1). The most salient similarity

Figure 9.1 Czech Heritage Language Programs in the United States

Note: CIRCLES—schools operating as part of a long-established cultural organization (LARGE CIRCLES—schools offering classes for children, SMALL CIRCLES—schools offering only classes for adults), STARS—newly established independent schools.

between the two types of programs is the fact that the program directors and managers are generally young Czech immigrant mothers or fathers, who are personally invested in children's HL learning (Patterson, 2014).

Educational Practices

A wide variety of educational practices is found across Czech HL programs in terms of age and proficiency of participants, number and qualifications of teachers, frequency and duration of classes, and intensity and rigor of the programs. While virtually all U.S.-based programs provide some classes for adults, it is instruction of children that typically constitutes the core of the schools' language offerings. All independent schools and about a half of the schools operating within an established cultural organization provide a variety of HL classes for children aged 3–15. The numbers of children enrolled vary between 5 and about 90 students per school. Classes usually meet once a week for one to two hours. Only two schools offer classes that meet for three or more hours each week: one in Chicago and one in San Francisco. The most common time to hold classes is Saturday morning; however, some schools prefer to meet on Saturday afternoons, Sundays, or on weekdays after school. Teachers are typically recruited from among parents of the students and often do not have pedagogical training. They are paid a small compensation for their time and effort.

Children are typically divided by age and proficiency into groups of 6–10 students. Depending on the demand, schools may offer classes for toddlers, preschoolers, elementary school children, or middle school children. Preschool and lower elementary classes have typically the most students, while middle school classes are less common. Most programs find it difficult to retain middle school children, and as a result, Czech HL classes for high school students are generally non-existent. However, it is also important to note that the new wave of immigrants began settling in the U.S. only recently. Therefore, most children currently growing up with Czech parents in the U.S. are younger than 15 years old. The majority of children enrolled in the HL classes come from families where at least one parent is a Czech-speaking immigrant, but exact data about the percentage of all-Czech versus mixed families is not available. Depending on the family situation and parental goals, children come to HL schools with varying degrees of familiarity with the Czech language. Some children are fluent, some have only a passive knowledge of Czech, and still others have almost no understanding of the HL.

Depending on the degree of children's familiarity with the Czech language, each school selects its own approach to instruction and uses language materials and textbooks of their choice. While language classes for toddlers and preschoolers tend to be similar across programs (incorporating arts, crafts, and storytelling in Czech), larger differences in instruction exist among classes for school-aged children. A few schools follow the Czech national curriculum and teach the language in the same way it is taught in public schools in the Czech Republic, using textbooks for native speakers of the language. One advantage of this approach is a large selection of textbooks available from the Czech Republic. These textbooks, however, are not suitable for most HL learners because the books contain morphologically complex and culturally specific vocabulary, the latter generally unknown to U.S.-born children. In addition, the way in which grammar is presented to native speakers is generally not appropriate for heritage speakers growing up abroad. For this reason, other schools opt for an approach and textbooks much closer to foreign language instruction. These programs often use a textbook called *Čeština pro malé cizince* [Czech for Little Foreigners] (Škodová, 2004, 2005), developed for immigrant children studying Czech as a second language in public schools in the Czech Republic. This textbook, however, is not challenging for children with prior exposure to the language because it presents basic terms and phrases, such as "ahoj" (hi), "maminka" (mother), "nahoře/dole" (up/down), or "Já se jmenuju . . ." (My name is . . .). Overall, neither pedagogical approach is appropriate for heritage learners (Valdés, 2005). Thus, many Czech HL schools in the U.S. struggle to find an instructional approach and language materials that would match the abilities and fit the needs of heritage speakers. Since textbooks suitable for Czech HL learners are virtually non-existent, teachers must combine materials from multiple sources and prepare their own materials.

The selection of materials depends upon the students' language proficiency and upon the goals of each program. Only a few schools aim to achieve a nearly native-like knowledge of Czech (such as San Francisco, Chicago, or Washington, DC), follow the Czech national curriculum, and use textbooks for native speakers of Czech consistently. Most Czech HL programs, however, do not expect native-like degree of proficiency. These programs aim to nurture the children's ability to communicate—and perhaps read—in Czech, and to cultivate children's positive relationship to the Czech language and culture. They use any engaging materials and focus only on a few major grammatical rules. This diversity of teaching goals is apparent not only across but also within individual schools. For example, a program in Washington, DC, provides classes that strictly follow the Czech national curriculum as well as classes that take a much more informal approach, focusing mainly on conversation and basic literacy skills.

In addition to language instruction, most programs include engaging activities, such as games, crafts, and music, in order to make the Saturday school more appealing to the children. Virtually all schools organize at least a few cultural events for children per year. The most popular are St. Nicholas Day [*Mikulášská*], Christmas Pageant [*Vánoční besídka*], Easter Celebration [*Velikonoce*], and Children's Day [*Den dětí*]. Additional programs may include family picnic days, costume parties, movie nights, cooking or baking workshops, camping, and various fundraising events. All these activities foster a sense of community and are also used to showcase children's projects.

Resources

Assuring sufficient funding is a challenge for most Czech HL programs. The main expenses include facility rental fees, insurance payments, costs of teaching materials, and compensation of teachers. The majority of labor connected with running an HL school, however, is voluntary. To reduce expenses and thus keep tuition low, all programs attempt to find affordable spaces for their classes and often make an agreement with local churches and use their classrooms for a reduced fee or in exchange for a small donation. Interestingly, Czechs are one of the least-religious nationalities in the world. Only 10% of all Czechs living in the Czech Republic identify as Roman Catholics, while 80% consider themselves non-religious (Czech Statistical Office, 2011). Thus, most of the churches renting their facilities to Czech HL programs have no significance or connection to the Czech Republic. Other facilities rented for Czech HL classes include public school classrooms, libraries, and community centers. Schools operating as part of a larger cultural organization usually have access to the organization's facilities free of charge.

The main sources of income for all schools include tuition fees, grants from the Czech government, donations by sponsors, support from a larger organization (if part of one), and gains from fundraising events. Tuition fees range from about $100 to $760 per school year (September–June) for a two-hour weekly class. An average fee is about $500 a year per child and most schools offer a sibling discount. The largest U.S.-based Czech school (in San Francisco) charges up to $1,300 per year, but it offers longer instructional time: three hours a week. In general, programs operating under a larger cultural organization charge much less tuition (between $100 and $400 a year) than the independent schools. This is possible not only because these programs use the organization's facilities for free but also because they may be covered under the insurance policy of the mother organization, which lowers their expenses even further. The Czech government supports HL schools by providing financial gifts and textbooks. Still, it is not possible for the schools to rely solely on these gifts. In addition to tuition fees and grants, many schools seek donations from private sponsors and organize fundraising events, which range from small bake sales and raffles to more grandiose events, such as the annual Czech Banquet and Gala in Palo Alto, California. This is perhaps the largest fundraising event organized by a recently established HL school. As for sponsors, the typical donor would be a wealthy entrepreneur with Czech roots or a local company with links to the Czech Republic.

4 Czech Heritage Language Education in Europe

In Europe, a noticeable increase in emigration from the Czech Republic was enabled in part by the fall of the Communist regime in 1989 but mainly by the country's accession to the European Union in 2004. Higher living standards and higher wages in Western European countries are among the main reasons for the increased migration from Central and Eastern Europe to the West. Today, most people with Czech heritage in Europe live in Austria (55,000), Germany (50,000), Slovakia (47,000), the United Kingdom (30,000–40,000), France (20,000–30,000), Switzerland (13,500), and Ireland (11,000) (Ministry of Foreign Affairs of the Czech Republic, 2011). While these young professionals settle in the given countries, they typically travel to the Czech Republic with their families at least once a year. This transnational mobility increases parents' motivation for Czech language maintenance (McCabe, 2016). Over the past decade, a network of Czech HL schools has grown steadily across Western Europe. At the same time,

Czech schools have long operated in a number of Eastern European countries, such as Croatia, Ukraine, and Romania. While these three countries served as historical destinations for Czech immigrants for over a century, the numbers of Czech people living in these communities are decreasing today, with the latest statistics listing 10,000 people in Croatia, 6,000 in Ukraine, and fewer than 1,000 people in Romania (Dům zahraniční spolupráce, 2015b; Ministry of Foreign Affairs of the Czech Republic, 2011).

Types and Locations of Czech Heritage Language Programs

At least 45 Czech HL programs operate across Europe today. As a result of the recent wave of emigration from the Czech Republic to the west, most new programs are located in Western Europe, such as in neighboring Germany (at least eight schools), France, and Italy. At the same time, at least 15 long-established schools operate in Croatia, Ukraine, and Romania. One country, Slovakia, represents a unique situation. While the number of people with Czech heritage in Slovakia is among the highest in Europe, not a single Czech school operates in this country. The two likely reasons are that most of this population are of an older generation and that because the Czech and Slovak languages are closely related, their speakers can easily understand one another without explicitly studying the language. Czech HL programs in Europe fall into three major categories: (1) eight programs in Western Europe fall under an umbrella organization called *Česká škola bez hranic* (CSBH) [Czech School without Borders]; (2) about 20 other schools in the West operate as independent organizations and maintain only loose connections with CSBH; and (3) at least 15 long-established schools provide Czech language education in Eastern Europe, mainly in Croatia and Romania. For details, see Figure 9.2.

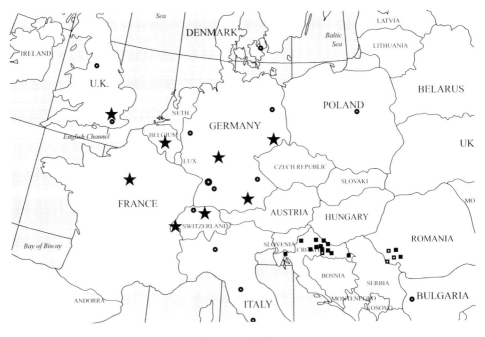

Figure 9.2   Czech Heritage Language Programs in Europe

Note: STARS—CSBH schools; CIRCLES—schools operating independently of CSBH (not all schools operating independently are shown); SQUARES—long-established schools in Eastern Europe.

The non-profit organization CSBH, with an accompanying school, was established in Paris in 2003. Affiliated schools were subsequently founded in Germany, Switzerland, Belgium, and the UK. The goal of the organization is to maintain the Czech language and culture in Czech communities living abroad. The schools independent of CSBH have generally been established even more recently, between the years 2011 and 2015. These programs are also located mainly in Western Europe, such as in Germany (5), Italy (4), the UK (2), Switzerland, Denmark, Portugal, and Spain, but are additionally found in Greece, Bulgaria, Poland, and Iceland.

In some Eastern European countries, on the other hand, many Czech schools have operated for decades or even centuries in villages inhabited largely by people of Czech origins. In Croatia alone, about 15 Czech schools are currently in operation. A number of these schools provide all-day instruction in the Czech language for grades first through eighth, according to a teaching plan approved by the Croatian government. Some Croatian public schools, including at least one high school, offer Czech language as an elective and provide up to four hours of instruction in Czech each week (Češi v Chorvatsku, n.d.; Dům zahraniční spolupráce, 2015a). The Czech community in Croatia is so well established that it even has a representative in the Croatian Parliament. The other two countries with a traditional Czech minority, Romania and Ukraine, both have a number of Czech villages that operate Czech schools. In some of these village schools, all subjects in grades first through fourth are taught in Czech. However, because the numbers of Czech people and especially children are markedly decreasing, Czech language has remained only an elective subject in most village schools in both countries (Člověk v tísni, 2013; Dům zahraniční spolupráce, 2015b, 2015c). For the purposes of this chapter, I will focus on CSBH schools as an example of a new, successful, and growing initiative in Czech HL education.

Educational Practices

CSBH schools offer systematic Czech language education for children 18 months to 15 years old living abroad. The educational program uses a total immersion method allowing only Czech to be spoken in the classes. Toddler and preschool classes meet for about one to two hours each week and integrate arts, crafts, music, and drama. Classes for elementary-school children typically meet for four to five hours every weekend and provide education in Czech language, literature, geography, and history.

The purpose of CSBH is to provide Czech language education comparable to the instruction in public schools in the Czech Republic. To reach the desired nearly native proficiency in the Czech language, CSBH schools: (1) provide longer hours of instruction (four to five hours a week plus homework) than is usual with other weekend schools; (2) follow the Czech national curriculum in the subjects of Czech language, literature, geography, and history; (3) use Czech elementary school textbooks; and (4) require that their teachers are highly qualified (i.e., receive pedagogical training from a Czech university). In return for this high-quality instruction, the Czech Ministry of Education may provide an accreditation to select CSBH schools to issue the same end-of-grade student report cards valid in the Czech Republic. These report cards serve as proof that a student has completed the requirements for each grade at a level comparable to any public school in the Czech Republic. The CSBH school in Paris was the first Czech heritage school to receive such accreditation from the Czech Ministry of Education in 2013 (Česká škola bez hranic, 2015), and although all CSBH schools hold a common vision of HL education, only three CSBH schools have received this accreditation so far.

While any Czech HL school in the world can apply for the accreditation to issue report cards valid in the Czech Republic, most independent HL schools in Europe and in the U.S. do not fulfill the required conditions regarding time allotment, rigor of classes, materials used, and teacher qualifications. In the U.S., only one school (in San Francisco) has successfully applied and received this accreditation. Considering the high language proficiency goals, ambitious curriculum, and qualified teachers, CSBH may be considered the most institutionalized form of Czech HL education. On the other hand, to maintain the high standard of instruction and the desired student outcomes, these schools generally do not accept children who are not fluent speakers of the Czech language by age six. To accommodate less-proficient students, many CSBH schools also provide supplementary classes in Czech as a foreign language for speakers "whose level of Czech skills is not sufficient for them to fully integrate into the regular 'Czech School without Borders' program" (Česká škola bez hranic, 2015). These classes focus more on communicative ability and less on explicit grammar instruction.

Resources

Similar to the U.S.-based schools, programs in Europe must cover expenses such as rental fees, insurance, and teacher salaries. They obtain financial resources from tuition fees and donations by sponsors and receive additional support from the Czech government through the Ministry of Foreign Affairs and the Ministry of Education. In addition, embassies, consulates, and Czech centers abroad sometimes provide a teaching space in their facilities and help promote the schools' activities (Česká škola bez hranic, 2015). CSBH, as an umbrella organization, handles most financial issues and donations for the associated schools, while independent schools apply for grants individually and organize their own fundraising events.

5 Forms of Collaboration

HL schools both in Europe and the U.S. thrive when interconnected and collaborating among themselves and with other institutions. The most frequent types of such partnerships include (1) Czech governmental support, (2) partnerships with educational institutions in the Czech Republic, and (3) collaboration between HL schools. While the Czech government has always supported the long-established Czech schools abroad, it is now beginning to pay increasing attention to the newly established HL schools. Similarly, Czech universities have always collaborated with U.S.-based universities offering Czech as a foreign language to adults. Today, however, Czech academic and non-governmental institutions take an interest in Czech as an HL and provide training, materials (although limited), and advice to HL programs.

Collaboration between Heritage Language Schools and the Czech Government

During the post-1989 wave of emigration from the Czech Republic, when many young and promising Czech professionals left the country, a "brain drain" occurred that went largely unnoticed until the country began experiencing a shortage of qualified doctors, scientists, and so on. Recently, the Czech government has begun paying attention to this new emigration wave and started working towards a comprehensive return policy (Brouček & Grulich, 2014). While the policy is by no means finalized, the support of Czech language education abroad is listed among the tools promising to enable an easier return for entire families to the Czech Republic. At present, three main governmental offices attend to the language needs of Czechs living abroad: (1) the Czech Ministry of Education, (2) the Office of a Special Commissioner for Czechs Living Abroad at the Czech Ministry of Foreign Affairs, and (3) the Commission on Compatriots Living Abroad at the Senate of the Czech Republic.

Most material support comes from the Ministry of Foreign Affairs in the form of financial donations for compatriot organizations (Ministry of Foreign Affairs of the Czech Republic, 2011). Grant money is provided to Czech organizations of all kinds, including about 40 HL schools worldwide. In fact, the Czech government has declared the support for HL schools as one of its top priorities for the upcoming funding cycle. At present, about $50,000 is divided each year among the HL schools that apply for support (Ciborová, 2014). Additional services are available through an educational program for Czechs living abroad funded by the Ministry of Education. This program provides scholarships for language courses for Czech compatriots and teachers as well as scholarships to study at Czech public universities (Ministry of Education, Youth, and Sports, 2013). The training courses are organized by Ústav jazykové a odborné přípravy (n.d.; UJOP) [Institute for language and preparatory studies] at Charles University in Prague. In addition, the Ministry of Education may also donate surplus textbooks to Czech HL schools, if requested. It also provides accreditation to schools reaching the highest instructional standards. Moreover, the Czech government sends up to 15 Czech language teachers to compatriot organizations every year. Currently, the one teacher working in the U.S. is based in Chicago. In Europe, Czech teachers serve in Croatia, Serbia, and Romania. As evident from the list of locations, the government sends teachers to the traditional Czech settlements, despite the fact that the number of Czech-speaking residents in these communities may be declining.

In addition, the Commission on Compatriots Living Abroad has organized an annual Prague-based conference of Czech HL schools. Since 2009, this conference serves as a venue for exchange of ideas and experiences among Czech HL schools worldwide. This conference stresses the role of HL maintenance in the preservation of Czech cultural heritage abroad and features a several-day training course for teachers (Česká škola bez hranic, 2015). A representative from UJOP, Charles University, is typically present to lead a workshop about teaching Czech as an HL. Finally, many Czech HL schools work in close collaboration with Czech consulates and embassies. Consuls are possibly the most valued allies in the effort to establish and successfully run an HL school. At least four Czech consuls have personally started or helped establish an HL school in the past three years, and other schools collaborate with consulates on events such as film screenings, Christmas celebration, National Day celebration, and so on.

Collaboration between Heritage Language Schools and Educational Institutions in the Czech Republic

Currently, HL schools are discovering new possibilities of collaboration with non-profit organizations in the Czech Republic and with Czech academia. For instance, researchers from Charles University's UJOP are developing teaching materials and methods suitable for heritage speakers and at least one school in the U.S. has developed an exclusive partnership with Charles University to collaborate on developing methodologies for teaching Czech in communities abroad. Lastly, a number of Czech HL schools have fostered collaboration with individual public schools in the Czech Republic. A school in Chicago, for instance, recently hosted a delegation of students and teachers from a public high school in Prague, providing enriching cultural and educational exchange for both parties.

Collaboration among Czech Heritage Language Schools

In contrast to CSBH in Europe, Czech HL schools in the U.S. have not formed an official organization. Yet, most school directors in the U.S. communicate via a Facebook forum and meet at an annual conference called Czech Schools in North America. Since 2012, this conference provides a space for Czech HL programs to exchange experiences, network, and plan joint events, such as visits by Czech artists or musicians. Representatives from the Czech Ministry of Education, Czech Embassy, and Czech consulates are typically present at this conference to offer their support. In addition, a number of U.S.-based schools have developed closer partnerships with the European-based CSBH. Because CSBH's mission extends beyond coordinating its eight member schools to representing all Czech HL schools to the Czech government, CSBH not only provides information to any Czech HL school worldwide but also negotiates a general legislative framework for Czech HL education with the Czech government. As an additional service, CSBH organizes an annual weeklong summer camp in the Czech Republic for children who are HL speakers of Czech.

It is interesting to note, however, that none of the new Czech HL schools, at least in the U.S., has developed any form of collaboration with mainstream public schools or universities in their host country. The situation is different in Croatia, Romania, and Ukraine, where Czech language instruction often takes place directly in public schools. For Czech HL schools in Western countries, by contrast, building partnerships with mainstream public schools remains the necessary next step in order to ensure greater visibility, recognition, and support from the educational system of the host country. While other HL programs in the U.S. collaborate with mainstream institutions quite successfully (such as the French program discussed by Jaumont, Le Dévédec, and Ross, this volume), Czech schools have much to learn in this regard.

Institutionalization of Czech HL Programs: Conclusions and Discussion

This chapter provided an overview of existing HL programs, both in the U.S. and in Europe, and demonstrated a variety of current approaches to Czech HL education. This section will draw on the findings and attempt to evaluate the level of institutionalization of these programs. To help determine whether institutionalization is taking place and to what degree, four major indicators of institutionalization proposed by Ekholm and Trier (1987, p. 17) are discussed: (1) negotiation, (2) resources, (3) rise in legitimacy, and (4) organizational conditions.

First, successful *negotiations* leading to the implementation of changes constitute the initial step toward institutionalization. This indicator is assessed by examining the outcomes of these negotiations, i.e., informal and formal agreements that result from successful negotiations about an innovation, both within the HL schools as well as between the HL schools and other entities. While many of the post-1989 Czech HL schools started rather unofficially, as gatherings of a few parents, all Czech HL schools and programs eventually obtained a legal status in the host country, operating either as independent non-profit corporations or as constituents of a larger heritage organization. Most schools have established governing boards and bylaws in which the rules of operation as well as the roles of the directors are specified. In addition to their legal status in the host country, Czech HL programs are recognized as compatriot organizations and supported by the Czech government. At present, five schools (one in the U.S. and four in Europe) meet very high standards, set the by the Czech Ministry of Education, and hold an accreditation as official providers of Czech language education abroad. One area for improvement for Czech HL schools, however, includes negotiations with and a rise in legitimacy within the dominant educational system of the host countries.

Second, sufficient material and instructional and personal *resources* constitute yet another indicator that an innovation is successfully becoming institutionalized. Material resources, such as sufficient funding and affordable classroom space, are usually the top concerns of each incipient program. To ensure financial stability, all schools collect tuition, although the amount varies greatly across programs. Most schools also receive grants from the Czech Republic to help with their expenses. On the other hand, the host country rarely helps with any expenses of Czech HL programs. Overall, most schools are able to run fairly low-cost operations. Instructional resources, on the other hand, constitute a major challenge as acceptable textbooks and teaching methodologies for Czech heritage speakers are largely non-existent. While some programs rely on materials intended for native speakers, other Czech HL programs use a textbook originally developed for children learning Czech as a second language in public schools in the Czech Republic. Still, neither solution meets the needs of heritage learners. Teachers in most programs prepare their own materials to supplement the existing options but they have yet to find out the way to share these resources across programs.

In addition to sufficient material support and appropriate textbooks, qualified teaching staff constitutes perhaps the most important resource for any successful HL program. Due to financial constraints and the overall shortage of qualified teachers, dedicated parents typically serve as teachers, with or without the necessary qualifications. As mentioned above, the Czech Ministry of Education offers training courses for teachers of Czech language from immigrant communities. Anyone can apply and participate in this professional development course in Prague provided space is available. Additionally, some European-based schools collaborate with teacher training programs at Czech universities and invite Czech college students to gain teaching experience at an HL school abroad. Such an experience is invaluable for the students and enriching for the HL schools.

In addition to acting as teachers, parents also take on the roles of school directors, managers, and general program volunteers. Even the most institutionalized form of Czech HL education, CSBH, was conceived and established by a dedicated immigrant mother. However, many of these parents do have qualifications crucial to the success of a program, such as managerial training, legal experience, grant-writing experience, or perhaps the needed connections to educational or governmental institutions in both the Czech Republic and the host country. Due to financial constraints, it is typically impossible to hire qualified professionals for any of the above posts. Therefore, each school attempts to draw on resources available within the local Czech community.

Moreover, involvement of representatives of the Czech government can boost the school's chances to evolve into a strong HL program. Many Czech schools have fostered collaborations with local consulates, ranging from using the facilities of the consulate to organizing joint events. A number of Czech consuls have personally established HL schools, and others serve on the board of directors in some of these programs. Regrettably, however, representatives of the host country's educational system are rarely involved in establishing or running HL schools, and systematic collaboration between the mainstream educational institutions and Czech HL schools is missing.

Rise in legitimacy constitutes a third major indicator of institutionalization, and it occurs when "there is a decreasing need to motivate people specially to use the new idea or practice" (Ekholm & Trier, 1987, p. 17). For newly established programs, a rise in legitimacy would mean a growing demand for their services. Currently, most Czech HL schools in Western countries are experiencing a new period of growth. Numbers of students are rising, new classes are being added, and instructional time is often being extended. In addition, entire new schools are being established in response to the growing demand for Czech HL classes, such as in Atlanta, Georgia, in 2013 and in Seattle, Washington, and Durham, North Carolina, in 2015. Overall, the recent growth in the number of Czech HL schools in both the U.S. and Europe reflects a rise in the legitimacy of these programs within local Czech immigrant communities.

Finally, stable *organizational conditions* constitute the fourth major indicator of institutionalization. An organization has reached this step if the existence of the new is "no longer dependent on specific persons or temporary special organizational or financial arrangements" (Ekholm &

Trier, 1987, p. 17). As non-profit organizations, many Czech HL programs have a distinct mission, a board of directors, and rules clearly defined in the bylaws. The most stable are certainly the largest schools with the most well-defined organizational framework, such as San Francisco, New York, and the CSBH schools in Europe. Membership in CSBH also boosts a school's chances of remaining strong exactly because of the organizational structure in place. By their nature, HL organizations that rely on volunteers have a high turnover of personnel, especially because volunteers are mainly parents who leave the school when their children do. Having organizational details encoded in bylaws makes them less dependent on specific people.

Overall, the recent increase in numbers and institutionalization of Czech HL schools across Europe and the U.S. is highly encouraging. These programs represent a needed and successful tool for Czech HL maintenance. Still, Czech HL programs face challenges more significant than securing sufficient funding or recruiting qualified teachers. Important next steps include retaining middle and high school students and building meaningful collaborations with mainstream educational institutions.

Even with the recent increase in Czech HL offerings, Czech language is by no means as widely used among Czechs abroad as it was 100 years ago (Eckert & Hannan, 2009). Today, especially in the U.S., children of immigrants do not necessarily consider Czech a practical language to learn (McCabe, in press), which brings back the crucial question of incentives and motivation. As discussed above in the U.S. context, most programs face high attrition rates among middle and high school students, partly because the programs fail to provide a credible reason for why teenagers should put so much effort into studying a language of a small country they might never live in. The children's "homeland," and a major frame of reference, is typically the host country and they need to see the applicability of the HL in this context. While parents may convince a younger child to attend HL classes, older children tend to have higher agency in terms of choosing their free-time activities. When a teenager is not internally motivated, it is very difficult to convince him/her to attend an HL program. Thus, while legitimacy of these programs is certainly well established among immigrant parents, the necessary next step is to provide sufficient motivation for children themselves, especially teenagers. Since these young people are typically U.S. citizens, most HL programs have yet to offer incentives that would legitimize HL learning as a reasonable goal for any U.S.-born teenager.

While Czech HL programs are generally well institutionalized (recognized, developed, and funded) with respect to the Czech Republic, they do not have the same degree of institutionalization with respect to the host country. Therefore, I suggest that in order to boost legitimacy and retain students at higher rates, HL programs need to claim their space within the educational system of the host country. However, Czech language is taught neither as elective nor as part of after-school programs in public schools in the U.S. and Western Europe, which makes it difficult for students of Czech to receive any high school credits for their proficiency in the language. While the Scholastic Aptitude Test (SAT) does not exist for the Czech language at present, a number of programs in the U.S. are working towards finding an official test to help high school students demonstrate their proficiency in Czech to the public schools and thus qualify for the Seal of Biliteracy Award.[1] Such official recognition of their effort might provide the necessary motivation for middle and high school students to devote more of their time to studying a language other than English. If language maintenance is to have a chance, HL education must become recognized and supported as a valid form of learning not only with respect to the country of origin but also within the educational landscape of the host country. Clearly, developing a meaningful collaboration between Czech HL programs and mainstream educational institutions represents the next important step towards a fuller institutionalization of these programs.

Note

1 In the U.S., the Seal of Biliteracy is an official award issued by a local education authority to students who study two or more languages to a certain level of proficiency by high school graduation.

References

Aravossitas, T. (2010). *From Greek school to Greek's cool—heritage language education in Ontario and the Aristoteles Credit Program: Using weblogs for teaching the Greek language in Canada* (Master's thesis). University of Toronto, Canada. Retrieved from https://tspace.library.utoronto.ca/handle/1807/25467

Brouček, S., & Grulich, T. (Eds.). (2014). *Nová emigrace z České republiky po roce 1989 a návratová politika.* Praha: Etnologický ústav AV ČR. Retrieved from http://www.iom.cz/files/Nova_emigrace.pdf

Češi v Chorvatsku—Nejorganizovanější česká komunita?. (n.d.). Slovensko-český klub. Retrieved from http://www.czsk.net/svet/clanky/svet/chorvatsko.html

Česká škola bez hranic [Czech school without borders]. (2015). Česká škola bez hranic [web site]. Retrieved from http://csbh.cz

Chumak-Horbatsch, R. (1999). Language change in the Ukrainian home: From transmission to maintenance to the beginnings of loss. *Canadian Ethnic Studies, 31*(2), 61–75.

Ciborová, K. (2014, June 9). Češi mizí v cizině. Lákáme je těžko. *Denik.cz.* Retrieved from http://www.denik.cz/z_domova/cesi-mizi-v-cizine-lakame-je-tezko-20140608.html

Člověk v tísni. (2013). Rumunsko—Banát [Web page]. Retrieved from https://www.clovekvtisni.cz/cs/humanitarni-a-rozvojova-pomoc/zeme/rumunsko

ČTK. (2014, June 5). Po Listopadu odešlo za hranice 200 tisíc Čechů, spočítali experti. *iDnes.cz.* Retrieved from http://zpravy.idnes.cz/po-listopadu-odeslo-z-republiky-na-200-tisic-cechu-fur-/domaci.aspx?c=A140605_163121_domaci_cen

Czech Statistical Office. (2011). Změny struktury obyvatel podle náboženské víry v letech 1991, 2001 a 2011. Retrieved from https://www.czso.cz/csu/czso/nabozenska-vira-obyvatel-podle-vysledku-scitani-lidu-2011–61wegp46fl

Dům zahraniční spolupráce [Centre for international cooperation]. (2015a). Chorvatsko [Web page]. Retrieved from http://www.dzs.cz/cz/program-podpory-ceskeho-kulturniho-dedictvi-v-zahranici/chorvatsko/

Dům zahraniční spolupráce [Centre for international cooperation]. (2015b). Rumunsko [Web page]. Retrieved from http://www.dzs.cz/cz/program-podpory-ceskeho-kulturniho-dedictvi-v-zahranici/rumunsko/

Dům zahraniční spolupráce [Centre for international cooperation]. (2015c). Ukrajina [Web page]. (2015). Retrieved from http://www.dzs.cz/cz/program-podpory-ceskeho-kulturniho-dedictvi-v-zahranici/ukrajina/

Dutkova-Cope, L. (2006). Discontinued intergenerational transmission of Czech in Texas: Hindsight is better than foresight. *Southern Journal of Linguistics, 30*(2), 1–49.

Eckert, E., & Hannan, K. (2009). Vernacular writing and sociolinguistic change in the Texas Czech community. *Journal of Slavic Linguistics, 17*(1–2), 87–161.

Ekholm, M., & Trier, U. P. (1987). The concept of institutionalization: Some remarks. In M. B. Miles, M. Ekholm, & R. Vandenberghe (Eds.), *Lasting school improvement: Exploring the process of institutionalization* (pp. 13–21). Leuven, Belgium: Acco.

Ference, G. C. (1993). Slovak immigration to the United States in light of American, Czech, and Slovak history. *Nebraska History.* Retrieved from http://www.nebraskahistory.org/publish/publicat/history/full-text/Czech_04%20_Slovak_Immig.pdf

Fillmore, L. W. (1991). When learning a second language means losing the first. *Early Childhood Research Quarterly, 6*(3), 323–346.

Gibson, C., & Jung, K. (2006). Historical census statistics of the foreign-born population of the United States: 1850 to 2000 [Working Paper No. 81]. Washington, DC: U.S. Census Bureau. Retrieved from https://www.census.gov/population/www/documentation/twps0081/twps0081.html

Hrouda, S. J. (2011). Czech Language Programs and Czech as a Heritage Language in the United States. *Center for Applied Linguistics.* Retrieved from http://www.cal.org/heritage/pdfs/briefs/czech-language-programs-in-the-united-states.pdf

Kouritzin, S. G. (1999). *Face[t]s of first language loss.* Mahwah, NJ: Lawrence Erlbaum.

Kozminska, K. (2015). Language contact in the Polish-American community in Chicago. *International Journal of Bilingualism, 19*(3), 239–258.

McCabe, M. (2016). Czech and Slovak as heritage languages in the southeastern United States: The potential of parental transnationalism for language maintenance. *International Journal of the Sociology of Language, Thematic Issue: Multilingualism and Minorities in the Czech Sociolinguistic Space, 238*(2), 169–191.

McCabe, M. (in press). Parents struggling to maintain children's heritage language: Stories from 10 Czech and Slovak mothers in North Carolina. In X. L. Rong & J. Hilburn (Eds.). *Immigration and education in North Carolina: The challenges and responses in a New Gateway State.* Boston: Sense.

Ministry of Education, Youth, and Sports. (2013). Support for vompatriot communities abroad [Web page]. Retrieved from http://www.msmt.cz/eu-and-international-affairs/support-for-compatriot-communities-abroad

Ministry of Foreign Affairs of the Czech Republic. (2011). Czechs abroad [Web page]. Retrieved from http://www.mzv.cz/jnp/en/foreign_relations/czechs_living_abroad/

Nesteruk, O. (2010). Heritage language maintenance and loss among the children of Eastern European immigrants in the USA. *Journal of Multilingual & Multicultural Development, 31*(3), 271–286.

Otcu, G. B. (2009). *Language maintenance and cultural identity construction in a Turkish Saturday school in New York City* (Doctoral dissertation). Teachers College, Columbia University. Retrieved from ProQuest Dissertations and Theses database: Linguistics (UMI No. 3368361).

Patterson, M. (2014, June 3). Česky v USA zakládají školy. *Lidové Noviny.* Retrieved from https://www.scribd.com/fullscreen/228217393?access_key=key-JweoWq0Zjdt5g79846q9&allow_share

Petruscu, M. C. (2014). *Minority language acquisition & retention: A study of Canadian-born Romanian-speaking bilingual children* (Doctoral dissertation). University of Toronto, Canada. Retrieved from https://tspace.library.utoronto.ca/handle/1807/68416

Škodová, S. (2004). *Čeština pro malé cizince* 1 [*Czech for little foreigners 1*]. Prague, Czech Republic: Euromedia Group.

Škodová, S. (2005). *Čeština pro malé cizince* 2 [*Czech for little foreigners 2*]. Prague, Czech Republic: Euromedia Group.

Tamošiūnaitė, A. (2013). Lithuanian Saturday schools in Chicago: Student proficiency, generational shift, and community involvement. *Heritage Language Journal, 10*(1), 108–133.

U.S. Census Bureau. (2015). Language use. [Detailed Tables: Table 1. Detailed languages spoken at home and ability to speak English for the population 5 years and over for the United States: 2009–2013]. Retrieved from http://www.census.gov/data/tables/2013/demo/2009-2013-lang-tables.html

Ústav jazykové a odborné přípravy. (n.d.). Kurzy [Web page]. Retrieved from http://ujop.cuni.cz/kurzy/vzdelavani-pedagogu

Vaculík, J. (2009). *České menšiny v Evropě a ve světě* [*Czech minorities in Europe and in the world*]. Praha: Nakladatelství Libri.

Valdés, G. (2005). Bilingualism, heritage language learners, and SLA research: Opportunities lost or seized? *The Modern Language Journal, 89*, 410–426.

10

The Role of Informal Heritage Language Learning in Program Building

Persian Community School Language Learners in Australia

Mojgan Mokhatebi Ardakani and Robyn Moloney

1 Introduction

Significant migration into Australia, dating from the end of World War II and increasing in the last 20 years, has been a driving force in initiating Heritage Language (HL) research to investigate and promote understanding of issues in HL learning in the Australian context. Similar factors have also led to the development of the field in North America, which has seen a rapid proliferation of research, professional development projects, and meetings in the last two decades (Van Deusen-Scholl, 2014). Seeking to share resources and insights, in 2001, U.S. and Australian scholars gathered in Melbourne, Australia, to identify potential collaboration in developing, implementing, and evaluating Heritage/Community Language Education. Since then, the rapid development of the field has been characterized by an international outlook and a growing diversity of languages and issues (Hornberger, 2005).

However, even as the scope of the research continues to expand, the focus to this point has been primarily on the most commonly taught languages and has been largely dominated by research perspectives on adolescent, college-aged learners, and beyond (Kim, 2006; Kondo-Brown, 2003; Miremadi, 2014; Rohani, Christine, Amjad, Christal, & Christopher, 2014). Primary school HL learners, who are the focus of this chapter, have received less attention (Oriyama, 2011). Similarly, the institutionalization of HL teaching and learning, which is the focus of this volume, is also in need of further development, in particular, how to integrate current research findings with the design, implementation, and structure of HL programs.

This chapter is situated at the intersection of these two areas of priority. In particular, it probes the role of informal language learning experiences in HL acquisition and on the basis of the findings presented, calls for the incorporation of more of these types of experiences in community HL schools.

To the authors' knowledge, this is the first research study of Persian language learning in Australia. The first author's two case studies of Persian community language schools in Sydney,

Australia, inform this chapter's analysis. The first, a pilot study (Mokhatebi Ardakani & Moloney, 2010), identifies three general challenges that undercut the success of these schools. The second, a follow up study, was a doctoral dissertation (Mokhatebi Ardakani, 2015). This chapter critically examines one part of the data collected, to provide insight into how to address the challenges identified in the pilot study, through advocating the incorporation of informal learning experiences into the school context. Before delving into these issues, the next section examines the main theoretical frameworks behind the present analysis, namely, Sociocultural Theory and Institutionalization. Following that, we provide a brief overview of Persian as a world language and its status in Australia.

2 Literature Review

Sociocultural Theory and Language Learning

Originating in the work of Vygotsky and his colleagues, the principles and constructs of Socio-Cultural Theory (SCT) began to inform Second Language Acquisition (SLA) in the mid-1980s through the work of scholars such as Lantolf and colleagues (Lantolf, 2000; Lantolf & Thorne, 2007). SCT posits that language developmental processes are fundamentally socially mediated processes and that language learning is not solely about acquiring language systems, new sounds, and structures. Mediation occurs through language use in settings such as family life, peer groups, and schooling, and through interaction within these social environments (Lantolf & Thorne, 2007, p. 197). In the school environment, SCT emphasizes the social aspect of learning, calling for instruction that is premised on social interaction.

Within this framework, language learning emerges from the language resources that are made available to learners through socially mediated processes. According to Norton and Toohey (2011, pp. 418–419) "language learners must 'see' or be exposed to mature practice of language". With the focus being on the sociocultural contexts of language use, interaction is critical, both the language used by the learner as well as the language used by others to speak to the learner (Van Lier, 2000, p. 247). These "others" constitute a community of practice. Local analysis of the community is important as these vary regarding ease of access, opportunities for practice, and so on (Lave & Wenger, 1991). This chapter focuses on the home as a community of practice, using it as a departure point for understanding how to best structure HL community schools.

The concept of HL is an inherently sociocultural concept because it is both a means of communication by a group of people and a reflection of an affiliation with an ethnolinguistic group. Despite this, research on HL learning which explicitly focuses on sociocultural contexts of language use, is somewhat limited (He, 2008, p. 204). In particular, there is a need for research which uses qualitative methods and is sensitive and responsive to multiple sociocultural dimensions that frame input and interaction in the HL. A shift from focusing on the individual learner, to co-participants such as parents, siblings, peers, and community members can illuminate the process and inform instruction.

Institutionalization: Educational Program Improvement at the Initiation Phase

Educational program improvement begins by introducing new knowledge or new practices (Louis, 2006). Stakeholders' knowledge of the new practice and their collaboration and cooperation are then needed to obtain educational improvement outcomes. This improvement process, taking place in different sectors such as school and other community organizations, has different subprocesses, according to Ekholm and Trier (1987, p. 13).

The first subprocess, which is the main focus of this chapter, is called initiation. During this stage, an organization obtains the necessary knowledge about new practices and decides to adopt it (Eiseman, Fleming, & Roody, 1990). In the present case, the knowledge gained from the study of Persian community schools in Sydney underscores the importance of incorporating into the school context a wide range of informal learning experiences that build on certain home practices that are conducive to HL learning. Before discussing these practices, some background information on Persian, both as a world language and in the context of Australia is provided in the next section.

3 Background

Persian Language Status and the Iranian Community in Australia

Persian, also known as Farsi, is an Indo-Iranian language, a sub-branch of the Indo-European group of languages. It is spoken by some 150 million people worldwide (Australia National University, n.d.). It is primarily spoken in Iran, Afghanistan, and Tajikistan. It is also used in parts of Armenia, Azerbaijan, India, Iraq, Kazakhstan, Pakistan, Turkmenistan, Turkey, and Uzbekistan (Language Materials Project, n.d.).

Many Iranians have migrated to countries around the world, including Australia. Iranian migration to Australia started prior to the 1979 revolution and increased during the 1990s, when many Iranians emigrated under the Skilled and Family Streams of the Migration Program (Australian Government Department of Immigration and Citizenship, 2014). By comparison with other languages, the Persian language has a relatively modest presence both in Australia as well as in Sydney, where the four schools that constitute the focus of this study are located.

According to the 2011 census as reported in Community Profile (n.d.), Australia is home to approximately 34,453 Iran-born individuals, which represents an increase of 52.8% from the 2006 census. The state of New South Wales is home to the largest concentration, 15,463 Iranian Australians, particularly around Sydney, Canberra, Newcastle, and Wollongong. The age distribution of Iranian people in Australia showed that 6.9% were aged 0–14 years. Persian language was the main language spoken at home by 24,481 of Iran-born people in Australia. The Australian Persian Community has an active online presence featuring a wide range of services and products, as well as many prosocial organizations that promote Persian culture and arts, provide welfare and social services, and act as a liaison between the Australian government and local Iranian communities. There is however, limited information about Persian-language learning.

In Australia, the Persian language has been designated as a less commonly taught language by the Federation of Ethnic Communities' Councils of Australia (FECCA, 2011), a national organization that represents Australians from culturally and linguistically diverse backgrounds. FECCA is active in promoting issues of multiculturalism to the government, business and the broader community. Unfortunately, this status has not resulted in the promotion of the Persian language nor the creation of a unified curriculum. In 2009, only four Persian schools were registered by the Department of Education and Training (DET) in Sydney. These schools were the focus of the two studies that inform this chapter.

Persian community language schools in Sydney are examples of how a minority community engages and struggles to preserve their HL and its cultural values, in an English-dominant society. Education is highly prized amongst Iranians and children are pressured to succeed academically. Iranian culture is also adult oriented, which means that parents make major decisions for their children (Price, 2001). The words below, from one school's mission statement, capture the critical role played by the privileging of education and parental agency, in this institution's existence:

> We owe the existence of this cultural institution to the literacy intellectuals who persevered through the difficulties they faced at the time of inception and after much hard work they managed to establish a foundation in Australia that until today our children have had the opportunity to benefit from and enjoy.
>
> *(Ryde Persian School, n.d.)*

The Pilot Study

The first author of this chapter is a member of the Iranian community in Sydney, a mother of two children who were learning Persian, and was for a time a volunteer teacher in one of the focus schools in 2008. In that capacity, she was involved in Persian teaching and learning activities and she was familiar with the challenges learners, parents, and teachers were confronting. The findings of the pilot study reported here were the foundation for a doctoral research project that started in 2011. At the time of the pilot study, the number of Persian HL learners attending these four schools was greater compared to the time when the major study started, when the number of students had reduced by approximately one quarter. Overall, the pilot study identifies institutional factors that undercut HL learning, while the follow up study sheds light on potential solutions.

The pilot study was conducted by interviewing the four principals of the schools. Among its findings, this study (Mokhatebi Ardakani & Moloney, 2010) revealed that Persian community language schools, operating on Saturday mornings outside the mainstream school system, were organized and managed on an ad hoc basis by volunteer parents and members of the Persian community. Of the four schools, one was operating under the Ministry of Education and Training legislation in Iran, and the other three operated independently and had no connection to the Iranian government. The schools utilized resources prepared in Iran for native speakers of Persian, and some had also developed their own curricula, resulting in a lack of articulation between the schools' teaching programs.

A second finding related to the parents and the home environment. In the interviews, the principals expressed concern about the lack of parental involvement in activities at school and after school, such as mentoring their children's Persian-language learning at home. Moreover, they noted that a number of parents, especially fathers, spoke English at home, thereby limiting their children's exposure to the HL. In fact, practical opportunities to use the language at home and in the wider community were often neglected. At the same time, the principals recognized that parents were the driving force behind their children's participation at their school and efforts to learn the language. They also noted that students whose families took a serious approach to school study and provided home learning experiences that built on the activities of school were more successful language learners.

Finally, a third issue concerned the high rate of attrition and the phenomenon of students moving between the four Persian community language schools, which led to inconsistent language learning experiences and proficiency gained by the students.

The Follow-Up Study

The first author returned to the same schools to explore some common informal learning experiences in the home environment that students and their families engaged in. The data in this chapter are taken from that broader study, which also examined learners' identity and motivation. As will be discussed, three informal contexts play a prominent role in the development of HL proficiency in school-age children. In terms of institutionalization, we will argue that these contexts should inform how to structure curricula and activities in HL programs to maximize learning and address the three main findings of the pilot study.

4 Methodology

Research Design

A qualitative case study was chosen so that research participants could freely express their opinions (Hatch, 2002; Patton, 1990). Semi-structured interviews were employed as the best choice for the investigation (Ratner, 2002). Norton (2000, p. 5) focuses on both language learner and language learning context in order to investigate a learner's access to language resources. Therefore, the interview questions were designed to investigate the availability of Persian language resources at home. The research participants were asked about the available opportunities to (1) speak the language at home, (2) consume Persian-language media, in particular, movies at home, and (3) travel to Iran as an activity organized through the home. These questions were selected on the basis of the pilot study and the findings of a National Heritage Language Resource Centre survey (Carreira & Kagan, 2011, p. 43), which acknowledged the importance of input in the home environment and sought information on these elements.

Data Collection Procedure

The first group of research participants comprised 35 primary school Persian HL learners in the four Persian community language schools. These students were interviewed in focus groups. Other research participants comprised nine parents and seven teachers who were interviewed individually. The same interview questions were employed to explore similarities as well as differences among participants' views in semi-structured interviews. The interviews were conducted entirely in Persian upon participants' request and were recorded with a digital voice recorder and transcribed into English by an independent translator.

To ensure anonymity, students, parents, and teachers were identified with pseudonyms. Each of the schools was given a number and students were identified by using the school number, the focus group number, and the student number. For example, S1 FG2 St3 represented student number three from focus group number two and school number one. Similarly, parents and teachers were identified by the school number followed by the number given to them.

Data Analysis

Grounded theory (Charmaz, 2005) was chosen for data analysis in order to identify themes as they emerged from the research data. Data coding processes were conducted in accordance with the principles of a grounded theory approach. In order to do this, the transcriptions were coded line by line. The three basic types of coding, "open," "axial," and "selective" were employed for data analysis.

Through "open coding" (Strauss & Corbin, 1990) or "initial coding" (Saldaña, 2012, p. 100), the first author generated as many codes as was justified by the data. An iterative and inductive process was conducted during the data coding process, until new themes stop emerging and the project "levels off" (Richards, 2014). Then, the codes were compared against each other for similarities as well as differences. Codes which were conceptually similar were grouped together to form categories. Through axial coding, the core categories (and subcategories) essential to the research questions were identified. Using selective coding, all unified categories shaped a theme. After identifying different themes, the themes were integrated into a broader pattern or "theory" and a visual model of findings. While different participants' data were analyzed separately, triangulation of learners', parents', and teachers' data was employed (Dörnyei, 2007).

We acknowledge that subjective interpretations of data by the first author as the researcher (Glesne & Peshkin, 1992), can be influenced by personal bias (Russell & Kelly, 2002). Therefore, the researcher's role is recognized in interpretation of the data. In the following section, a summary of findings is provided.

5 Findings

During the process of data analysis, three broad themes were identified: Tendency to speak the HL, Opportunity to speak the HL, and Proficiency in the HL. The integration of the themes was developed into a TOP model, which is illustrated in Figure 10.1.

The TOP model shows the interrelationship between tendency, opportunity, and proficiency. Together, these three themes capture how the informal learning experiences of Persian HL learners play out in the areas mentioned earlier, namely, (1) speaking the language, (2) consuming Persian-language media, in particular, movies, and (3) traveling to Iran.

The TOP model acknowledges the work of Lo Bianco and Peyton and their development of the COD model (Lo Bianco & Peyton, 2013). According to COD theory, three conditions are necessary for language vitality and revitalization: capacity development, opportunity creation, and desire. "Capacity development" refers to the level of proficiency in the language; "Opportunity creation" refers to the development of domains in which use of the language is natural, welcome, and expected, and "Desire" is the creation of strong desire or investment in learning of the language.

The use of "tendency" in the TOP model instead of "desire" reflects our view that learners' willingness to learn the language may not be as strong as the term "desire" connotes. Within the

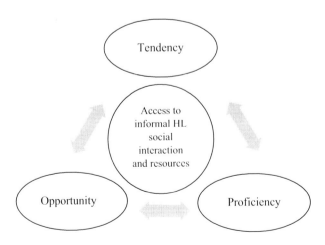

Figure 10.1 TOP Model of Access to Informal HL Social Interaction and Resources

TOP model, we define "tendency" as an attitude, habit, or situation that is starting to develop in a particular way. Tendency can be independent from desire, for example, it is possible to feel positive about speaking a language but not be in the habit of doing so. We will see an example of this in the data to be discussed. Another difference concerns the role of family and community members in the development of tendency. The TOP model, which emerged from the evidence from the study of young learners, demonstrates that community members, in particular parents, are integrally involved in the development of tendency. The COD model, on the other hand, emphasizes learners' motivation over the role of community members, such as teachers and adults, in influencing learners' desire.

Both the TOP and the COD models recognize the role of others such as family members in creating opportunity and proficiency. Like COD, the TOP model posits a relationship between the elements, whereby gains in the area of tendency, opportunity, or proficiency will likely yield gains in the other areas. Furthermore, it stands to reason that there is a spillover effect between contexts or domains, such that, for example, gains made in the home environment facilitate further gains in the school domain. These ideas are further elaborated in the sections that follow.

Access to Informal Heritage Language Resources at Home: Tendency, Opportunity, Proficiency

As noted earlier, Persian HL learners access informal language resources by means of three commonly mentioned activities, namely, speaking the language at home, watching Iranian movies, and visiting Iran. The data on these activities were triangulated and used to explore in greater depth how learning plays out within each of these contexts as viewed through the TOP model.

Speaking Persian Language at Home

In order to investigate home language practices, we asked research participants whether the Persian language was spoken at home. The analysis of data suggests an extremely diverse linguistic context within homes. In a number of cases, either Persian or English was spoken; in other cases, both languages were spoken equally; in yet other cases, one language was spoken more dominantly than the other. The research participants provided different reasons for this diversity.

Tendency

From the data, it appears that a number of mothers are very strict about speaking Persian and therefore force their children to communicate in this language at home. For instance, from the student perspective, S4 FG1 St4 stated: "*I speak English most of the time but my mom gets angry then I have to speak Persian too. So my mom wants me to speak Persian.*" Parent and teacher data also suggest this. For example, S1 P1 said: "*We actually prefer that they speak Persian with us.*" Thus, parental insistence on enforcing the use of the HL at home, increases the tendency to use and practice it.

Opportunity

In many homes the opportunities to use the HL are limited. For a number of students, English rather than Persian is spoken more frequently with and by their parents and siblings at home, which results in diminished opportunity to speak their HL. For example, S2 FG2 St3 said: "*We [the whole family] don't speak Persian at home but we like to speak it."* This is a case where the desire is present, but not the tendency. A teacher, S1 T1, also spoke to the widespread practice of speaking English at home: *"They (students) often speak in English. I think it is because they spend their whole week in an English-speaking environment at school. . . . Unfortunately they (parents) are Iranian but they speak English with their children at home, so it is hard for them to learn Persian."*

However, where there is opportunity, some students like to take advantage of it, as the teacher S2 P1 points out in reference to one of her students: *"She speaks Persian with adults who speak Persian."* Opportunities such as this increase learners' access to the language.

Proficiency

In a circular relationship, issues of proficiency, both that of the learner and their interlocutor, often play a role in determining the language of interaction. For example, S3 FG1 St3 said: *"My father knows English very well so I speak English with him. I speak Persian with my mom because her English is not good."* Another student, S1 FG3 St1, said: *"I came here, people don't know Persian so I should speak in English."* Apart from situations in which a Persian-dominant interlocutor is present, English is the preferred medium of interaction. Teacher S3 T1 describes the relationship between her students' proficiency and their choice of language as follows: *"They [the students] speak English because it is easier for them."* In keeping with this, student S2 FG1 St3 said: *"When I talk to my friends about a topic, for example, about football, it's easier to talk in English and I am more comfortable to talk in English."* The situation is not confined to students, as parent S1 P3 said: *"My husband mostly speaks English with my children at home because his English is better than Persian."* Issues of proficiency in both languages and with regard to both students and their interlocutors thus impact opportunity to engage in the HL. From this, it follows that HL proficiency is not just an end goal for HL-speaking children but also a catalyst in the tendency/opportunity/proficiency chain. That is, proficiency begets opportunities, which in turn beget tendency. This is true both within a given context (e.g., the home), as well as across contexts (e.g., the home and school).

Media Consumption and Preferences at Home

In order to investigate students' further access to language input and knowledge through informal transmission of language at home, the researcher asked participants about available opportunities to watch Iranian movies or listen to Iranian music. This opportunity, according to "Interaction" theory and Second Language Acquisition (Ellis, 1990; Long, 1981), is a form of interaction for further language development through fun and entertainment (Moloney & Oguro, 2015). The same themes of tendency, opportunity, and proficiency were identified through analyzing the data.

Tendency

The research participant data show that the learners regularly consume and enjoy Iranian media, particularly comic movies and TV series. For instance, S4 FG2 St2 stated: *"We watch Iranian movies especially the comedian ones, because they are very funny."* Similarly, in reference to his son, parent S1 P5 stated: *"He likes Iranian movies very much . . . and he himself watches them."* Furthermore, student and parental comments indicate a preference for Iranian movies over music, on the part of the students. Student S2 FG1 St2 asserted: *"We watch Iranian movies. My dad listens to Iranian music but I listen to English music more."* S1 P4 said: *"My kids love Iranian movies. . . . They don't actually like or listen to Iranian music."*

Opportunity

The data demonstrate that parents provide the opportunity for their children to watch movies. For example, they supply the devices such as satellite connections for watching Iranian movies. Moreover, parents are avid movie and television watchers themselves, which makes this a family activity that parents and children participate in together. For example, from the student perspective, S1 FG2 St3 said: *"When my parents watch Iranian series, I also join them."* S2 FG1 St1 said: *"Yes, we watch Iranian movies a lot because we have GLBOX and it has all Iranian series, so we watch them."* From the parent perspective, S1 P4 said: *"My kids love Iranian movies . . . we often watch family movies on DVDs during school holidays."* Teachers are also aware of this, S2 T1 said: *"They told me that they have GLBOX . . . they told me they watched it with their families."*

Although teachers are aware of students' desire to watch Iranian movies, they noted a number of restrictions that prevent them from including these language resources in their pedagogy. S2 T2 explained: *"Unfortunately here [at school] we don't have enough time and facilities."* S4 T2 also noted the lack of technical equipment: *"We only have our textbooks; we don't have other facilities in our school to watch movies."*

Proficiency

Research data illustrate that Iranian movies are used as a language resource and parents felt that watching movies helped their children's understanding and even speaking of the language. For instance, S4 P1 said: *"We used to watch more Iranian movies when we were in New Zealand. There was no Persian school there . . . he liked some series a lot as we watched them together and he became interested in them . . . watching movies has helped him a lot improve his understanding and speaking of Persian especially when he was very young."*

From the point of view of the TOP model, the data reveal that movie watching is valuable in three ways. First, it is enjoyable to students, which speaks to high tendency levels. Second, it is supported and facilitated by parents, which makes it an available opportunity. And third, it is valuable from the point of view of language learning, which means that it promotes proficiency. Nevertheless, this activity is not part of the school experience due to perceived practical limitations on the part of teachers. The discussion section considers different approaches to making movie watching part of the school experience.

Frequency of Family Visits to Iran

Visits to the HL country provide access to rich input and opportunities for interaction, thereby enhancing proficiency (Carreira & Kagan, 2011). In order to investigate learners' access to this opportunity, students and their parents were asked about the frequency of visiting Iran and teachers were asked if their students talked about their trips to Iran. The findings suggest that visiting Iran was a relatively frequent experience; more than half of the students (62.8%) visit every one to three years. However, because of the students' age, the frequency of visiting Iran was contingent on their parents' effort.

Tendency

Research data evidence a strong tendency on the part of parents to visit Iran with their children, and great enjoyment of this activity on the part of students. From a parent perspective, S4 P1 said: *"We attempt to go and we go as much as we can."* Similarly, parent S1 P5 said: *"I try to travel to Iran at least once every two years."* Finally, S1 P4 stated: *"My kids like to go to Iran very much."*

Opportunity

The data identify two primary linguistic benefits associated with visits to Iran. First, these visits provide rich and varied opportunities for the learners to speak Persian. In keeping with this perspective, parent S4 P1 asserted: *"When we get there he knows he should speak Persian and he easily shifts to Persian language."* Second, these visits are also associated with an increased tendency on the part of the students to learn and use the HL. Once again teachers evidence an awareness of this resource. For instance, S4 T2 said: *"Those who frequently go to Iran are more willing to learn the Persian language."*

Proficiency

A study by Shirazi and Borjian (2012) demonstrates that the relationship between language proficiency and frequency of visiting Iran is reciprocal. That is, visiting Iran was shown to have a positive impact on learners' language proficiency and, in turn, learners' language proficiency and ability to communicate with their relatives in Iran was a reason for their willingness to travel to Iran. The research data in this study corroborates this finding. For example, parent S1 P1 said: *"My daughter and son love to visit Iran because they can easily communicate with their cousins and enjoy playing with them."* Similarly, parent S1 P3 said: *"If she wants she can speak in Persian because we go to Iran several times each year. This has had a significant effect on her willingness to speak, and on her Persian speaking skills, and has caused her to have a better speaking performance."*

In short, significant numbers of students in the Persian schools visit Iran on a regular basis. These visits provide important opportunities for informal HL learning and quite likely lead to gains in tendency and proficiency. In the discussion that follows, we consider how this finding, as well as the others discussed in this section, bear on issues of teaching and learning in the focus schools, and more generally, how they bear on issues of institutionalization.

6 Discussion

If family connection is the sine qua non of HLL status, exposure to the HL, both through formal and informal learning experiences, is essential to the development of the HL. Formal learning, typically associated with the school context, leads to the development of literacy skills and the acquisition of the grammatical structures and vocabulary that are part of the formal and academic registers of language (Montrul, 2005). Informal learning experiences, typically associated with the home environment and other everyday contexts, are known to play a key role in the development of functional skills and practical cultural knowledge (Nunan & Richards, 2014). Also, as discussed earlier, informal learning experiences, such as watching movies and traveling abroad, generate positive attitudes towards the HL on the part of children, leading to increased tendency, opportunity, and proficiency.

The findings of the follow-up study indicate that Persian community language teachers are aware of the benefits of these informal learning experiences and, more generally, of the value of the language resources of the home. Yet, these experiences and resources are largely underutilized in the school context. This situation runs counter to the current understanding and best practices of the field of HL teaching, which is premised on the view that formal instruction should capitalize on the language resources of the family and the experiences of HL learners (Carreira & Kagan, 2011; Zentella, 2005)

For the schools in this study, capitalizing on experiences such as watching movies or traveling abroad can be surprisingly simple and does not involve overcoming the type of impediments mentioned by the teachers. For example, in the case of movies, it can involve having students survey their parents, teachers, and community members about their favorite movies and television series and posting their findings on the school site. As a follow-up activity, students can create a database of recommended movies for home watching and write a synopsis and review of the most popular ones. Other options include keeping a journal of movies watched at home (akin to a reading journal), having students perform a scene from a favorite movie, or playing a guessing game in the class involving popular movies. With regard to travel, students can design a virtual trip to Iran for their family focusing on places they have yet to visit. They can interview their parents and other adults for ideas and recommendations and by way of a final product they can create a detailed itinerary and description of the locations to be visited, which can be presented to their family. Alternatively, students can write up a description of a favorite place in Iran that they have visited with their family and share it with their classmates.

These activities make strategic use of the informal learning experiences of the home to teach literacy skills, promote authentic social interaction in the HL, and engage students in collaborative learning. Furthermore, because many involve family participation, these activities can also help address an issue that came up both in the pilot and the follow-up study, namely, the low levels of tendency and opportunity to use the HL in some of the children's homes. Of course, to fully address this issue schools must do more than employ activities such as these. They must also educate parents as to the importance of speaking the language at home and provide them with concrete strategies for increasing tendency and opportunity in the home context.

This general approach is in keeping with Epstein's (2010) six-step framework for increasing family involvement in the school context, in particular, the following two steps: (1) Learning at home, which is about "providing information and ideas to families about how to help students at home with homework and other curriculum-related activities," as well as giving students the "responsibility for discussing important things they are learning," and (2) Parenting, which is about helping families "establish home environments to support children as students," enabling families "to share information about culture, background, and children's talents and needs," and "understanding families' background, cultures, concerns, goals, needs, and views of their children" (pp. 15–16).

In addition to increasing family engagement, Epstein (2010) framework has been shown to be effective at reducing dropout rates (Epstein & Sheldon, 2002), which was a problem identified in the pilot study. We believe that anchoring instruction around topics and activities that are well-liked and familiar to students and that are supported by parents is likely to improve retention rates, since students and parents both will feel more vested in the activities of the school. This approach can also help address another problem identified in the pilot study, namely the lack of articulation between schools and the ad hoc structure of instruction (which resulted in inconsistent learning experiences when students moved between schools). The family-centered approach being proposed, which uses students' informal learning experiences at home as the foundation for formal learning in the school setting, provides a systematic and coherent way to approach instruction and curriculum design. For the schools in this study, such an approach involves tapping into three common and popular home activities, namely, speaking Persian language, watching movies and traveling to Iran, to build bridges to formal instruction, and to increase tendency and opportunity to use the HL in the home and school. Designing curricula along these lines would provide much needed articulation between schools, without imposing a singular teaching plan on all schools.

7 Conclusions

Our study of the informal learning experiences of students at the four focus schools underscores the importance of speaking the language, movie watching and visits to Iran as purveyors of rich linguistic input outside of the school context. We have argued that these learning experiences provide a rich foundation for formal learning in the school setting. They can also help address three main challenges identified in the pilot study, namely, (1) the ad hoc structure of the schools and curricula, (2) the underutilization of the home environment, particularly parents, as a source of HL input, and (3) students' inconsistent learning experiences and gains due to high attrition rates and switching schools.

More generally, this chapter has outlined a general approach to the design and development of HL community schools. As the initiation step in HL program improvement, which was a focus of this chapter, we have advocated for the inclusion of informal learning experiences in the school context and have put forward the TOP model as a framework for analyzing these experiences and conceptualizing the design of instructional practices and curricula that build on them. We hope that practitioners involved in HL program building will further investigate ways to encourage and integrate informal language learning experiences into formal classroom learning.

References

Australia National University. (n.d.). Persian program [Web page]. Retrieved from http://cais.anu.edu.au/programs/persian-program

Australian Government Department of Immigration and Citizenship. (2014, February). Community information summary: Iran born [Web page]. Retrieved from https://www.dss.gov.au/sites/default/files/documents/02_2014/iran.pdf

Carreira, M., & Kagan, O. (2011). The results of the National Heritage Language Survey: Implications for teaching, curriculum design, and professional development. *Foreign Language Annals, 44*(1), 40–64.

Charmaz, K. (2005). Grounded theory in the 21st century: Applications for advancing social justice studies. In N. K. Denzin & Y. S. Lincoln (Eds.), *The Sage handbook of qualitative research* (3rd ed., pp. 507–536). Thousand Oaks, CA: Sage.

Community Profile. (n.d.). Birthplace [Web site]. Retrieved from http://profile.id.com.au/australia/birthplace?WebID=250

Dörnyei, Z. (2007). *Research methods in applied linguistics: Quantitative, qualitative, and mixed methodologies.* Oxford, UK: Oxford University Press.

Eiseman, J., Fleming, D., & Roody, D. (1990). *Making sure it sticks: The school improvement leaders' role in institutionalizing change.* Andover, MA: The Regional Laboratory.

Ekholm, M., & Trier, U. P. (1987). The concept of institutionalization: Some remarks. In M. B. Miles, M. Ekholm, & R. Vandenberghe (Eds.), *Lasting school improvement: Exploring the process of institutionalization* (pp. 13–21). Leuven, Belgium: Acco.

Ellis, R. (1990). *Instructed second language acquisition: Learning in the classroom.* Oxford, UK: Basil Blackwell.

Epstein, J. L. (2010). School/family/community partnerships: Caring for the children we share. *Phi Delta Kappan, 92*(3), 81–96.

Epstein, J. L., & Sheldon, S. B. (2002). Present and accounted for: Improving student attendance through family and community involvement. *The Journal of Educational Research, 95*(5), 308–318.

FECCA. (2011, April). Enhancing and celebrating Australia's cultural diversity through language learning [Submission paper]. Retrieved from http://www.scoa.org.au/resources/FECCA%20-%20Enhancing%20and%20Celebrating%20Australia%E2%80%99s%20Cultural%20Diversity%20through%20Language%20Learning.pdf

Glesne, C., & Peshkin, A. (1992). *Becoming qualitative researchers: An introduction.* White Plains, NY: Longman.

Hatch, J. A. (2002). *Doing qualitative research in education settings.* Albany, NY: State University of New York Press.

He, A. W. (2008). Heritage language learning and socialization. In P. Duff & N. H. Hornberger (Eds.), *Encyclopedia of language and education* (2nd ed., pp. 201–213). New York, NY: Springer.

Hornberger, N. H. (2005). Heritage/community language education: US and Australian perspectives. *International Journal of Bilingual Education and Bilingualism, 8*(2–3), 101–108.

Kim, E. J. (2006). Heritage language maintenance by Korean-American college students. In K. Kondo-Brown (Ed.), *Heritage language development: Focus on East Asian immigrants* (pp. 175–208). Philadelphia, PA: Philadelphia John Benjamins Publishing Company.

Kondo-Brown, K. (2003). Heritage language instruction for post-secondary students from immigrant backgrounds. *Heritage Language Journal, 1*(1), 1–25.

Language Materials Project. (n.d.). Persian [Web page]. Retrieved from http://www.lmp.ucla.edu/Profile.aspx?LangID=63&menu=004

Lantolf, J. P. (2000). *Sociocultural theory and second language learning.* Oxford, UK: Oxford University Press.

Lantolf, J. P., & Thorne, S. L. (2007). Sociocultural theory and second language acquisition. In B. Van Patten & J. Williams (Eds.), *Theories in second language acquisition: An introduction* (pp. 201–224). Mahwah, NJ: Lawrence Erlbaum.

Lave, J., & Wenger, E. (1991). *Situated learning: Legitimate peripheral participation.* Cambridge, UK: Cambridge University Press.

Lo Bianco, J., & Peyton, J. K. (2013). Vitality of heritage languages in the United States: The role of capacity, opportunity, and desire. *Heritage Language Journal, 10*(3), i–viii.

Long, M. H. (1981). Input, interaction, and second-language acquisition. *Annals of the New York Academy of Sciences, 379*(1), 259–278.

Louis, K. S. (2006). *Organizing for school change.* London, UK: Routledge.

Miremadi, A. (2014). Why do Iranian heritage and no-heritage students show interest in learning Persian language. *Journal of ELT and Applied Linguistics (JELTAL), 2*(1), 1–48.

Mokhatebi Ardakani, M. (2015). *A case study of primary school Persian heritage language learners in Australia* (Doctoral dissertation). Macquarie University, Sydney, Australia.

Mokhatebi Ardakani, M., & Moloney, R. (2010). *Evaluating and developing curriculum design for Persian heritage learners in Persian community schools in Sydney, Australia.* Paper presented at The First International Conference on Heritage/Community Languages, UCLA, CA.

Moloney, R., & Oguro, S. (2015). "To know what it's like to be Japanese": A case study of the experiences of heritage learners of Japanese in Australia. In I. Nakane, E. Otsuji, & W. S. Armour (Eds.), *Languages and identities in a transitional Japan: From internationalization to globalization* (pp. 121–140). Melbourne, Australia: Routledge.

Montrul, S. (2005). Second language acquisition and first language loss in adult early bilinguals: Exploring some differences and similarities. *Second Language Research, 21*(3), 199–249.

Norton, B. (2000). *Identity and language learning: Gender, ethnicity and educational change.* London, UK: Longman.

Norton, B., & Toohey, K. (2011). Identity, language learning, and social change. *Language Teaching, 44*(4), 412–446.

Nunan, D., & Richards, J. (2014). *Language learning beyond the classroom.* New York, NY: Routledge.

Oriyama, K. (2011). The effects of the sociocultural context on heritage language literacy: Japanese–English bilingual children in Sydney. *International Journal of Bilingual Education and Bilingualism, 14*(6), 653–681.

Patton, M. Q. (1990). *Qualitative evaluation and research methods.* Newbury Park, CA: Sage.

Price, M. (2001). Codes of behaviour, Iranian experience. Retrieved from http://www.iranchamber.com/culture/articles/codes_behavior.php

Ratner, C. (2002). Subjectivity and objectivity in qualitative methodology. *Forum Qualitative Sozialforschung/Forum: Qualitative Social Research, 3*(3), Art. 16. Retrieved from http://www.qualitative-research.net/index.php/fqs/article/view/829/1800

Richards, L. (2014). *Handling qualitative data: A practical guide.* Thousand Oaks, CA: Sage.

Rohani, S., Christine, C., Amjad, R. N., Christal, B., & Christopher, C. (2014). Languages maintenance and the role of the family amongst immigrant groups in the United States: Persian speaking Bahais, Cantonese, Urdu, Spanish and Japanese: An exploratory study. *Articles and Papers: Student Papers.* Retrieved from http://tc-cmll.org/publications/articles-and-papers/

Russell, G. M., & Kelly, N. H. (2002). Research as interacting dialogic processes: Implications for reflexivity. *Forum Qualitative Sozialforschung/Forum: Qualitative Social Research, 3*(3), Art. 18. Retrieved from http://www.qualitative-research.net/index.php/fqs/article/view/831/1806

Ryde Persian School. (n.d.). History [Web page]. Retrieved from http://rydepersianschool.org.au/en/history/

Saldaña, J. (2012). *The coding manual for qualitative researchers*. Newbury Park, CA: Sage.

Shirazi, R., & Borjian, M. (2012). Persian bilingual and community education among Iranian-Americans in New York City. In O. García, Z. Zakharia, & B. Otcu (Eds.), *Bilingual community education and multilingualism: Beyond heritage languages in a global city* (Vol. 89, pp. 154–168). Briston, UK: Multilingual Matters.

Strauss, A. L., & Corbin, J. M. (1990). *Basics of qualitative research* (Vol. 15). Newbury Park, CA: Sage.

Van Deusen-Scholl, N. (2014). Research on heritage language issues. In T. G. Wiley, J. K. Peyton, D. Christian, S. C. K. Moore, & N. Liu (Eds.), *Handbook of heritage, community, and Native American languages in the United States: Research, policy, and educational practice* (pp. 76–84). New York, NY: Routledge.

Van Lier, L. (2000). From input to affordance: Social-interactive learning from an ecological perspective. In B. VanPatten & J. Williams (Eds.), *Theories in second language acquisition: An introduction* (pp. 245–259). New York, NY: Routledge.

Zentella, A. C. (Ed.). (2005). *Building on strength: Language and literacy in Latino families and communities*. New York, NY: Teachers College Press.

Part III
Community Initiatives
All-Day Pre-, Primary, and Secondary Schools

11

Opportunities and Challenges of Institutionalizing a Pluricentric Diasporic Language

The Case of Armenian in Los Angeles

Shushan Karapetian

1 Introduction

According to the 2010–2014 American Community Survey 5-Year Estimates, Armenian is the 21st most commonly spoken non-English language in the U.S., the 6th in California, the 5th in Los Angeles County, and the 1st in the city of Glendale (U.S. Census Bureau, 2015). The U.S., particularly Southern California, hosts one of the largest Armenian populations outside of the Republic of Armenia. Although this is a very robust linguistic community, it has been heavily sustained by continuing immigration from Armenia and other diaspora communities. Scholars, community activists, and school administrators have observed rapid language shift, the demotion of the Armenian language both inside and outside of Armenian day schools, and a strong degree of linguistic compartmentalization, particularly among second- and third-generation Armenian-Americans (Chahinian & Bakalian, 2016; Karapetian, 2014; Kouloujian, 2012; Peroomian, 2006). These observations, coupled with concerns over declining enrollment and unsuccessful methods of instruction in Armenian day schools, have led to the creation of three Task Forces in the last few years with varying degrees of outreach, working to reform language instruction as well as promote Armenian language use in the Los Angeles community (Chahinian & Bakalian, 2016; Karapetian, 2014).

As an active member of all three Task Forces and a researcher who specializes in Armenian as a heritage language (HL) in Los Angeles, I will take stock of the HL programs and practices related to language maintenance in this community, with a particular focus on its unique situation as a pluricentric minority language in a diasporic context. I will first present the overall landscape of Armenian by providing an introduction to the development of the two modern standards of Armenian, a brief history of Armenian immigration to the U.S., and the presence of Armenian in educational contexts. Finally, I will discuss the opportunities and challenges to institutionalizing new language practices and attitudes through the lens of the three Task Forces. I will be using the framework proposed by Ekholm and Trier (1987), which defines institutionalization as "a process through which an organization assimilates an innovation into its structure" (p. 13). Since the three Task Forces have different targets (one Armenian day school, all Prelacy Armenian day schools, the Los Angeles community at large) and are at various stages on the initiation, implementation, and institutionalization spectrum (Ekholm & Trier, 1987), the scope of the desired innovations is also different, ranging from improving classroom practices in one school to changing the organizational culture of a conglomeration of Armenian institutions (both academic and non-academic) across the community.

2 Development of Modern Armenian(s)

The Armenian language comprises its own unique branch in the Indo-European language tree, with the creation of its alphabet dating to the early fifth century. During fifteen centuries of written history, the spoken language evolved much faster than the literary standard, going through several main periods of development. By the mid-nineteenth century, the standardization of Modern Armenian, comprised of Eastern and Western Armenian, was accomplished. The pluricentric development of the language was triggered by historical and political factors in the history of the Armenian people as well as divergent linguistic developments (Cowe, 1992; Dum-Tragut, 2009). As a result of Armenia's unique geographic location on the highland between the Mediterranean, Black, and Caspian Seas, the Armenian plateau became the buffer and coveted prize of rival empires (Hovhannisian, 2004). On the major thoroughfare between East and West, the country was frequently partitioned between the great powers on either side (Cowe, 1992; Hovhannisian, 2004). The dynastic era of Armenian history, which spanned some two thousand years (with interruptions), came to an end with the fall of the last independent Armenian kingdom in the late fourteenth century. Thereafter, historic Armenia was eventually partitioned between the Ottomans and the Persians and later between the Ottomans and the Russians (Bournoutian, 2006). Some Armenians, mostly peasants and minor craftsmen, remained in historic Armenia, while many others lived outside of the homeland in diasporic communities, which formed, increased, or diminished as a result of invasions, massacres, revolutions, colonialism, and nationalism (Bournoutian, 2006).

The modernization of the Armenian language was the outcome of the rise of national consciousness as a result of the cultural and political enlightenment of the Armenian people from approximately 1700 to 1850 (Oshagan, 2004). Urban centers across diasporic communities served as bases for educated and liberal-minded intellectuals, who recognized the urgency of educating and informing the population, for which they needed an effective means of communication. This would require bridging the gap between the variety of spoken vernaculars and the written standard. By the second half of the nineteenth century, two modern standards were established across empires: the Armenian community in Constantinople, capital of the Ottoman Empire, became the vessel for the standardization of Western Armenian, while Eastern Armenian formed as the standard for Armenians living in the Russian Empire, as well as those living within the Persian Empire. Apart from some phonetic, morphological, and grammatical differences, the largely common vocabulary and similar rules of grammatical fundamentals allow users of one variant to understand the other somewhat easily with some exposure.[1]

The catastrophic historical events of the early twentieth century heavily impacted the developments of the modern standards. The 1915 genocide resulted in the annihilation of the Armenian intelligentsia in Constantinople and the mass deportations and slaughter of Ottoman Armenians. Western Armenian was exiled from its homeland and "forced to reinvent itself in cosmopolitan centers in Europe and the Middle East along the refugee trail" (Chahinian & Bakalian, 2016, pp. 39–40). The most notable community in this regard was Beirut, Lebanon, which functioned as the major center of the Western diaspora for the first three quarters of the twentieth century, providing institutionalized resources for the transmission and cultivation of Western Armenian.

On the eastern front, after the turmoil of the Russian revolution (1917) and a brief trial with independence (1918–1920), a small landlocked area, comprising about 10% of historic Armenia, became part of the Soviet Union (1921–1991). The collapse of the Soviet Union in 1991 ushered in the period of the current independent Republic of Armenia. In terms of language, Eastern Armenian secured its position as the national language of Soviet Armenia and the following independent Republic, although it went through an orthographic reform, leading to a gap between the official orthography of the Republic, commonly referred to as Reformed Orthography, and the Armenian literary languages outside Armenia, which employ Classical or Mesrobian Orthography (Dum-Tragut, 2009).

As it stands now, Eastern Armenian is the official language of the Republic of Armenia as well as the unrecognized Republic of Mountainous Karabagh. It is also traditionally the language of Armenians living in the former Soviet Union, Iran, and India. Until the first half of the twentieth century, Western Armenian was the language of the greater Armenian Diaspora throughout the Middle East, Asia Minor, Europe, Australia, and the Americas. As will be discussed in the following section, during the last few decades there has been a major exodus both from the Republic of Armenia and traditionally stable diaspora communities from the Middle East to the West, particularly to Southern California. The expansion and diversification of a novel (for those from Armenia) and second or third (for those from the Middle East) diaspora community in an entirely different political and sociolinguistic environment has created a completely new dynamic. In 2010, Western Armenian was officially designated in UNESCO's Atlas of the World's Languages in Danger as "definitely endangered" (UNESCO, n.d.) raising alarm throughout the worldwide diaspora. In this circumstance, "Armenian American communities provide a unique vantage point to examine the existential question of Western Armenian, because therein the state-less language shapes itself in direct interaction with its Eastern counterpart" (Chahinian & Bakalian, 2016, p. 38), creating the opportunities and challenges for a pluricentric language in a diasporic context.

3 Armenian Immigration to the United States

Armenian immigration to the U.S. can generally be categorized into three waves. The first major group of Armenian immigrants arrived to the U.S. at the turn of the twentieth century, escaping persecution and oppression in the Ottoman Empire, particularly the Hamidian Massacres of 1894–1896 and the Armenian Genocide of 1915–1923 (Mirak, 2004). A second wave of immigration began after World War II in 1948 with the arrival of a few thousand Armenians admitted under the Displaced Persons Act. After the immigration reforms of the 1960s that ended the discriminatory quota system in the U.S., larger numbers of Armenians began to arrive. Due to the political devastation caused by civil upheaval and war, the once prosperous and stable Armenian communities in Egypt, Turkey, Lebanon, and Iran were shaken, leading many Armenians to resettle in the U.S. (Mirak, 2004). Up until the 1960s, the largest Armenian American communities settled on the East Coast. The exception was a significant group who settled in the Central Valley of California in Fresno, where they engaged in agricultural work such as farming and grape growing. After 1975 and up to the late 1980s, smaller groups of Armenians annually left Soviet Armenia for the U.S., many of whom had originally repatriated to Armenia after World War II from Europe, the Middle East, and the U.S., but had found it impossible to adjust to the socialist regime (Mirak, 2004; Yeghiazaryan, Avanesian, & Shahnazaryan, 2003). Soon other Soviet Armenians followed, benefiting from American refugee legislation and Soviet easing of immigration restrictions (Mirak, 2004). Unlike former immigrants, those arriving after the 1970s mostly preferred to settle on the West Coast, particularly Southern California.

The third and continuing wave of immigration spans the last few decades during which difficult living conditions in Armenia and diasporic hostland countries have continued to bring thousands more immigrants to the U.S. The devastating 1989 Spitak earthquake, followed by the Nagorno-Karabagh conflict that erupted into a war between Karabagh and Azerbaijan, and the severe economic crisis after the collapse of the Soviet Union intensified emigration from Armenia (Yeghiazaryan et al., 2003). Over the past three decades, the majority of new Armenian immigrants to the U.S. have preferred the West Coast, particularly Los Angeles County.

Although there is a large concentration of Armenians in the Los Angeles area, it is misleading to assume that this is a homogeneous community. As the immigration patterns reveal, there is great diversity in terms of country of origin, wave of immigration, socioeconomic status, and linguistic standard or dialect. In her analysis of Armenians in the 1980, 1990, and 2000 U.S. Census, Claudia Der-Martirosian (2008) indicates that Armenians from the Middle East were the single largest sub-ethnicity among foreign-born Armenians before 1980. However, after that date, there has been a drastic shift to increasing immigration from Armenia. Armenians from the Republic, who are primarily from the third immigration wave, though often highly educated, tend to be refugee, working-class immigrants struggling to create a new life for themselves. In contrast, Armenians from Iran and Lebanon are largely comprised of second-wave immigrants, many of whom achieved material wealth in their countries of origin and are therefore more economically secure in the U.S. Furthermore, they have a two-decade lead and financial advantage over the newer immigrants from Armenia (Karapetian Giorgi, 2012). Most importantly, the second wave immigrants from the Middle East, with the exception of Iranian-Armenians, are Western Armenian speakers, whereas Armenians from the Republic of Armenia are Eastern Armenian speakers. Iranian-Armenians speak various dialects of Eastern Armenian and employ Classical Orthography. All of these sub-ethnic groups with their varieties of Armenian are in contact with one another and with English, creating a unique linguistic environment.

4 Armenian(s) in Educational Contexts

The establishment of Armenian schools and programs or lack thereof reflects the various immigration patterns, the economic and sociolinguistic background of the immigrants, as well as the sociolinguistic environment they arrived to in the U.S. The pioneering wave of immigrants, particularly those who arrived before the ethnic revival movement (mid-1960s—mid-1970s), encountered a larger American society that did not explicitly discourage bilingualism, but imposed cultural policies that did not support HL maintenance (Bakalian, 1993). Thus, the first wave of immigrants felt strong pressure to assimilate and did not have the economic means, support, or motivation to establish Armenian programs. Once the second wave arrived from the Middle East, they clashed with the already Americanized Armenians over language, shocked at the deprioritization of language in the composition of Armenian-American identity (Bakalian, 1993). The Armenian communities in the Middle East had encountered much more favorable conditions for HL maintenance in their particular historical contexts and extralinguistic environments. Factors such as the utility and acceptance of multilingualism, the prestige of and loyalty toward Armenian, the insular and close-knit milieus that Armenians occupied, complete with their churches, schools, community clubs, and marketplaces (Jebejian, 2010) created a favorable environment for the maintenance and fully functional use of Armenian. Thus the second wave immigrants who had attended Armenian schools in Lebanon, Syria, and other countries wanted to replicate the tradition for their U.S.-born children (Chahinian & Bakalian, 2016). Holy Martyrs' Ferrahian, the first Armenian all-day school in the U.S., was established in Encino in 1964, paving the way for many more.

Table 11.1 List of Armenian Prelacy Day Schools in California: Name, City, Year Established, and Grade Level

Prelacy Schools	City	Year Established	Grade Level
Ari Guiragos Minassian Armenian School	Santa Ana	1986	PreK–6
Armenian Mesrobian School	Pico Rivera	1965	PreK–12
Holy Martyrs Ferrahian High School	Encino	1964	6–12
Holy Martyrs Mari Cabayan Elementary School	Encino	1991	PreK–5
Krouzian Zekarian Vasbouragan Armenian School	San Francisco	1980	PreK–8
Levon & Hasmig Tavlian Armenian Preschool	Pasadena	1991	Pre-K–K
Richard Tufenkian Armenian Preschool	Glendale	1975	Pre-K–K
Rose & Alex Pilibos Armenian School	Los Angeles	1969	K–12
Vahan & Anouch Chamlian Armenian School	Glendale	1975	1–8

At present there are 24 Armenian schools in the U.S., the majority of which are in the Greater Los Angeles area (see Table 11.1). More than half of these schools are grouped under the auspices of the Western Prelacy of the Armenian Apostolic Church of America, governed by a Board of Regents, which is appointed by the Prelate and Executive Council. The remaining schools are typically independent (of one another and the Prelacy), many with their own religious or political affiliation, although they do come together on certain occasions, such as an annual staff development day hosted by the Board of Regents of the Prelacy Schools. Reflecting the immigration trends presented above, the student body at Armenian day schools is very diverse with regard to family background and linguistic form and dialect; however, traditionally the language of instruction for subjects that are taught in Armenian is Western Armenian. A few schools such as Chamlian and Pilibos offer an Eastern Armenian track as well to accommodate the new demographics of the community.

Armenian day schools function like regular private schools that in addition to a basic curriculum of general studies, teach Armenian language, history, literature, religion, and culture. It is crucial to highlight that these are not bilingual immersion programs, as students are taught all core subjects in English except for the Armenian subject classes. There is no content instruction in Armenian outside of these classes and the hours of Armenian instruction are quite limited. Tables 11.1 and 11.2 below provide a complete list of Prelacy and non–Prelacy Armenian day schools in California, along with their location, year of establishment, and grade levels.

The growing presence of the Armenian community over the last few decades (particularly Eastern Armenian speakers) in Los Angeles County is fittingly represented in the increasing number of Armenian language programs in the public education sector. In the last decade, Glendale Unified School District (GUSD), particularly at the elementary level, has stood out as a model district for bilingualism and biliteracy. In 2006, in response to strong community interest, the Armenian program at GUSD initially started as the Heritage Language Program at Jefferson Elementary in Glendale. The goal of this program was to maintain students' heritage language, culture, and traditions with daily instruction during which Armenian language was taught as enrichment, with literacy as a primary focus. In 2009, Jefferson Elementary School started the

Table 11.2 List of Non-Prelacy Armenian Day Schools in California: Name, City, Year Established, and Grade Level

Non-Prelacy Schools	City	Year Established	Grade Level
AGBU Manoogian-Demirgian School	Canoga Park	1976	PreK–12
AGBU Vatche and Tamar Manoukian School	Pasadena	2006	9–12
Armenian Sisters Academy	Montrose	1985	PreK–8
Charlie Keyan Armenian Community School of Fresno	Fresno	1977	PreK–6
Mekhitarist Fathers Armenian School	La Crescenta	1979	K–8
Merdinian Armenian Evangelical School	Sherman Oaks	1982	PreK–8
Sahag-Mesrob Armenian Christian School	Altadena	1980	PreK–8
St. Gregory Alfred & Marguerite Hovsepian School	Pasadena	1984	PreK–8

50/50 Armenian dual immersion program, also known as the FLAG Armenian Program, and in the fall of 2010, it expanded to include R.D. White Elementary School. The main objective of this program is to develop bilingualism and biliteracy with academic language in two languages; therefore, Armenian language is taught both for language acquisition and content instruction. Dual Immersion classes are taught by fully credentialed bilingual teachers who have additional preparation and expertise in teaching Armenian. Eastern Armenian (Reformed orthography) is the primary standard of instruction.

An additional development in terms of Armenian language instruction in Los Angeles County was the opening of Ararat Charter School in 2010, which currently enrolls 351 students in grades K–5 on two campuses in the city of Van Nuys. Though not an immersion model as defined above in the case of GUSD's FLAG programs, Ararat Charter School is the first school to incorporate two languages other than English into their core curriculum: Armenian (Eastern standard) and Spanish.

In terms of Armenian language programs or options beyond elementary school, Toll Middle School in Glendale offers an (Eastern) Armenian heritage course for more advanced learners, which only started in 2014 (A. Asatryan, personal communication, May 1, 2014). Over the last decade, both Glendale High School and Hoover High School in GUSD have also offered (Eastern) Armenian as a foreign language option, including four different levels with increasing difficulty (Armenian 1–2, 3–4, 5–6, 7–8). Classes are typically entirely comprised of 1.5 or second generation heritage learners, with a few non–native speakers as well (A. Asatryan, personal communication, May 1, 2014).

In addition to the host of K–12 Armenian language programs presented above, the Greater Los Angeles area truly stands out as the heart of Armenian Studies in higher education. At the community college level, Glendale Community College emerges as the leader, with over a dozen Armenian Studies courses offered, including multiple levels of Armenian language (Eastern Armenian) with both foreign and heritage language tracks. Nearby Pasadena Community College offers two semesters of Elementary (Western) Armenian. At the university level, California State University, Northridge (CSUN) boasts the largest population of Armenian college students outside of Yerevan State University, with 10% of its student body comprised of Armenians students. The program offers 14 different courses in a range of subjects—from Armenian language (Western) to culture and contemporary issues—as well as a minor in Armenian studies and a concentration for students majoring in liberal studies (Chandler, 2006). The University of California, Los Angeles, possesses the longest and richest history in Armenian Studies, with two endowed chairs in Armenian Language and Literature and Modern Armenian History. Since 1997, regular instruction in both Eastern and Western Armenian has been offered with a popular undergraduate minor in Armenian Studies introduced the following year. At the graduate level, students can pursue MA and PhD degrees in Armenian Studies. Moreover, since 2010 the Center for World Languages at UCLA has offered a summer (Eastern) Armenian language course for high-school-age heritage speakers as part of its Summer High School Heritage Language Program.

Outside of Armenian day schools and language programs in the public sector, there are a variety of supplemental programs such as Saturday/Sunday schools and extracurricular activities in both standards. The weekend programs are typically sponsored by the churches and the Armenian political parties, where children of Armenian descent learn the rudiments of the Armenian alphabet, history, and culture. There are secondary organizations such as summer camps, Boy and Girl Scout groups, dance troupes, and athletic organizations, "that are likely to maintain Armenian networks, but do not necessarily reinforce the language, especially among the U.S.-born" (Chahinian & Bakalian, 2016, p. 46).

5 Task Forces

Although the picture above presents a vibrant linguistic community with ample institutions and programs for HL maintenance, all of the opportunities to study Armenian in an educational context serve only 5–10% of the student population of the Armenian community in LA (Kouloujian, 2014). Moreover, the classification of Western Armenian as an endangered language in 2010, declining enrollment in Armenian day schools, and the unsatisfactory results of several proficiency assessments in Prelacy schools have rung alarm bells throughout the community. All of these factors contributed to the formation of three Task Forces with increasing degrees of outreach, actively working on enhancing Armenian language instruction in Armenian Prelacy and private day schools as well as revitalizing and promoting oral and written Armenian in the Los Angeles community at large.

The first of these, entitled the Saroyan Project (hereafter referred to as Task Force #1), was launched in July of 2011 by the administration of Chamlian Armenian School, following the concerns raised by Chamlian alumni, parents, teachers, and administrators, who were invited to participate in a one-day symposium in order to examine the condition of Armenian language instruction. The committee is comprised of the directors of the Eastern and Western Armenian tracks at the school and three UCLA researchers, including two who were Armenian day school alumni with experience teaching in Armenian schools and serving on similar committees, and myself, a specialist on Armenian as an HL in the Los Angeles community. After an initial phase of assessment, the committee decided that the school needed to adopt an HL model for instruction. This involved developing new and more fitting Armenian language standards as the existing ones were merely a translation of the English Language Arts standards and naturally not functional for this group of heritage learners. Moreover, the committee implemented a series of workshops designed to train the teachers in the fundamentals of HL instruction, objective-based teaching, lesson planning, and classroom management. Furthermore, in tandem with the teachers, the committee launched a new series of content-based and objective-driven unit plans for the first grade. These comprise the curriculum as currently implemented in the school, with an observation-based checks and balances system of providing consistent aid and feedback to teachers. The long-term goals of the project are to continue the instructional reforms for all of the additional grades (up to eighth grade). Thus, the level of innovation for this particular Task Force is limited to classroom practices in one Armenian day school.

The second Task Force (hereafter Task Force #2) was initiated in January of 2013 by the Executive Director of the Board of Regents of Prelacy Armenian Schools in order to enhance and promote Armenian education within Prelacy schools in Los Angeles. Committee members include Armenian language professors at UCLA and CSUN, Armenian Studies scholars, and current and former principals of Armenian schools. A process of data collection and assessment of the current situation of Armenian instruction began with a focus group meeting with 40 to 50 Armenian subject teachers from all of the Prelacy schools on February 9, 2013. The concerns highlighted at the teachers' meeting along with the evaluation of factors such as declining enrollment trends from the last decade, the assessments of former task forces and committees, and the input of the current Task Force members from their own varying areas of expertise led to the decision to create a progress report or plan of action. On February 4, 2014, the Task Force presented its diagnosis, work plan, vision, mission, core values, and short- and long-term strategies and action plans to the Board of Regents. After a two-year hiatus due to internal structural changes within the Board of Regents, the newly appointed board leaders expressed their acknowledgment and approval of the plan of action, and as of March 2, 2016, committed to begin implementing the recommended changes.

In terms of level of innovation, the scope here deals with changing classroom practices as well as the organizational culture in all Prelacy Armenian schools in Los Angeles. The latter entails updating the vision and mission of the schools in order to prioritize the role of the Armenian language and ensure that practices and attitudes both in and out of the Armenian subject classrooms reflect these. For example, the suggested vision statement by Task Force #2 during its presentation to the Board of Regents of Prelacy Armenian Schools reads: "To ensure the perpetual continuity of Armenian cultural heritage by creating its future Armenian–American consumers and producers through the means of the living and contemporary language" (Board of Regents Armenian Task Force, 2014). In opposition to the current mission statement of Prelacy Armenian schools, which de-emphasizes linguistic competence and instead accentuates goals such as "developing a strong sense of national and spiritual values," providing an "Armenian upbringing," and instilling a motivation and inspiration "to be actively involved in the pursuit of the Armenian cause" (Western Prelacy of the Armenian Apostolic Church of America, n.d.), the committee proposed a new statement that situates the successful transmission of Armenian at its core. The expectation is that such a language-centric shift in the vision and mission will be reflected at various organizational levels in the schools, including but not limited to the physical signage (walls, marquees, building signage), active and natural use of Armenian *outside* of the Armenian subject classroom (library, cafeteria, office, gym, events, during recess), use of Armenian in all forms of communications (internal, external, PR), and so on. The task is to guarantee Prelacy schools' commitment to the vision and mission so that they will align their internal structure, policies, and procedures accordingly.

On May 1, 2013, the "Armenian Language Revitalization Committee" (hereafter Task Force #3) was launched at the invitation of Prelate H.E. Archbishop Moushegh Mardirossian and the Executive Council of the Western Prelacy, with a focus on the revitalization and preservation of the oral and written Armenian language in the Los Angeles community. Similar to the other Task Forces, this committee is comprised of language professors, Armenian school principals, Armenian Studies scholars, and prominent community members. As articulated in the press release of the Western Prelacy Divan, during the initial meetings, "the committee concurred that the use of the Armenian language, both oral and written, is in decline, and that the ability to understand and communicate in Armenian is vital to the sustainability of Armenian identity and sense of belonging" (Western Prelacy of the Armenian Apostolic Church of America, 2014). The Committee concluded that it was essential to find a solution to remedy this critical situation and

> began to evaluate the root causes of this problem based on available research results and statistics, and to create a plan of action with a clear vision, mission, and strategic goals for spearheading a decentralized language revitalization program. Partnerships with schools, churches, organizations, political parties, media and interested individuals will be central to the program's success.
>
> *(Western Prelacy of the Armenian Apostolic Church of America, 2014)*

After two years of work, the Committee has drafted an in-depth plan of action that is currently in the process of being transformed into a series of short- and long-term projects. Of the three Task Forces, this one has the most far-reaching target—the entire Armenian community in Los Angeles. The desired level of innovation aims to introduce change in the organizational culture of all of the major Armenian institutions (both educational and non-educational) in their attitudes and practices, in order to prioritize and promote Armenian language use.

In the following section, I will discuss the challenges and opportunities for the Armenian community, incorporating the assessments, recommendations, and experiences from all the Task Forces.

6 Discussion: Challenges and Opportunities

There are several factors that must be considered when assessing the challenges and opportunities of maintaining Armenian for this particular community, particularly in the process of introducing innovation at various organizational levels.

Resistance to Change

As many of the contributors to this volume will corroborate, bringing about change is a very difficult and nuanced process. One of the key pre-requisites must be to account for resistance to change, as "the success of a strategy of institutionalization will depend to a large degree on a realistic approach to this dialectic of cultures and contra cultures involved in the process of change" (Ekholm & Trier, 1987, p. 21). It must be recognized that any type of improvement project involves not only an institutionalization process of the new, but along with it a "de-institutionalization of the old" (Ekholm, Vandenberghe, & Miles, 1987, p. 244), which can create conflict with the existing local culture. Unless this resistance is accounted for and dealt with, improvement efforts can be obstructed by a set of generally accepted and routinized norms, structures, and procedures.

The experience from the Task Forces, particularly the first two, as they were launched earlier and have a longer track record of activities, demonstrate that resistance might spring from diverse stakeholders and for various reasons. This was the case with Task Force #1, when some teachers resisted new HL pedagogical approaches because they did not want to invest the time and effort to learn and implement them, particularly when they did not believe that they were being sufficiently rewarded. The administration resisted supplying unanticipated time and resources to adequately prepare and reward teachers for innovative practices, which in turn augmented teachers' resistance even further. Additionally, in the example of Task Force #2, when we held a large focus group meeting with all the Armenian subject instructors in Prelacy schools, some teachers refused to participate, while others expressed explicit disbelief in the possibility of change. The impression was that some of the Armenian teachers were so resigned that they were apathetic and tired of being subjected to short-term "Band-Aid" solutions, which did not lead to long-term change and positive outcomes. Most importantly, in previous scenarios, any attempt at change or innovation had been dictated in a top-down way, without involving the teachers in the process. Finally, manifestations of resistance even sprung up within the committees themselves in the process of determining what kind of innovation was needed and how it should be implemented.

The experiences described above indicate the need to recognize that institutionalization is a process of "growing collective ownership" (Ekholm & Trier, 1987, p. 15), in which stakeholders need to be provided with "public opportunities to affirm and 'buy in' to the change" (Louis, 2006, p. 25). Especially if the targeted innovation deals with changing classroom practices, ensuring teachers' commitment and support cannot be underestimated. Moreover, teachers must feel that their involvement will be rewarded, whether that reward is symbolic in form or by some other means. The important point here is that the innovation project must be carefully and meticulously orchestrated to account for and tackle any resistance, even within the organizing committee itself. Staging activities for vision building that clarify the change involved enables stakeholders to develop meaningful organizational behavior during the institutionalization phase (Ekholm et al., 1987).

Demographics

The demographic profile of the Los Angeles Armenian community has drastically evolved over the past several decades, producing an extremely heterogeneous community in numerous respects. As the immigration patterns described above indicate, this is a highly diverse population in terms of generational status, country of origin, socioeconomic status, and linguistic standard or dialect. On the one hand, this may present difficulties in attempts to design, implement, reform, or institutionalize HL programs with a uniform approach, but on the other, it may also provide unique opportunities for HL maintenance. For example, in the case of Armenian day schools, which have been the backbone of HL institutionalization both for this community and diasporic Armenian communities worldwide, catching up to the rapidly shifting profile of their student body has lagged, both in terms of generational status and linguistic standard (Chahinian & Bakalian, 2016; Karapetian, 2014; Peroomian, 2006). Although the student body of Armenian schools is largely comprised of second- and third-generation students, who are no longer Armenian-dominant, the majority of schools implement an instructional model, based on the Middle Eastern approach, of treating and teaching Armenian as a dominant language, which they recognize is not working (Chahinian & Bakalian, 2016).

Moreover, despite the fact that Eastern Armenian is the language of the overwhelming majority of more recent immigrants, the dominant language of instruction in Armenian Prelacy schools is still Western Armenian (exceptions noted above). All day schools have reported an increasing presence of Eastern Armenian–speaking students, in some cases comprising half of the student body, yet only a small number offer tracks in both standards. As a result, for the Eastern Armenian speaking student, the language of the home is different from the language of the school, not to mention the differences in orthography for those from Armenia, as well as the complications brought about by the diglossic nature of Eastern Armenian (i.e., dialectal forms used by Iranian-Armenians or the large gap between spoken and literary Armenian for those from the Republic).

Given the potential difficulties of such a large and diverse population, the importance of demographic density, which is constantly fueled by the arrival of new speakers, cannot be emphasized enough in the opportunities it may hold for HL maintenance. Research has consistently demonstrated that generational status is the highest predictor of language maintenance and use (Bakalian, 1993; Karapetian, 2014). This means that continuing immigration is constantly replenishing and refueling the community with hosts of native speakers (or speakers from other diasporic communities) who, in addition to their linguistic wealth, bring with them new energy and cultural breadth. Moreover, the large concentration and number of Armenians, primarily with the expansion of Eastern Armenian speakers, has led to a strong response from the public domain, particularly in the GUSD (heritage and immersion programs, junior and high-school courses). Even though the need for such programs may be initiated by the community, numbers speak the loudest when seeking state support. As for Armenian day schools, with the passing of time the growing Eastern Armenian–speaking population, especially the cohort from the Republic, is slowly climbing the socioeconomic ladder and becoming a prominent target market that needs to be tapped. In order to do this, their needs must be met by offering tracks in both standards. The experience and wisdom of older generations, both from the U.S. and other diasporic communities, can be combined with the energy and linguistic vitality of newer immigrants to introduce and adapt HL models that are designed to meet all Armenian-American students' needs.

Multiple Variants

As a result of the changing immigration and settlement patterns described above, linguistic boundaries have become more fluid and blurred. In the case of Los Angeles, both standards and a host of dialects are not only present, but in contact with one another and with English. Moreover, a new generation of "hybrid" families increasingly uses both varieties of Armenian because the two parents speak varying standards (or dialects) and children are raised with *both* as their HL. Although a high degree of dialect bending and accommodation is prevalent (a fascinating area of study!), a new "LA Armenian" has not yet emerged as a viable literary standard.

As such, each standard faces its own set of unique challenges in terms of HL maintenance. There is no question that the situation of Western Armenian, a stateless diasporic language, recently categorized as endangered, is much more dire when compared to its Eastern counterpart, which enjoys official status and the backing of a state. "Western speakers are dwindling in the U.S. by lower immigration rates from the Middle East, by aging and death of the Western-speaking cohorts and by the assimilation of the second and third generations" (Chahinian & Bakalian, 2016, p. 47). It is viewed as a threatened language, not only by the dominant languages it coexists with in host countries, but also by its Eastern counterpart (Chahinian & Bakalian, 2016). The stakes are indeed much higher for Western Armenian as it stands on the threshold of language extinction.

Eastern Armenian, though obviously more secure in its status overall, is experiencing similar challenges of language shift in a diasporic setting, particularly in communities in the West. In some regard, it may even be argued that without the constant refueling of new immigrants, Eastern Armenian will succumb to language shift at an even quicker pace because of the unique sociolinguistic background of a large number of its speakers. The Armenians from Armenia, who are the fastest expanding cohort, represent the only subgroup transitioning from a majority status to a minority one. Naturally, they have led a very *unmarked* Armenian existence, without experiencing, much less acknowledging impending concerns of ethnic or linguistic assimilation. They are oblivious to ideas of identity and language preservation as these are taken for granted in an environment where one is accustomed to living in one's own homeland. As a result, members of this subethnic group are often less prepared for their change to a minority status and the complications that process entails (Karapetian, 2014).

Although efforts to preserve and revitalize the Western standard are critically important, linguistic conservatism and perspectives positioning the two standards in competition for resources may not be productive. In the face of community-wide decline and language shift, "the cultivation and safeguarding of Armenian as an immigrant heritage language should be the goal in the culturally and linguistically diverse Armenian American communities" (Chahinian & Bakalian, 2016, p. 54). More liberal views on language have indeed been adopted by the Task Forces, none of which single out either standard, recognizing the importance of maintaining and promoting Armenian in all its forms.

For example, in its presentation to the Board of Regents, Task Force #2 proposed as one of its core values the critical need not to discriminate against the demographic or linguistic composition of students in Armenian day schools (i.e., Eastern Armenian, Western Armenian, Armenian from Armenia, Iranian Armenian, etc.) coupled with an appreciation and pride in the language as beautiful and viable in all its variants.

Teachers

The issue of Armenian teachers is an extremely grave one, as the present cohort is almost entirely from Middle Eastern communities, often with limited or no professional education in teaching Armenian (or teaching in general), particularly in the American setting. Furthermore, many of the currently employed teachers are on the brink of retirement without viable candidates to take over, as there is no institution in the U.S. that produces Armenian teachers, nor is the job viewed as economically or socially prestigious by the community. As a result, most of the teachers are hired based on recommendations and previous experience teaching in *another* diaspora community (Syria, Lebanon, Iran). Consequently, there is no uniformity in the instructors' theoretical and methodological approach; on the contrary, each teacher comes from a different school of pedagogy (if they indeed have some kind of formal pedagogical education) and with very diverse attitudes about *what kind* of Armenian should be taught and *how* it should be instructed.

The assessments of all Task Forces identify the issue of training the present cohort and producing a new generation of Armenian teachers as one of the major challenges facing the community. Short-term activities in this direction are already on their way in the form of teacher training workshops and seminars. As mentioned above, Task Force #1 organized a series of workshops for the Armenian teachers at Chamlian ranging from an introduction to HL learners and best practices to backward design and content-based curriculum development. Moreover, in 2013 during its annual staff development day for all of the Armenian day schools, the Board of Regents invited two HL specialists to give workshops for the Armenian teachers on HL pedagogy.

Long-term goals proposed by the Task Forces include the creation of a program or institution with the purpose of preparing Armenian teachers by providing interested candidates with the opportunity to receive teaching credentials while pursuing a degree in Armenian Studies. Fortunately, in this regard, in October of 2015, CSUN received a $250,000 donation from the TF Educational Foundation to prepare future Armenian teachers (Chandler, 2015). The pledged money will be paid over five years "for the creation of an annual scholarship to liberal studies students in CSUN's Integrated Teacher Education Program (ITEP) who are also minoring in Armenian studies" (Chandler, 2015). Critically, this type of program will fill the large gaps in the profile of Armenian teachers by preparing a new cohort that will have a solid foundation both in Armenian studies and teaching methodologies appropriate for a classroom in an American setting.

Instructional Approaches

There is consensus among all Task Forces that Armenian instruction is failing, with Armenian "growing like a fruit in a greenhouse" (Peroomian, 2006, p. 1), limited to the boundaries of the Armenian language classroom, and viewed as an imposed subject by the students. Instruction of Armenian subjects is not standardized nor is it objective based. As noted in an earlier section, Task Force #1 discovered that the existing standards were unusable, as they were simply a translation of the GUSD Language Arts standards. Moreover, since instruction is not objective based there is no uniformity within and across Armenian schools on the curricula employed. Basically, curriculum development and pedagogical approaches are guided and executed by each instructor at their discretion and based on their experience (Chahinian & Bakalian, 2016). Consequently, having Armenian classes is one thing, but ensuring suitable and successful practices inside the classrooms is altogether another.

Classroom observations in the assessment stage of Task Force #1 revealed that instruction is overwhelmingly teacher-centered and grammar focused. Teachers are not trained in HL pedagogy, which is significantly different from both first-language and second-language pedagogy. All the Task Forces have recognized the need, and have in varying degrees proposed or already begun, to implement HL-specific instructional approaches. The teacher training workshops described in relation to the work of Task Force #1 above, for example, included sessions on identifying the profile of heritage students, recognizing, acknowledging, and validating students' background knowledge, as well as designing learner-centered activities. There was also extensive training and work on developing content- and theme-based curricula, which can be used as a means to teach grammar, culture, and a host of other important skills.

In the most recent meeting with members of the Board of Regents of Prelacy schools as part of the activities for Task Force #2, the need to improve not only Armenian instruction, but instruction in all subjects, was articulated in order to elevate the quality and prestige of Armenian schools and thus attract more students. Moreover, proposed changes in the organizational culture of Prelacy schools, which were focused on increasing the presence and use of Armenian both inside and outside of the classroom, were supported. These include simulating opportunities of pseudo-immersion, where students would be exposed to Armenian in atypical settings, such as during art class, P.E., after-school activities, and the cafeteria.

Language Attitudes

Among all of the factors mentioned thus far, impacting language attitudes is the most difficult yet most significant undertaking, as at the core of any major and meaningful change must be a shared ideology. With the passing of time and generations, the domains of Armenian language use have predictably contracted. Giving in to the reality that Armenian language use is declining, school and community leaders have re-evaluated the boundaries of Armenian identity, de-emphasizing the role of language in that formula and instead highlighting less tangible notions such as possessing an Armenian spirit or dedication to the Armenian cause (Bakalian, 1993; Karapetian, 2014; Kouloujian, 2012). In this process, the language's primary function and instrumental value as a vehicle of communication has narrowed in scope, while a new form of symbolic engagement with the language has emerged, in which socialization into affective sentiments *about* the language is prioritized over socialization *into* actual language use (Karapetian, 2014). As a result, heritage speakers have internalized feelings of moral responsibility and obligation for knowing Armenian, without the actual proficiency in the language. The heightened symbolic focus on language preservation instead of actual language cultivation has led to highly idealized sentiments about the language that conflict with language behaviors in which Armenian is essentially stripped of its utility (Karapetian, 2014).

The institutions in charge of language maintenance are often complicit in the demotion of the language. As noted above, Armenian day schools do not employ an immersion model that would involve content instruction in Armenian. On the contrary, Armenian is taught as a "specialized subject," consigned to the boundaries of the Armenian classroom, and lacking practical utility outside of the few hours dedicated to Armenian subjects (Armenian language, history, religion). Most importantly, Armenian is not the language of play, with English functioning as students' language of choice in most domains. This type of attitude exacerbates linguistic compartmentalization, in which the life and the context of Armenian youths quickly evolve into separate compartments based on thematic and temporal divisions. Armenian functions in spheres restricted to the home ("the kitchen"), daily interactions, the familial world, the elderly, and the past, while English marks current interests, higher education, abstract thought, and future endeavors (Karapetian, 2014; Kouloujian, 2012).

The fundamental goal for all Task Forces, regardless of their scope, is to change the existing attitudes about Armenian in order to restore the language as vital, relevant, and contemporary. At the core of this challenge is to shift the focus from language preservation to language cultivation, so that Armenian is viewed as an organic and dynamic element of everyday life by expanding its domains of use. Task Forces #2 and #3 aim to raise awareness about linguistic compartmentalization across a variety of domains in order to impact language policies in community institutions, both educational and otherwise. As one of its core values, Task Force #2 states: "The student should not have an 'Armenian language or Armenian world' and parallel with it, his/her own 'real' world, where the 'Armenian language and things Armenian' are missing. The world in its entirety must fit into Armenian" (Board of Regents Armenian Task Force, 2014). Khatchadourian (2014), in his presentation of the novel pedagogical philosophies of the successful Mgnig Armenian language workshop in Paris, France, echoes the notions above by stating that one of the fundamental conditions in this approach is the view of Armenian as "a language that encompasses all aspects of life" (p. 12). All of the Task Forces, particularly #2 and #3, which have broader targets, have incorporated multipronged strategic goals for making Armenian visible and present in the community's everyday life, in order to restore its role as a viable and relevant HL.

7 Conclusion

As the discussion above has highlighted, all the relevant factors in maintaining Armenian as an HL for this community are really complex, nuanced, and interdependent. The stakes are extremely high, particularly for Western Armenian, a stateless language entirely dependent on diasporic institutions and interventions for its very survival. Moreover, changes in the geopolitical profile of the Armenian diaspora have positioned Los Angeles as its new epicenter, endowing this community with a great deal of responsibility and opportunity. Consequently, the significance of the existence and work of such Task Forces cannot be understated, as they attempt to shape the various paths of HL maintenance.

The results are yet to be seen, as the Task Forces have a long road ahead, particularly since #2 and #3 are only now in the process of transitioning from their planning phase into actual implementation. Yet, there is reason to be hopeful. Diasporic communities all over the world have awakened to the need of maintaining Armenian as an HL, with major global collaborations across institutions and programs.[2] On the home front of Los Angeles, the activities of the Task Forces have already witnessed a trickle-down effect. Three Prelacy Armenian high schools have decided that their annual student gathering in April, traditionally dedicated to discussing ways of advancing the Armenian cause, will instead take the form of a student-led and student-run conference focusing on the issue of fostering Armenian in this community. What better proof of change in action.

Notes

1 "Western Armenian and Eastern Armenian are about as different from each other as Spanish from Portuguese or Russian from Ukrainian. A proficient speaker of one version can easily pick up the other with some exposure to it in natural language settings, that is, in the speaking community" (Hagopian, 2005: Introduction).
2 The Gulbenkian Foundation has emerged as a leader in this regard, organizing and supporting a variety of innovative conferences, workshops, and programs related to the development of strategic goals for Armenian language cultivation in the diaspora.

References

Bakalian, A. P. (1993). *Armenian-Americans: From being to feeling Armenian.* New Brunswick, NJ: Transaction Publishers.

Board of Regents Armenian Task Force. (2014, February 4). *Progress report.* Presentation made to Board of Regents, Prelacy Armenian Schools, Los Angeles, CA. Archives of the Board of Regents Armenian Task Force, Los Angeles, CA.

Bournoutian, G. A. (2006). *A concise history of the Armenian people.* Costa Mesa, CA: Mazda Publishers.

Chahinian, T., & Bakalian, A. (2016). Language in Armenian American communities: Western Armenian and efforts for preservation. *International Journal of the Sociology of Language, 2016*(237), 37–57.

Chandler, C. R. (2006, September 11). New head of CSUN's Armenian studies program looks to the future [News Release Archives]. Retrieved from http://www.csun.edu/pubrels/press_releases/fall06/armenianstudies.html

Chandler, C. R. (2015, October 26). CSUN Today: TF Educational Foundation gift to CSUN to support future teachers of Armenian studies [Web page]. Retrieved from http://csunshinetoday.csun.edu/arts-and-culture/tf-educational-foundation-gift-to-csun-to-support-future-teachers-of-armenian/

Cowe, P. S. (1992). Amēn tel hay kay: Armenian as a pluricentric language. In M. Clyne (Ed.), *Pluricentric languages: Differing norms in differing nations* (pp. 325–345). Berlin, Germany: Mouton de Gruyter.

Der-Martirosian, C. (2008). Armenians in US Census of 1980, 1990, 2000. *Journal of Society for Armenian Studies, 17,* 127–141.

Dum-Tragut, J. (2009). *Armenian: Modern eastern Armenian.* Amsterdam, The Netherlands: John Benjamins Pub. Co.

Ekholm, M., & Trier, U. P. (1987). The concept of institutionalization: Some remarks. In M. B. Miles, M. Ekholm, & R. Vandenberghe (Eds.), *Lasting school improvement: Exploring the process of institutionalization* (pp. 13–21). Leuven, Belgium: Acco.

Ekholm, M., Vandenberghe, R., & Miles, M. B. (1987). Conclusions and implications. In M. B. Miles, M. Ekholm, & R. Vandenberghe (Eds.), *Lasting school improvement: Exploring the process of institutionalization* (pp. 243–267). Leuven, Belgium: Acco.

Hagopian, G. (2005). *Armenian for everyone: Western and Eastern Armenian in parallel lessons.* Ann Arbor, MI: Caravan Books.

Hovhannisian, R. G. (Ed.). (2004). *Armenian people from ancient to modern times* (Vols. 1–2). New York, NY: St. Martin's Press.

Jebejian, A. (2010). Patterns of language use among Armenians in Beirut in the last 95 years. *Haigazian Armenological Review, 31,* 453–469.

Karapetian Giorgi, C. (2012). *Gender and migration: Armenian women's experiences 1990–2010* (Doctoral dissertation). Manchester, UK: University of Manchester.

Karapetian, S. (2014). *"How do I teach my kids my broken Armenian?": A study of eastern Armenian heritage language speakers in Los Angeles* (Doctoral dissertation). Retrieved from http://escholarship.org/uc/item/7jq085nr

Khatchadourian, K. (2014, February 28). *A new pedagogical approach to transmitting the Armenian language in the Diaspora: A case study of Mgnig educational workshop.* Paper presented at the Graduate Student Colloquium in Armenian Studies, UCLA, CA.

Kouloujian, H. (2012, April 19). *On the demotion of language as the virtual territory sustaining diaspora.* Paper presented at the Arpa 20th Anniversary Conference, Sherman Oaks, CA.

Kouloujian, H. (2014, May 8). *Linguistic compartmentalization in heritage language speakers: Observations in the Armenian diaspora.* Paper presented at the Second International Conference on Heritage/Community Languages, UCLA, CA.

Louis, K. S. (2006). *Organizing for school change.* New York, NY: Routledge.

Mirak, R. (2004). The Armenians in America. In R. G. Hovannisian (Ed.), *The Armenian people from ancient to modern times* (Vol. 2, pp. 389–411). New York, NY: St. Martin's Press.

Oshagan, V. (2004). Modern Armenian literature and intellectual history. In R. G. Hovannisian (Ed.), *The Armenian people from ancient to modern times* (Vol. 2, pp. 139–174). New York, NY: St. Martin's Press.

Peroomian, R. (2006). *An outlook on Armenian schools.* Unpublished article. Department of Near Eastern Languages and Cultures, UCLA.

UNESCO. (n.d.). Endangered languages [Web page]. Retrieved from http://www.unesco.org/new/en/culture/themes/endangered-languages/atlas-of-languages-in-danger/

U.S. Census Bureau. (2015). Table B16001: Language spoken at home by ability to speak English for the for the population 5 years and over [data tables for U.S., California, Los Angeles County, and Glendale City, California]. 2010–2104 American Community Survey 5-year Estimates. Washington, DC: Author. Retrieved from http://www.census.gov

Western Prelacy of the Armenian Apostolic Church of Armenia. (2014, February 21). Armenian language revitalization committee established under auspices of the Western Prelacy [Web page]. Retrieved from http://westernprelacy.org/armenian-language-revitalization-committee-established-under-the-auspices-of-the-western-prelacy/

Western Prelacy of the Armenian Apostolic Church of Armenia. (n.d.). Schools [Web page]. Retrieved from http://westernprelacy.org/schools/

Yeghiazaryan, A., Avanesian, V., & Shahnazaryan, N. (2003). How to reverse emigration? Retrieved from http://www.amerialegal.am/pdf/d5c0447534321fa8e3db55f97def1070.pdf

12

Education in the Cambodian Chinese Diaspora[1]

Dana Scott Bourgerie

1 Ethnic Chinese in Cambodia

There have been Chinese in what is now Cambodia for at least 700 years. The Chinese diplomat and Ming dynasty emissary Zhou Daguan documented in detail his visit to the Angor kingdom in 1296, where he reported a Chinese community in what is now Siem Reap (Harris, 2007). Others have postulated a Chinese presence in Cambodia as early as 140 BCE as part of a Han Dynasty conquest of the southern territories, including parts of Vietnam and Cambodia (Schliesinger, 2011a). Willmott suggests as least some Chinese contact with Cambodia from the time of the region's earliest written history. In fact, Chinese were the first to chronicle the Kingdom of Funan (first–sixth century CE), which included parts of present-day Cambodia. However, it is not clear that there was a significant Chinese settlement per se in Funan or that the presence was more than a trading mission (Willmott, 1967, pp. 3–4).

Whenever the first settlement, Chinese came to Southeast Asia from southern China in various waves throughout the centuries (Edwards, 2009, pp. 179–180), often induced to emigrate by tumult in the homeland. Song dynasty loyalists fled to Indochina for refuge in 1276 at the fall of the dynasty and there were exoduses from the strife of the Ming and Qing dynasties. In addition to the flow from the southern China mainland, Chinese also arrived in Cambodia after the Koxinga collapse in Formosa (present-day Taiwan) around 1683 (Edwards, 2009, p. 180). Migration continued in fits and starts though the nineteenth century and into the mid-twentieth century as many Chinese came as miners and traders. Until the nineteenth century these émigrés were considered traitors to the Chinese motherland (Edwards, 2009, p. 181; Yen, 1985, pp. 16–22) and for this reason it was difficult to return, giving more incentive to establish permanent residence in their newly adopted countries such as Cambodia (Pan, 1990). After 1952–1953, Chinese immigration to Cambodia was severely curtailed by new local immigration laws (Willmott, 1967, pp. 16–17).

Although in many places in Southeast Asia ethnic Chinese met with persecution and were targets of mass killings (Pan, 1990, Chapter 4), they have found relatively good acceptance in Indochina (Willmott, 1967). Two glaring exceptions to this positive reception was their treatment under the Khmer Republic of the Lon Nol regime (1970–1975) and during Pol Pot's Khmer Rouge (1976–79). During the former, Chinese were suspected of being communist

Table 12.1 Historical Timeline of Contact between China and Cambodia

---

- **140 BCE** (Han Dynasty, Emperor Wu conquered southern territories) Vietnam corridor (Schliesinger, 2011b)
- **1st–6th centuries** CE Funnan Kingdom
- **1276** Song loyalist refugees to Indochina (Yen, 1985)
- **1296** Zhou Daguan visit (Harris, 2007)
- **1609** Portuguese visitor to Cambodia (3,000 of Phnom Penh's 20,000 inhabitants reported as Chinese; Schliesinger, 2011b, p. 199)
- **Ming/Qing** refugees to Cambodia and Vietnam (Xia Ding, as cited in (Edwards, 2009, p. 180)
- **Circa 1683** Koxinga collapse (Formosa)
- **1860s** movement from Cholon, the Chinese enclave in Saigon
- **18th and 19th centuries** Immigration of miners, traders, plantation workers (Schliesinger, 2011b, p. 199)
- **Late-mid 19th century** Recognition of overseas Chinese by China (Yen, 1985)
- **1920s** Almost half the population of Phnom Penh said to be Chinese (Schliesinger, 2011b, p. 199)
- **1930s** economic crisis caused a surge in immigration from Chaozhou (also Romanized as Teochew) migration, supplanting the Cantonese.
- **1952–1953** Most Chinese immigration to Cambodia ceased due to new local laws (Yen, 1985, Chapters 5–6)

---

sympathizers; in the latter, they were singled out as capitalists and targeted for extermination (Edwards, 2009, pp. 177, 200–210; Pan, 1999, pp. 147–148; Suryadinata, 2013, pp. 280–281; Tea & Nov, 2009, p. 239).

From early times, the ethnic Chinese have played vital economic roles and have dominated the business and education sectors of Cambodia (Willmott, 2007) and elsewhere in Southeast Asia. The populations have been largely urban, though certain groups, such as the Hainanese (from the Chinese island of Hainan), have been involved in farming—especially pepper production (Willmott, 1967, p. 21). However, whether urban or rural, the Chinese role in Cambodia has been long-lasting and substantial.

2 Background of the Chinese Language

Terms for Chinese

Terms for the Chinese language vary by region and usage. For example, Modern Standard Chinese (MSC) is *Putonghua* 普通话 [common language] in the People's Republic of China (hereafter "Mainland China") and *Guoyu* 国语 [National Language] in Taiwan. *Hanyu* 汉语 [language of the Han] is also used in Mainland China for the Chinese language generally and the standard language by default. *Huayu* 华语 [language of China] is used in most areas of Southeast Asia to refer to any variety of Chinese, including the various dialect groups. *Fangyan* 方言 [dialect] is used to refer to any non-standard variety of Chinese, including mutually unintelligible forms (e.g., Cantonese, Taiwanese, etc.).

Classification of Chinese Varieties

Chinese is traditionally divided into seven or eight major dialect groups (Li, 1973), each group of which is largely unintelligible to the others. Nevertheless, because of cultural reasons and because

Table 12.2 Estimated Numbers of Chinese Dialect Speakers (2010)

Dialect Group	Speaker Number Estimates	%	Representative Locales in China
Mandarin	938,637,000	70.0%	
Northern	*450,545,760*	*48%*	Beijing, Tianjin, Shandong
Northwestern	*131,409,180*	*14%*	City of Baoji and through most of northwestern China
Southeastern	*65,704,590*	*7%*	Lower Yangtze, in an area centered on Nanjing
Southwestern	*290,977,470*	*31%*	Sichuan, Yunnan, Chongqing, Guizhou, most parts of Hubei
Wu	100,568,250	7.5%	Shanghai, Suzhou, Wuxi
Yue (=Cantonese)	60,340,950	4.5%	Western Guangdong, Hong Kong, Macau
Jin	50,954,580	3.8%	Shanxi Province
Min	49,613,670	3.7%	Eastern Guangdong, Fujian
Northern	*16,090,920*	*1.2%*	Fuzhou
Southern	*33,522,750*	*2.5%*	Taiwan, Chaozhou, Hainan Island
Xiang	46,931,850	3.5%	Hunan, Shuangfeng
Kejia (=Hakka)	33,522,750	2.5%	Guangdong Province
Gan	26,818,200	2.0%	Jiangxi
Other	33,522,750	2.5%	
TOTAL	**1,340,910,000**	**100%**	

Sources: Li (1973), National Bureau of Statistics of the People's Republic of China (2014), and Ramsey (1987).

all Chinese varieties share a common standard writing system, the term "dialect" is conventional when referring to these sub-varieties of Chinese. Despite China's huge population growth, the relative percentage of speakers of the various dialects has not likely changed much since Yuan (1983) carried out his landmark survey between 1955 and1958. Table 12.2 below gives the estimated number of dialect group speakers as extrapolated from the 2010 survey population figure (National Bureau of Statistics of the People's Republic of China, 2014) but based on Yuan's relative percentages of speakers.[2]

Terms for Chinese in Cambodia

In describing the Chinese language situation in Cambodia, it is important to understand the various terms that refer to the Chinese population. The choice of terms relates to perceived identity and has both political and cultural dimensions (Edwards, 2009, p. 176). The broadest term for ethnic Chinese in the Khmer[3] language is *Khmer-cen*, Cambodian-Chinese, or simply *cen*, Chinese. However, Cambodians can make specific distinctions in Khmer based on when a person or person's family immigrated, which, in turn, impacts their perceived place in the Chinese community:

Cen-daekook: "Dry land Chinese" newer term for temporary residents from the PRC, Hong Kong, Taiwan, and Singapore.
Cen-chiw: "Raw Chinese," i.e., new arrivals

Khmae-yeung: Long-term residents from China
Coul-Kmae: "Entered the Khmers," i.e., integrated Chinese
Koun-cen: Children of Chinese
Koun-ciw-cen: Grandchildren of Chinese
Koun-Kat Cen or Koun-Kat: "Cut child Chinese" i.e., "half and half"

Since the majority of Chinese have arrived in the last 100 years, most would fit into the last four categories. Additionally, even within categories, there are degrees of integration. For example, some *Coul-Kmae* may still belong to Chinese associations. There are no reliable figures on the numbers in each category.

Cen-daekook are regarded as foreigners and have their own schools and associations. *Khmae-yeung*, by contrast, are accepted as members of Cambodian society. Within Chinese Cambodian schools, one can find *Khmae-yeung* staff and teachers, many of whom came to work but eventually married local Cambodian women. In practice there is overlap between the terms, especially those who have been born in Cambodia (*Koun-cen, Koun-ciw-cen, Koun-Kat Cen*, and *Cen-Chiw*)—all are often simply referred to as *Cen* "Chinese." Nevertheless, the various terms for Chinese suggest an awareness of sub-identity.

Origins of the Sino-Cambodians

The Cambodia Chinese diaspora has its origins primarily in the province of Guangdong and Hainan Island. Nearly all of the local Sino-Cambodian population belongs to one of five ethnolinguistic subgroups: three Min dialects (Chaozhou, Fujianese, and Hainanese), one Yue (Cantonese), and one Hakka (Kejia). The romanized Khmer terms for these dialects are provided in Table 12.3, as well as the numbers for each group of speakers as a percentage of the Chinese population in Cambodia. Once the largest group, the Cantonese have been eclipsed by those originating from Chaozhou, which are now dominant in both numbers and influence.

Although the Cambodian Chinese populations originate in south China, they came by varying routes, though largely by sea and most coming through the Vietnamese port of Cholon (Steinberg, 1959, p. 43). The latter route necessitated secondary migrations by land as well from Cholon to Cambodia, a path especially favored by the Cantonese.

Table 12.3 Chinese Ethnolinguistic Groups Residing in Cambodia

EthnoLinguistic Group[4]	Dialect Group	Khmer	Est. % of Chinese Population[5]
Chaozhou 潮州 (Teochew)	Min	Cen-Teechiew	60
Cantonese 广东	Yue	Cen-Katang	20
Fujian 福建 (Hokkien)	Min	Cen-Hokkien	7
Hakka 客家	Hakka (Kejia)	Cen-Keh	4
Hainanese海南	Min	Cen-Hainan	4

Source: Steinberg (1959, p. 43).

3 Sino-Cambodian Organizations and Associations

As is true throughout most of the Chinese diaspora worldwide, one can find in Cambodia a wide range of Chinese organizations and institutions, including organizations based on place of origin (同乡会 *tongxianghui* or 会馆 *huiguan*, which align with the ethnolinguistic groups

Table 12.4 Chinese "Place of Origin" Associations in Cambodia

Association	Origin
柬华理事总会 The Foundation of Associations of Chinese in Cambodia	Umbrella Association
潮州会馆 Chaozhou Association	Chaozhou area of Guangdong
广肇会馆 Guangzhao Association	Western Guangzhou province, including 肇庆 Zhaoxing city area
客属会馆 Kejia (Hakka) Association	Guongdong Province
福建会馆 Fujian Association	Fujian Province
海南会馆 Hainan Association	Hainan Island

Source: The Foundation of Associations of Chinese in Cambodia 柬华理事总会 (2010).

in Table 12.3; see Table 12.4 for examples), or family names (e.g., the Lee Association), as well as Chinese language media. In 1891 the French colonial government co-opted these existing associations (called *congrégations* in French) for purposes of control and official reporting. From that time forth, Chinese in colonial Cambodia were required to join the congregation associated with their place of origin group.

Since the end of the colonial period in 1953, the place of origin associations have continued to serve the Chinese community, supporting business interests, family associations, Chinese language media, and Buddhist temples, all of which can be found in the capital city Phnom Penh and in most provinces. Most of these groups belong to an umbrella organization called The Foundation of Associations of Chinese in Cambodia (柬华理事总会 *Jianhua lishi zonghui*), which also co-publishes a Chinese language newspaper called Cambodia Chinese Daily (柬华日报 *Jianhua Ribao*). Table 12.4 lists the main place of origin associations organized by the Sino-Cambodian community. These organizations have historically established and operated Chinese language schools throughout Cambodia.

4 Population Estimates

According to The Foundation of Associations of Chinese in Cambodia (personal correspondence, October 2014), there are some one million ethnic Chinese among the country's approximately 14 million residents. But this estimate is probably in one sense too high and another much too low, because it is extremely difficult to determine who should be counted as Chinese. The most recent Cambodian census data do not include ethnicity and widespread intermarriage with the Khmer and Cham Muslim populations makes issues of identity problematic (Edwards, 2009, pp. 180–184; Tea & Nov, 2009, p. 235; Willmott, 1967, pp. xii–xiii). Various researchers and organizations have attempted estimates but the numbers vary drastically for definitional and methodological reasons. Estimated figures are given in Table 12.5.

Willmott's (1967, p. 13) summary of Chinese population estimates for the years 1857 to 1964 range between 90,000 and 400,000, and shows a pattern of steady increase. Lacking reliable statistics, he and others base their estimates on interviews with Chinese association leaders or on a combination of methods. Accordingly, there is a great deal of debate on the numbers, leading one writer to dub a 1998 census number of 47,180 Chinese as "statistical genocide" (Schliesinger, 2011b, p. 202). Ultimately, it is difficult to establish a reliable estimate of the Chinese populations

Table 12.5 Estimates of the Chinese Populations in Cambodia (1874–2014)

Date	Population Est.	Source/Note
1874	106,764	French account (Paulus, 1884) in (Schliesinger, 2011b, pp. 198–202)
1921	159,000	French account (Paulus, 1884) (Schliesinger, 2011b, pp. 198–202)
1921	91,200	French protectorate government census (Willmott, 1967, p. 12)
1931	148,000	French account (Paulus, 1884) in (Schliesinger, 2011b, pp. 198–202)
1936	106,000	French account (Paulus, 1884) in (Schliesinger, 2011b, pp. 198–202)
1955	275,000	"Pure" Cambodians (Steinberg, 1959, p. 42)
1967	425,000	(Willmott, 1967, p. 17)
1973	450,000	American University Foreign Areas Studies (Whitaker et al., 1973, p. 17)
1998	47,180	1998 census; (Schliesinger, 2011b, p. 202)
2006	300,000 to 340,000	Sino-Cambodia Association (Edwards, 2009, p. 174), 1995 estimate by the Association of Chinese Nationals in Cambodia
2014	~1 million	The Foundation of Associations of Chinese estimate (personal communication, October 2014)

in Cambodia at any given time. Recent government figures do not include questions on ethnicity and so many estimates are impressionistic. Moreover, the calculations are further complicated by questions of identity. Nevertheless, by examining various indirect institutional, commercial, and cultural indicators—including Chinese language education—one can begin to gain a sense of the role ethnic Chinese play in contemporary Cambodia.

5 Institutionalization

Institutionalization will not be examined as it pertains to the introduction of an innovation into an educational organization (Ekholm & Trier, 1987). Instead, the recent history and current characteristics of the system of Chinese schools in Cambodia will be examined, with a view to discussing the changing role of this education and its relevance to the lives of its students. Chinese schools in Cambodia differ from those found in the U.S.(and other parts of the world) in that they are primarily full-time, all-day schools. Prior to WWII, lack of funds and numbers meant that "Chinese school" in the U.S. became synonymous with after-school education that is supplementary to mainstream schooling, and has remained so into the present (e.g., Lai, 2004a, 2004b). The size of the Chinese community in Cambodia, on the other hand, has made the establishment of full-time schools viable.

Historical events of the twentieth and twenty-first centuries have significantly impacted Sino-Cambodian schools. Ekholm and Trier (1987) point out that the stability and robustness of an educational venture, i.e., its institutionalization, is tied to local histories, to "changes in the past, changes in the present and change expected" (p. 14). This chapter examines such changes in relation to Chinese education in Cambodia.

6 The Chinese School System

Historical Background

Modern Chinese language schools in Cambodia date to the early 1900s and were from the beginning affiliated with the various Chinese associations. As mentioned above, these schools are full-time and, before the 1990s, taught the curriculum in the language represented by the organizing place of origin association (see Tables 12.3 and 12.4). They range in levels offered, with some covering the equivalent of kindergarten to fifth grade and others covering all grades from kindergarten to twelfth grade. The larger of the schools are "public" in the sense that they operate under the jurisdiction of the Ministry of Education and have a minimal Khmer language requirement; these schools are classified as 公立 [gongli; public]. By 1938 there were over 4,000 students enrolled in schools nationwide (Edwards, 2009, p. 197). In 1967 there were a reported 170 Chinese schools throughout the country with an estimated total enrollment of 25,665. In Phnom Penh alone, Wu (as cited in Edwards, 2009, p. 197) estimates 11,350 Chinese students at 27 schools at the time. That same year the Cambodian government began to suppress Chinese education because of alleged Chinese interference in Cambodian affairs. Accordingly, the Ministry of Education attempted to impose Khmer language and culture curricula in the Chinese public schools, but with mixed success, and most graduates of the schools continued to be proficient in Chinese (Edwards, 2009, p. 198). The schools were largely shut down during the Lon Nol regime (1970–1975) and Khmer Rouge (1976–79) as part of a general purge of the education system and a specific targeting of the Chinese population.

Recent Context

After a 20-some-year hiatus in Chinese education due to its suppression under the Khmer Republic and the Khmer Rouge, Chinese schools began to re-open in the late 1990s (Tea & Nov, 2009, p. 264). However, this time with a crucial difference: The schools implemented Mandarin as the language of instruction, while still maintaining their place of origin affiliations. By the time Chinese education resumed in Cambodia, the global Chinese language context had changed dramatically, in several ways. In the first place, Mandarin is now seen as a useful language in light of Mainland China's economic growth. Secondly, the Mainland Chinese government has begun to exert a much larger influence on overseas Chinese education, including on heritage communities. The local Chinese associations still maintain control over the schools but, influenced by Mainland Chinese language policy, no longer use regional dialects in the classroom, although association business is still mostly conducted in the associated dialect. Students and teachers are no longer necessarily or even predominantly speakers of the association's dialect; for example, at the Guang Zhao School in Phnom Penh, Cantonese is not the background of many students and teachers. Instead of ethnolinguistic considerations, families often chose schools based on other factors such as educational reputation and location.

With the exception of several remote areas, most provinces have some sort of Chinese education for heritage Chinese. Some, such as Phnom Penh and Kampong Cham, have 10 or more schools. Table 12.6 outlines some of the various Chinese schools in Cambodia according to the Sino-Cambodian Business Information Handbook (Foundation of Associations of Chinese in Cambodia, 2014).[6]

Most provincial schools are limited to levels K–6 or K–5 (Tea & Nov, 2009, p. 267) and after grade 6, students need to either transfer to one of the larger Chinese schools in Phnom Penh or cease their formal Chinese education. Therefore, the general level of Chinese education is much weaker in the provinces and literacy is more limited.

In Phnom Penh, there are currently seven major Chinese language schools and many smaller ones. Table 12.7 provides a basic outline of the major Phnom Penh–based Chinese schools as currently constituted. Seven of the eight main schools are considered public schools (公立) and need to meet certain Ministry of Education standards, including minimum instruction for Khmer language.

Table 12.6 Chinese Schools in Cambodia, by Province

Name of Province	Schools	Name of Province	Schools
Phnom Penh Municipality	10	Mondulkiri	0
Banteay Meanchey	2	Oddar Meanchey	0
Battambang	1	Pailin	0
Kampong Cham	11	Preah Sihanouk	1
Kampong Chhnang	1	Preah Vihear	0
Kampong Speu	3	Prey Veng	3
Kampong Thom	3	Pursat	1
Kampot	5	Ratanakiri	1
Kandal	7	Siem Reap	2
Koh Kong	1	Stung Treng	1
Kep	1	Svay Rieng	1
Kratié	3	Takéo	0
		Tboung Khmum	1

Source: Sino-Cambodian Business Information Handbook (2014).

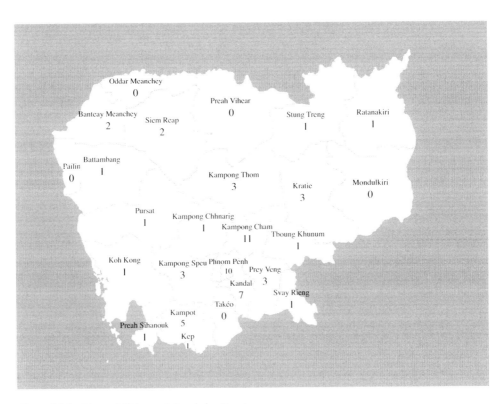

Figure 12.1 Map of Chinese Schools by Province

Source: Data from Sino-Cambodian Business Information Handbook (2014).

Table 12.7 The Major Chinese Schools of Phnom Penh

School Name	Affiliation	Notes
端华正校（公立） Duan Hua (Tuon Fa) Public Chinese School 端华分校（公立） Duan Hua School Branch Campus	潮州会馆 Chaozhou Association	*Established* 1914, reopened in the 1970s *Enrollment* K–12: ~13,000; Evening Chinese courses: ~2,700 *Teachers* 300 (2015)
集成学校（公立） Ji Cheng School (Public)	海南会馆 Hainan Association	*Established* 1932, Reopened 1992 *Enrollment* K–9: ~1,700 *Teachers* N/A
民生学校（公立） Min Sheng School (Public)	福建会馆 Fujian Association	*Established* 1927. Closed 1970–79 Re-established 1999 *Enrollment* K: ~600; 1–6: ~600; 7–10: ~200 *Teachers* 50
崇正学校（公立） Chhong Cheng School (Public)	客属会馆 Hakka Association	*Established* 1992 *Enrollment* K–12: ~3–4,000 students; student population 80% Sino-Cambodian, 20% Khmer *Teachers* 97
广肇学校（公立） Guang Zhao School (Public)	广肇会馆 Cantonese Association	*Established* ~1950, Reopened 1995 *Enrollment* K–12: ~1,600 *Teachers* 65
培华学校（公立） Pei Hua School (Public)	——	*Established* 1994 *Enrollment* K–5: ~100; student population ~10% Cham *Teachers* 12
华明学校（公立） Hua Ming School (Public)	铁桥头理事 Iron Bridgehead Association 福建 Fujian	*Established* 1966, reopened 2001 *Enrollment* K–5: ~100+; Evening classes: ~200; significant Cham and Vietnamese population *Teachers* 30
立群学校 Li Qun School (Private)	NA	*Established* 1964, Reopened 1994 *Enrolment* 3,000+ *Teachers* NA

Source: Interviews with members of The Foundation of Associations of Chinese in Cambodia and with six of the eight principals (excluding Ji Cheng and Li Qun schools), 2014–2015.

Duan Hua School is by far the largest school in Phnom Penh (and in Cambodia overall) with two campuses and approximately 13,000 day students throughout the full K–12 range. It also offers part-time, after-school, and weekend instruction. On the other end of the spectrum, Pei Hua School has just around a hundred students in the K–5 range and just 12 teachers.

Although the great majority of students in Phnom Penh Chinese schools are Sino-Cambodian, a small but growing segment of the student population is now non-Chinese. For example, the Chhong Cheng School principal (personal communication, October 2014) estimates about 20% are now Khmer. Moreover, Hua Ming and Pei Hua schools—which are adjacent to Phnom Penh's Muslim quarters—report significant numbers of ethnic Cham Muslims and some schools also note a growing number of ethnic Vietnamese students. Because of the increasing utility of

Chinese in the Asian business world and because of the relative strength of the Chinese schools' curriculum vis-à-vis Cambodian schools, these non-heritage students' families often see a Chinese language education as a competitive advantage.

Besides the eight main schools, there are a plethora of small, commercial schools (e.g., 精华中文学校 Jing Hua Chinese School, 明华中文学校 Ming Hua Chinese School, 文光 Wen Guang, 文生 Wen Sheng, and Hour Meng School). In terms of enrollments, Ming Hua School can serve as an example: It reports around 300 (200 evening, 100 daytime) students. These schools are mainly tutorial services housed in inferior facilities and staffed by untrained teachers.

7 Cambodia Chinese Student Profiles: A Four-School Sample

Between September 2014 and February 2015, I carried out a language use and language background survey in four of the major Phnom Penh Chinese schools: Duan Hua, Chhong Cheng, Min Sheng, and Guang Zhao. These schools represent a broad cross-section of the Chinese population in Phnom Penh and are affiliated with four separate Chinese associations.

The survey collected broad demographic information and language use data (see Bourgerie, n.d., for full survey) and was administered in higher-level high school classes (grades 11 and 12). The survey was bilingual (Khmer and Chinese) and was carried out in the classroom under the supervision of the teacher and researcher. Because it was done in class with the support of the principals, the response rate was 100% within participating classes. A version of the survey was also administered to a non-student group[7] to provide a point of comparison (Bourgerie, n.d.). Table 12.8 provides information on the number of respondents by participating school.

Survey Results: All Schools

Student Demographics

The overwhelming majority of students in the Phnom Penh Chinese schools were born in or near the city and all but one of the rest were born in another area of Cambodia, as shown in Table 12.9.

Table 12.8 Student Survey: Schools Attended by Survey Respondents

School	Number of Respondents	Affiliation
Duan Hua	56	Chao Zhou Association
Chhong Cheng	14	Hakka Association
Min Sheng	51	Fujian Association
Guang Zhao	25	Guang Zhao Association

Table 12.9 Student Survey: Birthplace of Survey Respondents

Individual's Birthplace	Phnom Penh	Kampong Cham	Kampot	Kandal	Katie	China	Taiwan	Cambodia—Non Specified
Percentage	85.7%	2%	2%	2%	0.7%	0	0.7%	5.4%
Count	126	3	3	3	1	0	1	8

Although students' parents are much less likely to be born in Phnom Penh (see Table 12.10), they were nonetheless mostly born in Cambodia. Hence, these are not the so-called *Cenchiw* "raw Chinese" or new arrivals, or even the *Kouncen* "children of Chinese," but typically come from established ethnic Chinese families. The data underscore the resiliency of Chinese language in Cambodia, despite significant political and social barriers of the last 50 years.

Family Language and Ethnic Identity

Although most of the students report Khmer as a primary language, all speak a Chinese dialect as well as the Mandarin that they use in school. The Chinese varieties spoken throughout the four-school sample (Figure 12.2) roughly mirror the estimates for the countrywide Chinese population (as shown in Table 12.3).

Table 12.10 Student Survey: Birthplace of Survey Respondents' Parents

Mother's Birthplace	Phnom Penh	Kampong Cham	Kampot	Kandal	Katie	China	Taiwan	Cambodia— Non Specified
Percentage	53.7%	8.8%	4.8%	7.5%	4.8%	0	0	12.9%
Count	79	13	7	11	7	0	0	19
Father's Birthplace	Phnom Penh	Kampong Cham	Kampot	Kandal	Katie	China	Taiwan	Cambodia— Non Specified
Percentage	49%	8.8%	5.4%	5.4%	4.1%	2%	2%	11.6%
Count	72	13	8	8	6	3	3	17

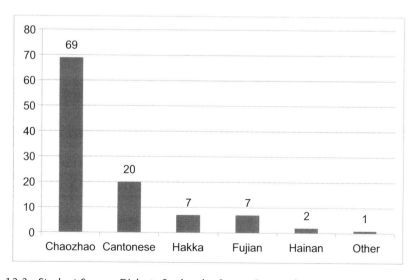

Figure 12.2 Student Survey: Dialects Spoken by Survey Respondents

Table 12.11 outlines the responses by students concerning their parents' language use. Parents were reported to be "primarily Khmer speakers" and at the same time speakers of "both Chinese and Khmer." For this reason, the percentages for "Father's language" and "Mother's language" in Table 12.11 add up to more than 100%. The contradiction in itself underscores the ambiguity of identity for Chinese in Cambodia. They are both bilingual and bicultural in many ways, and there are increasingly few ethic Chinese who would consider themselves purely *cen* [Chinese].

Ethnic Identity

Ethnic identity in Cambodia is a complex issue. The survey used two main ways to assess identity, one direct and one indirect. For Table 12.12, participants were asked "When you think of your family, do you think of yourself mainly as: Cambodian ___ Khmer ___ Chinese ___ Other: (please specify) _____ ?" (See full survey at Bourgerie, n.d.). The term "Cambodian" (in Chinese and Khmer) can refer to political or ethnic identity; "Khmer" refers only to ethnicity.

Table 12.12 suggests that ethnic Chinese students assume a dual identity in Cambodia, seeing themselves as both Khmer and Chinese. Indeed, only about 4.1% consider themselves primarily Chinese.[8] In preliminary questions asked prior to interviewing the non-student group (in addition to surveying them), participants were asked (in Khmer or sometimes English) whether or not they were Chinese. To these preliminary questions, the participants often responded in the negative, despite obvious clues to the contrary (e.g., Chinese family shrines, lunar New Year banners, and physical characteristics). They would often subsequently acknowledge their ethnicity, but only after clearly establishing their national identity. The survey data and these oral interviews support what Edwards (2009) and others have noted about the nature of Cambodian Chinese identity.

Table 12.11 Student Survey: Primary Language of Survey Respondents' Parents

Father's Language	Chinese Primary	Khmer Primary	Other Primary	Both Chinese & Khmer	English	Chao zhou	Canto nese	Thai/Viet	French
Percentage	15.6%	82.3%	0.7%	53.7%	7.5%	21.8%	6.1%	2.7%	0
Count	23	121	1	79	11	32	9	4	0
Mother's Language	Chinese Primary	Khmer Primary	Other Primary	Both Chinese & Khmer	English	Chao zhou	Canto nese	Thai/Viet	French
Percentage	6.8%	87.1%	1.4%	40.1%	4.8%	25.2%	4.1%	2.7%	0.7%
Count	10	128	2	59	7	37	6	4	1

Table 12.12 Student Survey: Family Ethnic Identity

Family Identity	Both	Chinese	Khmer
Percentage	79.6%	4.1%	14%
Count	117	6	22

Religion

Buddhism is the majority religion of Cambodia, with the Theravada being the dominant school. However, the Mahayana school is associated with many East Asian countries, including Japan, Korea, Vietnam, and China. Therefore, it was hypothesized that self-identification with one school or the other would be an indirect marker of cultural identity—those who practice Mahayana Buddhism and associated rituals (such as attendance at temple events) would be more likely to consider themselves Chinese. However, unlike the direct query concerning ethnic identify question, a relatively small percentage of students identified as Mahayana (13.9%) and an even smaller segment (9.5%) identified with both. Despite their feelings of mixed ethnic identity, a large majority saw themselves as Theravada along with their other countrymen.

Home Language Use

As can be seen in Table 12.14, a large majority of the students surveyed reported using Khmer as their primary language at home, but 14.9% (combined Chaozhou/Cantonese Primary) reported primary use of a Chinese dialect at home. A mixture of Khmer and a Chinese dialect in the home environment was reported by 38.1% (combined Khmer & Chaozhou/Cantonese) of respondents. These figures are in notable contrast to what was reported by the non-student participants, who were over 18. As can be seen from Table 12.15, 55% report using Khmer and 45% either Chaozhou or Cantonese as the primary home language. This difference in language practices may be a result of the Mandarin-medium school policy now general in Cambodia. Mandarin is not a native variety for the vast majority of Sino-Cambodians and so they would be unlikely to speak their school language at home with family members. Lacking the school support for

Table 12.13 Student Survey: Religious Identification

Religion	Both	Mahayana	Theravada
Percentage	13.6%	9.5%	75.5%
Count	20	14	111

Table 12.14 Student Survey: Primary Home Language

Language at Home	Khmer Primary	Chaozhou Primary	Cantonese Primary	Khmer & Chaozhou	Khmer & Cantonese	No Khmer	Unknown
Percentage	81%	12.9%	2%	34%	4.1%	6.8%	1.4%
Count	119	19	3	50	6	10	2

Table 12.15 Non-student Survey: Home Language Use

Language at Home	Khmer Primary	Chaozhou Primary	Cantonese Primary	Khmer & Chaozhou	Khmer & Cantonese	No Khmer	Unknown
Percentage	55%	32.5%	12.5%	17.5%	5%	27.5%	5%
Count	22	13	5	7	2	11	2

Table 12.16 Student Survey: Language Use with Friends

Language with Friends	Chinese	Khmer	Both
Percentage	4.5%	18.2%	74.2%
Count	6	24	98

Table 12.17 Student Survey: Self-Assessed Literacy Level (10-Point Scale) of Student Respondents

Reading/Writing Capabilities (Chinese)	Personal	Father	Mother
Reading (avg)	6.34	4.9	3.32
Writing (avg)	6.21	4.5	2.85

their family dialect, many appear to be more comfortable with Khmer at home or at least with a mixture of Khmer and Chinese.

In contrast with the home-use pattern, students overwhelmingly use both languages when speaking with friends, as shown in Table 12.16. This result is striking in that it implies the students' friends are primarily ethnically Chinese, yet they do not use Chinese exclusively with their Chinese-speaking social group. The use pattern also suggests some level of code mixing. Because I was not able to formally observe friend-to-friend interaction between students, I have no way of confirming this hypothesis. However, I did notice mixed use of Khmer and Chinese among students generally in school hallways and playgrounds.

Literacy

As part of the survey, each participant was asked to self-rate (on a 10-point scale) their reading and writing abilities in Chinese. Because standard written Chinese is mostly independent of dialect, we do not differentiate dialect group in the literacy part of the survey.

Student participant self-assessments are markedly higher than their parents. This is an expected result because during the 1970s and 1980s Chinese schools (and most other schools) were closed by the government. Moreover, in rural areas where many participants were raised, access to education was generally limited and support for school attendance was (and is) weak. Many of the students' parents only had a few years of formal education, though some were taught Chinese in the home.

8 Chinese School Classroom Context (Phnom Penh)

Teacher Background

The Chinese schools in Phnom Penh are staffed primarily by Sino-Cambodians who were educated in-country, though some received training in China or in other Chinese-speaking locations such as Singapore. Each of the participating schools also utilized teachers who were part of Mainland China's Hanban (汉办 [Office of Teaching Chinese]) and Qiaoban (桥办 [Bridge Office]) guest teacher programs.[9]

Table 12.18 Teachers from China in the Four Participating Schools (2014)

School	Enrollment	Hanban Teachers	Qiaoban Teachers	Total Teachers
Duan Hua	Day: ~13,000 Evening: ~2,700	12	22	250
Chhong Cheng	3–4,000	6	2	97
Min Sheng	~1,400	10	–	50
Guang Zhao	~1,600	10	6	55

The assistant director of the Foundation of Associations of Chinese in Cambodia reports approximately 100 Hanban teachers and around 50 Qiaoban teachers countrywide, who apply directly through the Foundation (personal communication, January 15, 2015). A smaller number of mainland teachers apply directly to individual schools. Moreover, although formerly a significant number of teachers from Taiwan taught in Cambodia, currently there are few. The trend toward China-based guest teachers follows a broader engagement with China and corresponding weakening of Cambodia-Taiwan relations. Moreover, because of low local salaries, few teachers from Taiwan, Hong Kong, or Singapore are attracted to jobs in Cambodia.

As Table 12.18 indicates, despite significant numbers of China-trained teachers within the school system, the majority of teachers are Sino-Cambodian. Because these teachers are native speakers of one of the five southern dialects predominant in Cambodia, they are non-native Mandarin speakers in ways that differ from their dialect speakers counterparts in China. Whereas, say, Cantonese speakers in Guangdong Province may use their dialect at home, their education from the beginning is conducted in Mandarin, as are many of their other professional and public activities. By contrast, Sino-Cambodians differ widely in their exposure to standard Mandarin. They may be in and out of the Chinese education system, and their daily use of Mandarin outside of certain narrow confines (e.g., school and some businesses) is limited. However, Mandarin has become the lingua franca in the Cambodian Chinese community, linking the various dialect speakers. The Mainland Chinese context by contrast more closely resembles a classic diglossic situation, where there are often just two varieties present—the local dialect at home and Mandarin in school and many professional situations. In Cambodia, Mandarin serves as a bridge for the Chinese community as a whole to bridge multiple dialects.

On the Chinese Language Classroom

The pedagogy of the Sino–Cambodian schools is "traditional" in the sense that it is in many ways similar to the approach used in Mainland China. Most of the instruction is teacher centered and based on rote demonstration of material. Additionally, there is also a strong literacy emphasis with an assumption of an existing level of oral skills that is not necessarily present in Sino-Cambodian students. With closer relations with Mainland China generally and with Chinese educational institutions specifically, simplified characters have become the norm in Cambodia, and textbooks published in China are typical. However, some schools use materials published specifically for the Southeast Asian Chinese market. For example, Duan Hua School makes use of materials from the Malaysia Chinese Association (e.g., 华 文高二 *Huawen Gaoer* [Chinese for second year high school]) as well as locally produced texts (Yang, 2015). The curriculum in all four surveyed schools contained elements of traditional studies, including classical reading selections, poetry, calligraphy, and traditional Chinese music.

Figure 12.3 Ming Sheng School Classroom, Phnom Penh
Source: Dana Scott Bourgerie.

As part of my general survey of the four schools, I observed classes in each school. The following is an outline of one such observation in Duan Hua School, Level 3 courses, on January 2, 2015:

1. Students stand to greet teacher
2. Recitation of Poem (孔雀东南飞 *kongque dongnan fei* [Peacock Flies Southeast])
3. Explication and discussion of poem, student participation
4. Character writing on whiteboard, work on stroke order
5. Performance of comic dialogue (相声 *xiangsheng*) by two "star" students

In addition to Duan Hua School, I observed classes at the other three schools where I conducted the surveys (Minsheng, Chhong Cheng, and Guang Zhao). Practices at these schools varied, but the Duan Hua School pattern was fairly typical, although as the largest school among the Phnom Penh schools, Duan Hua has the most resources and the most fully developed curriculum. The teaching approaches were similar to my observations in Mainland Chinese schools, although young guest teachers from China were more likely to experiment with interactive teaching not common in China. Besides foreign language instruction and the government-mandated Khmer language instruction, instruction in other classes was in Mandarin Chinese.

Outside of class (for example, in hallways and on the playground), I noted a good deal of code mixing (Mandarin, some dialect, and Khmer) by students, but teachers were scrupulous in use of Mandarin with students. Virtually all the outward communication and office communication (signage, bulletin boards, etc.) was nearly exclusively in Chinese, despite the fact that most teachers were bilingual Sino-Cambodians.

9 Conclusion

Chinese education in Cambodia has evolved and adapted to political and cultural changes. Yet, it remains vital to the Chinese community and enrolling in a Chinese school is a clear measure of Chinese ethnic identity. Enrollments are steady, and schools provide an immersion experience for their students, with innovative guest-teacher programs in place. The medium of instruction has shifted from dialect to Standard Mandarin, which is used in all classes other than Khmer language and foreign language instruction. In terms of institutionalization, the use of Mandarin can be seen as strengthening the schools and increasing their appeal, in that this has become a language of business and professional opportunity. At the same time, it denies home dialects support from educational institutions, a rich source of linguistic input. A writing system that is used across dialects, however, is present, and the connection to Chinese culture through curriculum content and school practices also remains strong.

Despite increasing use of Khmer in the home, Chinese dialects continue to be used, often in tandem with Mandarin. Younger Sino-Cambodians report using both Khmer and a Chinese dialect with their ethnic Chinese friends. Emerging from the Khmer Rouge era when many Chinese downplayed or even hide their ethnicity, many younger people are now proud of their heritage and see their identity as a status marker. Moreover, with the increased status of the Chinese language regionally and internationally, a Chinese education is increasingly perceived as a professional asset worth pursuing.

Notes

1 The author would like to thank Dr. Claire Hitchins Chik for her many substantial suggestions and her meticulous editing of this chapter.
2 The Chinese census does not provide numbers on dialect speakers; to estimate the current number of dialect speakers, the table assumes the relative percentages of speakers in Yuan's survey.
3 The terms "Khmer" and "Cambodian" are often used interchangeably when referring to language or ethnicity. Cambodian is also used to refer to citizenship. Hence, minority populations (e.g., Chinese, Cham, and Vietnamese) are also Cambodians.
4 Although it is now conventional to use standard Pinyin Romanization for Chinese words when representing Chinese words in English, certain words commonly follow dialect spelling, especially Cantonese, which was long the dominant form of Chinese in Western countries. For example, *Kejia* in English often follows the Cantonese pronunciation *Hakka*, whereas Fujianese is often rendered according its own dialect pronunciation *Hokkien*. The Chaozhou dialect is frequently spelled according to its dialect pronunciation *Teochew*.
5 There are various estimates for the number of each Chinese ethnolinguistic group in Cambodia. Filippi (2008, p. 57) give the following breakdown: Chaozhou, 181,000; Cantonese, 10,000; Hainan, 13,000; Hakka, 8,000; and Fujian, 5,000. Other surveys (Willmott, 1967, p. 18) suggest a larger percentage of Cantonese.
6 Tea and Nov (2009, pp. 264–265) give a somewhat different inventory based on 2006 interviews with Chinese Association leaders. Apart from some of the more major schools (see Table 12.7) such as those in the capital, the situation is fairly fluid, with schools opening and closing periodically.
7 The non-student group included 62 respondents, ranging in age from 20–80 years. Most of this group were small-business people and middle-class professionals.
8 It is important to note here that the survey used the Chinese term 华 *hua* for ethnic Chinese instead of the term 汉 *han*, used in mainland China, or 中国人 *zhongguoren*, which implies Chinese nationality. 华 *hua* is the most common term in Southeast Asia for Chinese ethnicity.
9 These two programs (Hanban, 2014a, 2014b) are part of China's Office of Teaching Chinese (国家汉办) overseas outreach program. Both programs allow Chinese as a Second Language teachers (mostly young teachers) to gain experience worldwide.

References

Bourgerie, D. S. (n.d.). Dana Scott Bourgerie [Web site]. Retrieved from http://bourgerie.byu.edu

Edwards, P. (2009). The Ethnic Chinese in Cambodia. In S. Hean (Ed.), *Ethnic groups of Cambodia* (Vol. 2009, pp. 174–280). Phnom Penh Cambodia: Center for Advanced Studies.

Ekholm, M., & Trier, U. P. (1987). The concept of institutionalization: Some remarks. In M. B. Miles, M. Ekholm, & R. Vandenberghe (Eds.), *Lasting school improvement: Exploring the process of institutionalization* (pp. 13–21). Leuven, Belgium: Acco.

Filippi, J-M. (2008). *Recherches préliminaires sur les langues des minorités du Cambodge.* Phnom Penh: UNESCO. Retrieved from http://unesdoc.unesco.org/images/0019/001901/190146f.pdf

Foundation of Associations of Chinese in Cambodia 柬华理事总会 (Ed.). (2010). *The Foundation of Associations of Chinese in Cambodia 柬华理事总会成立20周年.* Phnom Penh, Cambodia: Author.

Foundation of Associations of Chinese in Cambodia. (2014). *Sino-Cambodian business information handbook.* Phnom Penh, Cambodia: Author.

Hanban. (2014a). Confucius Institute Headquarters [Web site]. Retrieved from http://english.hanban.org

Hanban. (2014b). 汉语桥 [Hanyu qiao; Chinese Bridge] [Web site]. Retrieved from http://www.hanban. edu.cn/chinesebridge

Harris, P. (2007). *A record of Cambodia: The land and its people* (P. Harris, Trans.). Chiang Mai, Thailand: Silkworm Books.

Lai, H. M. (2004a). Chinese schools in America before World War II. In H. M. Lai (Ed.), *Becoming Chinese American* (pp. 271–308). New York, NY: Altamira Press.

Lai, H. M. (2004b). Chinese schools in America after World War II. In H. M. Lai (Ed.), *Becoming Chinese American* (pp. 309–362). New York, NY: Altamira Press.

Li, F. (1973). Languages and dialects of China. *Journal of Chinese Linguistics, 1*(1), 1–13.

National Bureau of Statistics of the People's Republic of China. (2014). Sixth National Population Census of the People's Republic of China. Retrieved from https://en.wikipedia.org/wiki/National_Bureau_of_Statistics_of_China

Pan, L. (1990). *Sons of the Yellow Emperor: A history of the Chinese diaspora* (1st U.S. ed.). Boston, MA: Little, Brown.

Pan, L. (1999). *The encyclopedia of the Chinese overseas.* Cambridge, MA: Harvard University Press.

Ramsey, R. (1987). *The languages of China.* Princeton, NJ: Princeton University Press.

Tournais, A., & Paulus, A. (1884). Le Royaume de Cambodge. *Revue Maritime et Coloniale, 82,* 517–590.

Schliesinger, J. (2011a). *Ethnic groups of Cambodia, Volume 1: Introduction and overview* (Vol. 1). Thailand: White Lotus.

Schliesinger, J. (2011b). *Ethnic groups of Cambodia, Volume 3: Profile of the Austro-Thai-and Sinitic-speaking peoples* (Vol. 3). Thailand: White Lotus.

Steinberg, D. (1959). *Cambodia.* New Haven, CT: HRAF Press.

Suryadinata, L. (2013). Southeast Asian policies toward the ethnic Chinese: A revisit. In C.-B. Tan (Ed.), *Routledge handbook of the Chinese diasopora* (pp. 274–289). New York, NY: Routledge.

Tea, V., & Nov, S. (2009). The Ethnic Chinese in Cambodia: Social integration and renaissance of identity. In C. F. A. Study (Ed.), *Ethnic Chinese of Cambodia* (pp. 235–280). Phnom Penh, Cambodia: Center for Advanced Study. Whitaker, D., Heimann, J., McDonald, J., Martindale, K., Shenn, R., & Townsend, C. (1973). *Area handbook for the Khmer Republic (Cambodia).* Washington, DC: Foreign Areas Studies of the American Univeristy.

Willmott, B. (2007). Varieties of Chinese experience in the Pacific. *Centre for the Study of the Chinese Southern Diaspora (CSCSD) Occasional Papers, 1,* 35–42.

Willmott, W. (1967). *The Chinese in Cambodia.* Vancouver, Canada: Publications Centre, University of British Columbia.

Yang, H. (2015). *A practical self-study course.* Phnom Penh, Cambodia: Author.

Yen, C. (1985). *Coolies and mandarins: China's protection of overseas Chinese during the late Ch'ing period (1851–1911).* Singapore: Singapore University Press.

Yuan, J. (1983). *Summary of Chinese dialects (Han yu fang yan gai yao)* (2nd ed.). Beijing, PR of China: 文字改革出版社: 新华书店北京发行所发行 Wenzi gaige chubanshe: Xinhua shudian Beijing faxingsuo faxing.

13

Innovation vs. Tradition in Language Education

A Case of Japanese Heritage Language Instruction in Chile

Saeid Atoofi and Francisco Naranjo Escobar

1 Introduction

This chapter examines two Japanese schools in Santiago, Chile, that cater to preschool and elementary school children of Japanese background. Following Ekholm and Trier (1987) and Miles and Louis (1987), we examine the factors that contribute to the stability of these schools. In this sense, we do not approach institutionalization as the introduction of an innovation into an institution (as do Ekholm & Trier, 1987, p. 13), but rather take the establishment of these institutions in Chile as an innovation that was accomplished in the past and has continued for several years. With that in mind, we examine some of the factors that have contributed to this continuity, particularly those factors that bear on HL teaching and learning. Specifically, we focus on the "ideologies, values, and beliefs" (Ekholm & Trier, 1987, p. 21) of participants as they pertain to the curriculum and teaching approach used in the schools, as well as the ways in which they impact issues of legitimacy in the eyes of the parents. In terms of the students, we examine the relationship between legitimacy and issues of fit or appropriateness of instruction. Additionally, we consider the role that foreign governments and other external entities play in institutionalizing heritage language (HL) instruction and defining what it means to be a speaker of the HL.

2 Literature Review

Teaching Japanese as a Heritage Language

Similar to other HL populations around the world, there is a wide range of profiles among Japanese HL speakers. While some speakers approach native speaker abilities, many do not. There is also another group that has only cultural ties to Japan and lacks any linguistic competency in Japanese. This relates to a difference described in the literature between "narrow definition" HL students who speak the language with varying degrees of proficiency, and "broad definition" HL students who have a familial connection to the language but did not grow up in a home where the HL was spoken (Polinsky & Kagan, 2007).

Japanese as an HL has a long history in many parts of the world, especially in the United States. Doerr and Lee (2009) report that in the U.S. alone there were about 86 weekend Japanese language schools, called *hoshuko* (supplementary schools), as of 2008, which these authors describe as follows:

> They are community-based schools that provide 'Japanese' children in the 1st to 9th grade (ages six to 15) who go to a local school or an international school during the week with part of the education they would have received in Japanese compulsory education, using the Japanese government-prescribed curriculum and the Japanese government-certified textbooks. The main subject matter is *kokugo* (language arts of Japanese national language).
>
> *(p. 426)*

Kokugo signifies a language arts approach to the study of Japanese (Doerr & Lee, 2009; Lee, 2010), and stands in contrast to *nihongo*, which denotes Japanese language as a linguistic system composed of grammatical rules, vocabulary items, and phonological features (Gottlieb, 2012). As such, while *nihongo* is usually involved when teaching Japanese as a second language, *kokugo* is reserved for native speakers of Japanese. Given that narrow-definition HLLs have been exposed to the language to some extent, though not as much as native speakers, the *nihongo* approach would be inappropriate. The *kokugo* approach is also inappropriate because children in Japan have developed their basic grammatical competence and age-appropriate oral proficiency (Basic Interpersonal Communication Skills) by the time they start schooling. Based on these already developed skills, the *kokugo* curriculum primarily teaches reading and writing using basal readers. In addition, Chinese characters that are introduced in each grade in *kokugo* textbooks were selected for children who live in Japan, based on their day-to-day experiences. For example, characters in the first-grade textbook such as "bamboo" and "rice field," are present in children's daily life in Japan and are therefore easy to understand and remember. This is not the case for JHL children living in foreign countries (Douglas, 2005; Masako Douglas, personal communication, May 10, 2016). For these and other reasons, for HL children living in other countries, an HL-specific approach is necessary. Since the 1990s such an approach, sometimes called Japanese Heritage Language (JHL) education, has indeed been developed and implemented in some schools (Doerr & Lee, 2009; Kano, 2013; Uriu & Douglas, this volume). Drawing on the best practices in HL teaching, JHL education aims to build on HL learners' bilingual and bicultural skills.

Many of the Japanese language schools around the world that adhere to *kokugo* receive their curricula directly from the Ministry of Education, Culture, Sports, Science, and Technology (MEXT) in Tokyo, and many even receive direct financial and administrative aid from this ministry. Primarily, MEXT seeks to streamline the education of children in the Japanese community abroad so they can fit into the system upon returning to Japan. As such, the content and goals of the curriculum are fixed for each level. In many MEXT-sponsored schools, learners not only learn the Japanese language, but also all other content areas of the MEXT curriculum, such as math, sciences, and history. In addition, there is an emphasis on cultural education to familiarize students with the Japanese lifestyle and cultural practices.

Not all Japanese schools abroad follow the MEXT curriculum; those who use a JHL approach work independently of the MEXT framework, and rather than viewing students as potentially returning to Japan, instead views them as bilingual, bicultural residents of the host country (Nakajima, 1997; see also Uriu & Douglas, this volume). JHL curricula and materials are developed independently of MEXT by individual schools to meet the linguistic and affective needs of their students (Doerr & Lee, 2009).

The Japanese in Chile

The Japanese have a long history of immigration in South American countries such as Brazil and Peru (see Zampaulo, this volume). By comparison, such a history is rather short and limited in Chile, which makes it interesting from the point of view of this chapter. The first documented presence of a small Japanese community in Chile appears in the census of 1903 (Masterson & Funada-Classen, 2004). This community grew steadily throughout the first half of the twentieth century, reaching its peak in 1940 with just under 1,000 individuals (Aróstica, 2012). However, Masterson and Funada-Classen (2004) point out that from an ethnic perspective many of these individuals were highly acculturated and of mixed Chilean-Japanese parentage, since most Japanese immigrants were males, and by some estimates as many as half of them at that time married Chilean women. Because of small numbers, the Japanese community in Chile did not develop the kinds of associations and community organizations that were characteristic of countries such as Brazil, Peru, and Argentina, which had much larger Japanese heritage populations (Masterson & Funada-Classen, 2004, p. 107).

The current Japanese population in Chile consists of roughly 1,500 expatriates (referred to as "residents" by the Japanese government) and 2,000 "Nikkei" (also called "descendants") who are permanent residents in Chile and includes second- and third-generation Japanese (Ministry of Foreign Affairs of Japan, 2015). Both groups share a common cultural identity, which they express through particular cultural practices that serve to differentiate them from mainstream Chileans as well as other communities, including those of Asian descent. Be that as it may, the Nikkei community has in many ways blended into Chilean society, while maintaining certain Japanese traditions and practices within their households. The essence of this biculturalism is captured in the following quote:

> In our case, we are **Chileans with a Japanese "something,"** just like other Nikkei who are North Americans or Cubans, but who also possess that same "something." For us to lose those special attributes and that typical Chilean idiosyncrasy would be a disaster in every way.
>
> *(Takeda, 2010, January 12; emphasis in original)*

Some Nikkei have an active presence in the Pan-American Nikkei Association (PANA), an organization that seeks to promote international cooperation among this community, supports research on Nikkei history, and promotes the dissemination of Japanese culture in each country (Hirabayashi & Kikumura-Yano, 2002). Also in line with these goals, a number of Chilean Nikkei are actively involved in the Nikkei Chronicles, an international writing project that seeks to document the experiences of the Nikkei community around the world (Discover Nikkei, n.d.). In contrast with Nikkei in other Latin American countries, Chilean Nikkei have low rates of participation in the recent phenomenon whereby people of Japanese heritage in different parts of the world return to Japan to work as *dekasegis* (Masterson & Funada-Classen, 2004). From the point of view of this chapter, this is significant in that it bears on the kind of language education that fits this population.

In terms of language, expatriates and Nikkei are different. Similar to many HL speakers across the globe, the second and third generations use the host language, Spanish in this case, as their language of choice, and if they know any Japanese, have problems switching into it. In an educational setting, the Chilean Nikkei largely fit the broad definition of HL learner. By contrast, the expatriates are largely native speakers, particularly the adults who are stationed in Chile for work reasons for a limited number of years.

3 Japanese Language Instruction in Chile

The first Japanese elementary school was opened in Santiago in 1939 offering three hours of instruction two days a week. World War II saw the closing of this school, which never reopened (Masterson & Funada-Classen, 2004, p. 105). But even while the school was operating, there was a sense that this was insufficient. In 1940, speaking at a conference for overseas Japanese organized by the Japanese government, Chozan Ota, a spokesman for the Chilean Japanese community, expressed worry that their children "were growing up without an opportunity to receive a genuine Japanese education or an appreciation for the culture of their ancestors" (Masterson & Funada-Classen, 2004, p. 105). This problem became more acute in the years following World War II.

Currently, Japanese instruction takes place in nine venues in Chile. These can be divided into institutes that teach Japanese as a foreign language, namely Universidad de Santiago de Chile, Universidad Austral de Chile, Universidad de Concepción, Universidad de La Serena, and the Tronwell Institute, and those that teach Japanese as a first or heritage language, namely Sociedad Japonesa de Beneficencia, Instituto Chileno-Japonés de Cultura, Sociedad Nikkei Valparaíso, Sanchago Nihonjin Gakkou (the Japanese School of Santiago, or JSS) and the Japanese Kindergarten (JKG). Only the last two institutions, namely JSS and JKG, will be the focus of the discussion that follows. Rather than the *hoshuko*, or supplementary schools discussed by Doerr and Lee (2009), which are found widely in the U.S., these are both full-time weekday schools.

4 The Settings

The information regarding JSS and JKG comes from direct observation made by the second author of this chapter and formal interviews with the schools' directors. At JSS, this author first worked as an intern and subsequently as an English language teacher, which gave him direct access as a participant/observer. At JKG, he was allowed to observe classroom interactions. The directors of JSS and JKG received a written interview questionnaire and were asked to send their responses by email. In the questionnaire, participants answered a battery of questions regarding the demography of their learners and teachers, the teaching methodology, cultural approaches, and assessment styles. Additional personnel were interviewed or contacted by email in order to supplement observations and clarify points; at JSS this included a secretary and some teachers, and at JKG, a teacher. We analyzed the data gathered from both institutions with particular reference to the framework of institutionalization, as discussed in a later section.

The Japanese School of Santiago

JSS is a K–8 school which runs from 8:30 in the morning until 4:30 in the afternoon on weekdays. Additionally, within the academic year the school runs workshops and social events aimed at replicating similar events in schools in Japan. Such events are exclusive to the Japanese community, and non-Japanese people require sponsorship to participate. Some of these events include the school's annual festival, the *undōkai* (sports festival), and the Japanese Bazar.

The school accommodates between 6 and 12 students per grade. Tuition is about 700 USD per month (calculated considering the USD/CLP exchange rate at the time of data collection), which is fairly expensive by Chilean standards. There is also a one-time enrollment fee of about the same amount and a bond of almost 500 USD, which is returned when the child leaves the school.

Many of the pupils' parents are expatriates who work for Japanese-owned companies with business relationships in Chile, while a very small group have parents who are residing indefinitely in Chile and have done so for more than one generation. At the time of this study, most of the students came from families where both parents were Japanese, though some also came from families with mixed backgrounds. The majority of students were Spanish dominant, including those whose families intended to go back to Japan. These families, like many affluent and even many middle-class Chilean families, employ Spanish-speaking nannies at home to look after their children. And of course, the children are widely exposed to Spanish via television, music, and so on. Hence, most of the students in JSS, expatriates and Nikkei alike, received significant linguistic input in Spanish. The expatriate children, in addition, received input in Japanese in the home environment from Japanese-speaking family members. As such, from a linguistic perspective they fit the narrow definition of HLLs. On the other hand, the Nikkei students mostly enter the school as broad definition HL learners, with an ancestral familial connection to Japanese, rather than a linguistic one. The expectation for these students is that they will fit in and do what it takes to keep up. This is in keeping with the egalitarian ethos of the Japanese educational system, whereby all children are assumed to have the potential to develop the necessary skills to succeed at school, without the need for tracking by ability (Ishikida, 2005).

Because JSS provides an immersion experience, children whose Japanese proficiency is low are eventually able to grow their skills and to a large extent integrate into the school, provided they start school early enough, preferably the first grade. Given the schools' all-Japanese curriculum, children who complete their elementary education at JSS and wish to enroll in a Chilean high school, will then need help with their Spanish, particularly in reading and writing, to keep up with their non-Japanese Chilean peers.

As discussed earlier, MEXT is directly involved in many Japanese schools worldwide, including JSS. In keeping with a strict plan of study assigned by MEXT, the JSS curriculum offers grade-appropriate instruction in all the relevant subjects up to eighth grade (per the Chilean and American educational systems, and equivalent to the second year of junior high school in the Japanese educational system, or *Chūgakkō*) and content materials are similar to those in Japanese schools utilized for the corresponding age group. Japanese is the medium of instruction in all classes except for Spanish and English, though at times Spanish is used by students to interact with the staff, such as administrators and janitors. Teachers were brought in from Japan to teach different subject matters for periods of three years at a time. The selection for teaching abroad is very competitive in Japan, and usually the best teachers will have the opportunity to teach in schools such as JSS. The Spanish subject language teachers were hired locally. The English subject teachers were native speakers of English, usually from Australia (with the exception of the second author of this chapter, who is a native Chilean; see Methodology section).

Regarding students, an observation by Kano (2013) may also be relevant in the context of JSS. This study of a Japanese after-hours school in the U.S. raises important concerns regarding the ways in which the MEXT curriculum positions both populations of children, expatriates and permanent residents, relative to their peers in Japan and to each other: "MEXT policy documents, such as the website, project a deficit discourse about overseas Japanese students who are compared with their monolingual peers in Japan, through such expression as 'they need to catch up with their peers in Japan'" (Kano, 2013, p. 104). Children residing temporarily overseas as part of an expatriate community are compared unfavorably with those residing in Japan, while children who are permanent residents in the host country are, in turn, compared unfavorably with expatriate students "within this same deficit model based on a monolingual standard" (Kano, 2013, p. 104). Thus a hierarchy of deficit is established, with monolingual children residing in Japan setting the standard, expatriate overseas residents falling short of this standard, and Nikkei students following behind both these groups.

The Japanese Kindergarten

Situated in Ñuñoa, one of the municipalities of Santiago, JKG serves 10 to 18 preschool children with profiles that are very similar to those of the students in JSS. Children attend school for five hours a day during the weekdays, occasionally complimented with another two hours of extra-curricular activity. The preschool children learned basic Japanese language and engaged in small projects related to Japanese arts and culture, such as practicing traditional Japanese calligraphy or making origami. Communications pertaining to school administration and interactions in the classroom were conducted mostly in Japanese, even though the director was fluent in Spanish. At the time of this study, the staff consisted of a mix of Chilean and Japanese teachers and administrators.

5 The Connection between Curriculum and Ideology

Research identifies autonomy of schools as one of the important factors contributing to the continuity and stability of innovations over time and across institutions (Fullan & Watson, 2000; Martinez & Quartz, 2012). However, dependence on governmentally funded and administered programs such as MEXT, in the case of Japanese schools, is one way to guarantee the fidelity of traditional practices of language learning and teaching over generations and across all learners. Furthermore, a school's direct educational and administrative relationship with MEXT is the most important way of ensuring that children who plan to return to Japan will be able to make a successful re-entry (see Wang, 2014, for a similar situation in early Chinese HL instruction in the U.S., where classical Chinese was taught in preparation for students to continue their education in China). The MEXT curriculum is also the most important way of insuring the legitimacy of a Japanese language program in the eyes of most Japanese parents, including those of Nikkei children. Thus, while adhering to the MEXT-prescribed curriculum can, at first, appear to be motivated primarily by financial considerations, in that it entails receiving funds from the Japanese government, it is more than that.

Based on an ethnographic study at a weekend Japanese-language school in the United States, Doerr and Lee (2009) observe that because many Japanese parents went to school in Japan and followed the government-prescribed curriculum, this is their point of reference and what they value and see as a legitimate educational experience for their children. A similar situation is described by Carreira and Rodríguez (2011) for an Argentine Spanish-language school in Los Angeles that follows a strict Argentine curriculum, and confers a high-school diploma that is accepted in a number of Spanish-speaking countries. Such examples are stark reminders that the institutionalization of HL programs may not so much depend on the assumed use of modern methods of language instruction as on the subjective language ideologies of the participating actors, particularly the parents. Crucially, the immersion approach used in JSS, which is geared to integrating the students into the Japanese educational system by ensuring that they are immersed in the same environment as their peers in Japan, is ideologically acceptable to all participants, those who are planning to return to Japan, and those who are not. To issues of institutionalization, this speaks to the importance of legitimacy as it relates to the ideology of the parents. If parents believe in the mission and practices of a school, they are more likely to send their children there, even if the teaching approach isn't the most appropriate. In the case of JSS and JKG, this belief connects to following accepted practices in the home country, regardless of whether there is the intention of returning to that country.

Such practices are not restricted to the purely linguistic and academic. In both JSS and JKG, classroom interactions between Japanese students and their teachers focused attention on gestures and body language as part of the interactional discourse. Students were not only routinely and explicitly instructed to communicate with adults in a courteous manner, but also to bow upon greeting, avoid direct gaze with their teachers, and abstain from kissing their peers or their teachers on the cheek. For HL students raised in Chile, this is not part of their experience in that it contrasts sharply with cultural practices in many South American countries where physical contact is an important part of communicating effectively in daily routines. In fact, Chileans, young and adult, routinely hug and kiss upon greeting, saying goodbye, and to show sympathy and affection (see Atoofi, 2015, for the role of body language in language teaching). Once again, the kind of attention given to teaching gestures and body language to HL students at JSS and JKG evidences an orientation toward the country of origin and immersing HL learners in the same environment as their peers in Japan. In keeping with this idea, the director of JSS outlined the curriculum as follows:

> In the first and second year the focus is on learning how to speak correctly and courteously with instructors and adults. In the third and fourth year, they learn expressions of courtesy [formulaic language]. In the fifth and sixth years they learn *keigo* and *sonkeigo* [honorific and respectful] language. In middle school, they study the grammar of honorifics and the way to use it in Japanese interactions.

This focus is also in line with the parents' idea of HL education, along with following the MEXT curriculum.

6 The Connection between the Curriculum, the Heritage Culture, and the Classroom Environment

Yoshimi (2009) argues that in the context of Japanese language pedagogy, even the most honest attempts to create pragmatically relevant curricula often fail to capture the interactivity and naturalness found in the encounters of everyday life. The separation between *kokugo* and *nihongo* indicates that for Japanese, there is a clear line between knowing a language (*nihongo*) and living it (*kokugo*). In our interview responses, both JSS and JKG participants stated that their main aim was the teaching of Japanese culture and the preservation of customs and ways of thinking of native speakers.

As has been systematically demonstrated in discourse analytical studies, all objects and spaces, including furniture, rooms, books, TV screens, tools, and so on, are part of any discourse (Nevile, Haddington, Heinemann, & Rauniomaa, 2014). Similarly, in our settings, Japanese patterns of communication were not solely present in the words and grammar being taught, or even the customs and cultural activities presented, but also in the material objects that formed part of the environment. For example, in JSS, the classroom furniture and layout matched those in Japanese classrooms. The students' chairs, the podium used by the teachers, and other classroom fixtures such as tables and wall decorations were similar to those found in typical Japanese classrooms.

By comparison to American classrooms, Japanese classrooms tend to be more teacher centered. According to one study, in Japanese classrooms teachers lead class activities 74% of the time, versus 46% in the U.S. (Stevenson & Stigler, 1994). In this educational context, the seating arrangement supports this interaction, with the podium establishing the leading role of the teacher. At JSS and JKG this arrangement and, more generally, pattern of behavior was also expected from non-Japanese teachers who worked at the school. For instance, English and Spanish language teachers were expected to use the same pedagogical approach as in the subject classes taught in Japanese and enforce cultural codes between teachers and students during classroom interactions.

Despite lack of any institutional connection between them, both JSS and JKG made extensive use of Japanese material objects in their establishments, which were brought in directly from Japan. By one account, even the pencils students used daily in the classes in JSS were exactly the same as those used by their peers in schools in Japan. According to the director of JKG, educational objects from Japan were supplemented with available materials in Chile that were adapted for the school environment due to budget considerations.

The educational materials used in these sites were also very similar in both content and form to those in Japan. Books were regularly shipped in from Japan for JSS, and Japanese animations and cartoon illustrations were used as supplementary educational materials as well as visual aids during classroom activities in both venues. Animation figures, comic illustrations, and visual aids are the hallmark of Japanese instructional discourse. Evaluation and feedback for students' work also followed those in mainstream Japanese schools. Teachers used the same marking style in students' work as those in Japan. For example, correct answers in the students' work were marked with circles or "maru," while incorrect responses were indicated with crosses or "batsu." Similar color types as in Japanese schools were used to highlight key information and to emphasize new content.

All in all, both JSS and JKG show great fidelity to Japanese cultural norms along a wide range of parameters that go beyond language. In both locations, administrators, teachers, and parents supported this general approach to HL education as instantiated in the class environment, interactions between students and faculty, use of materials, and pedagogical practices. Within each institution, this speaks to the existence of "congruence between people, processes and environment," which is one of the five factors that account for institutionalization according to Buller, Saxberg, and Smith (1985, as cited in Miles & Louis, 1987, p. 34).

7 Discussion of Issues of Institutionalization

JSS and JKG are well structured from the point of view of attending to the needs of the majority of the students, who expect to return to Japan. Though these students speak Japanese at home, they need the kind of rigorous educational experience provided by *kokugo* in order to acquire age-appropriate skills and knowledge that will make it possible for them to integrate into Japanese society. A second, and much smaller, population of students are Nikkei children, who are permanent residents in Chile. While these students receive limited input in Japanese in the home environment, if any, they manage to learn Japanese and keep up their studies, albeit with difficulty. However, the schools, particularly JSS, are not a good fit for them because the pedagogical focus is not on educating bicultural and bilingual individuals. Clearly, for Nikkei children, an HL pedagogical approach would be more suitable.

This raises two interrelated questions that are important to our study of institutionalization: (1) Given the imperfect fit between *kokugo*, as instantiated in JSS and JKG, and the objective needs of Chilean Nikkei, why do parents send their children to these schools? and (2) Why is JHL instruction not available in Santiago?

Regarding the first question, we believe that the legitimacy afforded by a MEXT-endorsed curriculum, in combination with a parental ideology that privileges a monolingual approach to language instruction, may lead parents to look past the shortcomings of *kokugo*. Lack of awareness of the concept of JHL education may also play a role in this regard. In effect, parents of Nikkei children may think that when it comes to teaching their children Japanese, there are only two options, *kokugo* or *nihongo*, and they may favor the former, by virtue of their familial connection to Japan.

Lack of awareness may also bear on the second question, that is, it may help explain why there are no JHL schools in Santiago. The existence of widely accepted, well-organized and well-supported *kokugo* schools such as JSS and JKG, may keep parents of Nikkei children from conceiving of other instructional options, let alone pursuing them. Effectively, these parents may not see a need for JHL education. A key concept in in the process of institutionalization, *need*, pertains to the "existence of a recognized problem, need, chronic service difficulty or crisis which an innovation may solve" (Miles & Louis, 1987, p. 39). The perception of need and the kind of action that follows from it is particularly important in the case of JHL. Developed independently of MEXT by individual schools, JHL schools require a great deal of parental initiative and investments of time, as well as know-how about pedagogical and administrative matters. They also require local leadership and resources (see Uriu & Douglas, this volume). Without an awareness of the need for JHL and its particular value for Nikkei children, the necessary ingredients needed to implement and sustain JHL schools may never materialize.

A logical starting point for gathering these ingredients are the Chilean Nikkei who are already actively involved in ventures such as PANA and the Nikkei Chronicles. These individuals have a sense of their uniqueness relative to the two populations they straddle, namely, Chileans and Japanese nationals, which is one of the foundational ingredients of an HL education. They also have access to key resources by virtue of their participation in these and other ventures.

All in all, this situation underscores the importance of further research on three issues of institutionalization. First, there is a need to better understand how parental ideologies surrounding language and education are formed and the role they play in implementing and sustaining instruction for HL-speaking children. Second, research on the concept of *need* as it applies to parents and other stakeholders in the schooling process, is also in order. In particular, it would be important to understand the conditions that give rise to an awareness of the advantages of JHL instruction and subsequently lead to its implementation. Further work is also needed on the role that foreign governments play in the institutionalization of instruction for HL learners.

In the framework of institutionalization, foreign governments are part of what Miles and Louis (1987) term the "external context," which includes variables that positively influence institutionalization (p. 39). In the present case, MEXT is a source of supporting infrastructure, legitimacy, and stability. With clearly defined and well-executed educational and administrative practices, MEXT also serves to codify Japanese instruction for children of Japanese ancestry in general; recall that JKG follows very similar practices to JSS despite lacking an official connection to MEXT. Furthermore, as the arbiter of what gets taught and learned, MEXT also helps define what it means to be a speaker of Japanese in the eyes of Chilean parents of Japanese heritage. As we have seen, this is often premised on a deficit perspective and a hierarchy where the Nikkei are below both their peers in Japan and the expatriate community in Chile. Oriented towards Japan, such a perspective is not optimal from the point of view of educating Nikkei children to function effectively in Chilean society nor is it oriented towards helping them develop their bilingual and bicultural identity. As Carreira and Kagan (2011) have shown, for such children, a community-based curriculum, rooted in local practices and perspectives, represents an effective way to achieve these goals.

So, given the differences between the expatriate students and Nikkei students, how can both populations have their needs met? Kano (2013) describes a program in the U.S. that offers a solution for the Chilean situation. She reports on a weekend Japanese school, the Princeton

Community Japanese School, that provides classes for a variety of learners. In order to serve these students effectively, the school is comprised of two divisions:

> Division 1 is hoshu-ko, an officially recognized supplementary school formally supported by MEXT. Division 2 is called the Princeton Course, which offers Japanese classes for English dominant bilingual children and adults who have had no exposure to Japanese. While Division 1 is in compliance with the MEXT regulations, including a principal sent and paid for my MEXT, Division 2, the Princeton Course, is entitled to exercise autonomy, which allows PCJLS to implement flexible and varied programs to serve learners with diverse needs. While Division 1 uses the same textbooks that are used in Japan, Division 2 draws on the original syllabi, and uses original teaching materials. In this way, Division 1 prepares students to return smoothly to a school or college in Japan. Division 2 prepares students to sit for US-based exams, such as the Japanese Advanced Placement test and the Japanese SAT II subject test.
>
> *(p. 107)*

8 Conclusions

As stated at the outset, our goal for this chapter was not to approach institutionalization as the introduction of an innovation into an institution (as do Ekholm & Trier, 1987, p. 13), but rather to take the establishment of these institutions themselves as an innovation that was accomplished in the past and has continued for several years. Our research suggests that JSS and JKG are highly stable and successful. From an institutional perspective, much of their success and stability connects to the expatriate population. In particular, both schools provide the kind of rigorous and immersive educational experience needed by children who are planning to return to Japan, and in the case of JSS, the MEXT curriculum also provides articulation with the Japanese educational system. Accordingly, both JSS and JKG show a great deal of fidelity to Japanese cultural norms and practices along a wide range of parameters, not just language. Administrators, teachers, and parents all support this approach, which is instantiated in the class environment, interactions between students and faculty, use of materials, and pedagogical practices.

For students of Japanese ancestry who are permanent residents of Chile, JKG and JSS present two significant benefits. First, given the limited choices for studying Japanese in Santiago, they offer children the valuable opportunity to develop their heritage language and culture and connect with others of similar background. And second, these schools enjoy a great deal of prestige and legitimacy, which makes them attractive—i.e., worth investing in. Recall that JSS and JKG are fairly expensive by Chilean standards. However, as we have seen, these schools are not a good fit when it comes to preparing children to function effectively in Chilean society and fostering a bicultural and bilingual sense of self. A better option in that regard is found in the JHL approach. In terms of creating the conditions associated with the implementation of this approach, Chileans who are active in Nikkei ventures such as PANA can play a leadership role in raising awareness of the need for specialized HL instruction and the development of local know-how and support.

All of this, of course, may not be confined to the present case or even to Japanese as an HL, but may apply to other languages that rely on the support of the homeland where the language is spoken. As we have seen, from the point of view of institutionalization, such support is immensely valuable, but it is not problem-free. In particular, for parents, the legitimacy enjoyed by the ideologies and practices endorsed by the home country may obscure issues of bad fit at the local level and may obviate the need for an alternative instructional model, along the lines of a JHL approach. Other key players, such as foreign governments, may find themselves in a similar situation: they may not see a compelling need for or find value in investing in an HL instructional model. In light of this, raising awareness of the value of such a model among parents and foreign governments (for example, in schools of education and among policy makers in the home country), may prove fruitful from the point of view of institutionalizing instruction that best responds to the needs of HL learners.

References

Aróstica, V. (2012). Un silencioso proceso de aculturación. Testimonios de inmigrantes japonesas en Chile, 1950–2010 [A silent acculturation process: Testimonials of Japanese female immigrants to Chile, 1950–2010]. *Journal of Hemisferic and Polar Studies, 4*(1), 1–31.

Atoofi, S. (2015). Second language acquisition: An edusemiotic approach. In M. A. Peteres (Ed.), *Encyclopedia of educational philosophy and theory*. Singapore: Springer. doi: 10.1007/978-981-287-532-7_23-1

Buller, P. F., Saxberg, B. O., & Smith, H. L. (1985). Institutionalization of planned organizational change: A model and review of the literature. In L. D. Goodstein & J. W. Pfeiffer (Eds.), *The 1985 annual: Developing human resources* (pp. 189–199). Tucson, AZ: University Associates.

Carreira, M., & Kagan, O. (2011). The results of the National Heritage Language Survey: Implications for teaching, curriculum design, and professional development. *Foreign Language Annals, 44*(1), 40–64.

Carreira, M., & Rodríguez, R. (2011). Filling the void: Community Spanish language programs in Los Angeles serving to preserve the language. *The Heritage Language Journal, 8*(2), 1–16. Retrieved from http://www.heritagelanguages.org/

Discover Nikkei. (n.d.). Nikkei chronicles [Web page]. Retrieved from http://www.discovernikkei.org/en/journal/chronicles/

Doerr, N. M., & Lee, K. (2009). Contesting heritage: Language, legitimacy, and schooling at a weekend Japanese-language school in the United States. *Language and Education, 23*(5), 425–441.

Douglas, M. O. (2005). Pedagogical theories and approaches to teach young learners of Japanese as a heritage language. *Heritage Language Journal, 3*(1), 60–82. Retrieved from http://www.heritagelanguages.org/

Ekholm, M. R., & Trier, U. P. (1987). The concept of institutionalization: Some remarks. In M. B. Miles, M. R. Ekholm, & R. Vandenberghe (Eds.), *Lasting school improvement: Exploring the process of institutionalization* (pp. 13–21). Leuven, Belgium: Acco.

Fullan, M., & Watson, N. (2000). School-based management: Reconceptualizing to improve learning outcomes. *School Effectiveness and School Improvement, 11*(4), 453–473.

Gottlieb, N. (2012). *Language policy in Japan: The challenge of change*. Cambridge: Cambridge University Press.

Hirabayashi, J., & Kikumura-Yano, A. (2002). The Pan-American Nikkei Association: A report on the tenth and eleventh meetings. *Amerasia Journal, 28*(2), 147–157.

Ishikida, M. Y. (2005). *Japanese education in the 21st century*. Lincoln, NE: iUniverse. Retrieved from http://www.usjp.org/jpeducation_en/jpEdContents_en.html

Kano, N. (2013). Japanese community schools: New pedagogy for a changing population. In O. García, Z. Zakharia, & B. Otcu (Eds.), *Bilingual community education and multilingualism: Beyond heritage languages in a global city* (pp. 99–112). Bristol, UK: Multilingual Matters.

Lee, Y. (2010). *The ideology of kokugo: Nationalizing language in modern Japan* (M. Hirano Hubbard, Trans.). Honolulu, Hawaii: University of Hawai'i Press.

Martinez, R. A., & Quartz, K. H. (2012). Zoned for change: A historical case study of the Belmont Zone of Choice. *Teachers College Record, 114*(10), 1–40.

Masterson, D. M., & Funada-Classen, S. (2004). *The Japanese in Latin America*. Champaign, IL: University of Illinois Press.

Miles, M. B., & Louis, K. (1987). Research on institutionalization: A reflective review. In M. Miles, M. Ekholm, & R. Vandenberghe (Eds.), *Lasting school improvement: Exploring the process of institutionalization* (pp. 25–44). Leuven, Belgium: Acco.

Ministry of Foreign Affairs of Japan. (2015). Chiri Kyōwa Koku; Kiso Dēta [Republic of Chile; Basic data]. Retrieved from http://www.mofa.go.jp/mofaj/area/chile/data.html#section6

Nakajima, K. (1997). Keishogo to shiteno nihongo joron [Introduction to Japanese as a heritage language education]. In K. Nakajima & M. Suzuki (Eds.), *Japanese as a heritage language: The Canadian experience* (pp. 3–20). Ontario, Canada: Soleil Publishing Inc.

Nevile, M., Haddington, P., Heinemann, T., & Rauniomaa, M. (Eds.). (2014). *Interacting with objects: Language, materiality, and social activity*. Amsterdam: John Benjamins Publishing Company.

Polinsky, M., & Kagan, O. (2007). Heritage languages: In the "wild" and in the classroom. *Language and Linguistics Compass, 1*(5), 368–395.

Stevenson, H., & Stigler, J. W. (1994). *Learning gap: Why our schools are failing and what we can learn from Japanese and Chinese education*. New York, NY: Simon and Schuster.

Takeda, A. (2010, January 12). Chilean Nikkei identity [Web page]. Retrieved from http://www.discover nikkei.org/en/journal/2010/1/12/copani-2009/

Wang, S. C. (2014). Being "critical": Implications for Chinese heritage language schools. In T. G. Wiley, J. K. Peyton, D. Christian, S. Moore, & N. Liu (Eds.), *Heritage and community language in the United States: Research, policy, and educational practice* (pp. 157–166). New York, NY: Routledge.

Yoshimi, D. R. (2009). From a! to zo: Japanese pragmatics and its contribution to JSL/JFL pedagogy. In N. Taguchi (Ed.), *Pragmatic competence* (pp. 19–39). Berlin, Germany: Mouton de Gruyter.

14

Rationalization of the First Language First Model of Bilingual Development and Education

The Case of Russian as a Heritage Language in Israel

Mila Schwartz

1 Introduction

Shohamy (2008) defines language policy as "concerned with issues of managing language, specifically focusing on motivations for and decisions of how language should be used in various entities" (p. 305). Language education policies address language policy specifically in schools and universities. This chapter illustrates the ways in which some of the challenges of Israeli language and educational policies have been approached practically and conceptually through the institutionalization of bilingual Russian-Hebrew preschool education.[1] Following Ekholm and Trier (1987), "institutionalization" is taken to be the introduction of an innovation into an organization such that the innovation becomes a stable part of the routine of the organization. More specifically, this chapter presents the challenges and non-linear processes (Miles & Louis, 1987) involved in the implementation and institutionalization of the First Language First (FLF) model of bilingual growth, an innovative program that was modified over time in order to respond to changing sociopolitical forces and thus remain stable (see also the FLF model in Schwartz, 2014).

The chapter focuses on the Russian-speaking community's establishment of a network of bilingual preschools and extracurricular non-mainstream activities aimed at preserving their cultural heritage and mother tongue in the context of Israel. This educational network enrolls second-generation children from the former Soviet Union (FSU) whose first language is Russian and whose second language is Hebrew—the majority language in Israel. The central discussion is on the less investigated model of one-way dual language education, the FLF model, and its implementation in a bilingual preschool, the site of data collection for this chapter, within the network.

Much is known about dual language educational programs in which children become bilingual by simultaneous exposure to both languages. However, little is known about the FLF model of children's bilingual development, which involves two steps: establishing a solid foundation in the L1, in this case Russian, through the initial teaching of literacy and curriculum content in the L1, and then gradually increasing the input of the L2, in this case Hebrew. The first step permits children to acquire the basic grammatical structures and vocabulary of their L1, which then serve as anchors for the mastery of the L2, supporting the early development of bilingual abilities. This process is related to the situation within immigrant families where a child initially receives L1 input at home, and is exposed to the second and dominant language of the host society only after entering a preschool educational setting (Montrul, 2008). The FLF model is not as common as models that follow a transitional strategy aimed at immersion in the L2. The chapter analyzes the application of the FLF model by addressing parents' and teachers' viewpoints.

Two main phases in the process of the preschool's institutionalization of the FLF model will also be discussed. The first involved the establishment of the Russian-Hebrew bilingual program, and in close proximity to this period, the setting up of the FLF approach, when teachers realized the importance of shifting from a transitional program to one that focuses on maintaining the home language from an early age as a goal in and of itself, and not simply as a means to help students' successful transition to Hebrew. The second phase emerged approximately 13 years after the introduction of the FLF model, when the sociocultural profile of parents in the program had undergone a major transformation as a result of changes in immigration patterns from the FSU to Israel. This development resulted in modifications to the program, including a rethink of the introduction of Hebrew only at age three within the FLF model.

2 Brief Description of the Educational Approaches to Teaching Heritage Languages within Community-Based Educational Settings

Immigrant parents, unless isolated from their community, do not work on L1 preservation all by themselves. Usually, they have the help of community resources such as community centers and churches. Some immigrant communities assign more value to learning a heritage language (HL) in a structured way and establish community schools and preschools for that purpose, in both full-time and after-hours formats. In terms of the latter, an example is provided by the Chinese community: Since first arriving in North America, Chinese immigrant communities have established HL schools wherever numbers have been large enough. In a study by Riches and Curdt-Christiansen (2010), Canadian Chinese parents deemed Chinese schools extremely important for their children's development because they believed in the advantages of bilingualism and biliteracy, thought that knowledge of an additional language was beneficial, and felt that only through learning to read in Chinese would the children be able to fully appreciate the rich Chinese culture.

In terms of full-time HL community-run programs, a change has occurred in recent years as perspectives toward bilingualism or even multilingualism have developed to include a global future that goes beyond the development of an HL as a single target (García, Zakharia, & Otcu, 2013). These programs often use the socially dominant language as well as the HL, either explicitly as a declared goal or implicitly in classroom language practices and in a rather flexible manner (Creese & Blackledge, 2011; García et al., 2013). This tendency extends beyond the classroom context, and will also be discussed by addressing negotiation between Russian as an HL and Hebrew as a dominant language in the wider society and sometimes within the home, a situation that is found in the target bilingual preschool.

3 Brief Overview of the Linguistic Situation and Language Policy in Israel

Israel's language situation is distinctive, representing one of the more complex cases of a modern multilingual and multicultural society (Leikin, Schwartz, & Tobin, 2012). In Israel, Hebrew (the majority language) and Arabic (the language of the largest ethnic minority in Israel) coexist as the two official languages. English is a semiofficial language used in numerous contexts (especially in academia, business and politics). Other spoken languages include Russian, Amharic, Spanish, and French, which are the native languages of large groups of immigrants, as well as scores of other languages. This diverse linguistic and cultural situation is not only interesting in itself, but also inspires research in different sociolinguistic and psycholinguistic domains and permits generalization of the data to other countries and societies.

Historically, Israel can be viewed as a classic case of a country of migration that has absorbed a large immigrant population from many and diverse origins. However, until recently, the dominant language policy in Israel was to support only one language: Hebrew (the revived national language of the Jewish people). Hence, there was a purposeful lack of interest displayed for the languages spoken by Jewish immigrants (except, perhaps, English because of its international character). Consequently, the active use of languages such as German, Polish, Yiddish, Ladino, and French was discouraged and ignored, and these have basically been lost in the communities that once spoke them. Nonetheless, significant changes in language policy and in attitudes toward languages other than Hebrew have occurred in the last two decades. As will be seen below, these changes were influenced, to a certain degree, by a major group of immigrants from the FSU (Spolsky & Shohamy, 1999).

4 Russian as a Language of Immigrants and Its Teaching and Learning in Israel

Between 1990 and 1999 over 835,000 people immigrated from the FSU to Israel. Unlike their predecessors, this recent wave of immigrants posed a cultural and social challenge to Israeli society. The process of psychological acculturation of this immigrant community was a "cultural shock produced by a move from more positive imagery [of the host country] to a more realistic and often negative reality" (Isurin, 2011, p. 64). Isurin (2011) found some immigrants had misconceptions about Israeli culture, expecting that Israeli Jews would have similar cultural values and traditions as the Russian Jewish immigrants.

The large-scale character of this immigration group together with a high demographic concentration in some areas might explain this community's declared policy of retaining its language of origin: Russian. This strong commitment to the HL can be regarded as an application of Fishman's (1991, 2001) Reversing Language Shift (RLS) theory concerning the positive role of community demographic density for its language vitality. Fishman (1991), an early proponent of proactive language maintenance research, put forward a model for RLS in which efforts to retain ethnic languages at the level of the family and the community are central. As part of this theory, an eight-level Graded Intergenerational Disruption Scale diagnoses the state of a particular language and presents a directive for worldwide attempts to support minority languages (such as Russian in Israel) by remedial actions.

Another factor strongly associated with Fishman's (1991) theory is the tendency of Russian Jewish immigrants to place great importance on their original culture, which has encouraged them to maintain their language of origin and promote its acquisition by their children, including those who were born in Israel (Ben-Rafael et al., 2006). Fishman's theory assigns a crucial role to intergenerational home-family-neighborhood transmission of the language in partnership with community schooling. Many Russian-speaking parents and grandparents passionately support a supplementary private education system (informal education outside of regular school hours) as well as bilingual private preschools (full time) designed to preserve the cultural heritage and the mother tongue in its literary standard form among Israeli-born Russian-Hebrew–speaking children (Horowitz, Shamai, & Ilatov, 2008; Kopeliovich, 2011).

How are these community efforts related to the official language education policy? In 1996, the Israeli Ministry of Education declared a new language education policy which, for the first time, reflected Israel's multilingual character, encouraging the study of additional languages (e.g., Russian) besides the two official languages and English (Ministry of Education, Culture and Sport, 1996). Unfortunately, the option to learn Russian as part of the mainstream curriculum in Israeli schools is limited mainly to high school matriculation students. In this case, as was stressed by Kopeliovich (2011), the legitimation of Russian as a matriculation subject occurred almost 10 years after the start of the last wave of immigration from the FSU, and "by that time many immigrant children had already lost their native proficiency in Russian" (p. 114). Thus, today, the linguistic vitality of Russian is supported only by private bilingual preschools and extracurricular non-mainstream activities. This chapter describes how the Russian-Hebrew–speaking preschools approach Russian maintenance by implementing the FLF model as the guiding principle of their language education policy.

Establishing an Alternative Type of Education for the Immigrant Community from the Former Soviet Union

FSU immigrants' main approach to acculturation is integration, combining maintenance of the culture of origin with adaptation to the host culture and relatively rapid and successful acquisition of Hebrew (Horenczyk & Ben-Shalom, 2006). To realize this approach, the recent wave of immigrants has developed an alternative type of education, aimed not only at preserving the cultural heritage of the immigrants from the FSU, but also at implementing the philosophy and pedagogical strategies of Russian education.

Horowitz et al. (2008, pp. 381–383) point to several factors favoring the establishment of this type of education in Israel. They draw attention to the growing unemployment rate among immigrant teachers, who were unable to find work in Israeli schools. Of these 50,000 certified teachers from the FSU, only 12% have found work in the mainstream education system. In addition, Horowitz et al. (2008) address factors such as immigrant parents' disappointment with the existing standard of Israeli education, from the point of view of both academic content (the teaching of science) and educational values (e.g., classroom behavior that includes respect for teachers, belief in education as the key to success). Some parents have dealt with this by sending their children back to the FSU to obtain a high school education. During my meetings with parents who had chosen the Russian-Hebrew preschools, they expressed their frustration with the low academic and professional level of the Israeli education system. This feeling was prominent especially among parents who had experienced schooling in both their home and host countries. They frequently stressed that one of the main reasons for their choice of these bilingual settings was their expectation that the preschool curricula would offer more cognitively enriching activities than in mainstream monolingual preschools in Israel.

The factors discussed above motivated community leaders and immigrant teachers to establish alternative educational networks. This motivation, together with the community's ability to take its fate into its own hands, was grounded in its rich human capital (Horowitz et al., 2008). The existence of an "army" of knowledgeable, experienced, and enthusiastic teachers, who were willing to implement their pedagogical ideas, was a stepping-stone to establishing these community educational networks.

The Union of Immigrant Teachers

The Union of Immigrant Teachers (hereafter UIT) was established in 1992 by a group of immigrant teachers who were aware of the special educational needs of the FSU community. This organization was supported by the Jewish Agency for Israel. UIT's primary aim was to provide a bridge between the needs of immigrant children and their families and the public education system in Israel. UIT intended to help children and their parents cope with the many hurdles and difficulties facing them in the new country.

UIT began by developing extracurricular activities in venues known as learning centers. By 1994, the UIT had decided to focus on preschool education. Today, this organization operates a network of more than 25 bilingual preschools and runs activities in 90 schools and cultural institutions throughout the country. During the 20 years since its foundation, the UIT has provided 3,000 employment opportunities for immigrant teachers from the FSU, and owes its success mainly to their professional experience and dedication. More than 20,000 children have benefited from this high-quality education.

Although the bilingual preschools described in this chapter are private institutions, they function under the supervision of the Israeli Ministry of Education. Teachers use the same curriculum as Hebrew monolingual preschools, but adapt them to the pedagogical approaches and needs of the network. The Ministry of Education provides clearly specified achievement standards, presented in a unified program for preschool teachers entitled *Tohnit Liba* [Core Program]. This program includes developmental standards and instructional directions in the following domains: emergent literacy (basis for reading and writing achievement in elementary school, as well as vocabulary expansion and acquisition of narrative skills), mathematics, athletics, and art education. More specifically, in the language domain, the everyday curriculum typically includes topic discussions (e.g., religious festivals, weather and climate, family, and so on), read-aloud sessions (questions about a story, predictions, discussions, vocabulary enrichment, and retelling), and music, rhythm, and art sessions.

The Ministry of Education's supervision of the bilingual preschools addresses only the program in Hebrew. The Hebrew program is delivered from around age three, by a native or non-native Hebrew-speaking teacher, who is responsible for Hebrew instruction and provides the language input during part of the daily classroom time. At age five, the children move on to compulsory municipal preschools. The Ministry of Education does not supervise the instructional program in Russian, which is planned and governed by the pedagogical staff of the network. This program is structured to match the Hebrew Core Program.

5 The Study of the Bilingual Preschool

The current study was conducted in one of the bilingual preschools that belongs to the UIT network: Radost[2] [Happiness]. This school was chosen because members of its pedagogical staff were happy to participate in the study. The preschool was established in northern Israel almost 15 years ago, and enrolls children ages six months to five years old. Its pedagogical approaches to language teaching have been formed through a collaboration between the preschool principal and pedagogical staff and are still undergoing changes, as will be shown later in the chapter.

The Bilingual Program

In addressing preschool bilingual education, our focus will be on Radost's dual language program. Freeman (2007) describes three types of dual language programs. The first type is the *two-way immersion program* such as those found in the U.S. for English-speakers and speakers of another language (e.g., Spanish). The main aim of this type of program is to increase inter-group communicative competence and cultural awareness (Freeman, 2007). In this type of dual language program, the language balance is a critical issue. Thus, at least 50% of instruction should be conducted in a minority language, with a balanced number of language minority and language majority-speaking students integrated in all classes. The second type is *the language immersion program* that exclusively targets speakers of the dominant societal language (e.g., English speakers who are immersed in a French program in the U.S. or Canada, or Finnish speakers in a Swedish program in Finland) and provides the second language for at least 50% of the curriculum. The rationale behind immersion is that students can learn a language effectively if it is used for significant periods and for substantive communication in school, much as children learn their native language in the home.

According to Freeman's (2007) classification, our bilingual preschool program could be defined as a third type of dual language program, namely *the one-way developmental bilingual program*, with the target children coming only from language-minority homes. This type of program views languages other than the majority language of a society (e.g., English in the U.S.; French in France) as resources to be developed (Ruiz, 1984). By supporting maintenance of the L1 as the children acquire the majority language, this language program provides an additive bilingual environment (Lambert, 1975).

The children in the one-way developmental bilingual program often come from language-minority homes where the minority language is the majority language of the local community (Baker, 2011; Freeman, 2007). When the first bilingual preschools were opened by the UIT, the one-way developmental bilingual program was the only type of dual language program that could be established. At that time, Israeli society was neither ready for nor interested in two-way programs such as those implemented in the U.S. and Canada. Hebrew as a majority and dominant language is a loaded concept in Israel, closely linked to ideological, political, and social issues, and Russian as a language of immigrants was not attractive to Israeli society. As a result, Hebrew-speaking families could not be expected to enroll their children in these bilingual preschools.

The Pedagogical Staff

In general, the network has a clear policy for staff selection with regard to both immigrant and host country teachers' engagement, with an emphasis on a high degree of professionalism. The immigrant Russian-speaking teachers make up most of the teaching staff in the network. The former general manager of the UIT explains this situation in the following excerpt:

> The Israeli teachers are often not well qualified. They are not committed to the profession; do not have inner individual standards. Russian teachers are well educated. They have internal dedication, and they aim to display the results of their work through the children's achievements. They arrive in Israel with a very good standard of higher education and influence Israeli society.
>
> *(Interview 2008, November)*

Both immigrant teachers and teachers trained in Israel were employed in Radost. All teachers had a preschool and first grade teaching diploma from a teacher training college or a university, either in the FSU or in Israel. Most of the immigrant teachers had more than five years of teaching experience in the FSU prior to their immigration to Israel. It is also worth noting that the principal and teachers in this preschool had received no professional training in bilingual teaching. However, they actively participated in professional development workshops and other professional meetings organized by the network and aimed to put into practice current theories on bilingual development and education, as well as sharing and reflecting on their personal experience.

Data Collection and Analysis

The study was part of a large-scale research project that I conducted from 2008 to 2014. In this project, the longitudinal ethnographic observations were conducted in Radost during circle time, outdoor activities, and spontaneous teacher-children communication. Six interviews were conducted with the staff by the author. This chapter includes sample quotes from the interviewers with the principal of the preschool, one of the Russian language teachers, and one of the Hebrew language teachers.

The semi-structured interviews took place in the preschool at a time convenient for the participants. They took the form of unstructured conversations, focusing on the interviewees' reflections on their bilingual pedagogical experience, perceptions, and language ideologies relevant to the teaching at the bilingual preschools. The teachers were also asked about their interaction with parents and, in particular, about parents' involvement in the development of the preschool's language curriculum. The interview with the general manager of the network addressed similar topics. Each interview lasted between 90 and 120 minutes, was audio-recorded with the interviewees' consent, and conducted in either Russian or Hebrew, according to the participant's mother tongue.

The interviews were transcribed, coded, and analyzed thematically by placing labels on themes and concepts that emerged from the data, open-coding, building connections between categories to form larger, core categories, and axial coding (Bogdan & Biklen, 1992; Braun & Clarke, 2006). The following three content categories will be addressed: (1) basic pedagogical approaches; (2) the FLF model; (3) parental feedback as impetus for change.

Basic Pedagogical Approaches

In the FSU, the aim of preschool education was to prepare children for elementary school. This means developing a certain set of skills within the cognitive, speech, literacy, socio-communicative, mathematic, and physical spheres (Čumičeva & Platohina, 2008). In this context, the question of how much teaching vis-à-vis play time to include in the daily schedule was important to the Radost curriculum. Mainstream Israeli preschools have on the whole fewer hours of structured teaching activities than the traditional Russian preschool system has. As noted above, Russian-speaking parents who choose this bilingual preschool have high expectations that preschool curricula will offer extensive instructional activities. This expectation accords with the preschool's general pedagogical approach to provide more educational activities than the monolingual settings. The principal of the preschool confirms this:

> We implement the same theme program and activities as regular preschools. However, we include other things that cannot be found in regular Israeli preschools. We do much more teaching. We want to impart more knowledge. Some say that we are depriving children of their childhood. We play with them while teaching. The child has to be engaged in learning by being interested. We spend less time outdoors, so we have more time for overt instruction. But we also work with smaller groups of children and that gives us more time.
>
> *(Interview 2008, November)*

The pedagogical conception of this network is based on Vygotsky's sociocultural theory (1978). Central to Vygotsky's view is the idea that children are social beings and that their development occurs on a social level within a cultural context. Furthermore, in Vygotsky's vision children's learning is determined by social functioning and the structure of an individual child's mental processes mirrors the social milieu from which they are derived. This idea is reflected in the UIT's objectives to provide children with a unique sociocultural environment incorporating cultural capital (e.g., educational values and principles, cultural traditions) brought from the home country with that of the Jewish and Israeli peoplehood, in order to build the foundation for multiple identities. Furthermore, Vygotsky (1962) suggests a distinction between learning and development, including the development of language. Learning is associated with formal education settings and contexts, whereas development occurs in a less controlled manner. This view was realized in the bilingual teachers' claim that Russian (L1) teaching needs to be structured in a similar way to the teaching of Hebrew (L2). Through their implementation of the FLF model, teachers provided scaffolding for L2 (Hebrew) acquisition.

The FLF Model

The Radost preschool applied a two-stage strategy model (Baker, 2011). The first stage aims to solidify children's L1, Russian. The second stage consists of gradually increasing the input of the second and majority language, Hebrew, with continued L1 instruction. This additional stage begins as basic grammatical structures (e.g., gender, number) and basic lexicon in L1 Russian are almost completely acquired around the age of three.

The first stage illustrates an application of Cummins' (2000) Linguistic Interdependence Hypothesis, which states that children's knowledge and skills transfer across languages, from the mother tongue acquired in the home to an L2 learned at school. From the point of view of children's development of concepts and thinking skills, the two languages are interdependent. Thus, concepts, language, and literacy skills that children learn in the L2 (within bilingual education programs) can transfer to the home language (L1) and vice versa. In short, each language nurtures the other when the educational environment permits children access to both languages (Cummins, 2003). Cummins (2000) points out that "the interdependence hypothesis is of critical importance in understanding the nature of bilingual students' academic development and in planning appropriate educational programs for students from both minority and majority language backgrounds" (p. 175). In the following example, the Russian language teacher illustrates an application of Cummins' views on linguistic interdependence in daily activities:

> In the beginning, my Hebrew-speaking colleague and I developed our joint plan for the next three months. We looked at our material that we were intending to use for teaching. All material discussed in Hebrew must also be discussed in Russian. Some of the material is mine, some was developed by the Hebrew teacher, and some material is shared; if we take the same theme, for example, holidays. I also have my special system of working with a book. At first . . . I read it with the children, I show them the pictures and tell them the story in Russian. Later, they work with the same book in Hebrew. Every new theme is explained first in Russian and then in Hebrew.
>
> *(Interview 2011, July)*

This description reflects the preschool's language ideology as well as the teachers' awareness of children's ability to transfer conceptual knowledge from the L1 to the L2, enhancing the role of the L1. While the teacher does not explicitly address Cummins' hypothesis, her understanding of a possible concept transfer from L1 to L2 supports it, encouraging her to continue this very effective practice (see Schwartz, 2014).

The FLF model maintains sequential exposure to a second language after the relative maturity of the L1. Thus, in Radost L1 Russian-speaking children began their immersion in Hebrew from around age three, taught by a native Hebrew-speaking teacher. Until age three, all teacher–child communication and instruction was conducted in Russian by a native Russian-speaking teacher.

Why was the FLF model chosen? In reflecting on the history of the preschool, the teachers reported that when the preschool first opened, both Russian and Hebrew were introduced concurrently and in a more or less balanced way. However, the teachers realized that it was more important to support Russian at an age at which its initial acquisition was still incomplete. Thus, it was decided that the children would initially develop awareness of the coexistence of two languages before being exposed to their L2. The initial role of the L1 as a transitional language was changed to that of the *language of instruction*. As a result, the teachers in fact promoted an *Enrichment Bilingual Education* approach, which involved the developmental maintenance of Russian. This educational approach is in contrast to the *Static Maintenance* approach, which aims to prevent the loss of L1 but does not attempt to increase L1 skills (Baker, 2011; Otheguy & Otto, 1980).

A gradual increase of L2 input from around age three was meant to avoid the stress involved in introducing an unfamiliar language. It was noted that a child's self-concept might suffer when their own language is not represented in an important institution of society (Baker, 2011; Cummins, 2000). Schwartz, Moin, and Leikin (2011) found that this assumption was reflected in Russian-speaking parents' beliefs in the potential traumatic effect of early immersion in Hebrew. For this reason, even parents who chose a monolingual Hebrew-speaking preschool searched for an educational setting with a "Russian-speaking staff member." They viewed it as critical to have a Russian-speaking staff person since "she/he can help and explain things" and understand what the child's essential needs are. Otherwise, as one parent put it, the child would "lose confidence" (Schwartz et al., 2011, p. 157).

In line with Bruner's (1986) and Vygotsky's (1978) theoretical assumptions, the teachers claimed that instruction in Russian provided earlier than instruction in Hebrew plays a *scaffolding role* that eases children's exposure to Hebrew. The teachers' perception of the facilitating role of the FLF model for the acquisition of Hebrew is consistent with growing empirical evidence from psycholinguistic research. Thus, in accordance with Paradis' (2008) maturational hypothesis, there is "the possibility that age of onset [of the L2] interacts with ambient language exposure time such that L2 children may acquire their L2 faster than children who have been acquiring this language from birth, either monolingually or bilingually" (p. 1). This hypothesis received support in the domain of vocabulary acquisition in a longitudinal study by Golberg, Paradis, and Crago (2008). In this two-year study, Golberg et al. followed vocabulary development in English (the L2 in this context) among nineteen minority-language children in Canada between the ages of nine months to three years at the beginning of the study. The onset of L2 acquisition occurred when the child entered an English-speaking (L2) educational setting. Children who were exposed to the L2 later, after age five, showed more rapid progress than children with younger age of onset of the L2 (before age five).

Parental Feedback as Motivation for Change

The interviews with teachers reflect the importance of parents' feedback in bringing about changes to program conceptualization and bilingual education practices. The analyses of the interviews demonstrate that the language program at Radost was evolving as a result of negotiations between parents and teachers with respect to the focus of the curriculum and components of the program. More specifically, the interviews reveal that, in the teachers' opinion, the parents, overall, supported their language ideology. In the following passage, the Russian language teacher explains the parents' expectations for the preschool:

> First of all, the goal is the maintenance of their first language, to nurture intergenerational connections. In some families, the grandparents speak Russian to the children, but the parents speak Hebrew, because many of the parents arrived here when they were very young and are more competent in Hebrew than in Russian.
>
> *(Interview 2011, July)*

Indeed, during the first few years of the preschool's existence, parents believed that the Hebrew linguistic environment would automatically provide L2 acquisition ("Kids will learn Hebrew anyway"; see Schwartz et al., 2011). Over time, their perceptions have changed, in part because of changes in the children's sociocultural landscape. When the Russian-Hebrew program based on the FLF model started about 15 years ago, the majority of children in the program were second-generation immigrants. As explained above, their parents had immigrated from the FSU as adults and thus tended to preserve their cultural heritage and language in the home. However, the sociocultural profile of the parents in the program has undergone a major transformation with time, as the quote above illustrates, and teachers have become aware of parents' growing concerns about what they perceive to be their children's slow progress in Hebrew.

At the time of this study, most of the parents in the program belonged to the 1.5 generation, i.e., young adults who immigrated to Israel prior to or during their early teens. Members of the 1.5 generation combine old and new cultures and traditions. They retain characteristics of their country of origin, but continue to be acculturated in the host country. As stated by the Hebrew language teacher and the principal, in some cases, these parents' dominant language has become Hebrew while Russian has become an HL. This generation of parents viewed providing Russian input at the beginning of preschool as giving the children "a good start," whereas they viewed learning Hebrew as a social and linguistic reality and necessity in their children's future. Hence, in recent years, this generation of parents has raised their concerns regarding introducing Hebrew only at age three. They were worried that children might not reach the expected level of Hebrew language when they were four to five years old and might not be able to adjust when they entered monolingual Hebrew preschools at that time. This change in the cultural makeup of the families in the program as a result of changes in the larger sociocultural landscape in Israel led to parents' different expectations of the program and thus prompted a modification of the language model used. This parental concern led to the second phase in the institutionalization of the FLF model, which brought changes to the curriculum and resulted in the earlier introduction of Hebrew into the program: 30 minutes of Hebrew instruction was introduced four times a week, at age two.

Another challenge for the preschool is related to the fact that very few native Hebrew speakers are enrolled in this dual program. In recent years, both teachers and parents noticed some difficulty in the children's communication with monolingual Hebrew-speaking peers. The principal of the preschool expressed her concern in her interview: "I really, really want to work on socialization. They [the children] do not have sufficient proficiency to communicate with other children . . . despite the fact that now we teach Hebrew from age 2" (Interview 2011, July). This issue was also addressed during my conversations with the parents; one mother reported her concern as follows: "I was very worried because he (her four-year-old son) refused to communicate with Hebrew-speaking children in the playground" (Interview 2011, June).

When applied to L2 learning, Blum-Kulka and Snow (2004) point out that L2-speaking peers as language teachers create the possibility in the classroom for an equal participant structure whereas teacher-child interaction is asymmetric and provides less opportunity for reciprocal exchanges (p. 298). It has been found that more knowledgeable peers can make meta-pragmatic and meta-linguistic comments to novice L2 learners, and as a result, promote their L2 acquisition

(Schwartz & Gorbatt, in press). As for our preschool, the principal offered one possible solution to this lack of natural input of Hebrew from peers during the preschool day:

I'm thinking—we have a *gan hova* [mainstream monolingual kindergarten] right across the street. Maybe we can invite [other] kids. Either [we can invite] older kids to play with our kids in the playground, or we can invite our older kids, or kids who already left our preschool, to come to play with the little ones. I think that would be great, too.

(Interview 2011, November)

6 Conclusions and the Limitations of the Study

In this chapter, I focused on the institutionalization process of a network of Russian-Hebrew bilingual preschools in Israel and, more narrowly, on the introduction of FLF into one of these preschools. This process included the UIT's establishment, which was supported by Russian-speaking community leaders and The Jewish Agency for Israel. The UIT aimed to take advantage of the rich human capital in the form of immigrant teachers from the FSU residing in Israel.

In the context of HL programs, especially those run by local communities, finding qualified teachers is more often than not an insurmountable challenge, leading to teachers with little or no training in language-teaching pedagogy, often parent volunteers, taking on the complex task of teaching HL students (e.g., Li, 2005, regarding Chinese community schools). The existence of a large pool of teachers who were not only well-qualified but also committed to FLF thus greatly contributed to the success of the network in general and the Radost preschool in particular.

This chapter took a close look at how the language policy of the Radost preschool and, specifically, the FLF model was executed by the pedagogical staff and the changes the program has undergone over the years. Once Hebrew instruction was added at an earlier age in response to sociocultural changes and linguistic expectations of parents, a major challenge was finding sufficient time to teach in both languages (Russian as the L1 and Hebrew as the L2). To address this challenge, the teachers modified the existing language model and the curriculum.

Miles and Louis (1987) maintain that we should be less concerned about the institutionalization of an innovation as reaching an end point, but rather "about school innovativeness and self-renewal" (p. 42). In other words, the ability to be flexible and make changes in response to changing circumstances, or to institute "second-order changes" (p. 42), is integral to maintaining the stability of a program.

Since this investigation was limited to a case study, its findings might not be fully generalizable. It is reasonable to assume that bilingual programs in other ethnolinguistic communities might take a different approach to solving the language issues involved. Nevertheless, within the broader context of community-based HL education, the data highlight the necessity for teachers to perform a critical examination of their own language ideologies and practices. Furthermore, in light of the central goal of the volume, this chapter documents the process of institutionalization of an HL program, informing other practitioners of the lessons learned, and allowing HL educators to view themselves as part of a "single community of interest, each learning from the other and correcting each other's experimental and attitudinal limitations" (Fishman, 1976, p. viii).

Notes

1 In this chapter the term "preschool" refers to a form of early childhood education which serves as a transition from home to the onset of more formal schooling. In Israel, preschool is part of the education system, usually catering to children between three and six years of age.
2 The name of the preschool has been changed to preserve anonymity.

Suggestions for Further Reading on Russian as a Heritage Language in Israel

Kopeliovich, S. (2009). *Reversing language shift in the immigrant family: A case study of a Russian-speaking community in Israel*. Saarbruken: VDM Verlag Dr. Muller.

Niznik, M. (2007). Teaching Russian in Israel—challenging the system. In M. Kenigshtein (Ed.), Русское лицо Израиля: Черты социального портрета. [*The "Russian" face of Israel: The features of a social portrait*] (pp. 403–417). Jerusalem/Moscow: Gesharim.

References

Baker, C. (2011). *Foundation of bilingual education and bilingualism* (5th ed.). Bristol, UK: Multilingual Matters.

Ben-Rafael, E., Lyubansky, M., Glöckner, O., Harris, P., Israel, Y., Jasper, W., & Schoeps, J. (2006). *Building a diaspora: Russian Jews in Israel, Germany and the USA*. Leiden, The Netherlands: Brill.

Blum-Kulka, S., & Snow, K. (2004). Introduction: The potential of peer talk. *Thematic Issue of Discourse Studies: Peer Talk and Pragmatic Development, 6*(3), 291–306.

Bogdan, R. C., & Biklen, S. K. (1992). *Qualitative research for education* (2nd ed.). Boston, MA: Allyn and Bacon.

Braun, V., & Clarke, V. (2006). Using thematic analysis in psychology. *Qualitative Research in Psychology, 3*, 77–101.

Bruner, J. (1986). *Actual minds, possible worlds*. Cambridge, MA: Harvard University Press.

Creese, A., & Blackledge, A. (2011). Separate and flexible bilingualism in complementary schools: Multiple language practices in interrelationship. *Journal of Pragmatics, 43*, 1196–1208.

Čumičeva, R., & Platohina, N. (2008). Problems and perspectives of preschool education in Russia and abroad [in Russian]. *Kindergarten from A to Z, 2*, 40–50.

Cummins, J. (2000). *Language, power, and pedagogy: Bilingual children in the crossfire*. Clevedon, UK: Multilingual Matters.

Cummins, J. (2003). Bilingual education: Basic principles. In J.-M. Dewaile, A. Housen, & L. Wei (Eds.), *Bilingualism: Beyond basic principles* (pp. 56–87). Clevedon, UK: Multilingual Matters.

Ekholm, M., & Trier, U. P. (1987). The concept of institutionalization: Some remarks. In M. B. Miles, M. Ekholm, & R. Vandenberghe (Eds.), *Lasting school improvement: Exploring the process of institutionalization* (pp. 25–44). Leuven, Belgium: Acco.

Fishman, J. A. (1976). *Bilingual education: An international sociological perspective*. Rowley, MA: Newbury House.

Fishman, J. A. (1991). *Reversing language shift: Theoretical and empirical foundations of assistance to threatened languages*. Clevedon, UK: Multilingual Matters Ltd.

Fishman, J. A. (2001). From theory to practice (and vice versa): Review, reconsideration and reiteration. In J.A. Fishman (Ed.), *Can threatened languages be saved?* (pp. 451–483). Berlin, Germany: Mouton de Gruyter.

Freeman, R. (2007). Reviewing the research on language education programs. In O. Garcia & C. Baker (Eds.), *Bilingual education: An introductory reader* (pp. 3–18). Clevedon, UK: Multilingual Matters.

García, O., Zakharia, Z., & Otcu, B. (Eds.). (2013). *Bilingual community education for American children: Beyond heritage languages in a global city*. Bristol, UK: Multilingual Matters.

Golberg, H., Paradis, J., & Crago, M. (2008). Lexical acquisition over time in minority first language children learning English as a second language. *Applied Psycholinguistics, 29*, 1–25.

Horenczyk, G., & Ben-Shalom, U. (2006). Acculturation in Israel. In D. Sam & J. Berry (Eds.), *The Cambridge handbook of acculturation psychology* (pp. 294–310). Cambridge, UK: Cambridge University Press.

Horowitz, T., Shamai, S., & Ilatov, Z. (2008). The Russian immigrant community vs. the Israeli educational establishment: From extra-curricular activities to systematic change. In A. Stavans & I. Kupferberg (Eds.), *Studies in language and language education: Essays in honor of Elite Olshtain* (pp. 379–394). Jerusalem, Israel: The Magnes Press, Hebrew University.

Isurin, L. (2011). *Russian diaspora: Culture, identity, and language change*. Berlin, Germany/New York, NY: Mouton de Gruyter.

Kopeliovich, S. (2011). How long is "the Russian street" in Israel? Prospects of maintaining the Russian language. *Israel Affairs, 17*(1), 108–124.

Lambert, W. E. (1975). Culture and language as factors in learning and education. In A. Wolfgang (Ed.), *Education of immigrant students: Issues and answers* (pp. 233–261). Toronto, Canada: Ontario Institute for Studies in Education.

Leikin, M., Schwartz, M., & Tobin, Y. (2012). Current issues in bilingualism: A complex approach to a multidimensional phenomenon. In M. Leikin, M. Schwartz, & Y. Tobin (Eds.), *Current issues in bilingualism: Cognitive and socio-linguistic perspectives* (pp. 1–18). New York, NY: Springer.

Li, M. (2005). The role of parents in Chinese heritage-language schools. *Bilingual Research Journal, 29*(1), 197–207.

Miles, M. B., & Louis, K. S. (1987). Research on institutionalization: A reflective review. In M. B. Miles, M. Ekholm, & R. Vandenberghe (Eds.), *Lasting school improvement: Exploring the process of institutionalization* (pp. 25–44). Leuven, Belgium: Acco.

Ministry of Education, Culture and Sport. (1996). מדיניות חינוך לשוני במערכת החינוך בישראל [Policy for language education in Israel] [Policy document]. Jerusalem, Israel: Office of the Director-General.

Montrul, S. (2008). *Incomplete acquisition in bilingualism.* Amsterdam, The Netherlands: John Benjamins.

Otheguy, R., & Otto, R. (1980). The myth of static maintenance in bilingual education. *The Modern Language Journal, 64,* 350–356.

Paradis, J. (2008, October). *Are simultaneous and early sequential bilingual acquisition fundamentally different?* Paper presented at Models of Interaction in Bilinguals: International Conference of Centre for Research on Bilingualism in Theory and Practice, Bangor University, Bangor, UK.

Riches, C., & Curdt-Christiansen, X. L. (2010). A tale of two Montréal communities: Parents' perspectives on their children's language and literacy development in a multilingual context. *Canadian modern language review, 66*(4), 525–555.

Ruiz, R. (1984). Orientations to language planning. *NABE Journal, 8,* 15–34.

Schwartz, M. (2014). The impact of the First Language First model on vocabulary development among preschool bilingual children. *Reading and Writing, 27*(4), 709–732.

Schwartz, M., & Gorbatt, N. (2016). "Why do we know Hebrew and they do not know Arabic?": Children's meta-linguistic talk in bilingual preschool. *International Journal of Bilingual Education and Bilingualism, 19*(6), 668–688.

Schwartz, M., Moin, V., & Leikin, M. (2011). Parents' discourses about language strategies for the child's preschool bilingual development. *Diaspora, Indigenous, and Minority Education: An International Journal, 5*(3), 149–166.

Shohamy, E. (2008). Language policies and language realities in Israel: A critical view. In A. Stavans & I. Kupferberg (Eds.), *Studies in language and language education: Essays in honor of Elite Olshtain* (pp. 305–323). Jerusalem, Israel: The Magnes Press, Hebrew University.

Spolsky, B., & Shohamy, E. (1999). *The languages of Israel: Policy, ideology and practice.* Clevedon, UK: Multilingual Matters.

Vygotsky, L. S. (1962). *Thought and language.* Cambridge, MA: Harvard University Press.

Vygotsky, L. S. (1978). *Mind in society: The development of higher psychological processes.* Cambridge, MA: Harvard University Press.

Part IV

Language Minority Communities and the Public School System

Opportunities and Challenges

15

Multilingual Los Angeles

Do Immigrant Language Communities Make an Impact on Language Education in Public High Schools?

Olga E. Kagan

"I learned so much about my culture. Now I am proud to be bilingual and bicultural."
From a heritage learner's language course evaluation

1 Introduction: The Purpose and Setting of the Study

Even a cursory look at recent demographic tables published by the U.S. Census Bureau shows convincingly that the country is not mono- but multilingual. As the Census shows, almost 21% of the U.S. population currently speak a language other than English at home (U.S. Census Bureau, 2013), and residents of many regions and often even different neighborhoods speak a wide variety of languages. As a language educator working in second and heritage language (HL) acquisition, I became intrigued as to whether national and state K–16 education systems attend to the linguistic diversity of local communities and respond to their needs by teaching languages represented locally. To address this question, I set out to explore the metropolitan area of Los Angeles, which includes Los Angeles County and Orange County, where I have lived and taught at the university level since the early 1980s. Metropolitan Los Angeles serves as a highly appropriate environment for such a study because its multilingual composition is both visible and extensive. The linguistic diversity is marked, from billboards and store signs to neighborhoods like Little Armenia, Little Ethiopia, Koreatown, Filipinotown, and so on. All these names attest to a multilingual and multicultural scene so vibrant that, in some cities that constitute Metro LA, English either shares equal territory with other languages or takes a second place.[1]

At any school or college campus in Metropolitan LA, you will certainly hear multiple languages as well. But what languages are offered for instruction? I wanted to conduct a study to see whether there was any parity between the languages of local ethnic communities and those offered in the local high schools. As will be shown in this chapter, the investigation has documented some successes and some failures. Many languages spoken by local residents in their homes are not typically offered in the region's high schools. There are some notable exceptions, however, where schools and local communities have collaborated to provide foreign language instruction, and other examples where languages of the communities are taught as both foreign and heritage languages. In what follows, I present these findings and make some recommendations to address the imbalance between languages spoken by the region's residents and language offerings in regional educational institutions.

Tables 15.1–15.3 present the results of the 2010–2014 Community Survey (U.S. Census, 2015) and detail the demographics of the U.S., California, and Los Angeles County with regard to the 10 languages other than English most spoken at home.

In all three tables, the Spanish-speaking community is the largest, followed by Chinese (in the Census, Chinese includes Mandarin, Cantonese, and other languages of China), and Tagalog in

Table 15.1 Ten Languages Other Than English Spoken at Home in the United States

United States	Estimate
Total	294,133,373
Speak only English	232,724,203
1 Spanish or Spanish Creole	38,098,698
2 Chinese	2,989,785
3 Tagalog	1,646,110
4 Vietnamese	1,427,194
5 French (incl. Patois, Cajun)	1,291,863
6 Korean	1,126,356
7 German	1,029,222
8 Arabic	981,070
9 Russian	889,707
10 French Creole	765,942

Source: Adapted from "Table B16001: Language Spoken at Home by Ability to Speak English for the Population 5 Years and Over" for United States. American Community Survey 2010–2014 five-year estimates, U.S. Census Bureau.

Table 15.2 Ten Languages Other Than English Spoken at Home in California

California	Estimate
Total:	35,545,621
Speak only English	19,992,432
1 Spanish or Spanish Creole	10,217,938
2 Chinese	1,083,029
3 Tagalog	775,347
4 Vietnamese	533,437
5 Korean	376,306
6 Armenian	195,501
7 Persian	193,721
8 Arabic	160,243
9 Hindi	157,604
10 Russian	154,001

Source: Adapted from "Table B16001: Language Spoken at Home by Ability to Speak English for the Population 5 Years and Over" for California. American Community Survey 2010–2014 five-year estimates, U.S. Census Bureau.

Table 15.3 Ten Languages Other Than English Spoken at Home in Los Angeles County

Los Angeles County, California	Estimate
Total:	9,329,565
Speak only English	4,032,116
1 Spanish or Spanish Creole	3,678,805
2 Chinese	354,501
3 Tagalog	227,733
4 Korean	183,483
5 Armenian	171,484
6 Vietnamese	82,707
7 Persian	73,447
8 Japanese	51,723
9 Russian	51,529
10 Arabic	43,105

Source: Adapted from "Table B16001: Language Spoken at Home by Ability to Speak English for the Population 5 Years and Over" for Los Angeles County. American Community Survey 2010–2014 five-year estimates, U.S. Census Bureau.

third place. However, the similarities break down after language number 4. Nationally, the fourth largest community is comprised of the combined languages of India: Hindi, Gudjurati, Urdu, and others. In California the fourth largest language community is Vietnamese; in LA County it is Korean. Other comparisons may be even more striking: Armenian, Persian, and Japanese are not among the 10 largest languages spoken in the country as a whole, but in California, Armenian is the seventh largest language, and in Los Angeles County it occupies the fifth place. Persian is eighth in California and seventh in Los Angeles County. Japanese is not among the 10 largest communities in the U.S. or California, but it is the tenth most spoken language in Los Angeles County. The comparison shows clearly that the language makeup of Los Angeles County differs substantively from the national distribution, creating a unique linguistic geography. While this study does not aim to propose any particular policy, it points out that geography may be an important but frequently ignored factor in determining the needs and opportunities in language instruction.

2 Foreign and Heritage Languages

Tables 15.1–15.3 show that many of the students in K–16 are speakers of home languages other than English, i.e., that if these students take foreign languages classes in high school or in college, these languages may not be foreign to them, but may in fact be the languages spoken in their homes. Fee, Rhodes, and Wiley (2014) analyze recent immigration patterns nationwide and conclude that foreign language offerings mostly do not meet the needs of HL students. For example, they note that even with the large numbers of Spanish-speaking students in K–12, "most Spanish foreign language courses are not designed for Spanish heritage speakers" (p. 15). The problem is twofold: inability to offer languages to HL learners and also a decline in foreign language enrollments. The authors come to the uneasy conclusion that there has been an overall "decline in language offerings from 1997 to 2008" (p. 9), and argue that if the current trends continue, "the United States will not only have fewer students with proficiency in another language but will also experience a continuation in the decline of language proficiency among heritage speakers" (p. 17).

In this chapter I attempt to demonstrate ways in which this decline could be slowed by school districts and school administrators. To begin with, trends that indicate increased numbers of HL speakers need to be viewed as positive, and schools should try to capitalize on them. More offerings of local languages could potentially be a cure for the declining language enrollments. Languages of local communities could be offered both as HLs for the children of immigrants who grow up speaking and hearing their home language and also as foreign languages for all other students in the neighborhood. The World-Readiness Standards for Learning Languages (American Council on the Teaching of Foreign Languages, 2014) stress the role that both local and virtual communities can play in language learning. However, the languages of local communities are not offered at all in many areas and, as pointed out above, when they are offered and heritage learners bring their home-gained proficiencies into the language class, they are often taught in a way that meets the needs of foreign language learners but not those of their HL classmates (Carreira, 2014; Ducar, 2012). Helmer (2014) stresses that HL speakers may not benefit from instruction that does not have "meaningful activity and authentic materials" that connect "curriculum to students' linguistic strengths, target-culture knowledge, and the communities from which they came" (p. 186). A connection to the communities can thus be central to HL learners, and can at the same time also strengthen language instruction for foreign language learners.

3 The Study

Rationale for Choosing Metropolitan Los Angeles for the Study

In this chapter, I provide a brief overview of the state of foreign and heritage language instruction in Metropolitan LA which can be regarded as a provocative test case because it is one of the most multilingual metropolitan areas in the U.S., that, according to Waldinger (2007), "offers a distinctive . . . cross section of the U.S. foreign born population" (p. 349) and can be seen as "the capital of twenty-first century immigrant America" (p. 367). Moreover, with a population of over 13 million people in the Metro LA area, this area not only displays a multiplicity of language representation, but also a density of languages in close contact with each other. These features make Metropolitan LA a highly suitable site to explore problems and opportunities in language education in a multilingual environment.

To underscore language diversity in the area, Table 15.4 compares the number of speakers of languages other than English in the United States with the number of speakers of languages other than English in California, Los Angeles County, the City of Los Angeles, and Orange County.

As Table 15.4 shows, speakers of languages other than English in California and the Los Angeles area are at least double the figure for the U.S. as a whole.

Table 15.4 Speakers of Languages Other Than English by Percent

United States	California	Los Angeles County	City of Los Angeles	Orange County
20.9%	43.8%	56.8%	60.1%	45.6%

Source: Adapted from "Table S1601: Language Spoken at Home" for United States, State of California, Los Angeles County, Los Angeles city, and Orange County. American Community Survey 2008–2012 five-year estimates, U.S. Census Bureau.

I begin by using as an example the school district that serves the largest number of school children in Metropolitan LA (hereafter "the largest school district"). I have focused on public high schools within this and other school districts in Metropolitan LA, excluding K–9 because their language offerings are sporadic while all high schools offer foreign languages. I have also excluded private schools, as the argument I try to make is that it is important for local governments, school boards, and school administrators to meet the needs of local communities in their own "backyard" by offering languages spoken in these communities. I have, however, included a charter school in Granada Hills that is loosely affiliated with its local school district.[2] This school offers several languages, both as foreign and heritage language options.

Research Questions and Data Collection

The research questions were as follows: Do public high schools take advantage of the rich linguistic landscape of their multilingual city by offering foreign and heritage courses for languages spoken in the local community? If HLs are offered, are they taught differently from foreign languages? And, finally, do teachers have sufficient preparation and resources to handle classes that are exclusively heritage or mixed (i.e., heritage and non-heritage students)?

Data were collected from the most recent U.S. Census and Community Surveys as well as school district and high school websites, the *Los Angeles Times* "Mapping L.A. Neighborhoods" website, and the Heritage Alliance website maintained by the Center for Applied Linguistics (CAL). I also collected data from email and phone interviews with participants from high schools within the largest school district as well as others in Metropolitan LA and the charter school: seven teachers, a director of a language program at a high school, and a school district language instruction coordinator. I also analyzed a survey filled out by five additional teachers. I am grateful to everyone who generously provided information by answering my questions.

The study is small because the goal is exploratory and serves as a pilot for a larger and more detailed study (this will be discussed at the end of the chapter). It was also kept small out of necessity: Finding information about language offerings and getting in touch with instructors and administrators took an enormous amount of time. None of the information is easily accessible.

The first part of the project was carried out in 2012; information from the charter school was added in 2015. I started by determining what languages were offered in Metropolitan LA high schools and whether the major languages of the local communities were well represented. I was especially interested in the offerings of less commonly taught languages (LCTLs). Additionally, during the interviews I tried to understand whether teachers of world languages received training to help them meet the needs of HL learners.

In this study I use the definition of HL suggested by Polinsky and Kagan (2007) who describe a heritage language as the first "in the order of acquisition" but it not "completely acquired because of the individual's switch to another dominant language" (pp. 369–370). A typical HL speaker belongs to the 1.5 generation (born abroad and brought to U.S. at an early age) or second generation (born in the U.S.), grew up speaking English, and has at least one immigrant parent (Carreira & Kagan, 2011; Kasinitz, Mollenkopf, Waters, & Holdaway, 2008). These students frequently elect to study their home language in a formal setting in order to gain literacy, to find out more about their heritage culture and linguistic roots, and to be able to talk to relatives in the U.S. and abroad who may not speak English well (Carreira & Kagan, 2011).

4 Metropolitan Los Angeles as a Multilingual Region

Omnipresent multilingual billboards and signs indicate the linguistic diversity of Los Angeles. Figure 15.1, for example, is written in English, Spanish, Russian, and Armenian.

Some neighborhoods house more speakers of an immigrant language than speakers of English. For example, in the City of Glendale, more residents speak Armenian than English as their home language, and 40% of students in high schools are of Armenian background. In the City of Alhambra, 72% of residents are Asian, as stated on the city's official website, and the predominant language is Cantonese, followed by Mandarin. The City of Los Angeles, the largest city of the metropolitan area, is home to large Tagalog- and Korean-speaking communities. Spanish, of course, is spoken everywhere by immigrants from a large number of Latin American countries, the main source country being Mexico, followed by El Salvador and Guatemala (Pew Research Center, 2012, September 6).

The largest school district serves a population of over 3.5 million people, where 1.5 million residents are speakers of Spanish, 90,000 speak Tagalog/Filipino, and almost 90,000 speak Korean. Additionally, there are 62,000 speakers of Armenian, 58,000 speakers of Chinese (the census does not distinguish between Chinese languages), 43,000 of Persian, and 32,000 speakers of Russian. (California Department of Education, n.d.) Given these large populations within a single school district, it could be expected that neighborhood schools would offer at least some of the local languages, in both foreign and heritage instructional models. This would allow both groups of students to take advantage of formal instruction and community resources. However, while all

Figure 15.1 Multilingual Sign: English, Spanish, Russian, and Armenian

Table 15.5 Ten Largest Language Communities vis-à-vis Languages Offered in Public High Schools in the City of Los Angeles

Language	City of LA: Speakers of Languages Other Than English (age 5+)[a]	Number of Schools Offering the Language[b]
Spanish	1,515,409	94 (all high schools)
Tagalog	90,484	None
Korean	89,183	14
Armenian	62,673	None in the City of LA, but taught in Glendale
Chinese	54,660	17
Persian	43,516	None
Russian	32,527	1
Between 10,000 and 20,000 speakers		
Vietnamese		None in the City of LA, but taught in Orange County
Arabic		3 non-heritage; 1 heritage (charter school)
Japanese		9

Sources: [a]Adapted from "Table B16001: Language Spoken at Home by Ability to Speak English for the Population 5 Years and Over" for United States, State of California, Los Angeles County, Los Angeles city, and Orange County. American Community Survey 2010–2014 five-year estimates, U.S. Census Bureau; [b]adapted from California Department of Education (n.d.); [c]adapted from "Multilingual Los Angeles: The Impact of Immigrant Language Communities on FL/HL offerings in High Schools" by O. Kagan (2014a).

schools offer Spanish, and some offer a heritage track in addition to the foreign language track, many of the languages spoken in the community are not represented.

Table 15.5 shows the number of residents in the 10 largest language communities vis-à-vis the number of schools that offer instruction in those languages in the County of Los Angeles. As can be seen from the table, two languages with large immigrant communities—Tagalog/Filipino and Persian—are conspicuously absent from any school offerings. Russian is only offered in one school. Japanese is offered at nine schools, which may be attributed to its perceived importance in the 1980s. Vietnamese is not offered in the City of Los Angeles, but it is offered in Orange County (this will be discussed later in the chapter). Arabic is a recent addition to the district's curricula. It was first offered in a summer program at Bell High School in 2008, and since then has become a regular offering as stated on the school website (Bell High School, n.d.). It is now also offered in other schools.

5 How Are Decisions Made?

Table 15.5 is limited to the 10 largest populations of speakers and shows a curious, almost random, dynamic that led me to ask: How are decisions regarding language course offerings made? Through interviews, I have discovered that the decision to teach a certain language primarily depends on the principal's vision, community interest (see the example of Vietnamese below), and the availability of resources, in particular whether there is a teacher available to instruct the class. While teachers can teach subjects in which they are not credentialed, they are usually expected to work toward credentialing in the subject or, if no credential is available (as is often the case with LCTLs), some kind of training in the non-credentialed subject is required or recommended. While all of these reasons are significant, the principals' vision and willingness to take risks in their decision making may be the single most decisive factor that determines the language offerings. It does not appear that many principals in the largest school district are risk-takers. By contrast, smaller school districts are more willing to meet the needs of local populations by offering locally spoken languages. For example, congruent with the density of the language communities, Armenian is offered in Glendale, Mandarin Chinese is taught in Alhambra, Khmer in Long Beach, and Vietnamese in the cities of Garden Grove and Westminster, Orange County. Recent history shows, however, that it is neither simple nor quick to introduce the instruction of a new language in public schools, even if that language is supported by a large ethnic community.

The example of Vietnamese in the City of Westminster, Orange County, is instructive. The city population is close to 84,000, and almost 33,000 speak Vietnamese at home (U.S. Census Bureau, 2015). The Vietnamese first settled in the area in the mid-1970s; it took almost 25 years, however, for the school district to provide instruction in Vietnamese. An article in the *Los Angeles Times* observes:

> Vietnamese parents and students had clamored for such a course since the mid-1980s. Westminster High School was the first to respond, in 1999.
>
> *(Yi, 2002, September 22)*

At the time of writing, Vietnamese is taught in three high schools in Westminster School District (WSD) and seven in Garden Grove School District (GGUSD), thus clearly responding to community needs.

As I investigated this case, I interviewed two teachers teaching Vietnamese at different schools in GGUSD. In the first school, almost 80% of the students are of Vietnamese background. Some of them are new immigrants (the largest group from Vietnam immigrated following the end of Vietnam War in the mid-1975, but there is a new wave of immigration at present). The school offers four levels of Vietnamese: Levels 1 and 2 enroll U.S.-born students; Level 3 is mixed (i.e., those born in the U.S. and Vietnam), and students in Level 4 are the newcomers who are basically native speakers of Vietnamese, though they may lack formal or academic language, and are in need of English language instruction. In the group of students who were born in the U.S., many parents are 1.5 generation Vietnamese who do not speak the language well, but there are also families who maintain Vietnamese at home and some that send children to Vietnamese community schools. Thus, as is typical for HL learners, students' proficiencies vary widely, and the teacher needs to meet the challenge of offering instruction at many levels within one class (Telephone interview, 2012, with teacher from La Quinta High School).

The second school also offers four levels of Vietnamese. The teacher stressed that even though most of the students are of Vietnamese ancestry (only about 10% are not from Vietnamese families), over 80% hear Vietnamese from their grandparents alone, because many parents do not speak Vietnamese at home. As a result, the teacher believes that Vietnamese can be taught as a foreign language and there is no need to offer a specialized HL-focused curriculum. Students with an advanced proficiency take a diagnostic exam to place into higher level classes. It seems, however, that these students are offered a foreign language curriculum as well (email interview, 2012, with teacher from Bolsa Grande High School). The results of these two interviews with the teachers working in the same region indicate that teachers may understand the needs of similar populations of students differently and offer them different kinds of instruction.

6 Examples of Successful Programs

For the purposes of this study, I define a successful language instruction program on the following terms: First, schools must offer language instruction in an area in which the community speaks that language. Second, classes should offer instruction targeted not only for foreign language learners but also for heritage speakers. This second qualification is especially important because, as both research and practice show, heritage speakers have different needs and learning targets from students acquiring a new language (see, for example, Helmer, 2014.)

To determine which schools teach HLs to heritage learners, I relied on interviews with teachers because information on course offerings is not listed on school websites for languages other than Spanish; in other words, while many school websites indicate that they offer courses for heritage speakers of Spanish, information regarding LCTLs is typically absent. The lack of publicized information regarding HL instruction can be seen to indicate the general lack of resources allocated to such courses or curricula development. For example, though teachers I interviewed clearly understood that their HL students were different from foreign language learners, in some cases the curriculum was the same for both groups. All teachers said that their classes were highly heterogeneous. Several of the respondents mentioned that lack of materials created difficulties as they had to either adapt existing materials designed for foreign language learners or create their own materials for HL learners. Finally, and disturbingly, teachers have little contact with colleagues and little opportunity to discuss the challenges they face in the classroom. As one teacher said while answering my questions, "This is the first time anyone asked me about my classes" (Arabic teacher, summer 2012). I discuss my interviews with several teachers in some detail below, keeping my respondents anonymous according to the IRB requirements of the study.

Instructor concerns with addressing the differential needs of heritage speakers and foreign language students are pronounced and cut across the various languages represented in Metropolitan LA. For example, a teacher of Mandarin at a high school in an area with a large Chinese population stated: "The curriculum [for heritage students] is more challenging and the students learn about Chinese culture more in depth than the regular students" (email interview, 2012). Similarly, a teacher of Armenian was clearly aware of her students' language needs when she observed that while all her students could speak Armenian, they need instruction in literacy. Similarly, she noted the lack of appropriate instructional materials; the school uses textbooks from Armenia that are not suitable for students who have grown up speaking English as their dominant language in the U.S. According to this teacher, much of the material used in the classroom is developed by teachers at the school on an ad-hoc basis (email and telephone interviews, 2012).

These challenges appear ubiquitous: A Korean teacher in a high school close to Koreatown reported that, in the beginning Korean 1 course, foreign language learners are taught together with heritage learners, and that the course includes instruction in the alphabet and in simple language routines. Although the latter would be very familiar to HL learners and for this reason not challenging, the teacher writes that, "It's ok for them to review." Levels 2 and 3 offer separate classes for HL and foreign language learners; however, the curriculum does not speak to the points made by Helmer (2014) regarding HL pedagogy: grammar and spelling are stressed and, in Korean 3, which enrolls mostly or only heritage students, literature (email and telephone interviews, 2012). Though the school offers four levels of Korean, these are taught by a single instructor who makes all curricular decisions on her own without any input from colleagues or administrators.

As we can see, "successes" in these cases are not without their own limitations. While these schools meet some local needs and provide instruction that can differentiate between heritage speakers and foreign language learners, they may have difficulty fully meeting the demands of different categories of students. Often, limited resources play a role.

These limitations are also evident in the case of a Khmer program in the Long Beach Unified School District. Teaching Khmer for Khmer speakers can be seen like an example of successful collaboration between the community and the school district. With over 17,000 Cambodian speakers, the City of Long Beach, California, "has the largest Cambodian population outside of Cambodia" (Wright, 2010, p. 123). To meet the instructional needs of this sizable population, the school district has provided the only program in California to cater to Khmer speakers at Wilson High School. The success of this program seems to be largely due to a single teacher's preparation and creativity. The teacher has about 100 students a year and offers four levels of Khmer.

According to the Khmer teacher, 90% of students who enroll in this course were born in the U.S., "meaning they understand spoken Khmer but have difficulty speaking" (email interview, 2012). The teacher is trained in teaching ESL, and he reports that he uses "the models and samples in ESL materials" because there are limited Khmer materials available. He also stresses that he has "to create many of the teaching materials/lessons" himself (email interview, 2012). Wright (2010) notes that it is difficult to find qualified teachers of Khmer who have fulfilled all teacher certification requirements. The same of course is true of many LCTLs.

As my interviews with the teachers of Armenian, Korean, Mandarin, Vietnamese, and Khmer show, while each school's language instruction can be deemed a success on the basis of responding to the local community and maintaining a distinction between foreign and heritage learners, these teachers, for all of their dedication and creativity, have limited ability to provide a comprehensive and targeted educational environment. Training in language pedagogy and certification examinations target foreign language teaching, but do not typically include strategies for HL instruction, or classroom contexts that includes both HL and foreign language learners, leaving teachers such as these to improvise on an ad-hoc basis.

7 A School Offering Several Languages of Local Communities

At this juncture, I turn my focus from schools that address a single linguistic community to schools with multiple regional languages. The charter school in Granada Hills is illustrative: This campus is able to offer Spanish, Korean, Arabic, and Mandarin Chinese as both foreign and heritage languages. The school used to teach Armenian but had to discontinue the program since there was no instructor who could teach both Armenian and another subject. There is also an interest in Persian and Tagalog/Filipino, but so far the school has not been able to find teachers who would either teach part-time or could teach one of these languages and another subject.

The level of institutional investment in the programs that are offered is notable. With a Language Program Coordinator who is an expert in foreign and heritage language teaching, the school is able to provide more comprehensive curricula than in the case of schools whose responsibilities for curricular development fall upon a single teacher with limited resources. The program coordinator explained in an interview that HL classes 1) build on the knowledge and skills that heritage speakers bring to the classroom; 2) provide students with language-use experiences that move them beyond informal situations; 3) increase student control of the formal linguistic register; 4) highlight heritage cultures within and beyond the U.S.; 5) use authentic materials to expose students to a variety of contents; and, 6) prepare them to function in the world beyond the classroom (email interviews, 2012, 2014).

Differences between this developed program and the ad-hoc instruction provided at the schools discussed above are marked. For example, the charter school's Department of World Languages and Culture has a clear separation between the foreign and heritage language tracks. The department's manual, *Framework-Aligned Instruction in Action: Teaching Heritage Languages*

(Department of World Languages and Cultures, n.d.), reinforces the importance of distinguishing heritage from foreign language learners. To this point, the handbook states:

> Effective heritage language programs build upon the knowledge and skills heritage speakers bring to the classroom. They provide students with language-use experiences that move them beyond the informal situations in which they function. Structured activities enable students to perform successfully in formal, academic, professional and other real-world situations. In addition, systematic support is provided to increase student control of the formal linguistic register necessary to function in the broadest range of situations.
>
> *(p. 3)*

In such an explanation, the handbook clearly indicates the needs of HL learners. In recognition of these different learning needs, the school has developed a placement program in which students are tested for proficiency and then placed into the most appropriate track and level. The program pays attention not only to students' linguistic abilities, but to their affective needs as well by addressing such features of learning as self-esteem, which research has shown to be pronounced with HL learners (Carreira, 2003, 2004; He, 2004, 2010; He & Xiao, 2008; Helmer, 2014; Tallon, 2009; Weger-Guntharp, 2008). According to the manual, "Topics are chosen in order to develop a strong sense of identity and a corresponding high level of self-esteem as students develop the broadest possible worldview and begin to see themselves in professional roles" (p. 3). Furthermore, curriculum goals are constructed in response to students' motivations and identities and built in a top-down (macro) fashion to respond to students' interests and needs (Carreira & Kagan, 2011; for a further discussion of identity's influence on language instruction, see a special issue of the *Heritage Language Journal*, Fall 2010). Indicating the extensive attention to HL instruction, the school's manual explains that heritage speakers are often able to understand the main ideas when listening, but may have difficulties understanding formal situations. It also elaborates that HL learners "reading ability is substantially below their performance in listening" (p. 3) thus paving the way for using listening as a springboard for reading instruction. Finally, the manual makes a point that students' "writing mirrors their speech" (p. 3), i.e., certain kinds of errors should be expected and anticipated. Building on these guidelines, teachers create a curriculum fitting their heritage students' requirements.

After examining the materials offered by the school, I also collected data from the teachers themselves. An online survey completed by the five teachers in the program shed additional light on their instructional processes. In particular, the respondents specified the differences that they perceive between the two groups of students. To them, heritage learners bring to the classroom "better command of the language such as speaking, writing, understanding" and "a great deal of in-built vocabulary and cultural knowledge." Moreover, heritage learners "have linguistic proficiency (receptive and/or productive) cultural and content knowledge and are connected to a heritage language family and potentially community." The teachers believe that the needs of heritage learners include: "Writing formal essays, grammar in general, accents, spelling"; some of these students also need "to acquire vocabulary and many need to make their receptive knowledge productive." All teachers mentioned a need to improve literacy.

Analyzing the comparison between the two groups of students, teachers commented that, "Instructional points for heritage learners focus on language acquisition, topic development and analysis. Foreign Language Learners focus on structure, basic writing communication, speaking abilities and vocabulary development." One of the respondents put it succinctly: "They are totally different." Another teacher mentioned different "cultural experiences" that the two groups bring to the classroom. One of the teachers reported the following:

They converge in some areas and are different in others. Students need to develop literacy skills and need to acquire grammatical elements that are not present in their linguistic repertoire. Additionally, there are objectives for content/culture and the content connected to living "between worlds" that is appropriate to heritage and not for non-natives.

All teachers expressed an interest in finding out about available textbooks and current research on heritage learners and seeing "materials used by other programs as well as student products and determine how programs/materials lead to successful outcomes." The respondents were also asked whether they thought the two groups of students should be taught together or separately. They unanimously responded "separately."

The language programs at the charter school described in this section will be the site for the second stage of the study. This will include observations of foreign language and HL classes as well as interviews with teachers and students over the course of a year. It is my hope that when the project is complete, it will generate concrete recommendations that may benefit other high school programs.

8 Limitations of the Study

This is a small study. It includes one, albeit a very large, metropolitan area, a small number of interviews with teachers (seven), and two interviews with administrators. It also includes five additional responses from teachers of the charter school who filled out an online survey. I would be the first to say that the study is too small to come to any robust conclusions. My justification for the chapter is that the results I describe are supported by other published work. For example, Carreira (2014) conducted a study of 300 language programs around the country and found that few offer special tracks for HLs or professional development for teachers. Ducar's recent study (2012) shows that fewer than half of Spanish programs in the U.S. offer special tracks for heritage speakers, no matter where they are located. These conclusions are also supported by my work as a director and instructor in the STARTALK/NHLRC[3] summer workshops where 30–40 teachers have met for a week every summer since 2009. We receive close to 100 applications every year, which underscores the need teachers feel for professional development in HL methods. Participants express a need for more professional development focusing on HLs which they have not received in their professional development as teachers of foreign languages. The workshop participants are as eager for more materials and heritage-specific curricula as the teachers I interviewed for this study. And they also strive for contacts with other teachers in similar situations.

9 Conclusions and Recommendations

At the beginning of this chapter, I asked whether immigrant language communities make an impact on language education in public high schools. The question must be answered in the negative: The ethnic language communities of Metropolitan Los Angeles have very little impact on the language offerings in high schools. As has been shown, Spanish is offered at all public high schools, but such prevalence may be unsurprising since Spanish is the most commonly taught foreign language in the U.S. By and large, the linguistic geography of Metropolitan LA seems mostly ignored in the public educational system, especially in the large school district featured in the study. On the whole, schools do not seem to take advantage of the surrounding communities and their linguistic and cultural richness.

Despite a paucity of targeted language instruction programs, examples of successful programs for HL learners can be found, indicating that there is in fact a way to connect the community with neighborhood schools, as well as a way to implement heritage-specific methodologies in teaching. In terms of the institutionalization framework as described by Ekholm and Trier (1987), factors that advance these two conditions can contribute to the implementation and eventual institutionalization of HL programs within a metropolitan area. In this context "institutionalization" refers to the incorporation of these programs such that they become permanent and stable curricular offerings that respond to their communities and meet the needs of all students.

The schools that make use of HL strategies and integrate with their surrounding communities tend to be found in smaller school districts or, in one example, in a charter school. These successful examples show even more poignantly, however, that there is no coherent policy of language offerings across districts or even between schools within the same district. As a result, school districts and individual schools often miss opportunities to increase their offerings of heritage or foreign languages spoken in local communities. Inter- and intra-district communication on this topic is clearly needed for offerings in HLs not only to grow but to grow in a coherent way. This approach would also lessen the risk factors for individual schools and their principals, making the process less dependent on the vision of isolated school principals.

My data also indicates that teachers rarely receive professional development in the area of HL teaching. A study by Lee and Oxelson (2006) demonstrates that, if teachers of all subjects are aware of the needs of HL speakers, they may be more supportive of HL instruction. The lack of training or awareness is not limited to teachers: It would be helpful for school administrators to understand the needs of students from homes where languages other than English are spoken.

While the field of HL education is relatively new, sufficient research and curriculum guidelines have become available in the past fifteen years[4] to indicate where the focus of HL curricula ought to be (Beaudrie, Ducar, & Potowski, 2014; Benmamoun, Montrul, & Polinsky, 2008.) As Schwartz Caballero (2014) notes, the resources "available to HL teachers are impressive" (p. 368) but they may not be easily available. This next step—making the material available and accessible—needs to be taken by those who are in charge of preparing foreign language teachers so that teaching HLs becomes part of teacher preparation.

Communities themselves could be more proactive in seeking collaborations with schools; however, although this would be helpful, most communities lack the know-how or organizational capacity to initiate such collaboration. For these reasons, it seems more appropriate and realistic for school districts and public schools to take on the task of engaging local communities in decision making regarding language offerings. There is also the need for more flexibility in the process of introducing course offerings so that the implementation of a future HL program can be expedited. Such flexibility would help avoid the case of Vietnamese instruction discussed earlier in the chapter, which took almost 20 years to implement.

As can be seen from the chapter, the data are limited and would not yield robust and unequivocal conclusions. However, the difficulties I have experienced in trying to collect data together with information from my interviews with instructors all indicate a need to enhance offerings for HL learners and to make preparation in HL teaching part and parcel of language instructor preparation. These measures, in its turn, will lead to greater language capacity in the country and may slow the sad trend of the "decline in language offerings from 1997 to 2008" noted by Fee et al. (2014, p. 9). Instituting heritage and foreign language programs in areas where there are large communities speaking the language will benefit all students and will improve language instruction. One step at a time locally can truly lead to huge changes in language teaching and language competence nationally.

Notes

1 Both Los Angeles County and Orange County consist of several cities. For instance, the cities of Alhambra, Glendale, and Long Beach are located within Los Angeles County, while Garden Grove and Westminster are located in Orange County. Los Angeles County also includes the City of Los Angeles. Typically, these cities each have their own school districts, though city boundaries and those of school districts do not always match exactly.
2 Charter schools vary a great deal: Some are dependent, under district control but free to follow their charter educational plan; some are independent, loosely affiliated with local school districts that have limited oversight. Some independent charter schools are start-ups and do not serve students within a specific geographic region; others are conversion schools that change the status of a district school from dependent to independent schools governed by their charter document. All charter schools are public schools and do not charge tuition. (B. Zaslow, personal communication, May 10, 2016).
3 For more information about the workshops, see NHLRC (2015).
4 The interest in heritage language instruction can be traced back to the first National Conference on Heritage Languages (Peyton, Ranard, & McGinnis, 2001) and the research agenda (UCLA Steering Committee, 2000.)

References

American Council on the Teaching of Foreign Languages. (2014). World-readiness standards for learning languages. Retrieved from http://www.actfl.org/publications/all/world-readiness-standards-learning-languages

Beaudrie, S., Ducar, C., & Potowski, K. (2014). *Heritage language teaching: From research to practice.* New York, NY: McGraw Hill.

Bell High School. (n.d.). Arabic language [Web page]. Retrieved from http://www.arabic-socal.com/

Bennamoun, E., Montrul, S., & Polinsky, M. (2008). White paper: Prolegomena to heritage linguistics. Retrieved from http://www.international.ucla.edu/media/files/HL-whitepaper.pdf

California Department of Education. (n.d.). DataQuest [information portal about California schools and districts]. Retrieved from http://data1.cde.ca.gov/dataquest/

Carreira, M. (2003). Profiles of SNS students in the twenty-first century: Pedagogical implications of the changing demographics and social status of U.S. Hispanics. In A. Roca & M. C. Colombi (Eds.), *Mi lengua: Spanish as a heritage language in the United States* (pp. 51–77). Washington, DC: Georgetown University Press.

Carreira, M. (2004). Seeking explanatory adequacy: A dual approach to understanding the term "heritage language learner". *Heritage Language Journal, 2*(1), 1–25. Retrieved from http://www.heritagelanguages.org

Carreira, M. (2014). Teaching heritage language learners: A study of program profiles, practices, and needs. In P. Trifonas & T. Aravossitas (Eds.), *Rethinking heritage language education* (pp. 20–44). Cambridge, UK: Cambridge University Press.

Carreira, M., & Kagan, O. (2011). The results of the National Heritage Language Survey: Implications for teaching, curriculum design, and professional development. *Foreign Language Annals, 44*(1), 40–64.

Department of World Languages and Cultures. (n.d.). Department of World Languages and Cultures notebook. Retrieved from http://spanish-for-spanish-speaker.granadahills.groupfusion.net/modules/locker/files/get_group_file.phtml?fid=26098254&gid=1782571

Ducar, C. (2012). SHL learners attitudes and motivations: Reconciling opposing forces. In S. Beaudrie & M. Fairclough (Eds.), *Spanish as a heritage language in the U.S.: State of the science* (pp. 253–282). Washington, DC: Georgetown University Press.

Ekholm, M., & Trier, U. P. (1987). The concept of institutionalization: Some remarks. In M. B. Miles, M. Ekholm, & R. Vandenberghe (Eds.), *Lasting school improvement: Exploring the process of institutionalization* (pp. 13–21). Leuven, Belgium: Acco.

Fee, M., Rhodes, N.C., & Wiley, T. G. (2014). Demographic realities, challenges, and opportunities. In T. G. Wiley, J. K. Peyton, D. Christian, S. K. Moore, & N. Liu (Eds.), *Handbook on heritage, community, and Native American language education in the United States: Research, policy and practice* (pp. 6–18). London, UK: Routledge.

He, A. W. (2004). Identity construction in Chinese heritage language classes. *Pragmatics, 14*(2–3), 199–216.

He, A. W. (2010). The heart of heritage: Sociocultural dimensions of heritage language learning. *Annual Review of Applied Linguistics, 30,* 66–82.

He, A. W., & Xiao, Y. (Eds.). (2008). *Chinese as a heritage language: Fostering rooted world citizenry.* Honolulu, HI: National Foreign Language Resource Center, University of Hawai'i at Mānoa.

Helmer, K. A. (2014). "It's not real, it's just a story to just learn Spanish": Understanding heritage language learner resistance in a Southwest charter high school. *Heritage Language Journal, 11*(3), 186–206.

Kagan, O. (2014a, April). Multilingual Los Angeles: The impact of immigrant language communities on FL/HL offerings in high schools. In *A Forum on Internationalization of U.S. Education in the 21st Century.* Symposium conducted by U.S. Department of Education, Williamsburg, VA.

Kagan, O. (2014b). Russian heritage language learners: From students' profiles to project-based curriculum. In T. Wiley, J. Peyton, D. Christian, S. Moore, & N. Liu (Eds.), *Handbook of heritage, community, and Native American languages in the United States: Research, policy, and educational practice* (pp. 177–185). New York, NY/Washington, DC: Routledge and Center for Applied Linguistics.

Kasinitz, P., Mollenkopf, J., Waters, M., & Holdaway, J. (2008). *Inheriting the city: The children of immigrants come of age.* New York, NY: Russell Sage Foundation.

Lee, J. S., & Oxelson, E. (2006). "It's not my job": K–12 teacher attitudes toward students' heritage language maintenance. *Bilingual Research Journal, 30*(2), 453–477.

NHLRC. (2015). STARTALK/NHLRC Teacher Workshop. Retrieved from the National Heritage Language Resource Center website: http://www.nhlrc.ucla.edu/nhlrc/events/startalkworkshop/2015/home

Pew Research Center. (2012, September 6). Population distribution of Hispanic origin groups by county, 2010 [Web site]. Retrieved from http://www.pewhispanic.org/2012/09/06/population-distribution-of-hispanic-origin-groups-by-county/

Peyton, J. K., Ranard, D. A., & McGinnis, S. (2001). *Heritage languages in America: Preserving a national resource.* McHenry, IL: Delta Systems Company Inc.

Polinsky, M., & Kagan, O. (2007). Heritage languages: In the "wild" and in the classroom. *Languages and Linguistics Compass, 1*(5), 368–395. Retrieved from http://scholar.harvard.edu/files/mpolinsky/files/Offprint.pdf?m=1360038879

Schwartz Caballero, A. M. (2014). Preparing teachers to work with heritage language learners. In T. Wiley, J. Peyton, D. Christian, S. Moore, & N. Liu (Eds.), *Handbook of heritage, community, and Native American Languages in the United States: Research, policy, and educational practice* (pp. 359–369). New York, NY: Routledge.

Tallon, M. (2009). Foreign language anxiety and heritage students of Spanish: A quantitative study. *Foreign Language Annals, 42*(1), 112–137.

UCLA Steering Committee. (2000). Heritage language research priorities conference report. *Bilingual Research Journal, 24*(4), 475–488.

U.S. Census Bureau. (2013). Table S1601: Languages spoken at home for the population 5 years and over, United States, State of California, Los Angeles County, Los Angeles City, and Orange County, California [data tables]. *American Community Survey 2008–2012 5-year Estimates.* Retrieved from http://www.census.gov

U.S. Census Bureau. (2015). Table B16001: Language spoken at home by ability to speak English for the population 5 years and over, United States, State of California, Los Angeles County, Los Angeles City, Orange County, California, and Westminster city, California [data table]. *American Community Survey 2010–14 5-year Estimates.* Retrieved from http://www.census.gov

Waldinger, R. (2007). The bounded community. *Ethnic and Racial Studies, 30*(3), 349–367.

Weger-Guntharp, H. D. (2008). The affective needs of limited proficiency heritage language learners: Perspectives from a Chinese foreign language classroom. In K. Kondo-Brown & J. D. Brown (Eds.), *Teaching Chinese, Japanese, and Korean heritage students: Curriculum needs, materials, and assessment* (pp. 211–234). Mahwah, NJ: Lawrence Erlbaum Associates Inc.

Wright, W. (2010). Khmer as a heritage language in the United States: Historical sketch, current realities, and future prospects. *Heritage Language Journal, 7*(1), 117–147. Retrieved from http://www.heritagelanguages.org/

Yi, D. (2002, September 22). Vietnamese classes set a new course. *The Los Angeles Times.* Retrieved from http://articles.latimes.com/2002/sep/22/local/me-vietclass22

16

Overcoming the Obstacles

Vietnamese and Khmer Heritage Language Programs in California

Claire Hitchins Chik and Wayne E. Wright

1 Introduction

Few schools offer heritage language (HL) programs in less commonly taught languages (LCTLs), even when large numbers of heritage speakers of these languages are present in surrounding communities (see, e.g., Kagan, this volume). A wide range of constraints plus a lack of institutional support make it difficult to start and sustain HL programs in LCTLs. Nonetheless, these challenges are not insurmountable. To illustrate, this chapter focuses on two school districts located in the Los Angeles metropolitan area, Long Beach Unified School District (LBUSD) and Garden Grove Unified School District (GGUSD), which have overcome these obstacles and have long-established, successful HL programs for their Cambodian (Khmer)[1] and Vietnamese students, respectively.

The Khmer and Vietnamese languages are rarely taught in U.S. schools, despite the fact that speakers of these Southeast Asian languages have been in the U.S. for over 35 years and continue to make up a large percentage of students in many schools in California and around the country (Boun & Wright, 2013). The Cambodian population in the U.S. began to grow significantly due to refugee resettlement beginning in the late 1970s. The City of Long Beach is widely recognized as having the largest population of Cambodians outside of Cambodia, with about 20,000 making up about 5% of the city's population (U.S. Census Bureau, 2015). A section of the city has been officially designated as "Cambodia Town." Of the school district's total population of about 79,709 students, about 7% (5,921) are Asian students,[2] the majority of whom are Cambodian (California Department of Education, 2014–2015). A wave of Vietnamese refugees began arriving in the U.S. in the second half of the 1970s, with one of the highest densities settling in Orange County, where GGUSD is located. A section of the county has been officially designated as "Little Saigon." Of the nearly 48,000 students enrolled in GGUSD, 14,567 are Vietnamese, that is, about 30% (James, 2013).

LBUSD and GGUSD have proven to be responsive to their students and local communities through their innovative Khmer and Vietnamese HL programs. The experiences of these districts in ensuring the success and longevity of the programs provide an example of the ways in which HL programs for other LCTLs can be developed and supported, and are thus worthy of study.

2 Institutionalization and Heritage Language Education

The Khmer and Vietnamese programs are analyzed with reference to the institutionalization framework proposed by Ekholm and Trier (1987). These authors use the term "institutionalization" to mean "a process through which an organization assimilates an innovation into its structure" (p. 13). In the first instance, the establishment of the programs themselves is an innovative step, and the Khmer and Vietnamese programs have gone through stages of initiation, implementation and, according to some of the indicators provided by Miles and Louis (1987, p. 26), institutionalization. In terms of these indicators, each program is accepted as an integral part of the curriculum by teachers, counselors, and administrators, is stable and expected to continue, and has routine allocations of resources. However, institutionalization never consists of arriving at a stable end state, and once initial hurdles are overcome, there is an "ongoingness" in the process that involves programs responding to new challenges in order to remain current, successful, and accepted (Miles & Louis, 1987).

In addition, Timmermans (1987) argues that "a distinction should be made between institutionalization at the school level and at the classroom level" (p. 134). The latter involves the uptake of innovations by individual teachers, and requires an intellectual effort that leads to changes in teaching practices. This focus is certainly apt with regard to programs that include heritage language learners (HLLs).[3] The formation of an HL program at the organizational level of a school and its incorporation into course offerings is the first step, but the learning environment for HLLs will be unsatisfactory if this is not accompanied by a second step: a change in teaching practices that encompasses HL pedagogy and the creation of HL-specific syllabi for use within each class. Researchers and practitioners point out that HL pedagogy is significantly different from second language pedagogy (e.g., Carreira, 2004; Kagan & Dillon, 2001/2003, 2009; Valdés, 2005). Students who have grown up in homes where the HL is spoken arrive in our classrooms with a measurable proficiency in the language and extensive knowledge of the culture, and a pedagogy that builds on these competencies is required. In other words, the establishment of HL programs is initially demographically driven, but cannot remain simply a response to student numbers (Beaudrie, 2011; Carreira, 2014).

In comparison to more commonly taught languages, the establishment of an LCTL program involves yet another layer of complexity in the institutionalization process. LCTL programs are almost always de facto HL programs, given that typically the vast majority of students that enroll are HLLs. This is certainly the case with both the Khmer and Vietnamese programs discussed in this chapter. More commonly taught languages such as Spanish or French have well-established fields of foreign language teaching and accompanying programs, and the incorporation of an HL track or the adoption of HL pedagogy is thus placed within this established field (M. Carreira, personal communication, May 13, 2016). LCTLs, on the other hand, do not have the resources of an established foreign language field to draw upon, and rather than the introduction of an HL track into an already existing program, the establishment of the program itself, together with an HL pedagogy, is typically required. For this reason, in order for an LCTL program to become stable and institutionalized, numerous factors need to be present at both the school and classroom levels.

School-level factors include those that are local to the institution, namely support from school and district administrators and the local community, as well as those that lie further afield, namely pathways to teacher certification and the establishment of student examinations by national or state entities. The discussion of the Khmer program focuses on these factors as they impinge on the institutionalization of the program at the school level. By contrast, the discussion of the Vietnamese program focuses on the introduction of an HL pedagogy at the classroom level, and discusses ongoing training efforts to support teaching practices that enhance the learning environment for HLLs.

3 Methodology

In this study we seek to answer the following research questions:

1. What are the past histories and future goals of the Khmer and Vietnamese programs?
2. What processes were, and are, used to overcome structural constraints in order to establish, maintain, and develop the Khmer and Vietnamese programs?
3. What institutional supports have been key to ensuring the longevity and success of the Khmer and Vietnamese programs?

Data for the Khmer HL program were collected by means of semi-structured interviews conducted between January and April 2015 with the Khmer HL teacher, the department head of the world languages program at the high school, the Assistant Superintendent of Curriculum, Instruction, and Professional Development (hereafter "district administrator"), and the former District Curriculum Leader for High School English Language Development/World Languages (hereafter "district curriculum leader"). Observations of all levels of the Khmer HL program were conducted in January 2015. In addition, the district curriculum leader provided surveys completed by 65 students who participated in the Khmer HL program in 2006. These anonymous surveys were part of a study on HL education in the district presented at the 2006 UC Language Consortium Conference. Interview transcripts, field note observations, and open-ended survey items were imported into NVivo 10.0 for coding and analysis.

For the Vietnamese program, data were collected by means of semi-structured interviews between December 2014 and December 2015 with:

a   Dzung Bach,[4] a teacher of Vietnamese I, III, and IV Honors, who was interviewed three times for approximately one hour each time.
b   Gabriel Magaña, one of two Teachers on Special Assignment (ToSA) for the Department of 7–12 Instruction/World Languages. His duties include: supporting new and tenured teachers, serving as a resource for effective research-based instructional strategies, and conducting professional development training, including a monthly professional learning community (PLC) meeting with the Vietnamese teachers. In all, Mr. Magaña was interviewed eight times for approximately half an hour each time.

Classroom observations were conducted in two high schools in November 2015: Mr. Bach's Vietnamese I class and Robert Nguyen's Vietnamese IV Honors class. An email interview was subsequently conducted with Mr. Nguyen. In addition, the Vietnamese teachers' PLC meeting was observed in November 2015. Nine teachers completed a follow-up survey asking three open-ended questions regarding the PLC and its impact on teaching practices. Interview transcripts, field notes from observations, and survey data were coded into themes using the constant comparative method (Glaser, 1969).

4 Program Histories

Khmer HL Program

Wilson High School, located near the heart of "Cambodia Town," is the only secondary school in LBUSD offering a Khmer-for-Khmer speakers program. There had been a few early attempts to create Khmer classes at other schools in the 1980s and early 1990s, including

Marshall and Franklin Middle Schools and Lakewood High School, but each program only lasted a year or two due to challenges recruiting and retaining qualified instructors. Long Beach also had a thriving Khmer bilingual program at two elementary schools from 1993 to 1999, which unfortunately came to an end following the passage of Proposition 227 in 1998 (Wright, 2003).

In the mid-1990s, a popular afterschool Khmer class at Wilson associated with the Cambodian students' club was taught by the school's Cambodian Community Worker. The club received some teaching and material support from the district's Program Assistance for Language Minority Students (PALMS). During this time, the district curriculum leader had been directed by an associate superintendent to create course outlines for the district's growing Spanish HL programs, the reason being that students could then receive proper credit for meeting foreign-language requirements when applying to California universities. Seeing an opportunity, she asked if she could create course outlines for Khmer HL courses as well. Permission was granted on the condition that no additional costs were incurred. Using her connections with Cambodian staff members in the PALMS office, the course outlines were completed and approved. The district curriculum leader described how she was motivated by her past experience as an ESL teacher working with Cambodian refugee students at Hoover Middle School, how she felt like she was never able to give them enough of what they needed, and how she wished an HL program had been available for them.

The Khmer HL afterschool program at Wilson was moved to seventh period and overseen by an official teacher of record because the Cambodian community worker was not a certified teacher. With the class offered as part of the school day, and students earning credits for college admissions, the Khmer HL program was given immediately legitimacy, equal to other world languages taught at the school. As the class became more formalized, however, the community worker felt less comfortable teaching it, plus it was well beyond his job description. In 1997, PALMS searched among existing Cambodian staff members and recruited an elementary school community worker, Darith Ung, who had the requisite educational background, qualifications, language skills, and a desire to teach Khmer and seek teacher certification. PALMS assigned him to Wilson in the mornings to teach one period of Khmer-for-Khmer speakers (Level 1–2), under the supervision of an official teacher of record.[5] The class grew in popularity, with higher levels added each year up to Level 7–8 by the fourth year. In addition to focusing on oral proficiency and literacy skills, the program also featured a strong focus on Cambodian history and traditional culture. Nearly two decades later, the program is stable, strong, and still taught by Mr. Ung, who remains highly committed to the program. He is now fully certified to teach high school Khmer and is a ToSA through the district office, teaching three periods of Khmer classes each day at Wilson.[6] He spends the rest of his time providing translation services and overseeing Title III projects at the district level. Getting to this point, however, required overcoming several structural constraints and receiving strong institutional support, as will be discussed below.

Vietnamese HL Program

Although Vietnamese immigration into the U.S. began to accelerate at the end of the 1970s, with a large portion of these immigrants settling in Orange County, it took approximately 20 years before Vietnamese classes were introduced into two of GGUSD's high schools, La Quinta and Bolsa Grande High Schools. Two teachers were hired in 2000, including Mr. Bach. The program has grown, and is now offered in all GGUSD high schools and four intermediate (middle) schools, as seen in Table 16.1.

Table 16.1 Vietnamese Classes Offered in GGUSD as of the 2015/16 School Year

High Schools	Vietnamese I			Vietnamese II			Vietnamese III			Vietnamese IV-Honors		
	sec-tions	stud-ents	teach-ers	sec-tions	stud-ents	teach-ers	sec-tions	stud-ents	teach-ers	sec-tions	stud-ents	teach-ers
Bolsa Grande	3	167	1	3	107	1	1	42	1	1	34	1
Garden Grove	3	108	1	2	74	1	2	53	1	1	30	1
La Quinta	4	143	3	4	147	1	2	77	1	1	37	1
Rancho Alamitos	2	70	1	2	61	1						
Santiago	1	34	1	1	26	1						
Los Amigos	2	51	1									
Pacifica	1	28	1									

Intermediate Schools	Vietnamese I		
	sections	students	teachers
Irvine	1	20	1
Jordan	1	18	1
McGarvin	1	29	1
Walton	1	18	1

Source: These figures were compiled by Gabriel Magaña from the GGUSD database. In total, there are 18 Vietnamese teachers; some teachers teach more than one level.

Three high schools offer Vietnamese I through IV Honors, two high schools offer Vietnamese I and II, and two high schools offer Vietnamese I. The programs that do not offer the full range of levels are expanding, and each year another level of Vietnamese is added as students move up the school. In addition, four intermediate schools offer Vietnamese I, which counts for high schools credit.

5 Essential Institutional Supports for Overcoming Structural Constraints

Khmer Program

Teacher Credentialing Challenges

As noted in the history of the Khmer HL program, a major challenge involved finding individuals qualified and committed to teaching Khmer. Even after such a teacher was found, a major constraint was the lack of state certification for Khmer language teaching at the secondary level. Mr. Ung—with substantial support from the district curriculum leader, the district administrator, and other district leaders—worked for many years taking courses and tests, trying to find a pathway for legitimate certification. The district curriculum leader noted that his Khmer skills were evaluated and certified by university faculty, and California had a Khmer test for bilingual teachers at the elementary level; however, the state would not accept any of these for secondary single-subject certification. At one point he was advised to simply get a credential in another subject such as Physical Education, but he insisted that he wanted to be certified to teach Khmer.

Ultimately, district officials in collaboration with HL scholars from UCLA and other educators around the state seeking similar certification in LCTLs worked with a local state legislator, Alan Lowenthal, who subsequently introduced legislation to address the issue. These efforts resulted in the California Commission for Teacher Credentialing establishing a California Subject Examination for Teachers (CSET) for Khmer and other LCTLs in 2009 (currently there are CSET exams for 22 languages). In addition to passing the CSET Khmer exam, Mr. Ung had to complete other requirements—including student teaching. With support from his district and school administrators, a flexible work schedule was established enabling him to complete these requirements without having to temporarily suspend his teaching of the Khmer classes. Ultimately he was able to become the first fully certified high school Khmer language teacher in the state. It is unknown if anyone else in the state has taken the exam and completed the certification. Mr. Ung described how he felt to finally earn this credential after many years of frustration and fights:

> It gave me a sense of security that I have a clear professional credential . . . it's something that fulfilled my life-long dream since I started working for the district. . . . And on a personal note, yes, that's an achievement that I can be proud of.

Having a fully certified teacher further added to the legitimacy of the Khmer HL program.

Other Challenges

Strong support from district and school administrators was essential to overcoming constraints associated with simply getting the Khmer HL program started. Through flexible and creative uses of staff members and funding, the Cambodian club's informal afterschool class became an official credit-earning world language course. Substantial support for Mr. Ung led to a long but ultimately victorious fight for a pathway to legitimate teacher certification. This strong support was also instrumental in saving the Khmer HL program when it was placed on a list of proposed cuts during a serious budget crisis. When asked how it got removed from the list, the district administrator laughed and said, "Screaming and yelling!" Mr. Ung and the district administrators argued that the program was the only one if its kind in the district and perhaps the state and country, and that the school was obligated to continue serving students who had completed the lower levels as they needed to take the higher levels to earn credits for college admissions. The district curriculum leader also noted that at one point the Khmer HL program was used as strong evidence in a school accreditation review that the school was serving the local community.

The Khmer HL program itself has other features that have helped ensure its longevity. One key feature is the use of combined level classes. For commonly taught languages such as Spanish, French, and German, the school has multiple teachers and multiple levels are available each period. For Khmer, with only one teacher, this is not possible, and thus it is difficult for students to fit the needed level into their schedule. To overcome this institutional constraint, Mr. Ung combines multiple levels into the same period. For example, for the three periods of classes observed, two periods were a combination of Levels 1–2 and 3–4, and the other period was a combination of Levels 5–6 and 7–8. Thus, at least for Levels 1 to 4, there are two potential periods when students can take the class. This arrangement has the full support of the department head and school administrators. Mr. Ung noted that the head counselor is very supportive in rearranging students' schedules so they can take the class. These combined classes, however, mean a lot more work for Mr. Ung. Students are divided into level groups seated on opposite sides of the classroom. During class Mr. Ung moves back and forth between the two groups, providing a bit of instruction, giving a specific task, and allowing students time to work on it while he goes to work with the other group, repeating the same process. He then returns to follow up on the work each group has done. During one observed class period, he moved back and forth between the two groups about four times. When asked about this in the interview, Mr. Ung admitted with a laugh, "It's hard because I have to jump around a lot! By the end of the day, I'm uuuuuuhhhhhhh! [exhausted]"

The department head has great respect for Mr. Ung and admires his strong commitment to the program and his students. He stated, "For my part, he has all the support that I can give." He also noted the school administrators know Mr. Ung well and strongly support the program. Mr. Ung also mentioned that the Assistant Principal overseeing world languages regularly visits his classroom to offer her support.

Another important support the school offers is space for the classes. In the past, the program was taught in various classrooms—whichever happened to be empty at the periods needed. But since 2011, the school has provided a dedicated classroom. Mr. Ung described this as a very positive change:

> It makes a huge difference! It gives [students] a sense of belonging. Now they are coming into their classroom, not somebody else's classrooms. It makes a huge difference for me as well too. I feel like if it's my classroom, I can decorate the way I like. When I was roaming, I don't dare even touch a computer. I don't dare even to post a paper on the wall, because you feel like you are in a guest's house. It's a huge difference. I hope it stays like this.

This change has enabled Mr. Ung to establish a clear space on campus for students to be Khmer, to celebrate their culture, and to be secure in their identity. A large Cambodian flag adorns the front window, a bilingual sign on the door welcomes students to the "Khmer Class," walls are covered floor to ceiling with colorful student posters on Cambodian history and culture alongside maps of Cambodia and other cultural artifacts, and student-made 3D models of a Cambodia village are displayed atop filing cabinets. A mini-fridge with an open container of money on top allows students to buy cold water in support of Mr. Ung's humanitarian work in Cambodia. Many students eat and hang out in the classroom during their lunch period.

However, a constraint that Mr. Ung faces is instructional materials—a common problem with less commonly taught HLs. Over the years, Mr. Ung has used a combination of materials developed for the (now defunct) elementary school Khmer bilingual program and Khmer literacy readers developed by the district in the early 1980s. While these materials are abundant, Mr. Ung began making annual trips to Cambodia each summer to engage in volunteer humanitarian work[7] and to search for newer supplemental materials for use in his class. The district administrator provides a small amount of funding to pay for the materials, but Mr. Ung has to pay his own travel expenses.[8] Mr. Ung typically purchases a few copies of current textbooks used in Cambodian schools, then makes copies of selected pages to supplement his lessons.

Finally, equally if not more important than district and school support is the strong support of the Cambodian American students in the Khmer HL program. Indeed, Mr. Ung described the students as the secret to the program's success:

> The success is that the students keep wanting to take it, because I think if there are no students, then that is the end, the failure of the program. So, I always have students that want to take the class, and that is a success.

An HL program cannot survive unless there are sufficient numbers of HL speakers in the school who want to take it. Despite the fact that the number of Cambodians living in the "Cambodia Town" section of the city is declining as families improve their economic situation and move to more prosperous neighborhoods, Wilson fortunately has a large school boundary inclusive of many of these neighborhoods. In addition, some students elect to transfer from other high schools to Wilson just to take the Khmer class. Mr. Ung described how students encourage their Cambodian friends to take the class, how much fun the class is, and how much they benefit from improving their Khmer proficiency and cultural knowledge. The teacher mentioned that when the program was threatened with budget cuts, the students were fully prepared to protest, write letters, and testify at school board meetings to fight for their program.

A new incentive for students is the opportunity to earn California's Seal of Biliteracy on their high school diploma. This outstanding recognition of bilingual skills is available for students who complete all four years of the Khmer program and who meet other criterion. A few students from the Class of 2015 were the first in the state to earn the Seal of Biliteracy for Khmer.

The surveys conducted by the district curriculum leader in 2006 provide strong evidence of how much students have enjoyed and benefited from the course. In the opened-ended questions about why they took the class, most described a desire to improve their Khmer language proficiency and to learn to read and write. One student wrote he took the class, "Because I was born in Cambodia but I [have] almost forgotten my own language, I felt that [the] Khmer class would be a great opportunity for me to bring back my language." Many also talked about wanting to connect with and learn more about their history and culture. As one student wrote, "I decided to take Khmer-for-Khmer Speakers to understand my culture better." In response to a question on what they liked best about the class, over half of the students commented that the class helped them improve their Khmer language skills and was also fun, and that they enjoyed being with other Cambodian American students. As one student stated, "It's where all the Khmer students are able to come and speak our native language and have fun and progress at our home language." In response to a question about how the class would help them in their future, most students described being able to communicate better with family and friends in the U.S. and in Cambodia, and several described how it would help them translate for others and in their future careers. For example, one student wrote, "It will help me communicate better with my family and other Cambodians. I can get jobs better if I'm bilingual. When I visit Cambodia one day I will be fluent and blend in with everyone."

Mr. Ung described receiving letters from former students thanking him and sharing ways their Khmer language skills were helping them in their careers. His Facebook page also features posts from former students thanking him with examples of how they are putting their Khmer skills to good use.[9] During observations of the class it was clear the students were highly engaged and enjoying the class. In fact, the graduating seniors (Class of 2015) presented Mr. Ung with a beautiful clock with the following engraving:

> Thank you for investing your time in us through your teaching of Khmer culture and language these past four years. We love you. Class of 2015

In summary, the Khmer HL program has been successful for nearly two decades first and foremost because there is a highly committed teacher who has earned the respect of the students and of his school and district administrators. By creating a fun class that provides students with valuable and desirable skills in the heritage language and culture, by going out of his way to find appropriate materials, by being willing to teach combined-level classes, he has created classes that students

Claire Hitchins Chik and Wayne E. Wright

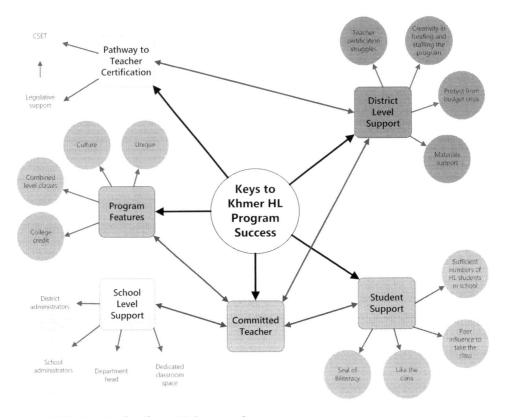

Figure 16.1   Keys to the Khmer HL Program Success

want and are able to take. With key allies at the school and district levels, he was able to become fully certified and receive needed support to stave off threats from budget cuts.

Remaining Challenges

Despite the successes, challenges and institutional constraints remain. As noted above, one of the biggest challenges is instructional materials. Mr. Ung's students are sometimes discouraged when they notice the supplemental materials from Cambodia are designed for lower grade levels. Another area of great need is technology. Mr. Ung mainly uses an old overhead projector and transparencies, along with worn-out white boards. He would love to have a SmartBoard and an Elmo-like document projector. Another challenge is that despite the combined level classes and counselor support, there are still far-fewer time slots for Khmer as there are for other world languages, thus there are students who want to take the class but can't due to schedule conflicts.

Other constraints include a general lack of opportunities for professional development (particularly in HL pedagogy) and Mr. Ung's status as a ToSA rather than as full-time faculty at Wilson. This arrangement means Mr. Ung has to spend time on district administrative tasks and translation and interpretation, which takes time away from preparing lessons and creating materials and removes him somewhat from the rest of the faculty at the school. Many former

Khmer community workers and paraprofessionals have been laid off as the demand for translation and linguistic accommodations for parents have declined. But Mr. Ung would like to see more Khmer staff hired, which would free him to focus on his teaching. It would also enable him to offer additional classes at the school, perhaps even a Khmer class for non-HL students if there was enough interest.

Finally, while the program has been highly successful at Wilson, the program has not been expanded to other high schools in the district. The district curriculum leader noted that changes in bussing has led to decreased enrollment of Cambodian American students at other high schools. However, Poly High School, also located near the heart of Cambodia Town, has a much larger Cambodian American student population than Wilson. Poly has shown interest in the past in creating its own Khmer HL program, but staffing, funding, and other issues have so far prevented this from happening. Mr. Ung said he would love to see the program expanded to Poly, believes it would be highly successful there, and said he would be willing to do whatever is needed to help the program get started. Indeed, expanding the program to other schools in the district and giving Cambodian American students in those schools the same opportunity as students at Wilson would likely bring even greater stability to the district's Khmer HL program.

Vietnamese Program

Hiring Challenges and Professional Development

The Vietnamese program, by contrast, has expanded to all high schools in GGUSD and to four intermediate schools. Like the Khmer program, it is supported by key personnel in the district and has routine allocations of resources and funding, not only for existing classes but also for the addition of new levels in high schools that currently only offer Vietnamese I or I and II. As a consequence of past and ongoing expansion, finding teachers that have the necessary credentials, experience, and Vietnamese language skills is a challenge, a common problem with LCTLs. Most of the Vietnamese teachers are not trained in HL pedagogy, and many do not have basic language teaching pedagogy when they start out. Their teaching credentials are in areas such as math, history, or English, and in addition to, or instead of, teaching these subjects, they teach Vietnamese classes. Once hired, all teachers of Vietnamese are required to take a language teaching methods class and also to pass the CSET in Vietnamese; however, these requirements only target second language, as opposed to HL, pedagogy.

For this reason, GGUSD has not relied entirely on external training and measures of language teaching proficiency. Professional development is available in summer workshops that focus on a variety of teaching issues. Monthly/weekly meetings at schools that have several Vietnamese teachers are also organized. This chapter, however, focuses on the PLCs led by Mr. Magaña that meet once a month from 3:30 to 5:00 pm. These are centralized meetings to which all the Vietnamese teachers are invited, including those who teach at intermediate schools. Attendance is voluntary, but a majority of teachers attend; in the meeting observed by the researcher, 12 of the 18 Vietnamese teachers were present. For those that do not attend, the resources and ideas from the meeting are available online, and they can also add their own materials for others to view.

Various topics related to the teaching of HLLs are covered, with the aim of supporting the Vietnamese teachers in their efforts to develop the language skills of these learners. For instance, the group has focused on the American Council on the Teaching of Foreign Languages' (2015) "can-do" statements as applied to Vietnamese I, analyzing and adapting them in order to clarify the functions that HL students at this level should be able to perform by the end of the year. In this way, expectations for Vietnamese I are streamlined, and better coordination between the schools is achieved. Another topic that has been addressed is how to deal with mixed abilities, a common challenge in classes that contain HL students.

For the academic year 2015/2016, the focus was on best practices in the teaching of writing to Vietnamese HLLs. In the observed meeting, some teachers had brought high, intermediate, and low writing samples of student work in order to discuss assessment strategies. After a very brief introduction by Mr. Magaña, the teachers worked in groups that were divided by level, and exchanged ideas in an informal and lively way. In addition to sharing and describing assessments, items on the agenda included reviewing writing rubrics and sharing essential vocabulary lists. Ideas on many other topics were also shared: lesson flow, i.e., how to divide class time (just under an hour) between a variety of activities targeting a variety of skills, ways to adapt textbooks, how to "build up" a project, use of technology, when to use English. As Mr. Magaña says, the PLC provides a setting in which all aspects of instruction can be discussed and veteran and novice teachers can exchange ideas.

Innovations at the Classroom Level: The Role of the Teacher on Special Assignment

Mr. Magaña sees his role as that of keeping abreast of current research-based pedagogies, in particular those relating to HL instruction, introducing these to teachers in workshops, and then providing opportunities by means of the PLCs to discuss the application of these approaches to the Vietnamese language classroom. In terms of the focus on writing, Mr. Magaña, in conjunction with the veteran teacher Mr. Bach, introduced Chevalier's (2004) framework for sequencing writing instruction for HLLs. This was presented in a three-hour summer workshop just before the beginning of the academic year. PLC meetings, such as the one observed in November 2015, subsequently provided a forum for discussing the framework and the practicalities of implementing it. Mr. Magaña noted that teachers are "more apt to want to try new things because they are doing it as a group."

Louis (2006) would agree. She argues that exposing teachers to innovative research-based pedagogies does not necessarily result in their incorporation into classroom practices. Instead, classroom uptake depends on opportunities for interpersonal interactions, which Louis terms the "social processing" (p. 3) of knowledge. This is crucial for the institutionalization of novel pedagogies, where discussion among colleagues allows for a shared understanding of the finer points of the innovation to emerge, and also for its adaptation to the local environment. The characteristics of the local environment at GGUSD include both the unique features involved in teaching the Vietnamese language as well as teaching it to HLLs.

Because of the importance of social processing, a central role of school leaders is to provide opportunities in which a communal exchange of ideas can occur. Louis (2006) sees their role as "'greasing the wheels' of social interaction" (p. 3), primarily through the organization of "dissemination events" (p. 8). Through the PLCs, Mr. Magaña establishes a routinized monthly event that fits this description. He describes his responsibilities as follows, "My position allows a big picture view and allows me to make connections and reach out and begin conversations and establish relationships." In "beginning conversations," Mr. Magaña encourages the social processing of new ideas for classroom application. The combination of Mr. Magaña's "big picture" role and the PLC meetings provides both a "top-down" introduction of research-based pedagogies from outside the local environment together with the "bottom-up" processing of these ideas by local practitioners in a social context (Louis, 2006, p. 8).

Innovations at the Classroom Level: Teachers' Experiences

From the perspective of the teachers, the bottom-up processing of pedagogical ideas was seen as very useful. In the surveys, teachers spoke to the important role the monthly PLCs played in supporting their classroom teaching. As one teacher pointed out, interactions that would not occur spontaneously were facilitated, "We have an opportunity to collaborate with other teachers from other schools within the district." Regarding this collaboration, teachers were overwhelmingly positive. Two of the teachers summed up the benefits as follows:

> The PLCs have impacted my teaching practices a great deal. . . . Communicating and collaborating with other teachers give me a clearer picture on how to improve my lessons as well as how to deliver them effectively.
>
> I find it extremely useful to interact with my other colleagues and PLC facilitators [Mr. Magaña and the other ToSA] regarding to our teaching practices. The interaction gives me a valuable opportunity to learn from their specific strengths in teaching to incorporate them to my own teaching.

In addition to the general benefits of the PLCs, four teachers mentioned the joint development of assessments as being particularly advantageous. These included the writing assessments shared in the November 2015 PLC as well as assessments targeting other skills discussed in earlier meetings. One example is:

> I've been able to get more ideas from my counterparts to apply in my classrooms. I enjoy the fact that we're working towards a common assessment.

In the email interview, Mr. Nguyen pointed out that as a veteran teacher he serves "as a resource and support for the new teachers" during the PLC meetings. In terms of Chevalier's (2004) writing framework for HLLs, this involved sharing insights such as the following:

> What is great about Chevalier's framework is that I can almost pinpoint where each individual student falls in this framework. I use that to help fill in whatever gaps they may have while moving them forward to the next stage. This is probably where teachers may struggle when they teach a heritage class. The ability level of their students may be all over the place.

PLCs, in short, provide a venue for the exchange of practical instructional ideas and the discussion of innovative approaches such as Chevalier's (2004) framework, instantiating the social processing of new ideas within a dissemination event as envisioned by Louis (2006). The results of these discussions influence classroom practices and, beyond this, encourage teachers to be analytical with regards to their teaching. As one teacher put it, "The PLCs have impacted my teaching practices a great deal. They give me an opportunity to deeply reflect on my strengths and weaknesses in terms of lessons and instructional strategies."

6 Conclusion

The Khmer and Vietnamese HL programs in LBUSD and GGUSD are strong, stable, and have lasted for many years due to substantial support and creative solutions that have overcome common institutional constraints in offering HL instruction in LCTLs. The discussion of the

Vietnamese program at GGUSD has focused on the intellectual and social efforts needed for the uptake of HL-specific teaching practices in the classroom. The monthly PLC meetings provide a venue for professional development that helps with this process. One of the challenges faced by the Khmer program is lack of access to such professional development. Mr. Ung noted that departmental-level meetings feature some informal exchange of ideas, "We share ideas, best practices, and stuff like that." But there are no district-level trainings and few opportunities to attend professional conferences.

Professional development that supports ongoing efforts to respond to HLL needs is particularly important with regard to LCTLs. Compared to programs that cater to larger populations such as Spanish, LCTLs are much closer to demographic vicissitudes that impact student profiles and therefore classroom dynamics. In both Long Beach and Orange County, the Khmer and Vietnamese communities are no longer primarily made up of first-generation immigrants, but rather of their second-generation children. In terms of family language practices, parents are increasingly English-dominant and tend to use this language regularly with their children, although interactions with grandparents ensure that the HL is still present in many homes. Mr. Bach points out that, "The parents go to work, and then it is the grandparents who take care of their grandchildren." As a result of these changes, a challenge that both programs face is the changing nature of the students they serve. Both Mr. Ung and Mr. Bach report that over the years they have noticed a decline in their HL students' language abilities. Mr. Ung says that while his students still have some receptive skills in Khmer, he has found the need to include a greater focus on developing their speaking skills. These students are still HLLs, but their needs are changing, and both programs face the possibility that they will gradually become more like foreign language rather than HL programs. In addition, both Mr. Ung and Mr. Bach have one or two non-HL students in their classes each year and, in the case of the Vietnamese program, students recently arrived from Vietnam are increasingly enrolling in the program. Ongoing training, such as that provided by the PLCs, can give teachers the tools needed to manage these as well as other challenges, and in so doing contribute to the continued success and stability of a program.

The discussion of the Khmer program has focused on the organizational effort that has been required to maintain a Khmer-for-Khmer speakers program in one Long Beach high school. Miles and Louis (1987) argue that one indicator of the institutionalization of a program at the organizational level is "person-independence" (p. 26), where the program depends on organizational structures and procedures rather than on specific individuals. In the context of LCTLs, this indicator can be elusive. The Khmer program has been sustained by a committed teacher, and searching for a replacement would likely prove demanding, though not impossible. The materials, resources, and other structures a new teacher would inherit, as discussed in this chapter, would provide a strong foundation, but this only goes so far in supporting a new teacher. Finding teachers who not only have the skills in both English and the target language but also the requisite qualifications is often challenging. Again, ongoing professional development would to some extent mitigate this problem, and a model such as the one provided by GGUSD in the form of a ToSA who leads regular PLCs is useful.

Despite these remaining challenges, GGUSD and LBUSD provide excellent examples of how school districts can and should be responsive to local language minority communities and offer innovative and successful HL programs, even in LCTLs. With the growing popularity of the Seal of Biliteracy, which to date has been adopted or is under development in over half the states, this is an opportune time for districts around the U.S. to afford students an opportunity to further develop and maintain their HLs, and to have their bilingual skills honored and recognized in a manner that can facilitate college admissions and future careers.

Notes

1 Cambodian and Khmer are often used interchangeably to refer to both the language and members of the ethnic group. However, Khmer is the proper name of the language and will be used in this chapter.

2 The percentage of Asian students does not include Filipino or Pacific Islander students.

3 These programs could consist of HLLs only or they could include both HLLs and non-HLLs, i.e., traditional foreign language learners. In both the Khmer and Vietnamese programs, the vast majority of students are HLLs, with one or two non-HLLs enrolling each year. For this reason, they will be referred to as "HL programs."

The California Department of Education (2012–2013) provides statistics for foreign language courses in California, including "X language for native speakers." Aside from Spanish for Native Speakers (3,035 classes in 644 schools), only a very limited number of courses "for native speakers" appear. The Vietnamese program in GGUSD does not appear as a "for native speaker" class because it is not formally designated "for native speakers." The Khmer class is designated "for native speakers" but it, too, does not appear in the listings because, presumably, it is subsumed in the "Other language course for native speakers" category. However, the composition of both the Khmer and Vietnamese programs is very similar.

4 The names of the schools, districts, and participants are used in this chapter with permission from GGUSD and LBUSD and all those who so kindly agreed to participate.

5 Each level corresponds with a semester; thus Level 1–2 refers to semester 1 and 2 (year 1), Level 3–4 refers to semester 3 and 4 (year 2), and so forth.

6 Note that the role of a Teacher on Special Assignment differs in the GGUSD and Wilson High School contexts.

7 Mr. Ung's humanitarian work is through a volunteer NGO called Hearts Without Borders. Two of the board members are former district administrators associated with the PALMS office.

8 The cost of a round-trip ticket to Cambodia ranges from $1,500 to $2,500.

9 One of these posts on Mr. Ung's Facebook page reads, "Today I was able to host a Cambodian Community Forum completely in Khmer! I was so nervous I was certain that I'd be using my Khmerenglish but I didn't! Though I said a lot of uhm's but cracked a few jokes in Khmer and everyone actually laughed. Khmer karaoke and 4 years of class in Wilson really paid off!!! Thank you!!!!! :)"

References

American Council on the Teaching of Foreign Languages. (2015). Can-do statements: Performance indicators for language learners. Retrieved from http://www.actfl.org/sites/default/files/pdfs/Can-Do_Statements_2015.pdf

Beaudrie, S. M. (2011). Spanish heritage language programs: A snapshot of current programs in the southwestern United States. *Foreign Language Annals, 44*(2), 321–337.

Boun, S., & Wright, W. E. (2013). K–12 schooling experiences of Southeast Asian American students. In R. Endo & X. L. Rong (Eds.), *Educating Asian Americans: Achievement, schooling, and identities* (pp. 75–101). Charlotte, NC: Information Age Publishing.

California Department of Education. (2012–2013). Course Listing, State of California 2012–2013 [data table]. Retrieved from http://dq.cde.ca.gov/dataquest/coursereports/CourseReport.aspx?CDSCode=0 0000000000000&cChoice=StCrse&cYear=2012–13&cLevel=State&cTopic=Course&myTimeFrame=S&submit1=Submit&VE=on&Self=on&Subject=on&IB=on&AP=on

California Department of Education. (2014–2015). DataQuest: Enrollment by ethnicity for 2014–2015 [data table], Long Beach Unified School District. Retrieved from http://data1.cde.ca.gov/dataquest/Enrollment/EthnicEnr.aspx?cChoice=DistEnrEth&cYear=2014–15&cSelect=1964725—Long%20 Beach%20Unified&TheCounty=&cLevel=District&cTopic=Enrollment&myTimeFrame=S&cType=ALL&cGender=B

Carreira, M. (2004). Seeking explanatory adequacy: A dual approach to understanding the term "heritage language learner". *Heritage Language Journal, 2*(1), 1–25. Retrieved from http://www.heritagelanguages.org

Carreira, M. (2014). Teaching heritage language learners: A study of programme profiles, practices, and needs. In P. Trifonas & T. Aravossitas (Eds.), *Rethinking heritage language education* (pp. 20–44). Cambridge, UK: Cambridge University Press.

Chevalier, J. F. (2004). Heritage language literacy: Theory and practice. *Heritage Language Journal, 2*(1), 1–19. Retrieved from http://www.heritagelanguages.org

Ekholm, M., & Trier, U. P. (1987). The concept of institutionalization: Some remarks. In M. B. Miles, M. Ekholm, & R. Vandenberghe (Eds.), *Lasting school improvement: Exploring the process of institutionalization* (pp. 13–21). Leuven, Belgium: Acco.

Glaser, B. G. (1969). The constant comparative method of qualitative analysis. In G. J. McCall & J. L. Simmons (Eds.), *Issues in participant observation* (pp. 216–228). Reading, MA: Addison-Wesley.

James, E. (2013, May 1). Vietnamese immersion program could be state's first. *Orange County Register*. Retrieved from http://www.ocregister.com/articles/vietnamese-506665-immersion-program.html

Kagan, O., & Dillon, K. (2001/2003). A new perspective on teaching Russian: Focus on the heritage learner. *Heritage Language Journal*, *1*(1), 76–90. Retrieved from http://www.heritagelanguages.org (Reprinted from *Slavic and East European Journal*, *45*(3), 2001, 507–518.)

Kagan, O., & Dillon, K. (2009). *Preparation of teachers of heritage languages: A matrix*. Proceedings of the Teacher Preparation Conference, University of Minnesota. Retrieved from http://www.international.ucla.edu/media/files/kagan_dillon-xz-gkt.pdf

Louis, K. S. (2006). *Organizing for school change*. New York, NY: Routledge.

Miles, M. B., & Louis, K. S. (1987). Research on institutionalization: A reflective review. In M. B. Miles, M. Ekholm, & R. Vandenberghe (Eds.), *Lasting school improvement: Exploring the process of institutionalization* (pp. 25–44). Leuven, Belgium: Acco.

Timmermans, R. (1987). Institutionalization of the MAVO-project—a Dutch case study. In M. B. Miles, M. Ekholm, & R. Vandenberghe (Eds.), *Lasting school improvement: Exploring the process of institutionalization* (pp. 125–142). Leuven, Belgium: Acco.

U.S. Census Bureau. (2015). *2010–2015 American Community Survey 5-year estimates*. Washington, DC: Author.

Valdés, G. (2005). Bilingualism, heritage language learners, and SLA research: Opportunities lost or seized? *Modern Language Journal*, *89*(3), 410–426.

Wright, W. E. (2003). The success and demise of a Khmer (Cambodian) bilingual education program: A case study. In C. C. Park, A. L. Goodwin, & S. J. Lee (Eds.), *Asian American identities, families, and schooling* (pp. 225–252). Greenwich, CT: Information Age Publishing.

17

Institutionalization of French Heritage Language Education in U.S. School Systems

The French Heritage Language Program

Fabrice Jaumont, Benoît Le Dévédec, and Jane F. Ross

1 Introduction

Long before the recent developments in research that focus on and promote Heritage Languages (HLs), HL learning took place in communities throughout the United States in multiple formal and informal settings (Fishman, 2001; Kloss, 1998). HL education was usually sponsored and sustained by immigrant and expatriate communities, and sometimes extended into the public and private school systems in the form of bilingual, dual language, or immersion programs. In most cases, these immigrant communities were cut off from their countries of origin, often having migrated for political or economic reasons. With a few notable exceptions, they received little or no support from their former national governments in these efforts to maintain their languages. In addition, governmental support for HL learning in the United States has experienced ebbs and flows, from extensive support for German in schools prior to World War I, for example, to more recent laws rendering bilingual education illegal in some states.

Similarly, French HL speakers in the United States experienced ebbs and flows in governmental support for language maintenance, both from France and from local American governments (Lemaire, 1966). This chapter examines the recent progress towards the establishment, expansion, and ultimately institutionalization of French HL learning in New York public schools through the development of the French Heritage Language Program (FHLP), launched in New York in 2005 as an educational non-profit in a partnership between the French government, a network of New York City public schools, and private foundation support from the French American Cultural Exchange (FACE) Foundation and the Alfred and Jane Ross Foundation. FHLP's mission is to provide free French classes to underserved schools and French-speaking communities, and to advocate for the teaching of HLs in the United States through research and curriculum development.

French HL speakers in the United States are a diverse group that includes historically French-speaking communities (Louisiana and Maine), European expatriates in major urban centers, and more recently, large Francophone immigrant communities from Haiti and West Africa (Valdman, 2010). Overall, over 8.4 million citizens claim French ancestry (U.S. Census

Bureau, 2015a), and more than 1.29 million people report speaking French at home (U.S. Census Bureau, 2015b). In fact, French is the fifth most commonly spoken home language in the country after English, Spanish, Chinese, and Tagalog, excluding English (U.S. Census Bureau, 2015b). French additionally enjoys a privileged status in the U.S., where it is the second most commonly studied foreign language in schools and universities after Spanish (Goldberg, Looney, & Lusin, 2015).

However, access to classes that teach French is often difficult for HL speakers. French may be the second most commonly taught foreign language, but the actual number of U.S. schools offering French instruction, and foreign language instruction in general, has declined over the past 30 years (Rhodes & Pufahl, 2010), making it harder for heritage speakers of French to access instruction in their own language, and especially challenging to find classes designed specifically for HL students. This was the motivation for the creation of FHLP. In the fall of 2004, the Embassy of France to the United States, through its Cultural Services department in New York, began to explore possible partnerships that would extend its already existing mission to promote the French language in the United States to a "new population" of underserved students who would not otherwise have access to French classes. The Embassy organized a series of meetings that included two of the authors, Jaumont and Ross, to discuss possible collaborations with a university school of education or a high school with significant numbers of French HL speakers. In the spring of 2005, the group proposed a pilot project to the principal of the Manhattan International High School, a school that serves only recent immigrants and included at the time about 40 French-speaking students primarily from West Africa. This turned out to be especially serendipitous timing, as the Manhattan International High School had just become part of the newly created Internationals Network for Public Schools (INPS), founded in early 2005 by Dr. Claire Sylvan, for the purpose of establishing a network of schools devoted to serving new immigrants. This chapter argues that the ensuing partnership between FHLP and INPS, in which FHLP was accepted into several high schools within the INPS network, has been an essential component of the successful expansion and institutionalization of FHLP and its various programs and a catalyst to eventually broaden its mission and geographic range.

2 Framework and Background

By "institutionalization" we mean "a process through which an organization assimilates an innovation into its structure" (Ekholm & Trier, 1987, p. 13). Ekholm and Trier (1987) argue that an innovation goes through several stages: to begin with, it is proposed or initiated, steps are then taken to implement it and, once it is accepted and stable, becomes part of an organization's routine and can be viewed as institutionalized. The innovation is often introduced from the outside, by actors that do not belong to the institution, and through processes that include negotiation, resource allocation, and the establishment of organizational arrangements that allow continuity independent of specific people, the innovation becomes an integral part of an institution (p. 17). In this chapter, we focus not only on these factors, but additional factors, in particular the partnerships mentioned above.

The success of these efforts by the FHLP in New York is the fruit of multiple partners. In addition to the initial impetus from the combined external support of the French government, private foundations and the partnership between FHLP and INPS, much of the success has relied on a solid tri-partite partnership: strong commitment from education leaders within INPS schools and local institutes of higher education, qualified teachers who understand the needs of heritage speakers, and ceaseless interest from the students and their respective Francophone communities, which continue to incentivize ongoing governmental support necessary to sustain the effort. The enthusiasm of the students themselves is especially notable as many of these new Francophone immigrants have limited parental or family support. Some have traveled to New York on their own or with other relatives, and for many of these students French is already a second language, one learned in school in their native countries, but not necessarily the language spoken in their own homes. As the FHLP entered its tenth year in 2015, some alumni have even begun to return to the program as teaching assistants and mentors.

In addition, innovative work by FHLP to develop suitable curricula has led to the acceptance of their courses by both students and educational leaders. In other words, it is not only the creation of FHLP classes that has received attention from educational backers, public or private, but also the incorporation of innovative HL pedagogy into their courses and their alignment with the school curriculum in general. In what we have characterized as "New York's French Bilingual Revolution" (Ross & Jaumont, 2012), the presence of a large and diverse Francophone population in New York City has facilitated the incorporation of heritage-speaker-oriented French programs into public programs, while extending the mission of afterschool programs to include HL education. In 2015, FHLP served 225 students in 10 INPS high schools and counted about 2,000 alumni in New York City.

3 Methodology

All three authors have been closely associated with the FHLP, and our collective 10 years' experience informs this case study and the ways in which it has approached institutionalization of French HL programs in multiple New York public schools within the INPS network. Two of the authors were involved in the initial moves to establish FHLP, and all three have played and continue to play a significant role in the development and operation of its programs.

From its inception, FHLP determined that to be sustainable and able to expand, the mission needed to incorporate not only classroom teaching, but also substantial research and curriculum development so that its model could be easily replicated in other French-speaking communities as well as in other HL programs. Reaching out to the Center for Applied Linguistics (CAL) in Washington, DC, and the National Heritage Language Resource Center (NHLRC) at the University of California, Los Angeles, the authors sought advice and collaboration in order to expand the mission of the FHLP beyond the initial classroom partnership with the INPS. The authors have continuously researched outcomes for the program's French-speaking immigrant students, conducting annual surveys of French HL students in New York that provide data as evidence that current French and Francophone immigrants to the United States have increasingly sought to maintain cultural and emotional ties to the French language. For example, these surveys have demonstrated that French is not merely an academic subject for these students, but also a fundamental aspect of their adaptation to life in the United States, providing a connection to their own extended families and influencing the way they view their future plans. These students indicate that they are able to use French not only in school and at home, but also via the Internet through accessing music, books, newspapers and, in some cases, connecting directly with family and friends in their home countries. Our research has led to additional publications that examine French heritage families who are making considerable efforts to ensure that French continues to be spoken within the family, schools, cultural centers, community centers, and local organizations (Ross & Jaumont, 2012, 2013, 2014). This has reinforced public policies that have revived and encouraged the preservation of French in many social and economic contexts (Ross & Jaumont, 2014).

4 French HL Education: Historical Background

As noted previously, Francophone communities in the United States have many different historical and geographic origins. Some trace their lineage as far back as the seventeenth and eighteenth centuries. These early settlers and refugees from Europe and Canada, most notably the Acadians of Maine and Louisiana, passed their language down through several generations. Others immigrated more recently, mainly from France, Haiti, Senegal, Côte d'Ivoire, and other African countries. Lately, these multiethnic communities have begun to work together in order to develop language training and economic prospects in order to encourage the transmission of French to new generations of speakers and ensure the long-term vitality of the French language in the United States (Ross & Jaumont, 2013). Earlier efforts to support French HL education in the traditionally French-speaking areas of Maine and Louisiana helped shape the mission of the FHLP, especially demonstrating the critical role of government support, or opposition, in determining the success of these efforts.

Louisiana was one of the first states to embrace French HL education. As a former French colony, Louisiana shares a rich cultural heritage with France and Canada, and during the early years of statehood, was technically bilingual with French being de facto the official second language. However, in 1921, the Louisiana Constitution prohibited the use of any language other than English in Louisiana's public schools. Social stigmatization of French speakers led to the further decline of the French language until 1968, when a state agency, the Council for the Development of French in Louisiana (CODOFIL), was created to "preserve" and promote the French language. CODOFIL's purpose is to represent and meet the cultural and educational needs of all of Louisiana's French language populations. Its mission is to support the development of French immersion programs in schools across the state, as well as generate greater sociocultural economic development in French-speaking communities through legislation and institutional development. The FHLP in New York recognized the importance of government support, both from France and from the state of Louisiana, and the creation of the institutional means of delivering the support through CODOFIL. This example also led the FHLP to include advocacy in its mission.

Efforts at HL maintenance have been less successful in New England, another historically French-speaking region. In the 1970s a Council for the Development of French in New England (CODOFINE) was created along the same lines of CODOFIL, with the goal of establishing French HL education in the Northeast. CODOFINE's mission was to organize and coordinate educational and cultural activities in agreement with French-speaking cultural centers and communities. The goal was to expand the use of French in all sectors, and multiply the number of bilingual education programs in order to meet the needs of local French heritage speakers. However, CODOFINE did not succeed as it was not able to find common ground among various pre-existing cultural organizations. More importantly, unlike CODOFIL in Louisiana, it did not receive financial support from the State, or any political support from influential individuals (Quintal, 1991). Nevertheless, today there are several initiatives to revitalize French, particularly in Maine, including public school programs with French HL classes, some initiated in collaboration with the FHLP in New York, and language revitalization efforts in several communities. Again, governmental support and institutional advocacy proved to be very important and helped shape the FHLP's approach in New York.

Contemporary French-speaking immigration is characterized by a flow of immigrants from French-speaking countries in Africa and Haiti. The Haitian diaspora in Boston, the New York area, and South Florida currently totals nearly a million people, many of whom speak Haitian creole as well as French. In the U.S. as a whole, there are over 750,000 Haitian creole speakers (Ryan, 2013), and Zephir (2004) estimates that 20% also speak French fluently. Similarly, several waves of immigration from Africa have brought more Francophones to the United States, many to the New York City area from countries where French has been the primary language of instruction (Senegal, Mali, Guinea, and the Ivory Coast, for example), even though many also speak other languages at home. For the FHLP in New York, these demographics meant that it was possible to reach the "critical mass" of French HL speakers in the partner schools. Francophone immigration has continued to grow over the past 10 years, allowing the FHLP to expand into 10 different schools in the INPS.

5 The French Heritage Language Program

Background

From its inception, FHLP has partnered with INPS to offer classes and develop curriculum and pedagogy in INPS' network of New York City public high schools, which by 2016 included 18 public high schools for new immigrants. All students in these schools are English Language Learners (ELLs), with sometimes up to 30% originating from French-speaking West Africa and Haiti. The schools offer intensive, content-based English language instruction through pedagogy that is based on, in the words of Dr. Sylvan, "the principle of heterogeneity and collaboration." (Grantee Spotlight, n.d.). Thus, these schools have developed pedagogical approaches to ensure academic success for students with very different educational backgrounds who speak up to 50 different languages—from students with interrupted formal education due to wars or disasters in their home countries, to students who might have been ready for university studies in their native languages. By adapting this kind of pedagogy, which includes heterogeneous learning groups, project- and content-based instruction, and culturally themed lesson plans (rather than specific linguistic or grammatical progressions), FHLP teachers address the tremendous diversity of the HL speakers in ways that traditional foreign or second language pedagogies could not. Because these high schools serve only immigrants, language instruction other than English was not included in their curricula. This posed a challenge in the initial launching of the French program, as no specific time slots or teacher salaries were allocated for French. For this reason, classes initially took place only after school and were paid for directly by FHLP.

Many of these schools were looking for ways to offer their students home language support in order to facilitate their integration at school and into their new environment. In the spring of 2005, the meetings among French Embassy representatives, school administrators, and private foundation supporters had also included students from INPS and they had contributed to the initial impetus to create the program. In June 2005, a group of students met with a representative of the French Foreign Ministry from Paris to express their eagerness to participate in such a program. Although interviews with students indicated that they were for the most part already in daily or weekly contact with their country of origin through the Internet and other media sources, many experienced the feeling of "losing" their French or of struggling to develop more advanced language skills that would enable them to succeed in a Francophone environment. Many wished to return to their country of origin in the future. All hoped to continue their education after high school. Fluency in French could be a decisive factor if they wished to study in Quebec, France, or their country of origin. These initial meetings also underlined INPS's awareness that developing their students' English skills could only be enhanced by a good command of the home language (García & Sylvan, 2011).

In July 2005, the French Ministry of Foreign Affairs announced the creation of a position for a New York–based coordinator to develop the FHLP, and FACE Foundation adopted FHLP under its not-for-profit umbrella to facilitate U.S.-based fundraising. With some initial seed money, the program began offering free language and culture classes in French after school, two hours a week, initially in the Manhattan International High School. Once launched, other schools in INPS also requested French classes, so that by the end of the first academic year, in June 2006, FHLP was delivering French HL classes in five of the network's schools, stretching from Manhattan to Brooklyn and eventually also to the Bronx.

Challenges and Achievements

This rapid early success of the program was not without difficulties, however. For community-based and other independent organizations such as FHLP, operating free afterschool activities in U.S. public schools poses many problems: financial dependence on external funding, low number of instructional hours, unstable attendance, severe competition from more recreational programs, and a lack of incorporation into the schools' own programming. Mostly financed by FACE Foundation, the Alfred and Jane Ross Foundation and individual donations, with the exception of the salary of the coordinator which is underwritten by the French government, the program had a clear incentive from the start to be progressively integrated and institutionalized within the public schools as part of the students' regular academic program. In order to reach that goal, one of the first priorities of FHLP was to define solid instructional content that could meet the needs of both students and their schools, and to establish research partnerships which could help the program in this task, including consultation with CAL and the NHLRC.

Without any existing teaching materials or curriculum specifically designed for French HL speakers in the United States, the program coordinator originally built a pedagogical approach for French HL education based on the methods successfully deployed by INPS for ELLs, as noted on the INPS website (Internationals Network for Public Schools, n.d.). Project-based teaching units were created using collaborative learning and differentiated instruction adapted for students from very different educational backgrounds. Group projects allowed students to work together on common themes, but at different skill levels, a method already familiar to INPS students in other subjects in their schools. New teaching material was published online on the FHLP website (French Heritage Language Program, n.d.) and presented at major research conferences and conventions including ACTFL and the International Heritage Language Conferences at UCLA in 2010 and 2014. Units were based on topics like self-portraits, the media, and literature, and relied on the use of authentic resources taken from a variety of sources from the French-speaking world.

The immediate benefits of these classes went beyond expectations; some of the schools began awarding high school credits to their French students and a few even started to offer the Scholastic Aptitude Test (SAT) in French, so students' skills in French could be officially validated on high school transcripts and college applications. Buttressed by this initial success, and the exposure at national conferences, the program was soon able not only to attract additional funding, but also to start hiring additional teachers to expand its classes in New York City as well as in new locations, including Florida and Maine. However, with this expansion of class offerings and increased teacher recruitment, the program faced new challenges. How to make teaching consistent throughout the classes? How to ensure that program quality and coherent objectives are met for every student? How to make such a program sustainable and fully incorporated (and funded) by the schools it serves? In other words, how to institutionalize the program?

Teacher Training and the Curriculum

Although teachers received training and continuing support from the FHLP, most classroom teaching continued to rely heavily on the teachers' own efforts. Lesson plans inspired by existing material, especially those shared on the FHLP website, still required individual adaptation by teachers who, because of the part-time nature of their assignments, experienced very high turnover. The program also lacked a unified curriculum with a common pedagogical progression to be followed by all staff and students, which often resulted in unequal quality of courses. In 2009, the program conducted an annual survey specifically to assess course efficiency and adjust its teaching method according to students' needs. Most students were happy being part of the French class and wanted to continue learning French. They also insisted that the courses remain fun and recreational because of the lack of time and energy they had to devote to afterschool activities, a demand that had to be balanced with FHLP's academic objectives.

In the fall of 2011, the FHLP launched a second phase of curriculum and pedagogical development to include more tools for assessment and increased support for teacher training. French teachers were invited to attend professional development institutes organized twice a year by the INPS so as to receive consistent training in project-based pedagogy and differentiated instruction as well as to learn best practices for working with ELLs. They were also invited to shadow INPS teachers and attend other subject classes at schools to experience these techniques in real context. While the FHLP coordinators had always participated in this shared professional development with the INPS, the inclusion of FHLP teachers was new, an added cost, but also a significant added benefit for all. During the same period, the program began developing a fully fledged curriculum designed to be implemented through a yearlong academic cycle, by all teachers and in all schools (Appendix 17A). Drawing on the training resources of INPS, feedback from conference sessions, and the work of other HL experts, for example, the work of Carreira and Hitchins Chik (in press) on differentiated teaching for Spanish HL learners, the FHLP coordinator could guide new teachers through new methodologies as well as new curriculum.

The curriculum contained hands-on teaching units with supporting material and was created by the coordinator and the whole teaching team. The FHLP also received further support from France's Jules Verne exchange program via the participation of two teaching fellows sponsored by the French Ministry of National Education. These teachers were selected because of their prior experience teaching new immigrants and developing original curricula. Responding to a growing demand by INPS principals, the program also gradually adapted curriculum to include cross-disciplinary content areas so that students could use their skills in French to reinforce other subjects like History and English.

New thematic units included Immigration and the American Dream, Black History and Discrimination, Human Rights and Freedom of Speech, Health and the Environment, all mirroring other content areas of the students' studies. French classes could then focus on building critical thinking and higher-order academic skills, including comparing and analyzing secondary sources, developing arguments, and defending one's point of view. According to Berena Cabarcas (2011), principal at International Community High School in the Bronx:

> The program helps students maintain their home language, which facilitates the acquisition of other languages like English, but it also helps them learn other subjects at school by building strong academic skills in their home language.

(p. 41)

The fun part of classes was preserved through increased participation of students in cultural outings, theater and writing contests, and recreational camps organized by FHLP around its curriculum themes throughout the school year. In doing so, the priority for FHLP was to improve the quality of its classes, but also to continue looking for new incentives to make its classes more engaging for students and appealing to schools, so it could extend weekly hours of instruction and better integrate them into the schools' regular programming. The goal was to create rewards for both students and their schools by enhancing the role that French could play in building academic success.

Format of the French Classes: Expanding Opportunities

Although many schools already recognized the quality of the French classes by awarding participating students with high school credits and offering SAT subject tests in French, the format of classes still primarily relied on the precarious two-hour-a-week afterschool arrangement, straining attendance and academic work, and making it hard to sustain the program's overall efforts. To change that situation, and in a defining step towards further institutionalization, FHLP was able to convince some principals that, by participating financially in the cost of French teaching (paying for the teachers and curriculum through FHLP), as well as logistically through added hours of French instruction integrated within their class schedules, schools could offer consistent preparation for the Advanced Placement (AP) French examination and so allow their students to gain college credits. This represented a strong incentive not only for students but also for the schools, because demonstrating a school's capacity to prepare students for college can boost their performance index report with local educational authorities.

Few of these schools had ever considered offering any AP exams, which are often seen as too difficult for recently arrived immigrants who are ELLs. Their HL, on the other hand, represents one area in which ELLs can excel. Furthermore, the newly designed FHLP curriculum contained topics and objectives aligned with the AP French requirements, and schools were willing to pay for AP French textbooks and additional materials that support teaching. In 2013–2014, three high schools co-financed the extension of their FHLP course to four hours a week, with two hours placed during elective scheduling within the school day, allowing the program to pilot its first AP French prep class. Out of the nineteen students who took the test, seventeen attained scores between three and five, making them eligible to receive credits at most U.S. colleges at present. As one student testified:

> When I applied to Antioch College, they asked me if I had any AP credits. And when I told them that I got a 5 in AP French, they said that's what they're looking for . . . and they even gave me money for it.
>
> *(Personal interview, May 29, 2015)*

Not only did this student succeed in the AP exam, the program helped her gain access to extra funding for college.

Encouraged by these results, FHLP was able to extend this model to six partner high schools in 2014–2015, with a record 65 students taking the test in May 2015. The International High School at Lafayette, one of the first schools to offer AP French classes through FHLP, even adapted this model for its Spanish- and Chinese-speaking students. Megan Williams, assistant principal at Bronx International High School, also confirms the benefits:

> Spanish speakers see French kids [taking the AP courses]. So they advocate for themselves, [asking] why do they get to do that? It's just great. For the language and native language

skills: Those skills transfer in their acquisition of English. And the benefit of the test [if they pass] is that's one more class they don't pay for in College.

(M. Williams, personal interview, May 29, 2015)

At Bronx International High School the elective scheduling model is unique in that it has made French classes compulsory for Francophone students, with four hours in the regular school schedule combined with one hour after school.

Capitalizing on the enthusiasm generated by college credits, FHLP developed another similarly innovative model by partnering with LaGuardia Community College through the City University of New York's College Now Program. In 2013, the French Department at LaGuardia Community College approached FHLP to see how they could increase enrollment by recruiting French HL high school students for their French courses. The mission of College Now is to offer college-level courses to high school students, making it possible for them to earn credits before enrolling in a higher education institution. In the spring of 2014, FHLP and LaGuardia combined their efforts to complement the existing FHLP afterschool class at Brooklyn International High School with an on-site College Now extension course directly run and financed by the LaGuardia French Department. The French College Now course was granted at no cost to students or the school, and augmented the existing two-hour FHLP afterschool class with a three-hour College Now course (based on LaGuardia's own curriculum). LaGuardia's French Department approved the FHLP curriculum, so that all students registered in the new course had to follow both curricula in order to gain credits.

The pilot project was met with outstanding success and all participating students received college credits at the end of the school year. The class was renewed in the spring of 2015 and increased its capacity by including FHLP students from another partner high school, the International High School at Union Square. Professor Habiba Boumlik sees great potential in the partnership between LaGuardia Community College and FHLP to create more College Now opportunities for high-schoolers:

> At LaGuardia Community College we see [these courses] for career purposes. Students should be helped and their skills valued [so they are able to] use their heritage language in a professional setting. . . . We have some great instructors and have been receiving good feedback this year to help develop the program.
>
> *(Personal interview, May 29, 2015)*

Kathleen Rucker, principal at Brooklyn International High School, agrees about the importance of offering such partnerships to help maintain and develop ELL students' linguistic skills. She says:

> Through this partnership we are able to offer French courses for college credit in our school building, which increases the participation and has allowed for cross collaborations with our sister school Union Square International High School. This is one of the few opportunities that students across different INPS schools have a chance to work together on a regular basis, building friendships and strengthening our inter-school community. The French Heritage Language Program has been integral to helping our Francophone students not only maintain their native languages, but also to further develop their language as they work on long-term projects directly tied to their lives in the United States.
>
> *(Personal interview, May 29, 2015)*

Our most recent survey confirms this point. It was conducted with 115 students registered in FHLP in New York and showed that 97% of respondents found it important for them to continue to learn and use French in the United States. Furthermore, 90% of the same students also declared that they were planning to continue taking French classes in college, and 73% said they were doing so for a future job or career. Finally, 69% of these students thought that their schools valued the fact they were speaking French.

Although not all problems are solved for FHLP, offering college credits has proven to be a very effective strategy for promoting the teaching and institutionalization of French HL classes (as well as other HLs) in American public high schools, especially in cases where these schools did not initially have any form of foreign language instruction. It also offers higher education institutions like LaGuardia Community College an innovative way to attract more students into their foreign language departments. The success of this partnership and program shows that far from being a liability, HLs can be a serious asset for new immigrants and the U.S. school system at large.

6 Conclusion

The experiences outlined in this chapter show that opportunities to incorporate HL learning within a broader context of educational opportunities have been instrumental in institutionalizing programs that can endure beyond an initial influx of French speakers into a community. When combined with long-established school-based academic programs, such as the College Board's AP French program, or with higher education institutions, like the City University of New York, HL classes can become an integral part of a school's mission and their students' futures. Acknowledgment of HL programs from established bodies such as these gives value and meaning to HLs in the context of the formal educational system. Within such programs, HL speakers can continue to develop their linguistic capacities beyond the goals of typical bilingual programs and, importantly, are motivated to do so. Students in HL programs are able to reinforce their bilingualism instead of abandoning their home language as they learn a new one after entering the country.

The benefits of this institutionalization of French HL education extend to a broad range of communities, sometimes joining together the needs of new immigrants with those of long-standing communities of French descent. This principle has been particularly well illustrated in Francophone communities in New York, where newly arrived participants and long-established French and American institutions have become the creators of educational opportunities for young Francophone immigrants to study French, and where outside funding may become less necessary as courses are progressively institutionalized within the schools that benefit from FHLP support and other similar initiatives in the United States. Institutions such as the French Government, through its Embassy, and its partners, FACE Foundation, the Alfred and Jane Ross Foundation, and INSP, have formed a unique partnership in introducing and moving forward French HL programs in New York schools, as well as institutionalizing FHLP by making it sustainable and fully incorporated (and funded) by the schools it serves. As such, this partnership has fostered strong commitments from education leaders within INPS schools and local institutes of higher education, qualified teachers who understand the needs of heritage speakers, and ceaseless interest from the students and their respective Francophone communities, incentivizing the collective and collaborative support necessary to sustain the effort.

References

Cabarcas, B. (2011, March–April). Aux Etats-Unis, le français trouve un nouveau public [In the U.S., the French language has found a new audience] [Online article]. *Le Français dans le Monde, #374.* Retrieved from http://www.fdlm.org/

Carreira, M., & Hitchins Chik, C. (in press). Differentiated teaching: A primer for heritage and mixed classes. In K. Potowski (Ed.), *The handbook of Spanish as a heritage/minority language*. Abingdon, UK: Routledge.

Ekholm, M., & Trier, U. P. (1987). The concept of institutionalization: Some remarks. In M. B. Miles, M. Ekholm, & R. Vandenberghe (Eds.), *Lasting school improvement: Exploring the process of institutionalization* (pp. 13–21). Leuven, Belgium: Acco.

Fishman, J. A. (2001). Heritage languages in America: Preserving a national resource. In J. K. Peyton, D. A. Ranard, & S. McGinnis (Eds.), *Heritage languages in America: Preserving a national resource* (pp. 81–89). McHenry, IL: Center for Applied Linguistics.

French Heritage Language Program [FHLP]. (n.d.). Teaching resources [Web page]. Retrieved from http://face-foundation.org/french-heritage-language-program/teaching-ressources.html

García, O., & Sylvan, C. E. (2011). Pedagogies and practices in multilingual classrooms: Singularities in pluralities. *The Modern Language Journal, 95*(3), 385–400.

Goldberg, D., Looney, D., & Lusin, N. (2015). Enrollments in languages other than English in United States institutions of higher education, Fall 2013 [Web publication of Modern Language Association]. Retrieved from https://apps.mla.org/pdf/2013_enrollment_survey.pdf

Grantee Spotlight. (n.d.). The W. Clement & Jessie V. Stone Foundation: An interview with Dr. Claire Sylvan of the Internationals Network for Public Schools. Retrieved from http://www.wcstonefnd.org/wp-content/uploads/2012/04/spotlight_sylvan.pdf

Internationals Network for Public Schools. (n.d.). Heterogeneity and Collaboration [Web page]. Retrieved from http://internationalsnps.org/about-us/internationals-approach/heterogeneity-and-collaboration/

Kloss, H. (1998). *The American bilingual tradition*. McHenry, IL: Center for Applied Linguistics.

Lemaire, H. (1966). Franco-American efforts on behalf of the French language in New England. In J. A. Fishman (Ed.), *Language loyalty in the United States* (pp. 253–279). The Hague, The Netherlands: Mouton & Co.

Quintal, C. (1991). Les Institutions Franco-Américaines: Pertes et Progrès [Franco-American institutions: Progress and loss]. In R. D. Louder (Ed.), *Le Québec et les francophones de la Nouvelle-Angleterre* (pp. 61–83). Laval, Canada: Les Presses de l'Université Laval.

Rhodes, N. C., & Pufahl, I. (2010). *Foreign language teaching in U.S. schools: Results of a national survey*. Washington, DC: Center for Applied Linguistics.

Ross, J., & Jaumont, F. (2012). Building bilingual communities: New York's French bilingual revolution. In O. Garcia, Z. Zakharia, & B. Otcu (Eds.), *Bilingual community education and multilingualism* (pp. 232–246). New York, NY: Multilingual Matters.

Ross, J., & Jaumont, F. (2013). French heritage language vitality in the United States. [Special Issue on Language Vitality in the U.S.]. *Heritage Journal Review, 10*(3), 316–327.

Ross, J., & Jaumont, F. (2014). French heritage language communities in the United States. In T. Wiley, J. Peyton, D. Christian, S. C. Moore, & N. Liu (Eds.), *Handbook of heritage and community languages in the United States: Research, educational practice, and policy* (pp. 101–110). Oxford, UK: Routledge.

Ryan, C. (2013, August). Language use in the United States: 2011: American Community Survey Reports. Retrieved from https://www.census.gov/prod/2013pubs/acs-22.pdf

U.S. Census Bureau. (2015a). Table B04006: People reporting ancestry [data table]. 2010–2014 American Community Survey 5-Year Estimates. Retrieved from http://www.census.gov

U.S. Census Bureau. (2015b). Table B16001: Language spoken at home by ability to speak English for the population 5 years and over, Westminster city, California [data table]. American Community Survey 2010–14 5-year Estimates. Retrieved from http://www.census.gov

Valdman, A. (2010). French in the USA. In K. Potowski (Ed.), *Language diversity in the USA* (pp. 110–127). Cambridge, UK: Cambridge University Press.

Zephir, F. (2004). *The Haitian Americans*. Westport, CT: Greenwood Press.

18

Engagement, Multiliteracies, and Identity

Developing Pedagogies for Heritage/Community Language Learners within the UK School System

Jim Anderson

This chapter examines how new understandings of language, literacy, and identity in the late modern era have provided a richer and more personalized basis for second/foreign language learning pedagogy and, in addition, greater space for the unique situation and needs of heritage language (HL) learners to be taken into account. It reports on two studies led by researchers based in the Department of Educational Studies at Goldsmiths University of London. The first investigated the potential of arts-based creativity, involving art, dance, drama, and story, to enrich the learning of HLs (Arabic, Chinese, Panjabi, and Tamil) in mainstream and complementary[1] school settings in London. The second examined whether a more meaningful and engaging context for language learning could be generated through a student-led, critical approach to multilingual digital storytelling, drawing on the power of the internet for online sharing and communication. This project involved mainly secondary level students studying a range of languages, European and non-European, in mainstream and complementary schools in and around London as well as overseas (Algeria, Palestine, and Taiwan).

Linking to research on pedagogies for HL learners in other countries, it is worth noting that the principles underpinning these projects resonate strongly with the macro model of HL teaching proposed by Kagan and Dillon (2001/2003), namely a curriculum driven by an experiential, task-based component that connects with ways in which learners use the language in real life contexts outside of class (Kagan & Dillon, 2001/2003, 2009; Wu & Chang, 2012). There are also strong links with work by Cummins and others on digital media and multiliteracies, including the notion of identity texts (Cummins, Brown, & Sayers, 2007; Cummins & Early, 2011). With regard to digital storytelling, there is a growing body of literature from various countries looking at how it can be used most effectively in the contexts of first and second language learning (Castañeda, 2013; Hafner & Miller, 2011; Robin, 2008; Skinner & Hagood, 2008; Vinogradova, Linville, & Bickel, 2011; Yang & Wu, 2012). Attention is now also starting to be drawn to its relevance for HL learning (Vinogradova, 2014).

In relation to the question of institutionalization, defined as "a process through which an organization assimilates an innovation to its structure" (Ekholm & Trier, 1987, p. 13), consideration is given to the model of teacher professional development underlying the two projects and how this can enable innovative practices to become sustainable.

1 New Perspectives on Second Language Learning Pedagogy

The changes in global relations which characterize the late modern era have made it increasingly hard to maintain the myth of one nation-one language ideology and the view that multilingualism and multilingual identities represent a threat to national unity. The relationship we have to our own language and culture and to others is now seen to be more multidimensional, dynamic, and interwoven than was previously understood. Moreover, forces of globalization and the increasingly diverse nature of many societies, particularly in the West, have altered the way we perceive both the purpose and means of language learning. Reacting against a utilitarian, tourist perspective and binary notions of self and other, language learning has been reconceptualized as an intercultural endeavor to do with navigating daily realities in the modern world and in the process developing new, multifaceted and flexible identities (Byram, 1997; Kramsch, 2014; Liddicoat & Scarino, 2013; Norton & Toohey, 2011). Importantly, in place of an unrealistic aspiration towards native speaker norms, has come an integrated and empowering view of the individual's "multicompetency" across a repertoire of language varieties (Cook, 2002a, 2002b). The implications of this multilingual turn in relation both to second language acquisition and language education are increasingly recognized (Conteh & Meier, 2014; May, 2014). This is reflected, for example, in the growing use of the term "translanguaging" (Garcia, 2009) to describe fluid movement between language varieties and a recognition that, instead of an exclusive focus on the target language in the classroom, a more flexible, though principled, bilingual approach may be advantageous.

Complementing the deeper engagement with intercultural understanding and skills in pedagogical thinking pointed out above, are cross-curricular/thematic and content based approaches to language teaching. These are referred to as Content and Language Integrated Learning (CLIL) in the European context. Strong arguments have been made for CLIL (Coyle, Holmes, & King, 2009; Coyle, Hood, & Marsh, 2010), backed up by a growing body of evidence that this approach can bring significant benefits for learning and its particular relevance in the context of HL teaching has also been noted (Anderson, 2009). There have been and continue to be attempts to introduce CLIL in primary and secondary schools across various languages in the UK, but in contrast with other European countries, government support to provide the infrastructure required for wider sustainable implementation has been lacking.

In tandem with the focus on content has come a greater realization of the importance of providing opportunities for learners to apply the language they are learning to "real life" tasks which involve interaction and team work with peers and promote learner agency and a sense of ownership. Developments in the areas of Task-Based Language Teaching (TBLT) and, more broadly, Project-Based Learning (PBL), are clearly relevant here. Both of these are learner-centered, dialogic, and process-oriented approaches, which are holistic in nature, promote student autonomy, and foster higher levels of creative and critical thinking. Importantly, they involve working towards some meaningful end goal, whether this be a presentation, performance, publication, or display. The emphasis on student empowerment permeating these approaches means that they can lend themselves easily to the development of active citizenship and student voice (Brown & Brown, 2003; Osler & Starkey, 2005)

Alongside a greater emphasis on content, learner agency, and authentic tasks, a more balanced view has been arrived at in relation to the teaching of grammar in language teaching. The neglect of grammar in earlier interpretations of communicative language teaching in the

UK, based on the view that it would be "picked up" by osmosis, was found to be counterproductive, and meant that many learners were left without an ability to manipulate the language system creatively and to move beyond basic phrase book utterances. Conclusions reached by government inspectors reporting on foreign language teaching as well as by examination boards in the UK were supported by a growing body of research evidence (Lyster, 2007; Spada, 1997). This indicated the importance of a balanced approach where attention to form is not seen as an end in itself, but is set within a broader communicative framework. Significantly, the studies by Lyster (2007) and Spada (1997) took place in the Canadian immersion context where exposure to the language is far greater than in the traditional language classroom. As far as HL students are concerned, there has also been recognition of the dangers that an overemphasis on grammar can have, in particular if this serves to undermine confidence in naturalistic, context-related communicative abilities (Anderson, 2008; Krashen, 2000; Lynch, 2003). At the same time, studies have shown that HL learners can benefit from form-focused instruction (Montrul & Bowles, 2010; Potowski, Jegerski, & Morgan-Short, 2009). A helpful approach in relation to the teaching of HLs is that proposed by Cummins (2000) for the development of academic expertise. Here classroom interactions between teacher and student are considered crucial in maximizing both cognitive engagement and identity investment, the latter referring to positive affirmation of students' cultural, linguistic, and personal identities. Central to the model of the teaching-learning process Cummins presents is an initial focus on meaning (comprehensible input, critical literacy), moving on to a focus on form (awareness and critical analysis of language forms and uses), and leading finally to a focus on use (i.e., a creative outcome to which the learner brings new and personal perspectives). This has commonalities with the proposal put forward by Carreira (2016) and Kagan and Dillon (2001/2003) that HL learners are best reached by a macro-based, i.e., top down, approach.

A development that has become more prominent within recent pedagogical thinking in the UK, partly in reaction to an increasingly regimented, test oriented education system, has been a focus on creativity. While subscribing to a democratic and universalized interpretation of creativity, the arts (including work around stories, poems, songs, films, and drama) are seen to have particular potential as a stimulus for language and cultural learning. Within language teaching, creativity is associated with a "humanistic" approach which focuses on the whole person and stresses the personal and affective dimensions of the learning process, including opportunities for control and a sense of ownership (Arnold, 1999; Stevick, 1996). Moreover, this approach offers opportunities for personal responses and self-expression as well as developing intercultural understanding and skills. It is worth noting here that for HL learners, many of whom have a foundation in speaking and listening skills, but limited literacy in the home language, drawing on creative works has been found to provide an effective means of bridging this gap. It should also be noted that stories lend themselves well to bilingual teaching approaches. This may involve drawing on both languages in presenting and working on different aspects of the story as well as for purposes of language comparison and analysis. Furthermore, we should remember that work on stories from different cultures forms part of students' broad literacy development, and sometimes texts can be worked on in bilingual versions with the involvement of parents and/or other community members (Datta, 2007; Kenner, 2004; Sneddon, 2009). Interestingly, in Wales there has been encouragement to pursue this comparative approach through a "triple literacies" model (Welsh Government, 2011).

Extending these developments in pedagogy have been the new possibilities and perspectives brought about by advances in digital media and the integration of language(s) within a much broader semiotic frame. With regard to language teaching pedagogy, use of Web 2.0 tools as an interactive, collaborative medium has greatly enhanced opportunities for online communication to include activities such as podcasting, blogging, and digital storytelling (Evans, 2009). It has also facilitated partnerships with schools abroad, bringing valuable opportunities for intercultural dialogue and collaboration (Evans, 2009).

There is increasing recognition that a multiliteracies view and the critical, dialogic pedagogy that it espouses has important implications for language teaching. On the one hand, it foregrounds the extended range of semiotic resources available for meaning-making and the ways language(s) fit within this. On the other, it recognizes that learning occurs in and across different contexts (inside and outside school), different modes (including multiple languages), as well as on and off line. It thereby builds awareness of the intersections between multilingualism and multimodality. It further recognizes how students' identities are inscribed within literacy practices in different spaces (Cope & Kalanzis, 2000, 2013; Cummins et al., 2007; Helot, Sneddon, & Daly, 2014; Lotherington & Jenson, 2011; Pahl & Rowsell, 2012). Importantly, this perspective has strengthened the case for investing in bilingualism in all its forms and for moving beyond the tokenism, i.e., the superficial and unsustained engagement, which has characterized national policy on HLs.

2 Recent Research Projects Involving Heritage Languages at Goldsmiths, University of London: Background and Methodology

A focus on HLs and multiliteracies has for many years featured strongly in the work of the Centre for Language, Culture, and Learning in the Department of Educational Studies at Goldsmiths. Following Norton's post-structuralist perspective on identity (Norton & Toohey, 2011), organizers of the two projects discussed in this chapter built on the idea that "investment" in developing a second language depends on students having a sense of their own agency, gaining the confidence to position themselves as multilingual subjects empowered to make sense of culture in their own terms (Leeman, 2015; Leeman, Rabin, & Román-Mendoza, 2011), and to construct a fluid, "syncretic" (Gregory, Long, & Volk, 2004) sense of self in the process. Moreover, both projects involved work in which language learning was subsumed within wider interdisciplinary aims, drawing in particular on the arts and on an aesthetic sensibility.

Theoretically, the two projects were grounded in a sociocultural and critical view of learning as well as current perspectives on second language acquisition and bilingualism, principles/methods of second and foreign/HL teaching and, particularly in relation to the second study, the multiliteracies framework based on developments in the field of social semiotics. An important aim within both of these projects has been to contribute to work taking place in the UK and elsewhere which recognizes the background and needs of bilingual learners and seeks to find a middle ground between mother tongue and foreign language teaching models (Anderson, 2008, 2011; Brinton, Kagan, & Bauckus, 2008). The challenge is to make this part of a strategic approach leading towards institutionalization whereby these approaches are incorporated into teacher repertoires. There are important implications here for teacher and, it should be added, for researcher professional development and this is an issue to which we return below.

The perspective proposed, it should be noted, emphasizes commonalities as much as distinctions between different forms of language education and is based on those principles of integration, interdisciplinary, and inclusion which are integral to an intercultural orientation towards the curriculum and to the multiliteracies approach (Anderson & Obied, 2011). It also recognizes the importance of digital media in communication and learning and the increasingly significant role they play in youth culture (Craft, 2011).

Methodologically, a critical ethnographic and collaborative approach was adopted in both studies, as this enabled processes of teaching and learning to be captured in a more differentiated and organic way and for wider ecological and ideological factors to be taken into account. It was also understood that researchers would be collaborating with teachers in the planning and evaluation of tasks as well as in broader analysis of the project and in the creation of professional development material. For both studies a range of data was collected:

- Video recordings of key lessons
- Field notes
- Semi-structured interviews with selected students, teachers, and some parents each term
- Teaching plans and resources
- Outcomes of students' work (paintings and collages, story books, comic books, play scripts, recordings of drama and dance performances, digital stories)
- Minutes of meetings of teachers, the research team, and the external advisor to the project

Triangulation of evidence drawn from these data sources enabled us to arrive at findings which were both realistic and balanced. Importantly, however, it should be recalled that both of these projects were complex and multifaceted involving, amongst other things, different languages, different contexts of learning, different participant profiles, and different subject combinations. This was consistent with the holistic view of language and literacy learning upon which both projects were based and a desire to uncover important connections between, as much as insights into, specific areas. This required a wide-angle lens to be used for much of the time when carrying out fieldwork. Given this, we were not surprised that analysis revealed multiple strands with overlapping features.

3 Findings from the Two Projects

Project 1 Creativity in the Community/Heritage Language Classroom

This two-year project, funded by the Nuffield Foundation, set out to investigate the potential of arts-based creativity to enrich the learning of community/heritage languages (Arabic, Chinese, Panjabi, and Tamil) in mainstream and complementary school settings. Drawing on the landmark "All Our Futures" report (NACCCE, 1999) and a sociocultural view of learning, four strands were identified as central to the way creativity was understood within this project (Anderson & Chung, 2011a):

1. Seeing new or other possibilities—including different linguistic/cultural perspectives;
2. Active participation in a collaborative process of generating, shaping, and evaluating ideas—drawing on prior knowledge and experience as well as "funds of knowledge" (Moll, Amanti, Neff, & Gonzalez, 1992) at home and in the community;
3. Personal investment and self-expression—taking ownership; and
4. Pursuing meaningful goals and presenting to others—affirming identity and challenging the marginalized status of HLs.

Following ethnographic research procedures set out above, a range of data was collected on arts-based tasks involving stories, drama, dance, song, and art work, as presented in Table 18.1 (Anderson & Chung, 2011a).

Table 18.1 Overview of Tasks Carried Out in the Different Settings

School	Task A	Task B	Task C
Sarah Bonnell School (SBS) (Mainstream secondary girls' school in Newham) Class: Year 7/8 (Students from diverse backgrounds, but mainly beginners in Arabic) (Age 11–12)	Art work integrating images and text (Exhibition)	Dual-language storybooks (Presentation in local primary school)	Puppet Show (Performance in class)
Downderry Primary School (DPS) (Mainstream, mixed sex, primary school in Lewisham) Class: Year 3–6 (After school) (Age 6–10, mainly 2nd generation) (Tamil)	South Indian Dance based on song stories (Complementary work carried out in language and dance lessons)	South Indian Dance based on song stories (Performance in school assembly and local Tamil community event)	Drama and digital film-making based on song stories (Presentation in class)
London Mandarin School (LMS) (Mixed sex, primary-secondary complementary school in Hackney) Class: Year 1–3 (Age 5–7, mainly 2nd–3rd generation) (Mandarin)	"Four Season Song" based on traditional three-word chant	Scrapbook: pages made up of drawings, natural garden material as well as Chinese characters representing spring and summer (Slide show posted on school website)	Drama adaptation of the Chinese classic "Journey to the West" (Performance in school talent show)
Rathmore Asian Community Project (RACP) (Mixed sex, primary-secondary complementary school in Greenwich) Class: Year 3–12 (Age 6–17, mainly 3rd–4th generation) (Panjabi)	Family drama conceived, scripted, and performed by students with support of teachers and parents (Performance for school and community members)	Wedding scene from drama expanded to incorporate traditional and modern dance (Performed for school and community members)	Dual language comic book based on the family drama (Presented to school and community members)

Source: Adapted from "Finding a voice: Arts based creativity in the community languages classroom," by J. Anderson and Y-C Chung, 2008, *International Journal of Bilingual Education and Bilingualism 14*(5), p. 556. Copyright 2008 by *International Journal of Bilingual Education and Bilingualism.*

In spite of differences in settings, student profiles, and the types of arts-based work, analysis revealed clear patterns clustering around language and literacy, cognition, intercultural understanding, and personal and social development. It also provided important insights in relation to pedagogy and teacher professional development.

While a detailed discussion of findings from the project as well as a related teacher professional development resource are available elsewhere (Anderson & Chung, 2011a, 2011b, 2014),

Jim Anderson

by way of exemplification here two tasks, one at the London Mandarin School and the other at Downderry Primary School will be discussed.

(1)   The scrapbook task at the London Mandarin School.

The school, which is based in a community college in East London, runs on Sunday afternoons. The young children in the Year 1–3 class were working on the theme of the seasons. The teacher first introduced the "Four Season Song" based on a traditional Chinese three-word chant, and this led on to a homework task to create a page for a scrapbook using any material they could find. The children used plants from their own gardens or from parks, personalized their work by drawing and sticking images incorporating elements from Chinese painting, and added labels written in basic Chinese characters that they were familiar with.

Both the class teacher and parents were impressed by the range and quality of work produced and the effort that had gone into it. One parent noted that the task had helped relate learning to real life for her child, commenting that:

> This project connects the books with practical things. Before, they only learnt these in the textbook. But now, those are in the real world for them. When they go out sometimes, they cannot stop looking for the things they want for the work. They kept on asking me what things are in Mandarin as well.
> (Mother, LMS)

Other parents commented that, while welcoming their interest and support, children were adamant that this was their work and they didn't want anyone else to do things for them. As one mother put it:

> I helped them when they didn't know how to write some words. They are full of their own ideas and they want the work to be in the way they like. They didn't even allow me to write the Chinese characters on their paper. I have to write them on another piece of paper and then they tried to copy them to their work.
> (Mother, LMS)

In order to celebrate and share the children's work, the teacher created a slide show made up of photos of the scrapbook pages and posted this on the school blog. In class, she went on to compare the seasons in England and China using the children's work as a stimulus and noted a high level of learner engagement. She also noted the longer-term impact on overall motivation, commenting that:

> The students who did this project are very confident in learning Mandarin now. They like to come to school. I also continue to do the scrapbook work.
> (Mandarin teacher, LMS)

(2)   The song stories and South Indian dance (Bharatha Natyam) at Downderry Primary School.

This school runs Tamil language and South Indian dance classes once a week after school with the support of a local complementary school, the Tamil Academy of Language and Arts. The two classes had been operating separately, but it was decided for this project to explore the possibility of collaboration. Discussion between to the two teachers quickly led to the realization that the song stories, upon which dances are based, could form a natural link to language learning. Thus it was agreed that work in languages lessons would focus on developing understanding of the

254

song stories and the messages underlying them, while in dance lessons the focus would shift to expressing the meaning of the stories through the medium of dance.

The integrated approach began with the Tamil language teacher telling a simplified story to the class in Tamil, drawing on visuals to convey the meaning of key words. She then introduced the song with a musical recording, modeling a number of gestures and facial expressions suited to the Bharatha Natyam dance style. Next, she had pupils sing the song while copying gestures and facial expressions. The teacher found that the incorporation of these kinesthetic and musical elements supported language development and led to greater enjoyment and better retention of new vocabulary:

> *All of the children are very happy. I can tell. They always like stories but this time, they learn more than just stories. They do movements and songs. They really like that.*
>
> *(Tamil language teacher, DPS)*

The dance teacher built on this work by drawing on students' increased awareness of how combinations of words, music, and gesture can combine to enhance communication and lead naturally into more extended expression through dance movement. As with the task set at the London Mandarin School, parental involvement was encouraged and important bridges built between school and home, as the language teacher noted:

> *Parents are very involved and very supportive. They work with me and Navaraj [the dance teacher] all the time. They help the students do the homework and printed out things for the students from the internet. They helped make invitation cards and sort out the costumes.*
>
> *(Tamil language teacher, DPS)*

Also similar to London Mandarin School, developing this more integrated approach with an emphasis on active learning and creative expression was found to provide a more stimulating and supportive context in which to develop both linguistic and dance skills.

Project 2 Critical Connections: A Multilingual Digital Storytelling Project

Building on the investigation of creativity described above, the Critical Connections project, a two-year exploratory, ethnographic study (2012–2014), funded by the Paul Hamlyn Foundation, sought to examine if and how a more engaging context for language learning could be generated through a student led, critical approach to storytelling, drawing on digital tools and the power of the internet for online sharing and communication. The project involved mainly secondary level (age 11–18) students studying a range of languages, European and non-European, in mainstream and complementary schools in and around London as well as overseas (Algeria, Palestine, and Taiwan). Figure 18.1 below illustrates how the vision of multilingual digital storytelling fits within a broader communication landscape and educational context.

To assist in preparing and supporting students with the project, team meetings attended by teachers and researchers were held each term, and these included some digital media training. As illustrated in the diagram above, pedagogically there was a strong emphasis on relating critical thinking and creativity to learner autonomy and use of technology. One way in which this was achieved in the project was by having students formulate their own set of criteria for what makes a good digital story, and then apply these at regular intervals as they engaged in peer review of each other's films, firstly within their own schools and then across schools, including overseas schools.

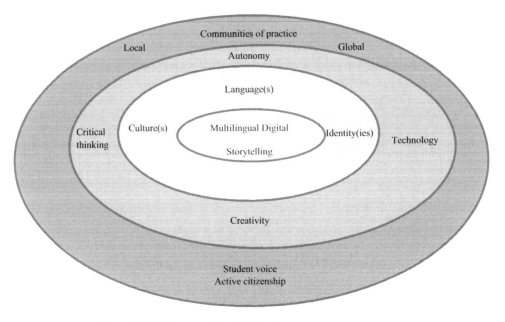

Figure 18.1 Multilingual Digital Storytelling in Context

Source: Reprinted with permission from *Critical connections: Multilingual digital storytelling project. Handbook for teachers*, 2014, by J. Anderson, V. Macleroy, and Y-C. Chung, p. 14. Copyright 2014 by Goldsmiths, University of London.

Data analysis pointed to the value of the project in a number of ways: for language and inter-cultural learning; for the development of digital literacy including multimodal composition; for fostering learner autonomy, creative and critical thinking, and student voice; for extending out-of-school learning and harnessing funds of knowledge in the home; for exploiting the online medium for sharing and building a community of practice; for increasing student engagement, pride in a bilingual identity, and motivation. It also provided valuable insights at the pedagogical and school policy levels. A detailed discussion of these findings as well as a related teacher professional development resource are available elsewhere (Anderson & Macleroy, 2016; Anderson, Macleroy, & Chung, 2014).

By way of example, here we describe digital stories created in complementary schools attended by a mix of heritage background and non-background learners, all having English as their dominant language. The schools, located in North London, are the Hua Hsia Chinese School (HHCS) and the Peace School (PS), and both run on weekends. The digital stories described here, as well as others created within the project, can be viewed on the dedicated project website (Goldsmiths, University of London, 2012).

(1) "The Chinese Zodiac" at Hua Hsia Chinese School.

This bilingual Mandarin–English digital story, based on a traditional Chinese tale, recounts the race of the 12 zodiac animals. The story was made by a group of older primary age children (9–11 years old) each of whom took on the role of one of the animals in the story. Li Hong, the class teacher, suggested the theme of the story, which she felt would be appropriate for several reasons: cultural significance (Chinese lunar calendar; Chinese new year and related elements of Chinese mythology, including moral dimensions as typical in Chinese folk tales: in this case, competition—doing well, but also helping others); students' familiarity with aspects of the story and associated vocabulary, e.g., names of animals; potential for students to develop in active, creative ways using language that would be appropriate for their level of competence in Chinese and English.

Work on the story was carried out over a number of weeks both in class and as homework. Guided through the multimodal composition process by the class teacher, students worked through a number of stages: researching their animals; producing a script; finding suitable images or making drawings; storyboarding; adding subtitles, background music, and credits; reviewing, editing, and improving. Although students were familiar with some of the vocabulary in the story, related to animals, landscapes, and food and drink, this was extended to include new items as well as some new grammatical structures.

Culturally students deepened their appreciation of the story of the Chinese zodiac and its moral significance. However, as was found generally within the project, learning extended beyond linguistic and cultural dimensions to include a range of cognitive and critical skills (planning, researching, drafting, reviewing) as well as broader social skills (teamwork, negotiating and problem solving, presenting to an audience). Importantly, composing their own bilingual, multimodal digital stories enabled children to make sense of culture in their own terms and ultimately to produce work which represented and affirmed their bilingual, bicultural identities. As in Project 1, digital storytelling was found to provide an effective means of harnessing "funds of knowledge" within the home setting and facilitating parental involvement. One parent explained this process:

> I feel that there are aspects of this project where parents really need to get involved. They need to help the children understand where they are going . . . the children love it. . . . It's not just going there, being dropped off, then that's it. After, then there's this follow up, this personal interest. I think it's very, very good because everyone's getting involved . . . because we choose subjects which are close to the children, the children get to choose their own topic so it may be something they enjoy doing with the parents, so it just takes it that one more step—it's fantastic. That's why I'm here.
>
> *(Parent, HHCS)*

(2) "The story of Ibn Battuta" at the Peace School.

In the first year of the project, skills were developed through work on a number of digital stories. Having completed this, students and the head teacher[2] decided for the second year to attempt a larger-scale piece focusing on the travels of the famous fourteenth-century Moroccan explorer, Ibn Battuta. This involved students with Arabic and non-Arabic background researching, scripting, rehearsing, performing, and assisting in the filming of a series of scenes reflecting the travels of Ibn Battuta, which also incorporated contextualizing images and video material. Focusing attention on dramatic and musical elements, and ideally drawing on the expertise of specialists in these areas, can greatly enhance the quality of digital storytelling, as both this study and others indicate (Charalambous & Yerosimou, 2015; McGeoch & Hughes, 2011). Again, in creating this digital story a high degree of parental participation was evident, not least in making costumes and providing props.

A further dimension to this work was provided by the Peace School's partner school in Algeria, the Lycée Ibn Sahnoun, also part of the Critical Connections project. This school made the travels of Captain James Cook the focus for one of their digital stories. This complementary work introduced an enriching comparative element with geographical, historical, and social dimensions.

Once again, the value of linking language learning to meaningful cross-curricular content was apparent, as well as the importance of students' active engagement in decision-making and in review processes. In this regard, the shift towards a more student-centered pedagogical approach over the two years of the project was evident. As one of the teachers involved in the project at the Peace School remarked:

> *The role of the teacher completely changed within this project . . . and students had the space to make their own decisions. It wasn't just us taking leadership of the class, the students were making decisions, they had the space to be creative, they had the space to take it on and lead it themselves.*
>
> *(Teacher, PS)*

4 Implications for Pedagogy

Most broadly, work across the two projects demonstrated the importance of an integrated and inclusive approach to language education, which gives value to all forms of language learning (foreign and heritage languages as well as English and English as an Additional Language), recognizing commonalities as well as differences between these. Arts-based creativity and multilingual digital storytelling, it was found, provided engaging contexts where language development occurred naturally as part of a wider communicative purpose. Both projects strongly supported intercultural perspectives on language teaching, allowing space for students to draw on their full linguistic and cultural repertoires. This could be seen within individual projects, but was greatly extended in the Critical Connections project through the sharing of work online and through annual film festivals.

Within both projects the importance of learner agency was increasingly recognized and teachers encouraged collaborative and critical processes to promote this. Learner agency was seen as an essential part of student engagement and the development of autonomy. This did not mean that the teacher became redundant and indeed some teacher-led skills training was found to be essential, as was the implementation of relevant scaffolding strategies. What was important, though, was that students maintained a sense of ownership through the work, a factor which was partly about active participation, but also, as already mentioned, about construction and performance of identity and investment in a community of practice. The significance of this for HL students was particularly great because it challenged the dominant monolingualizing ideology of the education system by affirming and celebrating bilingual perspectives.

Also emerging clearly from the data is the potential for learning across contexts within these kinds of projects: mainstream and complementary schools, home and community, online and offline. The projects provided a focus which drew parents in and allowed funds of knowledge in the home to become a resource for learning, validating the linguistic and cultural capital that this represents and supporting a harmonious bilingual identity construction (Conteh, Martin, & Robertson, 2007; Cummins & Early, 2011; Kenner & Ruby, 2012). Importantly, where synergies are seen to grow between school and home and community, where, in other words, there is a sense of "collective ownership," so the chances of sustainability are strengthened (Ekholm & Trier, 1987, p. 19).

5 Institutionalization through a Collaborative Professional Development Model

Institutionalization, it should be remembered, operates not just at an organizational level, but also at a classroom level in terms of how and to what extent teachers introduce innovations into their classroom practices. In seeking to implement educational change, all too often a top-down approach has been adopted, positioning the teacher as "technician," receiving training in and then delivering a ready-made package created by "experts" for any situation. This approach has been found to have fundamental flaws: Most significantly, it has not allowed space for teachers to make sense of an innovation in terms which relate to their experience and their classroom situation, thus new ways of working have not become embedded and sustained. A more effective approach, and the one adopted in the projects described in this chapter, is one based on a reflective practitioner model in which teachers and researchers engage in a collaborative and dialogic process of learning which takes account of personal and professional needs (Burley & Pomphrey, 2011; Edwards, 2009; Hawkins, 2004).

Within each of the two-year projects, teachers and researchers met on a regular basis, at least once a term to share and discuss experiences and to reflect on the development of ideas as the projects unfolded. This "social processing" of knowledge (Louis, 2006, p. 3), arrived at through interpersonal interactions, enabled grounded understandings to be reached which connected with the different participants and the different settings where the project took place. Within this trusting and supportive context, colleagues with differing levels of professional qualification and expertize felt able to engage with new ideas and explore how they worked in practice. It took some time for the shift in mindset to take hold, particularly the emphasis on a far more student-centered, inquiry-based pedagogy. However, the impact over time was profound and there was a real sense of growing into a new, positive teacher persona, as can be felt in the words of one of the complementary school teachers in the second project:

> Definitely for me it [the approach to pedagogy] has completely changed. It's not a quantum leap and it's not all of a sudden. Definitely throughout the months I've noticed a change even in the way that I'm thinking and the way I'm planning the lessons and putting the curriculum together. It's a tool that I can use to get the students to use the language in a different way and make it real for them, for them to speak about something that is important for them. . . . Whereas before, I thought that I was quite innovative, I thought that was really, really creative until this came along. All the other times I was thinking how I can get the message across . . . but this, they lead it and I correct it.

The deeper understanding and confidence teachers gained through collaboration in both these projects made a deep impact. Seeing the increased engagement of students and the way the projects developed students' linguistic, intercultural, cognitive, and social skills changed teachers' perception of their role and in some cases led to a rewriting of programs of study. It should also be mentioned that the confidence gained through the project has led to a number of teachers presenting their work at conferences and other professional development events. It is worth noting that findings from the two projects under discussion here clearly reflect the conclusion arising from Wu, Palmer, and Field's (2011) study, which examined the professional identity and beliefs of Chinese HL teachers in the U.S., that, "Rather than playing a role as knowledge transmitters, teachers displaying higher levels of professionalism become facilitators and focus on knowledge construction" (p. 48).

6 Conclusion

This chapter has looked at pedagogy for HL learning and teaching in the context of language education and research in the UK. Having mapped significant developments in pedagogical understanding in the late modern era, insights gained from projects related to arts-based creativity and multilingual digital storytelling carried out recently at Goldsmiths, were presented. Evidence showed that, when implemented with an appropriate pedagogy, the approaches described can engage learners and build strong multilingual and multiliterate identities. The implications for teacher professional development through a process oriented, reflective practitioner model have also been discussed and the significance of this for the institutionalization of innovation has been made clear.

Notes

1 The term "complementary" school (also referred to as "supplementary," "mother tongue," or "community" schools) is used here to refer to voluntary community-based schools which operate mainly at weekends.
2 The head teacher carries out the same role as the school principal in the United States.

References

Anderson, J. (2008). Towards integrated second language teaching pedagogy for foreign and community/heritage languages in multilingual Britain. *Language Learning Journal, 36*(1), 79–89.

Anderson, J. (2009). Relevance of CLIL in developing pedagogies for minority language teaching. In D. Marsh, P. Meehisto, D. Wolff, R. Aliaga, T. Asiakinen, M. J. Frigols-Martin, S. Hughes, & G. Lange (Eds.), *CLIL practice: Perspectives from the field* (pp. 124–132). Jyväskylä, Finland: CCN, University of Jyväskylä.

Anderson, J. (2011). Reshaping pedagogies for a plurilingual agenda. *Language Learning Journal, 39*(2), 135–147.

Anderson, J., & Chung, Y.-C. (2011a). Finding a voice: Arts based creativity in the community languages classroom. *International Journal of Bilingual Education and Bilingualism, 14*(5), 551–569.

Anderson, J., & Chung, Y.-C. (2011b). *Arts-based creativity in the community languages classroom: A professional development resource.* London, UK: Goldsmiths, University of London. Retrieved from http://www.gold.ac.uk/clcl/multilinguallearning/creativity/booklet/#d.en.26692

Anderson, J., & Chung, Y.-C. (2014). Transforming learning, building identities: Arts based creativity in the community languages classroom. In J. Conteh & G. Meier (Eds.), *The multilingual turn in languages education: Benefits for individuals and societies* (pp. 278–291). Clevedon, UK: Multilingual Matters.

Anderson, J., & Macleroy, V. (Eds.). (2016). *Multilingual digital storytelling: Engaging creatively and critically with literacy.* London, UK: Routledge.

Anderson, J., Macleroy, V., & Chung, Y.-C. (2014). *Critical connections: Multilingual digital storytelling project: Handbook for teachers.* London, UK: Goldsmiths, University of London. Retrieved from https://goldsmithsmdst.wordpress.com/handbook/

Anderson, J., & Obied (née Macleroy), V. (2011). Languages, literacies and learning: From monocultural to intercultural perspectives. *NALDIC Quarterly, 8*(3), 16–26.

Arnold, J. (1999). *Affect in language learning.* Cambridge, UK: Cambridge University Press.

Brinton, D., Kagan, O., & Bauckus, S. (Eds.). (2008). *Heritage language education: A new field emerging.* New York, NY: Routledge.

Brown, K., & Brown, M. (2003). *Reflections on citizenship in a multilingual world.* London, UK: CILT.

Burley, S., & Pomphrey, C. (2011). *Mentoring and coaching in schools: Professional learning through collaborative inquiry.* Abingdon, UK: Taylor & Francis.

Byram, M. (1997). *Teaching and assessing intercultural communicative competence.* Clevedon, UK: Multilingual Matters.

Carreira, M. (2016). Supporting heritage language learners through macro-based approaches. In S. Beaudrie & M. Fairclough (Eds.), *Innovative approaches in HL pedagogy: From research to practice* (pp. 123–142). Washington, DC: Georgetown University Press.

Castañeda, M. (2013). "I am proud that I did it and it's a piece of me": Digital storytelling in the foreign language classroom. *CALICO Journal, 30*(1), 44–62.

Charalambous, C., & Yerosimou, M. (2015). Drama, music and media in heritage language learning. *Journal of Education, Culture and Society, 2*, 370–381.

Conteh, J., Martin, P., & Robertson, L. (Eds.). (2007). *Multilingual learning: Stories from schools and communities in Britain.* Stoke-on-Trent, UK: Trentham Books.

Conteh, J., & Meier, G. (Eds.). (2014). *The multilingual turn in languages education: Benefits for individuals and societies.* Clevedon, UK: Multilingual Matters.

Cook, V. J. (2002a). Background to the L2 user. In V. J. Cook (Ed.), *Portraits of the L2 user* (pp. 1–28). Clevedon, UK: Multilingual Matters.

Cook, V. J. (2002b). Language teaching methodology and the L2 user perspective. In V. J. Cook (Ed.), *Portraits of the L2 user* (pp. 327–343). Clevedon, UK: Multilingual Matters.

Cope, B., & Kalanzis, M. (2000). *Multiliteracies: Literacy learning and the design of social futures.* London, UK: Routledge.

Cope, B., & Kalanzis, M. (2013). "Multiliteracies": New literacies, new learning. In M. Hawkins (Ed.), *Framing languages and literacies: Socially situated views and perspectives* (pp. 105–135). New York, NY: Routledge.

Coyle, D., Holmes, B., & King, L. (2009). *CLIL national statement and guidelines.* London, UK: The Languages Company.

Coyle, D., Hood, P., & Marsh, D. (2010). *CLIL: Content and language integrated learning.* Cambridge, UK: Cambridge University Press.

Craft, A. (2011). *Creativity and education futures: Learning in a digital age.* Stoke on Trent, UK: Trentham.

Cummins, C. (2000). *Language, power and pedagogy: Bilingual children in the crossfire.* Clevedon, UK: Multilingual Matters.

Cummins, J., Brown, K., & Sayers, D. (2007). *Literacy, technology and diversity: Teaching for success in changing times.* Boston, MA: Pearson.

Cummins, J., & Early, M. (Eds.). (2011). *Identity texts: The collaborative creation of power in multilingual schools.* Stoke on Trent, UK: Trentham Books.

Datta, M. (Ed.). (2007). *Bilinguality and literacy: Principles and practice* (2nd ed.). London, UK: Continuum.

Edwards, V. (2009). *Learning to be literate: Multilingual perspectives.* Bristol, UK: Multilingual Matters.

Ekholm, M., & Trier, U. P. (1987). The concept of institutionalization: Some remarks. In M. B. Miles, M. Ekholm, & R. Vandenberghe (Eds.), *Lasting school improvement: Exploring the process of institutionalization* (pp. 25–44). Leuven, Belgium: Acco.

Evans, M. (Ed.). (2009). *Foreign language learning with digital technology.* London, UK: Continuum.

Garcia, O. (2009). *Bilingual education in the 21st century: A global perspective.* Malden, MA: Blackwell/Wiley.

Goldsmiths, University of London. (2012). Critical Connections II: Moving forward with multilingual digital storytelling. Retrieved from https://goldsmithsmdst.wordpress.com/

Gregory, E., Long, S., & Volk, D. (Eds.). (2004). *Many pathways to literacy: Young children learning with siblings, grandparents, peers and communities.* London, UK: Routledge Falmer.

Hafner, C. A., & Miller, L. (2011). Fostering learner autonomy in English for science: A collaborative digital video project in a technological learning environment. *Language Learning & Technology, 15*(3), 68–86.

Hawkins, M (Ed.) (2004). *Language learning and teacher education: A sociocultural approach.* Clevedon, UK: Multilingual Matters.

Helot, C., Sneddon, R., & Daly, N. (Eds.). (2014). *Children's literature in multilingual classrooms: From multiliteracy to multimodality.* London, UK: IoE Press/Trentham Books.

Kagan, O., & Dillon, K. (2001/2003). A new perspective on teaching Russian: Focus on the heritage learner. *Heritage Language Journal, 1*(1), 76–90. Retrieved from http://www.heritagelanguages.org (Reprinted from *Slavic and East European Journal, 45*(3), 2001, 507–518.)

Kagan, O., & Dillon, K. (2009). The professional development of teachers of heritage language learners: A matrix. In M. Anderson & A. Lazaraton (Eds.), *Building contexts, making connections: Selected papers from the Fifth International Conference on Language Teacher Education* (pp. 155–175). Minneapolis, MN: Center for Advanced Research on Language Acquisition.

Kenner, C. (2004). *Becoming biliterate: Young children learning different writing systems.* London, UK: Trentham Books.

Kenner, C., & Ruby, M. (2012). *Interconnecting worlds: Teacher partnerships for bilingual learning.* Stoke on Trent, UK: Trentham.

Kramsch, C. (2014). Teaching foreign languages in an era of globalisation: Introduction. *The Modern Language Journal, 98*(1), 296–311.

Krashen, S. (2000). Bilingual education, the acquisition of English, and the retention and loss of Spanish. In A. Roca (Ed.), *Research on Spanish in the United States: Linguistic issues and challenges* (pp. 432–444). Somerville, MA: Cascadilla.

Leeman, J. (2015). Heritage language education and identity in the United States. *Annual Review of Applied Linguistics, 35,* 100–119.

Leeman, J., Rabin, L., & Román-Mendoza, E. (2011). Identity and activism in heritage language education. *Modern Language Journal, 95*(4), 481–495.

Liddicoat, A. J., & Scarino, A. (2013). *Intercultural language teaching and learning.* Hoboken, NJ: Wiley-Blackwell.

Lotherington, H., & Jenson, J. (2011). Teaching multimodal and digital literacy in L2 settings: New literacies, new basics, new pedagogies. *Annual Review of Applied Linguistics, 31,* 226–246.

Louis, K. S. (2006). *Organizing for school change*. New York, NY: Routledge.

Lynch, A. (2003). The relationship between second and heritage language acquisition: Notes on research and theory building. *Heritage Language Journal, 1*(1), 26–43. Retrieved from http://www.heritagelanguages.org/

Lyster, R. (2007). *Learning and teaching languages through content: A counterbalanced approach*. Amsterdam, The Netherlands/Philadelphia, PA: John Benjamins.

May, S. (Ed.). (2014). *The multilingual turn: Implications for SLA, TESOL and bilingual education*. New York, NY: Routledge.

McGeoch, K., & Hughes, J. (2011). Digital storytelling and drama. In M. Anderson, D. Cameron, & J. Carroll (Eds.), *Drama education with digital technology* (pp. 113–128). London, UK: Continuum.

Moll, L. C., Amanti, C., Neff, D., & Gonzalez, N. (1992). Funds of knowledge for teaching: Using a qualitative approach to connect homes and classrooms. *Theory into Practice, 31*(2), 132–141.

Montrul, S., & Bowles, M. (2010). Is grammar instruction beneficial for heritage language learners? Dative case marking in Spanish. *The Heritage Language Journal, 7*(1), 47–73. Retrieved from http://www.heritage languages.org/

NACCCE. (1999). *All our futures: Creativity, culture and education*. London, UK: Department for Education and Employment.

Norton, B., & Toohey, K. (2011). Identity, language learning and social change. *Language Teaching, 44*(4), 412–446.

Osler, A., & Starkey, H. (Eds.). (2005). *Citizenship and language learning: International perspectives*. Stoke on Trent, UK: Trentham Books.

Pahl, K., & Rowsell, J. (2012). *Literacy and education: Understanding the new literacy studies in the classroom* (2nd ed.). London, UK: Sage Publications.

Potowski, K., Jegerski, J., & Morgan-Short, K. (2009). The effects of instruction on linguistic development in Spanish heritage language speakers. *Language Learning, 59*(3), 537–579.

Robin, B. R. (2008). Digital storytelling: A powerful technology tool for the 21st century classroom. *Theory into Practice, 47*(3), 220–228.

Skinner, E. N., & Hagood, M. C. (2008). Developing literate identities with English language learners through digital storytelling. *The Reading Matrix: An International Online Journal, 8*(2), 12–38.

Sneddon, R. (2009). *Bilingual books—biliterate children: Learning to read through dual language books*. Stoke-on-Trent, UK: Trentham.

Spada, N. (1997). Form-focussed instruction and second language acquisition: A review of classroom and laboratory research. *Language Teaching, 30*(2), 73–87.

Stevick, E. (1996). *Memory, meaning and method: A view of language teaching* (2nd ed.). Boston, MA: Heinle and Heinle.

Vinogradova, P. (2014). Digital stores in heritage language education: Empowering heritage language learners through a pedagogy of multiliteracies. In T. Wiley, D. Christian, J. K. Peyton, S. C. Moore, & N. Liu (Eds.), *Handbook of heritage, community, and Native American languages in the United States: Research, educational practice, and policy* (pp. 314–323). New York, NY: Routledge & Washington, DC: Center for Applied Linguistics.

Vinogradova, P., Linville, H., & Bickel, L. (2011). "Listen to my story and you will know me": Digital stories as student-centered collaborative projects. *TESOL Journal, 2*(2), 173–202.

Welsh Government. (2011). *Supporting triple literacy: Language learning in key stage 2 and key stage 3*. Cardiff, UK: Author.

Wu, H., Palmer, D. K., & Field, S. L. (2011). Understanding teachers' professional identity and beliefs in the Chinese heritage language school in the USA. *Language, Culture and Curriculum, 24*(1), 47–60.

Wu, M.-H., & Chang, T. P. (2012). Designing and implementing a macro-approaches-based curriculum for heritage language learners. *Innovation in Language Learning and Teaching, 6*(2), 145–155.

Yang, Y., & Wu, W. (2012). Digital storytelling for enhancing student academic achievement, critical thinking, and learning motivation: A year-long experimental study. *Computers & Education, 59*(2), 339–352.

Part V

Maintenance of Heritage/ Community Languages in Public Schools

The Impact of Government Policy and Sociopolitical Change

19

Reforming Australian Policy for Chinese, Indonesian, Japanese, and Korean Heritage Languages

Examples from the Japanese Community

Kaya Oriyama

1 Introduction

In Australia, 23.2 % of the population (Australian Bureau of Statistics [ABS], 2013) speak at least one of over 340 languages other than English at home (Department of Immigration and Citizenship, 2008). Depending on the policy of each state, up to 46 languages are offered as subjects in the final two years of senior secondary school. Successful completion and total scores (from Years 11–12 internal assessments and Year 12 external final end-of-school exams) determine graduation, university entrance, and potential majors. In the state of New South Wales (NSW), 35 languages are offered as Higher School Certificate (HSC) courses by the Board of Studies, Teaching and Educational Standards NSW (BOSTES NSW) (known as "the Board of Studies NSW [BOS NSW]" until 2014), and many are offered at different levels, including heritage and non-heritage tracks, in each year. As high-stakes subjects, these languages retain special "symbolic value for individuals and minority communities" (Mercurio & Scarino, 2005, p. 146), and their availability as final-year subjects thus has important consequences for heritage language learners (HLLs).

However, in several states, including NSW, where concentrations of Asian language speakers are highest in the nation, most HLLs of the four Asian languages identified as key by the National Asian Languages and Studies in Australian Schools Strategy (NALSAS) 1995–2002 (NALSAS Taskforce, 1995, 1998), namely Chinese, Japanese, Indonesian, and Korean, were excluded from HSC courses between 2002 and 2011 due to eligibility criteria. This exclusion, applied only to these Asian languages, has led to years of struggle by the Japanese community in Sydney to assert their children's right to study their HL for HSC. Their struggle appeared to have ended successfully in late 2008 when the incoming Rudd Administration announced a new Asian language education policy, and gave its financial support for a national project to develop curricula for HLLs of these four Asian languages. However, many issues remain in relation to access and appropriateness regarding the new HL courses.

Using data from surveys and interviews with Japanese heritage students and their parents affected by the policy, along with information gained through personal involvement with the community movement, I critically analyze the "institutionalization" (Ekholm & Trier, 1987) of the first HL curricula in Australian schools for the four Asian languages, along with the language education policy reform behind it. I also explore social consequences of the policies before and after the reform, and discursive representations surrounding language maintenance issues, i.e., how they are "constructed, represented and positioned in political discourse" (Lo Bianco, 2008a, p. 53). I understand *institutionalization* as "a process through which an organization assimilates an innovation into its structure" (Ekholm & Trier, 1987, p. 13), and whose levels are measured by such indicators as "acceptance" of the innovation's legitimacy by participants and its organizational "widespread use" (Eiseman, Fleming, & Roody, 1990, pp. 12–13). Using this definition, this chapter addresses the following questions:

1. How did the curriculum changes occur?
2. What were the challenges and obstacles in bringing about such changes?
3. Since the curriculum implementation, what problematic issues remain or have emerged?

2 Language Education Policy and Planning: Unmasking Ideology

Education plays the most crucial role in language policy implementation, occasionally "bearing the entire burden" (Ferguson, 2006, p. 33). Moreover, language education policy implementation becomes a means to realize "*deliberate* language change" (Baldauf, 1990, p. 14, emphasis in original)—a strategy to solve language problems. However, such "problems" are ideological artifacts which tend to be constructed before language planning (LP) occurs, relying on persuasion as much as reality (Lo Bianco, 2008b). Ideology, although described as "taken-for-granted, common-sense understandings" (Jorgensen & Phillips, 2002, p. 189), encompasses more than ideas; it influences discursive practices, events and texts, social and cultural structures, relations, and processes (Fairclough, 1995). As discursive practices, language education policy and planning affect the structures and existing ideology of educational institutions.

Language education policy, moreover, represents the "particular political positions and cultural values" (Lo Bianco, 1990, p. 52) of those in power, legitimized in relation to national interests for "socially transformative goals and ideologies" (Lo Bianco, 2001, p. 212), such as young citizens' needs for language education in the global economy. As part of social and political planning, LP's success depends on incorporating "language facts in their social, political, economic, psychological and demographic contexts" (Baldauf, 1990, p. 14). However, decisions are usually made without input from those likely to be affected by the policy (Baldauf, Kaplan, & Kamwangamalu, 2010). As Ellis, Gogolin, and Clyne (2010) argue, "a monolingual mindset" such as believing in links between language and patriotism and distrusting intergenerational minority language transmission shapes an influential discourse that constructs language education policy, even in a multicultural nation like Australia. Yet, language "problems" addressed in policy, generally not even linguistic in nature, are perceived as neutral or not full of interest and ideology, and to be unrelated to the LP process (Lo Bianco, 2008b). Considering that LP is a discursive and political practice, we need to scrutinize recurring themes and expose questionable policy making (e.g., commitments inconsistent with rhetoric) to interpret intentions or uncover implicit messages of language policy (Lo Bianco, 2008b).

3 Japanese in Australia and NSW

The number of Japanese in Australia has increased dramatically over the last two decades from around 20,000 to over 80,000; Australia now has the third largest Japanese population in the world (Ministry of Foreign Affairs of Japan [MOFA], 2013). Permanent settlers now outnumber

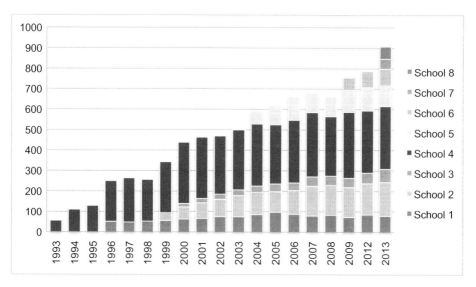

Figure 19.1   Enrollments in Japanese Community Language Schools in NSW

Source: Created from "Japanese CLS student numbers." Copyright 2014 by HSC Japanese Committee.

temporary residents in all major cities. Over 40% of Japanese nationals and permanent residents in Australia have settled in NSW, primarily Sydney, with their numbers increasing from around 3,000 in 1993 to nearly 18,000 in 2013 (MOFA, 2013). The numbers of Australian-born Japanese heritage children have increased, and now form the majority of the second generation, a point underscoring the demographic shift from temporary expatriates to permanent settlers.

The shift has led the community to open eight weekend Japanese schools in Sydney designed to develop and maintain children's Japanese language and cultural awareness, especially literacy. Reflecting the demographic change, student numbers grew from 56 in 1993 to 908 in 2013 (see Figure 19.1). The increase also indicates parental commitment to their children's Japanese education. However, within this upward trajectory, a noticeable drop in enrolment occurred in 2008, which may relate to the aforementioned HSC issue.

Method

I first investigated past HSC issues and background of the language education policy reform using digitally recorded and transcribed interviews with 30 Japanese heritage students (18 females and 12 males, including five pairs of siblings) and their mothers (23 Japanese and 1 Australian),[1] and a questionnaire the students filled out about their experiences of HSC Japanese (see Appendix 19.1; see also Oriyama, 2010). As Table 19.1 shows, these students have a variety of educational, sociocultural, and parental backgrounds. Then, 7 of the 17 students in the first HSC Heritage Japanese course (given pseudonyms for anonymity, see Table 19.2) were surveyed via email to examine current HSC issues, the course's suitability in terms of level and access, and its overall institutionalization. Language policy documentation, correspondence, and discussions between community representatives, key educational authorities, and the researcher were also analyzed to examine challenges and obstacles before and after the reform, and discursive representations in bringing about changes.

Table 19.1 Demographics of Japanese Heritage Participants Interviewed

Name	Age	Gender	Parentage[a]	Age of Leaving Japan[b]	Length of Residence in Japan[c]	Length of Community Schooling[d]	Length of Japanese Study in Australian/ International Schools[e]	Length of Formal Japanese Education
A1	21	M	1	AB	0	5.5 (Y2–7)	2 (Y11–12)C	0
A2	21	M	1	AB	0	8 (Y1–8)	4 (Y7–10)	0
A3	15	M	2	AB	0	11 (YK-10)	0*	0
A4	15	M	1	AB	0	11 (YK-10)	0*	0
A5	18	F	1	AB	0	5 (YK-4)	6 (Y7–12)E	0
A6	19	F	1	AB	0	6 (Y1–6)	6 (Y7–12)E	0
A7	17	F	2	AB	0	7 (YK-6)	0*	0
A8	15	F	1	AB	0	10 (YK-9)	0	0
B1	18	M	2	1	1	9 (Y1–9)	0.5 (Y11)B*	0
B2	18	M	1	AB	0	10 (YK-9)	1 (Y10) 0.5 (Y11)C*	0
B3	16	M	1	3	3	3 (Y1–3)	0*	0
B4	17	F	2	AB	0	10 (YK-9)	1 (Y9–10)*	0
B5	22	F	1	3	3	8 (Y1–8)	0*	0
B6	18	F	2	5	5	10 (YK-9)	0*	0
B7	19	F	2	2	2	4 (Y1–4)	0*	0
C1	17	M	1	AB	0	6 (Y1–6)	6 (Y1–6)SJ Int 4 (Y7–10) 0.5 (Y11)B*	0
C2	20	M	1	3	3	7 (Y1–7)	6 (Y1–6)SJ Int 4 (Y7–10)B	0
C3	18	M	2	3	3	9 (Y1–9)	5 (Y2–6)SJ Int 3 (Y8–10) 1 (Y11)E*	0
C4	17	F	1	1	1	10 (YK-9)	6 (Y1–6)SJ Int 6 (Y7–12)E	0
C5	18	F	1	5	5	4 (Y2–5)	1 (Y6)SJ Int*	0
C6	17	F	1	1	1	5 (YK-4)	2.5 (Y1–3) SJ Int 2 (Y7, 9)*	0.5 (Y3)SJ
C7	21	F	2	4	4	5 (Y5–9)	2 (Y11–12)B	4 (Y1–4)SJ
D1	15	M	2	10	10	3 (Y7-Y9)	0*	4 (Y1–4)
D2	16	M	2	USB	7	0	0*	1 (Y1)
D3	17	F	1	6&14	13	1 (Y1)	4 (Y5–8)Int. schl 4 (Y9–12)B	3 (Y2–4)
D4	19	F	2	1	1	2 (YK-Y1) Hong Kong 2 (Y11–12) Tut. School	0*	0

(Continued)

Table 19.1 (Continued)

Name	Age	Gender	Parentage[a]	Age of Leaving Japan[b]	Length of Residence in Japan[c]	Length of Community Schooling[d]	Length of Japanese Study in Australian/ International Schools[e]	Length of Formal Japanese Education
D5	16	F	1	5	5	0	1 (Y6)SJ Int*	0 Int.preschl
D6	14	F	1	AB	0	0	0	4 (Y1–4)SJ
D7	17	F	2	4	8 (0–4& 8–12yrs old)	0	1 (Y11)B*	5 (Y2–6)
D8	16	F	2	AB	0	4 (Y1–2&7–8)	0*	0

Note:
[a]1 = 1 Japanese parent (and 1 non-Japanese parent), 2 = 2 Japanese parents.
[b]AB = Australian Born, USB = U.S.A. Born.
[c]Length = length in years.
[d]Y = Year (Year levels vary among the community schools, as some do not follow the standard curriculum in Japan); Tut. School = Tutoring school.
[e]C = Continuers, E = Extension, B = Background Speakers; SJ = Sydney Japanese weekday (full-time) school, Int = International section; Int.schl = International school.
*Those who were refused to take or did not take the Continuers/Extension courses due to eligibility criteria.

Table 19.2 Heritage Japanese Survey Respondents' Demographics

Student	Age	Gender	Parentage[a]	Age on Arrival[b]	Length of Residence in Japan[c]	Length of Community Schooling[d]	Length of Japanese Study in Australian Schools[e]
Kate	16	F	1	AB	0	9 (Y1–9)	0
Yumi	17	F	2	AB	0	4 (YK-3)	0
Hanna	17	F	2	4	4	3 (YK-2)	0
Chloe	17	F	1	AB	0	11 (YK-10)	2 (Y7–8)
Riki	17	M	2	AB	0	10 (YK-9)	1 (Y7)
Nina	16	F	2	AB	0	9 (YK-8)	0
Lisa	17	F	2	AB	0	13 (YK-12) Tut. School	0

Note:
[a]1 = 1 Japanese parent (and 1 non-Japanese parent), 2 = 2 Japanese parents.
[b]AB = Australian Born.
[c]Length = length in years.
[d]Y = Year (Year levels vary among the community schools, as some do not follow the standard curriculum in Japan); Tut. School = Tutoring school.
[e]Study before Year 11.

4 Higher School Certificate Issues in the Past: How the Community's Struggle Began

In NSW, students can study languages from primary to senior secondary level. Until 2001, Japanese HLLs in Year 10 could select from three separate level HSC Japanese course streams: "Continuers" (post-"Beginners"), "Extension," and "Background Speakers." However, in 2001, ambiguous eligibility rules were introduced to exclude students from four key Asian languages' HSC Continuers and Extension courses if their target language knowledge derives from other than study as a second language or "more than one year's formal education . . . in the language, in a country where the language is the medium of instruction" (BOS NSW, 2001). Although Japanese HLLs were a minority in the Continuers and Extension courses before 2001, the eligibility rules were intended to distinguish *foreign* language learners from those with "*some background* in the language*" (BOS NSW, 2001, emphasis added), restricting most HLLs to the Background Speakers course. However, the targeted entry level of the Background Speakers course has always been much higher than most HLLs' proficiency levels: at least Year 9 of formal education (junior secondary school graduates) in Japan, i.e., native speakers (Oguro & Moloney, 2010). Moreover, "*failure* to adhere to the eligibility rule could *jeopardise*" (BOS NSW, 2001, emphasis added) award of a HSC, suggesting that students alone are responsible for jeopardizing themselves, although principals in consultation with BOS NSW have withdrawn some students from the courses even after they were accepted or had begun to study.[2]

In 2005, stricter and more detailed eligibility criteria were implemented to exclude students from the four Asian languages' HSC Continuers or Extension who "speak *or* write the language at home, or elsewhere outside the classroom, *in a sustained manner* with a person or persons who have a *background* in using the language" or have had "more than one year's *formal education* . . . in the language *in a country and/or school* where the language is the medium of education" (BOS NSW, 2005, p. 85, emphasis added). Accordingly, students who wished to take these languages for HSC had to fill out an application to determine eligibility, sign a statutory declaration, and provide supporting evidence such as birth certificates.

Several problems were apparent in the 2005 criteria: The exclusion of those who "speak *or* write" the language meant that HLLs who can speak but cannot write Japanese were placed in the same Background Speakers course as those with years of formal education in Japan. Furthermore, since the terms "sustained manner," "background," or "formal education" were unexplained, many principals considered a community language school attendance "formal education" and excluded students from the Continuers on this basis, which should not have been the case, as BOS NSW admitted (HSC Japanese Committee [HSCJC], 2008). Most HLLs, though Australian-educated, were placed in the Background Speakers, even though the course's targeted level was well beyond them, and subsequently had to give up Japanese study. The criteria discouraged parents' home Japanese use, as well as enrollment in a community language school (HSCJC, 2008) or a full-time Japanese school (Japanese Studies Association of Australia, 2007). This situation shook the community, and led in 2007 to the formation of the HSCJC, primarily composed of parents from Sydney's Japanese community.

The main issue of concern was the classification of Australian-educated HLLs in the same category as Japanese-educated "Background Speakers," i.e., "Native Speakers."[3] Yet, HLLs are not recently arrived, mostly Japanese-educated "Native Speakers." Valdés (2001) describes an HLL as one who "is raised in a home where a non-English language is spoken, who speaks or merely understands the HL, and who is to some degree bilingual in English and the HL" (p. 38). What characterizes HLLs' language is therefore generally more developed comprehension or conversational skills, acquired within the family, but limited or absent literacy. As Clyne (2005) states, many Australian studies have shown that children suffer from first language attrition; their insufficient monitoring of grammar often results in inferior language examination outcomes.

Clearly, then, placing primarily Australian-educated HLLs in the same course as those who have attended school mostly or for some time in Japan is inappropriate. This problem was also highlighted in the HSCJC's 2008 survey: 83% of 110 students (Years 10–12) lacked sufficient confidence for the Background Speakers course. Those who felt confident were likely to be the Japanese-educated children of expatriates. In addition, teachers who have taught Australian-educated Japanese HLLs in the Background Speakers course regard the linguistic and cognitive abilities as well as the cultural knowledge of these learners as inadequate (Oguro & Moloney, 2010).

The current study confirms that the Background Speakers course is unsuitable for most HLLs: Only 6 of 30 informants (including 5 with more than one year's formal full-time Japanese education) took the course, with three completions. Even those with several years of Japanese full-time education avoided this Background Speakers course since raw exam marks not in the top percentile are usually "scaled down," i.e., converted into lower scaled scores.[4] Therefore, these students lacked the confidence to earn top scores and thus minimize this procedure's impact. All HLLs schooled primarily in English found the course "TOO HARD!" as one wrote in the survey. They felt discriminated against because of their ethnicity; as one interviewee put it, "[I wasn't allowed to take the Continuers] because I've got a face like this."

This feeling of unfairness is exacerbated because HLLs of 26 other modern languages can study their HLs in the HSC Continuers or Extension courses, and indeed form the majority in most of these courses. Furthermore, the eligibility criteria apply only to languages, not subjects like music and math in which students might be advantaged if they have musician/mathematician parents or have been exposed to and trained in these areas since childhood (Clyne, 2005).

In 2010, BOS NSW justified the different regulations for the four Asian languages because of: (1) "an acknowledgement of the *difficulty for second language learners . . .* to acquire these Asian languages and to reach a level of proficiency commensurate with the level that can be reached by second language learners in European languages" (HSCJC, 2010, p. 2, emphasis added) using the U.S. Foreign Service Institute's (FSI) classification of languages in the 1960s according to difficulty for *adult native* English speakers (Jackson & Kaplan, 1999); and an unsubstantiated belief that (2) students with these Asian languages backgrounds "have *a distinct advantage . . . significantly greater* than that gained by students with a background in other languages, in particular in European languages" (HSCJC, 2010, p. 1, emphasis added). Here the learning of these Asian languages by second language learners, rather than HLLs, is the focus, and this perspective is also promoted by the government and other agencies through NALSAS (Erebus Consulting Partners, 2002).

However, BOS's above arguments are inconsistent and contradictory: For instance, the FSI categorizes Indonesian as being of low-medium difficulty and easier than most European languages, while Arabic, one of the most difficult languages in the FSI ranking (Jackson & Kaplan, 1999), is exempted from differential treatment. Moreover, at the time, one in four NSW school students had a language other than English (LOTE) background, many of whom were not native English speakers and elected to study Japanese (HSCJC, 2010). BOS never provided evidence supporting the argument of disproportionate advantage in these circumstances, despite the HSCJC's repeated requests. On the contrary, Elder's (1997) study of Italian, Greek, and Chinese HLLs suggests that irrespective of language, HLLs are not really advantaged relative to non-HLLs in educational settings; Their generally better listening skills prove less of an advantage in Year 12, as with each succeeding year an emphasis on literacy increases, an area where many non-HLLs perform as well as or even better than HLLs.

5 Solving Higher School Certificate Issues: Linking National and Community Interests

Seeking resolution to the HSC issues, the HSCJC sent three letters (the third included 1,423 signatures) to BOS NSW in 2007, explaining the eligibility problems and asking related questions. The Japanese Studies Association of Australia's and the researcher's letters followed, backing the HSCJC's claims with research and proposing a new course for HLLs. Much correspondence subsequently took place between HSCJC and BOS, and meetings were finally held in 2008 to discuss matters in detail, which BOS later admitted was "an important step" leading to the development of Heritage curricula. The discussions also made BOS members realize that HLLs differ from "Background Speakers" and that mostly Australian-born and Australian-educated HLLs are excluded from target language courses due to eligibility criteria. A national project was then established to investigate ways to accommodate HLLs in existing courses by making eligibility criteria consistent nationally, which proved difficult. While application forms were modified to clarify criteria terms, BOS still did not properly address eligibility issues.

A turning point came when the Labor Party took office and announced the formation of the National Asian Languages and Studies in Schools Program (NALSSP) in late 2008. The new national language policy for the 2008–2012 period aimed at doubling the percentage of secondary school graduates fluent in Chinese, Indonesian, Japanese, and Korean to 12% by 2020 (Department of Education, Employment, and Work Relation [DEEWR], 2010). The program attracted $62.4 million in funding, part of which became available to develop new Heritage curricula for HLLs of these strategically important languages, thus giving these HLLs options to take either Heritage or Background Speakers courses for HSC. In other words, the courses available for the four languages for HSC now consisted of "Beginners," "Continuers," "Extension," "Heritage," and "Background Speakers."

In 2009, a public national forum was held in Sydney to discuss the development of Heritage courses, where BOS stated that they realized that "just adjusting eligibility criteria [is] not going to be sufficient" to achieve the targeted fluency level of being able to "communicate in a business sense" after attending the NALSSP forum for stakeholders in 2008 (HSCJC, 2009, p. 1). What "most importantly" and "really helped" the Heritage course development, BOS emphasized, was government funding and support (HSCJC, 2009, p. 2). According to this perspective, community lobbying from "below" (non-governmental local agencies such as HSCJC; Alexander, 1992) to change language policy was pushing the "middle" (sub-national state governmental agencies such as BOS; my original) to move, but could not achieve much without the support of those "above" (national governmental agencies such as the Council of Australian Governments; Hogan-Brun, 2010).

6 Current Higher School Certificate Issues: The Community's Struggle Continues

While the decision to develop new Heritage courses was positive, the eligibility criteria remained. BOS "studiously avoided consultation about the eligibility criteria right through the consultation process about the course structure and content, even though eligibility is a critical issue in discussing structure and content" (HSCJC, 2011, p. 1). As pointed out by Baldauf et al. (2010), in relation to the usual process of language policy making, the community affected by the policy was excluded from decisions, and the inappropriateness of the newly developed criteria was never acknowledged, "despite the obvious evidence to the contrary" (HSCJC, 2011, p. 1).

Nevertheless, the Heritage courses were developed and implemented in 2011, and the Japanese Continuers' eligibility criteria now place those who "use the language for sustained communication outside the classroom," or have "had more than one year's formal education" in Japanese, or lived in Japan for "more than three years in the past 10 years" (BOS NSW, 2010) in either the Heritage or Background Speakers course regardless of proficiency. In addition, the Heritage course eligibility criteria exclude those who have had formal Japanese education after age 10 (Year 5 of primary school). While the criteria changed, the targeted entry levels for Heritage (Year 4 of Japan's primary school/lower-intermediate Japanese proficiency) or Background Speakers (Year 9 of Japanese junior secondary school/advanced Japanese proficiency) courses still exceed what many Australian-educated Japanese HLLs can reasonably be expected to achieve, especially due to their much stronger emphasis on literacy than Continuers or Extension.

What prevents most Japanese HLLs from reaching the targeted levels of these courses is inadequate knowledge of *kanji* and its associated vocabulary and expressions. Acquisition of these ideographs is essential to Japanese literacy, but *kanji* are complex, each usually read in at least two or three ways, and including 2,136 characters officially prescribed as in daily use (taught by Year 9 in Japan). As a result, learning *kanji* places an enormous burden on Australian-educated HLLs; *kanji* knowledge needs to be considered closely when placing students in a Japanese course.

Inevitably, HLLs' vastly different levels of literacy, especially in *kanji*, and the arbitrary eligibility criteria mean that the language background and proficiency levels of the Heritage course students vary greatly. Students could range from Australian-born who can use Japanese for daily family communication but cannot read or write, to those educated in Japan up to Year 5 of primary school who have learned up to 825 *kanji*. Included by default are non-HLLs who have 1.1 years of formal Japanese education during Years 1 and 2, or lived in Japan for 3.3 years even if they attended an English-medium school there. It is thus obvious that the criteria make proficiency levels within the Heritage course too diverse, and place unsuitable learners in the course.

7 Current Higher School Certificate Issues Identified by Heritage Course Students

The inadequacy of eligibility criteria for placement is further evident from an analysis of the Heritage Japanese course student survey regarding family and language background, proficiency levels, course evaluation, and course accessibility (see Table 19.2, Appendix 19.2). Only 15 HLLs (seven males and eight females) completed the first Year 12 Heritage course in 2012,[5] just around 4% of Japanese heritage children of appropriate age in NSW (ABS, 2006). These students form a minority who have developed higher levels of Japanese literacy with a genuine commitment. Unlike other Japanese courses, Heritage and Background Speakers courses are offered externally and only outside the normal school hours.[6] Many of these students spent three hours every Saturday or Sunday morning at a community language school in childhood, and subsequently as teens had to spend three hours every Saturday morning at Heritage classes.

Commuting and class time became an issue for many. Some spent up to two hours traveling to school for their Heritage classes. Until Open High School began offering the Heritage Japanese course via correspondence in 2014, the course had been offered only in the north of Sydney at the Saturday School of Community Languages (SSCL), a public secondary school which teaches 24 languages as official school subjects on Saturdays at 16 centers in NSW. These centers provide students with "the opportunity to study the language they speak at home" (SSCL, 2015), and they can study languages other than Chinese, Japanese, Korean, and Persian in either the Continuers or Extension courses for HSC. While face-to-face classes are preferable, sports classes on Saturday mornings are compulsory in most secondary schools, forcing many students to give up the Heritage course.

Moreover, a requirement for enrolling in the SSCL or Open High School is that the target language is not taught in students' weekday school, because it is assumed that schools can offer the Heritage course if they teach the target language. Most secondary schools, however, teach Japanese at the Beginner's level, and teachers are unable to teach the Heritage course because its level is beyond them and student numbers are too small. This issue seriously limits the number of students who can take the Heritage course. Also contributing to this problem is that preparatory courses for the Heritage course are rarely offered in Years 7 and 8, and the only preparatory courses offered for Years 9 and 10 are correspondence courses at Open High School that have no special curriculum and use the same material as Continuers or Extension courses.

Initially, 17 students attended the first Year 12 Heritage class. Only three were mixed Japanese/non-Japanese heritage, even though such students form the majority in NSW community Japanese language schools. This discrepancy suggests that reaching the level needed for the Heritage course is difficult when you have just one Japanese-speaking parent. One student in this course had no Japanese parentage, but attended primary school in Japan until Year 2 or 3. The vast majority attended only community language schools for many years, but two had discontinued after Year 2 and 3, respectively.

Nonetheless, the students' proficiency levels "vary A LOT," according to the survey response from Riki. Kate elaborated on this point: "some students have difficulty writing Yr [Year] 2 kanji, while others . . . have no difficulties reading japanese novels." The result of eligibility criteria that place students who "are in the *vague* range in between the continuer japanese and background japanese courses" (Chloe, emphasis added) in one Heritage course was detrimental to many. Students noted that several low proficiency students "have a very hard time keeping up with the lessons" and "evidently struggle when reading passages from Year 8 course materials from Japan," but top students find the course "too easy" and feel that their fluency has not increased with the course. For these reasons, most students judged the course in some way inappropriate for the majority of the class.

Furthermore, many saw a problem in the lack of a fixed syllabus and the limited resources, which often led content to be repeated. For example, Nina stated they "have been asked the same essay question four times." Also, the course does not "have any prescribed texts or past papers to set a standard for what we will be doing for our HSC" (Chloe). Most thought "the course content is really vague, mislead [sic] and uninteresting" (Riki) and thus "difficult . . . to learn" (Nina). Students particularly enjoy discussions and are interested in "learning about issues in Japan" (Yumi) and "real Japanese history, culture, tradition, opinions, perspectives and lifestyles in much depth" (Nina). Therefore, Nina identifies the need "to incorporate texts and other materials" such as "films, essays, novels, music, etc . . . that cover these topics," and discuss topics after reading or before writing essays for more effective learning. This recommendation is similar to approaches suggested for an HLL curriculum that build on students' existing proficiency and emotional, cultural, and instrumental motivation (Kagan, 2005). Clearly, their potential to achieve high proficiency cannot be realized "without a soundly designed curriculum" (Kagan, 2005, p. 214) and pedagogical approaches adapted to HLLs' needs (Carreira & Kagan, 2011). Carreira and Kagan (2011) recommend community-based curricula to connect the learner and the community, and Kagan (2005) proposes macro-approaches that use global tasks (i.e., negotiating meaning in a variety of situations) to teach specific elements like grammar, vocabulary, and spelling.

The core of the problem lies in placing HLLs in one standard course using arbitrary criteria, despite widely varying ranges of proficiency. As Kagan (2005) points out, "As with all students, HLLs should have access to instruction at their level of ability" (p. 214). Courses for HLLs should be offered at different levels to solve this issue, but if limited resources and student numbers do not allow this, HLLs should be placed in a course based on proficiency, not background. For placement, *kanji* knowledge would be a much better indicator of proficiency than background since HSC Japanese exams are mainly reading and essay writing, and literacy acquired in a set period of time is different for each student.

Those for whom the targeted level is roughly appropriate largely find the Heritage course a positive experience; Lisa appreciates "the comfort of learning within a community [I] belong to," and Chloe reports that "I have improved in terms of vocabulary and essay writing." For the majority, the course's best aspect is social, a sense of belonging to a community. They are mostly Australian-born, and value interaction with those of similar backgrounds "bound by the awareness that we're all Japanese teens in an Australian society" (Chloe). Unfortunately, however, most HLLs are losing the opportunity for a similar experience.

Overall, institutionalization of the Heritage course with regard to "acceptance" and "widespread use" are unsatisfactory. The ambiguous and arbitrary eligibility criteria seem to influence student perceptions of the course most. Many perceived the course objectives and content as "vague" and the wide proficiency gap among classmates as problematic. Issues of access in terms of time, place, and enrolment criteria, and the lack of a fixed syllabus, resources, and preparatory courses, also contribute to a sense of dissatisfaction and the low enrolments. Therefore, top-down institutionalization of HL education without attention to bottom-up concerns cannot solve the core issue of access to instruction at appropriate levels, and causes further issues. While the diversity of language backgrounds and proficiency in HL classes is indeed a common problem across languages, the nature of diversity is different in each language (Carreira & Kagan, 2011). Such diversity thus needs to be considered for successfully institutionalizing HL education, along with other practical issues.

8 Seeking Solutions to HSC Issues: Moving Forward

The issues surrounding eligibility criteria are not limited to NSW. Only in Victoria have Japanese course completion numbers not fallen significantly (de Kretser & Spence-Brown, 2010). In that state, notably, Japanese HLLs are eligible for the Second Language course (the Continuers' equivalent) if they have had "up to seven years of education in a school where Japanese is the medium of instruction" (Victorian Curriculum and Assessment Authority [VCAA], 2011). Moreover, until 2011, only Victorian Year 12 students who successfully completed LOTE studies received 10% bonus Australian Tertiary Admission Rank points that facilitate higher education entry (Group of Eight, 2007).[7] These incentives and the lack of strict eligibility criteria have contributed to relatively high enrolments in final-year Japanese in Victoria compared with other states and territories (de Kretser & Spence-Brown, 2010).

In NSW, only the University of NSW has introduced such bonus points for HSC languages studies for some degree programs since 2010 and currently also for Heritage courses, but bonus points for top performance in Heritage are lower than those for Continuers, Dance, or Drama courses. Although other NSW universities now offer similar bonus points for languages, they typically do not include Heritage courses. "Acceptance" (an institutionalization indicator; Miles & Louis, 1987, p. 26) of, and incentives to take, the Heritage courses are thus low at the institutional level.

The VCAA made a proposal as part of the 2009 national project to remove the eligibility criteria and provide incentives to study languages, but BOS NSW disagreed, and its eligibility criteria remained. It is noteworthy that, as with Japanese, enrolments in HSC Chinese, Indonesian, and Korean, where the eligibility criteria also apply, declined after criteria enforcement,

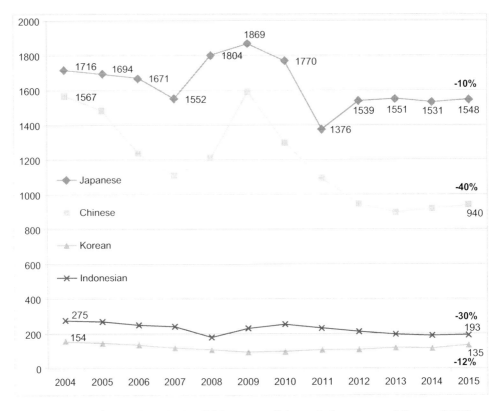

Figure 19.2 Total Year 12 Entries in HSC Japanese, Chinese, Indonesian, and Korean (NSW)

Source: Created from "Statistics archive." Copyright 2016 by Board of Studies, Teaching and Educational Standards, New South Wales.

especially Chinese, whose HLL numbers are the largest (see Figure 19.2). Heritage course enrolments remain low, especially in Indonesian and Japanese, while the gradual increase in Chinese reflects large demographic growth (see Figure 19.3). Yet, these Asian languages are the very ones that the government hopes to promote.

This contradiction resolves itself upon examination of NALSSP and its predecessor, NALSAS. An evaluation of NALSAS for the government states that "NALSAS was *never* about language or cultural maintenance for students from Asian backgrounds" (Erebus Consulting Partners, 2002, p. 99, emphasis added). HLLs were clearly not the target population for the program, despite their "linguistic capital" (Bourdieu, 1991) and potential to achieve advanced levels of target language proficiency.

While it is significant that the development of "specialist" (i.e., Heritage) curriculum for advanced language students became an NALSSP objective, unlike the total disregard of HLLs in the NALSAS, the stated primary objective of the NALSSP is "to significantly increase the number of *Australian* students becoming proficient at learning the languages and understanding the cultures of our *Asian neighbours*," which is important "in ensuring young *Australians* are equipped with the skills to compete in the globalised economy of the future" (DEEWR, 2010, p. 1, emphasis added). The argument of promoting "Australians" learning "Asian languages" in

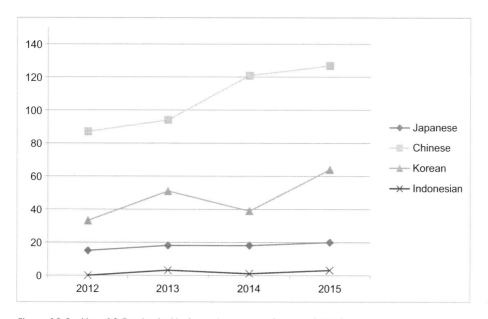

Figure 19.3 Year 12 Entries in Heritage Language Courses (NSW)

Source: Created from "Statistics archive." Copyright 2016 by Board of Studies, Teaching and Educational Standards, New South Wales.

the Australian Language and Literacy Policy (Department of Employment, Education and Training, 1991) and the NALSAS strategy is repeated in the NALSSP approach. That is, it follows the perspective that "frames all languages other than English as 'foreign'—separate from and alien to 'Australians'" (Moore, 1996, p. 480), with which they need to "become familiar" (DEEWR, 2010, p. 1), despite the increasingly diverse language backgrounds of Australian students.

Like its predecessors, NALSSP emphasized the economic value of priority languages and cultures for the majority and ignored personal and social values of multilingualism for all. In Moore's (1996) words, "the economic rationalist ethic had colonised social justice" (p. 491). Removal of "barriers to the study of Asian languages" to stimulate "student demand" was one of the NALSSP goals, but eligibility criteria—the real barrier for HLLs—were never removed, despite the HSCJC's repeated requests. BOS considered the presence of HLLs in the classroom a "barrier" for foreign/second language learners (a concern shared by Asia Education Foundation, 2010) because they "could be *flooded* by students with a high level of Japanese proficiency" (BOS NSW, cited in HSCJC, 2008, p. 8, emphasis added)—which evoked Hanson's 1996 statement that Australians "are in danger of being *swamped* by Asians" (Making Multicultural Australia, 2002, p. 1, emphasis added). However, as this chapter has demonstrated, such fear was unfounded, and removing this "barrier" did not stem the decline in foreign/second language learners' enrolment in non-heritage courses (BOSTES NSW, 2016).

Asian countries have become major sources of immigration over the last two decades, and Australia needs "young Australians . . . equipped with the [Asian language] skills to compete in the globalised economy" (DEEWR, 2010, p. 1). Why then, does Australia waste valuable human resources and discourage those who can most readily become a bridge between countries and contribute to Australian society? Why are HLLs of key Asian languages regarded as "specialists" who possess advanced abilities and are denied access to courses at their levels, unlike HLLs of other languages? When the goal of this "specialist" curriculum is to produce students who can "communicate in a business sense," the curriculum needs to train students toward such a goal. Clearly, HLLs' Japanese proficiency varies greatly even within the Heritage course: Only about one-third of the participants were around the targeted level of the course, while just a few were above the course level and the rest were struggling. This indicates that course placements by eligibility criteria are inappropriate, and that the single Heritage course cannot accommodate students with a wide range of proficiency. If limited resources allow only one Heritage course suitable for very limited numbers of HLLs, other HLLs should be placed in courses at or closer to their levels.

Australia needs to move forward with its growing multilingual population; as an urgent first step, eligibility criteria must be removed and replaced with incentives and proficiency-based placements to encourage enrollment in all key Asian language courses, and to provide courses that match students' abilities and needs.

9 Conclusion

This chapter has examined the language policy reform and resulting institutionalization of the first HL curricula in Australian schools as discursive practices, considering in particular: (1) how language education policies (and eligibility criteria in particular) affected Japanese HLLs' access to HL education in NSW; (2) how the community struggled to convince authorities that HL education meets the national interest so as to bring about the introduction of the HL courses; and (3) why issues remain after curriculum implementation. Consistent with previous studies, I have argued that language policy "problems" are ideological and created by political interest—in this case, with an additional economic incentive: to produce "Australians" proficient in "Asian" languages. Consequently, the need to place only HLLs of four Asian languages in separate one-size-fits-all courses regardless of proficiency by arbitrary criteria cannot be defended by research. Disregarding "language facts" (Baldauf, 1990) in LP has had significant negative consequences for the Japanese community, as the HLLs and their parents testify. Institutionalization of HL education cannot be truly successful or solve all the issues without considering such facts.

When a stated goal and policy have contradictory effects, implementation and institutionalization suffer, as do those negatively affected by the policy. Top-down LP cannot succeed without taking into consideration those at the bottom. In a globalized world, language education policies need to accommodate linguistic diversity and reality. Linguistic minorities should be able to actively participate in forming (and reforming) such policies not only for individuals and communities, but for the nation as a whole.

Notes

1 Both students and their mothers were interviewed except for two cases.
2 Principals made the decision regarding eligibility (unless they were unsure and asked BOS), depending on their interpretation of the rules and consideration of students' circumstances.
3 The Background Speakers syllabus implemented in 2000 replaced the existing syllabus in Japanese for Native Speakers with "a minor change" (BOS NSW, 1999, p. 1).
4 Scaled marks, used to make performance across different subjects comparable for the Universities Admissions Centre, show how much students' marks deviate from the mean/average cohort benchmark. Some subjects' marks tend to convert to much higher or lower scaled marks (scaled up or down), not depending on the difficulty of the subjects, but on how well the students in a certain subject perform relative to other subjects (better performance leads to higher scaling).

5 In 2015, 10 students were enrolled in the Year 12 Heritage Japanese course at the SSCL and 10 at the Open High School.
6 This is also the case for Indonesian. Some schools with large HLL numbers offer Chinese and Korean Heritage and Background Speakers courses internally.
7 In 2011, five universities in other states announced the introduction of various bonus points for tertiary entry.

References

Alexander, N. (1992). Language planning from below. In R. Herbert (Ed.), *Language and society in Africa: The theory and practice of sociolinguistics* (pp. 56–68). Johannesburg: Witwatersrand University Press.

Asia Education Foundation. (2010). *The current state of Chinese, Indonesian, Japanese and Korean language education in Australian schools: Four languages, four stories.* Carlton South, Victoria: Education Services Australia. Retrieved from http://artsonline.monash.edu.au/mcjle/files/2012/07/current_state_asian_langugae_overarching_report.pdf

Australian Bureau of Statistics (ABS). (2006). 2006 Census data. Retrieved from http://www.abs.gov.au/websitedbs/censushome.nsf/home/historicaldata2006?opendocument&navpos=280

Australian Bureau of Statistics (ABS). (2013). 2011 Census QuickStats. Retrieved from http://www.abs.gov.au/websitedbs/censushome.nsf/home/quickstats?opendocument&navpos=220

Baldauf, R. B. (1990). Language planning and education. In R. B. Baldauf & A. Luke (Eds.), *Language planning and education in Australasia and the South Pacific* (pp. 14–24). Clevedon: Multilingual Matters.

Baldauf, R. B., Kaplan, R. B., & Kamwangamalu, N. (2010). Language planning and its problems. *Current Issues in Language Planning, 11*(4), 430–438.

Board of Studies, New South Wales (BOS NSW). (1999). *An introduction to Japanese background speakers stage 6 in the new HSC.* Sydney, Australia: Author.

Board of Studies, New South Wales (BOS NSW). (2001). Official notice [BOS 75/01, 10(6)]: Eligibility rules for stage 6 languages continuers/background speakers courses. Sydny, Australia: Author.

Board of Studies, New South Wales (BOS NSW). (2005). *Assessment certification and examination manual.* Sydney, Australia: Author.

Board of Studies, New South Wales (BOS NSW). (2010, April 15). Eligibility for stage 6 languages courses. Retrieved from http://www.boardofstudies.nsw.edu.au/syllabus_hsc/lang-eligibility-criteria.html

Board of Studies, Teaching and Educational Standards, New South Wales (BOSTES NSW). (2016). Statistics archive. Retrieved from http://www.boardofstudies.nsw.edu.au/ebos/static/ebos_stats.html

Bourdieu, P. (1991). *Language and symbolic power.* Cambridge, MA: Harvard University Press.

Carreira, M., & Kagan, O. (2011). The results of the National Heritage Language Survey: Implications for teaching, curriculum design, and professional development. *Foreign Language Annals, 44*(1), 40–64.

Clyne, M. (2005). *Australia's language potential.* Sydney, Australia: UNSW Press.

de Kretser, A., & Spence-Brown, R. (2010). *The current state of Japanese language education in Australian schools.* Carlton South, Australia: Education Services Australia. Retrieved from http://artsonline.monash.edu.au/mcjle/files/2012/07/current_state_asian_langugae_overarching_report.pdf

Department of Education, Employment, and Work Relation (DEEWR), Australian Government. (2010). National Asian languages and studies in schools program: Program guidelines 2009–2012, v.3. Canberra, Australia: Author.

Department of Employment, Education and Training, Australian Government. (1991). *Australia's language: The Australian language and literacy policy* (Vols. 1–2). Canberra, Australia: Australian Government Publishing Service.

Department of Immigration and Citizenship. (2008). The people of Australia—Statistics from the 2006 Census. *Commonwealth of Australia.* Retrieved from https://www.dss.gov.au/sites/default/files/documents/01_2014/poa-2008.pdf

Eiseman, J. W., Fleming, D. S., & Roody, D. S. (1990). *Making sure it sticks: The school improvement leader's role in institutionalizing change.* Andover, MA: The Regional Laboratory.

Ekholm, M., & Trier, U. P. (1987). The concept of institutionalization: Some remarks. In M. B. Miles, M. Ekholm, & R. Vandenberghe (Eds.), *Lasting school improvement: Exploring the process of institutionalization* (pp. 13–21). Leuven, Belgium: Acco.

Elder, C. (1997). *The background speaker as learner of Italian, Modern Greek and Chinese: Implications for foreign language assessment.* (Doctoral dissertation). University of Melbourne, Australia.

Ellis, E., Gogolin, I., & Clyne, M. (2010). The Janus face of monolingualism: A comparison of German and Australian language education policies. *Current Issues in Language Planning, 11*(4), 439–460.

Erebus Consulting Partners. (2002). Evaluation of the National Asian Languages and Studies in Australian Schools Strategy: A report to the Department of Education, Science and Training. Retrieved from http://www.curriculum.edu.au/nalsas/pdf/evaluation.pdf

Fairclough, N. (1995). *Critical discourse analysis.* London, UK: Longman.

Ferguson, G. (2006). *Language planning and education.* Edinburgh, UK: Edinburgh University Press.

Group of Eight. (2007). *Languages in crisis: A rescue plan for Australia.* Turner, ACT: Author. Retrieved from https://www.go8.edu.au/sites/default/files/agreements/go8-languages-in-crisis-discussion-paper.pdf

Hogan-Brun, G. (2010). Contextualising language planning from below. *Current Issues in Language Planning, 11*(2), 91–94.

HSC Japanese Committee (HSCJC). (2008). Minutes of meeting between HSC Japanese Committee and the NSW Board of Studies, May 22. Retrieved from http://www.hscjapanese.org.au/

HSC Japanese Committee (HSCJC). (2009). "Opening Address" at the National Forum on 25th of February 2009 by Dr. John Bennett, the Board of Studies NSW. Retrieved from http://www.hscjapanese.org.au/

HSC Japanese Committee (HSCJC). (2010). Response to Mr. Hewitt's letter from 4/2010. Retrieved from http://www.hscjapanese.org.au/

HSC Japanese Committee (HSCJC). (2011). Letter to the Board of Studies NSW, August 20. Retrieved from http://www.hscjapanese.org.au/

HSC Japanese Committee (HSCJC). (2014). Japanese CLS student numbers. Retrieved from http://www.hscjapanese.org.au/

Jackson, F. H., & Kaplan, M. A. (1999). Lessons learned from fifty years of theory and practice in government language teaching. In J. E. Alatis & A. Tan (Eds.), *Georgetown university round table on languages and linguistics 1999* (pp. 71–86). Washington, DC: Georgetown University Press. Retrieved from http://digital.georgetown.edu/gurt/1999/gurt_1999_07.pdf

Japanese Studies Association of Australia. (2007). Letter to the Board of Studies NSW, December 21. Sydney, Australia: Author.

Jorgensen, M., & Phillips, L. (2002). *Discourse analysis as theory and method.* London, UK: SAGE Publications Ltd.

Kagan, O. (2005). In support of a proficiency-based definition of heritage language learners: The case of Russian. *International Journal of Bilingual Education and Bilingualism, 8*(2–3), 213–221.

Lo Bianco, J. (1990). Making language policy: Australia's experience. In R. B. Baldauf & A. Luke (Eds.), *Language planning and education in Australasia and the South Pacific* (pp. 47–79). Clevedon, UK: Multilingual Matters.

Lo Bianco, J. (2001). Policy literacy. *Language and Education, 15*(2–3), 212–227.

Lo Bianco, J. (2008a). Policy activity for heritage languages: Connections with representation and citizenship. In D. M. Brinton, O. Kagan, & S. Bauckus (Eds.), *Heritage language education* (pp. 53–70). New York, NY: Routledge.

Lo Bianco, J. (2008b). Tense times and language planning. *Current Issues in Language Planning, 9*(2), 155–178.

Making Multicultural Australia. (2002). Commonwealth Parliamentary Debate—Hanson's maiden speech. Retrieved from http://www.multiculturalaustralia.edu.au/library/media/Document/id/57

Mercurio, A., & Scarino, A. (2005). Heritage languages at upper secondary level in South Australia: A struggle for legitimacy. *The International Journal of Bilingual Education and Bilingualism, 8*(2–3), 149–159.

Miles, M. B., & Louis, K. S. (1987). Research on institutionalization: A reflective review. In M. B. Miles, M. R. Ekholm, & R. Vandenberghe (Eds.), *Lasting school improvement: Exploring the process of institutionalization* (pp. 25–44). Leuven, Belgium: Acco.

Ministry of Foreign Affairs of Japan (MOFA). (2013). 海外在留邦人数調査統計 [Annual Report of Statistics on Japanese Nationals Overseas]. Retrieved from http://www.mofa.go.jp/mofaj/files/000049149.pdf

Moore, H. (1996). Language policies as virtual reality: Two Australian examples. *TESOL Quarterly, 30*(3), 473–497.

National Asian Languages and Studies in Australian Schools (NALSAS) Taskforce. (1995). *NALSAS strategy implementation plan.* Brisbane: NALSAS Secretariat.

National Asian Languages and Studies in Australian Schools (NALSAS) Taskforce. (1998). *Partnership for change: The NALSAS strategy.* Brisbane: NALSAS Secretariat. Retrieved from http://www1.curriculum.edu.au/nalsas/reports/reports01.htm

Oguro, S., & Moloney, R. (2010). An alien from their own language: The case of Japanese in New South Wales. *Babel*, *44*(2), 22–31.

Oriyama, K. (2010). Heritage language maintenance and Japanese identity formation: What role can schooling and ethnic community contact play? *Heritage Language Journal*, 7(2), 76–111.

Saturday School of Community Languages (SSCL). (2015). About us: Saturday School of Community Languages. Retrieved from http://www.sscl.schools.nsw.edu.au/how-to-enrol/about-us1

Valdés, G. (2001). Heritage language students: Profiles and possibilities. In J. Peyton, J. Ranard, & S. McGinnis (Eds.), *Heritage languages in America: Preserving a national resource* (pp. 37–77). McHenry, IL: The Centre for Applied Linguistics and Delta Systems.

Victorian Curriculum and Assessment Authority (VCAA). (2011). Japanese second language. Retrieved from http://www.vcaa.vic.edu.au/Pages/vce/studies/lote/japanese2nd/jap2ndindex.aspx#H2N10090

20

Russian as a Heritage Language in Lithuania

Meilutė Ramonienė, Ala Lichačiova, and Jelena Brazauskienė

1 Introduction

The status, role, and place of the Russian language started changing radically in Lithuania toward the end of the twentieth century. The change began under Soviet rule, when an amendment including Lithuanian alongside Russian as the co-official language of the Soviet Republic of Lithuania was added to the Soviet Constitution in 1988. Since the restoration of the independent Republic of Lithuania in 1990, Lithuanian has been the only official state language in a de jure and de facto capacity. With these changes, the status of Russian has altered significantly, and rather than the dominant language of a political entity of which Lithuania was a part, it is currently a heritage language (HL) for people of Russian ethnicity and other ethnic groups of Russian speakers,[1] and a foreign language for other residents of Lithuania. The result has been a functional redistribution of the languages in Lithuania as well as changes in their higher or lower ranking in the country's linguistic environment. Russian functioned as a lingua franca among different ethnic groups for more than a century (in Czarist Russia and during Soviet times), but Lithuanian has now taken over this role. Russian was also important in many other areas in Lithuanian society (Pavlenko, 2008) but, like in most post-Soviet countries, since 1990 the place and status of the Russian language has drastically altered. This has had a considerable impact on the language policy in Lithuania as English, the most preferred international language, has gradually become the first foreign language selected by students at schools while Russian, which used to be compulsory at secondary schools and even universities in the Soviet era, is now included in the list of optional school curriculum subjects. By contrast, a native-like command of Lithuanian has become one of the main requirements for receiving or holding a good position at work.

Changes in the sociolinguistic situation in Lithuania with respect to the place of the Russian language have already attracted researchers' attention. Several studies focus on the general linguistic situation, language use, and social adaptation (e.g., Hogan-Brun, Ozolins, Ramonienė, & Rannut, 2009; Hogan-Brun & Ramonienė, 2005; Kasatkina & Leončikas, 2003), education (Bulajeva & Hogan-Brun, 2008; Leončikas, 2007), language usage at work (Ramonienė, 2011), language use and identity (Brazauskienė & Lichačiova, 2011; Ehala & Zabrodskaja, 2011; Lichačiova, 2015; Ramonienė, 2010) language use at home (Ramonienė & Extra, 2011a, 2011b), and family language policy and management (Ramonienė, 2013a).

Despite the decline in the status of Russian, an important dynamic remains, one that is created by the number of Russians and Russian speakers in Lithuania. The aim of this paper is to discuss and evaluate the level of institutionalization of the teaching and learning of Russian as an HL in this population, and the needs and priorities for the future. Institutionalization will be examined not only in terms of the availability of schools and programs offering Russian language and their stability going forward, but also in terms of beliefs and ideologies of Russian speakers towards the maintenance of Russian as an HL (Ekholm & Trier, 1987). In addition, the concept of institutionalization will not be confined to educational settings, but will be interpreted more broadly to encompass other types of organizations as well as the non-organizational HL maintenance practices of Russian-speaking inhabitants of different age groups. In sum, this approach includes:

1. Organizational: formal institutions of education at all levels, from kindergartens to universities, less formal educational organizations such as community-run Sunday schools, drama or music studios with Russian as the language of instruction, as well as official cultural organizations such as the Russian Drama Theatre, and also the media;
2. Non-organizational: family and any microsocium, e.g., a company of friends, colleagues at work, or leisure-time events created by participants themselves in a variety of formats, e.g., game evenings or public discussions (for more ideas, see Neshchimenko, 2000).

As a result, organizational sustainment of language and culture can be implemented both formally and informally, and this chapter will examine both areas. In order to do so, data from a variety of sources will be used: two sociolinguistic scientific projects, the 2011 Population and Housing Census (Statistics Lithuania, 2013a, 2013b; hereafter "the 2011 Census"), the Ministry of Education and Science, as well as information from a wide range of non-governmental organizations and other institutions. The sociolinguistic projects were carried out in various Lithuanian towns and focused on linguistic behavior and linguistic attitudes. The project *Language Use and Ethnic Identity in Urban Areas of Lithuania* (Ramonienė, 2010, pp. 15–21)[2] (hereafter "the Language Use project") was conducted between 2007 and 2009 in the three largest Lithuanian cities: the capital Vilnius, the second largest city Kaunas, and the port of Klaipėda. Two different surveys were conducted: The first covered primary schools in Vilnius, Kaunas, and Klaipėda, with 23,341 pupils being surveyed: 11,136 pupils in 92 schools in Vilnius, 8,479 in 60 schools in Kaunas, and 3,726 in 33 schools in Klaipėda. Methodology from the *Multilingual Cities* project (Extra & Yağmur, 2004, 2005; Ramonienė & Extra, 2011a, 2011b) was adapted to collect evidence on languages used in the private (home) domain. The second survey covered a representative sample of 1,742 participants aged 15 and older from the same three cities. The second project, *Sociolinguistic Map of Lithuania: Towns and Cities* (Ramonienė, 2013b, pp. 10–16)[3] (hereafter "the Sociolinguistic Map project"), was carried out between 2010 and 2012 in the urban areas of Lithuania inhabited by at least 3,000 people with urban occupations. Both projects aimed at a large-scale study of the sociolinguistic situation in urban Lithuania and involve both quantitative surveys and qualitative in-depth interviews, the data from which are cited in this chapter. The in-depths interviews were conducted in Russian or Lithuanian; excerpts are translated into English in the chapter.

2 Russians, Russian Speakers, and Russian as a Heritage Language in Lithuania

The proportion of residents of Russian ethnicity has undergone significant changes in Lithuania during the last several decades. According to data from the last Soviet Population Census, the

Table 20.1 The Percentage of the Largest Ethnic Groups (Lithuanians, Russians, and Poles) in Lithuania according to the Population Census

Ethnicity	Population census					
	1959	1970	1979	1989	2001	2011
Lithuanian	79.3	80.1	80.0	79.6	83.5	84.2
Polish	8.5	7.7	7.3	7.0	6.7	6.6
Russian	8.5	8.6	8.9	9.4	6.3	5.8

Source: The 2011 Population and Housing Census (%) (Statistics Lithuania, 2013a, p. 149).

percentage of Russians had increased from 8.5 % in 1959 to 9.4 % in 1989, but fell dramatically after the restoration of Lithuanian independence (see Table 20.1). The 2011 Census showed some changes in the country's ethnic composition because Russians, who used to account for an majority after Lithuanians, were outnumbered by the Polish minority and became the second largest ethnic group in Lithuania, constituting 5.8 % of the population.

As can be seen from Figure 20.1, the proportion of Russians and Russian–speaking residents varies across Lithuania. According to the data from the 2011 Census (Statistics Lithuania, 2013a, 2013b), the towns ranked by Russian population density are: Panevėžys (2.44 %), Kaunas (3.8 %),

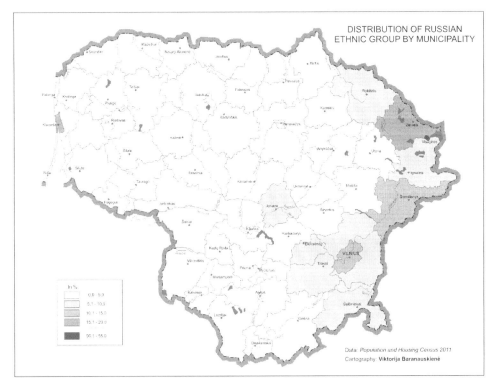

Figure 20.1　Map of Lithuania: Distribution of Russian Ethnic Group by Municipality

Source: The 2011 Population and Housing Census (%) (Statistics Lithuania, 2013a, pp. 160–163).

Table 20.2 Numbers of Russians and Russian Speakers according to the Data from the Language Use and Sociolinguistic Map Projects

Residents	Vilnius	Klaipėda	Visaginas
Ethnic Russians	14 %	21.3 %	52 %
Russian speakers (Russian as their mother tongue)	27 %	29 %	77 %

Source: Quantitative surveys of the sociolinguistic projects *Language Use and Ethnic Identity in Urban Areas of Lithuania* and *Sociolinguistic Map of Lithuania: Towns and Cities* (Ramonienė, 2010, 2013b).

Šiauliai (4.13 %), Vilnius (12 %), and Klaipėda (19.6 %); but the biggest numbers reside in Visaginas (52.4 %).

According to data from the 2011 Census, the vast majority of Lithuanian residents of Russian ethnicity, 87.2 %, consider Russian to be their native language. Other ethnic groups also claim Russian as their native language, for example, 56.3 % of Belarusians, 56.5 % of Jews, and 48.8 % of Ukrainians, as well as others (Statistics Lithuania, 2013a, 2013b). As can be seen from Table 20.2, in the most ethnically heterogeneous towns of Lithuania, the numbers of ethnic Russians and Russian speakers do not coincide since there are more Russian speakers than ethnic Russians.

Thus, it is possible to discuss the status/place of Russian as HL among Russians as well as people of other ethnicities who consider themselves native speakers of the Russian language.

In a heterogeneous linguistic and cultural environment, linguistic practices are complex. Take, for example, the linguistic environment in the private domain of one participant in the surveys, a student of Vilnius University, who was brought up in a family of Russians in Visaginas:

Researcher: *What language did you speak at home?* Interviewee: *Russian.* Researcher: *Is it still the language you use at home?* Interviewee: *Yes.* Researcher: *When you have guests, what language do you usually speak?* Interviewee: *Russian, well . . . it depends on the guests, whether they come to see my family or me. . . . If in Visaginas, my parents almost don't speak Lithuanian at all, they understand everything, but speak very bad Lithuanian, while my grandmother can't even understand, so only in Russian. But if I have guests, then we usually speak Lithuanian. Here in Vilnius the people I communicate with are Lithuanians.* (a 21-year-old female university student from Visaginas, who graduated from a Lithuanian school)

3 Russian HL Education

The Russian Language at Preschool and School Institutions

The Law of the Republic of Lithuania on Education (Republic of Lithuania: Law Amending the Law on Education, 2011) advocates the accessibility of education for national minorities in their mother tongue in preschools/kindergartens and schools of general education: primary schools (1st–4th forms), pro-gymnasiums (1st–8th forms), schools of basic education (1st–10th forms), secondary schools (1st–12th forms), and gymnasiums (9th–12th forms). In accordance with this law,

A state municipal preschool education and general education school shall provide opportunities for learners belonging to national minorities to have supplementary study of the native language, provided that there is a real need, [and] a specialist of that language is available.

(p. 22)

285

In other words, if ethnic Russian children study at schools teaching in Lithuanian, according to the law, they should be provided with opportunities to have supplementary study of their mother tongue. However, in reality such classes are not formed due to additional expenses that would be imposed on a school. As a result, such learners can study Russian as a second foreign language together with other pupils for whom Russian is not their mother tongue from the 5th or 6th to the 12th form (or shorter) for two hours per week in schools where this option is available. Recently, Russian as a second foreign language has been chosen by approximately 70–80% of pupils in schools where the language of instruction is Lithuanian (Užsienio Kalbų Mokymas, n.d.). While these options are available, the teaching methodology used is not geared towards HL speakers, a point that was revealed in the in-depth interviews:

Researcher: *But was the Russian language taught at school? Or did that fall outside the realm of the normal school curriculum?* Interviewee: *It was the second foreign language; well, you know, "Dima prishol v shkolu" ["Dima has come to school"], that was the level of the language taught for Lithuanians.* (a 21-year-old female university student from Visaginas, who graduated from a Lithuanian school)

There are, however, state-run schools in which Russian is the language of instruction, and high levels of proficiency are expected. At the time of writing, 33 Russian schools of general education, teaching primarily in the Russian language, operate in Vilnius, Klaipėda, Visaginas, and some other towns, and 28 schools that teach in Russian and at least one other language (AIKOS, n.d.) are also currently operating across Lithuania.[4] The latter category of schools teach in the following languages: Lithuanian and Russian (13 schools), Russian and Polish (9 schools), Lithuanian, Russian, and Polish (6 schools). Both types of institutions include schools of primary, basic, and secondary education as well as gymnasiums. In all of these schools, 14,354 learners are enrolled and have the opportunity to study curriculum subjects in Russian (Švietimo ir mokslo ministerija, 2013, p. 2). Education in Russian is also carried out in preschool institutions: four preschools in Vilnius and two kindergartens each in Klaipėda and Visaginas.

Not all learners in the Russian schools are of Russian ethnicity because children of different ethnic backgrounds enroll in these schools (e.g., Poles, Belarusians, Ukrainians, Jews, Armenians, Georgians, Tatars, and Romani people). Some Lithuanian students also study in the Russian schools, generally those who returned to Lithuania from Russia (approximately 1% of the 14,354 figure) or children from mixed Lithuanian/Russian families, (approximately 6%). The Language Use project gathered data from 1,707 learners in the Russian schools in Vilnius, of which approximately 35% indicated that they were not of Russian ethnicity.

In 1990–1991, there were more than 80 Russian schools in Lithuania, providing education for 76,000 pupils (Švietimo ir mokslo ministerija, 2013, p. 2). Thus, it can be seen that after the restoration of the Republic of Lithuania, the numbers of Russian schools started falling dramatically. However, since 2012 this tendency has more or less stabilized: about 40 Russian schools were operating in 2012 and 33 at the time of writing in 2016. There is an objective reason for the falling numbers of Russian schools, namely, a decrease in the numbers of school-age children who speak Russian at home. One cause of this trend is a falling birthrate in Lithuania, across all ethnicities. However, parents' decisions regarding education is another important factor contributing to falling numbers of Russian schools. After the restoration of Lithuanian independence, a large number of Russians, feeling concerned about the future of their children, wanted them to attend schools teaching in the state language, although recently this trend has decreased. Russians and Russian speakers still express their wish to learn and teach their children in their mother tongue, but families always express doubts about which school to choose for their children. Data from the Language Use project indicates that there is still a wish to teach children in their mother tongue in areas with significant ethnic minority populations such as Vilnius and Klaipėda (44 %) (Brazauskienė, 2010, p. 112).

Higher Education and the Russian Language

As mentioned above, higher education is conducted in Lithuanian, although study programs in Russian are implemented at the European Humanities University in Vilnius and Russian can be studied as a foreign language in all colleges and universities. In addition, institutions of higher education offer bachelor's programs in Russian Philology, Russian Language, and Russian Literature. For instance: English and Russian Languages at Vilnius University Kaunas Faculty of Humanities and Vilnius University Institute of Foreign Languages; Russian Philology and Intercultural Communication at The Lithuanian University of Educational Sciences; and English and Second Language (Russian) Teaching at Mykolas Romeris University. A master's program, Russistics, is offered by the Russian Philology Department at the Faculty of Philology at Vilnius University.

The Russian study programs are currently not very popular, with approximately 20 students enrolling to study Russian Philology and Russian Language annually at Vilnius University, resulting in little entrance competition. The students are typically graduates of Lithuanian and Polish schools, where Russian is taught as a foreign language. Graduates with Russian as their HL tend to choose those study programs that provide them with the opportunity to study two languages—English and Russian. Students of Russian ethnicity, after graduating from schools teaching in Russian, tend not want to pursue studies related only to the Russian language. They prefer to become bilingual specialists/linguists. Therefore, as few as one-two graduates from Russian schools opt for the Russian Philology program, whereas 10–12 such students choose the Russian-English Languages study program each year.

Russians graduating from schools where the curriculum subjects are taught in the state language quite often opt for Russian as a foreign language at colleges and universities or attend Russian language courses and study independently. The main reason for this trend is their wish to master written Russian, because they usually cannot write or even read in that language. Reading and writing skills are, however, necessary in work settings, and speaking skills mastered in the family to communicate in the private domain are frequently insufficient for the professional domain.

4 Maintenance of HL from an Intergenerational Perspective

Ethnic minority psychologists use the term "cultural transmission" when referring to three types of intergenerational learning and teaching mechanisms that promote an ethnic minority group's cultural transmission to its inheritors (Berry, Poortinga, Segall, & Dasen, 2002):

1. Vertical transmission: when cultural values, traditions, beliefs, and social experience are passed on from parents to children;
2. Horizontal transmission: when children learn in a peer to peer context;
3. Oblique transmission: when a person attains cultural and similar knowledge in specialized social institutions (schools, universities) or through communicating with non-parental adults, e.g., relatives, neighbors.

In a multicultural environment, cultural transmission might also refer to the influence exerted by the representatives of another culture or cultures (Stefanenko, 2004), so even parents frequently become transmitters of both cultures. The same could be said of language. Since language may be considered a part of culture (Smolicz, Secombe, & Hudson, 2001), cultural transmission also describes ways of HL transmission. In a multilinguistic environment, all three transmission types co-exist simultaneously, and will be discussed in the context of the organizational and non-organizational categories described earlier.

According to the Russian speakers who participated in the Language Use and Sociolinguistic Map projects, of the three types of HL transmission mentioned above, oblique transmission, specifically institutions of education with Russian as the language of instruction, ensures the best acquisition of Russian, because family efforts are typically insufficient to maintain one's mother tongue among speakers of another language. Below are two excerpts from in-depths interviews from the sociolinguistic projects which illustrate this point:

(1) Interviewee: *You can learn your mother tongue in the family, but not so well as at school. I mean if you aren't introduced to Russian literature and traditions, and history, that will be just colloquial language. . . . Definitely much worse than the language of those people who graduated from Russian schools.* (a 21-year-old male university student from Vilnius, who graduated from a Russian school);

(2) Interviewee: *Personally, I hope my kids graduate from a Russian school. You can certainly learn your mother tongue by speaking it at home but this is not the same as learning it at school, where you are also taught Russian literature and traditions. The language spoken at home is colloquial, it is certainly worse than the language spoken by people educated in Russian schools.* (a 24-year-old woman from Vilnius, who graduated from a Russian school and works for a pharmaceutical company)

The role of the family in HL maintenance research is frequently considered the most significant, for example: "In the case of HL maintenance, intergenerational family language practices are of vital importance" (Juan-Garau, 2014, p. 427). However, the majority of the Russian speakers in the studies believed that this type of HL transmission, while important, might lead to the acquisition of rather limited linguistic competence. They considered this reduced repertoire an inevitable consequence of living in the kind of linguistic environment in which they find themselves. For example:

(3) Researcher: *How well can Russians speak Russian? Well, normally? Do they forget, make a lot of mistakes, speak with an accent, what do you think?* Interviewee: *Well, it is obvious that with mistakes and . . . Lithuanian words start appearing . . . local dialects—Polish-Lithuanian. People put the stress in words in the wrong place, write with mistakes.* (a 24-year-old woman from Vilnius, who graduated from a Russian school and works for a pharmaceutical company)

For some participants, speaking Russian with "mistakes" was not viewed as problematic, and a good command of Russian was not viewed as necessary in Lithuania at all. For example:

(4) Researcher: *Do you think it is necessary to graduate from a Russian school if you want to learn to speak the language well in Lithuania? Can you learn Russian somewhere else, not in a Russian school?* Interviewee: *No, you can't.* Researcher: *So, only at school?* Interviewee: *Certainly.* Researcher: [If parents choose a Lithuanian school for their child] *does this mean they don't want their child to speak Russian well?* Interviewee: *Well, he can speak the language quite well. But if he lives in Lithuania, why does he need to speak Russian very well or if he is planning to live here in the future? It is not necessary.* (a 65-year-old female retiree from Visaginas, who studied in Russia)

Accompanying the belief that a limited command of Russian is adequate is the attitude that children's Lithuanian should be proficient. Data from the two sociolinguistic surveys indicates that 70% of the Russian-speaking respondents who graduated from Russian schools choose Lithuanian schools for their children, believing that a good command of Lithuanian is the most important consideration for a promising future (Lichačiova, 2010, 2015; Ramonienė, 2013a; on this point see also Leončikas, 2007). For example:

(5) Interviewee: *I know families whose children study in Lithuanian schools. . . . They study in Lithuanian schools only because it will be easier to adapt later, at work, for example, or in further studies.* (a 45-year-old female manager from Visaginas, who studied in Russia)

A participant who had studied in a Lithuanian school confirmed this perspective. Her parents, who could not speak Lithuanian at all, chose to send her to a Lithuanian school, which at first she felt was an act of torture. However, later she came to understand the value of her studies in the school, and even plans to make the same decision for her future family:

(6) Interviewee: *I was very much against it, well, when I went to school, I didn't know a word in Lithuanian and they kept convincing me every morning: "You need to speak it, you need to speak it, later it will be easier for you." Well, I was really convinced: in any Lithuanian environment I feel like I'm one of them. I don't even have an accent when I speak Lithuanian . . . and I think that if the parents behave in some reasonable way, do not exaggerate . . . that is, if they still give some Russian literature to read, of course, if that's important to them, preserve some bond, then everything is alright. . . . Well, if I have children, if one speaks Russian to them at home there is a chance they will be as Russian as me.* (a 21-year-old female university student from Visaginas, who graduated from a Lithuanian school)

Parents who send their children to Lithuanian schools usually intend to maintain their children's mother tongue by employing a similar range of means—communicating with them in Russian as much as possible, reading books and watching movies in Russian. For example:

(7) Interviewee: *I think that even if my children grow in Lithuania and go to a Lithuanian kindergarten and a Lithuanian school, I will ensure as much as I can that I will teach them Russian, too. Even though that might be colloquial Russian. . . . Since I was little, my parents have tried to give a lot as far Russian is concerned . . . at first I was forced, later I got to like it—I read a lot of Russian literature.* (a 22-year-old female university student from Visaginas, who graduated from a Lithuanian school)

The informants consider the decision to choose a Lithuanian school for children from Russian-speaking families as an act of reconciling with assimilation or even an attempt to assimilate, which is particularly obvious in families with different national backgrounds:

(8) Researcher: *Wouldn't your children call themselves half-Russians? Or would they?* Interviewee: *No, they wouldn't. They don't call themselves like this. They say they are Lithuanians, but if they are asked, they say that "our mom is Russian" . . . . Since we have always communicated in Lithuanian, the Russian language has remained in the background. They just understand it. They can speak, but very badly, very badly. . . . We just thought that our children live in Lithuania, besides, the surname is Lithuanian.* (a 45-year-old female keyholder of Klaipėda University, who graduated from a Russian school)

There is no doubt that young people from families such as these can study Russian as a second foreign language in schools, colleges, or universities. However, in English-speaking countries, relying on this course of action has been unfavorable for HL maintenance: "it has become apparent that educating HL speakers primarily—if not exclusively—in English and later on, at the secondary or tertiary level, instructing them in the HL through a foreign-language approach has neither been appropriate nor successful" (Juan-Garau, 2014, p. 427). The same situation is evident with Russian as an HL in Lithuania—Russian linguistic background and foreign language study does not lead to advanced levels of Russian acquisition, while this is achieved in Russian schools.

In the two surveys, Russian speakers of Lithuania mentioned just two ways of HL maintenance: institutions of formal education providing instruction in Russian and/or communication in Russian in the private (home) domain. Sunday schools or Russian art ensembles (as types of non-formal educational organizations) were never mentioned in any interview. This is surprising given that in Lithuania almost every Russian secondary or Sunday school has its own theatre studio, folk ensemble, or choir, the repertoire of which mostly consists of works in the Russian language.

Some of these ensembles, which later became independent institutions, originated in schools. For example, the Vilnius Russian folk theatre *Zelionyj fonar* [The Green Lantern] has been performing for children and youth in the Russian language since 1992, as well as giving theatre performance training sessions. Initially founded in a school in Vilnius, this theatre became an independent Russian children and youth organization in 1995 and was registered in the Vilnius municipality (Radzivilova, 2010). The theatre's mission is as follows: "Cherishing and maintaining the continuity of Russian culture and traditions. Broadening the knowledge of Russian culture, literature, and language. Promoting children's and youth's spiritual, aesthetic, and creative goals by means of the best examples of Russian cultural heritage" (Public Organizations of Russian Compatriots in Lithuania, n.d.). The theatre Harlequin, an amateur company of actors, was founded in Vilnius in 2007, growing out of the Russian theatre studio in the Vasilij Kachalov[5] Gymnasium in 1998. The actors are former pupils currently studying in universities and working (Pažemeckienė, 2014), while the theatre director orchestrates the mounting of theatre productions and delivers theatre training classes (Jasinskaja, 2012). Other similar school theatre studios have been founded in Russian secondary schools and gymnasiums in Vilnius and Klaipėda.

The importance of such studios in the life of the Russian community is highlighted on the official website of the Visaginas Center of Culture:

> Most of our performers choose Lithuanian institutions of higher education after school, but while on holiday in Visaginas they willingly participate in the rehearsals of the ensemble, various festivals, and concerts. . . . This is a special form of communication among young people as they get immersed into traditional folk culture while singing, playing, and dancing to Russian folk songs. . . . The concerts do not allow the Visaginas Russian community to forget their roots.
>
> *(Visagino kultūros centras, 2015)*

It is noteworthy that all the groups of performers clearly see the importance of their activity not only in the development of their creative skills, but also in the maintenance of their sense of ethnic identity and love for the Russian language and culture, as is stated on the websites of the aforementioned organizations.

Other types of Russian organizations are also present in Lithuania, several of which are supported by the Lithuanian Charity and Support Foundation's Non-Governmental Organisations' Information and Support Centre (n.d.), which brings together ethnic community-based organizations. Among these is the Russian Culture Centre (Vilnius), the House of National Communities (Vilnius), and Russian Sunday schools (one in Vilnius and three in other towns; on Russian schools in Israel, see Schwartz, 2008, this volume). The Vilnius Russian Sunday school was established in 1999 as an institution of informal education to serve the needs of two groups of inhabitants. The first group comprises children from Russian schools which do not teach Russian ethnocultural subjects (history, art). The second group consists of children from Lithuanian, Polish, Jewish, and Belarusian schools who want to study the Russian language. These two groups still make up most of the student population, but their numbers are decreasing at the same time as more and more children from Lithuanian families are enrolling in these schools (Zverko, 2013).

How could the slipping popularity of Russian Sunday schools among Russians in Lithuania be accounted for? The Polish community, by comparison, maintains 12–15 Sunday schools. Among the possible reasons is that Russian speakers, as represented by the participants in the two studies, have not experienced the loss of their linguistic environment, so they do not feel totally disconnected from the Russian language and culture, nor do they consider the linguistic situation in the country to be fatally unfavorable to the Russian language. The second or third generations of Russian speakers, who cannot speak or understand Russian, have not grown up yet—it is these people's HL which is usually lost when another dominant language is present (Carreira & Kagan, 2011; Seville-Troike, 2000), a development that often prompts the formation of weekend community schools.

One more reason for the unpopularity of supplementary Russian language and cultural studies can be traced to beliefs in the Russian community about the usefulness of high-quality Lithuanian-Russian bilingualism and the relative importance of each language, as discussed earlier. Additionally, rather than focus on Sunday schools, participants in the surveys emphasized the role of strong personal motivation in learning their HL well. For example:

(9) Researcher: *Is it possible to graduate from a Lithuanian school and to have a good command of the Russian language?* Interviewee: *Yes.* Researcher: *And how to achieve this?* Interviewee: *You have to be personally interested. . . . I used to read a lot in my childhood, and learnt to write on my own, because at first I learnt to write in Lithuanian, but later I felt very ashamed that I, a Russian lady, cannot write in Russian. I asked my mother to buy some notebooks for me and I learnt myself following the examples given.* (a 21-year-old female university student from Visaginas, who graduated from a Lithuanian school)

In addition to the amateur theatre groups mentioned above, Russian language usage is also promoted by the Russian Drama Theatre in Vilnius. Founded in 1864, when Lithuanians lived under the rule of the Russian Empire, this theatre is the only professional theatre staging performances not in the state language. Finally, one more mode of transmitting language and culture at the organizational level can be mentioned—the country's mass media. There are several Russian TV channels that broadcast in Lithuania, five nationwide newspapers for Russian readers, several local Internet portals in Russian, a half hour info-analytical radio program in Russian on a daily basis on national radio, the program *Rusų gatvė* [A Russian Street] on national television at weekends that provides information about the life of the Russian community.

As far as the non-organizational level beyond the context of the family is concerned, Russian as an HL is also promoted by various events in which Russian is the language of communication, although not for the purpose of maintaining ethnicity, because the Russian community in Lithuania is not ethnically homogeneous. Public meetings and discussions with Russian writers, journalists, theatre directors, actors, and similar people are among such events, which are organized several times per year by the international mass media club *Formatas A-3*, founded in 2009 on the initiative of Moscow journalists who decided to build a professional network with colleagues from neighboring countries (International mass media club *Formatas A-3*, n.d.). These meetings are not usually translated into Lithuanian, although they are moderated by famous Lithuanian journalists.

Additional examples are weekly quiz games and other intellectual competitions conducted among several leagues in Vilnius and other cities. Since around 2005, when such intellectual leisure time activities acquired increasing popularity in Lithuania, every evening hundreds of Lithuanian residents have participated in team games, the so-called brain fights, which take place in cafes and restaurants. As of the year 2012, the Association of Intellectual Games, which organizes games and consults about organizational issues, has been uniting people engaged in this type of leisure-time activity. According to its representatives, the local brain fights are a variant of pub quizzes which have been held in Great Britain for about 50 years. However, the Russian TV game show "What? Where? When?" (Žemaitis, n.d.), which has been well known for Lithuanian TV viewers since 1975 and which has inspired real-life competitions of the same format in many countries, might also explain the residents' interest in brain fights.

Dozens of Russian-speaking teams, the members of which are from a wide range of age groups, constantly compete in different leagues of intellectual competitions in Lithuania. Not only do such games make a good pastime activity, but they also maintain linguistic and cultural competence. The famous German Internet portal *Bilingual-Online,* which serves the needs of Russian speakers, started collaborating with instructors of the Moscow edition of "What? Where? When?" the aim being

> to contribute to the good cause of learning Russian as one of the cornerstones in the overall building of Russian culture. . . .The majority of questions deal not only with the facts of geography, physics, chemistry, history, and other school curriculum subjects, but are also related with the diversity of Russian culture—theatre, painting, cinema, music, literature, folklore, crafts.
>
> *(Heifets & Nechajev, 2015)*

Thus, it appears that the best and most reliable sustainment of the heritage culture and language should be carried out at all levels, when a person acquires knowledge of ethnic language and culture by means of the three transmission modes discussed above, and in both organizational and non-organizational settings which, taken together, provide rich opportunities to make use of the HL not only in the family or at school, but also in various other situations in life.

5 Concluding Remarks

The changes in the place and status of the Russian language after the establishment of the Republic of Lithuania have influenced the decisions of Russian-speaking and other ethnic minority families concerning the development of their children's linguistic competence. There has been a large increase in the attendance of Lithuanian schools by non-Lithuanian children, including those who speak Russian at home. Having experienced linguistic discomfort after the restoration of the Republic of Lithuania, a great number of Russian-speaking families have reconciled themselves to the sacrifice of Russian for the sake of a better future for their children. Thus, the

Russian linguistic competence of the two generations—parents brought up in the Soviet era and their Post-Soviet children—has become radically different. Most of the parents could not have predicted that the Russian language level of their children attending Lithuanian schools would drop so significantly, while the topics they could discuss would cover just family life as Lithuanian became the second or even first language for children from Russian-speaking families in Lithuania.

Nevertheless, opportunities to maintain Russian in both organizational and non-organizational venues are present in Lithuania. In terms of schools using Russian as a medium of instruction for all or part of the curriculum, the number of students has fallen since 1990–1991 from approximately 76,000 to 14,435, but the fall in enrollments has stabilized over time. In this case, institutionalization is associated with parental beliefs toward language maintenance. As Ekholm and Trier (1987) point out, the "ideologies, values, beliefs" (p. 21) of participants, in conjunction with changing local situations, impact institutionalization. In the case of Russian-speaking parents, beliefs about the relative value of Russian versus Lithuanian have influenced decisions about sending their children to schools that use Russian as a medium of instruction. These beliefs have been influenced not only by the political change in Lithuania, but also by the ethnic make-up of the area: in areas with higher densities of Russian speakers, parents are more likely to opt to send their children to schools that use Russian as a medium of instruction.

However, according to the sociolinguistic surveys, Russian speakers' attitudes towards preserving Russian as HL have started changing recently. Children who were born into Russian-speaking families after the restoration of Lithuanian independence and who graduated from Lithuanian schools have begun to feel a different type of discomfort: their poor knowledge of the Russian language. As this generation comes of age, motivation to send their children to Russian Sunday schools will increase. A sense of security in the preservation of Russian that existed pre-independence is giving way to a realization that unless families and communities takes steps, the next generation of children will have few skills in Russian. Like the Polish community, which has been in this position for longer than the Russian-speaking community, a greater number of Russian Sunday schools is likely to become established.

As the dominant position Russian enjoyed erodes, the availability of Russian media takes on a greater role in providing opportunities to maintain the language. At the time of writing, the availability of Russian media is robust in Lithuania, and appears stable for the immediate future. The same observations hold with regard to non-organizational activities that support Russian language skills. Clubs such as *Formatas A-3* and a widespread network of weekly quiz games and other intellectual competitions provide lively venues for Russian maintenance. While these cannot be described as "institutionalized" in the strict sense as applied to an organization, their existence and recent growth attests to bottom-up, organic activity that enhances Russian language use.

Despite these opportunities, according to HL researchers,

> the various volumes providing support and guidance to parents and teachers on raising and educating children with more than one language . . . attest to the fact [that] this is a challenge which may not be met unless a language policy that is well suited to the children's family and community circumstances is adopted.
>
> *(Juan-Garau, 2014, p. 431)*

Thus, the situation pertaining to HL preservation in Lithuania might improve if it received more attention, especially as Lithuania could be regarded as a natural laboratory of multilingualism. First, in order to ensure the continuity of a multilingual society in Lithuania, attention should be paid to understanding Russian-speaking and other minority families' private language planning and family language policy or ideology (Juan-Garau, 2014; Piller, 2001; Schwartz, 2008; Spolsky, 2004) for HL preservation. Second, an area in which HL maintenance is lacking is at the level of higher education, i.e., programs devoted to the sustainment of minority languages outside institutions of primary and secondary education.

Generally speaking, it cannot be asserted that the laws which regulate language policy with respect to ethnic minorities in Lithuania are inappropriate. On the contrary, the laws theoretically promote HL teaching, but practically there is minimal support. This is a problem not only in the educational system but in society at large, where an attitude prevails that an all-out effort should be made to protect the Lithuanian language due to the increasing speed at which English is spreading around the world. Public opinion articulated via the media supports a tendency towards limiting "threelingualism" (Lithuanian-Russian-Polish) to the sphere of primary/secondary education and home/family domains, which also influences the language ideologies of the majority of Russian speakers.

A language policy implemented at the state level to promote positive linguistic attitudes, tolerance of language diversity, and the preservation and development of mother tongues of all ethnic groups in Lithuania would help change attitudes. In the ideal case, national linguistic and educational policies should be oriented not toward assimilation, where learning a second language implies the loss of the mother tongue, i.e., subtractive bilingualism, but to an integrationist perspective that fosters additive bilingualism (for more ideas, see Berry et al., 2002). The Russian minority in Lithuania would benefit greatly if various HL-related services, which are currently given no or very little attention at the state level, such as native language classes and training courses for children and adults, language schools and camps, consultancy services for minority people concerned with the maintenance of their HL, and so on, were significantly improved.

Of course, the appearance and effectiveness of similar services first of all depend on Russian speakers' awareness and determination to preserve the Russian language in Lithuania.

Notes

1 In our projects and in this article, the term "Russian speaker," which is ambiguously used in other sociologists' and sociolinguists' works (see Kasatkina, 2007; Kasatkina & Leončikas, 2003; Pozdniakova, n.d.), refers to the residents of Lithuania who consider Russian as their mother tongue, regardless of whether they think of themselves as ethnic Russians or as belonging to other nationalities.
2 This project was funded by a grant from the Lithuanian State Science and Studies Foundation. One of the authors of this article, Ramonienė, was the initiator and supervisor of the project; Brazauskienė and Lichačiova were co-researchers in the project.
3 This project was funded by a grant (No. LIT-2–18) from the Research Council of Lithuania, with Ramonienė as the initiator and supervisor of the project, and Brazauskienė and Lichačiova as co-researchers.
4 For the sake of comparison, there are 1,192 schools of general education and 335,160 pupils in Lithuania.
5 Vasilij Kachalov is a famous Russian actor, who was born in Vilnius in 1875.

References

AIKOS. (n.d.). Švietimo ir mokslo institucijos—Pagrindinis [Education and scientific institutions—Home] [Web site]. Retrieved from http://www.aikos.smm.lt/Registrai/Svietimo-ir-mokslo-institucijos/Site Pages/Pagrindinis.aspx?ss=01d0faa8-e894-4a13-b068-af25e9ed18c2

Berry, J. W., Poortinga, Y. H., Segall, M. H., & Dasen, P. R. (2002). *Cross-cultural psychology: Research and applications* (2nd ed.). Cambridge, UK: Cambridge University Press.

Brazauskienė, J. (2010). Lietuvos miestų rusų gyventojų portretas [Lithuanian cities: Portrait of the Russian population]. In M. Ramonienė (Ed.), *Miestai ir kalbos* [*Cities and languages*] (pp. 125–151). Vilnius, Lithuania: Vilnius University.

Brazauskienė, J., Lichačiova, A. (2011). Русские в современной Литве: языковые практики и самоидентификация [Russians in contemporary Lithuania: Linguistic practices and self-identification]. *Диаспоры* [*Diasporas*], *1*, 61–85.

Bulajeva, T., & Hogan-Brun, G. (2008). Language and education orientations in Lithuania: A cross-Baltic perspective post-EU accession. In A. Pavlenko (Ed.), *Multilingualism in post-Soviet countries* (pp. 122–148). Bristol, UK: Multilingual Matters.

Carreira, M., & Kagan, O. (2011). The results of the National Heritage Language Survey: Implications for teaching, curriculum design, and professional development. *Foreign Language Annals, 44*(1), 40–64.

Ehala, M., & Zabrodskaja, A. (2011). Этнолингвистическая витальность этнических групп стран Балтии [Ethnolinguistic vitality amongst ethnic groups in the Baltics]. *Диаспоры / Diasporas, 1*, 6–60.

Ekholm, M. R., & Trier, U. P. (1987). The concept of institutionalization: Some remarks. In M. B. Miles, M. Ekholm, & R. Vandenberghe (Eds.), *Lasting school improvement: Exploring the process of institutionalization* (pp. 13–21). Leuven, Belgium: Acco.

Extra, G., & Yağmur, K. (Eds.). (2004). *Urban multilingualism in Europe: Immigrant minority languages at home and school.* Clevedon, UK: Multilingual Matters.

Extra, G., & Yağmur, K. (2005). Mapping immigrant minority languages in multicultural cities. *International Journal of the Sociology of Language, 175*(176), 17–40.

Heifets, B., & Nechajev, J. (2015, March 16). *Приглашают в игру: игроки московского клуба «Что? Где? Когда?»* [You're invited to a game: Players in the Moscow club "What? Where? When?"] [Email]. Retrieved from https://groups.google.com/forum/#!topic/bilingual-online/50ko_MKVVlA

Hogan-Brun, G., Ozolins, U., Ramonienė, M., & Rannut, M. (2009). *Language politics and practices in the Baltic states.* Tallinn: Tallinn University Press.

Hogan-Brun, G., & Ramonienė, M. (2005). The language situation in Lithuania. *Journal of Baltic Studies, 36*(3), 345–370.

International mass media club *Formatas A-3.* (n.d.). Международный медиа-клуб "Формат А-3" [International media-club "Format A-3"] [Web site]. Retrieved from http://www.format-A3.ru

Jasinskaja, T. (2012, January 18). *Татьяна Тимко и её «Арлекин»* [Tat'iana Timko and her "Harlequin"] [Review]. Retrieved from http://www.obzor.lt/news/n4260.html

Juan-Garau, M. (2014). Heritage language use and maintenance in multilingual communities. *Applied Linguistics Review, 5*(2), 425–440.

Kasatkina, N., & Leončikas, T. (2003). *Lietuvos etninių grupių adaptacijos kontekstas ir eiga* [*Adaptation of ethnic groups in Lithuania: Context and process*]. Vilnius, Lithuania: Socialinių tyrimų institutas/Eugrimas.

Leončikas, T. (2007). *Etniškumo studijos 1: Asimiliacija šiuolaikinėje Lietuvos visuomenėje: švietimo sektoriaus pasirinkimas* [*Ethnicity Studies 1: Assimilation in contemporary Lithuanian society: Choosing the language of education*]. Vilnius, Lithuania: Socialinių tyrimų institutas/Eugrimas.

Lichačiova, A. (2010). Vilniaus ir Klaipėdos rusų ir rusakalbių tapatybės savivokos ypatumai [Self-identification of the Russian and Russian-speaking population of Vilnius and Klaipėda]. In M. Ramonienė (Ed.), *Miestai ir kalbos* [*Cities and languages*] (pp. 125–151). Vilnius, Lithuania: Vilnius University.

Lichačiova, A. (2015). Дилеммы языковой и культурной самоидентификации в русских семьях Литвы: межгенерационный аспект [Dilemmas of linguistic and cultural self-identification in Russian families in Lithuania: An intergenerational aspect]. In K. Duda & A. Dudek (Eds.), *Русское детство. Rosyjskie dzieciństwo* [*Russian Childhood*] (pp. 205–214). Krakow, Poland: Księgarnia Akademicka.

Neshchimenko, G. (2000). Г. К постановке проблемы «Язык как средство трансляции культуры» [Posing a problem: "Language as a means of transmitting culture"]. In M. Jeshitch (Ed.), *Язык как средство трансляции культуры* [*Language as a means of transmitting culture*] (pp. 30–45). Moscow, Russia: Nauka.

Non-Governmental Organisations' Information and Support Centre. (n.d.). NGO data base [Web site]. Retrieved from http://www.3sektorius.lt/en/third-sector/ngo-data-base

Pavlenko, A. (Ed.). (2008). *Multilingualism in post-Soviet countries.* Bristol, Buffalo, Toronto: Multilingual Matters.

Pažemeckienė, A. (2014, July 21). Teatro mėgėjams—festivalis "Tautos sparnai". [For theater lovers—the festival "Wings of the nation" [Review]. *Penktadienio žemaitis*]. Retrieved from http://www.pzemaitis.lt/teatro-megejams-festivalis-tautos-sparnai/

Piller, I. (2001). Private language planning: The best of both worlds? *Estudios de Sociolinguistica, 2*(1), 61–80.

Pozdniakova, T. (n.d.). Русскоязычие и проблемы русскоязычной идентификации билингвов [Russian speaking and problems of identification of bilinguals as Russian speakers]. Retrieved from http://www.bilingual-online.net/index.php?option=com_content&view=article&id=831%3Aprobleme-der-selbsidentifizierung-der-bilingualen&catid=50%3Akabinet-psihologa&Itemid=47&lang=ru

Public Organizations of Russian Compatriots in Lithuania. (n.d.). Детский и молодежный центр «Зеленый фонарь» [Children and youth center "Green light"] [Web site]. Retrieved from http://www.rusorg.lt/teatrzf/

Radzivilova, Z. (2010, October 6). История театра "Зеленый Фонарь" 3 [History of the "Green light" theater] [Web site]. Retrieved from http://vk.com/topic-6417944_23205669

Ramonienė, M. (Ed.). (2010). Miestai ir kalbos [Cities and languages]. Vilnius, Lithuania: Vilniaus universiteto leidykla.

Ramonienė, M. (2011). Adaptation to Lithuanian as the second language among minor ethnolinguistic groups: In M. Lauristin (Ed.), Language space and human capital in the Baltic States. In Baltic way(s) of human development: Twenty years on (pp. 126–129). Estonian Human Development Report 201/2011. Tallinn, Estonia: Eesti Koostöö Kogu.

Ramonienė, M. (2013a). Family language policy and management in a changed socio-political situation: Russians and Russian speakers in Lithuania. In M. Schwartz and A. Verschik (Eds.), Successful family language policy: Parents, children and educators in interaction (pp. 127–143). Multilingual Education 7. doi: 10.1007/978–94–007–7753–8_6, New York, NY: Springer Science+Business Media Dordrecht 2014.

Ramonienė, M. (Ed.). (2013b). Miestai ir kalbos II. Sociolingvistinis Lietuvos žemėlapis [Cities and languages II: Sociolinguistic map of Lithuania]. Vilnius, Lithuania: Vilniaus universiteto leidykla.

Ramonienė, M., & Extra, G. (2011a). Multilingualism in Lithuanian cities: Aims and outcomes of a home language survey in Vilnius, Kaunas and Klaipėda. Kalbotyra, 3, 59–77.

Ramonienė, M., & Extra, G. (2011b). Multilingualism in Lithuanian cities: Languages at home and school in Vilnius, Kaunas and Klaipėda. Klaipėda, Lithuania: Klaipėdos universiteto leidykla.

Republic of Lithuania: Law Amending the Law on Education. (2011, March 17). Vilnius, Chapter 3, Article 30, No. XI-1281. Retrieved from http://planipolis.iiep.unesco.org/upload/Lithuania/Lithuania_Law_amending_Law-on-education_2011.pdf

Schwartz, M. 2008. Exploring the relationship between family language policy and heritage language knowledge among second generation Russian-Jewish immigrants in Israel. Journal of Multilingual and Multicultural Development, 29(5), 400–418.

Seville-Troike, M. (2000). Causes and consequences of language maintenance/shift. In E. Olshtein & G. Hornczyk (Eds.), Language, identity, and immigration (pp. 159–171). Jerusalem, Israel: The Magnes Press, Hebrew University.

Smolicz, J. J., Secombe, M. J., & Hudson, D. M. (2001, April). Family collectivism and minority languages as core values of culture among ethnic groups in Australia. Journal of Multilingual and Multicultural Development, 22(2), 152–172.

Spolsky, B. (2004). Language policy. Cambridge, UK: Cambridge University Press.

Statistics Lithuania. (2013a). Gyventojai pagal tautybę, gimtąją kalbą ir tikybą. Lietuvos respublikos 2011 metų gyventojų ir būstų surašymo rezultatai [Ethnic composition of the population, mother tongue, and religion: Results of the 2011 Population and Housing Census, Republic of Lithuania]. Retrieved from http://statistics.bookdesign.lt/dalis_04.pdf

Statistics Lithuania. (2013b). Gyventojai pagal išsilavinimą ir kalbų mokėjimą. Lietuvos respublikos 2011 metų gyventojų ir būstų surašymo rezultatai [Population by education and language skills: Results of the 2011 Population and Housing Census, Republic of Lithuania]. Retrieved from http://statistics.bookdesign.lt/esu_05.htm?lang=lt

Stefanenko, T. (2004). Этнопсихология [Ethnic psychology]. Moscow, Russia: Aspect Press.

Švietimo ir mokslo ministerija [Ministry of Education and Science]. (2013, December). Tautinių mažumų švietimas [Ethnic minorities in education]. Švietimo problemos analizė [Educational Analysis of the Problem], 19(105). Retrieved from http://www.sac.smm.lt/wp-content/uploads/2016/01/bs_Tautiniu-mazumu-svietimas-Lietuvoje-2013–12.pdf

Užsienio Kalbų Mokymas. (n.d.). Institucijos savivaldybė: Visos, 2014–15 [Foreign language instruction for all institutional municipalities, 2014–15]. Švietimo valdymo informacinė Sistema [Education management information system]. Retrieved from http://rsvis.emokykla.lt/cognos8/cgi-bin/cognosisapi.dll?b_action=cognosViewer&ui.action=run&ui.object=%2fcontent%2ffolder%5b%40name%3d%27Bendrasis%20ugdymas%27%5d%2ffolder%5b%40name%3d%271-mokykla%27%5d%2freport%5b%40name%3d%274.%20U%C5%BEsienio%20kalb%C5%B3%20mokymas%27%

5d&ui.name=4.%20U%C5%BEsienio%20kalb%C5%B3%20mokymas&run.outputFormat=&run.prompt=true&cv.toolbar=true&cv.header=false

Visagino kultūros centras. (2015, January 23). Rusų folkloriniai ansambliai "Bylina" ir "Žavoronok". [The Russian folklore ensembles "Folk tales" and "Lark"] [Web site]. Retrieved from http://visaginokultura.lt/apie-vkc/etnokulturos-skyrius/folkloro-kolektyvai/rusu-folkloriniai-ansambliai-bylina-zavoronok/[c1]

Žemaitis, A. (n.d.). Protų žaidimų istorija [The history of mind games]. [Web site]. Retrieved from http://www.protu.lt/protu-zaidimu-istorija

Zverko, N. (2013, June 27). Русские воскресные школы в провинции привлекают литовцев [Russian Sunday schools in the provinces attract Lithuanians]. Retrieved from http://ru.delfi.lt/news/live/russkie-voskresnye-shkoly-v-provincii-privlekayut-litovcev.d?id=61722679

21

Pasifika Heritage Language Education in New Zealand[1]

Corinne A. Seals

1 Introduction

The status and presence of heritage language (HL) education in New Zealand varies widely across the country, depending largely on the degree to which each language community is recognized and/or supported by the national government, particularly by the Ministry of Education. For example, the New Zealand government has supported Māori language education on a wide, though varied, scale nationally. However, in addition to the Māori language for which New Zealand is known, there are over 150 languages other than English spoken regularly by more than 20% of residents (Statistics New Zealand, 2013). This chapter focuses on the largest HL-speaking community in New Zealand—Pasifika.

Pasifika is the term that will be used in this chapter for Pacific peoples because it comes from and is embraced by the people who it describes. Ferguson, Gorinski, Wendt Samu, and Mara (2008) define *Pasifika* as follows:

> The terminology includes those peoples who have been born in New Zealand or overseas. It is a collective term used to refer to men, women, and children who identify themselves with the islands and/or cultures of Samoa, Cook Island, Tonga, Niue, Tokelau, Fiji, Soloman Islands, Tuvalu, and other Pasifika or mixed heritages.
>
> *(p. 5)*

As part of Pasifika cultures, an emphasis is placed on maintaining the HLs and cultures associated with each community. This chapter will focus specifically on HL education (HLE) for the top six most spoken Pasifika languages in New Zealand: Samoan, Cook Islands Māori, Tongan, Niuean, Fijian, and Tokelauan (Advisors to the Education and Science Select Committee, 2012, p. 4). Pasifika HLE in New Zealand has gained much support over the past 30 years, as the Pasifika languages are widely recognized nationally and even have dedicated support from the Ministry of Pacific Island Affairs. Furthermore, this chapter will explore how Pasifika language education has historically focused on HLE, but this is beginning to change to include Pasifika foreign language education for second language speakers (non-HL speakers) in New Zealand as well.

This chapter begins with an introduction to the importance of HLE and the importance of officially recognizing HLs through approaches that support institutionalization. Then, HLs and HLE in New Zealand are discussed broadly, followed by a discussion of the discourse surrounding New Zealand's responsibility towards Pasifika HLs. The discussion following this focuses specifically on Pasifika HLE, including examples from two different Pasifika HLE programs. Finally, the nation's current goals and future directions for HLE are discussed.

Literature Review of Heritage Language Education

HLE has increasingly become of interest to researchers, educators, communities, and families over the past two decades. In particular, research into HLE has empowered HL speakers and their families, contradicted common beliefs that HLE has negative effects, and instead showed its *many* positive effects (e.g., Lao & Lee, 2009; Lo Bianco, 2008; Tucker, 2008; Valdés, 2005; Wiley & Lee, 2009). For example, Wang and García (2002) found that through HLE, HL speakers feel that their HL is a valuable part of their identity, which then can contribute to language maintenance and revitalization. Menard-Warwick (2009) further found that learning in general is enhanced when heritage and native language identities are recognized. The contribution of HLE to increased educational performance broadly has also been confirmed by a number of researchers, including Cenoz (2015) and Gorter (2015) in the Basque country, as well as by Seals (2013, 2014, 2015) and Seals and Kreeft Peyton (2016) for East-European American schoolchildren.

In addition, particular to the context of the current chapter, empirical studies in Pasifika language schools have shown that continued support for Pasifika languages is of great importance for HL maintenance. For example, in their longitudinal study of language development among 49 Samoan and Tongan–speaking children in Auckland, Tagoilelagi-LeotaGlynn, McNaughton, MacDonald, and Farry (2005) found a great difference between the children's bilingual abilities while attending a Pasifika immersion preschool compared to a year later when they had begun attending a mainstream English-speaking school. Over the course of enrollment in the Pasifika immersion preschool centers, the children steadily developed increasing verbal and literacy proficiency in both their HLs and English, without detriment to either language. However, after their first year in English mainstream schooling, the children began to quickly lose HL skills as they continued to develop English language skills. This study, and all those previously mentioned, highlight the importance of continuing access to HLE throughout all levels of schooling.

Framework for Chapter Discussion

In line with the theme of the present volume, it is important to consider the degree to which institutionalization of HLE practices and policies has occurred/is occurring in terms of Pasifika languages in New Zealand. Ekholm and Trier (1987, p. 17) provide a framework for determining institutionalization through a set of given indicators—namely, *negotiation, resources, rise in legitimacy, organizational conditions,* and *diminishing visibility.* These indicators will be drawn upon throughout the current chapter; however, an additional focus, namely the impact of "ideologies, values, beliefs" (Ekholm & Trier, 1987, p. 21) on institutionalization, will also be explored.

First, *negotiation* practices can allow government ministries to seek input and advice from relevant stakeholders, including educators and community members, when they create guidelines for educational programs. Official negotiations that follow this pattern have taken place with regard to most, but not all Pasifika HL programs (see section 4.3 below for a counterexample). As this official negotiation and recognition has taken place, the government has also established *resources* for programs in the form of sample lessons and some funding and meeting spaces. The Community Languages Association of New Zealand (CLANZ) has also initiated the ongoing development of workshops for HL teachers and community parents. This resource development adds further to Pasifika HLE's *rise in legitimacy*, which this chapter extends to mean a growth in its ideological acceptance as a necessary and valued subject of study. Because these programs have only fairly recently received this official recognition, however, there is still much variability in terms of *organizational conditions*, i.e., procedures that are stable enough to ensure the continuation of these programs independent of specific personnel. This situation has, in turn, prevented the *diminishing visibility* of these new systems, in the sense that their inclusion in educational programs is not taken for granted and routinized.

All of these indicators will continue to appear throughout the remainder of the chapter. While the indicators occur in different forms and to different degrees depending on the program being examined, several of them are applicable to all Pasifika HL programs in New Zealand.

2 Heritage Languages in New Zealand

As previously mentioned, New Zealand is a "super diverse" country with over 150 languages spoken among its 4.6 million residents (Statistics New Zealand, 2015). However, despite this rich diversity, there is no written policy for most HLs, which results in little educational support for most communities, and uneven distribution of what there is of it. Exceptions to this include the officially recognized languages Te Reo Māori (i.e., New Zealand Māori) and New Zealand Sign Language, as well as Pasifika languages, which receive government support though they are not officially recognized in legislation.[2]

Te Reo Māori was recognized as an official language of New Zealand in 1987, and the recent national document *Tau Mai Te Reo: The Māori Language in Education Strategy 2013–2017* (2013) advocates for further support for Te Reo Māori language education. Likewise, the *Pacific Languages Framework* (2012) outlines national goals for HL support of the Pasifika languages, and the Royal Society paper *Languages in Aotearoa New Zealand* (2013) speaks to the need for establishing a national languages strategy that supports HLE for all communities. With growing interest in HLE, supporting this education across communities has become a major focus for academics and many of the ministries in recent years. The author, who advises New Zealand governmental organizations on HL policy support, is also the Academic Advisor to CLANZ, a non-profit volunteer-led organization, which has now included advocacy for HLE in their mission at the author's urging.

Relatedly, one of the growing conversations in New Zealand has targeted the definition of *heritage languages*, as New Zealand has traditionally focused on *community languages*. As a result of discussions with New Zealand academics, educators, researchers, community representatives, and ministry officials around the country, the following definitions are used in this chapter:

1. *Community languages*: broadly refers to those languages "spoken by members of minority groups or communities within a majority language context" (The National Centre for Languages, 2011, p. 1). The focus is on the *community's* role in maintaining and revitalizing languages. In New Zealand, this includes every language other than English, New Zealand Sign Language, and Te Reo Māori.
2. *Heritage languages:* refers to languages spoken by "individuals with familial or ancestral ties to a language other than [the dominant societal language] who exert their agency in determining if they are [heritage language learners] of that language" (Hornberger & Wang, 2008, p. 6). The focus is often on the *individual* in self-identifying with a language through

heritage (recent or distant). In New Zealand, these languages include Te Reo Māori, New Zealand Sign Language, Pasifika languages, and all other community languages.

Both definitions, taken together, are now used by the Community Languages Association of New Zealand,[3] which is a volunteer-led organization supporting the teaching and learning of both community and HLs through the free dissemination of printed resources, delivery of teacher development workshops, and government advocacy on behalf of community and heritage languages. When discussing HLE throughout this chapter, the above definition of *heritage languages* will be used.

HL and community language advocates have very recently come together in a shared goal to promote minority language education. This goal was further fueled by the publication of a misinformed and widely damaging document by the Office of Ethnic Affairs in 2014,[4] which resulted in a massive outcry from minority language advocates from around the country. Most worrying from the document were statements such as:

> There is a negative correlation between the conditions that are favourable to English language acquisition and those that promote heritage language maintenance. Consequently, very few migrants or their descendants born in New Zealand will be able to read, write and speak proficiently in both English and their heritage language.
>
> *(Office of Ethnic Affairs, 2014, p. 1)*

Fearing that this document would result in a loss of legitimacy for HLs and incorrectly lead people to assume that HLE negatively affects English language acquisition, statements were produced from around the country denouncing the above-referenced paper. For example, Dr. Arianna Berardi-Wiltshire, an academic and advocate for HLE in New Zealand, was quoted widely as stating in a press interview:

> It's crucial for [non-English speaking] parents to feel vindicated in speaking their own language with their children. We're talking about the transfer of cultural knowledge, which can be crucial to the healthy development of children of immigrant background. Language carries deep cultural roots and the foundations of identity.
>
> *(Massey University, 2014)*

Moreover, there has been increasing recognition in New Zealand of the severely negative impacts that occur when HLs are not offered in mainstream education. In particular, New Zealand scholars have candidly discussed the problematic historical positioning of speakers of languages other than English as deficient, when these speakers should have been provided with resources to foster their multilingual and multicultural development (e.g., May, 2002a; McCaffery & McFall-McCaffery, 2010; Tuafuti & McCaffery, 2005). Such historical positionings have had a highly negative impact on minority language speakers, including Pasifika language speakers, with overall literacy levels significantly dropping for these populations due to historical subtractive language education (May, 2002a, p. 7).

As a result of such research-based awareness-raising efforts, New Zealand's stance towards multilingualism has significantly changed, with an increasing amount of negotiation between stakeholders and an increasing number of resources being devoted to minority language education. Pasifika language speakers, the largest population of HL speakers in New Zealand, are now among the most recognized language minority groups in education in the country, resulting in a significant rise in legitimacy.

3 New Zealand's Responsibility

Alongside discussions of language education in New Zealand, the very visible discourse of "New Zealand's responsibility" is routinely found, occurring in both unofficial and official documents and campaigns surrounding the issue of government support for the teaching, learning, and maintenance of Pasifika languages. This discussion highlights a critical awareness on the part of HL stakeholders of their government's role in providing the necessary symbolic and material support that HLE needs in order to be seen as legitimate and to succeed.

An often cited official document supporting stakeholders' position in the negotiation of New Zealand's responsibility towards Pasifika HLE is the New Zealand Bill of Rights Act 1990, Section 20, which states that,

> a person who belongs to an ethnic, religious, or linguistic minority in New Zealand shall not be denied the right, in community with other members of that minority, to enjoy the culture, to profess and practise the religion, or to use the language of that minority.
>
> *(Ministry of Justice, 1990, p. 6)*

Furthermore, drawing upon international law, New Zealand linguist May (2002b) makes the argument that minority language speakers with significant populations in the host country, such as Pasifika language speakers in New Zealand, "have a reasonable expectation to some form of state support" including language support (p. 30).

There is an additional ongoing issue, however. According to recent research by de Bres (2015), who interviewed representatives of language and cultural organizations in New Zealand, there are differing levels of support, and thus unstable organizational conditions, from within minority communities. Investing governmental resources into the preservation of Pasifika languages depends on each organization's own goals, challenges, and the power they can access in negotiations. For example, groups such as Multicultural New Zealand, the Community Languages Association of New Zealand, and the Office of Ethnic Affairs (all with symbolic but not monetary capital) have stated that Pasifika languages are a special part of New Zealand, and "regarded the government as having a role in supporting Pacific languages as a result of its ex-colonial/administrative relationships with Pacific countries" (de Bres, 2015, p. 9). However, representatives of other minority language advocate groups that hold more power in negotiations were not convinced that government resources such as money, space, and time should go to Pasifika HLE because they argued that "Pacific languages could continue to be used in the Pacific Islands" (de Bres, 2015, p. 10; see this work for an extended discussion of these groups).

4 Pasifika Language Education in New Zealand

The position adopted by groups that feel Pasifika languages are rooted in the Pacific Islands does not align with the fact that the vast majority of Tokelauan, Niuean, and Cook Island Māori speakers now live in New Zealand. According to Komiti Pasifika (2010), "91 per cent of Niueans, 83 per cent of Tokelauans, and 73 per cent of Cook Islanders now live in New Zealand. Their languages are at risk of becoming extinct" (pp. 3–4). In fact Auckland, New Zealand's largest city, has the highest concentration of Pasifika language speakers in the world. For this reason, efforts to support the use of these languages among HL speakers is essential, and Pasifika HLE is particularly relevant in the context of New Zealand.

The increase in educational resources and visibility for Pasifika languages, and their uptake within mainstream schools in particular, is reflected in statistics for 2014, as shown in Table 21.1.

Table 21.1 All Mainstream Schools in New Zealand Offering Pasifika Languages 2014

Hours of Pasifika language use per week[5]	Samoan	Tongan	Cook Islands Māori	Niuean	Tokelauan	Other	Total
20+ hours	11	0	2	0	0	0	12
12.5–20 hours	7	4	1	0	0	0	9
7.5–12.5 hours	4	2	0	0	0	0	4
3–7.5 hours	12	2	3	1	0	0	14
As a separate subject[6]	46	10	9	2	0	4	53
Total	80	18	15	3	0	4	92

Source: Adapted from "Table 21.1: Number of schools offering a Pasifika Language by Immersion Level and Language as at July 2015" [Data table] and "School data dimension notes: Level of learning," [Data table] by *Pasifika language in education: Statistics.* Copyright 2016 by Education Counts, New Zealand Government. (New Zealand Government: Education Counts, 2016a, 2016b).

Ninety-two mainstream schools (out of 2,400) utilized Pasifika languages in their curriculum in 2014. Of these, 53 present Pasifika languages in the context of "a separate subject," that is, as a foreign language, in which both HL speakers and FL speakers may enroll. The remaining 39 mainstream schools offered a second model in which the Pasifika languages are integrated in some (undefined) way into the regular school subjects. Of the 39 using this second model, 12 schools use a system closer to two-way immersion (though not defined as such) for Samoan or Cook Island Māori during the majority of the 25-hour school week.

However, this is not to say that Pasifika languages are becoming regularized in mainstream classrooms. Of the 92 schools offering Pasifika language instruction, Samoan is present in 80 of them, Tokelauan is present in none of them, and Fijian is not even reported on. Thus, there is still much work to be done, especially within mainstream education in terms of the allocation of resources and standardizing organizational conditions across languages. Furthermore, while the available statistical information is useful, there is much missing in terms of how the programs operate and exactly what they include, so that a detailed composite analysis is nearly impossible. This is an area in need of improvement by Statistics New Zealand and the Ministry of Education.

Primary School and Early Childhood Education

New Zealand has an increasingly active interest in supporting Pasifika HLE, which is manifested in the form of both mainstream and community school programs. For example, there are currently 462 early childhood education services (both government- and community-run) supporting the learning of Pasifika languages, with 93 of them (over 3,000 children) using Pasifika languages over 50% of the time (Education and Science Committee, 2013, p. 9). It is important to note that for all educational sectors, there is no clear evidence as to how much these programs were historically directed towards HL speakers or FL learners, as this distinction has not previously been seen as important in New Zealand.

Between early childhood education and primary school there is a reduction in available educational programs. Table 21.2 shows that in 2014, 74 primary schools were teaching the six most spoken Pasifika languages to 8,873 students.[7] For students in Year 1 to Year 6, the most common

Table 21.2 Primary School Students Enrolled in Pasifika Language Education in 2014 by Hours per Year

Language		Enrollment (Student Numbers)						Total	Number of schools
		Year 1 to Year 6			Year 7 and Year 8				
		Up to 15 hours	15–30 hours	More than 30 hours	Up to 15 hours	15–30 hours	More than 30 hours		
Pasifika Languages	Samoan	418	702	87	1,487	482	333	3,509	38
	Cook Island Māori	1	534	55	863	56	61	1,570	11
	Tongan	198	492	66	938	9	70	1,773	13
	Niuean	0	473	19	881	9	4	1,386	7
	Fijian	0	473	0	70	9	0	552	3
	Tokelauan	49	0	0	34	0	0	83	2
Total		666	2,674	227	4,273	565	468	8,873	74

Source: Adapted from "Primary Languages by Year and Hours 2000–2015" [Data table], in Primary School Languages (Year 1 to 8). *Pasifika language in education: Subject enrolment.* Copyright 2016 by Education Counts, New Zealand Government. (New Zealand Government: Education Counts, 2016c)

programs had between 15 and 30 hours of language education per year (2,674 of 3,567 enrollments; note that Education Counts makes the following information available in hours per *year*, while the previous information was in hours per *week*). However, primary school Tokelauan programs only exist at a level of 15 hours of language education or less per year, primarily as elective programs. This speaks, once again, to persistent disparities between languages with regard to the allocation of resources and organizational conditions. Furthermore, language education continues decreasing as students progress, with the majority of Year 7 and Year 8 students enrolled in 15 hours or less per year (4,273 of 5,306 enrollments).

Secondary School Education

While enrollments decrease as students age, secondary schools have nonetheless historically contributed greatly to the rise in legitimacy for Pasifika languages in New Zealand. This is first noted in the context of the first Pacific Islander conference, convened in 1974, at which time several secondary schools in New Zealand began planning the incorporation of Samoan language teaching into their curricula, given that Samoan was the most widely spoken Pasifika language in the country (Fetui & Mālaki-Williams, 1996, pp. 232–233). The first mainstream secondary school to officially plan, implement, and continue the use of Samoan in the curriculum was Sir Edmund Hillary Collegiate (formerly Hillary College), which did so in the early 1980s; by the mid-1980s, several secondary mainstream schools were running Samoan language programs (Fetui & Mālaki-Williams, 1996, pp. 234–235). Today, Auckland secondary schools (including Sir Edmund Hillary Collegiate) run an annual Pasifika and Māori languages and cultures festival, with stages devoted to Samoan, Tongan, Niuean, Cook Islands Māori, New Zealand Māori, and a "diversity" stage for over 60 additional cultural groups. Currently, over 60 schools (of a variety of types), 9,000 students, and 100,000 attendees take part (Tapaleao, 2014).

At the time of writing, Samoan, Tongan, Cook Islands Māori, Niuean, and Tokelauan are taught in mainstream secondary schools, with Samoan and Tongan having credit-bearing

Table 21.3 Secondary School Students Enrolled in Pasifika Language Education, 1998–2014

Year	Samoan	Tongan	Cook Islands Māori	Niuean	Tokelauan	Fijian	Total
1998	432	17	26	9	14	NA	498
2002	994	90	70	NA	198	NA	1,352
2006	2,168	65	192	22	46	NA	2,493
2010	2,047	376	375	59	29	NA	2,886
2014	2,422	577	267	62	36	NA	3,364

Source: Adapted from "Secondary Languages by School & Subject Name—1 July 1998–1 July 2015" [Data table]. From *Subject Enrolment: Secondary School Subjects (Year 9 and Above); Secondary Subjects Time Series Downloads.* Copyright 2016 by Education Counts, New Zealand Government. (New Zealand Government: Education Counts, 2016d)

programs in these schools. This has led noticeably to Samoan attracting over 2,000 HL and FL combined enrollments in 2013 (Harvey, 2014; Statistics New Zealand, 2013). In addition to raising the social profile and legitimacy of the Samoan and Tongan languages, such credit-bearing educational programs also provide more opportunities and resources for Samoan and Tongan students to learn their HLs. Though they are not the direct target of these programs, HL speakers make up a large percentage of the enrollments (see Table 21.3).

When looking at secondary school enrollments in Table 21.3, it appears that Pasifika language enrollments increased steadily for the most part from 1998 until 2014. However, no data exists for Fijian language education, which suggests these programs may no longer be active in secondary schools.

Pasifika Junior Language Programme

An example of a particularly notable new educational resource is a program under development by a mainstream secondary school for Pasifika HL speakers in New Zealand's South Island. The Pasifika Junior Language Programme (a pseudonym) is being piloted in 2015 for secondary school students of any Pasifika heritage. Classes are held together for all Pasifika students within the school for two hours every Wednesday after school, and include both culture and language (a full account of the program can be found in Bland, forthcoming). By holding heritage classes within mainstream schools for all Pasifika HL speakers (even those from very small minority communities), the languages and cultures are given visibility and normalized, thereby imbuing them with social and cultural capital (Seals, 2013, 2014), as well as increasing their rise in recognized legitimacy.

Additionally, drawing upon linguistic literature showing the important relationship between supporting all of a student's languages in order to for them to best succeed, the program was proposed with the specific goals of "develop[ing] and enhanc[ing] the bilingual abilities of Pasifika students to improve both languages and literacies . . . and academic achievement" (Bland, forthcoming). Finally, the program encourages empowerment of the communities by strengthening connections between parents and the mainstream school, thereby providing more direct lines of contact and contributing to the stability of the program. With its success thus far, the program is anticipated to be expanded in the coming years.

While secondary school enrollments in Pasifika languages have been increasing over the years, there is still a rapid decrease of enrollments over the course of students' entire educational trajectories. Educators need to be mindful of this decrease in future endeavors, if students are to maintain multilingual proficiency. New initiatives at the secondary level, such as the Junior Language Programme, are one way that ongoing HLE can be encouraged.

Governmental HLE Initiatives

In regards to the instructional content delivered in Pasifika language programs, whether weekend community-led or within mainstream or private schools, the Ministry of Pacific Island Affairs developed a strategy meant to empower all Pasifika communities with the skills and tools needed to maintain and teach HLs within all possible programs. The strategy drew upon Hornberger's (1998) research on language maintenance and revitalization and Spolsky's (2009) research on language management.[8] The Pacific Languages Framework (2012) was developed specifically in response to community concerns about the declining use and eventual loss of their HLs, which had been raised in governmental forums and during community-led events. The guiding principles of the framework are as follows:

1. ***Support for language should be led and owned by communities***: Leadership and ownership of the protection and promotion of Pacific languages lies with Pacific communities. The role of Government agencies is primarily to support Pacific communities to achieve their language aspirations.
2. ***The decline in language skills should be reversed***: The decline of Pacific languages must first be slowed, stopped and then reversed to achieve revitalization.
3. ***Language is vital to vibrant Pacific cultures***: Pacific languages are an integral part of Pacific culture, are vital for the expression of Pacific identity, and an important part of New Zealand's culturally diverse identity.
4. ***Heritage language skills will contribute to positive outcomes***: Vibrant Pacific languages are necessary to efforts to improve social and economic wellbeing, and to strengthen Pacific families and communities.

(Ministry of Pacific Island Affairs, 2012, p. 4)

Crucially, in addition to encouraging access to HLE, the Pacific Languages Framework (2012) highlights the importance of empowering Pasifika communities to lead language revitalization and development efforts. This is meant to reflect findings by Tuafuti and McCaffery (2005) from a 10-year longitudinal study with Pasifika HL speakers in Auckland, which argued that language education in itself is not enough—Pasifika speakers and communities must be empowered through active involvement as administrators and teachers in establishing and developing Pasifika language education, as well as "challeng[ing] and disrupt[ing] existing dominant power, hegemonic discourses and silences" (p. 488). However, the guidelines themselves do not provide access to educational programs—this is still left to the communities and individual schools to resource for themselves. Thus, the impact of the guidelines is minimal. At the current time, the impact is mostly in recognizing the value of Pasifika HLE in schools and opening forums for community members to discuss HLE with school administrators and educators.

While all of the Pasifika languages in New Zealand fall under the Pacific Languages Framework (2012), each language also has its own guidelines as set forth by the Ministry of Education. These guidelines, and the state of each language, are discussed in the following sections. This is followed by examples of a government-sponsored program and a mainstream school initiated program.

Samoan

Samoan is the most spoken Pasifika language in New Zealand, with 86,403 people stating they could hold a basic conversation in Samoan in 2013 (Statistics New Zealand, 2013). As we have seen, there are also more Samoan language programs than any other Pasifika language. Given the high demand from families, both of Samoan descent and of other backgrounds, for Samoan language exposure in schools and the number of students enrolling in these programs, the Ministry of Education established guidelines for the teaching of Samoan in New Zealand in all educational contexts.[9] The newest version of these guidelines was published in 2009 as *Ta'iala mo le Gagana Sāmoa (The Gagana Sāmoa Guidelines)* (Ministry of Education, 2009b). Modified versions of these guidelines have been issued for the teaching of all other Pasifika languages.

In terms of institutionalization, the establishment of these guidelines is seen by HL speakers, communities, and educators as a necessary and positive step in legitimizing HLs in New Zealand, which will then allow increased access to funding and a community advisory presence in governmental affairs dealing with HL issues. The guidelines show a rise in legitimacy and symbolic investment in Samoan by the government, encourage ongoing education in the language, provide recognition of variation in the language and contexts in which it is used, recognize that there are different types of learners, and encourage community involvement and learner empowerment. Additionally, the *Ta'iala mo le Gagana Sāmoa (The Gagana Sāmoa Guidelines)* document further investments in the practical teaching of Samoan by providing tangible resources for educators, including recommended sample activities for levels 1 through 8, approaches to assessment, learning objectives, and even targeted activities for oral language (i.e., speaking and listening), written language (i.e., reading and writing), visual language (e.g., performances and crafts), and cultural learning (e.g., customs and cultural lifestyle), all of which are important resources for HLE. While most of the teaching material is based on traditional foreign language approaches used in L2 classrooms, there is also recognition of the importance of culturally immersive approaches to teaching the Samoan language, and recommendations are made for carrying this out, which aligns with HL instruction. However, while the basic lesson samples are provided, any further development of them required financial investment by the individual educational institutions, which is a difficult undertaking for some schools.

Furthermore, there has been an increasing focus on Samoan HLE, in particular, given the release of recent statistics showing that despite an increasing number of Samoan language enrollments, the actual number of Samoan speakers is decreasing relative to Samoan population growth (Bedford & Didham, 2015). In particular, the difference in Samoan speakers is noticeable between overseas-born speakers and New Zealand-born speakers (i.e., HL speakers). There has been a decrease in the number of people born in Samoa who have moved to New Zealand, with the largest immigration point being about 50 years ago. Those born overseas generally tend to retain Samoan language abilities in contrast to those born in New Zealand. While there has been a great increase in New Zealand-born individuals of Samoan ethnicity, less than half of this heritage speaking group has Samoan language abilities (and the percentage is decreasing over time).

These figures are particularly worrying, as there has long been a hope that Samoan HL transfer between generations would be successful, given the positive attitudes many Samoan immigrants in New Zealand have displayed towards their native language and the supportive home language policies that many families have in place (Fairburn-Dunlop, 1984; Roberts, 1999). Therefore, language efforts will need to be geared towards HL speakers in particular for the language to be maintained in New Zealand in the future.

Cook Islands Māori

There are also a notable number of speakers of Cook Islands Māori in New Zealand, with 8,124 people stating that they could hold a basic conversation in the language in 2013 (Statistics New Zealand, 2013). There are 15 mainstream school programs teaching Cook Islands Māori, and 1,837 primary and secondary school students were enrolled in mainstream or private school language programs in 2014 (Education Counts, 2015a, 2015b). Similar to Samoan, the Ministry of Education developed guidelines for teaching Cook Islands Māori, including sample resources to be used in teaching, with the most recent document being published in 2012. The listed aims are the same as for Samoan, but there is the addition of two goals that connect "ideologies, values, beliefs" (Ekholm & Trier, 1987, p. 21) to the institutionalization of HLE, namely, affirming kinship ties with the Māori of New Zealand, and recognition of the rights of HL speakers to develop and use their language in their education (Ministry of Education, 2012b, p. 9)

Additionally, there is a great opportunity to foster and develop Cook Islands Māori as an HL in New Zealand. Bell, Davis, and Starks reported in 2000 that the average age of individuals in the Cook Islands diaspora in the Auckland region is 23 years old, and most migration from the Cook Islands to New Zealand has taken place during the past 50 years (Davis & Starks, 2005, p. 299). Such a young average age of residents and a relatively short period of migration to New Zealand means that it is possible to show support for Cook Islands Māori early in the diaspora's settlement, hopefully leading to increased HL maintenance. However, this of course is dependent upon the social capital (Bourdieu, 1986) associated with Cook Islands Māori—thus the need for the continuing development of strong governmental and educational support for HL resources and of instantiating *negotiation* practices that will allow government ministries to seek input and advice from relevant stakeholders, including educators and community members, when they create guidelines for educational programs.

Tongan, Niuean, Tokelauan, and Fijian

Tongan, Niuean, Tokelauan, and Fijian together had over 45,000 language speakers as of 2013. Tongan alone has 31,839 speakers, which is significantly more than Cook Islands Māori. Despite this, there has been less per capita development of Tongan language programs, with about the same amount developed as for Cook Islands Māori. Likewise, Niuean, Tokelauan, and Fijian have seen an underdevelopment of programs and resources, with only seven, two, and three mainstream programs, respectively. However, Niuean has 4,548 speakers, Tokelauan has 2,469 speakers, and Fijian has 6,273 speakers (Statistics New Zealand, 2013), which shows that a need for such programs exists.

The Ministry of Education developed guidelines along with sample lessons for Tongan, Niuean, and Tokelauan, with the goals of each sharing the same wording as that of the Samoan guidelines shown above in Section 4.1 (Ministry of Education, 2009a, 2012a, 2012c). However, there has been no development of teaching guidelines or resources for Fijian language education. As shown in Table 21.3 above, programs that offer Fijian are also often not reported, suggesting less government and educational investment in these programs, as well as little to no recognized legitimacy. However, with over 6,000 speakers, visibility for and investment in these programs is crucial if the language is to survive among HL speakers in New Zealand. Overall, this speaks to significant disparities between the Pasifika languages, as it pertains to government support and the level of legitimacy they enjoy.

Pasifika Education Centre

As an example of a very successful HL program utilizing the new resources and guidelines provided by the Ministry of Education, this section discusses the government-sponsored after-school/work Pasifika Education Centre (PEC). In response to the vast, and growing, number of immigrants to New Zealand from Pasifika countries, the Tertiary Education Commission developed the PEC in Auckland in 1978 (originally called the Pacific Islanders Education Resource Centre; Pasifika Education Centre, 2013). Now, with over 60% of Pasifika New Zealanders born in New Zealand (Pasifika Education Centre, 2013), a large part of the lessons provided at the PEC involve HL speakers, while first generation Pasifika immigrants to New Zealand and foreign language learners are also welcome.

Currently, the PEC teaches weekly two-hour classes in Samoan, Tongan, Cook Islands Māori, Niuean, and Fijian, with Tokelauan, Tuvaluan, and English as a Second or Other Language (ESOL) under development. Native-speaking tutors teach each class, which are free of charge. Students only purchase their books, which are kept at a low, affordable rate. Additional paid services are also available, such as one-on-one tutoring, translation services, cultural consulting services, and workplace language classes. Uptake of the free classes offered by the PEC is quite high, with 15 tutors and 743 students enrolled in 2013 and 15 tutors and 721 students in 2014 (Pasifika Education Centre, 2015, p. 11), which they report "exceeded our annual target of 650 adults learners at four venues around Auckland" (Pasifika Education Centre, 2015, p. 6). Such demand for these courses further underlines the need for continuing resource development by educational and government institutions and speaks to progress in the area of institutionalization.

5 Concluding Remarks

New Zealand is a "super diverse" country, not just with regard to the number of languages spoken, but, to the focus of this chapter, with regard to factors that bear on the institutionalization of Pasifika HLE education—namely, *negotiation, resources, rise in legitimacy, organizational conditions,* and *diminishing visibility,* as well as the impact of "ideologies, values, beliefs" (Ekholm & Trier, 1987, p. 21).

This chapter speaks to the importance of formally recognizing communities' roles in heritage language education. The institutions and systems involved in HLE must evolve with communities' and speakers' changing circumstances, and to do so, they must have ongoing communication and negotiations with the communities themselves. For example, the Office of Ethnic Communities (previously the Office of Ethnic Affairs) held the *Lining Up Language: Navigating Government Policy* conference in 2015, which brought together government representatives, educators, researchers, and community representatives to discuss needs and possible strategies. Such efforts to formalize negotiations between community and government organizations are necessary for HLE to succeed.

Furthermore, the multitude of programs detailed in this chapter (including early childhood, primary, secondary, and after-school, making use of immersion, bilingual, and elective systems) depict the wide range of efforts and strategies that are going into Pasifika heritage language education in New Zealand. As such, it is important to recognize that no single system of institutionalized organizational conditions could respond to the variety of contexts that are present. Similarly, examining any single educational institution would not give an accurate picture of the complex institutional situation throughout the country. Rather, there are many different contexts nationwide that contribute to supporting Pasifika languages, and institutionalization needs to be thought of in terms of two levels: what is happening nation-wide and at the local level.

Notes

1 My deepest thanks to the kind assistance of the Ministry of Pacific Island Affairs, Statistics New Zealand, and the Ministry of Education. Additionally, thank you to the editors and reviewers of the present volume.
2 There are mixed opinions in New Zealand as to whether all of these languages should be considered HLs. However, representatives from within each community have strongly advocated for their inclusion in HL discussions in recent years, especially with the growing number of second- and third-generation speakers learning and/or reclaiming the languages in each community.
3 For further information, see www.communitylanguagesnz.weebly.com.
4 The Office of Ethnic Affairs was reformed as the Office of Ethnic Communities in 2015. At the time of this chapter, the OEC was working towards an official statement in support of home HL use, to be delivered in 2016.
5 A school week averages 25 hours of instruction.
6 A minimum of 15 hours per year for primary school, or a minimum of 20 hours per year for secondary school
7 No distinction is made in the official statistics between program/school type.
8 In New Zealand, the involvement of communities is promoted in both community-led and mainstream schools, meaning that guidelines set forth by ministries are applicable to all programs.
9 The official establishment of ministry guidelines is a common practice in New Zealand and brings official recognition to the programs/endeavours for which they are established.

References

Advisors to the Education and Science Select Committee. (2012). Pasifika languages in ECE—introductory briefing. Retrieved from http://www.parliament.nz/resource/en-nz/50SCES_ADV_00DBSCH_INQ_11371_1_A270335/812364afd6fac0d9d34e1608716e4eeda8a93a07
Bedford, R., & Didham, R. (2015, May). National ethnic projections. Presentation at the Languages and Super Diversity in Aotearoa New Zealand Workshop, Wellington.
Bell, A., Davis, K., & Starks, D. (2000). Languages of the Manukau region: A pilot study of use, maintenance and educational dimensions of languages in South Auckland. Report to the Woolf Fisher Research Centre. New Zealand: University of Auckland.
Bland, A. (forthcoming). The implementation of a Samoan junior language programme in a South Island, New Zealand secondary school (Unpublished PhD dissertation). University of Canterbury, Christchurch.
Bourdieu, P. (1986). The forms of capital. In J. Richardson (Ed.), Handbook of theory and research for the sociology of education (pp. 241–258). New York: Greenwood.
Cenoz, J. (2015, November). Translanguaging and minority languages: A threat or an opportunity? Keynote presented at the Language, Education and Diversity Conference, Auckland, NZ.
Davis, K., & Starks, D. (2005). Four factors for Cook Islands Māori language maintenance. In A. Bell, R. Harlow, & D. Starks (Eds.), Languages of New Zealand (pp. 298–321). Wellington: Victoria University Press.
De Bres, J. (2015). The hierarchy of minority languages in New Zealand. Journal of Multilingual and Multicultural Development, 36(7), 677–693.
Education and Science Committee. (2013). Inquiry into Pacific languages in early childhood education: Presented to the House of Representatives. Retrieved from http://www.parliament.nz/resource/mi-nz/50DBSCH_SCR6016_1/58901894ca7314cece165273904eda601ad39934
Education Counts. (2015a). Pasifika language in education: Number of schools offering Pasifika language in education. Retrieved from http://www.educationcounts.govt.nz/statistics/pasifika-education/pasifika-in-schooling/6044
Education Counts. (2015b). Subject enrolment. Retrieved from http://www.educationcounts.govt.nz/statistics/schooling/student-numbers/subject-enrolment
Ekholm, M., & Trier, U. P. (1987). The concept of institutionalization: Some remarks. In M. B. Miles, M. Ekholm, & R. Vandenberghe (Eds.), Lasting school improvement: Exploring the process of institutionalization (pp. 13–21). Leuven, Belgium: Acco.

Fairburn-Dunlop, P. (1984). Factors associated with language maintenance: The Samoans in New Zealand. *New Zealand Journal of Educational Studies, 19*, 99–113.

Ferguson, P. B., Gorinski, R., Wendt Samu, T., & Mara, D. (2008). Literature review on the experiences of Pasifika learners in the classroom: A report prepared for the Ministry of Education. Retrieved from http://www.educationcounts.govt.nz/__data/assets/pdf_file/0017/28016/887_Pasifika_Lit_Review.pdf

Fetui, V., & Mālaki-Williams, A. M. (1996). Introduction of the Samoan language programme in New Zealand. In F. Mugler & J. Lynch (Eds.), *Pacific languages in education* (pp. 228–244). Suva, Fiji: Institute of Pacific Studies.

Gorter, D. (2015, November). *Translanguaging, experimenting and assessing: The case of a multilingual basque school.* Paper presented at the Language, Education and Diversity Conference, Auckland, NZ.

Harvey, S. (2014, July). *Where are community languages in schools? Mapping current practice and future possibilities.* Paper presented at the Conference on Community Languages and ESOL in New Zealand, Wellington, NZ.

Hornberger, N. H. (1998). Language policy, language education, language rights: Indigenous, immigrant, and international perspectives. *Language in Society, 27*, 439–458.

Hornberger, N. H., & Wang, S. C. (2008). Who are our heritage language learners? Identity and biliteracy in heritage language education in the United States. In D. M. Brinton, O. Kagan, & S. Bauckus (Eds.), *Heritage language education: A new field emerging* (pp. 3–35). New York: Routledge.

Komiti Pasifika. (2010). 'Mind your language': Our responsibility to protect and promote Pacific Islands languages in New Zealand as part of a National Languages Policy. Retrieved from http://www.ppta.org.nz/index.php/resources/publications/doc_download/953-mind-your-language-our-responsibility-to-protect-and-promote-pacific-islands-languages-in-nz

Lao, R. S., & Lee, J. S. (2009). Heritage language maintenance and use among 1.5 generation Khmer college students. *Journal of Southeast Asian American Education & Advancement, 4*, 1–21.

Lo Bianco, J. (2008). Policy activity for heritage languages: Connections with representation and citizenship. In D. M. Brinton, O. Kagan, & S. Bauckus (Eds.), *Heritage language education: A new field emerging* (pp. 53–70). New York: Routledge.

Massey University. (2014, July). Linguist's concern at heritage language report. Retrieved from http://www.massey.ac.nz/massey/about-massey/news/article.cfm?mnarticle=linguists-concern-at-heritage-language-report-24-07-2014

May, S. (2002a). Accommodating multiculturalism and biculturalism in Aotearoa/New Zealand: Implications for language education. *Waikato Journal of Education, 8*, 5–26.

May, S. (2002b). Where to from here: Charting a way forward for language and education policy in Aotearoa/New Zealand. *TESOLANZ Journal, 10*, 22–35.

McCaffery, J., & McFall-McCaffery, J. T. (2010). O tatou o aga'i i fea?: 'Oku tau o ki fe?: Where are we heading? Pacific languages in Aotearoa/New Zealand. *AlterNative: An International Journal of Indigenous Peoples, 6*(2), 86–121.

Menard-Warwick, J. (2009). *Gendered identities and immigrant language learning.* Tonawanda, NY: Multilingual Matters.

Ministry of Education. (2009a). *Gagana Tokelau (The Tokelau language guidelines).* Wellington: Ministry of Education.

Ministry of Education. (2009b). *Ta'iala mo le Gagana Sāmoa (The Gagana Sāmoa guidelines).* Wellington: Ministry of Education.

Ministry of Education. (2012a). *Ko e Fakahinohino ki he Lea Faka-Tonga (The Tongan language guidelines).* Wellington: Ministry of Education.

Ministry of Education. (2012b). *Te Kaveinga o Te Reo Māori Kūki 'Āirani (The Cook Islands Māori language guidelines).* Wellington: Ministry of Education.

Ministry of Education. (2012c). *Tau Hatakiaga ma e Vagahau Niue (The Niue language guidelines).* Wellington: Ministry of Education.

Ministry of Education. (2013). *Tau Mai Te Reo: The Māori language in education strategy 2013–2017.* Wellington: Ministry of Education.

Ministry of Justice. (1990). *New Zealand Bill of Rights Act 1990.* Wellington: Ministry of Justice.

Ministry of Pacific Island Affairs. (2012, October). *The Pacific languages framework.* Wellington: Ministry of Pacific Island Affairs.

The National Centre for Languages. (2011). What are community languages? Retrieved from http://www.naldic.org.uk/Resources/NALDIC/Initial%20Teacher%20Education/Documents/Whatare communitylanguages.pdf

New Zealand Government: Education Counts. (2016a). Table 1: Number of schools offering a Pasifika language by immersion level and language as at July 2015 [Data table]. *Pasifika language in education: Statistics*. Retrieved from http://www.educationcounts.govt.nz/statistics/pasifika-education/pasifika-in-schooling/6044

New Zealand Government: Education Counts. (2016b). School data dimension notes: Level of learning [Data table]. *Pasifika language in education: Statistics*. Retrieved from http://www.educationcounts.govt.nz/statistics/pasifika-education/pasifika-in-schooling/6044

New Zealand Government: Education Counts. (2016c). Primary languages by year and hours 2000–2016 [Data table]. Primary school languages (Year 1 to 8). *Pasifika language in education: Subject enrolment*. Retrieved from http://www.educationcounts.govt.nz/statistics/schooling/student-numbers/subject-enrolment

New Zealand Government: Education Counts. (2016d). Secondary languages by school & subject name— 1 July 1998–1 July 2015 [Data table]. Secondary school subjects (Year 9 and above). Subject enrolment: Secondary school subjects (Year 9 and above), secondary subjects time series downloads. *Pasifika language in education: Subject enrolment*. Retrieved from http://www.educationcounts.govt.nz/statistics/schooling/student-numbers/subject-enrolment

Office of Ethnic Affairs. (2014). *Language and integration in New Zealand*. Wellington: Office of Ethnic Affairs.

Pasifika Education Centre. (2013). About us. Retrieved from http://www.pacificislandeducation.co.nz/about-us/

Pasifika Education Centre. (2015). *Annual report for the year ending 31st Dec. 2014*. Auckland: Pasifika Education Centre. Retrieved from http://www.pacificislandeducation.co.nz/files/8614/2766/1282/PEC_Annual_Report_-_low_res.pdf

Roberts, M. (1999). *Immigrant language maintenance and shift in the Gujarati Dutch and Samoan communities of Wellington* (Unpublished PhD dissertation). Victoria University of Wellington, Wellington.

The Royal Society of New Zealand. (2013). Languages in Aotearoa/New Zealand. Retrieved from http://www.royalsociety.org.nz/media/Languages-in-Aotearoa-New-Zealand.pdf

Seals, C. A. (2013). *Multilingual identity development and negotiation amongst heritage language learners: A study of East European-American schoolchildren in the United States* (Unpublished PhD dissertation). Georgetown University, Washington, DC.

Seals, C. A. (2014). *Making heritage language speakers visible in the mainstream classroom*. Washington, DC: Alliance for the Advancement of Heritage Languages, Center for Applied Linguistics.

Seals, C. A. (2015, November). *Investment in translanguaging and the social, educational and linguistic outcomes*. Paper presented at the Language, Education and Diversity Conference, Auckland, NZ.

Seals, C. A., & Kreeft Peyton, J. (2016). Heritage language education: Valuing the languages, literacies, and cultural experiences of immigrant youth. *Current Issues in Language Planning*. Early View: http://www.tandfonline.com/doi/full/10.1080/14664208.2016.1168690

Spolsky, B. (2009). *Language management*. Cambridge: Cambridge University Press.

Statistics New Zealand. (2013). 2013 Census totals by topic. Retrieved May 20, 2014, from http://www.stats.govt.nz/~/media/Statistics/Census/2013%20Census/data-tables/totals-by-topic/totals-by-topic-tables.xls

Statistics New Zealand. (2015, July 1). Population clock. Retrieved from http://www.stats.govt.nz/tools_and_services/population_clock.aspx

Tagoilelagi-LeotaGlynn, F., McNaughton, S., MacDonald, S., & Farry, S. (2005). Bilingual and biliteracy development over the transition to school. *International Journal of Bilingual Education and Bilingualism*, 8(5), 455–479.

Tapaleao, V. (2014, March 12). From Tiny Start to world's biggest. New Zealand Herald. Retrieved from http://www.nzherald.co.nz/entertainment/news/article.cfm?c_id=1501119&objectid=11217894

Tuafuti, P., & McCaffery, J. (2005). Family and community empowerment through bilingual education. *International Journal of Bilingual Education and Bilingualism*, 8(5), 480–503.

Tucker, G. R. (2008). Learning other languages: The case for promoting bilingualism within our educational system. In D. M. Brinton, O. Kagan, & S. Bauckus (Eds.), *Heritage language education: A new field emerging* (pp. 39–52). New York: Routledge.

Valdés, G. (2005). Bilingualism, heritage language learners, and SLA research: Opportunities lost or seized? *The Modern Language Journal*, 89(3), 410–426.

Wang, S.C. & García, M.I. (2002). *Heritage Language Learners*. National Council of State Supervisors of Foreign Languages: Position Paper. Retrieved from http://theblvdgroup.me/papers/NCSSFLHLLs0902.pdf

Wiley, T. G., & Lee, J. S. (2009). Introduction. In T. G. Wiley, J. S. Lee, & R. W. Rumberger (Eds.), *The education of language minority immigrants in the United States* (pp. 1–34). New York: Multilingual Matters.

22

Heritage Language Education in Norway and Sweden

Sunil Loona and Mats Wennerholm

1 Introduction

Education in the heritage language (HL) of immigrant students has been a part of the public school system in Norway and Sweden for the past 40 to 50 years. These two Scandinavian countries in Northern Europe, with a total population of about 15 million people, are comparable in size to the province of Ontario in Canada. While there are many similarities in HL education in Ontario and these two Scandinavian countries, one major difference is that twice as many students receive HL instruction in Sweden and Norway as in Ontario. Roughly 150,000 students in elementary schools in Norway and Sweden receive education in their HLs. Such education encompasses approximately 150 different languages.

Sweden has a total population of 9.8 million, of whom roughly 1.43 million, or 15%, are foreign-born (Statistics Sweden, 2015). Norway has a total population of 5.16 million, of whom 512,000, or 9.9%, are categorized as being foreign citizens (Statistics Norway, 2015). Sweden, in other words, not only has a larger population, but also has a higher percentage of foreign-born citizens compared to Norway. Labor migration to Sweden started much earlier than labor migration to Norway. Sweden's industry, which emerged intact at the end of World War II, had a strong demand for labor during the postwar years of European reconstruction. Initially, most of this labor was recruited from the south of Europe and from Finland. Since the 1970s, migration has mainly consisted of refugees and asylum seekers from countries in the third world. In contrast, labor migration to Norway first gathered momentum in the late 1960s and early 1970s following the discovery of oil in the North Sea.

In this chapter on HL education in Sweden and Norway, we start by briefly describing the educational systems in these two nations. We then go on to describe national policies for HL education in each country; how HL education was first introduced in the 1960s and 1970s; how it was organized and incorporated into the school-system, and how it has evolved since then. We then examine the interplay of several factors, which we believe have contributed to national reforms in the education of immigrant children and the institutionalization of HL educational programs. In so doing, we focus on the important roles played by minority organizations, teacher unions, parental organizations, and communities of researchers in creating political pressure for a more pluralistic and inclusive HL educational policy. Our main area of concern here is with the public debates and political processes that have influenced, and continue to influence, the development of instruction in HLs. Finally, we describe some of the challenges still existing in the development of infrastructures to support HL instruction in Sweden and Norway. This section also focuses on attempts being made to resolve issues related to the development of learning materials, teacher training, and other instructional areas. We conclude by discussing some research findings on the impact HL instruction is having on the identities and processes of language development among students enrolled in these programs.

The term "heritage language" will be used interchangeably with the term "mother tongue" in this chapter. We are aware of the controversy surrounding the use of "mother tongue" (García, 2009), but choose to use this term because it is most commonly used in both Norway and Sweden. Official documents in Norway no longer use the term "Norwegian as a second language" but refer rather to teaching in "adapted Norwegian." Finally, when discussing mother tongue education, our emphasis will be on education in preschool as well as primary and lower secondary school levels, the latter referring to students aged 6 to 16 in Norway and 7 to 16 in Sweden, rather than on upper secondary schools.

2 Education Systems in Sweden and Norway

There are many similarities in the Swedish and Norwegian education systems. Education in both these countries is mainly organized within the public sector and is compulsory and free for all school-age children. In both countries the state (represented by parliament and governmental ministries) formulates national education policy and stipulates educational objectives in the form of laws, statutes, and curriculums. A common standard is ensured through legislation and through national curricula. Education is based on principles of equality. The Swedish school system stresses the right of all pupils to an equivalent education (Sweden, n.d.). The Norwegian school system is based on the principle of adapted learning for everyone within an inclusive environment (Government.no, 2014).

While the parliaments and governments in Sweden and Norway define broader goals and decide the budgetary frameworks for education, the municipalities in these countries are responsible for running pre-, primary, and lower secondary schools, and both Sweden and Norway share well-established traditions of decentralization and school autonomy. With the exception of a small private school sector in both countries, 290 municipalities in Sweden and 430 municipalities in Norway have responsibility for running schools.

While there are many similarities in the Swedish and Norwegian educational systems, there are also some differences regarding HL education. Whereas the education law in Sweden has consistently stressed the importance of language maintenance since 1977, Norway's policy has shifted from a policy of language maintenance in the 1980s to a policy of transitional bilingualism since the 1990s.

3 Heritage Language Education in Sweden: An Emphasis on Language Maintenance

The period from 1960 to 1998 has been described as a period of political consensus on issues related to migration in Sweden. Immigration issues were not on the agenda in election manifestos. Neither were they discussed at party leader debates. All ministers responsible for immigrant affairs in Sweden supported the same idea of integration of immigrants, independent of their party affiliation (Dahlström, 2006).

This political consensus on the integration of immigrants also meant a general consensus among researchers, practitioners, and politicians that knowledge of the HL contributes to the student's self-esteem and identity, and strengthens their participation in their own language community. There was also agreement that instruction in the HL enhances the student's opportunities for knowledge development and contributes to society's need for a knowledge base for many different languages. In 2006, the Swedish National Agency for Education wrote the following:

> It is through language that pupils express their culture and values. Language gives them self-esteem. Language is the bearer of knowledge and forms the basis of meetings with other people. Pupils need language to be able to think, dream, ask questions, and solve problems. More languages give more opportunities.
>
> *(Beijer, 2006)*

The Swedish state recognized the right of immigrant children to maintain and to develop their mother tongue languages as early as 1962 (Hyltenstam & Arnberg, 1988, p. 487). Four years later, in 1966, the municipalities received earmarked funds from the national government to arrange a Tutorial Program for immigrant and stateless children, as well as for Swedish children who had studied in foreign schools. The Tutorial Program of 1966 consisted of two parts: instruction in Swedish as a foreign language, later changed to instruction in Swedish as a second language, and instruction in school subjects through the medium of the mother tongue (called *studiehandledning* in Swedish).

Though the municipalities were not obliged by law to arrange for instruction in the mother tongue, they accepted the government's recommendations, probably because the core curriculum of 1969 (Skolöverstyrelsen, 1969) had already made the municipalities responsible "for providing the children of migrants with the best possible conditions for their education" (p. 111). In theory, this meant that all immigrant children were given the opportunity to study their mother tongue from as early as 1968 (Hyltenstam & Tuomela, 1996, p. 44).

In 1977 the Home Language Reform Act (HLRC) was passed making it mandatory for the municipalities to arrange for mother tongue education for immigrant children in primary and lower secondary schools in the country, that is to say for children between the ages of 7 and 16 years. The HLRC was based on three objectives: 1) Equality between immigrants and the Swedish people; 2) Cultural freedom of choice for immigrants; and 3) Cooperation and solidarity between Swedes and ethnic minorities. The basis for the HLRC was a resolution passed by the Swedish parliament in 1975 stressing the importance of integrating rather than assimilating minorities into society (Hyltenstam & Tuomela, 1996, p. 29).

It was left to the municipalities to decide whether HL instruction was to be given during school hours or after school hours. For practical reasons most municipalities choose to organize HL instruction after school hours, but in some inner-city schools, where there is a large concentration of students with a common HL, instruction in the subject is given during school hours. *Studiehandledning* is, however, given only during school hours.

Although minority students have a statutory right to mother tongue education, it is not compulsory for them to attend mother tongue classes. Only if a minimum of five students in a municipality ask for instruction in their mother tongue is the local school administration obliged to arrange this, provided a suitable teacher can be engaged. When this occurs, the mother tongue of minority students is taught as a separate subject in primary and lower secondary schools, with its own syllabus and grading criteria. Teaching in the subject emphasizes the importance of language as a tool for preserving and developing the student's cultural heritage and multicultural identity.

In addition to instruction in their mother tongues, students can also be given help and guidance in the different school subjects through the medium of their mother tongue. Study guidance in the mother tongue, or *studiehandledning*, is particularly important for students who have recently arrived in Sweden. Because of lack of proficiency in the Swedish language, they are often unable to understand academic subject matter if it is taught solely in Swedish. *Studiehandledning* is not as widespread as mother-tongue instruction, is not obligatory, and is given on an individual basis to students whom the school judges as having difficulties following lessons. Normally, a mother tongue teacher or study guidance teacher comes into the classroom and supports the student by explaining subject matter to him/her while lessons are being carried out in Swedish.

Legislation in Sweden also gives minority children an opportunity to develop their mother tongue in preschool. Since 1989, the Swedish government has provided financial support to municipalities so that all immigrant children ages 0–6 can be given mother tongue support in daycare centers and preschools (Arnberg, 1996, p. 189). Such support was however neglected during the 1990s when Sweden was facing an economic crisis. Though still available in most municipalities, mother tongue support consists of only an hour or so every week. Since 2002, guidelines for providing support for children in both their mother tongue and Swedish have been strengthened. However, the state does not regulate how the local school administrations implement such policies. Consequently, there are major differences in how local school administrations in the different municipalities provide support in the mother tongues to children in preschools.

In summary, there are good institutionalized structures for HL development in Sweden, in the sense that laws have been passed at the national level that support HL instruction. However, ever since the reforms took effect, there has been a widening gap between the intentions with regard to mother tongue education and the actual implementation of the reforms in the municipalities. A number of loopholes in the legislation allow local school administrations to interpret the rules and regulations according to their own priorities. Consequently, many students are not offered teaching or tutoring in their mother tongue. This has led to a hollowing out of instruction in heritage languages.

At present, only 54% of all students entitled to mother tongue instruction in primary and lower secondary schools are receiving this service (Skolverket [Swedish National Agency for Education], 2015). There are many reasons for these low figures. As mentioned before, mother tongue classes are usually held immediately after regular school hours because they are not supposed to encroach on teaching in other obligatory subjects. Teaching after school hours is generally unpopular among students, and teachers often complain about tired, unmotivated students.

The percentage of preschool children receiving support in their mother tongues is significantly lower than those receiving this support in primary and lower secondary schools. Whereas in 1990, 6 out of 10 children were provided with support in their mother tongues in kindergartens, the numbers had dropped in 2002 to 1 in 10 (Skolverket, 2002). This drop in HL support happened at the same time as research findings were increasingly pointing to preschool years as being critical and sensitive for language development, and therefore optimally suited for laying the foundations for an active bilingualism (Bialystok, 1999, 2001).

A study undertaken by the Swedish National Agency for Education entitled *With another mother tongue* (Skolverket, 2008) describes mother tongue instruction as being peripheral and external to activities at school—but at the same time, significant for students' performance. Students who participate in mother tongue programs have on average a higher merit rating than students who only receive instruction in Swedish as a second language. The fact that one hour's tuition in the subject should have such a noticeable effect on students' academic performances is described in the study as being "remarkable." The study sums up its findings as follows:

Mother tongue instruction appears . . . on the one hand to have possible importance for the students' general knowledge development and, on the other hand, to be an activity that for the most part takes place outside of other school activities and that can almost be described as marginalized.

(Skolverket, 2008, pp. 19–20)

In conclusion, that national policy on mother tongue education in Sweden is both positive and ambitious in its scope, but at the same time policy makers have hesitated in demanding that local school administrations in the municipalities organize, fund, and implement mother tongue teaching programs adequately.

4 Heritage Language Instruction in Norway—an Emphasis on Transitional Bilingualism

Initially, in the 1970s and early 1980s, with the arrival of labor migrants in Norway, there was a consensus among researchers, practitioners, and politicians that mother tongue knowledge was important for students' self-esteem and conceptual development. Of all the political parties in Norway, only the anti-immigration Progress Party, then a small and insignificant populist party, was against mother tongue instruction.

In 1978 the first of many bicultural classes for students from first to third grade were established in Oslo. A bicultural class was composed of children from both the majority Norwegian community and from a minority language community, for example, Turkish speakers. Both groups of children received instructions in reading and writing in their respective mother tongues. Lessons in all subjects, such as mathematics and the natural sciences, were carried out through a bilingual two-teacher system, with both a Norwegian teacher and a mother tongue teacher present in class. In addition, the minority students received lessons in Norwegian as a second language and instruction in their mother tongue (Loona, 2001). These bicultural classes were in part financed by the Council of Europe, which considered the bicultural class model as a good example of how the teaching of linguistic minorities could be organized in the rest of Europe.

The consensus on the importance of mother tongue education was also reflected in the core curriculum of 1987 (Mønsterplan for grunnskolen, 1987), which defined functional bilingualism as an important goal in the education of minority students. Similar to Sweden, the mother tongue was to be taught as a separate subject in schools during school hours.

However, this consensus on the importance of mother tongue education began breaking down toward the end of the 1980s as a direct consequence of increased public support for the Progress Party's anti-immigration and pro-assimilation policies. In 1989 the Conservative Party abandoned its earlier position on mother tongue instruction and started arguing for a model of transitional bilingualism in the education of minority students. Two years later, during the municipal elections in Oslo in 1991, the leader of the Oslo Labor Party, under increasing pressure from the right, and contrary to articles in his party's program, described mother tongue instruction as a form of misplaced "kindism" that was hindering the integration of minorities. The Labor Party won a resounding victory in the Oslo municipal elections.

Two years later, in 1993, the Oslo City Council passed a resolution redefining the goal of minority education: "The goal for the student is to learn the Norwegian language as fast as possible so that he/she can participate in the ordinary teaching." In other words, the goal of functional bilingualism was abandoned in favor of a model of transitional bilingualism. Consequently, teaching in the mother tongue was assigned a new role: "As a teaching method, schools can use the students' mother tongue as a tool, an aid to learning Norwegian and in the teaching of subjects" (Aktstykker, Oslo kommune, 1992, Item 1. Oslo City Council Resolution of 3/24/93). At the same time, the remaining bicultural classes in Oslo were terminated (Loona, 2001).

During the national elections in 1993, the largest political party, the Labor Party, which had earlier been a proponent of strengthening mother tongue teaching, did not address this topic in its party program. Interestingly, both the Conservatives and the Labor Parties were now embracing a standpoint similar to the one which the Progress Party alone had held in the early 1980s. The new model for teaching minorities in Oslo, also known as the "Oslo model," eventually became the model for the whole country when the Norwegian parliament approved a new Education Act in 1998 (Norwegian Education Act, 1998).

The shift in focus from the 1980s when bilingualism was viewed positively as a resource to a focus on students' limited grasp of Norwegian in the 1990s has led to a gradual movement away from a policy of linguistic diversity in the education of immigrant students to one of "worthy assimilation" (Ozerk, 1993). The Norwegian Education Act (1998) states the following on adapted language education for pupils from language minorities:

> Pupils attending the primary and lower secondary school who have a mother tongue other than Norwegian or Sami have the right to adapted education in Norwegian until they are sufficiently proficient in Norwegian to follow the normal instruction of the school. If necessary, such pupils are also entitled to mother tongue instruction, bilingual subject teaching, or both.
>
> *(Section 2–8)*

Consequently, instruction in the mother tongue and/or bilingual subject teaching is not treated as a right in and of itself, but follows from and is dependent on the right to adapted language education in Norwegian. If a student has sufficient skills in Norwegian to follow regular classes, he/she does not have a right to mother tongue and/or bilingual subject teaching. Besides, the formulation, "If necessary, such pupils are also entitled to mother tongue instruction, bilingual subject teaching, or both" leaves much to the discretion of the local school administrations in the municipalities to decide whether mother tongue instruction and bilingual subject teaching are necessary for students. In this context, many municipalities opt out of giving mother tongue instruction and/or bilingual subject teaching to minority students.

Earlier we quoted a study undertaken in Sweden describing mother tongue education as being external to other activities in schools and with only 54% of students participating in mother tongue classes. In comparison, mother tongue instruction and bilingual subject teaching in Norway seems to be even more marginalized than in Sweden. Statistics for the school year 2014–2015 show that of a total of 43,380 students attending adapted Norwegian language classes in Norway, only 2,482 (5.7 %) are being offered both mother tongue instruction and bilingual subject teaching. An additional 1,623 of these students (3.7 %) are receiving only mother tongue instruction, and finally, 8,830 students (20.35 %) are receiving only bilingual subject instruction (Grunnskolens Informasjonssystem, 2015).

There are also big differences in mother tongue instruction in the largest municipalities in Norway. In 2013, while 88–89%of students who attended classes in adapted Norwegian in the municipalities of Trondheim and Bergen were offered some form of mother tongue and/or bilingual subject instruction, only 20% of students were offered such instruction in the municipalities of Oslo and Drammen (Store forskjeller i morsmålsopplæringen i Norge [Major differences in mother tongue education in Norway], 2013). Many small municipalities in Norway, who neither have mother tongue teachers nor resources necessary to implement mother tongue instruction and bilingual subject teaching in local schools, often choose to opt out of providing these services.

5 Factors Leading to the Current Policies Regarding HL Education in Sweden and Norway

A policy of assimilation prevailed in much of Europe from the mid-1800s to the 1950s, including Norway and Sweden. During this period, nation-building was seen as essential to national unity and schools were seen as key sites for the cultural and linguistic assimilation of minorities. Up through the 1950s, it was forbidden for children of national minorities to speak Finnish or Sámi in classrooms, even during recess.

May (2002), an international authority on language rights, language policy, and bilingualism, says that demographic diversity, which has increased markedly in recent years due to increased migration and the forced relocation of refugees, has placed increasing pressure on the public policies of nation-states. In discussing the degree to which the languages and cultures of so-called "minority" groups can and should be accorded recognition in the public domain in nation states, May differentiates between rights of national minorities and rights of ethnic minorities. According to May, national minorities, who have always been associated historically with a particular territory, can lay claim to what he terms "self-government rights." Ethnic minorities and immigrants, on the other hand, ought to claim "polyethnic rights," which he defines as rights that seek to protect rather than eliminate cultural and linguistic differences, and the right to some form of state support, including the right to educational provision in their first language (May, 2002).

Sweden has granted its ethnic minorities many of the "polyethnic" rights mentioned above. Sweden's model of mother tongue instruction has been described as being unique among the major immigrant-receiving countries of the world (Reath Warren, 2013). Norway's model of mother tongue instruction and bilingual subject teaching as students transition to Norwegian seeks neither to protect nor to eliminate cultural and linguistic differences. This model has been established within the school system and has been accorded recognition in the public domain, but only during a transitional period in the schooling of immigrant students. Nonetheless, from a historical point of view, the mere existence of mother tongue instruction in both Sweden and Norway is an indication of the expansion of minority rights within these nation states. In this section of the chapter we therefore briefly discuss what kind of pressures have led Norway and Sweden to grant these rights to ethnic minorities and immigrants.

After World War II, and right up to the 1970s, both Sweden and Norway were marked by reconstruction, optimism, and a gradual expansion of the welfare state. However, from the end of the 1960s onwards, an increasing numbers of groups, such as women, students, and minorities, began to express their displeasure at the policies of the government. In 1968 the Norwegian Sámi Association was formed in Kautokeino. (The Swedish Sámi Association had already been established in 1950.) The Sámi uprisings that followed in the 1970s in both Sweden and Norway were movements that not only demanded the right to self-government for indigenous minorities, but also the right to preservation of Sámi cultural and linguistic identity. The mere fact of existence of these movements, after decades of harsh cultural and linguistic repression, were powerful reminders to state authorities that policies of forced assimilation of minorities had failed, and that the continuation of such policies would only lead to conflict and disharmony in society.

These developments meant that the principle of cultural and linguistic homogeneity, long espoused by the nation state as necessary for the maintenance of national unity, was no longer tenable and had to be replaced by a more multilingual approach when formulating policy on the integration of labor migrants and their children into society.

Greater awareness among immigrant parents regarding the benefits of education in the mother tongue for their children has played an important role in influencing national education policy toward immigrant children in Sweden and Norway. For example, toward the end of the 1970s, many immigrant parents in Norway, unhappy over the poor performance of their children at school, started an organization called the Immigrant Children's Parents Union. They demanded an improvement in the schooling of their children, including more hours of instruction in the children's mother tongue. The organization was behind several reports in the media critical of the ways in which their children were being taught in schools in Oslo.

In 1980 the local school authorities in Oslo issued a circular, F-90/80, stating that when offering classes in Norwegian as a second language and in the mother tongue, schools should give priority to students from "distant" lands and cultural backgrounds rather than to students from cultural backgrounds "similar" to Norwegian culture. This was not an easy task for principals at schools in Oslo to resolve. It is impossible to categorize some ethnic groups as culturally "distant" and others as "close" without resorting to some kind of "imaginative geography" (Said, 1978). This circular caused an outbreak of public anger among parents and teachers who believed that all students should get equal opportunities to learn their mother tongues, regardless of their language backgrounds (Bergan, 2014).

In May 1982, the Immigrant Children's Parents Union organized a general strike for one day for all immigrant students in Oslo schools and 1,700 students stayed home from school. The demand by these parents for an improvement in mother tongue education was supported by two of the largest teachers' unions in Norway—the Norwegian Union of Teachers and the Norwegian Union of School Employees. Reviewing the development of education in the mother tongue for minority students in Norway during the period from 1980 to 1999, Bergan (2014) describes this general strike as being a watershed in the development of mother tongue education in Norway. According to him, this was the starting point of a public debate on the importance of mother tongue education for immigrant children in Norway. Similarly, the Finnish school strike in Stockholm during February of 1984, when Finnish parents kept their children out of school in support of their demand for Finnish medium schooling, was later to lead to a debate on bilingual education as an option within the Swedish school system.

Finally, it is important to keep in mind the important role that academic research has played in supporting mother tongue teaching in Norway and Sweden. Prior to the 1950s, bilingualism was associated with poor intellectual performance and described as causing confusion and anomie in the minds of bilingual speakers. By documenting the positive effects of bilingualism/multilingualism on children's cognitive and identity development, academic research has contributed to a change in public attitudes toward mother tongue teaching. Within the Scandinavian context, research carried out by Tove Skutnabb-Kangas (e.g., 1981), Kenneth Hyltenstam (e.g., 1996), Anne Hvenekilde (e.g., 1998), and many others, has been influential in creating pressure from below for a more pluralistic and inclusive education policy.

6 The Institutionalization of Mother Tongue Instruction and Bilingual Subject Teaching

Ekholm and Trier (1987) define institutionalization as "a stabilized modification, aiming at improvement of an institution or parts of it—its process, products or capacities" (p. 13). In this section of the chapter, we describe some of the factors that have influenced the institutionalization of HL education at the state and local levels, including the development of an infrastructure to support HL instruction in Norway and Sweden, as well as the development of resources to support the teaching of mother tongues. Ekholm and Trier point out that the availability of resources is an essential building block in sustaining innovative educational programs and furthering the process of institutionalization. In the Swedish and Norwegian contexts, these resources include the creation of learning materials, opportunities for teacher training, and the development of forums, both on and off line, for the sharing of instructional tools.

Most of the textbooks and teaching materials available in the different mother tongues, whether in print or on the Internet, are designed for use in the countries of origin of the different immigrant groups. Using imported learning materials places great demands on mother tongue teachers: Searching for adequate learning materials in public libraries or on the Internet, and then adapting the material for use in Swedish and Norwegian contexts—a task that can be both tedious and time-consuming. In the long term, if a language is to become an active and permanent resource in any society, this requires that learning materials in that language should be developed and adapted for use in that particular society. However, developing and publishing learning materials locally in Sweden or Norway, especially in languages with few speakers, is often not commercially viable, especially for small, private publishing houses. Consequently, the state in both Sweden and Norway has had to step in and provide grants to publishers willing to develop learning materials in the different mother tongues, and some learning materials have become available in the mother tongues of larger groups, such as Arabic, Kurdish, Polish, and Somali. In addition, the state, especially in Sweden, has allocated considerable funding over several years for the development of general learning resources such as online multilingual dictionaries, language assessment, tools and information on the Internet.

In accordance with legislation on mother tongue support in kindergartens and schools, many municipalities in both Sweden and Norway have recruited bilingual teachers and bilingual assistants to work in local schools and kindergartens. Many of these bilingual teachers are not qualified as teachers, let alone as language teachers, though most of them have academic backgrounds from universities in their home countries. Having qualified teachers to teach the mother tongues improves the quality of HL teaching and at the same time contributes to a higher status for the subject.

It is possible for mother tongue teachers and bilingual assistants to qualify as teachers by enrolling in ordinary teacher-training programs, and many do so. However, very few choose their mother tongue as a subject during their teacher training. They argue that the mother tongue has a low status and is not offered within a school's timetable but is taught after school hours. For a great many, this means that they would rather choose a combination of subjects that can increase their chances of obtaining permanent employment in a single school instead of teaching the mother tongue at several different schools in the municipality.

In order to encourage mother tongue teachers and bilingual teachers to seek supplementary education that can formally qualify them to teach in schools, since 2003 the state in Norway has been running a scholarship scheme for teachers who wish to study at teacher-training institutes that offer courses adapted to their needs. Only teachers who teach in mother tongues other than Norwegian, Sámi, Danish, Swedish, English, French, and German can apply for such scholarships.

Lack of training opportunities for mother tongue teachers and lack of teaching materials in their subject has led the Swedish government to establish a website to support mother tongue teachers. The Swedish website, *Tema Modersmål* [Theme Mother Tongue] (Skolverket, n.d.), was launched in 2001 and is run by the Swedish National Agency for Education. The purpose of the website is threefold: Firstly, to provide school administrators, teachers, and parents with easily accessible information on ongoing developments in the field of minority education. Secondly, to establish a countrywide forum for communication between mother tongue teachers, and to provide them with a platform for finding information and exchanging experiences relevant to their work in schools. Thirdly, the project also aims at providing an arena where mother tongue teachers would not only be able to develop methods and skills, but also have access to teaching materials in their languages in the form of texts, images, audio, videos, and links to various information databases. Editorial boards in the different languages taught in Swedish schools have been established in collaboration with local school administrations. Each editorial board, which consists of a team of two to three well-qualified mother tongue teachers, have been asked to publish regular bilingual teaching-materials in their respective languages on the website. The content has to be in accordance with the national core-curriculum. All published materials are freely available to users and can then be downloaded by mother tongue teachers all over the country and adapted for use in classrooms.

The Theme Mother Tongue project was so successful in Sweden that the Norwegian government decided to initiate a similar project in 2009. The Norwegian Directorate for Education and Training was asked to collaborate with the Swedish National Agency for Education in establishing the project in Norway. Today the project in Norway, also called *Tema Morsmål* [Theme Mother Tongue] (n.d.), is run by the National Centre for Multicultural Education. The two projects collaborate with each other and hold yearly conferences, alternatively in Sweden and Norway. Both websites regularly publish updated articles on research on bilingualism/multilingualism and pedagogical innovation. One section on both websites provides information and guidelines for parents as to how they best can support their children in a multilingual setting.

Multilingual dictionaries presented in a multimedia-format on the websites have proven to be extremely popular. Here students can see texts and pictures, and listen and compare words in different languages. Younger children can hear multilingual stories on the websites. These are stories that alternate between two languages, for example, Norwegian and the mother tongue. The multilingual stories provide many opportunities for multilingual work in kindergartens and schools, and like all other material published on the site, this service is freely available for users.

The two Theme Mother Tongue websites have similar layouts and navigating between them is easy. At present, the Swedish website (Skolverket, n.d.) publishes learning resources in 30 different languages and the Norwegian website (Tema Morsmål, n.d.) publishes learning resources in 13 different languages. Altogether, more than one hundred mother tongue teachers and school administrators from Norway and Sweden contribute regularly to the development of the two websites.

The Swedish National Agency for Education and the National Centre for Multicultural Education in Norway hold regular workshops, seminars, and conferences for mother tongue teachers in their respective countries. At these meetings, competence-building takes place through lectures, presentations, dialogue, and discussion, as well as by establishing formal and informal networks among the teachers.

Mother tongue education is an optional subject in Sweden and requires that parents must register their children for instruction in the mother tongue. To do so, they need to make informed choices on behalf of their children. Many parents face a dilemma when making decisions about their children's education. On the one hand, they want their children to learn their mother tongue, but on the other hand, they are afraid that mother tongue education might hinder learning the majority language. Publication of multilingual brochures, like "Two languages or more? Advice for multilingual families" in Sweden (Skolverket, 2004) and "Children in Multilingual Families" in Norway (Nasjonalt senter for flerkulturell opplaering [National Center for Multicultural Education], 2014), are meant to help parents and teachers find information about children's language development as well as provide information about the benefits of being bilingual or multilingual. This is especially important since bilingualism has earlier been associated with poor intellectual performance (e.g., Hakuta, 1986). The role of ideologies and beliefs on the part of parents is thus also important with regard to the institutionalization of programs that include mother tongue instruction (Ekholm & Trier, 1987).

7 Concluding Remarks

Ideally, the aim of educating minority students in their HL should be language maintenance. It is primarily through the institutionalization of education in HLs in schools that linguistic diversity in a society can be maintained. Transitional models of instruction in the mother tongue, such as the one practiced in Norway, cannot serve this purpose. In this concluding section of our article we discuss the impact that HL education is having on language development and cultural identity of minority students in Sweden and Norway.

In Sweden, the aim of education of immigrant students is not only to encourage them to acquire a high level of competence in the Swedish language, but also to facilitate the maintenance and development of their mother tongues. Have policies regarding mother tongue maintenance been successful, and if not, what factors are impeding their success? Do minority students, who receive one hour of tuition in their mother tongue every week in elementary schools, manage to maintain and develop their mother tongues, or are they undergoing a language shift, which will eventually result in Swedish becoming their dominant language? Will they become balanced bilinguals, with literacy skills in both their languages, or will their language situation be characterized by subtractive bilingualism, in which case they will acquire only rudimentary oral skills in their mother tongues?

Surprisingly, there are very few studies undertaken on language maintenance and language loss among immigrant children growing up in Sweden. One exception is a study entitled *Iranians in Sweden: A Study of Language Maintenance and Shift* by Namei (2012).

Namei's results on the language socialization of 188 Persian–Swedish bilinguals showed that the second generation was being socialized to a much greater extent in Swedish than in Persian. They were also more competent in their second language. Persian was the main instrument of communication in the families; however, the younger children in particular also used some Swedish when speaking to other family members. These patterns of language use found among second-generation Persian students seem to indicate that a shift in language is under way in the families studied. While the parents are trying to pass on their mother tongue to their children by using it in their home, it is unlikely that the children will pass on the language to their own children. As is known from earlier research, the HL will be lost by the third generation (e.g., Fishman, 1991).

This language shift is taking place despite the students receiving mother-tongue instruction at school. Namei (2012) herself suggests that the cause of the language shift seems to be sociopsychological factors rather than just psychological factors. In other words, language shift is taking place because both the mother tongue and its speakers have low status in society and because there are very few domains in Swedish society where the mother tongue can be used.

Does mother tongue instruction have low status among minority students because of the way in which it is structured and organized within schools in Sweden? In a study analyzing the syllabus for mother tongue instruction in Sweden, Reath Warren (2013) finds a significant gap between what the subject aspires to do and what it is able to achieve. According to her, as a subject, Mother Tongue Tuition (as named in the curriculum) both has an intended curriculum and a hidden curriculum. While the intended curriculum is internally consistent and is constructively aligned with the overall values, tasks, and goals of the Swedish school system, the hidden curriculum plays an important role in impeding successful implementation of the intended curriculum. The hidden curriculum has been defined as "the one that no teacher explicitly teaches but that all students learn . . . that powerful part of the school culture that communicates to students the school's attitudes towards a range of issues and problems" (Banks, 2001, p. 23).

In her study, Reath Warren (2013) found that the hidden curriculum of Mother Tongue Tuition in Sweden has the following features:

- Mother Tongue Tuition is non-essential (elective);
- Mother Tongue Tuition is less important than other languages (one hour per week as opposed to three or four hours per week in English, Swedish, and modern languages);
- Mother Tongue Tuition is inconvenient (after-hours, sometimes held in another school, always in another classroom);
- Mother Tongue Tuition is low status (short on resources, books and qualified teachers);
- Mother Tongue Tuition is disconnected from every other aspect of school life.

This has interesting implications for institutionalization in that the formal introduction of a curriculum is one step, but the way it is implemented—details such as those described above—can contribute to a hidden culture that impacts the robustness of a program going forward.

In her conclusion, Reath Warren (2013) says that the right step for future implementation of the Mother Tongue Tuition syllabus in Sweden would be to uncover and challenge the negative effects of the hidden curriculum. By changing the conditions surrounding the implementation and organization of mother tongue instruction, she feels it will become easier to realize the values, tasks, goals, and guidelines of the subject's intended curriculum.

The challenges facing mother tongue instruction in Norway are even greater than the challenges facing mother tongue instruction in Sweden. There is a need for a renewed debate on the importance of HL education in Norway. In 2004, the Norwegian government launched a strategic plan entitled *Equal Education in Practice! A Strategy for Increasing Learning and Better Participation by Language Minorities in Kindergartens, Schools and Education 2004–2009*. In the preface to the strategic plan, the then Minister for Education and Research, Kristin Clemet, said the following:

> Unfortunately we do not have equitable education for all. There are major differences between speakers of minority languages and speakers of the majority language. With regard to participation in and learning outcomes of education, speakers of minority languages, whether they are born and raised in Norway or have come here later, perform consistently poorer than speakers of the majority language. Why is it so?
>
> *(Norwegian Ministry for Education and Research, 2004, p. 3)*

The answer is because, in the words of Professor Jim Cummins, we are still seeing culturally and linguistically diverse children as "a problem to be solved" (Cummins, 2001, p. 20). Cummins, one of the world's leading authorities on bilingual education, maintains that "the cultural, linguistic, and intellectual capital of our societies will increase dramatically" when we "open our eyes to the linguistic, cultural, and intellectual resources they [minorities] bring from their homes to our schools and societies" (p. 20).

References

Aktstykker, Oslo kommune [Legal documents, Oslo municipality]. (1992, November 27). Bystyrets forhandlinger, protokoll referat 1993, sak 1–215, bind 1, sak nr 106, [City council protocol, report 1993, issue 1–215, case number 106], Undervisning av elever fra språklige minoriteter i grunnskolen. [Instruction of students from language minorities in primary school]. Byrådssak 699 av 27.11.92 [City government case 699].

Arnberg, L. N. (1996). Invandrarbarn i förskolan–den svenska modellen [Immigrant children in nursery school—the Swedish model]. In K. Hyltenstam (Ed.), *Tvåspråkighet med förhinder? Invandrar- och minoritetsundervisning I Sverige* [*Bilingualism with obstacles? Immigrant and minority education in Sweden*] (pp. 187–223). Lund, Sweden: Studentlitteratur.

Banks, J. A. (2001). Multicultural education: Characteristics and goals. In J. A. Banks & C. McGee (Eds.), *Multicultural education: Issues and perspectives* (4th ed., pp. 3–30). New York, NY: John Wiley and Sons.

Beijer, M. (2006). Växelvis på modersmål och svenska [Moving between languages]. *Myndigheten för skolutvecklingen* [*Swedish National Agency for School Improvement*]. Stockholm, Sweden: *Myndigheten för skolutvecklingen* [*Swedish National Agency for School Improvement*].

Bergan, A. B. (2014). Språklige minoriteter og morsmålsopplæring i grunnskolen 1980–1999 [Linguistic minorities and language teaching in primary schools]. Universitetet I Oslo. Retrieved from https://www.duo.uio.no/bitstream/handle/10852/40135/bolstadbergan_master.pdf?sequence=1&isAllowed=y

Bialystok, E. (1999). Cognitive complexity and attentional control in the bilingual mind. *Child Development, 70,* 636–644.

Bialystok, E. (2001). *Bilingualism in development: Language, literacy, and cognition.* New York, NY: Cambridge University Press.

Cummins, J. (2001). Bilingual children's mother tongue: Why is it important for education? *Sprogforum. nr, 19,* 15–20. Retrieved from http://inet.dpb.dpu.dk/infodok/sprogforum/Espr19/CumminsENG.pdf

Dahlström, C. (2006, March 29–April 2). *The Rhetoric and practice of institutional reform: Modern immigrant policy in Sweden.* Paper presented at the Biannual Meeting of the Council for European Studies, Chicago, IL. Retrieved from http://councilforeuropeanstudies.org/files/Papers/Dahlstrom.pdf

Ekholm, M., & Trier, U. P. (1987). The concept of institutionalization: Some remarks. In M. B. Miles, M. Ekholm, & R. Vandenberghe (Eds.), *Lasting school improvement: Exploring the process of institutionalization* (pp. 13–21). Leuven, Belgium: Acco.

Fishman, J. A. (1991). *Reversing language shift.* Clevedon, England: Multilingual Matters.

García, O. (2009). *Bilingual education in the 21st century: A global perspective.* Oxford, UK: Wiley Blackwell.

Government.no. (2014, November). The Norwegian education system [Web page]. Retrieved from https://www.regjeringen.no/en/topics/education/school/the-norwegian-education-system/id445118/

Grunnskolens Informasjonssystem [Primary school information system]. (2015). E. Særskilt språkopplæring for minoritetsspråklige elever [E. Special language education for minority students]. Retrieved from https://gsi.udir.no/application/main.jsp?languageId=1#

Hakuta, K. (1986). *Mirror of language: The debate on bilingualism.* New York, NY: Basic Books.

Hvenekilde, A. (1998). Literacy training for linguistic minorities in Norway. In A. Y. Durgunoglu & L. Verhoeven (Eds.), *Literacy development in a multilingual context* (pp. 147–166). Mahwah, NJ: Lawrence Erlbaum.

Hyltenstam, K. (Ed.). (1996). *Tvåspråkighet med förhinder? Invandrar- och minoritetsundervisning i Sverige.* Lund: Studentlitteratur [Bilingualism with obstacles? Immigrant and minority education in Sweden]. Lund, Sweden: Studentlitteratur.

Hyltenstam, K., & Arnberg, L. (1988). Bilingualism and education of immigrant children and adults in Sweden. In C. B. Paulston (Ed.), *International handbook of bilingualism and bilingual education* (pp. 475–513). New York, NY: Greenwood Press.

Hyltenstam, K., & Tuomela, V. (1996). Hemspråksundervisning [Immigrant language teaching]. In K. Hyltenstam (Ed.), *Tvåspråkighet med förhinder? Invandrar- och minoritetsundervisning i Sverige.* Lund: Studentlitteratur [Bilingualism with obstacles? Immigrant and minority education in Sweden] (pp. 9–109). Lund, Sweden: Studentlitteratur.

Loona, S. (2001). En flerkulturell skole? I Voksne for barn (Ed.), Barn i Norge: Årsrapport om barn og unges psykiske helse. Oslo: Voksne for barn. Retrieved from http://www.vfb.no/filestore/Publikasjoner/Barn_i_Norge/BarniNorge2001.pdf

May, S. (2002). Where to from here? Charting a way forward for language and education policy in Aotearoa/New Zealand. *The TESOLANZ Journal, 10,* 22–35.

Mønsterplan for grunnskolen: M87 [Master plan for primary school]. (1987). Retrieved from http://www.nb.no/nbsok/nb/2aef891325a059851965d5b8ac193de5?lang=no#0

Namei, S. (2012). *Iranians in Sweden: A study of language maintenance and shift.* Uppsala, Norway: Institutionen för nordiska språk, Uppsala universitet [Institute for Norweigian language, Uppsala University].

Nasjonalt senter for flerkulturell opplaering [National Center for Multicultural Education]. (2014). Children in multilingual families: Informational booklet. Retrieved from http://morsmal.no/images/Barn%20i%20flerspraklige%20familier%20Engelsk.pdf

Norwegian Education Act. (1998). Retrieved from https://www.regjeringen.no/contentassets/b3b9e92cce6742c39581b661a019e504/education-act-norway-with-amendments-entered-2014-2.pdf

Norwegian Ministry for Education and Research. (2004). Equal education in practice! A strategy for increasing learning and better participation by language minorities in kindergartens, schools and education 2004–2009. Retrieved from https://www.regjeringen.no/globalassets/upload/kilde/ufd/pla/2004/0002/ddd/pdfv/212768-strategiplan_eng.pdf

Ozerk, K. Z. (1993). En verdig assimilasjon er nodvendig [A worthy assimilation is necessary]. *Norsk skoleblad* [*Norweigian School magazine*], *15*(93).

Reath Warren, Anne. (2013). Mother tongue tuition in Sweden: Curriculum analysis and classroom experience. *International Electronic Journal of Elementary Education*, *6*(1), 95–116.

Said, E. (1978). *Orientalism*. New York, NY: Routledge and Kegan Paul.

Skolöverstyrelsen [Board of Education]. (1969). *Läroplan för grundskolan* [*Curriculum for primary school*]. Stockholm, Sweden: Liber Ab.

Skolverket [Swedish National Agency for Education]. (2002). Flera språk—fler möjligheter—utveckling av modersmålsstödet och modersmålsundervisningen 2002 [More languages—more opportunities—the development of mother tongue assistance and mother tongue teaching in 2002]. Retrieved from http://www.skolverket.se/om-skolverket/publikationer/visa-enskild-publikation?_xurl_=http%3A%2F%2Fwww5.skolverket.se%2Fwtpub%2Fws%2Fskolbok%2Fwpubext%2Ftrycksak%2FBlob%2Fpdf1019.pdf%3Fk%3D1019#page=1&zoom=auto,-209,848

Skolverket [Swedish National Agency for Education]. (2004). Två språk eller flera? Råd till flerspråkiga familjer [Two languages or more? Advice for multilingual families]. Retrieved from http://www.skolverket.se/om-skolverket/publikationer/visa-enskild-publikation?_xurl_=http%3A%2F%2Fwww5.skolverket.se%2Fwtpub%2Fws%2Fskolbok%2Fwpubext%2Ftrycksak%2FBlob%2Fpdf1919.pdf%3Fk%3D1919

Skolverket [Swedish National Agency for Education]. (2008). With another mother tongue:Students in compulsory school and the organisation of teaching and learning. Retrieved from http://www.skolverket.se/om-skolverket/publikationer/visa-enskild-publikation?_xurl_=http%3A%2F%2Fwww5.skolverket.se%2Fwtpub%2Fws%2Fskolbok%2Fwpubext%2Ftrycksak%2FBlob%2Fpdf2181.pdf%3Fk%3D2181

Skolverket [Swedish National Agency for Education]. (2015). Skolor och elever i grundskolan läsaret 2014/15 [Schools and pupils in primary schools in the 2014/15 school year]. Retrieved from http://www.skolverket.se/statistik-och-utvardering/statistik-i-tabeller/grundskola/skolor-och-elever

Skolverket [Swedish National Agency for Education]. (n.d.). Tema Modersmål [Theme mother tongue]. Retrieved from http://modersmal.skolverket.se/sites/svenska/

Skutnabb-Kangas, T. (1981). *Bilingualism or not: The education of minorities* (Vol. 7). Briston, UK: Multilingual Matters.

Statistics Norway. (2015). Folkemengde og befolkningsendring, Q3 2015 [Population and population changes, third quarter, 2015]. Retrieved from http://www.ssb.no/befolkning/statistikker/folkendrkv/kvartal

Statistics Sweden. (2015). Population statistics: Number of persons 31 August 2015. Retrieved from http://www.scb.se/en_/Finding-statistics/Statistics-by-subject-area/Population/Population-composition/Population-statistics/

Store forskjeller i morsmålsopplæringen i Norge [Major differences in mother tongue education in Norway]. (2013, July 17). *Aftenposten*. Retrieved from http://www.aftenposten.no/nyheter/iriks/Store-forskjeller-i-morsmalsopplaringen-i-Norge-7254951.html

Sweden. (n.d.). Education in Sweden [Web page]. Retrieved from https://sweden.se/society/education-in-sweden/

Tema morsmal [Theme mother tongue] [Web site]. (n.d.). Retrieved from http://modersmal.skolverket.se/sites/svenska

23

"The Right to Mother-Tongue Education for Migrants in This City"

Factors Influencing the Institutionalization of a Two-Way Bilingual Immersion Program in Berlin

Gabriela Meier and Birgit Schumacher

1 Introduction

"If Berlin sees itself as an international metropolis, if Berlin is one of Germany's cities with the highest proportion of foreign migrants from East and West, and if Berlin wants to provide incentives for foreign investment, then the city will have to improve its education for bi- and multilingual children. Does Berlin want to become pedagogically provincial?"

(Document from 1986: 1IniEU [see Table 23.1], p. 1)

This quote is from a 1986 document indicating the beginning of a two-way immersion (TWI) program in Berlin, whose history we trace in this chapter. TWI unites learners of two different first languages in one classroom, and uses these two languages for instruction. Half (or some proportion) of the lessons are conducted in an official or dominant language, such as English in the U.S., and the remainder in another locally spoken language, such as Spanish in the U.S. context. Thus, schools include the home languages of children with a non-dominant language background, often referred to as heritage languages (HLs), making these languages a valuable asset and a useful skill in the school setting—rather than a deficit. At the same time, this model teaches children with a dominant-language background another locally relevant language, using the two languages as a resource for learning. Thus, it enables children to learn two languages from and with each other, and to develop bilingualism and biliteracy (e.g., Baker, 2006; Cummins, 1981).

While TWI programs have existed for several decades, the institutionalization of these programs, or their official acceptance as options within mainstream school systems such that they are viewed as "normal" and "expected to continue" (Ekholm & Trier, p. 13), has hardly been researched to date. Knowing more about the institutionalization process, however, is important as this is associated with program sustainability and resilience. We begin to fill this gap by examining documents relating to this process in the largest TWI program in Europe, the *Staatliche*

Europa-Schule Berlin (State Europe School Berlin; SESB), during the period from the 1986 to 2012. The document analysis is supplemented and interpreted with the help of informal conversations with two individuals involved in the founding of SESB. The first-named author conducted the document analysis and provided the theoretical framework, while the second-named author held informal conversations with the two SESB founders in her role as SESB primary coordinator and former SESB teacher.

The research question examined in this study is: What factors have facilitated or hindered the institutionalization of SESB? We see *institutionalization* as distinct from *implementation* which, in the case we discuss, takes the form of a trial or pilot project that is of a more experimental nature. In the context of SESB, we interpret *institutionalization*, initially at least, as occurring at the end of the trial period with the formal incorporation of the program into Berlin's state school system as part of the permanent options open to local pupils.

The next section will introduce TWI in general and in Berlin in particular, and look at the institutionalization process of TWI programs and school innovation more generally. The following section will then outline the research design and analytical process, before findings are reported. We conclude by suggesting factors that may indeed facilitate or hinder the institutionalization process.

2 Two-Way Immersion Education

TWI or dual-language programs that include HLs exist above all in the U.S., where they have been implemented from the 1960s onwards and currently include over 458 programs; these mostly combine English and Spanish, but also other locally spoken languages, such as Cantonese, French, German, Italian, Japanese, Korean, and Mandarin (Center for Applied Linguistics, 2015). They also exist in Israel/Palestine (Bekerman & Horenczyk, 2004) and Macedonia (Tankersley, 2001) as peace projects. In Europe, there has been interest in TWI programs since the 1960s, which accelerated in the 1990s. In Germany, TWI programs have been offered in many cities, combining at least 10 locally spoken languages with German (Meier, 2014; for an overview of TWI in Europe, see Meier, 2012a). Based on international literature, Meier (2014) summarized benefits (e.g., bilingualism and biliteracy in all learners, grade-level subject learning, social cohesion) and challenges (e.g., recruitment of balanced language groups, political acceptance, strict language separation) encountered by TWI programs.

SESB is a state-maintained program that is fully integrated into the Berlin public school system and runs from Year 1 to the end of upper secondary school or of high school, at the age of 19, with approximately 7,000 students enrolled at any one time. Although SESB is centrally coordinated, it does not hold TWI classes in one location, but rather exists as streams in several regular schools across the city. In this way, SESB has been able to respond to the different languages spoken in different neighborhoods by offering those languages at local schools. At the time of writing, there were 31 SESB locations providing TWI education, of which 17 were at primary and 14 at secondary level. For the most part, SESB follows the Berlin educational curriculum and pupils earn bilingual school leaving certificates upon graduation. Alongside German, SESB incorporates nine HLs as languages of instruction: English, French, Greek, Italian, Polish, Portuguese, Russian, Spanish, and Turkish.

3 The Institutionalization of TWI Programs

Looking at the literature on institutionalization of educational innovation, Ekholm and Trier (1987) describe initiation, implementation, and institutionalization as the main sub-processes that lead to new educational programs becoming permanent features in schooling settings. Turning to

TWI models in particular, factors that play a role in the initiation (or planning, which will be used interchangeably with "initiation"), and implementation phases of these programs can be summarized as follows (based on Howard & Christian, 2002; Howard, Sugarman, Christian, Lindholm-Leary, & Rogers, 2007; Meier, 2011; Meier, 2012b; Montone & Loeb, 2000; Williamson, 2012):

Planning a TWI Program

- Context of proposed program
- Support available from stakeholders
- Stakeholder attitudes
- Contact with existing programs
- Time allowed for planning
- Local demographics and staffing
- Legal frameworks

Implementing and Developing a TWI Program

- School model (e.g., proportion of time for each language) and type of instruction, including curriculum, instructional approach, location
- School leadership
- Development and sustainability through teacher cooperation, including regular meetings, ongoing reflection, and self-evaluation
- Cooperation between stakeholders

With regard to factors that can facilitate or hinder the next step, namely institutionalization of a program, Ekholm and Trier (1987) point to several dimensions that potentially play a role in the different phases of this process. Factors include those that are both independent of the project and provide a wider historical and social context in which the process is embedded, and factors that are dependent on the specific project and the organization in which it is being introduced. In terms of the independent factors, the following (pp. 14–15) will be considered in this chapter:

Unique history	Changes in the past, present, and anticipated in the future;
Cultural dimension	Tensions between the established culture and a new contra culture;
Social dimension	Participants and persons with decision-making power develop a sense of ownership of the innovation.

In terms of the dependent factors, the following (p. 17) will be considered:

Negotiation	Formal and informal between persons and groups in and outside school;
Resources	Allocation of time, material, and personnel;
Rise in legitimacy	Growing habit of acceptance and use;
Organizational conditions	Sustainability—no longer dependent on specific persons or temporary financial arrangements;
Diminishing visibility	The new "loses its provocative flavour" and is "simply there" (p. 17), i.e., normalization.

Taken together, the factors detailed above will inform the following discussion.

4 Document Analysis

We collected 34 documents that were associated with the history and institutionalization of SESB, dating from 1986 to 2012, and we had informal conversations with two members of the SESB planning group, both former employees of the Senate Department for Education, Science, and Research in Berlin (hereafter "Berlin Education Ministry"), Dr. Höttler and Ms. von Loh (hereafter "informants"). Dr. Höttler (then leader of the department for cross-school, international, and super-regional affairs) and Ms. von Loh (then leader of the working group for preschool and primary schools) were both involved in negotiations leading up to the formation of SESB.

This section introduces the groups that produced the documents we use, and explains the political system in Berlin. As can be seen from Table 23.1, each document was given a unique reference, composed of a number as well as abbreviations for phase and author as explained below. These references will be used in the following sections.

Table 23.1 Information about Documents Analyzed That Were Associated with the History and Institutionalization of State Europe School Berlin (1986 to 2012, in Chronological Order)

Unique doc. reference					
Doc. No.	*Sub-phase Id*	*Author Id*	*Year*	*Authors*	*Title and/or function of document*
1	Ini	EU	1986	Europa-Union Berlin	Minutes of Meeting: European School for Berlin
2		COM	1989	Berlin Parent Association	An international School for Berlin: Proposal
3		EU	1991	Europa-Union Berlin	Concept for European School in Berlin
4	Found	BEM	1992	BEM	Legal questions relating to SESB
5		BEM	1992	BEM	Structure and problems of comprehensive SESB streams
6	Trial	EU	1992	AG-ISFE	SESB school trial application.
7		GOV	1993	Local Berlin Government*	Communication from BEM to Local Berlin Government
8		POL	1993	Local mayor	Letter to Europa-Union Berlin
9		POL	1993	SPD local delegates	Letter to Europa-Union Berlin
10		EU	1993	Europa-Union Berlin	Recognition of vocational qualifications
11		EU	1993	Europa-Union Berlin	Forty years of multilingualim in Luxembourg schools. Experiences, problems, solutions.
12		BEM	1993	BEM	Comprehensive SESB secondary streams (transition model)
13		COM	1994	Parent representation	Letter to Berlin Education Minister Mr. J. Klemann
14		COM	1994	Planning committee	Proposal for SESB secondary streams
15		EU	1994	Europa-Union Berlin	Crucial prinicples for SESB secondary streams
16		EU	1996	Europa-Union Berlin	Letter to BEM

Unique doc. reference			Year	Authors	Title and/or function of document
Doc. No.	Sub-phase Id	Author Id			
17		POL	1996	Member of local Berlin government	Letter to Europa-Union Berlin
18		COM	1997	Principal of primary school and parents	Letter to BEM
19		COM	1997	Parent group	Initiative related to secondary streams submitted to BEM
20		BEM	1997	BEM	Invitation to 2nd planning committee meeting re SESB secondary streams
21		EU	1998	Europa-Union Berlin	Statement re secondary planning committee results to date
22		EU	2001	Europa-Union Berlin	SESB: Obsolete or future model?
23		EU	2002	Europa-Union Berlin	All-day concept in SESB primary streams
24		EU	2002	AG-ISFE	Continuation of SESB at secondary level. Conceptual proposal.
25		EU	2004	Europa-Union Berlin	Development of SESB secondary streams in German system
26		EU	2004	AG-ISFE	Outlining role of AG-ISFE
27		EDU	2006	SESB teacher	Speech on the occasion of the graduation of the first SESB cohort
28	Inst	GOV	2010	Local Berlin Parliament*	Communication: Evaluate SESB and end school trial!
29		GOV	2011	Berlin advisory committee for schools	Statement about SESB implementation order
30		GOV	2011	Coalition SPD/CDU*	Coalition agreement
31		BEM	2012	BEM*	Implementation order for SESB
32	Rem	EDU	2012	Academic*	Speech on the occasion of SESB's 20th anniversary
33		EU	2011	Europa-Union Berlin	History of SESB
34		EDU	2012	SESB teacher and member of AG-SESB**	Article about the history of SESB

Note: Abbreviations: Ini = initiation; Found = foundation; Trial = school trial; Inst = institutionalization; Rem = remembering; BEM = Berlin Education Ministry; EU = Europa-Union (not be confused with the political organization of a similar name, the European Union); GOV = Berlin government; COM = Support from the community; EDU = support from teachers/academics; POL = involvement of politicians.

Sources: * provided by Berlin Education Ministry; ** published article (Pěček, 2012); all other documents available from SESB (n.d.).

Some of the documents were available from the SESB online document archive offered by *Europa-Union Berlin* (2011a). This is a sub-organization of *Europa-Union Germany*, which describes itself as the largest non-governmental citizen initiative in Germany. A quote from their website might give the reader a flavor of their ideology, which underpins one of their missions, namely, to promote a European dimension in schools:

> "**Europe** [meaning the European Union] **is the best answer to the problems of our time!** We work towards a peaceful, free and federalist Europe, which is democratic, transparent and able to act. These have been our aims for over 60 years."
>
> *(Europa-Union, 2013, emphasis in original)*

Europa-Union Berlin incorporates an SESB working group, which existed under the name of *AG-ISFE* (Arbeitsgemeinschaft [Working group]—Internationale Schule für Europe) from 1986 to 2010, and renamed itself as *AG-SESB* (Arbeitsgemeinschaft—Staatliche Europa-Schule Berlin) in 2010. This working group has included members from all walks of life, including members of the local, national, and European Governments. Europa-Union Berlin and AG-ISFE/AG-SESB share a stake in SESB, and documents were issued under both names (abbreviation = EU). Further informal SESB campaign groups existed, such as parent organizations and members of the public that could be seen as community support/campaign groups (abbreviation = COM), a well as teachers and academics who also played a role as campaigners (abbreviation = EDU) or as analysts of SESB's history.

Some documents were provided directly by the Berlin Education Ministry (abbreviation = BEM). It may be worth noting that education policy in Germany is determined by the *Länder* (similar to the state-level in the U.S.). Each *Land* has its own local government and education ministry, which determines educational law, curriculum, and school organization. As the capital of Germany, the city of Berlin is the seat of the *Bundestag*, the national government, and as a *Land* in its own right, it has an *Abgeordnetenhaus*, a local parliament (hereafter "Berlin Government"; abbreviation = GOV). Educational policy is determined by the education ministry of each Land, guided by the political majority in the local government. Some documents were authored by individual local politicians (abbreviation = POL), who represent Berlin constituents. At a national level, there is a standing conference of education ministers—the *Kultusministerkonferenz* (KMK)—which coordinates national directives. For Berlin this means that, based on agreements drawn up by the KMK, the Berlin Government and the Berlin Education Ministry determine school policy for Berlin, including the language curriculum.

A thematic analysis, following Braun and Clarke (2006, p. 78), was adopted to analyze the documents with the help of Nvivo software, which entailed "finding, selecting, appraising (making sense of), and synthesizing data contained in documents" (Bowen, 2009, p. 28). This resulted in categories related to overarching themes, which are reported in the next section. While the original documents are in German, all quotes are given in their English translation. Information from the informal conversations complements the documentary analysis, as documents can only provide a limited understanding on their own.

Categorizing the documents

On their website, AG-SESB divides the history of SESB into four phases: the beginnings, the foundation phase, the school trial, and institutionalization (Europa-Union Berlin, 2011b). This loosely overlaps with Ekholm and Trier's (1987) sub-processes, namely initiation, implementation, and institutionalization, or Williamson's (2012) phases of institutionalization in Chile: prior to institutionalization (historical-social process), the implementation phase, consolidation phase, and expansion phase. Guided by the above divisions, we categorized the documents as belonging to four phases (Table 23.1): **Initiation** (1986–1991; abbreviation = Ini); **Implementation** (1991–2010; abbreviation = Imp), including the two sub-phases of foundation (1991–1992; abbreviation = Found) and school trial (1992–2010; abbreviation = Trial); **Institutionalization** (i.e., the end of the trial and the establishment of official status; 2010–2012); and **Remembering** (2006–2012; abbreviation = Rem). The last phase relates to speeches and reviews, celebrating milestones or charting the history of SESB.

5 Results

Four main themes were identified deductively (Table 23.2), guided by Ekholm and Trier (1987) and the other authors cited above; these serve as headings in the discussion that follows. Under each heading, a number of categories or sub-themes are listed, some of which were identified inductively, i.e., they were developed during the document analysis guided by data. In order to answer the research question, the focus centered on the institutionalization process and factors facilitating or hindering this.

Table 23.2 Coding Results from Thematic Analysis of the Documents

Themes and Categories	Total Sources
Institutionalization	
• *Negotiation*	20
• *Organizational conditions/sustainability*	4
• *Resources*	23
• *Legal frameworks*	21
Historic dimension	
• *Unique historic situation*	6
• *Necessity of change*	3
• *Opportunity for change**	4
• *Previous similar projects**	3
Cultural dimension	
• *Beliefs, ideologies*	12
• *Vision*	7
• *European orientation**	14
• *Migrant orientation**	13
• *Equality orientation**	7
Conflict dimension	
• *School model**	15
• *Political support**	11
• *Financing**	11
• *Institutionalization**	10

Note: * = inductively identified categories.

Institutionalization

Between 1992 and 2010, a trial of SESB programs was conducted in several Berlin schools. This started with three language combinations and incorporated nine by 1998. In 1992, before the school trial started, Berlin Education Ministry documents already envisaged that SESB would be institutionalized and become a "school with particular pedagogic character" (4FoundBEM, 5FoundBEM, p. 5) as part of the Berlin public school system. In 1999, AG-ISFE applied to have SESB become a formal part of this school system (33RemEU). However, it was not until 2012, 20 years after the start of the trial, that the Berlin Government recommended that the Berlin Education Ministry end the school trial following a final report issued in 2010 (28InstGOV). The report was based on a survey of parents and teachers conducted at the SESB trial locations (33RemEU). Finally, in March 2012, SESB was formally institutionalized through a document (31InstBEM) recognizing its official status.

Negotiation

A narrative emerged, based on the data that details the negotiation process leading from first initiatives in the early 1980s to the institutionalization of SESB in 2012. The phases that AG-SESB use (given in italics below) provide a loose framework for reporting the negotiation process in a chronological way.

The beginnings date from the early 1980s. The president of the Parent Association of Berlin school children and a member of the Berlin Government repeatedly urged the Berlin Education Ministry to take into consideration the increasing numbers of migrant families from the former Yugoslavia, Turkey, and Poland (34RemEDU). In 1986, representatives of several groups met (34RemEDU) and founded the working group AG-ISFE, (1IniEU, 34RemEDU) to move forward the ideas for a new school model. It is unclear to what extent the advocacy of AG-ISFE was responsible for policy makers becoming active, as our informants suggest that policy makers developed ideas alongside these more grassroots initiatives in 1987/1988. It is clear, however, that in 1990, Jürgen Klemann was the first Berlin Education Minister to provide political support for the SESB project (26TrialEU). Although the Berlin Education Ministry's planning group, set up in 1991, and AG-ISFE agreed that such a school model ought to have a supra-national orientation, the former preferred a European dimension while the latter suggested an International School of Europe to be established in Berlin (informants).

Moving to the *foundation phase,* SESB was founded after the reunification of East and West Germany in 1989 and during the re-instatement of Berlin as the German capital. Our informants point out that while the model had been approved by the Berlin Education Ministry at the beginning of the 1990s, around two years of preparation were necessary before SESB welcomed its first pupils in 1992. Following a conference between AG-ISFE, the Berlin Education Ministry, the European Center for the Development of Vocational Training,[1] the then Commission of the European Community (predecessor of the EU), and senior figures from the European School system[2] (26TrialEU), the Berlin Government approved the foundation of SESB as a school trial, starting with pre-school classes in 1992 (33RemEU, 34RemEDU). To begin with, this comprised three language combinations: German-English, German-French, and German-Russian. It was based on immediate needs stemming from the presence of the four Allied Forces (26TrialEU, 27RemEDU, 32RemEDU, 34RemEDU) at the end of the Cold War. Conversations with our informants indicate that this was considered a gesture of thanks to the four Allied Forces for their postwar presence. However, the inclusion of "Europa" in SESB's name was chosen at the time to emphasize a European dimension and, additionally, enhance fundability.

Documents from Europa-Union Berlin indicate that, in their approval, the Berlin Government mandated that the Berlin Education Ministry had to consult with AG-ISFE in the development of this new school model (33RemEU), thus continuing a culture of negotiation between interest groups and government authorities, a pattern that had been present from early on. Indeed, according to our informants, a close collaboration between the Berlin Education Ministry and AG-ISFE, and other stakeholders, was crucial at the foundation stage. The informants further argue that SESB came about as a product of tensions between pedagogic requirements, visions of a sustainable future, as well as legal and political feasibility.

As mentioned above, the *institutionalization phase* lasted from 2010 to 2012, but included repeated earlier requests for making SESB a formal part of the Berlin school system (e.g., 4FoundBEM, 18TrialCOM, 19TrialCOM, 21TrialEU). Soon after 1992, expansion of the model to include secondary education (19TrialCOM) was also requested. These two requests, however, remained without response from the authorities for some time. In 2002, AG-ISFE presented a conceptual proposal to develop the legal foundation for the upper-secondary streams (25TrialEU) for the attention of the Berlin Education Ministry, in order to formally integrate secondary education into SESB. This was part of the negotiations that eventually enabled the first SESB cohorts to start secondary school in 1999/2000, but institutionalization still remained off the agenda at that time.

In 2010, there was a renewed push towards institutionalization, triggered by the survey commissioned by the Berlin Education Ministry, which urged both formal incorporation into Berlin's school systems and a scientific evaluation of the trial program (28InstGOV). In 2011, there was an additional statement by an educational advisory committee, established by the Berlin Education Ministry in 1994,[3] (29InstGov) which recommended the transition from school trial to permanent fixture in the Berlin school system. Thus, the documents indicate that the institutionalization process, was a lengthy partly bottom-up process initiated from within the community, and negotiated between different stakeholders. This took 20 years from implementation of the school trial to its formal institutionalization in March 2012 (31InstBEM).

The above narrative shows that a lengthy negotiation process preceded the official normalization or institutionalization of SESB. It indicates that Europa-Union Berlin and AG-SESB, and a certain amount of tenacity on their part, played an important facilitating role throughout this process. The working group AG-SESB still exists today (34RemEDU), and still takes a close interest in the running of SESB in 2016. This narrative shows that various groups were active in the negotiation and collaboration that brought about and led to the institutionalization of SESB.

Organizational Conditions and Sustainability

By 2004/2006, SESB was seen as a success (26TrialEU, 27RemEDU) and a model to be adopted beyond Berlin (27RemEDU). Based on the experience of the second author, we must not forget that this success was above all due to work by teachers and learners who trialed and developed the SESB model in practice, as well as the trust parents placed in the model. In 2011, the educational advisory committee (29InstGOV) praised the cooperation between the Berlin Education Ministry and AG-SESB as a valuable organizational instrument. Furthermore, it was argued in 2004 that institutionalization would not make AG-SESB obsolete (27RemEDU), since the cooperation above all between Governmental entities (GOV), Ministerial personnel (BEM), politicians (POL), AG-SESB (EU), the schools (EDU) and community stakeholders (COM), all working together for the future of Berlin's children, was seen as an indicator of its future sustainability. Looking to the future, cooperation is deemed to be of continued importance beyond the initial institutionalization process or official recognition (28InstGOV, 27RemEDU).

The discussion above has indicated that a crucial factor related to the success of SESB in the past, and one that is predicted to continue to be so in the future, is good cooperation between stakeholder groups as described above. Europa-Union Berlin and AG-SESB seemed to act as a pivotal body facilitating this cooperation.

Resources

The category of *resources* (see Table 23.2) consists of the sub-categories *school materials*, *premises*, and *teachers*. Of these, the category related to teachers seemed to be most relevant to the institutionalization process and will be discussed in this section. Another category of resource, namely financial resources, is discussed under Conflict Dimension below.

In 2009/2010, 300 foreign teachers were working in SESB; some of them were paid by their respective embassies (Greece, Portugal, Italy) during the school trial. The involvement of the embassies in teacher recruitment, remuneration, and teacher development during the trial phase was a further facilitating factor. Nevertheless, staff turnover among non-German teachers was reported to be high (28InstGOV), a finding explained to some extent by the fact that these teachers were paid less than their German colleagues in SESB, on the basis that they had no German teacher qualification (15TrialEU, 22TrialEU, 23TrialEU). This issue will be further discussed in the next section.

Legal Frameworks

Initially, TWI instruction was possible based on existing national curricula that provided for the introduction of a first foreign language in Year 1 and a second in Year 5 (7TrialGOV). Following this schedule, SESB started with two languages of instruction per class in Year 1, and then introduced English or French in Year 5, in compliance with existing public law (2IniCOM) and directives for primary schools (7TrialGOV). However, in other areas it was repeatedly pointed out that SESB needed *new legal structures* as it worked toward institutionalization (3IniEU, 7TrialGOV, 18TrialCOM, 22TrialEU), relating to: catchment areas (7TrialGOV), teacher recruitment and remuneration (10TrialEU, 18TrialCOM, 22TrialEU), as well as curricula development (28InstGOV). The documents suggest that new legal provisions had been in preparation from 2001 (22TrialEU), and shortly following its institutionalization, the SESB curricula had to be adapted according to a new framework curricula for Berlin in 2012/2013.

The area that seemed to cause most problems was the treatment of foreign teachers. Although foreign teachers were seen "to be an indispensable pre-requisite" for SESB (10TrialEU, p. 1), new legal regulations were required to employ them, especially those from non-EU countries such as Russia and Turkey (22TrialEU). Therefore a revision of employment criteria was requested (22TrialEU) as well as the creation of appropriate conversion courses to avoid a requirement for full German teacher qualifications (10TrialEU). This has since been addressed in two ways: In 1995/1996 a simplified recruitment procedure for newly qualified teachers was implemented for SESB (23TrialEU, 28InstGOV) and, furthermore, the legal basis for remunerating foreign SESB teachers was changed in 2008, in line with EU directives, enabling equal pay with their German colleagues (28InstGOV). Another notable development was that increasingly German-educated teachers with a migrant background (rather than foreign-educated teachers) took up positions in SESB (28InstGOV), particularly in the German-Turkish SESB location.

The documents suggest that the existing legal situation was a facilitating factor in the implementation phase. However, in order to enable SESB to function effectively and sustainably, the legal basis needed adapting, which required authorities to take note and work out solutions.

Institutionalization may not have been a direct consequence of solving legal issues surrounding SESB, but ultimately it may have facilitated the process, and it was a sign of growing political support. The legal recognition of SESB in 2012, based on paragraph 18 of Berlin School Law (31InstBEM), we have used as a marker of the moment of formal institutionalization.

Historic Dimension

The *unique historic situation* of Berlin was a theme that included the necessity for change (e.g., 2IniCOM), opportunities for change (e.g. 1IniEU), and the histories of previous similar projects (e.g., 3IniEU), which show that there were a number of historic circumstances unique to Berlin that initially prohibited the implementation of SESB, for instance Berlin's, and Germany as a whole's, division into East and West, and then later enabled its formation, for instance: the 750-year celebration of the founding of Berlin as a city in 1987, its designation as the European City of Culture in 1988, the reunification of Germany—and Berlin as a city—in 1989, and closer integration of Europe through the Maastricht Treaty, establishing the European Union in 1992.

The *necessity of change* was argued from various related perspectives. A Europa-Union Berlin initiative in 1986 (1IniEU) and a parent initiative in 1989 (2IniCOM) suggested that there was an increasing number of international organizations in Berlin (1IniEU, 2IniCOM), which meant that there was a "steadily increasing number of bilingual families [which] urgently necessitates a school that enables bilingual education" (2IniCOM, p. 2). The AG-SESB (26TiralEU) suggested that after several rejections, "SESB was approved by the Berlin Government due to a historic necessity: It was seen as an answer to the historic situation of Berlin" (26TrialEU, p. 1).

A speech on the occasion of the 20th anniversary of SESB in 2012 given by an academic (32RemEDU) emphasized the great political changes in Berlin in the 1980s and early 1990s that necessitated a new school model for Berlin, and the increasing need to promote an international and European awareness through education. Informants argue that the Berlin Education Ministry had been aware since the early 1980s that new answers were required in relation to these historic changes in Berlin.

SESB was founded at a historically unique juncture in Berlin's history, bringing with it *opportunities for change*. It was the unification of the country in 1989 and the establishment of the EU in 1992 that seemed to have brought about the impetus to begin the trial program, after more than a decade of campaigning. In 1989, parents (2IniCOM) anticipated the EU's trade integration, and according to the anniversary speech (32RemEDU), it was the reunification in 1989 that changed the "framework conditions for the initiative" (33RemEU, website) to trial SESB. There is also the argument that it was the re-instatement of Berlin as the German capital (moving from its provisional postwar location in Bonn), and the new coalition government that was formed in 1990, that enabled political support for the project (32RemEDU, 34RemEDU). The latter will be discussed separately below.

Another factor that may have eased political change is that Berlin has a long history of *previous similar projects*. Berlin has had various models of bilingual education for migrant families since the seventeenth century. Based on the 1986 document 1IniEU, a German-French school was founded in 1689 (sic!) for the children of protestant French families who fled persecution in France. Most of these previous initiatives included French and, in some cases, also English. An example of the latter is the J.F. Kennedy primary and secondary school, on which SESB was ultimately modeled (34RemEDU). However, SESB expanded this to include a wider range of HLs, including languages that, unlike French and English, are not traditionally used as languages of instruction in Germany.

In this section, the findings suggest that dramatic historical developments in Berlin acted as both detrimental and facilitating factors, and that the resident multilingual population, and the need for further migrant workers for international organizations and industry, may also have played a role. This dual local and international outlook, especially in view of the EU, seems to have been a facilitating factor in the case of Berlin, which leads to the next theme.

Cultural Dimension

Beliefs and ideologies underpin the values that motivated the campaign for bilingual education and all phases of the institutionalization process (Ekholm & Trier, 1987). Based on informal conversations, the ideas underlying the foundation of SESB initially incorporated an international orientation. As the latter did not seem to spark enough support, the idea of a European orientation eventually took its place.

Interestingly, both the international and the European orientations were present in the 1986 document 1IniEU. This document refers to UNESCO's 1974 resolution which emphasizes international understanding, cooperation, and world peace in view of human rights and basic freedoms as educational aims. In addition, the document includes a quote from a 1978 KMK resolution recommending a European dimension as an important pedagogic focus (1IniEU, 3IniEU). This KMK resolution emphasized and strengthened the European orientation, and focused attention not only on the relationship between national, societal, and individual experiences, but also on the European community of member states, with a view to reducing prejudice and respecting diversity. Supporting this view, a report on a visit to Luxembourg's multilingual schools (11TrialEU) argues that languages have indeed a role to play in respecting diversity, and that ways have to be found to understand languages as a means of enabling encounters between diverse communities. This is in line with Europa-Union's wider ideology, as shown by the quote above (in *Document analysis*).

These influences supported and shaped the concept behind SESB, whose motto is "learning together, from one another, for one another"[4] (10TrialEU, p. 1). *The vision* for SESB was thus above all to enable intercultural encounters (5FoundBEM, 6TrialEU, 23TrialEU, 25TrialEU) and tolerance (5FoundBEM, 33RemEU), and to view the HL as an enrichment for migrant children and their German peers (34RemEDU), bringing social, economic, and cultural benefits (34RemEDU).

Eventually, SESB was given, as the name suggests, a *European orientation* or dimension (4FoundBEM, 7TrialGOV, 10TrialEU, 32RemEDU). This encompasses not only instrumental perspectives such as geographic mobility and language skills that make learners "fit for Europe" (28InstGOV, p. 24), but also affective perspectives such as the development of European identity (19TrialCOM, 26TrialEU, 28InstGOV, 31InstGOV) and awareness (28InstGOV, 32RemEDU). As shown above, the European orientation has shaped SESB since the early stages, based on the aims and ideology of Europa-Union and the KMK.

As regards the *migrant orientation,* the documents refer to the international population in Berlin, namely migrants from former Yugoslavia, Turkey, and Poland (34RemEDU), and to "the implementation of the right to mother tongue education for migrants in this city" (17TrialPOL, p. 1), which inspired the title of this chapter. The integration of migrants was indeed a motivational factor for the SESB campaign (2InstCOM, 22TrialEU, 29InstGOV, 34RemEDU). This relates to the vision of an inclusive, cosmopolitan Berlin, as discussed above. Our informal conversations indicate that the initial idea was to unite all language combinations in one school. This, however, was rejected and separate SESB streams were established in different schools in neighborhoods where the respective languages were spoken by resident families (34RemEDU), thus SESB was conceived as a project for the whole city.

The analysis also identified an *equality orientation*, which refers to the equality between partner languages and their speakers in schools (23TrialEU, 28InstGOV, 32RemEDU, 34RemEDU). Thus, "German and the relevant non-German partner language have equal status as languages of instruction" (28instGOV, p. 6), and "the schools should open their doors to children who live in Berlin, foreigners and Germans" (34RemEDU, p. 184). Additionally, SESB has aimed to recruit equal numbers from each language group (e.g., 24TrialEU, 29InstGOV, 32RemEDU). Equality also concerns working conditions for teachers (22TrialEU, 24TrialEU), as discussed above.

In this section, the argument starts to develop that the vision for SESB was three-fold, which may have been a facilitating factor: 1) The values which underlie the conception and development of SESB relate to human rights, peace, respect for diversity, equality, and intercultural understanding through learning languages from, for, and with one another, and to support the European dimension in the classroom; 2) a vision to meet the needs and rights of children with a migrant background resident in Berlin; and 3) SESB was to support international links with European member states.

Conflict Dimension

Perhaps not surprisingly, there were several references to what can be interpreted as sources of political conflict in the journey from planning to institutionalization. These were related to the school model (content), political support, financing, and institutionalization itself.

There were two main conflicts relating to the *school model* in the earlier stages. One of these was the question as to whether SESB should be for linguistically more able students or provide inclusive education of a comprehensive nature (19TrialCOM, 21TrialEU, 26TrialEU). In 2007, Meier (2010) identified some uncertainty among SESB teachers in this respect. Another important conflict that was identified related to secondary education. While the German education system used to stream learners in secondary education according to their ability into more vocational (Hauptschule und Realschule) and more academic streams (Gymnasium), parents, schools, and AG-ISFE argued for a comprehensive secondary model (18TrialCOM, 24TrialEU, 26TrialEU, 33RemEU), as streaming would reduce the secondary cohorts to smaller and therefore unviable classes. SESB secondary streams now exist either as Gymnasia (academic streams) or as integrated comprehensive secondary streams.

A second conflict related to *political support and finances*, which affected the institutionalization phase. A document from 1996 shows that politicians had changed their mind (17TrialPOL) from being skeptical to becoming supportive of SESB during the implementation phase. This skepticism may have been related to a perceived lack of administrative planning (16TrialEU, 21TrialEU), political decision making (16TrialEU), and financing (2IniCOM, 19TrialCOM, 21TrialEU, 22TrialEU, 27RemEDU). Our informal conversations, however, point to other possible reasons for the change of mind, which was apparently related to the fact that the SESB trial had been implemented during a time when the Christian Democratic Union (CDU) dominated the Berlin Government (1990–2001), and indeed several members of AG-ISFE belonged to CDU at the time (informants). This means that when the Social Democratic Party (SPD[5]) gained a majority in 2001, the government was reluctant to support a CDU-approved initiative.

The idea of *institutionalization* itself also caused conflict in the form of two related issues: independent evaluation and ending the school trial. SESB campaign groups pointed out during the trial that SESB needed a systematic and scientific evaluation (21TrialEU, 25TrialEU, 27RemEDU). However, apart from individual research projects covering one or several SESB locations (see Meier, 2010, for a summary), there had not been any systematic scientific evaluation before the Berlin Education Ministry initiated a study in 2014 (Baumert, Hohenstein,

Fleckenstein, & Möller, in press). In terms of ending the school trial and thus formally institutionalizing SESB, this had been anticipated since 1992 (4FoundBEM, 5FoundBEM), and openly requested from 1997 by parents (18TrialCOM) and from 1998 by the Europa-Union (21TrialEU, 33RemEU). The second author reminds us that it is a condition for all school trials in Berlin to be evaluated before they can be institutionalized as a school with a particular pedagogic character. She argues that in the case of SESB, the reason this was done only after institutionalization was partly due to the financial situation in Berlin.

In this section, factors that hindered institutionalization were identified. The documents suggest that political skepticism meant that the call for institutionalization remained off the agenda. The skepticism seemed to have started to recede after 2001, but it was not until 2010 that it seemed to have finally been overcome, when the Berlin Education Ministry initiated the final phase of the institutionalization process. Furthermore, government funding was made available in 2014 for an independent scientific evaluation.

Rise in Legitimacy

While the documents did not yield much information in relation to legitimizing SESB (no such theme was identified), the informal conversations reminded us that it is often the undocumented work by the parents, teachers, and learners who prove through their daily engagement that the SESB concept works. On the basis of this we argue that day-to-day practice in school was necessary to legitimize the model through ongoing development, innovation, and above all results. The second author's personal experience as SESB primary coordinator indicates that parents, teachers, and learners are quite capable of moving the program forward. However, it was the survey (28InstGOV) that formally confirmed the success of the model and thus legitimized it. Interestingly, SESB caters to higher and lower status languages and their communities, with the result that stakeholders from different socioeconomic backgrounds and varied social status work together. Thus, *integrating both higher and lower status languages* may well be another legitimizing factor often absent in TWI models elsewhere. This integration may make TWI more acceptable to the wider society. However, questions such as how teachers of different languages work together in SESB, and to what extent the different languages are accepted, would be worthy of further research.

6 Important Factors in the SESB Institutionalization Process

Based on 34 documents and conversations with founder members, we traced approximately 30 years of efforts by various bodies and individuals to institutionalize SESB in Berlin. In line with previous research, the SESB case study confirms that there are three main phases—initiation, implementation, and institutionalization—that constitute the institutionalization process, similar to those suggested by Ekholm and Trier (1987) and Williamson (2012). In this chapter, the main focus was the third phase, which in Berlin was clearly marked by ending the school trial that started in 1992 and making it a permanent feature of Berlin state education in 2012.

With a view to answering the research question, the themes discussed in the *Results* section provide a framework to help understand the institutionalization process, but this does not enable us to rank the factors in any way. Indeed, a document analysis alone, which draws heavily on one source (Europa-Union Berlin), can only make visible a part of the process. We complemented this with informal conversations with two of the founder members, whose recollection and interpretation of events enhanced and expanded our understanding of the findings. While the focus in this chapter is on the institutionalization of a TWI model, which in the case of SESB only came at the end of a lengthy process (Ekholm & Trier, 1987), one of our main contributions is to make visible possible factors that facilitate or hinder this process throughout, or in one or two of the three phases.

Similar to other contexts, *support* (Howard & Christian, 2002; Howard et al., 2007) and the backing of power holders (Ekholm & Trier, 1987) was important in SESB, but not only in one phase, as is suggested by previous literature, but in all three phases. In Berlin we have seen that *political support* seemed to first hinder and then facilitate implementation as well as institutionalization. The documents suggest that the Berlin Education Ministry at different times provided or withdrew support, eventually supporting the end of the school trial. This illustrates the fickle nature of politics and the effect that political support, or lack thereof, can have on school projects which are by nature long-term. Politics are also related to the *legal framework*, which first facilitated implementation and then needed adjustment to facilitate the last step of formal institutionalization. The act of formal institutionalization, establishing stable internal organizational structures (Ekholm & Trier, 1987), might make programs more resilient to political changes. This confirms the importance of the legal framework as a facilitating factor in planning (Howard et al., 2007) and institutionalization (Williamson, 2012). Indeed, it is assumed that once a suitable legal framework is established, political changes have less impact on an organization.

In the case of SESB, *support* was provided throughout by a multi-stakeholder working group, namely Europa-Union Berlin/AG-SESB, which seems to have played a pivotal role in negotiating institutionalization throughout. Based on the documents, *cooperation* between stakeholder groups is deemed an important facilitating factor in all phases, adding to previous literature (Howard & Christian, 2002; Howard et al., 2007; Meier, 2012b) that looked at implementation only. Another important factor in facilitating or hindering institutionalization seemed to be the (lack of) *formal recognition* of the achievements realized by the teachers and learners, who proved that SESB works through their continued commitment to and development of the program. From this follows that supporting or preventing an *evaluation of a school model* may well be an important facilitating or hindering factor, as this provides or withholds evidence regarding to what extent the program may be successful and fully developed, which according to Ekholm and Trier (1987) is an indicator of institutionalization. Based on this, the results of the study conducted by Baumert et al. (in press) are anticipated with much interest. It is not surprising that, in line with Ekholm and Trier's (1987) theory, a series of *conflicts* arose that needed to be solved to facilitate institutionalization, such as evaluation and adjusting the legal framework.

Other findings from this study that may be of interest to individuals or groups working in, or planning, TWI programs, namely those that are of an ideological/cultural or historical nature not specifically associated with institutionalization. Clearly, the historic/political situation of Berlin in the late 1980s and early 1990s cannot be compared with other contexts. However, it shows that certain sociopolitical developments may be more facilitative than others. In Berlin, a dual focus was present. First, the recognition of changes in local demographics and needs (linguistic, economic, equality, and integration) and, second, the desire or need to integrate Germany into a wider supra-national network comprised by the EU. Furthermore, while there was some political skepticism, there was no evidence of open societal or political opposition to the program, as has been the case in some states in the U.S. This raises the question of whether a TWI model that includes (or starts with) high-status HLs (e.g., English, French), such as was the case with SESB, strengthens and legitimizes the inclusion of other languages (e.g., Polish, Turkish) that are not normally considered languages of instruction in in the country. The inclusion of several languages also means that stakeholders from different language groups work together with the aim of providing education for many language communities.

From a language education perspective, we argue that SESB does indeed offer an alternative way of learning and teaching languages, in line with the founders' initial ideas. In fact it does more than that, as it meets the linguistic needs of resident families of German *and* heritage backgrounds, making all learners trilingual (two partner languages plus English or French), and enables integration within the classroom as well as across linguistic groups in the wider framework of SESB. Furthermore, the high linguistic achievements at SESB (see Fäcke, 2007; Reich & Roth, 2002) have resulted in universities in a number of countries admitting SESB graduates without further language tests, thus enabling student mobility beyond SESB (see Meier, 2009).

In conclusion, we argue that the factors that ultimately facilitated the final phase of institutionalization of SESB included support of the TWI concept through school evaluation, support by power holders and campaign groups, as well as cooperation between stakeholders. Factors that hindered this process were largely the absence of one or more of these factors. Additional findings showed that the situation in Berlin is clearly unique, but that it may be an advantage to develop a TWI concept that responds to local needs and fosters supra-national links at the same time. Furthermore, the initial inclusion of high-status HLs may increase the acceptability and legitimization of further HLs as languages of instruction and as valuable resources for all learners in mainstream schools.

7 Acknowledgments

We would like to thank Dr. Rainer Höttler and Ms. Dagmar von Loh for informally sharing their memories with us, and for their insightful feedback on early drafts of this chapter. Additionally, we are grateful to Beate Schöneburg (Berlin Education Ministry) and AG-SESB for making available relevant documents. Thanks also go to Claire Hitchins Chik and Ralph Openshaw whose constructive feedback helped finalize this chapter.

Notes

1 CEDEFOP: Centre européen pour le développement de la formation professionnelle
2 This is a school model established specifically for expatriate workers of the EU.
3 This committee was called Landesschulbeirat.
4 The original German motto is: Miteinander—voneinander—füreinander lernen!
5 Sozialdemokratische Partei Deutschlands

References

Baker, C. (2006). *Foundations of bilingual education and bilingualism* (4th ed.). Clevedon, UK: Multilingual Matters.

Baumert, J., Hohenstein, F., Fleckenstein, J., & Möller J. (Eds.). (in press). *Die EUROPA-Studie—Eine Evaluation der Staatlichen Europa-Schule Berlin [The EUROPA study—an evaluation of the Staatliche Europa-Schule Berlin]*. Münster, Germany: Waxmann.

Bekerman, Z., & Horenczyk, G. (2004). Arab-Jewish bilingual coeducation in Israel: A long-term approach to intergroup conflict resolution. *Journal of Social Issues, 60*(2), 389–404.

Bowen, G. A. (2009). Document analysis as a qualitative research method. *Qualitative Research Journal, 9*(2), 27–40.

Braun, V., & Clarke, V. (2006). Using thematic analysis in psychology. *Qualitative Research in Psychology, 3*(2), 77–101.

Center for Applied Linguistics. (2015). Directory of two-way bilingual immersion programs in the U.S. Retrieved from http://www2.cal.org/jsp/TWI/SchoolListings.jsp

Cummins, J. (1981). The role of primary language development in promoting educational success for language minority students. In California State Department of Education (Ed.), *Schooling and language minority students: A theoretical framework* (pp. 3–50). Los Angeles, CA: National Dissemination and Assessment Center.

Ekholm, M., & Trier, U. P. (1987). The concept of institutionalization: Some remarks. In M. B. Miles, M. Ekholm, & R. Vandenberghe (Eds.), *Lasting school improvement: Exploring the process of institutionalization* (pp. 13–21). Leuven, Belgium: Acco.

Europa-Union. (2013). Europa-Union Deutschland [Web site]. Retrieved from http://www.europa-union.de/

Europa-Union Berlin. (2011a). Archiv zur SESB [SESB archive]. Retrieved from http://www.europa-union-berlin.de/europa-schule/archiv/

Europa-Union Berlin. (2011b). Geschichte der SESB [History of SESB]. Retrieved from http://www.europa-union-berlin.de/europa-schule/geschichte/

Fäcke, C. (2007). Sprachliche Bildung und zweisprachige Erziehung. Überlegungen zum Partnersprachen-modell der Staatlichen Europa-Schule Berlin (SESB) [Thoughts on the partner-language model in SESB]. In D. Elsner, L. Küster, & B. Viebrock (Eds.), *Fremdsprachenkompetenzen für ein wachsendes Europa: Das Leitziel Multiliteralität* (Vol. 31, pp. 241–256). Frankfurt: KFU, Peter Lang.

Howard, E. R., & Christian, D. (2002). Two-way immersion 101: Designing and implementing a two-way immersion education program at the elementary level (Educational Practice Report 9) Retrieved March 4, 2009, from https://escholarship.org/uc/item/7cm4v2f5

Howard, E. R., Sugarman, J., Christian, D., Lindholm-Leary, K. J., & Rogers, D. (2007). *Guiding principles for dual language education.* Washington, DC: Center for Applied Linguistics.

Meier, G. (2009). Can two-way immersion education support the EU aims of multilingualism, social cohesion and student/worker mobility? *European Journal for Language Policy, 1*(2), 145–164.

Meier, G. (2010). *Social and intercultural benefits of bilingual education: A peace-linguistic evaluation of Staatliche Europa-Schule Berlin (SESB)* (Vol. 12). Frankfurt, Germany: Peter Lang.

Meier, G. (2011). Wandsworth Bilingual Education Conference March 19, 2011: Report. Retrieved August 1, 2013, from http://elac.ex.ac.uk:8080/bien_elgg/pg/file/read/31/wandsworth-bilingual-education-conference-1932012-report

Meier, G. (Ed.). (2012a). *Éducation bilingue en Europe et ailleurs: statu quo et itinéraires de recherche possibles [Bilingual education in Europe and beyond: Status quo and possible research agenda]* (Vol. 7). Sylvains les Moulins, France: Gerflint.

Meier, G. (2012b). Enseignement bilingue et amélioration scolaires: les conclusions de l'expérience Wix Primary School / École de Wix à Londres [The role of bilingual education in school improvement: Findings from Wix Primary School/École de Wix]. (Translated into French by Laurent Battut). *Synergies Europe, 7,* 53–76.

Meier, G. (2014). Multilingualism and social cohesion: Two-way immersion education meets diverse needs. In J. Conteh & G. Meier (Eds.), *The multilingual turn in languages education: Opportunities and challenges* (pp. 179–208). Bristol, UK: Multilingual Matters.

Montone, C. L., & Loeb, M. I. (2000). Implementing two-way immersion programs in secondary schools. Retrieved from http://www.carla.umn.edu/immersion/acie/vol6/bridge-6(3).pdf

Pěček, C. (2012). L'École Publique Européenne de Berlin (EPEB)—Staatliche Europa-Schule Berlin (SESB). *Synergies Europe, 7,* 183–185.

Reich, H. H., & Roth, H.-J. (2002). *Spracherwerb zweisprachig aufwachsender Kinder und Jugendlicher: Ein Überblick über den Stand der nationalen und internationalen Forschung [Language acquisition of children growing up bilingually: An overview of national and international research].* Hamburg, Germany: Local Government Authority for Education and Sport.

SESB. (n.d.). InfoPortal SESB. Materialien der AG-ISFE/AG-SESB zur SESB [Materials about SESB made available by AG-ISFE/AG-SESB]. Retrieved from http://www.sesb.de/ueberuns/materialiensesb/materialiensesb.html

Tankersley, D. (2001). Bombs or bilingual programmes? Dual language immersion, transformative education and community building in Macedonia. *International Journal for Bilingual Education and Bilingualism, 4*(2), 107–124.

Williamson, G. (2012). Institucionalización de la educación intercultural bilingüe en Chile. Notas y observaciones críticas [Instutionalization of intercultural and bilingual education in Chile: Critical notes and observations]. *Perfiles educativos, 34*(138), 126–147.

343

Part VI

Heritage/Community Languages in Higher Education

24

The State of Institutionalization of Heritage Languages in Postsecondary Language Departments in the United States

Maria M. Carreira

1 Introduction

This chapter examines the institutionalization of heritage language (HL) teaching in postsecondary institutions in the U.S., including what are known as "four-year colleges and universities," as well as two-year colleges (typically called community or junior colleges).[1] In keeping with the thrust of this volume, this chapter takes as its point of departure Ekholm and Trier's (1987) definition of institutionalization as "an assimilation of change elements into a structured organization, modifying the organization in a stable manner" (p. 13). The "change element" (or innovation), to be examined here is HL-specific instruction or pedagogy, which, broadly speaking, is an approach to language teaching premised on the idea that heritage language learners' (HLLs) linguistic and socio-affective needs are different from those of second language learners (L2Ls) and warrant specialized instructional attention. Though typically associated with HL courses, HL-specific instruction can also be implemented in other instructional contexts, such as mixed classes, i.e., classes with HLLs and L2Ls, independent studies, etc. The primary "structured organization" to be examined here are postsecondary foreign-language programs or departments that teach HLLs.

Informing this discussion is a survey of foreign language programs conducted by the National Heritage Language Resource Center (NHLRC) at UCLA and analyzed by Carreira (2014). Survey findings provide important insights into the state of institutionalization of HL teaching. Before delving into these issues, a brief review of the literature on HL teaching in higher education is in order.

2 Overview of the Research on Institutional Practices

Relative to other strands of research in HL teaching, institutional practices have received modest attention. At the postsecondary level in particular, Spanish is the sole language with a body of research on this topic. Demographics and history have much to do with this. With over 50 million speakers, Spanish is the most widely spoken HL language in the U.S. (Ennis, Ríos-Vargas, & Albert, 2011) and the most widely taught foreign language at all levels of education (American Council on the Teaching of Foreign Languages [ACTFL], 2007; Goldberg, Looney, & Lusin,

2015). Spanish also has the historical distinction of being the maiden language in HL teaching and research in the US, with a record spanning several decades (Carreira, 2012). A review of this record as it pertains to institutional practices is a good starting point for understanding key factors in institutionalization that apply to the field of HL teaching at large.

Wherritt and Cleary's (1990) nationwide survey of college-level Spanish HL programs sought information about courses and assessment, particularly placement. Of the 126 institutions that responded to the survey, 18% offered specialized instruction for HL speakers. Ingold, Rivers, Tesser, and Ashby (2002) obtained strikingly similar results in their nationwide survey: 17.8% of the 146 Spanish programs that participated in the survey offered separate courses for HLLs. This study also pinpointed a number of challenges surrounding HL teaching. Among these, programs with HL courses cited a lack of student interest and inadequate course-placement procedures, while programs with no such courses identified low enrollments, insufficient funding, inadequate training for instructors, and lack of administrative and faculty support as serious impediments to offering such courses.

Two regional studies shed light on the relationship between demographics and the availability of HL courses. Focusing on California, the state with largest population of Latinos in the country (Ennis et al., 2011), Valdés, Fishman, Chávez, and Pérez (2006) found strikingly higher rates of HL course availability in postsecondary programs (62%), pointing to the importance of demographics. Likewise, Beaudrie's (2011) comprehensive study of universities in the Southwest—the region with the largest concentration of Latinos—found higher rates than reported in national surveys, with 38% of institutions offering HL courses. This study cautions however, that the mere existence of more HL classes does not necessarily translate into well-crafted pedagogical experiences that are likely to lead to successful learning on the part of HLLs.

In terms of impediments to institutionalization, Valdés et al. (2006) found room for improvement in the areas of placement, teacher education, and curriculum design. Beaudrie (2011) documents similar deficiencies, as well as others. In particular, she found that terms such as *beginning, intermediate,* and *advanced* were used differently from one program to another, making articulation between programs and placement difficult. Also, she found that HL curricula were targeted largely at students around the midpoint of the bilingual continuum, to the neglect of those at the two ends of this continuum. Beaudrie (2012a) reports on a comprehensive nationwide survey of Spanish programs in four-year universities with a Latino student population of 5% or higher. Of 422 such institutions, 40% (169) were found to offer specialized Spanish HL courses. For the most part, such programs offer one or two HL courses. As was the case with earlier studies, programs without an HL track cited low student numbers, limited resources, and lack of training for faculty as primary obstacles. Comparing the finding of 40% availability of HL courses to those of earlier studies, Beaudrie (2012a) concludes: "This finding provides ample evidence that the call for special courses for HLLs has received an overwhelming response from postsecondary institutions with sizable populations of Hispanic students" (p. 207).

The overall pattern that emerges from the above studies, points favorably in the direction of institutionalization. This is true in the sense that these studies indicate that there has been a steady assimilation of HL pedagogy over time, as measured by the increasing presence of HL courses in Spanish departments. At the same time, the studies identify persistent impediments to institutionalization.

What about other HL languages? Beyond Spanish, information of this type is scant, both of in terms of having an inventory of departments offering HL courses at any point in time, as well as in terms of having a record over time by which to trace the assimilation and stabilization of HL instruction. Carreira's (2014) NHLRC survey, discussed in the remainder of this paper, is a first step towards addressing this gap.

The existence of this gap points to two weak links in the process of assimilation of HL pedagogy, one in the area of monitoring, or "tracking of progress of implementation and institutionalization," and the other in visibility of program-related activities (Miles & Louis, p. 39). In the foreign languages, enrollments and institutional trends are monitored on a regular basis by the Modern Language Association (MLA), the principal professional association in the U.S. for language and literature scholars. Published in 2015, the most recent MLA survey tracked enrollments in nearly all (98.3%) institutions of higher learning in the country, across 16 languages (Goldberg et al., 2015). Tellingly, although many of these languages have sizable numbers of HL speakers, the MLA survey report does not make any mention of the term "heritage," let alone examine enrollments or institutional practices in this area (Goldberg et al., 2015).

Besides the MLA, ACTFL, the principal professional association of teachers of languages other than English, also monitors and tracks institutional trends in the US. Its most recent survey of higher education is also telling with regard to monitoring and visibility of HL pedagogy.[2] This study sampled foreign-language high school students and teachers for purposes of transmitting information to colleges and universities "so they can better identify and serve high school students who meet their needs" (ACTFL, 2007). The survey report does not reference the term "HL" but does touch upon related issues. In particular, the survey queried students about their ethnicity as well as their motivations for studying a foreign language and by way of a conclusion the report notes that "Asian–American students, overall, indicated a very strong desire to study languages that correlated with their ethnic heritage." It also queried teachers about their reasons for choosing a career in foreign language teaching and found that family background was a factor for 10% of respondents.

In terms of better serving HL students, there's very little to work with in this report. Asian American students—the only population for which the report makes a connection between family background and language learning—are all lumped together. No actual information is given about their language background—or that or any other population of students—which would be important to know for curriculum design. As to the only other finding somewhat connected to HL, namely that family background can be an impetus for pursuing a career in language teaching, it's not obvious how it bears on the report's goal of helping departments better serve students. All in all, the report fails to draw attention to, let alone make the case for, HL teaching.[3]

Despite this, it would be a mistake to conclude that the MLA and ACTFL are blind to the importance of HL teaching. In fact, both organizations have put forth position statements in support of HLs. ACTFL's statement is particularly noteworthy for its detailed treatment of the attendant issues and its concrete recommendations. It is cited in its entirety below in anticipation of a point to be made later about the importance of having an expansive view of HL that goes beyond just offering HL classes.

The American Council on the Teaching of Foreign Languages (ACTFL) and its members encourage learning environments that support heritage and native speakers of languages other than English. It is critical that these students be able to continue to develop their heritage linguistic and cultural skills in order to become fully bilingual and biliterate in today's global environment. By doing so, they will be well-positioned to live and work in an increasingly multilingual environment in the U.S. Native speakers (those raised in an environment using mainly a language other than English) and heritage speakers (those raised in an environment where the language was most likely spoken in the home) benefit from instruction that draws on and enhances their native or heritage language skills and cultural knowledge. In addition, research has shown that continuing to learn their native and heritage language benefits them in their acquisition of English language proficiency.

In keeping with the goal of an educated citizenry that reflects the rich multicultural and multilingual nature of U.S. society, ACTFL encourages the active recruitment, training, and retention of heritage and native speakers as teachers. ACTFL further supports pre-service training and ongoing professional development for all language teachers to help them address the unique learning needs of heritage and native speakers. Successful language programs ensure the academic success of heritage and native speakers by providing:

- curriculum design that reflects the fact that the needs of native speakers and heritage students are often significantly different from non-native and non-heritage speakers;
- challenging curriculum that builds upon the existing linguistic skills and the cultural heritage and knowledge of the students;
- assessments that integrate language, culture and literature for all students Pre-K through 16;
- opportunities for heritage and native speakers to become involved in their language communities beyond the classroom; and
- systems to award credit or appropriate placement for oral and written proficiency and prior learning for native and heritage speakers.

(ACTFL, 2010)

All in all, a review of the literature on institutional practices at the postsecondary level underscores the need for monitoring and greater visibility of HL teaching, particularly for languages other than Spanish. With that in mind, the remainder of the chapter reports on the NHLRC survey of programs that teach HLLs (Carreira & Kagan, 2011).

3 The NHLRC Survey of Higher Education Programs: Methodology and Overview

A project of the NHLRC, the survey of higher education programs reported on by Carreira (2014) was an online survey designed to gather information from a wide range of languages on institutional practices that impact HLLs.[4] The goal, however, was not to track every program teaching HLLs, but rather, to collect representative information on the practices of programs that have HLLs.

Like the surveys discussed earlier, this one collected information on HL course availability. In addition, it identified and collected information on two other contexts that enroll HLLs, namely mixed classes and customized options such as independent studies and internships. As will be discussed, the latter two options are important barometers of the state of institutionalization of HL instruction.

The NHLRC piloted the online survey with a number of instructors during the design stage, running through iterative cycles of pilot testing and revising. The final product consists of 21 content questions, including discrete-point questions as well as open-ended ones. Several follow up interviews were also conducted with selected respondents to assess further information on particular issues or to seek clarification on some responses.

The survey was launched in October of 2010. Respondents were recruited through a variety of methods, including through listserv announcements, general advertising of the survey on the NHLRC website, announcements and booths at national conferences, and through personal contacts. Given these recruitment methods, it is impossible to tabulate a response rate for the survey. As of the writing of this paper, there are 296 programs in the database, representing a range of geographic locations, institution types, and languages.

In terms of location, 34 states with different immigrant population profiles are represented in the survey. All states with immigrant populations that exceed the national average of 12.9% are represented (Arizona, California, Colorado, Connecticut, Florida, Hawaii, Illinois, Massachusetts, Maryland, Nevada, New Jersey, and New York, as well as the District of Columbia). Also included are 5 out of the 10 states with the highest growth rates in their immigrant population (Alabama, Georgia, Indiana, Kentucky, and South Carolina). In addition, a number of states that do not meet the above conditions are included as well (e.g., Washington, Ohio, Wisconsin, Michigan) (Kandel, 2011).

In terms of institution type, roughly two-thirds (202/296) of the institutions are public and the rest are private. One-third (99) are PhD-granting institutions, 21.9% (65) are terminal M.A. granting institutions, 16.2% (48) are terminal B.A. granting institutions, and 11% (34) are community colleges.[5]

A total of twenty-seven languages are represented in the survey. Listed in descending number of respondents, they are: Spanish (76), Chinese (50), Arabic (44), Russian (36), Hindi/Urdu (32), Korean (13), Farsi (11), Vietnamese (5), Japanese (4), Tagalog (3), Hebrew (2), Portuguese (2), Punjabi (2), Serbo-Croatian (2), Yoruba (2), Armenian (1), Bulgarian (1), French (1), Greek (1), Hmong (1), Hungarian (1), Indonesian (2), Italian (1), Polish (1), Tamil (1), Thai (1), Yiddish (1).

The remainder of this chapter considers selected survey findings pertaining to institutionalization. In particular, it looks at the three instructional contexts where HLLs study their HL, namely, HL courses, customized options, and mixed classes, and examines common impediments to the implementation, assimilation, and stabilization of HL pedagogy in foreign language programs. For other findings, readers should consult Carreira (2014).

4 Survey Findings and Their Implications for Institutionalization

HL-Specific Instructional Contexts: HL Courses and Customized Options

In contrast to mixed classes, the two instructional contexts examined in this section, namely, HL courses and customized instructional options, have the distinction of being HL-specific. The term "HL class" is used here in reference to classes that enroll only HLLs and that report using instructional practices associated with HL teaching. "Customized options" is an umbrella term used in reference to a variety of alternative instructional formats such as independent studies, internships, tutoring, etc. Though as a general practice these formats are not restricted to HLLs, this survey reports only on customized practices created for HLLs.

Close to half of the programs surveyed (47.6%, 141/296) have separate instruction for HLLs in the form of one or more HL courses, with notable differences between languages, as shown in Table 24.1.

These results indicate significantly higher rates of HL course availability than would be expected by the nationwide surveys discussed earlier. Though such surveys were only for Spanish, it makes sense to consider them as benchmarks, albeit imperfect ones. This is particularly true for Beaudrie (2012a), which overlaps in time with the present study and which has a very large dataset (422 programs).

What could account for the discrepancy between that study, which puts the number of programs with an HL track at 40%, and the present one? It will be recalled that Beaudrie (2012a) was a comprehensive nationwide survey of all Spanish programs in four-year colleges. By comparison, the present survey is comprised of self-selected participants. As such, a self-selecting bias in the present study may overstate the frequency of programs with specialized HL courses. Be that

Table 24.1 Percent of Programs Offering HL Classes, by Language[6]

Language	Programs offering one or more specialized HL courses
Spanish	80.2% (61/76)
Korean	69% (9/13)
Chinese	54.9% (28/51)
Russian	47.2% (17/36)
Farsi	33.6% (4/11)
Hindi/Urdu	25% (8/32)
Arabic	6.8% (3/44)

Source: Adapted with permission from "Teaching heritage language learners: A study of programme profiles, practices, and needs," by M. Carreira, 2008. In P. Trifonas & T. Aravossitas (Eds.), *Rethinking heritage language education*, p. 26. Copyright 2008 by Cambridge University Press.

as it may, the fact that the present results compare favorably to those of other nationwide surveys which also involved self-selection (i.e., Ingold et al, 2002; Wherritt & Cleary, 1990) is supportive of Beaudrie's (2012a) appraisal that postsecondary institutions as a whole have responded favorably to the call for more HL courses.

Three categories of programs stand out for their particularly strong response. One such category consists of programs that offer four or more levels of HL instruction. A second category consists of programs that offer HL courses, despite having very few HLLs. A third category includes programs that use customized formats to meet the needs of HLLs. Each of these types of programs sheds light on critical factors in the area of institutionalization.

Programs That Offer Four or More Levels of HL Instruction

Mirroring the findings of Beaudrie (2012a), the present survey found that the large majority (92/142, 65.2%) of programs with an HL track offer one or two levels of instruction. Programs with four or more levels are significantly less common. As shown in the second column of Table 24.2, the present survey registers only 20 such programs, which amounts to 14% of programs with an HL track or 7% of all programs in the survey.

As shown in the third column, the large majority of programs with four or more HL courses have healthy enrollments in these courses. In particular, 15 programs have enrollments of 20 or more and 3 have between 11 and 20. Furthermore, as shown in the fourth column, many programs also have proportionally large HLL populations: in 15 out of 20 programs HLLs are 25% or more of the student population. Crucially, most programs with four or more HL courses have a critical mass of HLLs, as defined in terms of enrollments in HL classes and/or overall program representation.

However, numbers alone don't account for the curricular richness of these programs. After all, many other programs in the survey with similar demographic profiles have much more modest course offerings. What distinguishes many of the programs in Table 24.2 is their special access to institutional resources and faculty with initiative and expertise. For example, the Vietnamese and Spanish programs are connected with leading researchers in the field of heritage languages. The Russian program is at UCLA, which is home to the NHLRC. Directed by Olga Kagan, a Russian professor herself at UCLA and also a leader in the field of heritage languages, the NHLRC offers many professional development opportunities and sponsors research and conferences in the area

Table 24.2 Selected Characteristics of Programs with Four or More HL Courses

I	II	III	IV
Language	Programs with 4 or more HL courses/ total number of programs with HL courses	Typical HL class size	Percent of HLLs in the program (number of programs)
Chinese	14/28	20+ (for 13/14 programs)	10%–25% (2) 25%–50% (4) 50%–75% (4) > 75% (2)
Korean	1/9	20+	25%–50%
Russian	1/17	11 to 20	25%–50%
Spanish	3/61	20+	10%–25% (1) 25%–50% (1) >75% (1)
Vietnamese	1/3	5–10	50%–75%

Source: Adapted with permission from "Teaching heritage language learners: A study of programme profiles, practices, and needs," by M. Carreira, 2008. In P. Trifonas & T. Aravossitas (Eds.), *Rethinking heritage language education*, p. 30. Copyright 2008 by Cambridge University Press.

of heritage languages. UCLA is also home to two other language programs in this table, namely the Korean program and one of the Chinese programs. To the issue of institutionalization, many of the programs in Table 24.2 don't just have a critical mass of HL students. They also have "astute project leadership and supporting infrastructure" (Miles & Louis, 1987, p. 38).

Programs That Offer HL Courses Despite Having Very Few HLLs

As a general rule, programs need a critical mass of HLLs to be able to offer HL courses. Programs that manage to get around this impediment underscore the critical role that faculty leadership, collective ownership of the innovation, and institutional resources play in the process of institutionalization (Miles & Louis, 1987).

Only five programs in the survey offer HL courses with average enrollments of five or fewer students. One such program, the Japanese program at La Guardia Community College of the City University of New York, is the product of remarkable faculty initiative, as explained in a follow-up interview:

Our college administrators are probably the primary reason why we were able to run HL courses with low enrollment. As for Japanese, I tried to convince our president and provost that LaGuardia could serve as a hub of HL instruction in NY because no other colleges in the area offer HL Japanese courses. They were persuaded by my argument and decided to make HL as one of the college's goals this year. . . . We also actively sought external grants. With both internal/external funding, we tried to offer professional development events on HL frequently so that we can reach out our college community. Finally, HL worked quite well as a common theme among our colleagues' research interests. . . . Our colleagues have been very supportive in our initiative in HL for this reason.

(Carreira, 2014, p. 11)

In terms of institutionalization, this professor's efforts evidence the pivotal role that administrative support and a sense of collective ownership of the innovation can play in overcoming impediments related to low enrollments.

Another program is the Indonesian program at the University of Wisconsin at Madison, Wisconsin. Tellingly, this program's home institution is a national leader in South and Southeast Asia studies, hosting a yearly summer language institute (University of Wisconsin-Madison, n.d.a), outreach K–12 programs, and other projects that promote the study and teaching of the languages of this region (University of Wisconsin-Madison, n.d.b).

Programs with Customized Formats for HLLs

As noted earlier, alternative instructional formats such as independent studies, tutoring, seminars, and internships are some of the most common ways in which HLLs receive instruction that is tailored to their needs. Programs with HL courses often use these customized options to supplement their HL track, for example, to give HLLs the opportunity to use their HL in the community or in professional settings.

Programs that are unable to offer HL courses use them as a viable alternative for serving the specific needs of HLLs. Among such programs, roughly half (48%) offer one or more of these options. This means that if customized options are counted as a type of HL instruction (along with HL courses) then the percentage of programs that offer HL-specific instruction, in one form or another, rises to 73% (215/296). This points to widespread *implementation* of HL pedagogy at the postsecondary level, where implementation "involves putting new ideas, procedures, or a program of activities into practice" (Ekholm & Trier, 1987, p. 13).

The question remains whether the widespread implementation of HL pedagogy has been accompanied by a deep acceptance of this innovation at the program level. The next section addresses this question in the context of examining the third context in which HLLs study their HL, namely mixed classes.

Mixed Classes

There is general consensus that HLLs are best taught separately from L2Ls, particularly at the lower levels of instruction where the differences between the two populations are most pronounced, and are therefore most likely to interfere with teaching and learning. Against this backdrop, the presence of HL courses is commonly taken to be an indicator of the acceptance within language programs of HL-specific instruction or pedagogy, and the aggregate of programs reporting HL courses has been taken to be a measure of the acceptance of this innovation in the field at large. However, as a stand-alone metric (as used in previous surveys) the approach of tallying the number of departments that offer HL courses can underestimate the level of acceptance of HL pedagogy and its legitimacy. To this point, in an earlier discussion, we saw that many departments that are not able to offer HL courses use customized options to serve the needs of their HLLs. This is a clear embrace of the innovation, in the absence of HL courses.

With this in mind, this section utilizes another indicator of the state of institutionalization, namely, the workings of mixed classes, and more specifically, how they deal with HLLs. This type of information sheds light on institutionalization at two levels, the classroom and the department level (Timmermans, 1987).

Survey results suggest that mixed classes may function as traditional L2 classes. Regarding pedagogical materials, most of the descriptions of mixed classes provided in the survey referenced textbooks and other materials that are specifically designed for L2Ls. This was true even in mixed classes with a majority of HLLs, where HL-specific materials would have been just as appropriate, if not more so. Indeed, although mixed classes are more common than HL classes, survey results indicate that to date there are no textbooks for mixed classes. Further supporting the contention that mixed classes function as L2 classes, the comments below evidence a lack of attention to HL issues in mixed classes with few HLLs:[7]

1) I did not give particular consideration to HL—they are usually a very small segment of the class.
2) In the past five and half years of our program, we only had 2 heritage speakers. So we focus on true beginners, and we don't address the needs of the HLLs.
3) (Name of book) does not address the needs of HL but it does a good job at the beginning level where the majority of our students take the (name of language) as a general language requirement and where we have less HL (15%) than at more advanced levels.

(Carreira, 2014, p. 28)

Attending to the needs of learners as different as HLLs and L2Ls is a very difficult task under the best of circumstances. Doing so without the benefit of specialized materials and established pedagogical practices for mixed classes is nearly impossible. Despite pressing needs on this vital front, solutions for the mixed context have been surprisingly slow to emerge, perhaps because to date much of the attention of specialists has been on HL classes. Under these circumstances, it is not surprising that teachers in mixed classes should reach for what is familiar and accessible, namely L2 methods and materials.

If the findings of this survey are correct and many mixed classes actually function as de facto L2 classes, what does this say about the state of institutionalization of the field of HL teaching? This question connects to issues of scope and depth. Scope relates to how widespread an innovation is, that is "how many persons, resources, regulations, etc. are affected by the institutionalization" (Ekholm & Trier, p. 15). Depth has to do with the level of penetration of the innovation: whether it is a "mere addition to the existent", "a substitute for former patterns", or "even change the whole organization" (Ekholm & Trier, p. 15). Miles and Louis (1987) frame this difference in terms of whether an innovation leads to change *in* the organization versus change *to* the organization, which is a deeper type of change.

Change *to* the organization can be conceived of as the espousal of a broad vision of HL pedagogy that permeates all aspects of a program. In the area of instruction, this vision leads to the purposeful implementation of the core tenets of HL pedagogy throughout the curriculum, from language classes to upper-division content classes in literature, culture, linguistics, etc. Beyond instruction, this vision advances HL issues across the program in areas such as advising, professional development, hiring, etc.

The fact that mixed classes—the most common point of contact between HLLs and foreign language programs—proceed largely in accordance with L2 practices across many programs at the postsecondary level, suggests that the scope of HL pedagogy is largely confined to HL classes and the customized options. Seen in this light, the existence of HL classes and customized instructional options are more in keeping with change *in* foreign language teaching and learning rather than change *to* this field.

To bring about change to the field, an important first step is to address the need for teaching practices and materials for the mixed context. In light of the fact that so many programs cannot support HL classes, this is critical to increasing the scope or reach of HL pedagogy. With this in mind, the NHLRC is creating an online certificate in HL teaching that specifically addresses the mixed context, among other issues. A growing body of research on HLL-L2L interactions also stands to contribute on this front (Bowles, 2011; Henshaw, 2015; Potowski, Jegerski, & Morgan-Short, 2009).

Beyond instruction, vision clarity (Ekholm & Trier, 1987, p. 21) surrounding the place of HL issues in language programs is also of the essence. The ACTFL position statement cited earlier serves by way of example of what that vision might look like from the point of view of serving HL students. From the point of view of serving programs, the inclusion of a value proposition addressing the benefits of HL instruction *for programs* might help bring about change to the field. Among other benefits, such a proposition might alert programs as to the potential for increasing enrollments by tapping into HLLs, as well as the potential to diversify course offerings and increase visibility at the institutional level, through collaborations with other programs or departments. Having a value proposition connects with Ekholm and Trier's (1987) notion of incentives:

> The balance of individual and collective benefits and costs, gains and losses is one of the fateful issues in implementation. The balance is also decisive for institutionalization. The anticipation of rewards (material o immaterial), the nature of the personal investment—all these will facilitate or hinder—even prevent—institutionalization.
>
> *(p. 20)*

Miles and Louis (1987) cite work by Wallace (1979) suggesting that the formulation of a code or vision happens as part of the process of revitalization. One of three change processes associated with institutionalization, revitalization involves "deliberate social movement efforts to change a culture, often through multiple innovations" (p. 31). Revitalization also entails "cultural transformation, often involving capture of the infrastructure" (p. 32).

In the following discussion, issues of infrastructure—or the lack of it—figure prominently in the discussion of impediments to HL instruction.

5 Impediments to the Institutionalization of HL Pedagogy

There is a great deal of consensus across program types and languages surrounding needs in the area of HL teaching. This was somewhat unexpected, given the range of languages and program types represented in the survey. Respondents were asked to rank order seven areas of need identified in the research literature. The results are listed in Table 24.3, from most pressing to least. The discussion that follows examines each of these, focusing on issues of institutionalization.

Table 24.3 Areas of Need Identified by Respondents

1 Inadequate or lacking course options for HLLs
2 HL teaching and research are not on the path to tenure
3 Inadequate professional training opportunities
4 Inadequate or lacking placement tools
5 Inadequate or lacking pedagogical materials
6 Low enrollments
7 Low retention

Source: Adapted with permission from "Teaching heritage language learners: A study of programme profiles, practices, and needs," by M. Carreira, 2008. In P. Trifonas & T. Aravossitas (Eds.), *Rethinking heritage language education*, p. 37. Copyright 2008 by Cambridge University Press.

Inadequate or Lacking Course Options for HLLs

Table 24.4 below, compares programs with and without HL courses, with respect to the size of their HL student population. A comparison of the first and third columns shows that the likelihood of having HL courses goes up with the percentage of HLLs in a program. The converse is also true: the smaller the presence of HLLs the lower the likelihood of HL courses. This is depicted in the last column.

These findings come as no surprise. As noted earlier, programs need a critical mass of HL students to support HL courses. For many, if not all programs, this seems to be an immutable reality. However, an important finding of this survey is that low enrollments need not be an insurmountable impediment to serving the needs of HLLs.

As previously discussed, one way in which departments serve the needs of HLLs in the absence of HL courses is through customized instructional formats. These formats have two advantages. One, they are typically not subject to the type of minimal enrollment requirements that prevent departments from offering HL courses. That is, they can get around the critical mass problem. And two, because they are personalized, these options can be very effective at attending to the needs of HLLs.

Of course, this solution is far from perfect. If used as the primary means of teaching HLLs, it effectively leads to the creation of a phantom HL track functioning parallel to the mainstream track, but without the kind of support, oversight, and visibility associated with the latter.

Three issues of institutionalization merit particular attention here: voluntarism, person-independence, and visibility. Regarding the first, Ekholm and Trier (1987) note:

> Voluntarism, often present in the initiation-phase of a process of change, and needed during the implementation-phase, must usually decrease during institutionalization, and be replaced by new behavior-patterns, stable social arrangements in the organization, administrative regulations, etc.
>
> *(p. 21)*

Due to lack of monitoring, we have no way of knowing whether voluntarism in HL instruction is decreasing. However, the results of the present study point to current high levels of voluntarism, which, in turn, speak to low levels of administrative support and also perhaps low levels of legitimacy of the innovation at the department and university levels.

Volunteerism is closely connected to "person-independence," which, as Miles and Louis (1987) argue, is an indicator of institutionalization of an innovation (p. 26), To the extent that

Table 24.4 Relative Size of the HL Student Population of Programs with and without HL Courses Worksheet Developed for the Hindi-Urdu Song "Bazigaar"

I	II	III	IV
Percentage of HLLs in program	**Total programs N=294*	*Programs that offer HL courses N= 140*	*Programs that do not offer HL courses N= 154*
<10	69	24.6% (17)	75.3% (52)
10–25	77	42.8% (33)	57.1% (44)
25–50	68	55.9% (38)	44.1% (30)
50–75	41	63.4% (26)	36.5% (15)
>75	39	66.6% (26)	33.3% (13)

Note: *Two programs did not respond to this question.

Source: Adapted with permission from "Teaching heritage language learners: A study of programme profiles, practices, and needs," by M. Carreira, 2008. In P. Trifonas & T. Aravossitas (Eds.), *Rethinking heritage language education*, p. 29. Copyright 2008 by Cambridge University Press.

the customized instructional options rely on the presence and voluntarism of specific individuals, they undercut institutionalization.

Regarding visibility, Ekholm and Trier (1987) propose that with institutionalization comes diminishing visibility. This is because once assimilated, the innovation ceases to be seen as exceptional and becomes part of the status quo. This type of positive invisibility is very different from the kind of negative invisibility that characterizes the customized instructional formats. Negative invisibility speaks to low levels of administrative support and also perhaps low levels of legitimacy of HL pedagogy.

Seen in this light, the widespread use of alternative formats may be more of a case of infiltration, rather than assimilation, of HL pedagogy. To be sure, from the point of view of addressing the needs of HLLs, these formats are likely to be very good, for the reasons put forward earlier. However, they may not be on the pathway to assimilation and stabilization of HL teaching, due to their invisibility, person dependence, and low levels of administrative support.

HL Teaching and Research Are Not on the Path to Tenure

Survey results indicate that HL teaching is largely in the hands of non-tenure-track faculty (mostly lecturers, graduate students, and visiting fellows). The significance of this finding does not reside in what it says about the quality of HL teaching. Indeed, there is no evidence that contingent faculty are less effective HL teachers than tenure-track faculty. Rather, the importance of this finding lies is what it indicates about institutional commitment to HL teaching and how the absence of tenure-track faculty undercuts the assimilation and stabilization of HL pedagogy.

One of the main reasons why tenure-track faculty are so important to institutionalization (and their absence, so detrimental) is because they are available for long-term institutional and curricular planning, for hiring and mentoring new faculty, and other functions that support HL teaching in language programs. Another reason is that they have *supportive capacity,* or "access to decision making structures" (Miles & Louis, 1987, p. 38) crucial to obtaining organization-wide commitment. The comment below by an Arabic professor who participated in the survey speaks to this point. His knowledge of institutional issues and resourcefulness enable him to clear institutional obstacles that stand in the way of offering instructional options for HLLs:

> First, I built the program methodically and realistically. . . . Second, I have spread out expenditures by, say, offering certain courses through the evening program, which is another budget. Or, I open sections of courses . . . specifically through the Honors Programs. . . . Partially, I also frequently take on students in independent studies, usually graduate students or upper class students, to accommodate the need for advanced language, literature, and culture courses.
>
> *(Carreira, 2014, p. 38)*

Once again, this example speaks to the essential role of faculty leadership in the institutionalization of HL instruction.

Inadequate Professional Training Opportunities

Considerable numbers of programs have special speakers, workshops, and courses focusing wholly or in part, on HL issues and offering some pedagogical training. In addition, many survey respondents reported taking advantage of external sources of training and information, such as professional conferences, summer workshops, and online resources.

Given the variety of training options identified, it would be valuable to understand what types of professional development opportunities and how much training or instruction enable good HL teaching and promote faculty initiative. In this regard, it is important to remember that questions about the adequacy of professional training opportunities don't just bear on the current state of HL teaching, but also on the sustainability of the innovation. If today's graduate students are not instructed on the principles of HL teaching and learning, they will not have the knowledge or see the need to push forward an HL agenda when they enter the profession as faculty members, administrators, textbook editors, etc.

A more immediate concern surrounding inadequate training is that it may reduce teaching effectiveness in HL classes, leading to low retention rates of students. The mixed context is particularly worrisome in this regard.

Placement

Placement is an area where significant progress has been made in recent years. The NHLRC has a substantial database of references, proficiency assessments, background questionnaires, and other research tools developed by researchers and practitioners that may be utilized for assessing HLLs (National Heritage Language Resource Center, n.d.). Another contribution is the special issue of the Heritage Language Journal on Spanish assessment (Beaudrie, 2012b). What is not clear about placement—and what may explain its prominence among critical areas of concern in the survey, despite discernable advances—is whether teachers and programs are actually able to apply the existing information and resources on placement to their own circumstances. For mixed classes, this is a particularly daunting task due to lack of alignment in the knowledge base of L2 and HLLs and a lack of pedagogical materials for this context.

Placement connects to institutionalization in similar ways as teacher training. That is, gaps in this area have the potential to reduce teaching effectiveness and thereby undercut student retention rates. Though speaking to a different set of circumstances (namely, differentiation at the elementary level), Delisle's (2015) comment below elucidates the connection between teaching effectiveness and sensible class configuration, which is achieved by placement.

> The biggest reason differentiation doesn't work, and never will, is the way students are deployed in most of our nation's classrooms. Toss together several students who struggle to learn, along with a smattering of gifted kids, while adding a few English-language learners and a bunch of academically average students and expect a single teacher to differentiate for each of them. That is a recipe for academic disaster if ever I saw one.

Inadequate or Lacking Pedagogical Materials

Survey results indicate that there is a need for more textbooks and materials for HL courses across all languages, including Spanish, Chinese, and Russian, which already have a variety of HL textbooks. There is a particularly dire need for materials for mixed classes, without which such classes cannot adequately address the needs of HLLs. Once again, the availability of quality pedagogical materials for HLLs connects to teaching effectiveness and by extension, to retention rates.

Low Enrollment and Retention Rates

As made abundantly clear, enrollments and retention rates are inexorably linked to the other areas of concerns. While for the most part, low enrollments are out of the control of departments, survey findings point to strategies that may help with enrollments. The strategy described below by one of the survey respondents of investing in HL courses first, and waiting for HL enrollments to follow, proved fruitful from the point of view of generating enrollments:

> At UCLA we noticed an increase in the heritage speakers of Russian in the mid-90s. . . . All of these students, including the lowest proficiency group, were so different from our traditional foreign language or L2 students that the department felt they needed their own curriculum. . . . If we could offer these students the kind of instruction they would benefit from they would continue taking Russian, thus increasing the numbers of students in the department. A new course, Literacy in Russian, was launched that enrolled 10 students in the first year. This course has now been offered for 10 years. The enrollments have grown and the student population changed.
>
> *(Carreira, 2014, p. 23)*

Another strategy is to offer so called "language for specific purposes" courses, such as Spanish for business or healthcare. Though not HL courses per se, these types of courses align well with HL teaching and learning because their focus is on serving local speakers of the HL. From the point of view of enrollments and budgetary considerations, these classes have the advantage that they tend to be very popular with HLLs and, as indicated in the survey, are sometimes co-sponsored by the professional schools.

Finally, the Arabic professor cited earlier in this section identifies the strategy of offering HL courses through programs that are funded through a different budget and which presumably allow for smaller classes. In his program, offering HL classes through the evening program and the Honors Program proves useful in this regard.

To summarize, the impediments to institutionalization are significant, both in the sense that they are numerous, and also that they are interconnected. The situation of a Hindi/Urdu program in the survey illustrates how missing just one of these components undercuts the ability of programs to serve HLLs. With large numbers of HLLs, a working placement test, and a director with initiative and expertise, this program is nevertheless unable to offer HL courses (including a fully developed online tutorial for HLLs designed to be used in a variety of instructional contexts) due to the lack of trained faculty.

Thus, the impediments to institutionalization are dependent variables and must be treated as such.

6 Summary and Conclusions

Survey results paint a mixed picture of the state of institutionalization of HL pedagogy at the postsecondary level in the United States. On the positive side, the availability of HL courses and of customized options in many language programs is consistent with the view that the innovation is perceived as legitimate by many practitioners and enjoys a measurable level of assimilation in language programs. Also on the positive side, the survey identifies a striking number of strategies by resourceful faculty to implement HL-specific instruction, even when institutional conditions do not favor such courses.

On the negative side, the impediments to institutionalization are significant, not only because they are so numerous but also because they are interconnected, which means that departments must attend to them in a coordinated fashion. Mixed classes emerge as a top priority for the field. As currently configured, these classes are not serving HLLs as well as they could. Addressing this situation will require creating effective methods and materials for the mixed context and training instructors in all areas of the curriculum—from language to linguistics and literature courses—to use these methods in their mixed classes. Along these lines, there is also a need for a more encompassing vision of HL pedagogy that permeates all components of language programs, not just individual classes, and that elucidates the value proposition of HL teaching for programs.

Finally, greater visibility and monitoring of institutional practices involving HLs are critical to advancing the institutionalization of HL pedagogy.

Notes

1 Four-year colleges and universities both award bachelor degrees. Universities also have graduate programs and, in some cases, professional schools. Two-year colleges award associate degrees and offer basic freshman- and sophomore-level courses that can be applied toward a bachelor's degree at a four-year college or university.
2 This survey was conducted in conjunction with the National Research Center for College and University Admissions.
3 As of the writing of this chapter, the American Councils for International Education is conducting a survey of foreign language enrollments. The survey questions do not reference HLs (American Councils for International Education, n.d.).
4 Team members are: Afaf Nash (UCLA), Tri Tran (UC Irvine), and this author (Maria Carreira, UCLA and California State University, Long Beach).
5 A number of respondents indicated that they were uncertain as to the answer; the remainder failed to answer this question.
6 Only languages with 10 or more programs are included in this table.
7 These quotes have been modified to remove all identifying information.

References

American Council on the Teaching of Foreign Languages [ACTFL]. (2007). 2007 post-secondary planning survey: Final summary. Retrieved from https://www.actfl.org/sites/default/files/ACTFL_summary_2007_final.pdf

American Council on the Teaching of Foreign Languages [ACTFL]. (2010). Language learning for heritage and native speakers [Position statement]. Retrieved from http://www.actfl.org/news/position-statements/language-learning-heritage-and-native-speakers-0#sthash.TGFFBoRA.dpuf

American Councils for International Education. (n.d.). Survey of foreign language enrollment in the U.S. [Web page]. Retrieved from http://www.americancouncils.org/ForeignLanguageSurvey

Beaudrie, S. (2011). Spanish heritage language programs: A snapshot of current programs in the southwestern United States. Foreign Language Annals, 44(2), 321–337.

Beaudrie, S. (2012a). Research on university-based Spanish heritage language programs in the United States: The current state of affairs. In S. Beaudrie & M. Fairclough (Eds.), Spanish as a heritage language in the United States: State of the field (pp. 203–221). Washington, DC: Georgetown University Press.

Beaudrie, S. (Ed.). (2012b). Spanish assessment [Special issue]. Heritage Language Journal, 9(1), 1–138. Retrieved from http://www.heritagelanguages.org

Bowles, M. (2011). Exploring the role of modality: L2-heritage learner interactions in the Spanish language classroom. Heritage Language Journal, 1(8), 30–65. Retrieved from http://www.heritagelanguages.org

Carreira, M. (2012). Spanish as a heritage language: The state of the field. In J. H. Antxon Olarrea & E. O'Rourke (Eds.), The handbook of Hispanic linguistics (pp. 765–782). Hoboken, NJ: Wiley-Blackwell.

Carreira, M. (2014). Teaching heritage language learners: A study of programme profiles, practices, and needs. In P. Trifonas & T. Aravossitas (Eds.), Rethinking heritage language education (pp. 20–44). Cambridge, UK: Cambridge University Press.

Carreira, M., & Kagan, O. (2011). The results of the National Heritage Language Survey: Implications for teaching, curriculum design, and professional development. Foreign Language Annals, 43(3), 40–64.

Delisle, J. (2015). Differentiation doesn't work. Education Week, 34(15), 28–36. Retrieved from Education Week website: http://www.edweek.org/ew/articles/2015/01/07/differentiation-doesnt-work.html

Ekholm, M., & Trier, U. (1987). The concept of institutionalization: Some remarks. In M. B. Miles, M. Ekholm, & R. Vandenberghe (Eds.), *Lasting school improvement: Exploring the process of institutionalization* (pp. 13–21). Leuven, Belgium: Acco.

Ennis, S. R., Ríos-Vargas, M., & Albert, N. (2011, May). The Hispanic population: 2010. 2010 Census Briefs. C2010BR04. Retrieved from http://www.census.gov/prod/cen2010/briefs/c2010br-04.pdf

Goldberg, D., Looney, D., & Lusin, N. (2015). Enrollments in languages other than English in United States institutions of higher education, Fall 2013. Retrieved from Modern Language Association website: https://www.mla.org/content/download/31180/1452509/2013_enrollment_survey.pdf

Henshaw, F. (2015). Learning outcomes of L2-heritage learner interaction: The proof is in the posttests. *Heritage Language Journal, 12*(3), 245–270. Retrieved from http://www.heritagelanguages.org/

Ingold, C., Rivers, W., Tesser, C. C., & Ashby, E. (2002). Report on the NFLC/AATSP survey of Spanish language programs for native speakers. *Hispania, 85*(2), 324–329.

Kandel, W. A. (2011). The U.S. foreign born population: Trends and selected characteristics (CRS Report for Congress). Retrieved from Library of Congress, Congressional Research Service website: http://www.fas.org/sgp/crs/misc/R41592.pdf

Miles, M. B., & Louis, K. S. (1987). Research on institutionalization: A reflective review. In M. Miles, M. Ekholm, & R. Vandenberghe (Eds.), *Lasting school improvement: Exploring the process of institutionalization* (pp. 25–44). Leuven, Belgium: Acco.

National Heritage Language Resource Center [NHLRC]. (n.d.). Research and proficiency assessments tools. Retrieved from http://www.nhlrc.ucla.edu/nhlrc/category/data

Potowski, K., Jegerski, J., & Morgan-Short, K. (2009). The effects of instruction on linguistic development in Spanish heritage language speakers. *Language Learning, 59*(3), 537–579.

Timmermans, R. (1987). Institutionalization of the MAVO-project—a Durch case study. In M. Miles, M. Ekholm, & R. Vandenberghe (Eds.), *Lasting school improvement: Exploring the process of institutionalization* (pp. 125–142). Leuven, Belgium: Acco.

University of Wisconsin-Madison. (n.d.a). The South Asia Summer Language Institute, University of Wisconsin-Madison [Web site]. Retrieved from http://www.sasli.wisc.edu/

University of Wisconsin-Madison. (n.d.b). Center for South Asia [web site]. International Division, University of Wisconsin-Madison. Retrieved from http://southasia.wisc.edu/

Valdés, G., Fishman, J. A., Chávez, R., & Pérez, W. (2006). *Developing minority language resources: The case of Spanish in California*. Buffalo, NY: Multilingual Matters.

Wallace, F. C. (1979). *Culture and personality* (2nd Ed). New York, NY: Random House.

Wherritt, I., & Cleary, T. (1990). A national survey of Spanish language testing for placement of outcome assessment at BA-granting institutions in the United States. *Foreign Language Annals, 22*(2), 157–165.

25

"Arabic-as-Resource" or "Arabic-as-Problem"?

Arab Heritage Language Learners in Danish Postsecondary Education

Helle Lykke Nielsen

1 Introduction

Denmark is a small and highly globalized welfare state favoring a language policy which sets English as a top priority and, at least ideally, focuses on the need for other foreign languages. From this perspective, the growing presence of immigrant languages offers an important contribution to the country's globalization efforts. In practice, however, the situation for immigrant and heritage languages (HLs) in Denmark is highly complex and much less straightforward than official language policies would lead one to believe. Even though continuous efforts are made to adapt language educational policies to the changing global context, including the teaching of a few immigrant languages in schools and universities, there are also tensions, barriers, and resistance to these, which are not only expressed through political discourse and in the public media, but also at the level of institutions and among individual stakeholders.

The aim of this chapter is to analyze the educational arena for HL learners of Arabic at the university level in Denmark, and to show how clashes between top-down policies and bottom-up educational choices are dealt with at the institutional level. Ekholm and Trier (1987) point out that, "Institutionalization always occurs in a broad political context, where both macro- and micro-political processes are in action. It often emerges from controversial streams of ideology" (p. 14). In other words, beyond technical and administrative considerations that contribute to "establishing a relatively stable new pattern of sanctioned norms and activities in an organization" (p. 14) is a political and ideological element that impinges on the process, either supporting or undermining factors that lead to institutionalization. The discussion that follows sheds light on these points.

The analysis of this dynamic is based on data from three undergraduate interdisciplinary study programs which pair Arabic with business management, communication studies, and intercultural pedagogy, respectively, at the University of Southern Denmark (SDU), where young Danes and HL learners in Arabic have been trained for more than 20 years. These programs were suddenly closed by the university administration at the beginning of 2015 as a result of government requirements to reduce the number of students in higher education. From being a dynamic and well-integrated part of the university's foreign language portfolio with an annual intake of 75 first-year students, these programs were suddenly considered a liability due to a range of economic indicators. The closure raised a number of questions regarding, among other things, the role of HL learners in the university, and made it necessary to reconsider retrospectively the institutionalization processes of these programs in an attempt to understand what went wrong.

To understand the dynamics behind the university's decision and the implications for Arab HL learners in Denmark, I shall first identify the status of Arabic in Danish society, by showing how the language is framed in public and political discourse, and how the teaching of Arabic is implemented in the Danish educational system. Then I shall outline the profile of Arab HL learners in the university—who they are, why they choose to study Arabic, and what challenges they face—followed by a profile of the teachers and their role as language educational managers. And finally, I analyze the decisions made at the administrative level, discuss their implications for the HL learners, and outline the lessons learned.

Just a short note on the term "heritage language learner" as it is used in this chapter. Being aware that the term is contested in the research literature, as shown by Doerr and Lee (2013), I use it here as a social concept to categorize a group of learners whose language learning profile distinguishes them to a large extent from native speakers on the one hand and foreign language learners on the other. In Europe, and certainly in the Scandinavian countries, the term most often used in the research literature for the education of HL learners at the primary-school level is "mother tongue education," a term by no means less complex than "heritage language learning" (p. 31). In this context, I shall use, again for pragmatic reasons, the term "heritage language" and "mother tongue" interchangeably, though there are important differences between the two sets of terminology.

2 The Context: Arabic in Denmark

Arabic is the largest non-Western immigrant language in Denmark. In 2015, 92,641 migrants and their descendants had an Arabic-speaking background out of a population of 5.7 million (Statistics Denmark, 2015a). Arabic is a relatively new language in the Danish linguistic landscape. Even though the first Arab labor migrants from Morocco came to Denmark in the late 1960s, Arabic only gained currency with the many Palestinians who arrived between 1985 and 1992 in the wake of the Lebanese civil war, and later with the Iraqi refugees who came in large numbers between 1998 and 2003, and again from 2006. The Syrian civil war beginning in 2011 and later the rise of Islamic State in a number of Arab countries further increased the number of Arabic-speaking refugees with the result that Arabic is increasingly present in the Danish public sphere. The Arabic spoken by these migrants and refugees varies depending on their country of origin, but alongside these spoken varieties there is a common written variety, modern standard Arabic, which is taught in formal educational settings, including the programs discussed in this chapter.

Public Discourse in Danish Media and Politics

Every now and then politicians, interest groups, and NGOs are reported in the Danish media arguing that, as a small globalized nation, Denmark should make better use of the languages brought to the country by migrants and refugees. They argue, among other things, that Arabic is one of the world's largest languages, that the Arab world is Europe's closest neighbor, and that Denmark's numerous political and economic interests in the area are best taken care of by people who can communicate in Arabic (The Danish Government Council of Globalization, 2006; Deichmann, 2010; Nielsen, 2009). In contrast to this "language-as-resource" discourse is another that frames Arabic as a problem: The fact that Arabs in Denmark on average earn less money, have lower employment rates, have more children, are more poorly educated, receive a larger share of social benefits, and have a higher crime index than both Danes and Western and quite a few non-Western migrants reflects negatively on the language status of Arabic (Statistics Denmark, 2015b, pp. 7–9). The difficult socioeconomic situation of Arabs in Denmark is partly explained by the fact that Arab migrants and refugees have arrived later than, for example, Turks and Pakistanis, and therefore have not yet gained a foothold in the Danish labor market to the same extent. Moreover, a very large proportion of Arabs in Denmark are refugees and therefore more likely to have been exposed to physical and emotional suffering than labor migrants, which in turn affects their and their children's chances of doing well in Denmark.

The link between the average socioeconomic status of Arabs in Denmark and the language they speak is reflected in the Danish media's coverage of Arabic. A study of seven national Danish newspapers in 2009 showed that Arabic was characterized predominantly by three general attributes: Arabic was referred to as a simple language unfit for expressing the complexity of modern society; as a religious language used in mosques and other religious contexts to exclude outsiders; and as a language spoken only by people living in poor immigrant areas where the average income was low, unemployment high, and social problems significant. In these ways, the media indicated that Arabic was a low-status language as well as an expensive one, since the welfare state had to cover high interpreting costs for immigrants in hospitals, schools, and social services (Nielsen, 2009).

The negative press coverage of Arabic is reinforced by the attempts of some politicians to pursue policies with symbolic value through critical statements and proposals targeting immigrant languages. In particular, members of the Danish People's Party (DPP), which got 21% of the votes in the 2015 parliamentary elections, have proposed several times to restrict the use of Arabic and other immigrant languages in the public sphere. In 2010, the party suggested prohibiting any conversation in class and during recess in elementary schools in languages other than Danish (Schøler, 2010), and later the same year, the head of the DPP suggested banning satellite dishes for immigrants to prevent them from watching *al-Jazeera* and *al-Arabiya* which "promote hatred of the continent they live in" (Schjørring, 2010). In 2011, the DPP was behind a high-profile amendment of the health bill which required a user fee for the assistance of interpreters for immigrants who had lived in Denmark for more than seven years (Kristiansen, Nørredam, & Krasnik, 2010). More recently, in 2015, the party's integration spokesperson publicly argued that putting up business signs in Arabic in Danish stores should be prohibited (Kloster, 2015). Such proposals usually attract great media attention despite the fact that most of them could never be implemented due to Denmark's commitment to international agreements.

Language Educational Policies

The antagonism of "Arabic-as-resource" versus "Arabic-as-problem" in the Danish media and politics is found also in education, a sector considered to be very important for language policy and language status (Spolsky, 2004). There has long been a strong political focus on promoting "pattern breakers"[1] in Danish higher education through a policy which aims explicitly to attract and retain more young people from non-academic families, particularly young immigrants and descendants from non-Western countries (Vilhelmsen, 2014). In 2014, the Danish Ministry of Higher Education and Science made this a priority area for action in government educational policy (Ministry of Higher Education and Science—Denmark, 2014a, 2014b, p. 2), with a number of Danish universities following by prioritizing support of such students (Organization for

Economic Co-operation and Development, Higher Education Program, 2014, p. 10; University of Southern Denmark, 2013).

Immigrant languages from non-Western countries suffer, nonetheless, from differential treatment in the educational system, if they are offered at all. As the largest non-Western immigrant language, Arabic has formally gained ground in the education system. Until the mid-1970s Arabic was offered only in two Danish universities as philology studies with a focus on classical Arabic language, literature, and Islamic history, but labor migration led to the teaching of Arabic and other immigrant languages in primary schools from 1975. (In the Danish context, "primary school" refers to grades 1 to 10 and "secondary school" to grades 11 to 13.) Classes were offered free of charge, took place outside normal school hours, but suffered from a lack of qualified teachers (Daugaard, 2015, p. 14; Kristjánsdóttir, 2006, p. 84ff). At the end of the 1900s, however, as public debates on integration of immigrants into Danish society grew steadily, mother tongue education became a hot political issue, and this led to the loss of state subsidies for mother tongue education in 2002 and thus to a dramatic drop in the number of primary schools offering mother tongue education in Arabic (Daugaard, 2015, p. 16; Nielsen, 2007a, 2007b). In 1992, for the first time in Denmark, Arabic was offered as a modern foreign language at the university level due to a grant from the Danish Ministry of Education and Research, and from 1995 onward, Arabic has been offered as an optional modern foreign language at secondary school level, first as a provisional subject in a few schools to see if there was a demand for it, and from 2005, on a permanent basis (Nielsen, 2012).

Although Arabic is offered at all levels of Danish education, it is subject to a number of limitations. At the primary school level, it is the local municipality, not the schools, which decides if Arabic is offered as mother tongue education, and if so, whether to do it for free. As a result, Arabic is only offered by a few municipalities with high numbers of Arab immigrants and mostly for a fee—something very exceptional in the Danish school system where education is financed through general taxes and thus considered "free of charge" (Daugaard, 2015, pp. 16–17). And if students continue their mother tongue education until grade 9 or 10—again something very exceptional, since most municipalities only offer mother tongue education until grade 5 or 6—students cannot have their proficiency assessed through an examination, as is the case with other foreign languages (Danish Ministry of Education, 2014, Article 14, Section 3). Thus, Arabic proficiency is not an asset which is taken into account when students apply for secondary school. At the secondary school level, only around 10 schools in Denmark offer Arabic, again mostly in areas with many Arab immigrants. Danish secondary school curricula and exams, which in this case include Arabic, are managed nationally by the Ministry of Education and Research, and their policy is to frame Arabic as a foreign language, despite the fact that more than 90% of the students who register for the subject and 99% of those who sit for exams are HL learners.[2]

Hence, Arabic is offered only as an HL in primary school, and there is no pedagogical alignment with the teaching of Arabic in secondary school, where it is taught as a foreign language to mostly HL learners. Furthermore, Arabic in primary school is subject to a number of limitations which, taken together, makes it a second class subject compared to other foreign languages. The educational landscape of Arabic in Denmark is thus characterized by contradictory messages: On the one hand, there is a clearly stated policy aimed at supporting young Arab immigrants and children of immigrants in the educational system under the label of "pattern breakers," but on the other, their mother tongue or the language of their parents is considered to be of less value than other foreign languages (see Anderson, this volume, for a further discussion). So, how do HL learners of Arabic react to this mixed message once they finish secondary school?

3 Arab Heritage Language Learners in the University

The interest in studying Arabic at university level in Denmark has increased steadily since the turn of the millennium, from about 50 students per year in the late 1990s to the highest number so far in 2013 when 271 students applied for Arabic as their first priority in the national enrollment for Danish universities. One can add to this about the same number of students who applied for Arabic as their second or third priority (Ministry of Higher Education and Science—Denmark, 2015). Since Danish universities do not register students according to race, ethnicity, or religion, not much is known at the national level about the number of these students who actually qualify for the term HL learners. From classroom experience in the Arabic programs at SDU, statistics show that the number of HL learners has risen considerably over the past 10 years, as can be seen from Figure 25.1. Please also note that until 2007, students were enrolled only every second year.

Not much is known either about why HL learners want to study Arabic at university level in Denmark, but a survey conducted at SDU from 2007 might give an indication. By means of a questionnaire distributed in the first week of their study program, all first-year students of Arabic were asked, among other things, about their reasons for studying Arabic, if they studied Arabic prior to entering university, and what they wanted to do after graduation. In an attempt to make at least some of the results comparable to an earlier survey on Arabic students in the U.S., we used many of the same questions on student motivation as Belnap (2006, pp. 174–175).[3]

In a number of cases, heritage and foreign language learners seem to share a common motivation for studying Arabic. More than 80% of both groups stated that their main objective was to get a job working with or in the Middle East. This suggests that HL learners' major reason for studying Arabic, in Denmark at least, is of the same job-focused nature as that of most other students, whereas heritage-related motivations, such as religion or learning the language and culture of their parents, seem to be of less importance. The survey also indicated that only 15% of the heritage learners had studied Arabic prior to entering university, either in mother tongue

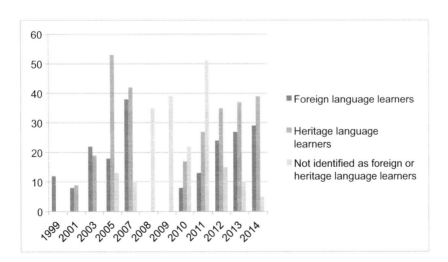

Figure 25.1   Number of First-Year Students of Arabic at the University of Southern Denmark, 1999–2014

Source: "KOT: Den koordinerede tilmelding [The National Admission Website]," by Ministry of Higher Education and Science—Denmark, 2015; and "White book: Statistics" by University of Southern Denmark, 2015a.

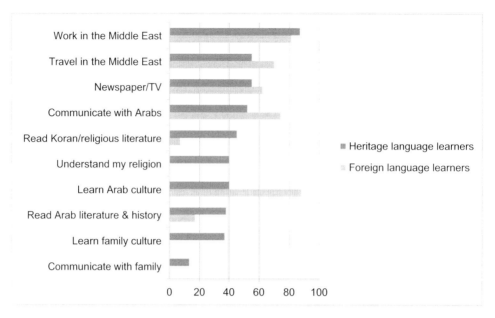

Figure 25.2   First-Year Students' Reasons for Studying Arabic at the University Level (%), 2007 (n=80)

classes in primary school or religious classes organized by a local mosque. The results of the survey correspond to opinions heritage learners often express during discussions in the Arabic classroom: They want to "turn their disadvantage into an advantage," to cite a heritage student, and have a clear expectation that Arabic can open doors to the labor market, despite the negative public discourse in Danish society. This indicates, among other things, that heritage learners choose university studies in Arabic at SDU mainly as a pragmatic approach to social mobility. This is further supported by a number of public statements by Arab HL learners who graduated from the three interdisciplinary Arabic programs. A former student, who is currently pursuing a career in music, wrote a feature in the Danish national newspaper *Information*, in which he stated:

> When I told my school counselor that I wanted to go to university, she gave me brochures on everything else. "Be realistic," she said. No one in my family had an education, they were more focused on getting away from the war [in Lebanon] alive than sitting in the classroom. . . . Today I stand with a bachelor's degree in international business communication and language from the University of Southern Denmark in hand and cannot help but think "Wow! How?!" I am still speechless and proud. It feels so surreal.
>
> *(Ismail, 2014)*

After graduating in Arabic and business management, another heritage student wrote on Facebook:

> At about the same time, 12 years ago, an almost illiterate Mohammed arrived in Denmark. Today, I am happy to announce that I have completed my undergraduate education, a bachelor (BA) in business management and language. Thanks to Denmark which has changed my life. Thanks to all the wonderful people who have supported me all the way through.

Thanks to those who offered me 100,000 [kroner] to leave the country as they have motivated me to be better than them. This is only the beginning . . . now the master program is waiting in September.

(Eid, 2015)

It bears noting that although both students value the professional advantages obtained from their degrees, neither mentions the Arabic component explicitly. This may stem from an awareness on the part of the students of the negative public discourse surrounding Arabic in Danish society.

Although heritage learners have varied language proficiency profiles in Arabic when they enter university, the vast majority have linguistic advantages over foreign language learners when it comes to listening comprehension, pronunciation, acquisition of vocabulary, etc. Therefore, it was surprising for us to discover that at least some HL learners took longer to complete their BA studies in the Arabic programs than foreign language learners. A recurrent explanation mentioned by the affected heritage learners pointed to the academic literature being in English. Danish academia today is strongly influenced by English, to the extent that regardless of their field of studies, students have to read most of the academic course literature in English, while discussing it, orally and in writing, in Danish. Although it is mandatory to study English in Danish primary and secondary schools, this diglossic-like situation puts pressure on most students, but it seems to be a heavier burden for some HL learners, particularly if they arrived in Denmark in their teens. Not only do they have to cope with a bilingual situation of a spoken Arabic variety and Danish, but for each of these languages they have to master a superposed variety, that is modern standard Arabic, and English, respectively, in order to succeed in their university studies. These students are thus affected by what could be termed "double hierarchical diglossia"—hierarchical in the sense that modern standard Arabic and English are both prestigious varieties learned through formal education (Badawi, 1973; Bassiouney, 2009; Ferguson, 1959). Having to read extensively in English thus imposes an additional language acquisition task for academic purposes on top of their bilingualism and their acquisition of modern standard Arabic.

4 Teachers as Language Planning Agents

From a language policy perspective, teachers in public education serve as implementers of macro language policies at the same time as they are actively engaged in the micro planning process of responding to learner needs and language problems in the classroom (Baldauf, 2006; Cabau, 2014). This dual role enables them to consciously take on language-planning agency. Instead of just seeing their role as mere dependent practitioners of top-down language orders from the governmental and university level, they can choose to take relatively autonomous actions which meet students' needs and demands, and thus develop measures to enhance their educational opportunities (Lo Bianco, 2014, p. 319). This language planning agency among teachers was an important factor in accommodating the growing number of HL learners who began to study Arabic at SDU from around the turn of the millennium.

The faculty's language planning agency has taken two interlinked directions over the years: to find solutions to the challenges involved in teaching heritage and foreign language learners within the same courses, and to develop interdisciplinary programs involving Arabic that are suited to HL learners' needs and demands. When the number of heritage learners rose dramatically in 2005, the Arabic faculty first asked for permission to create an HL track, but it was refused by the administration and the head of the study board on the grounds that it would make the organization of courses less flexible. They argued that in cases where HL learners had a higher proficiency level than the average foreign language learner in a given course, they could simply skip classes and sit for the mandatory exam at the end of the semester. Subsequently, the faculty suggested holding diagnostic proficiency tests at the beginning of each semester for interested students, and if their results corresponded to one of the four proficiency levels set across the Arabic programs, the students would earn credits for the corresponding course, which would allow them to register for a higher proficiency level. This suggestion, intended to optimize the course of study for HL learners and ease the pedagogical challenges of teaching heritage and foreign language learners in the same classroom, was initially accepted by the administration and added to the course curriculum, the official document governing all rules and regulations of a study program. However, it was removed some years later on the grounds that holding these additional exams was not allowed.

A second direction for the faculty's language planning agency was to develop new programs and curricula to accommodate HL learners' needs. When the first BA program in Arabic was established at SDU in 1992, it was agreed that Arabic should be combined with a second field of studies in order to keep the focus on communicative teaching of Arabic, enhance students' job opportunities, and adopt a different profile from the existing university programs in Arabic. The first program offered by SDU was a combined study of Arabic and international business management which included courses in mathematics and statistics, among other things. This proved to be a challenge for those students, heritage and foreign learners alike, who had chosen the study program out of interest for Arabic, and many of them dropped out within the first year. Subsequently, the Arabic faculty developed a second and more humanities-style program of Arabic and international business communication which began in 2005 with a very large influx of HL learners, as can be seen from Figure 25.1. Though this program continued to attract significant numbers of HL learners in the following years, it also involved a new challenge. As a mandatory part of both Arabic programs, students were supposed to spend their third year of study in an Arab country, and while this was considered a major attraction for most students, it also challenged some of the female HL learners, a majority in the programs, who were either married with children or had other family reasons preventing them from studying abroad. In an effort to cater to these students as well as to attract more HL learners, the faculty, together with researchers in educational pedagogy, developed a third combined program consisting of Arabic and intercultural pedagogy, this time without a mandatory study abroad component. This program started in September 2011 and aimed at a job market in the Danish immigrant sector.

A common denominator for the language planning agency of the Arabic faculty during this period was the desire to create educational opportunities at the university level which catered to HL learners' needs and demands and, at the same time, attracted more students. This deliberate strategy "from below" was based on the understanding that as a relatively new field of studies, the Arabic programs would be firmly rooted in the university's foreign language portfolio, and would continue provided that the numbers of students remained high enough.

5 From Growth to Closure: How and Why?

How did the administration respond to the HL learners' educational choices and the teachers' language planning agency in favor of these students? At first, positively in the sense that they approved and supported the implementation of the two new Arabic programs in 2005 and 2011 and changed the timeframe for registration of new students from every second year to every year. This lead to an increased number of Arabic students in a rather short span of time, and hence forced the university to set a cap on intake at 75 new students a year from 2011, which in turn led to higher entry requirements for students due to increased competition. This situation convinced the faculty that the Arabic programs had now entered a period of stabilization. At a time when the demand for foreign languages other than English had been declining steadily in Danish universities over the previous 10–15 years, and with a clear political focus on the need for pattern-breakers, the attempts to build up attractive university programs in Arabic for heritage and foreign language learners alike had proved successful and contributed to the important task of supporting social mobility for immigrants (Ministry of Higher Education and Science, 2011, pp. 44–48). Therefore, it came as a huge surprise to everyone when the Dean of Humanities decided, in January 2015, not only to cut back the number of Arabic students, as he did in other subjects, but to outright close the three Arabic programs as a result of a new government requirement to reduce the number of students in higher education. To understand how this change of strategy came about, it is necessary to distinguish between the structural conditions which all Danish universities are subjected to, and the decisions taken by local university agents within the framework of these structural conditions.

Structural Growth and Arabic-as-Resource

More than 90% of the university grants in Denmark come from the state, while the rest originate from private or foreign sources, mainly from the EU (Oddershede, 2009, p. 5). This makes Danish universities heavily dependent on political agendas and demands, and this was very clearly illustrated through the first decade of the twenty-first century, where growing youth unemployment made successive governments argue that more young people should have access to higher education. In this period, the number of university students grew significantly, as can be seen from Figure 25.3. It was during this period that the Arabic programs at SDU expanded. The increasing number of HL learners who wanted to study Arabic together with the faculty's language planning agency supported by centrally organized university initiatives to promote pattern breakers, met with virtually no resistance at any level of the university (University of Southern Denmark, 2013). Rather, the prevailing discourse was that of "Arabic-as-resource," which matched the profile of SDU as being the university with the highest number of students with immigrant backgrounds in Denmark, as illustrated in Figure 25.4.

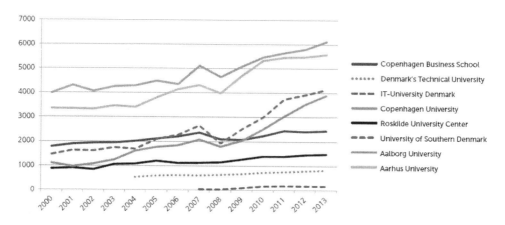

Figure 25.3 Undergraduate Students Admitted in Danish Universities 2000–2013 (n=243.753)

Source: Adapted from "*Fordeling af det stigende optag på universiteterne*" [The distribution of the increasing intake of students in Danish Universities], by Danish Evaluation Institute, 2015, p. 8. Copyright 2015 by EVA.

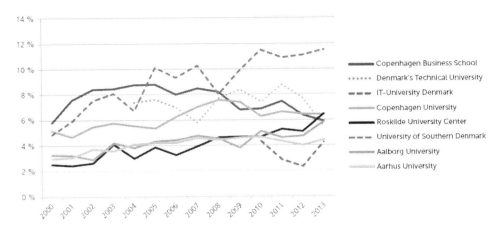

Figure 25.4 Students with Immigrant Background or Descendants of Immigrants Admitted in Danish Universities, 2000–2013 (n=14.692)

Source: Adapted from *"Fordeling af det stigende optag på universiteterne"* [The distribution of the increasing intake of students in Danish Universities], Danish Evaluation Institute, 2015, p. 14. Copyright 2015 by EVA.

Not opposing the programs is, however, not the same as supporting them. Universities have a complex hierarchical structure where different stakeholders may have conflicting interests, and policy choices do not necessarily pull in the same directions. A recurrent point of discussion during these years was the number of research faculty that underpinned the BA programs. In addition to a foreign lecturer, an administrative term for a native speaker teaching full time, the plan laid out by the department was to staff the programs with three senior faculty members with a research profile in Arabic as a foreign or second language. Over the years, two junior and three senior positions were announced, and though the number of applicants were rather high, only a few were qualified given the required research profile. In 2011, in the wake of the new Arabic program in intercultural pedagogy, the Arabic section was staffed with an associate professor, two assistant professors, and a foreign lecturer. As for the tenure process for the assistant professors, once their three-year contract ran out, it was not renewed, leading to a faculty reduction in this crucial area. To remedy the situation, the administration decided to employ a new assistant professor with a profile in HL learning, a doctoral student, as well as some part-time teachers that could fulfill the program's teaching needs. The research-based faculty was thus reduced to one associate and one assistant professor and a doctoral student. This obviously made the Arabic programs more vulnerable to staffing issues and led to increased teaching pressure and less research output, but had the benefit of reducing costs.

Socioeconomic Turbulence and Arabic-as-Barrier

Starting in 2012, the political signals began slowly to change, and in the fall of 2014, the government finally put forward specific demands to make universities "dimension their student population"—a euphemism for cutting back the number of students so that, in the words of the minister for Higher Education and Research, "universities no longer educate young people for unemployment" (Nielsen, 2014). The ministry grouped university programs across the country according to specific indicators of which unemployment was the single most important one, outlined targets for how much each group of programs had to cut back, and subsequently left it to the universities to decide the details and implement the cut backs. At SDU, it was decided not only to cut back the number of students of Arabic, but to close down the programs entirely by admitting no new students beginning in 2015. It was all the more surprising given that, in the spring of 2014, the deans of the Faculties of Humanities and Health Sciences had supported the establishment of a fourth program in Arabic and health communication. The administration argued for the decision by using three indicators: students' unemployment rate after graduation, students' completion and dropout rate, and "depth of research" measured, among other things, by number of researchers employed in the field as well as research output.

In subsequent discussions with the administration, it quickly became clear that unemployment figures were not available for students of Arabic; they simply could not be singled out from the pool of unemployment figures for graduates in foreign languages as a whole. As for the completion and dropout rate, the following statistics from 2009–2011 were used by the dean's office: In September 2009, 31 students were admitted into the program of Arabic and International Business Communication, but only five had graduated by December 2014, and in the following year, the numbers was 32 admitted and 6 graduated. And from the 49 students who were accepted in 2011, 28 students had dropped out by December 2014. Figures like these were not satisfactory, as the dean claimed in a local news story (Torp & Binnerup, 2015). As for the depth of research, no quantitative measures were given, only vague statements about "the importance of high quality research as a sound foundation for educational university programs" (Torp & Binnerup, 2015, p. 21). At a later meeting in March 2015, presented with figures for research output from the two researchers involved, the dean acknowledged the output as satisfactory.[4] More research output would have required more researchers, but the administration's decision in 2011 had actually prevented this by not employing more senior faculty.

With no unemployment figures from SDU graduates in Arabic and a "depth of research" which was satisfactory compared to the number of researchers employed, the crucial issue on which to justify the closing of Arabic became the number of students who actually completed the programs within the given timeframe. This indicator, which is used nationwide, stems from a political reform adopted in the Danish parliament in 2013, which links economy, both in terms of money for universities and scholarships for students, to the completion of studies in the stipulated time (Study Completion Reform, 2013, 2015). According to university statistics, 39.2% of the students who were admitted into the program of Arabic and International Business Communication—the program used by the dean's office to illustrate the low completion rate of Arabic students—between 2005 and 2011 actually graduated after 3.5 years (the BA programs of Arabic being seven semesters), compared to, for example, 34.5% of students admitted into Religious Studies, 37.9% of students admitted into German Studies and 47.9% of students admitted into History, as shown in Figure 25.5. The numbers presented by the Dean's office in January 2015 to argue the low completion rate of Arabic students—only 5 graduate students out of 31 admitted in 2009, and 6 out of 32 the following year—were thus not accurate and at best, very selective.

Students of Arabic might have a higher dropout rate and might take somewhat longer to complete their studies than students in some of the other programs, but the differences are by no means significant, as can be seen from Figure 25.5. Due to the administration's decision to close the three Arabic programs with reference to these indicators, we examined a number of exam protocols to see if we could identify the factors behind the dropout rate and length of completion data, and a rather clear pattern emerged from this scrutiny. It turned out that HL learners frequently had to be reexamined once or even twice in subjects not related to Arabic, but rather in economics, business communication, and intercultural pedagogy. This pattern does not occur in other foreign language studies at the university, where HL learners are an unknown phenomenon. However, the pattern is not surprising given that bilingualism and social background are

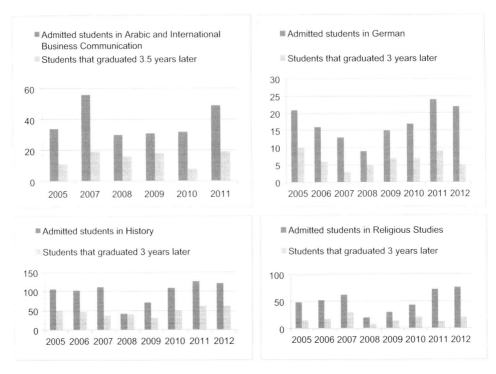

Figure 25.5   Number of Admitted and Graduate Students in Various BA Programs at the University of Southern Denmark, 2005–2011

Source: "White book: Statistics" by University of Southern Denmark, 2015a.

known to influence completion rates as well as exam results, as abundantly shown in Danish and international research literature (see e.g., Haahr, Nielsen, Hansen, & Jakobsen, 2005). If we add to this the "double hierarchical diglossia" which Arab HL learners have to cope with in Danish universities, it is certainly not surprising that the completion rates are lower and slower among HL learners than other university students.

The decision to gradually close the Arabic programs was criticized in many places by referring to the current political focus on pattern breakers. How could the university promote a policy of pattern breakers on the one hand, and close down Arabic on the other, knowing that these programs provided fertile ground for HL learners' educational and social mobility? But none of the decision makers wanted to take up this issue. The minister of Education and Research argued consistently that it was the university's sovereign decision to select the studies to be "dimensioned" and the administration claimed that the ministry did not leave them any choice. And in this void the university administration continues to brand SDU as a pattern breaker university, as the following citation from the vice-chancellor, dated November 15, 2015, shows:

> We can actually be proud of our ability to accomplish what we do. . . . SDU is the university in Denmark with students whose parents have the least education and the lowest-paying jobs. At the same time, we have more students with an immigrant background. As such, we work particularly to ensure that youth who come from non-academic homes have the chance to receive a university education, and through this we are performing an important duty for society.
>
> *(University of Southern Denmark, 2015b)*

6 Lessons Learned

What are the lessons learned from Arab HL learners in Danish postsecondary education and the institutional management of programs involving these learners in a Danish context?

First, there seems to be a raised awareness among Arab HL learners in Denmark that their language skills can be used for professional ends. By investing their linguistic capital into formal university education, the students intend to transform their language skills into educational capital which in turn could be converted into social mobility. This choice was made despite the ambivalent status of Arabic in Denmark, and is best described as "language pressure from below." By exploring and choosing from available educational resources, Arab HL learners located opportunities and planned their educational progress, thus acting as micro language planners who based their decisions on a heritage discourse of "language-as-resource." This bottom-up process, which stems from HL learners' desire for social mobility, was sustained by a faculty who actively supported them by acting as language planning managers and thus helped implement the top-down policy of supporting pattern breakers. The fact that the HL learners quoted above preferred labeling their BA degrees in public forums as in business management or communication studies, without mentioning the Arabic component (although this represented approximately 60% of their degree), might reflect the students' awareness of the predominantly negative attitudes toward Arabic in Danish society. It might also reflect a concern that, as Arab HL learners, a BA in Arabic would diminish their academic achievement in the eyes of the Danish public.

Secondly, from an institutional point of view, the pressure exerted by HL learners from below was embraced by the university administration in times of expansion and growth, whereas in times of socioeconomic turbulence, as happened in 2014–2015, the Arabic programs were the first to be closed down. This highlights a dual use of the Arabic programs, and thus Arabic HL learners, on the part of the administration. On the one hand, they are employed as a "strategic buffer" in the sense of being revenue-generating initiatives in times of growth, and also a means of instantiating governmental policies such as those that target pattern breakers. On the other hand, they become expendable areas in times of economic turbulence, even though the decision to dismantle the Arabic programs was taken at a time when Danish society had an urgent need for Arabic skills given the pressure from refugees and migrants entering Europe as a consequence of the Syrian civil war and the general political unrest in the area sparked by the Arab Spring in 2011. The Arabic programs, in short, were utilized for specific short-term economic goals rather than more long-term aims and policies, and were never viewed as fully integrated elements within the university. Ekholm and Trier (1987) argue that a crucial indicator of successful institutionalization is legitimacy, i.e., the acceptance of an innovation as "valuable and natural" (p. 17). Despite the best efforts of students and faculty, the Arabic programs did not rise to the level of legitimacy in the eyes of the administration. Put differently, top-down pressure prevailed over bottom-up forces, illustrating the point that in introducing an innovation, political and ideological factors can be determinate in the process of its institutionalization.

Other indicators of institutionalization detailed by Ekholm and Trier (1987) are more concrete, and focus on resource allocation. The role of "strategic buffer" is illustrated in this area as well. To begin with, HL learners' pedagogical needs were never fully taken into account. The university never established targeted courses for HL learners, although it would have benefited heritage and foreign learners alike and could have led to higher and faster completion rates for the HL learners. Placement initiatives instituted by the faculty that could have alleviated the teaching of this mixed population were also dismantled. The reluctance to employ permanent research faculty to support the programs also attests to their marginality.

Lastly, not only did Arab HL learners serve as a "strategic buffer" in the university, but they were also punished for their multilingualism. As bilinguals they had to cope with the challenges of mastering high levels of fluency in reading and writing Danish, acquiring English for academic purposes, and adding standard Arabic to their spoken variety. Instead of acknowledging these academic and linguistic challenges, the administration used dropout and completion rate "production targets" that reflected these challenges as a reason for closing down the programs. In this way, the administration underwent a marked change in attitude toward Arabic from "language-as-resource" to "language-as-problem" and at the same time prevented future Arab HL learners from leveraging their linguistic skills into educational capital and social mobility. This made the university discourse on pattern breakers and social responsibility sound rather hollow, and illustrates to what extend Danish universities choose short-term economic considerations over social responsibility, not only toward HL learners but society as a whole. While Danish universities are obliged to navigate in a neoliberal educational landscape based on completion rates and other production targets laid down by Danish politicians, they must also take account of the fact that they have to contribute to the solution of refugee problems and integration challenges, support Denmark's competitiveness on the international arena, and serve the country's complex foreign policy interests in a globalized world—tasks which many university graduates with an Arab heritage background are particularly qualified to take on.

Notes

1 Pattern breakers (in Danish: *Mønsterbrydere*) are students who break social patterns by achieving a higher level of education than that of their parents, thus improving their opportunities for upward social mobility. In higher education, pattern breakers are defined as university students whose parents did not attend university.
2 No public statistics are available at this level, but as an external examiner and member of the ministry's commission on Arabic for more than 10 years, I am well acquainted with these figures.
3 Belnap's survey, however, does not primarily focus on differences in student motivation between HL learners and non-HL learners.
4 From 2011 to 2015 the output from the associate and the assistant professors amounted to 17 research articles, 31 articles in newspapers and magazines, and 145 public lectures and interviews in media outlets (Dhahir, n.d.; Nielsen, n.d.).

References

Badawi, S. M. (1973). *Mustawayiat al-'arabiyya al-mu'asira fi misr* [*The levels of contemporary Arabic in Egypt*]. Cairo, Egypt: Dar al-Ma'arif.
Baldauf, R. B. (2006). Rearticulating the case for micro language planning in a language ecology context. *Current Issues in Language Planning*, 7(2–3), 147–170.
Bassiouney, R. (2009). *Arabic sociolinguistics: Topics in diglossia, gender, identity, and politics*. Washington, DC: Georgetown University Press.
Belnap, A. K. (2006). A profile of students of Arabic in U.S. universities. In K. Wahba, Z. Taha, & L. England (Eds.), *Handbook for Arabic language teaching professionals in the 21st century* (pp. 169–178). Mahwah, NJ: Lawrence Erlbaum.
Cabau, B. (2014). Minority language education policy and planning in Sweden. *Current Issues in Language Planning*, 15(4), 409–425.
The Danish Evaluation Institute. (2015). *Fordeling af det stigende optag på universiteterne* [*The distribution of the increasing intake of students in Danish universities*]. Copenhagen, Denmark: EVA. Retrieved from https://www.eva.dk/eva/projekter/2015/det-stigende-optag/hent-notater/fordeling-af-det-stigende-optag-pa-universiteterne
The Danish Government Council of Globalization. (2006). Fremgang, fornyelse og tryghed. Strategi for Danmark i den globale økonomi [Progress, renewal and security: Strategy for Denmark in the global economy]. Retrieved from http://www.stm.dk/multimedia/Fremgang_fornyelse_og_tryghed.pdf

Danish Ministry of Education. (2014). *The Folkeskole Act* [Danish public school, primary and lower secondary education] of December 11, 2015 Retrieved from https://www.retsinformation.dk/forms/r0710.aspx?id=176327#id73c451e7-10bb-40dc-8fac-311fbc943490

Daugaard, L. M. (2015). Sproglig praksis i og omkring modersmålsundervisning [Linguistic practices in and around mother tongue teaching] (doctoral dissertation). University of Aarhus. Retrieved from http://edu.au.dk/fileadmin/edu/phdafhandlinger/Daugaard_2015_protected.pdf

Deichmann, C. (2010). Dansk Industri: Folkeskolen bør også undervise i arabisk [Danish Industries: Primary schools should also teach Arabic]. *Folkeskolen.dk*, November 17, Retrieved from https://www.folkeskolen.dk/65230/dansk-industri-folkeskolen-boer-ogsaa-undervise-i-arabisk

Dhahir, O. (n.d.). Omar Dhahir [Website]. Retrieved from http://findresearcher.sdu.dk/portal/da/persons/omar-dhahir%2847fb287f-c37e-4815-8893-142cfd3fe8c1%29.html

Doerr, N., & Lee, K. (2013). *Constructing the heritage language learner: Knowledge, power and new subjectivities.* Hawthorne, NY: De Gruyter Mouton USA.

Eid, M. (2015, January 22). Samme tid for ca. 12 år side . . . [At the same time 12 years ago] [Facebook post]. Retrieved from https://www.facebook.com/mohammed.eid.161?pnref=friends.search

Ekholm, M. R., & Trier, U. P. (1987). The concept of institutionalization: Some remarks. In M. B. Miles, M. Ekholm, & R. Vandenberghe (Eds.), *Lasting school improvement: Exploring the process of institutionalization* (pp. 13–21). Leuven, Belgium: Acco.

Ferguson, C. A. (1959). Diglossia. *Word, 15,* 325–340.

Haahr, J. H., Nielsen, T. K., Hansen, M. E., & Jakobsen, S. T. (2005). Explaining student performance: Evidence from the international PISA, TIMSS and PIRLS surveys. Retrieved from OECD: https://www.oecd.org/edu/school/programmeforinternationalstudentassessmentpisa/35920726.pdf

Ismail, M. (2014, May 31). Først fik jeg ni knivstik, så tog jeg en universitetsuddannelse [First I got nine stab wounds, then I took a university degree]. *Information.* Retrieved from http://www.information.dk/499345

Kloster, C. (2015, January 22). DF-ordfører: Arabisk Føtex-skilt er et knæfald for islam [DPP spokesperson: Arabic Føtex sign is submission to Islam]. *Ekstrabladet.* Retrieved from http://ekstrabladet.dk/nyheder/samfund/df-ordfoerer-arabisk-foetex-skilt-er-et-knaefald-for-islam/5410051

Kristiansen, M., Nørredam, M., & Krasnik, A. (2010). Brugerbetaling for tolke i sundhedsvæsnet [User fees for interpreters in health care]. *Ugeskrift for læger, 172*(24), 1856–1857. Retrieved from http://mesu.ku.dk/publications/New_interventions_in_health_care/Kristiansen__N_rredam__Krasnik_2010.pdf

Kristjánsdóttir, B. (2006). *Evas skjulte børn. Diskurser om tosprogede elever i det danske nationalcurriculum* [*The hidden children of Eve: Discourses on bilingual students in the Danish national curriculum*] (Doctoral dissertation). Danmarks Pædagogiske Universitet, København.

Lo Bianco, J. (2014, March). A celebration of language diversity, language policy and politics in education. *Review of Research in Education, 38,* 312–331.

Ministry of Higher Education and Science—Denmark. (2011). Sprog er nøglen til verden [Language is the key to the world]. Retrieved from http://ufm.dk/publikationer/2011/filer-2011/sprog_er_noeglen_til_verden.pdf

Ministry of Higher Education and Science—Denmark. (2014a, July 7). Vær med i uddannelses- og forskningsministerens mønsterbryderkorps [Join the Education and Research Minister's Corps of Pattern-Breakers]. Retrieved from http://ufm.dk/aktuelt/nyheder/2014/vaer-med-i-uddannelses-og-forskningsministerens-moensterbryderkorps?searchterm=m%C3%B8nsterbryder

Ministry of Higher Education and Science—Denmark. (2014b). Anbefalinger fra Mønsterbryderkorpset [Recommendations from the Pattern-Breakers' Corps]. Retrieved from http://ufm.dk/publikationer/2014/filer-2014/anbefalinger-fra-monsterbryderkorpset-pdf.pdf

Ministry of Higher Education and Science—Denmark. (2015). KOT: Den koordinerede tilmelding [The National Admission Website]. Retrieved from http://ufm.dk/uddannelse-og-institutioner/statistik-og-analyser/sogning-og-optag-pa-videregaende-uddannelser/grundtal-om-sogning-og-optag/kot-hovedtal

Nielsen, H. L. (2007a). Har regeringen en sprogpolitik? [Does the government have a language policy?]. *Information om Indvandrere, 11*(4), 12–15.

Nielsen, H. L. (2007b). Ikke et ord om minoritetssprog [Not a word about minority languages]. *Sprogforum, 40,* 5–9.

Nielsen, H. L. (2009). Arabisk i den offentlige debat: Tabersprog eller politisk symbol? [Arabic in the public debate: Looser language or political symbol?]. *Mellemøstinformation, 29*(3), 1–7.

Nielsen, H. L. (2012). Arabisk er selvskrevet i gymnasiet [Arabic plays a natural role in secondary schools]. *Gymnasieskolen, 10,* 38–41.

Nielsen, H. L. (n.d.). Helle Lykke Nielsen [Website]. Retrieved from http://findresearcher.sdu.dk/portal/da/person/hellelykke

Nielsen, S. C. (2014). Vi kan ikke være bekendt at uddanne til arbejdsløshed [We cannot allow ourselves to educate for unemployment]. Retrieved from http://ufm.dk/minister-og-ministerium/ministeren/artikler-og-indlaeg/arkiv/tidligere-minister-sofie-carsten-nielsens-kronikker-og-debatindlaeg/2014/vi-kan-ikke-vaere-bekendt-at-uddanne-til-arbejdsloshed

Oddershede, J. (2009, February 2). Danish universities—a sector in change. Universities Denmark, 1–15. Retrieved from http://dkuni.dk/English/~/media/Files/Publikationer/A%20sector%20in%20change.ashx

Organization for Economic Co-operation and Development Higher Education Programme, Institutional Management in Higher Education. (2014). Fostering equity in higher education: Compendium of practical case studies. Retrieved from http://www.oecd.org/edu/imhe/Fostering-inclusion-of-disadvantaged-students.pdf

Schjørring, E. (2010, October 29). Har Lokke afblæst værdikampen? [Has Lokke called off the battle over values ?] [interview with Pia Kjærsgaard]. Berlingske. Retrieved from http://www.b.dk/kommentarer/har-loekke-afblaest-vaerdikampen

Scholer, P. (2010, February 5). DF vil forbyde arabisk i frikvartererne [DPP will prohibit Arabic during recess]. Politiken. Retrieved from http://politiken.dk/indland/politik/ECE894036/df-vil-forbyde-arabisk-i-frikvartererne/

Spolsky, B. (2004). Language policy. Cambridge, UK: Cambridge University Press.

Statistics Denmark. (2015a). Statistikbanken [Statbank Denmark]. Retrieved from http://www.statistik-banken.dk/1002

Statistics Denmark. (2015b). Indvandrere i Danmark 2015 [Immigrants in Denmark 2015]. Retrieved from http://www.dst.dk/Site/Dst/Udgivelser/GetPubFile.aspx?id=20703&sid=indv2015

Study Completion Reform. (2013, April 18). Fremdriftreformen [Reform of the student grant system and the framework for study completion, agreement text]. Retrieved from http://www.altinget.dk/misc/reform-af-su-systemet-og-rammerne-for-studiegennemfoerelse.pdf

Study Completion Reform. (2015, November 20). Fremdriftreformen [Reform of the student grant system and the framework for study completion, revised text]. Retrieved from http://ufm.dk/lovstof/politiske-aftaler/aftale-om-justering-af-fremdriftsreformen

Torp, S. M., & Binnerup, L. G. (2015, January 30). Malet: God uddannelse og relevant job [Good education and relevant jobs]. Fyns Stiftstidende, p. 21.

University of Southern Denmark. (2013, September 13). SDU will help pattern breakers through student life. Retrieved from http://www.altinget.dk/forskning/rssitem.aspx?id=927868

University of Southern Denmark. (2015a). White book: Statistics from University of Southern Denmark. Retrieved from http://www.sdu.dk/om_sdu/dokumentation_tal/whitebook

University of Southern Denmark. (2015b, November 5). News about SDU: Newsletter for employees: Vice-chancellor's comment. Retrieved from http://newspublicator.dk/e10/parker/nl/147d4e50c80dd132/mc2133503/view/

Vilhelmsen, J. (2014). Stigning i monsterbrydere blandt ikke-vestlige efterkommere [Increase in pattern breakers among non-Western descendants]. Arbejderbevægelsens Erhvervsråd, p. 1–7. Retrieved from http://www.ae.dk/sites/www.ae.dk/files/dokumenter/analyse/ae_stigning-i-monsterbrydere-blandt-ikke-vestlige-efterkommere_0.pdf

26

Adoption, Implementation, and Institutionalization of Spanish Heritage Language Programs at Two U.S. Regional Comprehensive Universities

Alegría Ribadeneira and Alejandro Lee

1 Introduction

Across the United States, institutions of higher learning are adopting and implementing innovative heritage language (HL) pedagogies into their traditional language curricula. There is undoubtedly great diversity with regard to what these institutions are doing to serve their Spanish heritage language (SHL) learner population. While some programs have begun to consciously serve heritage language learners (HLLs) alongside second language learners (L2s) in mixed classrooms, other programs are able to offer separate courses for HLLs. The future seems promising. Programs offering special tracks have grown in the last two decades from 18% (Wherritt & Cleary, 1990) to 40% (Beaudrie, 2012). The leap is extremely encouraging when set within the historical timeline of SHL education, which can be traced back to the 1970s when a group of concerned educators began a grassroots effort to meet the unique needs of HLLs (Valdés, Lozano, & García-Moya, 1981). Currently, whether programs are able to offer separate tracks or have to serve their students in mixed classroom settings, each situation inspires the implementation of innovative pedagogies both in specific courses and across the curriculum. Adding to this diversity of approaches, we can also find different stages in progress as the process of development and implementation of the innovative programs moves toward possible institutionalization.

As Rogers (1995) noted in his study of the general diffusion of innovation, the adoption of any innovation is a complex process that goes through various stages (knowledge, persuasion, decision, implementation, confirmation), while dealing with the gradual adhesion of key players to the cause. Following this same pattern, the case of adopting, implementing, and eventually institutionalizing an educational program can also be a lengthy, complex process and, as noted by Ekholm and Trier (1987), will not be linear, but instead it "is extended over time and will contain characteristic features of developmental processes, including dialectic, tensions, gradual shifts, freezing and unfreezing moments, etc." (p. 14).

This chapter analyzes the process of adoption, implementation, and institutionalization of innovative pedagogical approaches in SHL teaching at two small regional comprehensive universities that serve sizable Hispanic[1] populations: Colorado State University, Pueblo, and Central Washington University, Ellensburg.

The analysis presents an overview of the institutions and their Spanish programs, and then examines the processes through which each organization has assimilated innovation into its structure. In order to understand the process we present two sections for each institution. The first section includes a discussion of the various practices that have been adopted and implemented into the curriculum. We look at the history, challenges, issues of resistance, and facilitative conditions that permitted the programs to integrate these innovations.

The second section analyzes the issue of institutionalization defined by Ekholm and Trier (1987) as "an assimilation of change elements into a structured organization, modifying the organization in a stable manner" (p. 13). In order to gauge the level of institutionalization, we look at a set of indicators that we have adapted from Ekholm and Trier, and Eiseman, Fleming, and Roody (1990). The indicators we include are:

a) Negotiations—Formal and informal agreements have been reached about the continuation of the innovation.
b) Resources—Time, materials, and personnel have been routinely allocated.
c) Legitimacy—The innovation has become a habit in the sense that it is no longer controversial and has become standard and customary.
d) Organizational processes—Procedures and structures that aim to preserve the innovation are officially in place.
e) Stability—The continuation of the innovation does not depend on the initiative of specific people.

This investigation tries to determine the level of institutionalization achieved thus far in these two programs, but, most importantly, it illustrates the challenges and triumphs of introducing innovation in the context of small regional comprehensive universities. Our hope is that this analysis serves to encourage colleagues to initiate or persist in the process of implementing HL pedagogies into their language programs. As the analysis below shows, the innovations in both institutions have achieved a great level of stability, yet neither author will claim that full institutionalization has taken place. Throughout the chapter, it becomes evident that some aspects of the programs are now strongly grounded, while others are caught between implementation and institutionalization. In order to better understand these gray areas, we should consider Louis's (2006) observation that "institutionalization is part of the implementation process and it is not possible to determine exactly where implementation ends and institutionalization starts" (p. 28).

2 Colorado State University, Pueblo: Incorporating HL Pedagogies across the Curriculum

Program Overview

As a regional comprehensive university with moderately selective standards, Colorado State University, Pueblo, mainly serves the population of Pueblo County and its surrounding areas, while also attracting some out-of-state and international students. The university enrolls about 5,000 students, of which more than 25% are of Hispanic descent, granting the institution the designation of a Hispanic-Serving Institution.

CSU-Pueblo articulates a clear mission of being an educational resource for the area, and it states in its catalog that it is "strongly committed to providing access to members of all minority groups, particularly the Hispanic populations" (Colorado State University, Pueblo, 2014, p. 13). As an educational resource for southeastern Colorado the university plays a crucial role. Unlike the metropolitan areas, or many of the picturesque tourist mountain towns that boast strong economies and high levels of education, Pueblo, and much of its surrounding agricultural areas, show below-average income and education indicators. According to the 2015 U.S. Census Bureau, Pueblo, which is 50.7% Hispanic (U.S. Census Bureau, 2015a), has a median income of $34,889 (U.S. Census Bureau, 2015b) and only 19.5% of its population holds a BA degree or higher (U.S. Census Bureau, 2015c). In some of the surrounding areas the percentage of people living under the poverty line is well above the state average of 13.1% (U.S. Census Bureau, 2015b), as illustrated by Crowley County, east of Pueblo, where 28.3%of people live in poverty (U.S. Census Bureau, 2015b).

These economical and educational disparities make CSU-Pueblo a most critical and valuable institution when it comes to improving the lives of people in the region who want access to education. Many Hispanic students come to the university as first-generation students with low academic preparedness, and have been affected by what Valenzuela (1999) has labeled "subtractive schooling" and Carreira and Beeman (2014) have recognized as the "Latino achievement gap." The institution offers various support services including TRiO (Student Support Services), the Southern Colorado Educational Opportunity Center, and the College Assistance Migrant Program (CAMP). While these services are helpful, academic units, such as the Spanish program, also play a crucial role in student success. As Carreira and Beeman have noted, courses that serve HLLs tend to their affective and pedagogical needs in ways that build confidence and academic skills, all of which transfer to overall academic experience and performance (p. 21). Furthermore, growth in Spanish proficiency gives students an edge in their professions of choice when they market themselves as educated bilingual and bicultural individuals.

This critical role was not clearly recognized until 2006, when the Spanish program began a radical change out of necessity in response to dwindling student numbers. Up to this point, the Spanish program at CSU-Pueblo was a traditional foreign language program that followed the two-tiered configuration found in many similar universities, i.e., a focus on grammar-based language teaching in the first two years of study and literature courses in the upper division. That year the program had 38 majors and 19 minors, while enrolling only 8.5% of all university students in a Spanish course. The program was in crisis and its future seemed uncertain. Changes began by implementing a proficiency-based approach to language teaching. Two years later it became obvious that a focus on HLLs and further rethinking of the curriculum was crucial to the program's success.

Now almost 10 years later, what began as a sometimes contentious innovation has become normalized and institutionalized to a degree where it is no longer controversial, and the program has seen a dramatic increase in enrollment numbers. In the last five years it has served an average of 87 majors and 43 minors every year, while enrolling 18.3% of all university students in a Spanish course. The program enlists the help of three ranked faculty members, one half-time ranked faculty member, two full-time lecturers, and three adjuncts. At the head of the program is the Associate Chair for Foreign Languages, who is the first author of this chapter.

Currently 77% of majors and 65% of minors are HLLs. With this reality, it is imperative to have a program that serves this population well by integrating the best SHL teaching practices into the entire curriculum. In this program, like many others in the nation, there are no separate tracks dividing L2 learners from HLLs; because of enrollment numbers and budget realities this is neither practical nor economically feasible. So the challenge stands as one of mixing HLLs and L2Ls in the same classrooms while acknowledging and attending to the fact that each group has unique pedagogical and affective needs that stem from their different linguistic and cultural backgrounds.

Consciousness about and action toward these important considerations were not always present. Effective pedagogies for mixed classes had to be initiated and implemented in order to avoid the common mistake of turning the mixed class to a de facto L2 course. As more research emerges in this area, the program continues to integrate cutting edge pedagogical tools that allow both populations to be served well. What follows is an account of the process of adoption and implementation of the changes that have benefited the program, together with an overview of some of the most important practices that have enhanced the program to better serve HLLs.

3 Adoption and Implementation

At the beginning of the millennium CSU-Pueblo, along with many other institutions around the nation, was suffering from low enrollment numbers in language courses. In 2004 the Modern Language Association established an ad hoc committee charged with making recommendations regarding the challenges and opportunities facing language study in higher education. The report, *Foreign Languages and Higher Education: New Structures for a Changed World*, became one of the leading documents that would inform changes to the CSU-Pueblo program and help educate the administration. There was a definite need for the program to innovate if it was to survive and be relevant, and the MLA presented a compelling argument:

> The two-tiered configuration has outlived its usefulness and needs to evolve. . . . Replacing the two-tiered language-literature structure with a broader and more coherent curriculum in which language, culture, and literature are taught as a continuous whole, supported by alliances with other departments and expressed through interdisciplinary courses, will reinvigorate language departments.
>
> *(MLA Ad Hoc Committee on Foreign Languages, 2007)*

The first proposed innovation for CSU Pueblo's language program was the creation of a broader and more coherent curriculum. The goal was to craft a program that would be appealing and useful for anyone who wanted to apply second language skills to any field of interest: business, social work, mass communications, law, nursing, English, psychology, health, political science, history, etc. In addition, standards of achievement that would translate to student-learning outcomes were also needed. For this task, the clear choice was integrating the World Readiness Standards for Learning Languages, known as the 5C's (World Readiness Standards for Learning Languages, n.d.), together with the American Council on the Teaching of Foreign Languages' (ACTFL) guidelines of proficiency (American Council on the Teaching of Foreign Languages [ACTFL], 2012). While the 5C's would help expand our focus to include not only communication but also culture, connections, comparisons, and communities, the ACTFL guidelines would help establish language proficiency goals for every course and for the program as a whole.

The adoption of ACTFL guidelines also meant a strong shift in philosophy since the focus would no longer be on what students knew about the language (the more traditional grammar approach), but rather what they could actually do with the language. Furthermore, the guidelines helped with placement of students who already had functional abilities, especially HLLs. This became possible because, as ACTFL states,

> Guidelines present the levels of proficiency as ranges, and describe what an individual can and cannot do with language at each level, regardless of where, when, or how the language was acquired. . . . They neither describe how an individual learns a language nor prescribe how an individual should learn a language.

> (ACTFL, 2012, p. 3)

Persuading upper administration to allow the adoption of these two innovations was easy since most of the concern over low enrollments was coming from them. In fact, they initiated the change by hiring a person from the outside to implement a program overhaul. Persuading the existing faculty became more challenging when it came time to make decisions as to what changes to implement and who should be in charge. As Ekholm and Trier (1987, pp. 14–15) have observed, every institution will have to contend with invariants such as its unique history and varying political, cultural, and social dimensions when trying to implement change. The degree of dialectic tension between the established ideologies and the new ideas can become a great challenge, and this program was no exception. Variants regarding content, depth, and scope of the change (Ekholm & Trier, pp. 15–17) aggravated the situation since the changes being sought were structural, organizational, procedural and, more importantly, philosophical. Achieving faculty buy-in was a slow process as there was no sense of collective ownership and the change, to some, felt as a top-down imposition. Without full resolution of this challenge the two innovations were adopted, and within a year enrollment numbers doubled. This positive result began to create an understanding and acceptance by most of the existing faculty, and with this began the social processing, i.e., discussions on an interpersonal level (Louis, 2006, p. 3) from the bottom-up that helped move the innovation forward. This dynamic coincides with Louis's observations that a mixture of top-down and bottom-up approaches is needed to move innovations toward institutionalization.

Among the new students signing up for classes were a higher number of HLLs. The program had become more appealing to them now that the revamped and expanded upper-division curriculum included several non-literature courses that could engage those interested in applying their Spanish skills to areas outside teaching or graduate school. The strong emphasis on proficiency, and the use of proficiency guidelines, appealed to those who had stayed away because their lack of explicit knowledge of grammar had made them feel inadequate. Now that the emphasis was in favor of valuing functional abilities, the Spanish skills students brought from home were highly valued. Furthermore, the ACTFL scale created a roadmap for those who believed they already knew Spanish and there was no more to learn.

With the increase of HLLs in the program it became evident more HLL pedagogies would have to be incorporated in every classroom. For this third innovation buy-in was instantaneous. There was no denying the previous two innovations had brought more HLL students to the program and instructors wanted to help. By this time many structural, organizational, procedural, and curricular innovations were already in place, but there was no clear understanding of how they were benefiting the HLL population. In order to better understand how the innovations intersected with the needs of HLLs, key personnel participated in a weeklong workshop with the National Heritage Language Resource Center (NHLRC) at UCLA. Participation in the NHLRC and further research confirmed that the changes implemented were HLL friendly. The new knowledge acquired at the workshop also inspired new practices. What follows is an overview of some of the most important practices that have been adopted and implemented, resulting in an enhanced program that better serves HLLs.

Curriculum Redesign

The curriculum previous to the redesign centered on grammar and literature. For example, second-year Spanish courses were named "Spanish Grammar and Composition 1 & 2," while the description for the conversation course for that level stated, "Students use short stories and essays designed to provide a fundamental literary vocabulary. . . . Students are introduced to basic literary terms as a foundation for their upper division studies" (Colorado State University, Pueblo, 2005, p. 255). At the 300 level, 7 out of 10 courses were literature, and at the 400 level, 7 out of 8 courses were literature.

In the new curriculum some changes were introduced right away while others have been introduced gradually and are still in progress. Second-year courses were renamed "Intermediate Spanish 1 & 2" and the books selected displayed a communicative approach that seemed to align better with the new proficiency philosophy. The second-year conversation course was renamed "Intermediate Proficiency Building" and adopted an HLL-friendly book. This course was designated as a gateway course for HLs who are not yet at intermediate level but do not need to take previous courses. In this course and all others that follow, the main goal became to develop students' oral and literacy skills through a macro approach (Kagan & Dillon, 2003), where task-based and project-based activities would expose students' individual learning needs, so they could be addressed through differentiation (Tomlinson, 1999).

Following this goal, the third-year curriculum was completely overhauled. All third-year level literature courses but one (Introduction to Literature) were removed. A series of conversation and composition courses based on different geographic areas were created. Faculty were encouraged to approach these courses through cultural studies, targeting high and low culture while having students engage in conversations, discussions, presentations, compositions, and projects. The courses covered South America, The Caribbean, Mexico and Central America, Spain, and Spanish in the U.S. Also, the old "Advanced Grammar Course" was redesigned as a grammar course for advanced speakers and became the gateway course for HLLs who enter the program at an intermediate high or higher proficiency level. The course uses an HLL textbook and supplements instruction for L2s.

In the next few years other 300-level courses were created. Among these were Business in the Spanish-Speaking World and Health and Well-Being in the Spanish-Speaking World. Unlike traditional courses of Business Spanish and Medical Spanish that devote a significant part of the course to explicit grammar teaching, these courses concentrate on building language skills through the use of authentic materials. In these courses students engage in conversations, projects, presentations, and community interactions that explore the topics of business and health. Other courses at the 300 level include "Special Topics," which allows professors to try out new ideas and themes, and "Field Experience," which allows students to participate in the Hispanic community at home or abroad while creating a portfolio and a campus wide presentation.

Four hundred–level offerings have been the hardest to change. The curriculum at this level still revolves predominantly around literature; however, professors are reminded, and students are reassured, that the ultimate goal of these courses is to help them expand their communicative skills. Beyond the literature offerings we have been able to offer courses on the Mexican Revolution, Contemporary Cinema of Spain, Contemporary Cinema of Latin America, and Representations of Migration. Future courses will include Politics and Power in the Spanish-Speaking World and Gender and Society in the Spanish-Speaking World.

Professional Development

To further the process of faculty buy-in and ensure the success of the adoption and implementation of the innovations, it became paramount to encourage faculty participation in professional development. The goal was to give everyone the background to understand the new goals of the program. Every ranked professor was sent to participate in a four-day ACTFL Oral Proficiency Interview (OPI) Assessment Workshop. With the knowledge acquired, faculty could now plan courses, assess students, and share a common set of terms that would facilitate conversations. The dean and the department covered the expenses for the workshops, which were not insignificant. Lecturers have also gone through various degrees of training in ACTFL workshops, while adjuncts have received training through in-house workshops. Two key players attended the weeklong NHLRC workshop in UCLA on specific HL teaching.

Placement Policies

Our placement policies are directly intertwined with students' functional abilities as outlined by the ACTFL guidelines (ACTFL, 2012), therefore oral proficiency is the main criteria for placement. By using the OPI we are able to determine our students' strengths and weaknesses. This in turn creates a roadmap on how to help HLLs develop the abilities needed for reaching the next level (Swender, Martin, Rivera-Martinez, & Kagan, 2014). HLLs who are not at intermediate mid go into our second-year intermediate proficiency building course, while those who are at intermediate high go into our third-year gateway course.

Targeted Recruitment

HLLs find their way into the program in many ways. One of the most successful is our targeted recruitment through First Year Advisors, CAMP, and Chicano Studies. Every year, advisors in these programs receive a packet teaching them how to recognize HLLs through a short questionnaire, explaining our placement policies, and outlining the advantages HLLs can receive from studying their HL. This practice, now in its sixth year, brings dozens of students to our placement interviews where we further explain our program and its advantages.

Program Assessment

Since the inception of all these innovations, all our faculty has been required to participate in completing a program assessment report every year, and a comprehensive program review every five years. Both practices involve all instructors in analyzing outcomes and thinking about our philosophy and objectives. These assessment exercises have proven invaluable for buy-in as faculty see where their efforts fit into the program as a whole and have the opportunity to implement changes to their classes when outcomes are not reached.

The comprehensive five-year program review takes the assessment process one step further by aggregating the yearly assessments and analyzing successes and failures. The program review also contains sections where our program philosophy and objectives have to be explained to upper administration. One of the most important pieces of the program review is the external reviewer assessment. For this piece we have invited HLL teaching experts to conduct a thorough analysis of our program and make recommendations. The five-year program review goes through the university's Curriculum Committee, which on both occasions has approved the track the program has taken.

Instructor Guide

In 2010 it became obvious that in order to have all incoming instructors be on the same page and understand our program philosophy and policies, we needed to have an official instructor's guide. The guide is updated as needed and includes sections on program philosophy, ACTFL guidelines as they pertain to each of our courses, syllabi templates with set learning outcomes and ACTFL proficiency goals for each course, strategies for recruitment and retention, placement policies, common rubrics for the lower-level courses, and general guidelines for day-to-day operations. In the latest installment of the instructors guide we have added "Guidelines for addressing HL/L2 mixed classrooms" which includes a list of practices that can help instructors conduct a successful class where HLLs' affective and pedagogical needs are met (Appendix 26.1).

4 Institutionalization

As we look at issues of institutionalization of the different innovations mentioned above, we can see that while some practices are developing, most have now become institutionalized.

Negotiations

Many of the agreements reached at the beginning of the program transformation required much diplomacy, as they were informal and arose during meetings and discussions. It wasn't until the first program review in 2010 when the Curriculum and Academic Programs Board reviewed programmatic changes and student outcomes that the program was officially ratified and allowed to continue on its chosen path. The most recent program review in 2015 solidified this ratification, and the program is now strongly established.

Resources

This area is perhaps one of the most vulnerable as budget cuts and limited resources become commonplace. Despite these challenges, the position of Associate Chair for Foreign Languages has been maintained since 2006, when upper administration realized it was imperative to have a person dedicated to overseeing the program. The Associate Chair position receives one course release per semester to allow for the time it takes to ensure the quality of program. The course release translates to a financial commitment that supports the structure. Likewise, every tenure track professor has received money to participate in training in ACTFL workshops. Every person trained becomes personnel allocated to the needs of the program. It remains to be seen if these commitments can continue in the future as faculty come and go, and budgets shrink.

Legitimacy

One of the most encouraging facts noted by some individuals who were present at the onset of the program's overhaul is how normalized and natural so many of the once highly controversial practices and curriculum changes have become. A good example is the assessment requirements for graduating seniors. Before the changes, senior assessment consisted of a 40-page paper on a literary topic, and there was profound discontent when the new assessment was presented, namely an oral proficiency interview, a written proficiency test, a portfolio of student sample work, and an exit survey. Some faculty felt these were not as rigorous or valuable as the previous assessment. Now, after eight years, the new approach has become a non-issue, and all faculty routinely participate in the assessments.

Organizational Processes

Every year more processes and procedures become solidified by the act of repetition. Most have been formally established by finding their way into official documents. Program philosophy, placement policies, program learning objectives (5Cs and ACTFL guidelines), course offerings, and program requirements are present in the official university catalog, the program review documents, and the instructor's manual. As mentioned above, the manual also now includes the "Guidelines for addressing HL/L2 mixed classrooms." All these documents spell out organizational procedures and practices that aim to preserve the innovations for years to come.

Stability

Having detailed and systematic organizational processes in place have made the innovations less dependent on a group of reformers. In the last few years the president, provost, dean, and chair who supported the initial changes have moved on. There have also been changes in faculty, with the person hired to institute the changes and one of the major detractors gone. As personnel come and go, the strength of the organizational processes in place have been put to the test and so far have endured.

5 Central Washington University: Creating a Special Track for HL Students

Program Overview

Central Washington University (CWU), founded in 1891 as the Washington State Normal School in Ellensburg, Washington, is one of three regional comprehensive universities in the state. It enrolls approximately 13,000 students on the main campus and eight satellite locations housed in community colleges, and "serves more students on-line than any other comprehensive university in Washington" (Central Washington University, n.d.a). It attracts students mainly from coastal counties (King, Pierce, and Snohomish) and Yakima County. The enrollment numbers for 2014–15 reveal 92% are in-state students, 30% are students of color, and 12.5% of undergraduates are of Hispanic/Latino descent (Central Washington University, 2014–2015, n.d.b). As of 2014, the state of Washington has a population of about seven million, of which Latinos comprise 12% (Brown & Lopez, 2013).

As the only four-year institution of higher education in the center of the state with a sizable Latino population, CWU's vision and core values highlight "inclusiveness" by stating it "believes that diversity of peoples, cultures, and ideas is essential to learning, discovery, and creative expression" and it aims to distinguish itself "for its efforts to advance the social and economic health of the region" (Central Washington University, n.d.c). Many Latino students who attend CWU are first-generation students of Mexican descent, and are served by the Student Transitions and Academic Resources and two main academic units that address Latino issues: the Center for Latino and Latin American Studies and the Spanish program in the Department of World Languages. The latter offers majors and minors in French, Japanese, Spanish, and Russian, and minors in American Sign Language, Chinese, and German. The Spanish program currently enlists six tenured faculty and one adjunct, when needed.

Between 2013 and 2015, the number of students in world languages slowly dwindled. As of summer 2015, there were 47 Spanish majors and 54 minors, of which 32% and 37% were heritage students, respectively.

6 Adoption and Implementation of the HL Program

In 2001 two sequential third-year courses for HLLs, Spanish 345 and 346: Composition and Grammar for Heritage Speakers, were incorporated into the Spanish program to counteract the increasing tendency of HLs to enroll in composition courses designed for L2 learners, which created problems. On one hand, HLs' oral skills intimidated the L2 learners, creating an uncomfortable classroom dynamic; on the other, the HLs expressed their frustration at not having their educational goals and needs met. While the faculty supported the curriculum changes aimed at addressing these problems, there was no general interest in teaching or developing the new courses, with the exception of two faculty members who volunteered to teach most of them. While the courses, at first, had mostly healthy enrollments, Spanish 346 was canceled twice due to low enrollments.

Contributing to the problem of enrollments was the placement examination that had been adopted for both L2Ls and HLLs, namely the College Level Examination Program (CLEP).[2] Many HLLs who took the Spanish CLEP and were placed into upper-division courses, including Spanish 345 and 346, lacked the necessary metalinguistic knowledge and writing skills to succeed in them. Thus, in 2013 the program stopped accepting the CLEP results and instead decided to offer three second-year courses for HLLs in order to address their needs and increase the number of HLLs in the program. The chair and the second author volunteered to work together to create and teach the second-year courses, and both attended the NHLRC HL teaching workshop in the summer of 2012. In 2012, a committee began to create a new placement instrument to take the place of CLEP, which captured the needs and strengths of HLLs better and aligned better with course offerings in Spanish. This started out as a group enterprise but was, in the end, completed by the chair, working in his free time.

In contrast to the effort to create the third-year courses and the new placement examination, the development and implementation of the second-year series had administrative support. In order to research, develop, and implement the new series for the 2013–14 academic year, the second author applied for and received a course reduction, as well as a competitive summer innovation teaching grant. In the first year, the three second-year courses enrolled an average of 11 students each, while the second year saw a decline in enrollment (an average of 7 students) and a reduction to two courses because of budget constraints and staffing. As of 2015, only two second-year courses, and the original two third-year courses, were being offered for HL students.

Since Spanish 345 and 346 enroll HLLs with widely varying degrees of linguistic proficiency, and other upper-division courses at the third and fourth year levels are even more diverse in that they enroll both L2Ls and HLLs, some faculty have found creative and effective ways to incorporate differentiated teaching and other HL-friendly strategies into their teaching. As new research that focuses on HL pedagogy continues to come out, curriculum redesigns for Spanish 345 and 346 have also become necessary. The next section highlights these and other unique elements of the heritage program.

Curriculum (Re)Design

In 2012 the content of Spanish 345 and 346 was revamped to reflect current practices in HL education. Specifically, the following were included or expanded: macro-approaches to teaching grammar and culture (Kagan & Dillon, 2003); a diverse range of teaching materials that contain literary and non-literary texts; involvement with the community; and, perhaps most importantly, identifying opportunities to address students' socio-affective needs (Carreira, 2012).

In terms of the latter point, heritage students' evaluations reveal they welcome targeted HL courses because they help to create a sense of belonging and community other courses cannot offer. Within a few weeks of getting to know each other in the HL classroom, students form strong bonds and a community—a "big family," to use their terminology, is created. The HL program and both second- and third-year courses reinforce these bonds through various means, both in and out of the classroom:

- Instructors and students find opportunities for volunteer work in the community; attend or organize cultural events, potlucks, movie nights, get-togethers, etc.; and present at conferences and workshops, in which they share their experiences with re-learning their HL with local teachers and administrators.
- Instructors make concerted efforts to showcase heritage students' accomplishments by, for instance, sending the best essays and poetry written in the classroom for publication outside of the university.
- Instructors and students create a safe space in the classroom where they support each other and share personal stories related to immigration, family and work.

In addition, HLLs' socio-affective needs have been addressed through the creation of new courses. The second author has proposed and taught special topic courses at the 300 level that incorporate more cultural content, U.S. Latino authors, and themes of interest to bicultural students. In all these ways, HLLs' bicultural and bilingual identities are validated, and their sense of linguistic self-confidence is developed.

Like most programs, upper-division courses other than Spanish 345 and 346 enroll a mix of L2 and HL students. For instance, *Translation and Interpretation* enrolls both groups of students. In the case of HLLs, this is a popular course because it values their functional abilities and strengthens their interpreting skills. The phonetics course is also popular with a growing number of HLs, and because they already present a native-speaker-like pronunciation, the instructor has implemented differentiated instruction so they can draw other benefits from the course. For instance, the instructor trains HLLs on how to identify, transcribe, and evaluate their L2 classmates' recorded speech. The training and practice fine-tune HLLs' ears to listen for accents, interference from English, and subtle nuances such as the prosodic stress. The difficulties in identifying the syllabic stress vary widely in the HL population, and thus, the instructor can address it individually.

Professional Development

The second author, who has been actively involved with the NHLRC since 2010 as a faculty mentor, attends their workshops every summer as well as national and regional conferences on HL education, and, as noted earlier attended the workshop with the chair of the department in 2012, to prepare for redesigning the curriculum. Ideas and approaches from these contexts have been shared with colleagues and have informed the HL-focused curriculum changes. The second author and his colleagues have implemented activities such as formative assessments with exit cards, interviewing family, and identity-relevant readings in both English and Spanish.

Placement Policies

The program relies on the placement examination put into effect in 2013; however, there is much flexibility. Students who have taken second-year Spanish courses at the community college level can enroll directly into Spanish 345. Since courses for HLs are taught only once a year, we do our best to accommodate them on a case-by-case basis. Also, whenever potential HLs enrolled in L2 courses are identified during the first week of classes, they are asked to consult with a Spanish advisor or the instructor of record to determine if they should be placed in HL courses. Finally, not all HLLs take the placement examination because some transfer from other institutions, or their general academic advisors tell them to enroll in an L2 course.

Targeted Recruitment

HLLs learn about the HL program through their academic advisors, Spanish advisors, CAMP, TRiO, peers, and through outreach programs like Gaining Early Awareness and Readiness for Undergraduate Programs. In addition, information about all the programs is available at summer orientation days for new and transfer students, and fall open houses for prospective students.

One reason our HL courses are attractive is because HLs who are placed into the third year need to complete only three upper-division courses for the Spanish minor. This makes Spanish a desirable minor for HLLs. Furthermore, several students go on to declare a Spanish major before or after finishing the minor requirements.

Program Assessment

There has not been a formal program assessment for the second- and third-year HL courses. This is an area that needs to be developed in the near future, as the program matures into a fully developed and functioning HL program.

7 Institutionalization

Following the indicators that suggest institutionalization is taking place as described in Ekholm and Trier (1987), we can state there is an ongoing development of practices, and some could be seen as institutionalized. The foundations of the program, firmly established, bring a relative level of stability that allows for more fine-tuning.

Negotiations

By and large, the negotiations for the creation and implementation of both second- and third-year HL courses were conducted, informally and formally, in program and departmental meetings. The changes were primarily the purview of the second author and the chair, both of whom had an interest in HL teaching and learning, and who took on the project and worked together to accomplish the innovations. The remaining faculty welcomed and supported the changes, while not being centrally involved in the decisions or negotiations or in the teaching of the new courses. Given that the changes at CWU were confined to the introduction of a limited number of HL courses and a placement instrument for HL students, rather than a program-wide revamping of the curriculum as was the case at CSU-Pueblo, negotiations to effect the changes were relatively straightforward. The changes were also subsequently supported by the administration, which is receptive to all innovative strategies that address student needs and increase enrollment numbers campus wide.

Resources

Resources for curriculum redesign and HL teaching have been unevenly distributed. As mentioned earlier, the creation of the second-year series had administrative support in that the second author requested and received a course reduction and a summer innovation teaching grant. The chair and second author were also partially funded by the NHLRC to attend the HL teaching workshop. However, no resources were provided to create and implement the third-year courses in 2001, or to write the placement examination put into operation in 2013. The departure of the chair to an administrative position in 2013 reduced to one the number of instructors professionally trained in HL pedagogy, namely the second author. As of 2015, only two instructors (including the second author) are assigned to teach these courses. Additionally, recent budgets that are shrinking disallow assigning personnel to direct or coordinate the HL program.

Legitimacy

There is no doubt the HL courses are accepted as valuable to both students and the program. While the third-year courses are now seen as a natural and habitual component of the Spanish program curriculum, the second-year courses are in the process of becoming part of it. Recent student evaluations reveal that the students find that the HL courses address both their academic and socio-affective needs. In addition, the separate tracks for HL and L2 populations make it easier for instructors to focus on learners' specific learning needs.

Organizational processes

While some policies for the HL track are officially in place, there are instances where procedures have to be improvised in order to help students advance in their studies. This flexibility benefits the students, however, it also reduces the stability of the organizational process. One of the challenges is placement and course sequencing. Second- and third-year courses appear in the catalog yet the process of course placement and selection is sometimes modified. Changes have been made to the Spanish major program requirements to accommodate HLLs on a case-by-case basis so they can complete their studies and graduate in a timely fashion. Some students declare their Spanish minor or major late in their studies, by which time there are not enough courses they can take to fulfill their requirements. This situation forces advisors to find course substitutions from other departments or to offer them independent studies. Given that there is no written policy, advisors and faculty first discuss accommodation requests and proposals informally with each other and then ask the chair for approval.

Stability

While it may be too early to discuss the stability of the second-year program inaugurated in 2013, we can safely state that the third-year heritage courses, which have continually been taught since 2001, have become standard and customary in the program. Although there are established syllabi and textbooks for all HL courses, the curriculum allows instructors to change and select reading materials, projects, or films in order to address evolving student needs.

In order to create more stability, there is a need to motivate and engage faculty not directly associated with the HL program to teach the already established HL courses or to introduce HL-friendly strategies in their upper-division mixed elective courses.

8 Conclusion

As evidenced by these program overviews, CSU-Pueblo and CWU have approached the needs of their HLL populations in different ways, and face different challenges in adopting pedagogical innovations and achieving a solid degree of institutionalization with regard to HL-focused innovations. The two programs present examples of different scopes of change. CSU-Pueblo

391

integrated HLL pedagogies across the whole program, while CWU created separate courses specifically designed for HLLs. Interestingly, though the latter approach is preferable from a pedagogical standpoint, it has presented challenges such as achieving enough enrollment for HL courses, and persuading faculty not involved in these courses to have as much buy-in as the HL faculty. On the other hand, while CSU-Pueblo is no longer experiencing these hurdles, other challenges remain, primarily that of making sure all faculty are well trained to deal with the complexity of mixed classrooms without shortchanging either L2s or HLLs.

As Ekholm and Trier (1987) have asserted, institutionalization is "a process of affirming the collective ownership of an element of change. Consequently, the degree to which collective ownership is established throughout the implementation phase is important for the success or failure of institutionalization" (p. 19). Both institutions are fortunate to have faculty and administrators that genuinely care to serve students well, and ultimately want to implement needed innovations. This seems more easily achieved in a program where numbers of HLLs are larger such as CSU-Pueblo. When HLLs represent more than one-half the population in every classroom, teaching to their needs is inescapable.

What has perhaps become most evident is that the institutionalization of pedagogical innovations for HLL teaching and learning does not happen overnight, but is a lengthy and complex process that, even when achieving stability, needs constant vigilance to maintain. CSU-Pueblo and CWU began implementing changes nine and fourteen years ago, respectively. Each institution engaged in persuasion and negotiation with faculty and administration to institute the innovations and allocate resources. They have experienced tensions, gradual and rapid shifts, periods of stagnation, and setbacks. For these institutions the biggest challenges have been the adhesion of all players, budget constraints, and maintaining the stability of the programs when key players leave the institutions. The hope is that the procedures and structures that are now officially in place, together with the fact that most practices have been reiterated for so many years, will sustain the innovation to the point where it could be argued it has fully institutionalized.

Serving HLL populations in higher education is essential. It is in our hands to enhance these students' futures and that of society as a whole. It is also incumbent upon professionals involved in the process to remain steadfast, despite any challenges or setbacks. Perseverance is key, together with diplomacy and the understanding that this valuable innovation is a complex and sometimes challenging process, yet the rewards are immeasurable and worth every effort.

Notes

1 The U.S. Census defines "Hispanic" or "Latino" as "a person of Cuban, Mexican, Puerto Rican, South or Central American, or other Spanish culture or origin regardless of race" (Humes, Jones, & Ramirez, 2011). In this chapter we use both terms interchangeably.
2 The CLEP is a credit-by-examination program developed by the College Board.

References

American Council on the Teaching of Foreign Languages [ACTFL]. (2012). ACTFL proficiency guidelines 2012. Retrieved from http://www.actfl.org/sites/default/files/pdfs/public/ACTFLProficiency Guidelines2012_FINAL.pdf

Beaudrie, S. (2012). Research on university-based Spanish heritage language programs in the United States: The current state of affairs. In S. Beaudrie & M. Fairclough (Eds.), *Spanish as a heritage language in the US: State of the field* (pp. 203–222). Washington, DC: Georgetown University Press.

Brown, A., & Lopez, M. H. (2013, August 29). Mapping the Latino population, by state, county and city. Retrieved from http://www.pewhispanic.org/files/2013/08/latino_populations_in_the_states_counties_and_cities_FINAL.pdf

Carreira, M. (2012). Meeting the needs of heritage language learners: Approaches, strategies, and research. In S. Beaudrie & M. Fairclough (Eds.), *Spanish as a heritage language in the United States: The state of the field* (pp. 223–240). Washington, DC: Georgetown University Press.

Carreira, M., & Beeman, T. (2014). *Voces: Latino students on life in the United States.* Westport, CT: Praeger.

Central Washington University. (2014–2015). Common data set 2014–2015. Retrieved from https://www.cwu.edu/oe/sites/cts.cwu.edu.oe/files/CDS_2014–2015.pdf

Central Washington University. (n.d.a). History [Web page]. Retrieved from https://www.cwu.edu/about/history

Central Washington University. (n.d.b). Quick facts [Web page]. Retrieved from http://www.cwu.edu/about/quick-facts

Central Washington University. (n.d.c). Mission, vision, and values [Web page]. Retrieved from http://www.cwu.edu/strategic-planning/cwu-mission-vision-and-values

Colorado State University, Pueblo. (2005). Colorado State University, Pueblo, 2005–06 catalog. Retrieved from http://www.csupueblo.edu/catalog/Documents/Catalog2005–2006.pdf

Colorado State University, Pueblo. (2014). Colorado State University, Pueblo, 2014–15 catalog. Retrieved from http://www.csupueblo.edu/catalog/Documents/Catalog2014–2015.pdf

Eiseman, J. W., Fleming, D. S., & Roody, D. S. (1990). *Making sure it sticks: The school improvement leader's role in institutionalizing change.* Andover, MA: The Regional Laboratory.

Ekholm, M., & Trier, U. P. (1987). The concept of institutionalization: Some remarks. In M. B. Miles, M. Ekholm, & R. Vandenberghe (Eds.), *Lasting school improvement: Exploring the process of institutionalization* (pp. 13–21). Leuven, Belgium: Acco.

Humes, K. R., Jones, N. A., & Ramirez, R. A. (2011, March). *Overview of race and Hispanic origin: 2010.* Washington, DC: U.S. Census Bureau. Retrieved from http://www.census.gov/prod/cen2010/briefs/c2010br-02.pdf

Kagan, O., & Dillon, K. (2003). Heritage speakers' potential for high-level language proficiency. In H. Byrones & H. Maxim (Eds.), *Advanced foreign language learning: A challenge to college programs* (pp. 99–112). Boston, MA: Thomson & Heinle.

Louis, K. S. (2006). *Organizing for school change.* New York, NY: Routledge.

MLA Ad Hoc Committee on Foreign Languages. (2007). Foreign languages and higher education: New structures for a changed world. Retrieved from http://www.mla.org/flreport

Rogers, E. M. (1995). *Diffusion of innovations* (4th ed.). New York, NY: Free Press.

Swender, E., Martin, C. L., Rivera-Martinez, M., & Kagan, O. E. (2014). Exploring oral proficiency profiles of heritage speakers of Russian and Spanish. *Foreign Language Annals, 47*(3), 423–446.

Tomlinson, C. A. 1999. *The differentiated classroom: Responding to the needs of all learners.* Alexandria, VA: Association for Supervision and Curriculum Development.

U.S. Census Bureau. (2015a). Table DP05: ACS demographic and housing estimates [Data table], for Pueblo city, Colorado. 2010–2014 American Community Survey 5-year estimates. Retrieved from http://www.census.gov

U.S. Census Bureau. (2015b). Table DP03: Selected economic characteristics [Data tables], for Pueblo city, Colorado; Crowley County, Colorado; and State of Colorado. 2010–2014 American Community Survey 5-year estimates. Retrieved from http://www.census.gov

U.S. Census Bureau. (2015c). Table DP02: Selected social characteristics [Data table], for Pueblo city, Colorado. 2010–2014 American Community Survey 5-year estimates. Retrieved from http://www.census.gov

Valdés, G., Lozano, A. G., & García-Moya, R. (1981) *Teaching Spanish to the Hispanic bilingual: Issues, aims and methods.* New York, NY: Teacher's College Press.

Valenzuela, A. (1999). *Subtractive schooling: U.S. Mexican youth and the politics of caring.* Albany, NY: State University of New York Press.

Wherritt, I., & Cleary, T. (1990). A national survey of Spanish language testing for placement of outcome assessment at BA-granting institutions in the United States. *Foreign Language Annals, 22*(2), 157–165.

World Readiness Standards for Learning Languages. (n.d.). Retrieved from https://www.actfl.org/sites/default/files/pdfs/World-ReadinessStandardsforLearningLanguages.pdf

27

The Hindi-Urdu Heritage Language Stream

Institutional and Pedagogical Challenges

Shobna Nijhawan

1 Introduction

York University, located in the city of Toronto (Ontario), is one of the largest public postsecondary educational institutions in Canada. The university counts 53,000 undergraduate and graduate students, including 5,462 international students from 157 countries (York University, n.d.a), and prides itself for its "cross-discipline programming, innovative course design, diverse experiential learning and a supportive community environment" (York University, n.d.b). The Department of Languages, Literatures and Linguistics at York University is housed within the university's large Faculty of Liberal Arts and Professional Studies. In terms of heritage language (HL) teaching, HL streams in a number of language programs have gone through processes of initiation, implementation, and institutionalization, i.e., have been proposed, had initial steps or sub-processes implemented, and subsequently become a stable, well-established part of the department (Ekholm & Trier, 1987, p. 13). The department has also witnessed the closure of HL streams that have failed to become long-lived. Currently, the Arabic, Korean, and Spanish programs[1] offer separate streams for heritage language learners (HLLs) in some or all of the introductory, intermediate, and advanced language levels. The German, Greek, Japanese, Russian, Swahili, and Yiddish programs teach HLLs and second-language learners (L2Ls) in mixed classrooms. Some of these and other language programs, for various academic, pedagogical, and administrative reasons, never opted for the heritage stream or let go of it in the initiation phase. They instead accommodate the needs of a diversity of different student learners in one classroom.[2] Others, whose heritage streams had already been well established, decided to close them down due to administrative challenges. This applies to Chinese, Italian, and Portuguese. Language planners in the department have in the process engaged in scholarly debates revolving around different aspects of HL acquisition and bilingual learning, as well as institutional and administrative challenges associated with the implementation of alternate streams. This chapter draws from experiences of teaching Hindi-Urdu to primarily, but not exclusively, HLLs at three levels. After one decade of teaching HLLs and L2Ls in mixed classrooms, in 2015–16, the recently launched Hindi-Urdu HL stream is moving from the implementation to the institutionalization phase. The development of this stream will be reflected upon in this chapter.

The transition from the implementation of the Hindi-Urdu heritage stream to its institutionalization is embedded in larger efforts of internationalization of York University's faculties and departments. This process aims to bring an international and intercultural perspective to the curriculum and the university's faculty (Green Paper Working Group, 2009, p. 9). Centering specifically on the importance of non-Western languages, literatures, and cultures in instruction, a number of tenure-track appointments in the 2000s have been established for Arabic, Hindi, Korean, and Portuguese, amongst others. The Hindi tenure-track position dates back to 2008. Three years prior to this, Hindi language, literature, and culture courses were introduced at the first- and second-year undergraduate levels. Hindi (at that time without Urdu) was conceptualized as a foreign language to be taught to L2Ls. After one decade, introductory Hindi-Urdu is now offered in dual streams to HLLs and L2Ls. Placement for the first-year language level is through an interview and a biographical questionnaire, in which students describe their places of residence and schooling (formal and informal) for the past 10 years. Hindi-Urdu for heritage speakers is not only designed to meet the specific needs of HLLs, but also to increase the pool of students who will advance to the subsequent second-year (intermediate) language course, in which both streams from the first-year language level merge. This intermediate course is taught in alternate years in the mixed classroom format. Placement for students who have not enrolled in one of the introductory language courses is through a written test (if the student has received formal education) or an interview (for heritage students in particular who have no knowledge of the script, but are willing to self-learn it along with basic grammar). Third-year Hindi-Urdu is offered on demand as an independent reading course for either L2Ls or HLLs. This arrangement for advanced-level Hindi and/or Urdu is particularly suited to students from across departments who choose Hindi-Urdu to fulfill language requirements for degrees such as the International BA and International Business BA. All Hindi-Urdu language courses also count towards the degree requirements of the South Asian Studies Program and are open to graduate students who may use them to fulfill language degree requirements of the graduate diploma in Asian Studies or other programs of graduate studies.

Despite the fact that the creation of the separate Hindi-Urdu HL stream lies only two years back, I use the term "institutionalization" because the stream has been established with the expectation of being offered and expanded in the long term alongside Hindi-Urdu for L2Ls. I thus subscribe to an understanding of "institutionalization" that involves a program that is stable, but evolves and progresses over time (Miles & Louis, 1987, pp. 26–27). Furthermore, my understanding of institutionalization applies to the program level as well as to the classroom level (Timmermans, 1987), the latter of which will be the focus of this chapter.

The Hindi-Urdu HL stream at York University received administrative and pedagogical (classroom level) support from the Department of Languages, Literatures and Linguistics during the initiation and implementation phases, and from the Faculty of Liberal Arts and Professional Studies, who approved the innovation. As *Introductory Hindi-Urdu for Heritage Speakers* enters its second year, it may be described as a "stable and routinized" innovation in the Hindi-Urdu course offerings (Eiseman, Fleming, & Roody, 1990, p. 13; Miles & Louis, 1987, p. 26). In terms of resources, this course, like other language courses, relies on smart classrooms and the resource and space allocations from the Multimedia Language Center, which students are expected to visit on a weekly basis to complete class and home assignments. It is "person independent," another of Miles and Louis' indicators of institutionalization, in that a pool of experienced course instructors is able to teach this course and the future of the program does not depend upon the only tenured, full-time faculty member in charge of the Hindi-Urdu language, literature, and culture courses. Beyond the fact that it is offered with regularity and that there is a pool of experienced instructors, it is increasingly beginning to rely on pedagogies and teaching materials that are being specifically developed and codified by the instructor, indicating institutionalization processes at the classroom level. In fact, the course received an award for research in teaching from the York University Faculty Association for the development of generic pedagogical materials designed to meet the specific needs of HLLs in and beyond the Hindi-Urdu classroom. Lastly, the course has found acceptance from undergraduate and graduate students as well as South Asian student organizations, and receives full course enrollment.

2 Hindi, Urdu, and Hindi-Urdu

Hindi-Urdu at York University is conceptualized in a manner that acknowledges Hindi and Urdu as one language despite the difference of script. Hindi is written in the Nagari script (introduced in the first-year class) and Urdu in the Perso-Arabic Nastaliq or Naskh scripts (introduced in the second-year class).[3] Hindi and Urdu share a grammatical structure, syntax, and basic vocabulary. Hindi is even closer to Urdu than to its so-called literary predecessors, Brajbhasha and Avadhi (Trivedi, 2003, p. 960). In addition to the linguistic commonalities, Hindi and Urdu form a composite literary culture. Both languages share literary genres as well as eminent writers such as Premchand (1880–1936), the "father" of the modern Hindi *and* Urdu novel and short story. In the nineteenth century, this shared culture fell prey to British colonial language policies, as well as Hindu and Muslim communal quests for a distinct literary canon and a separate linguistic genealogy. Consequently, in the twentieth century, Urdu was increasingly defined as the language of Muslims and Hindi as the language of Hindus, notwithstanding South Asian realities that testify to a shared linguistic and cultural tradition.

Against this background, several universities in the United States and Canada hyphenate their language courses as 'Hindi-Urdu' or mark them with a diagonal as 'Hindi/Urdu'.[4] These language-planning choices are to be understood in the context of a tradition of academic engagement with Hindi-Urdu language and literature teaching that seeks to shed "communal baggage" (Bedi, 2002, p. 176) and that emphasizes the intertwined history and shared linguistic tradition of both languages and cultures, rather than the politically motivated rift carried forth in nationalist ideologies of both India and Pakistan (as well as, to a certain extent, in the South Asian diaspora). This language-planning decision extends into the classroom, where students are introduced to what is considered common vocabulary, and where heavily Sanskritized Hindi vocabulary and heavily Arabicized and Persianized Urdu vocabulary is consciously avoided. HLLs are furthermore made aware that a choice of a specific word may well be connected to a cultural and political statement. While Hindi in India and Urdu in Pakistan may be clearly defined as official languages that draw on their respective linguistic genealogies and etymologies, the use of Hindi-Urdu in the popular media borrows freely from different lexica (most commonly Hindi, Urdu, English, and Punjabi) and students are made aware of these manifestations of Hindi, Urdu, and Hindi-Urdu.[5]

3 The HL Classroom

Just as in the mixed classroom where HLLs and L2Ls bring a conglomerate of cultural and linguistic knowledge into the classroom, the HLL classroom is not a homogenous one. Neither is it monolingual in terms of the HL spoken. Especially in the South Asian diaspora context, multilinguality prevails (Ghaffer-Kucher & Mahajan, 2013, p. 76) and students enrolled in Hindi-Urdu for the most part also speak, read, and write one or more regional languages such as Punjabi, Gujarati, Bengali, or Marathi. The heritage-land connection is moreover not limited to the South Asian "mainland": students at York University also hail from the Caribbean and

Caribbean coastline, Mauritius, East Africa (Uganda, Kenya), South America (Guyana, Suriname), and occasionally from Europe. A diversity and variety of South Asian languages (and English) including Hindi and Urdu is spoken in their homes.[6] As a matter of practice, language instructors can reference students' bilinguality or even multilinguality (including Western languages such as French) when introducing the Hindi Nagari and Urdu Nastaliq scripts, practicing pronunciation and intonation, as well as introducing grammatical concepts and conducting conversations. As Cummins (2014) has so aptly commented, "When educators choose to ignore the linguistic competencies that students bring to school, they are also choosing to be complicit with the societal power relations that devalue the linguistic and cultural capital of their students" (p. 1). In this sense and along the lines of Gounari (2014), the challenge then is *not* to fall into the trap of reproducing monolingualism as the norm and everything other than that, such as prior exposure to a language other than English or exposure to an HL that is not the presumed standard, as a deviation. Instead, it is to reinvent the term "heritage language" in order to acknowledge it as a "living and relevant category" (Gounari, 2014, p. 266). This may be achieved with a specific HL pedagogy that actively involves students and *their* languages and cultures in classroom practices. I will describe such practices in the second part of this chapter.

Before the formally recognized heritage stream was created, approximately 90% of the students enrolled in introductory and intermediate Hindi-Urdu were HLL in the sense of having linguistic or cultural South Asian and South Asian diasporic allegiances (Polinsky & Kagan, 2007, p. 369) and varying linguistic and cultural proficiencies (Hornberger & Wang, 2008, p. 13). Out of these 90% of HLLs, who now enroll in the HL stream, about one-third enter the classroom not only as hearers and speakers of Hindi and/or Urdu, but also as writers and readers of one of the scripts. Polinsky and Kagan (2007, p. 370) would refer to these as HLLs in the narrow sense. However, in the case of Hindi-Urdu, the picture is more complex with regard to *broad*-definition HLLs. While this term is usually used to refer to students who have a familial connection to the HL, but speak the dominant societal language at home, it is important to realize that in Hindi-Urdu classes, many students who are identified as HLLs in the broad sense due to South Asian (most prominently Indian, Pakistani, Nepali, and Bangladeshi) or South Asian diasporic cultural allegiances, hail from families in which different regional languages are spoken. Whereas the South Asian languages Hindi and Urdu as well as Bengali, Punjabi, and Gujarati belong to the Indo-Aryan language family (although all have their own scripts), South Indian languages such as Kannada, Malayalam, Tamil, and Telugu are classified as Dravidian languages. They are not related to Hindi and Urdu with regard to lexicon, grammar, or script. Correspondingly, in a Hindi-Urdu language class, Gujarati heritage speakers self-identify as Hindi-Urdu HLLs more frequently than South Indian HL speakers.[7] Both groups, however, can be subsumed under the term "broad" HLL.

For these reasons, in the 2015–16 academic year at York University the HLL population in Hindi-Urdu could be described as follows: approximately one-third were hearers and speakers of Hindi and/or Urdu, two-thirds could be defined as HLLs in the broad sense of the term, but with the important caveat that they spoke different regional languages, some of them not related to Hindi-Urdu and, in many cases, self-identified as HLLs of Hindi-Urdu. Given this complex composition, the proficiency level ranges widely, from near-native proficiency with regard to aural comprehension and conversation skills in Hindi-Urdu, with or without literacy, to familiarity with a regional South Asian language, but no skills in Hindi-Urdu as such. Students who may be defined as HLLs in the broad sense and who self-identify as HLLs jointly determine their eligibility for the HL stream in consultation with the course instructor.

All these HLLs, however, are undoubtedly advantaged in their phonological abilities and their pronunciation of long and short vowels, dental and retroflex consonants as well as aspirated and non-aspirated ones, to name just a few particularities of Hindi–Urdu phonetics. In some cases, students from both groups of HLLs have advantages in morphosyntactical skills, but are generally insecure when it comes to identifying and applying formal grammatical rules. If Hindi–Urdu instructors recognize that both types of learners are legitimate HLLs, they will expect their students to interrelate the linguistic and cultural knowledge they bring into class with what they learn in class.

Identifying HLLs' Pedagogical Needs

The recognition that HLLs are a separate category of learners from L2Ls and require a specific HL pedagogy was a prime consideration that led to the establishment of the Hindi-Urdu heritage stream at York University. Acknowledging that HLLs are a highly divergent population further informed the structure and content of the stream. These two points relate to Ekholm and Trier's (1987) idea regarding the "necessity of change" (p. 18), in that the pedagogical needs of HLLs became apparent and provided the initial impetus for the introduction of the innovation.

In the field of HL studies, the idea that HLLs and L2Ls should be taught separately is well established.[8] To fill this need, the field has developed pedagogical models for teaching HLLs in separate HL classrooms and, to a lesser extent, in mixed classes. Carreira (2014) has argued for "customized options" (p. 40) for the mixed classroom and provided learner-centered recommendations for teachers of HL students. Recognizing the advances that have been made in the field of HL teaching over the past decades, she calls for tenure-track faculty to actively and responsibly build the curriculum and take a role in its implementation. Along similar lines, Parra (2014) proposes the creation of a "signature pedagogy" and "pedagogical spaces" (p. 214) for HLLs to develop their linguistic and cultural abilities—be it in the separate HL learning stream or in the mixed classroom—while Carreira and Chik (in press) recommend "differentiated teaching" as a way to approach language instruction of HLLs in HL only or in mixed HL/L2 classrooms. Given the diversity of backgrounds that make up the student body in the Hindi-Urdu classroom, such an approach is specifically relevant.

This discussion relates to Trifonas and Aravossitas' (2014) argument for keeping the term "heritage learner" and against its replacement with the category of the "bilingual learner," which is not as inclusive as the former. The term "heritage learner" emphasizes the span and flexibility of the category, which may include bilingual, multilingual, and even native speakers (Hornberger & Wang, 2008, p. 3). Regardless of whether a language is offered in an alternate HL stream or not, scholars have pointed to the responsibility of educators at schools and in postsecondary institutions to encourage HLLs to proudly and confidently bring bilingualism and multiculturalism into the center of their classroom experiences, rather than keeping their prior knowledge of an HL at the doorstep of their educational institution.[9] I extend this call even further in demonstrating how language instructors can actively involve HLLs in the course design of the classes, as explained in the next section.

4 Classroom Practices and Approaches

Given the heterogeneous student body even within the HL classroom, the challenge then, along the lines elaborated by Carreira and Chik (in press) and Parra (2014) on "signature pedagogy" and "differentiated teaching," respectively, is to acknowledge linguistic and cultural diversity as potential, and out of this recognition to develop a pedagogical approach that neither homogenizes nor stigmatizes the individual HLL. The course needs to accommodate the student and not vice-versa (Carreira, 2004, p. 21) and the "one-size-fits-all" approach has significant shortcomings (Carreira & Chik, in press). HLLs in the L2 classroom have long been considered more of a problem than an opportunity as the term "false beginner" suggests (Hornberger & Wang, 2008, p. 22). Such categorizations may extend into the HL classroom if the course instructor does not actively consider the different levels of (linguistic and cultural) expertise and allegiances that define HLLs. As Polinsky and Kagan (2007, p. 390) and Hornberger and Wang (2008, p. 23) suggest, students' prior linguistic and cultural knowledge, as much as it may differ from standard varieties and formal knowledge taught in the classroom, is a resource that needs to be recognized and incorporated into the classroom as well as into the curriculum. An ideal and distinct HL curriculum, according to Kagan and Dillon (2001/2003, p. 80), focuses simultaneously on linguistic, communicative, and cultural aspects of HL instruction. It distinguishes itself from L2L pedagogical needs in that it approaches HL teaching through a macro approach (Kagan & Dillon, 2001/2003, p. 82) and not through case-by-case introductions of grammatical concepts. The emphasis in the HL classroom is placed more on "skill development" of grammar, vocabulary, and cultural knowledge rather than on "error eradication" (Kagan & Dillon, 2009, p. 165). The skills are introduced with the intention that they may be immediately transferred and used outside the classroom (Kagan & Dillon, 2009, p. 168). Appealing to HLLs' creativity and encouraging students to draw from their cultural and linguistic backgrounds for classroom practices, as will be shown further below, draws them into the course design and turns them into agents in the classroom. They cease to be merely the "receivers" of language.

In building the Hindi-Urdu program over the past decade, I have built on what I have in a previous publication called a linguistically and culturally informed language pedagogy for the mixed classroom (Nijhawan, 2011). This demand continues to be center stage for the development of teaching materials and classroom practices that suit the pedagogical needs of HLLs in all learning contexts, whether HL-only or mixed classes. From my experiences with the mixed classroom, I have come to realize that HLLs are often reluctant to become proficient with the language in a formal linguistic way through learning grammatical rules, especially as these are introduced in textbooks designed for what used to constitute the "traditional" North American L2 classroom (see endnote v). They instead seek a working knowledge of what they understand as colloquial variants of either Hindi or Urdu through a "sounds-right" approach. In fact, HLLs have severe difficulties navigating conventional grammar books, and I no longer attribute this to indifference and lack of motivation or commitment on the part of students, but to the fact that HLLs' pedagogical needs are not being met through this approach.

To meet these pedagogical needs, specialized materials and classroom activities are needed, and a discussion of these topics is included in the next section. This speaks to a point made by Miles and Louis (1987, p. 31, quoting Merton) regarding the importance of providing alternative structures when replacing previous ones. Without concrete alternatives to previous practices, it is difficult for any innovation to take hold.

5 Teaching Materials and Activities

While I have in the past worked with conventional textbooks in the mixed classroom, I realize that they are inadequate for use in the HL classroom.[10] HLLs need not be sheltered from authentic linguistic and cultural subject matter that can be quite complex. In fact, they should from the outset be confronted with the language as they encounter it outside the classroom. Adjusting the classroom approach to meet the needs of the student, as mentioned above, requires that students are made aware that they are being introduced to an aspect of the language that they already make use of. They are not introduced to "new grammar," but asked to *recognize* and *identify* grammatical concepts that they know implicitly, but do not have the metalinguistic vocabulary or concepts to discuss explicitly. They are also asked to *apply* these concepts, sometimes in isolation, but mostly within a certain linguistic and cultural context that takes account of their everyday language. In terms of materials, postsecondary teaching materials for Hindi-Urdu HLLs do not exist, and I currently rely on readings, exercises, assignments, quizzes that I have designed for use in the HL classroom in general. In keeping with this approach, the following suggestions for classroom activities are not restricted to Hindi-Urdu, but may be transferred to the HL classroom more generally.

In the HL classroom, I wish to turn students into pronounced linguistic and cultural agents of the learning process. The materials and activities that I suggest differ significantly from materials for L2Ls in that they freely include vocabulary, grammar, and expressions from authentic sources. They draw from proverbs, sayings, songs, stories, and newspaper articles that are not adjusted other than the possible inclusion of a glossary. This approach would be difficult to instantiate in the mixed classroom, because L2Ls are generally overwhelmed by rapid or indistinct pronunciation, the amount of unknown vocabulary, grammar, and sentence structure when authentic sources are introduced aurally or by means of text. Whereas L2Ls may require case by case introductions to grammar and vocabulary (Kagan & Dillon, 2001/2003, p. 82), HLLs display more confidence in dealing with linguistic variety and variation.

When introducing a grammatical convention, HLLs are first of all made aware of their pre-existing knowledge of this convention (such as a certain verb tense or declination and conjugation particularities). Once they understand that they are revisiting a concept they already know through the approach of formal grammatical conventions, they are much more willing to familiarize themselves with this new approach. They understand that knowledge of a grammatical rule will alleviate their difficulties with spelling and enhance their overall grasp of the language and its culture, especially when it comes to written contexts. Handouts for group work and quizzes conducted in groups are valuable reinforcement tools to ingrain the recognition that learning a grammatical rule can indeed be a very useful exercise to enhance speaking and writing.

Visuals

Conducive to enhancing HLLs' linguistic and cultural skills simultaneously—while not limited to or exceptional for the HL classroom—are visuals, which prove beneficial in every class meeting. Visuals can be used to target both linguistic and cultural topics. Images arranged as slide shows through Prezi or PowerPoint, for example, may be used to practice grammatical features such as interrogatives or different verb tenses, expand vocabulary areas such as those related to colors, nouns, and adjectives, or they may be used to preview vocabulary at the beginning of a lesson. One single visual—such as a tea stall frequented by customers or passengers traveling in a train—is used to initiate a conversation or an interview between two or more students as they visualize themselves in the displayed setting. A variety of South Asian and non-South Asian foods (vegetables, fruits, sweets, festive dishes, everyday food, snacks) and clothing styles (from a diversity of festive and everyday South Asian, non-South Asian, as well as South Asian diasporic contexts) can be used as the basis for class discussions that bring to the fore the diversity of the HL population, and allow for the comparison of different life experiences that the image brings to mind. Generally, visuals appeal to students and spark their creativity in conversational, interpretative, and linguistic ways.

Visuals are not only prepared by the course director; students are asked to contribute to the pool of slides by selecting images from the internet or by sharing photographs of their own from visits to South Asia, the South Asian diaspora, or from encounters and interactions with South Asian and non-South Asian friends and families at home, at religious, cultural, and festive gatherings or at a university campus, the cricket field, or the skating rink. Such exercises allow for active inclusion of students' cultural background and individual interests.

Songs and Proverbs

Bollywood songs are perhaps the most appealing way of catching students' attention in the Hindi-Urdu classroom, both aurally and textually. From early on in the academic term, HLLs are asked to bring songs that they are already familiar with and connect with. In keeping with a macro approach, the first step would be to react to it as an authentic item—as a song to be enjoyed. Discussions that follow could examine the content of the song, looking at themes and cultural specificities. In terms of classroom management, one way to begin is by listening to the song as a whole class, without the lyrics. A discussion of why students like/dislike the song (or an aspect thereof) could follow. This can be organized as a whole class discussion, or first discussed in small groups and then reported back to the class as a whole.

As a last step, grammar is targeted. The purpose of this step is to train students' listening skills in recognizing grammatical concepts (future tense, plural formation, progressive and habitual tenses) that have been introduced in a previous class. This exercise depends mainly on students' involvement and aims to make them linguistic and cultural agents of recognizing and familiarizing themselves with Hindi-Urdu grammar. To enhance the learning experience, the instructor may prepare an accompanying worksheet such as the one developed for the Hindi-Urdu song "Baazigar" (Magician):

> *Refrain*
> ये काली काली आँखें (These black eyes)
> ये गोरे गोरे गाल (These round cheeks)
> ये तीखी तीखी नज़रें (These sharp looks)
> यह हिरनी जैसी चाल (These deer-like movements)

Exercise

With your group, listen to the refrain and translate it. Then, fill out the table by following the instructions given below:

1. Determine the gender (masculine or feminine) and number (singular or plural) of the word by looking at the ending.
2. Try to draw conclusions on *why* the word is/has to be an adjective or noun.
3. Determine whether the words are marked or unmarked nouns or marked or unmarked adjectives by applying the rules learned in class.

Word	Gender: Masculine or feminine?	Type: Marked or unmarked?	Number: Singular or plural?	Grammatical designation: Adjective or noun?
काली				
आँखें				
गोरे				
गाल				
तीखी				
नज़रें				
हिरनी				
चाल				

Now check the word agreement between the nouns and adjectives of each row. Respond to the following questions in your discussion group:

1. What are the rules for marked/unmarked nouns and adjectives (draw a chart outlining these rules)?
2. How were you able to determine number (singular or plural)? Draw a chart once again.
3. How were you able to determine gender (masculine or feminine)?

Apart from the identification of specific grammatical concepts, the lyrics may be used to point to the usage of specific vocabulary as well as cultural connotation and context (such as vocabulary relating to love and friendship or second-person pronouns' use for specific social and intergenerational relationships), allowing for a holistic learning experience that includes linguistic, literary, and cultural elements (see the follow-up exercise listed later in this section).

Songs suggested by students as well as proverbs and sayings may also be used for Hindi Nagari and Urdu Nastaliq script-reading exercises. For instance, students are given a handout with 10 commonly used proverbs, which they are then asked to read.[11] While students may still struggle with deciphering individual characters and making out specific sounds, they cherish the moment in which they identify an individual word and the meaning of the text as a whole. They particularly enjoy performing small skits with the proverb they just read used as the punch line. Because proverbs are culturally specific, not only within South Asian regional contexts but also within Western ones, they lend themselves to bringing in the diverse linguistic and cultural backgrounds of learners into the classroom. For example, one activity may involve a comparison of how different proverbs from the various regions represented in the classroom express the same idea.

Once students gain confidence in identifying individual characters of the script, they are introduced to little stories (short fables and tales). Such readings prove suitable to alert students towards spelling conventions that are often not identifiable in aural and oral contexts, which is particularly important for HLLs. Students proficient in spoken Hindi-Urdu, for example, often neglect to indicate the nasalization that is required for plural formations in the written context. It is through such classroom practices that they begin to realize that the knowledge of a grammatical rule or convention potentially prevents recurring grammatical mistakes.

6 Creativity, Collaboration, and Conversations

While certain components of classroom practices focus on learning grammatical forms of language that constrain, as Kramsch (1993, p. 76) would phrase it, "the context to its linguistic dimensions," other components of the same exercise or handout focus on enhancing collaborative learning, creativity, imagination, and a sense of experimentation. Following the identification and application of grammar rules through exercises such as those provided in the section on songs and proverbs, students are asked to prepare their own song stanza or to integrate a proverb into their own dialogue. Focusing entirely on linguistic aspects stifles communication and creativity (Kramsch, 1993, p. 74), which is particularly important to avoid for HLLs given their close personal connection to the HL and its intimate connection to their homes.

For this reason, an informal conversation prepared and initiated by one student in turn begins every class meeting. In this conversation, a student introduces a topic of their choice and concludes with a question. Each student is then asked to respond. This component of classroom learning is entirely oriented towards comprehension and conversation. Even in the context of such conversations, students are asked to become linguistic and cultural agents when making choices about the three available second-person pronouns, for example. Their usage depends on the relationship between speaker and addressee as it is determined by age and sociocultural relationship, among other determinants. Within the classroom and beyond, students are asked to investigate their own choices of second-person pronouns and to explore how these are employed in popular media.

7 Future of the Program

Apart from laying out the institutionalization of the Hindi-Urdu heritage stream at the organizational level, this chapter has mostly concerned itself with institutionalization at the classroom level. In the Hindi-Urdu program at York University, teaching materials have been created, introduced and implemented for routine usage in the HL track, the assumption being that HLLs require separate materials based on pedagogical practices that distinguish HL learning from L2 learning. The chapter has provided examples of HL classroom practices and activities with the purpose of exemplifying concrete ideas that may constitute "adequate alternative structures" (Miles & Louis, 1987, p. 31) to take the place of previous classroom practices that fell short of meeting the needs of HLLs.

Framing this discussion is the recommendation made by scholars that language instructors and program builders carry a special responsibility to offer HLLs suitable instruction, be it in the mixed classroom or in a separate HL stream. Positing that implementing and institutionalizing a separate HL stream provides students the necessary space to unfold (rather than hide) their potential as HLLs, this chapter has shown how the Hindi-Urdu program draws on an HL pedagogy that is in the process of being institutionalized at the classroom level, and that contributes to the internationalization of the curriculum. Central to the argument of this chapter has been the active involvement of HL speakers in designing the HL curriculum. The inclusion of jointly developed teaching and learning materials by students and instructor may be an approach for all language instructors who seek to improve the HLL experience in the HL or mixed classroom.[12]

The implementation and institutionalization of HL courses at the second and third year level depends on enrollment numbers and on resources allocated towards the teaching of languages. As York University's internationalization plans reach out towards the recruitment of students from India and Pakistan, these international students, who may not necessarily be native speakers of Hindi and/or Urdu and thus qualify as HLLs, may emerge as the new students of the Hindi-Urdu HL stream in the Canadian postsecondary educational setting.[13] The future presence of these students further underscores the need for the type of pedagogy outlined here, namely, one which is inclusive of a wide range of home languages and cultures and which calls for an HLL-centered teaching approach.

8 Acknowledgments

I thank my students from the introductory, intermediate, and advanced Hindi-Urdu language levels—HLLs and L2Ls—for their enthusiasm and dedication towards Hindi-Urdu and for stimulating my thinking about heritage and second-language acquisition. I also thank Claire Hitchins Chik for her invaluable feedback on earlier versions of this chapter. Research on this chapter was made possible through a York University Faculty Association Teaching Release Time Fellowship in the 2015–16 academic year.

Notes

1 While I use the word "program" for all languages offered by the department, not all languages are full-fledged, degree-granting programs, but may be languages offered at first- (introductory), second- (intermediate), and third-year (advanced) levels.

2 I thank the participants of the roundtable on HL streams in the Department of Languages, Literatures, and Linguistics at York University (February 28, 2015): Themis Aravossitas, Walid El Khachab, Roberta Sinyor, and Danielle Thomas, as well as Shanna Lino for the fruitful discussion on the topic.

3 Nastaliq and Naskh are different styles of writing: Nastaliq words slant downward while Naskh words are written horizontally (on the line).

4 These universities include the University of California (Berkeley, Los Angeles), the University of North Carolina (Chapel Hill, Raleigh), Columbia University, Princeton University, and the University of Toronto. The Hindi-Urdu Flagship at the University of Texas (Austin) is named as such, but offers separate Hindi and Urdu classes. University of Wisconsin (Madison) also offers separate Hindi and Urdu streams. The University of Chicago offers special "Devanagari Intensive" courses for HLLs Hindi and subsequently determines their appropriate entry level. It has a separate Urdu stream.

5 Even the use of the Hindi-English translation from Google Translate promotes Hindi as it is envisioned as an official language, i.e. purged of Arabic and Persian-derived and oftentimes also of Urdu word options. Students are usually not aware of the stylistic, linguistic, and ideological gradations when they search for vocabulary in such online databases. Furthermore, Google Translate offers translations of the individual word without grammatical markers such as gender. Searching for words in the plural does not yield accurate formations, which students need to be made aware of.

6 Gambhir (2008, p. 6), in her study on Hindi heritage learners, distinguishes between ancestral and associate heritage learners, the former being those who speak Hindi at home and the latter being divided into cognate and non-cognate learners. For the purposes of this chapter it may suffice to note that being an HLL does not imply certain proficiency levels in Hindi-Urdu, Hindi and/or Urdu. The category merely distinguishes HLLs from "traditional learners" of Hindi-Urdu, who come from non-South Asian backgrounds and constituted the bulk of American university language course students until the 1980s (Gambhir, 2008, p. 1).

7 Information on self-identification stems from two surveys conducted by the author among students enrolled in Introductory Hindi-Urdu and in Introductory Hindi-Urdu for Heritage Speakers (February 2015, October 2015).

8 See, for example, the essay collections on HL learning in community and postsecondary settings edited by Brinton, Kagan, and Bauckus (2008), García, Zakharia, and Otcu (2013), and Trifonas and Aravossitas (2014). For Canadian case studies, see Danesi, McLeod, and Morris (1993). See also the collection on bilingual and multilingual education edited by Abello-Contesse, Chandler, López-Jiménez, and Chacón-Beltrán (2013).

9 See Carreira (2014), Cummins (2014), and Lacorte and Canabal (2003). An entire conference entitled "Changes and Challenges in Language Teacher Education" has recently been organized by the Centre for Advanced Research on Language Acquisition at the University of Minnesota/CARLA (2015), where questions concerning research, theory, and best practices for the mixed and HL classroom were addressed.

10 One such textbook is *Introduction to Hindi Grammar* by Usha Jain.

11 Such as the proverbs बन्दर क्या जाने अदरक का स्वाद (What does the monkey know about the taste of ginger), दूर के ढोल सुहावने लगते हैं (In a distance, large drums sound pleasant), घर की मुर्गी दाल बराबर (At home, chicken tastes like lentils), यहाँ तुम्हारी दाल नहीं गल सकती (Your lentils won't cook like this), घरजने वाले बादल बरसते नहीं (Thundering clouds don't fall in showers), ओखली में सिर दिया तो मूसल से क्या डरना (First you lay your head in a mortar and then you fear the pestle).

12 In two written surveys conducted in February 2015 and October 2015 about HLLs' needs and the relationship of HLLs to L2Ls, HLLs of Introductory Hindi-Urdu in the mixed classroom unanimously opted *against* separate classrooms for HLLs and L2Ls. They pointed to the advantage for L2Ls of encountering more vocabulary from heritage speakers. They also pointed to the advantages of working through grammar together, as non-HLLs were considered to have developed useful learning strategies. Even though in the mixed classroom HLLs and L2Ls seated themselves in two groups spatially apart from each other, they all were in favor of collaborative learning and participated enthusiastically and were very focused in mixed group activities. HLLs in the HL classroom, however, favored separate classrooms over the mixed classroom (survey conducted in October 2015). While they recognized the heterogeneity of the HL classroom in and of itself, they had concerns about L2Ls' level of comfort and

feelings of being disadvantaged in a language class conducted in a mixed classroom format with HLLs. Arguably, while non-HLLs are at first threatened or intimidated by HLLs' seeming proficiency in their receptive and productive skills as well as their excellent pronunciation, over time they get to appreciate the functional proficiency of HLLs while also recognizing the advantages they have as L2Ls.

13 A total of 1.456 international students from India and Pakistan enrolled at York University in the 2009 academic year (Wright, 2010, p. 5). A sizable number of these students qualify as HLLs of Hindi-Urdu.

References

Abello-Contesse, C., Chandler, P. M., López-Jiménez, M. D., & Chacón-Beltrán, R. (Eds.). (2013). *Bilingual and multilingual education in the 21st century: Building on experience.* Bristol, UK: Multilingual Matters.

Bedi, S. (2002). Two sides of a coin: Linguistic and cultural aspects of a language. *Hindi: Language, Writing, Discourse, 2*(4), 165–180.

Brinton, D., Kagan, O., & Bauckus, S. (Eds.). (2008). *Heritage language education: A new field emerging.* New York: Routledge.

Carreira, M. (2004). Seeking explanatory adequacy: Understanding the term 'heritage language learner'. *Heritage Language Journal, 2*(1), 1–25. Retrieved from http://www.heritagelanguages.org

Carreira, M. (2014). Teaching heritage language learners: A study of program profiles, practices and needs. In P. Trifonas & T. Aravossitas (Eds.), *Rethinking heritage language education* (pp. 20–44). Cambridge, UK: Cambridge University Press.

Carreira, M., & Hitchins Chik, C. (in press). Differentiated teaching: A primer for heritage and mixed classes. In K. Potowski (Ed.), *The handbook of Spanish as a heritage/minority language.* Abingdon, UK: Routledge.

Cummins, J. (2014). Mainstreaming plurilingualism: Restructuring heritage language provision in schools. In P. Trifonas & T. Aravossitas (Eds.), *Rethinking heritage language education* (pp. 1–19). Cambridge, UK: Cambridge University Press.

Danesi, M., McLeod, K. A., & Morris, S. V. (1993). *Heritage languages and education: The Canadian experience.* Oakville, Ontario: Mosaic Press.

Eiseman, J. W., Fleming, D. S., & Roody, D. S. (1990). *Making sure it sticks: The school improvement leader's role in institutionalizing change.* Andover, MA: The Regional Laboratory.

Ekholm, M., & Trier, U. P. (1987). The concept of institutionalization: Some remarks. In M. B. Miles, M. Ekholm, & R. Vandenberghe (Eds.), *Lasting school improvement: Exploring the process of institutionalization* (pp. 13–21). Leuven, Belgium: Acco.

Gambhir, V. (2008). The rich tapestry of heritage learners of Hindi. *South Asia Language Pedagogy and Technology, 1*(1), no pagination. Retrieved from http://www.international.ucla.edu/media/files/salpat.pdf

García, O., Zakharia, Z., & Otcu, B. (Eds.). *Bilingual community education and multilingualism: Beyond heritage languages in a global city.* Toronto, ON: Multilingual Matters.

Ghaffer-Kucher, A., & Mahajan, A. P. (2013). *Salaam! Namaste!:* Indian and Pakistani community-based efforts towards mother tongue language maintenance. In O. García, Z. Zakharia, & B. Otcu (Eds.), *Bilingual community education and multilingualism: Beyond heritage languages in a global city* (pp. 74–86). Toronto, Ontario: Multilingual Matters.

Gounari, P. (2014). Rethinking heritage language in a critical pedagogy framework. In P. Trifonas & T. Aravossitas (Eds.), *Rethinking heritage language education* (pp. 254–268). Cambridge, UK: Cambridge University Press.

Green Paper Working Group. (2009). Internationalization. Retrieved from http://vpap.info.yorku.ca/files/2012/09/Internationalization.pdf

Hornberger, N. H., & Wang, S. C. (2008). Who are our heritage language learners? Identity and biliteracy in heritage language education in the United States. In D. Brinton, O. Kagan, & S. Bauckus (Eds.), *Heritage language education: A new field emerging* (pp. 3–35). New York, NY: Routledge.

Kagan, O., & Dillon, K. (2001/2003). A new perspective on teaching Russian: Focus on the heritage learner. *Heritage Language Journal, 1*(1), 76–90. Retrieved from http://www.heritagelanguages.org (Reprinted from *Slavic and East European Journal, 45*(3), 2001, 507–518.)

Kagan, O., & Dillon, K. (2009). The professional development of teachers of heritage language learners: A matrix. In M. Anderson & A. Lazaraton (Eds.), *Bridging contexts, making connections: Selected papers from the Fifth International Conference on Language Teacher Education* (pp. 155–175). Minneapolis, MN: Center for Advanced Research on Language Acquisition.

Kramsch, C. (1993). *Context and culture in language teaching.* Oxford, UK: Oxford University Press.

Lacorte, M., & Canabal, E. (2003). Interaction with heritage language learners in foreign language classrooms. In C. Blyth (Ed.), *The sociolinguistics of foreign-language classrooms: Contributions of the native, the near-native, and the non-native speaker* (pp. 107–129). Boston, MA: Thomson/Heinle.

Miles, M. B., & Louis, K. S. (1987). Research on institutionalization: A reflective review. In M. B. Miles, M. Ekholm, & R. Vandenberghe (Eds.), *Lasting school improvement: Exploring the process of institutionalization* (pp. 25–44). Leuven, Belgium: Acco.

Nijhawan, S. (2011). 'I got the point across and that is what counts': Transcultural versus (?) Linguistic competence in language teaching. *Journal of the National Council of Less Commonly Taught Languages, 9*(1), 59–81.

Parra, M. (2014). Strengthening our teacher community: Consolidating a 'signature pedagogy' for the teaching of Spanish as heritage language. In P. Trifonas & T. Aravossitas (Eds.), *Rethinking heritage language education* (pp. 213–236). Cambridge, UK: Cambridge University Press.

Polinsky, M., & Kagan, O. (2007). Heritage languages: In the 'wild' and in the classroom. *Language and Linguistics Compass, 1*(5), 368–395.

Timmermans, R. (1987). Institutionalization of the MAVO-project—a Dutch case study. In M. B. Miles, M. Ekholm, & R. Vandenberghe (Eds.), *Lasting school improvement: Exploring the process of institutionalization* (pp. 125–142). Leuven, Belgium: Acco.

Trifonas, P., & Aravossitas, T. (2014). Introduction. In P. Trifonas & T. Aravossitas (Eds.), *Rethinking heritage language education* (pp. viii–xxi). Cambridge, UK: Cambridge University Press.

Trivedi, H. (2003). The progress of Hindi (Part 2). In S. Pollock (Ed.), *Literary cultures in history: Reconstructions from South Asia* (pp. 958–1022). Berkeley, CA: University of California Press.

University of Minnesota/CARLA. (2015). LTE 2015: Changes and Challenges in Language Teacher Education [Website]. Retrieved from http://carla.umn.edu/conferences/past/LTE2015/speakers.html

Wright, Lorna. (2010). Internationalization at York University. Retrieved from http://www.yorku.ca/health/documents/InternationalizationatYorkUniversitySeptember2010.pdf

York University. (n.d.a). About York University [Web page]. Toronto, Canada: Author. Retrieved from http://about.yorku.ca

York University. (n.d.b). Our faculties [Web page]. Toronto, Canada: Author. Retrieved from http://about.yorku.ca/our-faculties/

Part VII

Heritage/Community Language Maintenance from a Lifespan Perspective

Formal and Informal Contexts

28

Chinese Heritage Language Learning

Negotiating Identities, Ideologies, and Institutionalization

Patricia A. Duff, Yongcan Liu, and Duanduan Li

1 Introduction

Given the vitality, migration patterns, and transnationalism of large numbers of speakers of Chinese languages over many centuries, education in Chinese as a heritage language (CHL) in diaspora communities, with its attendant desires, efforts, and successes, on the one hand, and challenges and disappointments, on the other, is not a new phenomenon or aspiration. Indeed, it may be idealistic to imagine that successive generations living in non-Chinese ethnolinguistic, sociocultural, and geopolitical contexts will either want to or manage to retain proficiency and affiliation with their heritage languages (HLs) and cultures in the midst of other languages and cultures, each with a different social and political status in their communities. For centuries, parents have asked themselves such questions as: Why do so many children in the Chinese diaspora *not* learn, use, or retain Chinese—and, more specifically, the language and cultural traditions of their parents or grandparents? Why do some Chinese dialects and writing systems have greater legitimacy, power, or utility than others? And what accounts for changes in their status over time? Which approaches to Chinese teaching and socialization are, or should be, adopted at home and in community schools to support children's (or parents') Chinese linguistic and cultural traditions without undermining their success in the dominant language and culture (and thus status and opportunities) in society? And what kinds of instructional materials are—or should be—used to represent language and literacy forms, ideologies, genres, topics, and interests?

Such questions are naturally related to wider issues surrounding how migrants and their ancestors have negotiated multiple ethnolinguistic and national identities, practices, ideologies, and lives across diverse sociolinguistic contexts in the worldwide Sinosphere (McDonald, 2011). These sorts of questions and phenomena have been on the minds of Sinophone parents and educators in North America for more than a century already (e.g., Chik, 2010; Jiang, 2010; Wang, 2014), although couched in very different kinds of (non-academic) discourse, and on the part of researchers in the past two decades. They have been explored in the UK (e.g., Hancock, 2014; Li & Zhu, 2011, 2014; Zhu & Li, 2014) and Australia as well (e.g., Chen & Zhang, 2014; Mu, 2016).

In the twenty-first century, the situation is changing, however, due to a number of converging factors: (1) the sheer scope and scale of Chinese people's migration and mobility; (2) the affordances of new, high-speed, and relatively low-cost information, communication, and transportation technologies allowing people to connect with Chinese communities and languages near and far; (3) the financial means, political will, and efforts that many communities are able to mobilize in support of CHL education; and (4) the increasing visibility and economic and political clout of China and, by extension, changing perceptions regarding the utility and importance of Mandarin in particular (Duff, Anderson, Doherty, & Wang, 2015; Mu, 2016; Wang, 2014). As a consequence, many applied linguists internationally are now turning their attention to Chinese language learning and use in CHL settings, and are examining the policies, programs, learning processes, and outcomes of CHL (linguistic and nonlinguistic) for individuals and social groups—as well as for nations, in terms of their economic, political, and security interests.

The concept of *institutionalization* is closely related to transformative change processes associated with attempts to improve education (Miles & Louis, 1987). In the case of CHL, it refers to rethinking the way HL education is understood, discussed, and implemented through such institutions as the family/home, community schools, public or private K–12 schools, and higher education as well as in public discourse.

In this chapter, we consider areas of CHL research that have received the greatest attention to date and then highlight topics for further study, especially in conjunction with the theme of institutionalism of HL education. We approach CHL from a lifespan perspective, starting with young children in the home, then school-aged learners' experiences through community (also known as heritage or complementary) schooling. Next, we discuss the experiences of young adults in postsecondary programs or other learning contexts, and finally consider older adults with young or school-aged children reflecting on challenges faced in their lifetimes in terms of Chinese language learning and retention themselves and now with their own children. Throughout, we consider insights and advances in research on CHL. We also suggest areas for improvement as part of further institutionalization of CHL education across the various domains in which it occurs.

2 Overview: Research Directions in Chinese as a Heritage Language

Linguistically oriented studies of CHL, as in Chinese as a foreign language (FL), often look cross-sectionally at learners' abilities in various aspects of speech (e.g., tones, grammar) or writing (e.g., Chinese character use, orthographic or morphological errors) at just one point in time or over a few weeks or a semester. However, increasingly research is also (or instead) attending to more sociocultural and sociolinguistic issues: learners' linguistic *trajectories* as speakers/writers of Chinese (or as bi/multilinguals), their multifaceted *identities* (including questions of "Chineseness," or "hybridity," or multiple communicative repertoires and allegiances), their *contexts* and *communities* of language learning, and the manner in which educators and parents try to *scaffold, mediate, or socialize* HL learning and retention (e.g., Curdt-Christiansen & Hancock, 2014; Duff, 2014; Duff & Li, 2013, 2014; He & Xiao, 2008; Li & Duff, 2008, 2014; Tsung & Cruickshank, 2011).

Agnes He (2006, 2012) illustrates this general trend by providing the typical trajectory of a young CHL learner in the U.S.—a "composite" character, Jason, who represents the cumulative experiences of CHL students with whom she has conducted research at various stages of their experiences from childhood to young adulthood. Similarly, Li and Duff (2014) describe the distinct trajectories of four transnational CHL learners located (at least while the study was conducted) in Canada. With a focus on trajectories, researchers are examining CHL across the lifespan and intergenerationally. These developmental linguistic pathways are typically *nonlinear*, interspersed with languages other than English or Chinese (and multiple varieties, such as Mandarin and Cantonese), with waves of learning and non-learning of Chinese, use and disuse, ambivalence toward or rejection of Chinese (or particular dialects) in some cases, and/or revitalization of Chinese within their lifetime or in subsequent generations as their circumstances change. A lifespan perspective should not, however, minimize the importance of learners' *concurrent* fields of socialization at any given point in their lives across the different social contexts they find themselves in (e.g., home, school, community) and the sometimes contradictory ways in which their linguistic identities, abilities, and practices are positioned therein.

In addition, sociolinguistic and ethnographic studies are documenting the manner in which CHL learners perform, contest, transgress, or playfully manipulate aspects of their language(s) and identity(ies) through various "translanguaging" practices (e.g., García & Li, 2014; He, 2013). They illustrate how language users can artfully move across semiotic systems to create meanings and perform identities in novel, personally relevant, often non-standard-language ways or in contravention of classroom language policies such as "No English." Another emerging focus is not just "Chinese" as an abstract concept—or *Chineses* (varieties of Chinese)—in CHL research (Duff & Doherty, in press). Researchers are beginning to show more awareness of the importance and ubiquity of multilingualism and polycentricity in Sinophone contexts (Li & Juffermans, 2016), involving competing linguistic varieties and "standards" (i.e., Standard Languages/dialects/registers) in different geosocial hubs (e.g., Cantonese vs. Mandarin; or traditional vs. simplified scripts systems in Vancouver, London, New York, or Melbourne). Enactment of, or affiliation with, the many possible oral or written codes depends on learners' histories and current contexts and purposes but also on the circulating ideologies about which varieties are most prestigious or significant in a given community or institutional setting.

All of these ways of framing CHL have implications for how society, educators, families and learners themselves engage with Chinese (generically), or with particular varieties of Chinese, and in turn with Chinese education. With the growing recognition by scholars (if not politicians or publics) that multilingualism in schools and society has cognitive, social, affective, and economic benefits, greater efforts are being made to further institutionalize and develop Chinese in community programs, as well as in credit-bearing Pre-K to adult programs. These programs may take many forms, ranging from second/foreign/heritage language classes to content-based, dual-language, or immersion/bilingual programs.

Discourse representing—and commodifying—Chinese as a "new, must-learn" *global language* (Duff et al., 2015) also confers on CHL the legitimacy or importance it might have lacked previously outside of Sinophone communities. With such developments comes the need to better understand learners' interests in CHL, their motivation to learn (or not to learn) it, and their concerns, experiences, and opportunities to continue their engagement with "Chinese" over the longer term. Even more pressing, though, is the need to think about how to make CHL a more meaningful, creative, engaging process for younger generations and provide effective institutional support to make that possible.

National and local language policies and ideologies, together with the manner in which these are implemented through pedagogy, can easily mitigate against an investment in HLs by families, communities, and individuals (e.g., Chik, 2010). This is particularly the case when conservative or xenophobic agendas promote more homogeneous, monolingual education or favor other languages instead of Chinese. In Canada, for example, where hundreds of thousands of school-aged children participate in bilingual (immersion) education programs involving English and French (the official languages of Canada) each year, there has been much less support in some parts of the country for schooling in non-official languages, such as Mandarin, despite the dramatically changing national and regional demographics (see Duff & Becker-Zayas, this volume; Mizuta, 2016). Therefore, policy contexts and circulating discourses surrounding Chinese—and different varieties of Chinese and geopolitical interests connected with those varieties—are important to understand.

411

In this chapter, we draw principally on research conducted in Canada, the U.S., UK, and Australia, while acknowledging that CHL issues are equally relevant, and often acute (albeit understudied), in many Asian, European, African, and South American contexts, among others. We do not aim to present a comprehensive review of all relevant research, but rather a synthesis of some of the main research directions and foci in Anglophone countries that have a substantial Chinese immigrant population and, thus, growing numbers of (prospective) CHL learners.

3 CHL in the Home

In discussions of institutionalizing HL education, it is important to consider the crucial formative institution of the home/family in terms of language policies and practices in relation to CHL (Curdt-Christiansen, 2009, 2014). Some families establish policies quite formally vis-à-vis expectations surrounding monolingual, bilingual, or even trilingual oral and written practices in the home. Others have only implicit or informal expectations and these may be mediated by multi-generational family structures in which, for example, monolingual Chinese grandparents interact with their children and grandchildren in a Chinese language, whereas the children and their parents move across languages in the household/community repertoire.

A common scenario is that parents (if both are Chinese-speaking, particularly among first generation immigrants and their young children in Canada) impose a Chinese-first family language policy, which is strengthened and enforced by the presence of Sinophone grandparents. However, if one parent is not Chinese-speaking or speaks a different dialect, and grandparents or other relatives are not close at hand, and children's friends outside the home are English-dominant (in English-speaking societies), it is predictable that with the onset of formal schooling outside the home, rapid shift to English or whichever language is most powerful in the wider society will be underway (Fishman, 2001; He, 2012; Jedwab, 2014; Jia, 2008).

If, however, it is anticipated that the family may engage in return (or serial) migration to or from a Chinese-speaking region, home language policies and patterns may reflect those prospects, with an orientation to Chinese-medium public school readiness, for example, even while in a diaspora context (e.g., Li, 2006). Indeed, in the absence of such exigencies, parents, over time, may simply relent as their children shift toward English, the language of dominant public institutions (in Anglophone contexts)—or, alternatively, may actively enforce a language policy privileging English at all costs, thinking that, given the status of English in the wider community, promoting Chinese at home is not in their children's best long-term interests academically, socially, or professionally.

4 CHL in Community Schools

CHL education has long been established, and thus "institutionalized," in diaspora contexts through community schools. These have been established, in large part, because of the lack of accommodation of HL learners and support for their multilingualism through mainstream public schooling, often for blatantly racist reasons (Chik, 2010; Jiang, 2010). Yet, despite the plethora of Chinese HL schools that exist worldwide outside of mainstream education, CHL learning through community schools is often fraught with challenges, many of which are shared by programs for other HLs: suitable and affordable space, funding, sufficient time to support learning to advanced levels (e.g., with once-weekly classes), the quality and training of teachers, curriculum and materials, language ideologies that have a political basis, and so on (see a recent review by Lee & Wright, 2014, in the context of U.S. heritage/community schooling across various language communities). Here we focus on several of these considerations in relation to CHL specifically.

Curriculum and Textbooks

CHL education through community schools has a long history in Anglophone countries (e.g., Chen & Zhang, 2014; Chik, 2010; Jiang, 2010; Li & Wu, 2008; Liu, 2010; Wang, 2014) going back to the early twentieth century (or even earlier) in Australia, Canada, and the U.S., and mid-twentieth century in the UK. Because of the many challenges associated with effectively mediating language and literacy socialization in CHL homes, parents often turn to community schools as a means of supporting and regularizing their children's oral and, especially, written language development. This also helps foster children's familiarity with long-established Chinese cultural values and traditions, and allows the children—and their parents—to become part of valuable social networks in the local Chinese community.

These schools, often staffed by untrained but well-intentioned parents or other volunteers, rely heavily on textbooks donated by foreign governments (e.g., in Beijing or Taipei), if available, that become the de facto curriculum and are used to help cultivate privileged linguistic and cultural forms of knowledge. Research on textbooks in CHL contexts therefore provides insights into ideologies, identities, genres, and content used in the socialization of CHL learners and students' reactions to these (Chiu, 2011; Curdt-Christiansen, 2008; Jiang, 2010). Chiu (2011), for example, analyzed two CHL textbook series widely used in North American (and Australian) CHL weekend schools, noting how the materials position CHL learners and their lifeworlds. She reported that the "ideal Chinese child" depicted in dialogues or other texts was expected to learn Chinese, to be respectful, diligent, and filial, and, especially in the materials from China, to be familiar with iconic Chinese heroes and monuments (e.g., the Great Wall). Learners were also expected to use Chinese within their extended families. The textbooks were filled with ideologies of patriotism, conservatism, and familism, among other dominant themes, and allegiance to tradition, though there were also some sharp differences in emphasis across the two series.

That textbooks are replete with ideological messages and meanings is not unique to CHL. However, the nature and objectives of the messages are interesting to examine in both contemporary and earlier materials. For example, a century ago one of the most important reasons for ensuring that young Chinese-heritage children in British Columbia, Canada, became literate in Chinese was to ensure that they could write letters on behalf of their sometimes illiterate elders in Canada to their relatives back in China. This would assure them that life in the diaspora was good and that the families were still closely connected with their communities back in China. For that reason, children's textbooks and their school-based instruction or extracurricular tutoring at the time focused on formal Chinese letter writing (Jiang, 2010), to prepare them to be effective literacy brokers on behalf of their relatives on both sides of the Pacific. Also instilled was the notion that at some later point the children/families would return to China, thus requiring a certain level of language proficiency. Different political ideologies were explicitly cultivated in the CHL materials used in Canada throughout the twentieth century as well (Jiang, 2011).

Classroom Instruction and Interaction

Other research examining discourse and interaction in CHL classrooms has also documented the means by which teachers and schools attempt to socialize children into "Chinese" identities and Chinese ways of schooling. He (2003, 2004), for example, shows how teachers attempted to downplay if not erase children's identities as (Chinese) Americans who had quite different experiences of schooling through their American schools, which included activities such as games, competitions, and prizes used in conjunction with instruction. The Chinese teachers created a strict classroom environment more in keeping with traditional Chinese education—but one that was resisted by students in various ways. Indeed, this combination of a strict instructional approach, a relentless focus on tradition and on Chinese literacy development (see also next section), and the dogmatic content of textbooks has often been reported as the reason many CHL students drop out of CHL programs (Chiu, 2011; Li & Duff, 2008; Mizuta, 2016). Some return to the study of Chinese later, in high school or university programs (Li & Duff, 2014), but more do not. They then may be left with a deep sense of regret or embarrassment, facing questions from themselves and others about their "Chineseness" (e.g., Duff, 2014). Alternatively, for others, the wholesale shift from Chinese to English, and possibly other languages, may be viewed as inevitable, strategic, or more conducive to successful integration and advancement in local communities.

Languages, Dialects, and Ideologies

Another crucial and complex dimension of CHL schooling is which Chinese language is to be taught (e.g., Mandarin or Cantonese) and whether that variety is the same as the one spoken by the students' families and communities (Duff & Doherty, in press; Li & Zhu, 2011, 2014). Different schools have in the past catered to parents' preferences in this regard, with parents establishing and choosing schools on the basis of their ethnolinguistic and philosophical allegiances. Language choice—and thus HL school choice—is also influenced by the perceived status of the language to be taught relative to others at the time, based on factors such as: number of speakers locally and in the worldwide diaspora or source regions, number and influence of new immigrants speaking that language locally, relationship between that language and the variety taught in public schools and postsecondary institutions, and other indices of prestige or power. A clear trend at present, given the "rise of China" (Duff et al., 2015) and the rise in Mainland Chinese emigration, is for complementary schools to offer Mandarin, if not exclusively, then with Cantonese as another option. The UK still seems to have a greater balance of both Cantonese and Mandarin schools than the U.S., Canada, or Australia (Hancock, 2014; Li & Zhu, 2011, 2014).

A related consideration is whether the script system (traditional or simplified) taught in a community school is the one parents or grandparents (if literate in Chinese) want their children to learn. This preference has a geopolitical and ideological basis and not simply a psycholinguistic (e.g., in terms of learnability) or pragmatic basis (i.e., one or other of the script systems is used in available reading materials). Students' writing may be corrected when the characters they use are not part of the script system favored by the teacher or institution (see He, 2004, for an example of this). The positioning of students and their heritage communities accordingly—for example, as speakers or writers of an institutionally dispreferred, different, or less prestigious or less "global" variety, or a non-Standard (e.g., southern) variety of Mandarin—is based on linguistic ideologies. Such ideologies are associated with the stratification of languages and connected with factors that include their perceived "beauty" (e.g., of traditional characters compared with simplified ones), utility, economics, and changing demographics (Duff & Doherty, in press; Li & Zhu, 2011). These circulating discourses, in turn, naturally affect CHL learners and communities deeply and make CHL education in community schools all the more political and complicated.

A third consideration related to language ideology, as well as teaching methodology and issues of teacher/student identity, is teachers' policies about language "purity," for instance maintaining a monolingual Chinese classroom ostensibly to maximize Chinese practice and reduce the confusion of working in two languages at once. This policy contrasts with allowing or encouraging code-switching in Chinese and English, which is now often studied in terms of "translanguaging" (e.g., García & Li, 2014). Students, and teachers themselves, often subvert or fail to comply with "Chinese only" policies in any case, despite their convictions and self-reports of their practices, thereby reproducing ideologies of English dominance through their linguistic behaviors (Chik, 2010).

Another powerful ideology surrounding what it means to "know" Chinese (and be an "educated Chinese person") in CHL programs is the preoccupation with *being highly literate* in Chinese above all else (as in many FL programs as well) (Duff et al., 2013; McDonald, 2011). This ideology typically drives the Chinese curriculum and instructional priorities, in spite of the difficulty of mastering Chinese writing, with thousands of characters to memorize and produce, four-character idioms, and myriad written genres and conventions. Yet CHL learners usually have infrequent occasions to engage in Chinese literacy practices in the wider society outside of CHL schooling. Evidence of this pervasive ideology is presented in research by Li and Zhu (2011), where parents of CHL students made comments such as the following (translated from the original Chinese):

> If you want to understand the Chinese culture, you must understand the Chinese language. If you can't read Chinese characters, how can you understand the Chinese culture? Traditionally we call those who can't read "word blind" (illiterate), like blind men [sic]. Also call them "uncultured." Illiterate people are of course uncultured.
>
> *(Parent 10) (p. 16)*

An additional ideology that may work against CHL is the somewhat defeatist (if also realistic/pragmatic) notion that trying to maintaining an HL such as Mandarin in predominantly Anglophone countries, with the hegemony of English as both a local and international language, is "a losing battle," as suggested by certain parents in Chik's (2010) study in California. For some CHL families, that realization or perspective may be reason enough not to try to promote Chinese learning; others may opt to make the effort and persevere (often against the wishes of their children) regardless, fearing the consequences of inaction. By doing so, and by involving their families in community-based CHL, parents may also claim new roles and a sense of belonging in local organizations where they are part of a collective with (mostly) shared goals and convictions despite their disparate backgrounds. The agency of these parents, individually and collectively, expressed in the form of participation in community schools often well after their own children have completed their studies, is itself an important phenomenon worthy of further attention (see Mizuta, 2016, for one such study).

Maguire and Curdt-Christiansen (2007) explore many of the aforementioned ideologies and others—which they differentiate as dialogically constructed *authoritative discourse* (typically external in origin based on official policies and traditions) and *internally persuasive discourse* (children's own beliefs). They analyzed ideologies in relation to students' various positionings and identities. Their research, situated in a large CHL community school in Montreal, Canada, identifies the macro-micro interplay of ideologies in that trilingual (English, French, Mandarin) socio-educational context, in part related to children's comparisons of their mainstream (French or English) schools with their CHL schools. Through their analysis of the short written Chinese compositions of 48 children, they observed several ideologies at play. These were often connected with the relatively recent arrival (less than three years earlier) of some students in Canada. Children's statements such as, "I will continue learning Chinese so that I can serve my motherland [PRC] when I grow up" (p. 6), or "I miss China," reflected this enduring affiliation with their homeland. The authors conclude: "Many [participants] see learning Chinese as an ideological obligation towards their families and an important part of their identity. They draw on the socio-cultural resources of the three languages to construct their own language systems, affiliations and ideological becomings" (pp. 74–75).

5 CHL in Public Schools

There appears to be scant research on language learning and use among CHL learners in public, credit-based school courses—either those designed to teach Chinese or in other mainstream subject areas in which students might be encouraged to produce multilingual texts. This gap in research exists despite the growing number of school-age students studying Chinese in Anglophone countries, which nonetheless remains quite small, relative to the number of students studying European languages. In Edmonton, Canada, for example, there has been a regrettable lack of research on a very large and successful K–12 Mandarin-English bilingual school program offered through public schools for decades. It was established and is sustained largely by the advocacy of Chinese-background parents, though it now has a good balance of Chinese and non-Chinese-background students.

One explanation for this lacuna in CHL research may simply be that CHL learners with a home background in Chinese are in some contexts ineligible to take Chinese courses designed for Anglophones without Chinese heritage/proficiency (cf. Mizuta, 2016). This kind of policy is problematic on several grounds, not least because it denies CHL students opportunities to build on and obtain official credit for their existing knowledge, interests, and genuine aspirations for reaching advanced levels of proficiency as officially recognized and eligible Chinese language students (Kelleher, 2010; Mizuta, 2016). However, such forms of exclusion may also stem from the inability of language programs and teacher education programs to equip teachers with the tools and approaches to effectively teach highly diverse, multi-level learner groups in the same classroom and program, or to offer distinct tracks for students with different backgrounds, needs, and interests.

Furthermore, no systematic research, to our knowledge, has examined the movement between or participation of students in *both* weekend and mainstream school Chinese programs and how they navigate those distinct learning spaces and how they are positioned within each. Learning concurrently in non-credit CHL schools and credit programs at school appears to occur in some contexts, such as Australia, but in the research this phenomenon is described mainly in terms of state funding, language education policy, curriculum, and teaching methodology. Chen and Zhang (2014), for example, describe how Australia has promoted and strengthened Chinese instruction in both community schools (for CHL *and* non-HL students) and in mainstream schools at both primary and secondary levels. They describe the development of Chinese curriculum and materials in the states of Victoria and New South Wales from the 1980s that supported mainstream and community school instruction in Mandarin, specifically, using simplified characters. However, in the K–12 mainstream education context, the curriculum framework for Chinese was the same as the one for European languages, and it did not have distinct provisions for CHL and non-CHL learners. A curriculum that includes different streams for those with and without Chinese backgrounds now exists both in community and mainstream schools, providing different options for students.

Chen and Zhang (2014) detail the strengths and weaknesses of the streaming, the curriculum, and the available instructional resources. Student attrition has been a major issue, though, beyond compulsory language study (100 hours total in one continuous 12-month period in grades 7–10). Low retention rates among both CHL and non-heritage students in mainstream programs are attributed to unreasonable expectations regarding learning outcomes (e.g., vocabulary size, number of characters), and are perhaps also exacerbated by teachers' backgrounds. Quite simply, teachers educated in China who teach in Chinese community and mainstream schools have different beliefs and approaches to instruction than those educated in Australia. And where programs do cater to CHL students, it is these teachers born and educated abroad—and not highly proficient Australian teachers of Mandarin with English as a first language—who tend to be assigned to teach the CHL learners due to their native proficiency in Chinese.

The topic of teacher education calls for a broader discussion of the preparation of teachers for CHL contexts (as distinct from contexts that do not include HL students or that focus on European languages), since most modern language teacher education programs we know of do not effectively prepare teacher candidates specifically for differentiated curriculum and instruction for CHL learners—or even for Chinese. As in the Australian example, much teacher preparation in modern language education is generic and is not differentiated according to the specific language to be taught (i.e., teachers of Spanish, Japanese, and Mandarin take the same methodology courses; the same is true in parts of Canada we are familiar with, apart from French teacher education). In the context of community schools, it may not be surprising that teachers lack training, but even in mainstream schools that employ trained language teachers, the content of this training typically excludes either an HL focus or a Chinese-specific focus.

6 CHL in Postsecondary Programs

Naturally, given the proximity of most university-based researchers to university courses, the majority of studies not dealing with young children's multilingualism and biliteracy practices in homes or community programs focus on postsecondary learners. This observation of a bias toward university-based studies in the U.S., especially, holds for Chinese SLA in general as well as for other languages. Not surprisingly, then, postsecondary learners are the population that He and Xiao (2008) and Tao (2006) feature in their edited volumes on CHL. He and Xiao examine CHL in terms of the habitus learners are being socialized into, learner characteristics (e.g., emotional investment in CHL), and language/literacy development. These topics are addressed in other research as well, with studies on attitudes, motivation, and identities (e.g., Comanaru & Noels, 2009; Li & Duff, 2014) and CHL students' writing (Zhang, 2014). Li and Duff (in press) and Xiang (2016) review current trends in postsecondary CHL education and research. Here we note several key themes that arise at this level.

Programmatic Priorities and Research in Postsecondary CHL: Problematizing Tracks, Categories, and Binaries

Li and Duff (2008, in press) and Xiang (2016) discuss many of the issues connected with differentiating instruction (or not doing so) for CHL learners at the postsecondary level, and the implications for institutionalization of the programs. Of particular salience is the general lack of accommodation of the specific needs, interests, backgrounds, and goals of (and even among) CHL versus non-CHL learners and thus curriculum and assessment that is appropriate for the students involved. Only programs with large enrolments are normally able to provide separate tracks for CHL students. Those that do so may still have reasonably proficient CHL students with significant prior exposure to Chinese enrolled in lower-level courses designed for non-HL learners if not screened well, or at all; students may simply choose to under-report their proficiency (Weger-Guntharp, 2006), or may not enroll or stay in the track that was designed for them for other reasons (Kelleher, 2008, 2010).

Patricia A. Duff et al.

However, such binaries of "CHL" and "non-CHL" are too stark and essentialist, masking vast differences among students within a category; for example, non-CHL learners who have lived or worked in a Chinese-speaking region or have substantial prior education in a variety of Chinese, usually Mandarin, entering first-year university courses; CHL learners who can speak (some) vernacular Cantonese or Mandarin, but cannot read or write Chinese; and then every other possible combination of abilities and experiences, such as Japanese learners of Chinese whose Sinographic heritage, if they are literate in Japanese, has given them a significant foundation in Chinese characters. As noted earlier, Li and Duff (2014) provide profiles of four very distinct "CHL" learners—from Beijing/PRC, Hong Kong, Indonesia, and Canada—each with an elaborate multilingual repertoire and pathway to learning Mandarin to an intermediate to advanced level. We are not aware of CHL research focusing on populations from other non-Chinese, yet Sinographic, language backgrounds learning Mandarin at the postsecondary level.

Another phenomenon to be considered in research and pedagogy is not program distinctions, but how students are positioned—by themselves, their programs, instructors, and classmates. CHL learners in a non-HL track may choose or be asked to underperform their competence because it would be frustrating for their non-HL classmates, as one of Weger-Guntharp's (2006) CHL participants explained in her study: "I definitely do [limit the vocabulary I use during class]. . . . My professor actually gets really mad when we use vocab that's not in the lesson" (p. 38). Or, as noted earlier, students' prior learning of their HL may not be relevant or even helpful if it is a different dialect than the one being taught and may be interpreted as nonstandard, accented, or illegitimate (Duff & Doherty, in press).

The plight of "dialect" speakers in university Mandarin courses and how they are positioned and placed, institutionally, was investigated by Kelleher (2008, 2010) in California. Her study was framed, in part, in terms of department categories and tracks, on the one hand, and how CHL students exercise their agency to negotiate their enrolment in either "regular" (non-HL) or accelerated "bilingual" (HL/dialect, with some oral proficiency) courses, often against the institution's expectations and program design. The two tracks eventually merged at higher levels in the program Kelleher focused on, which is not uncommon for programs with dual or multiple tracks. The HL students joined advanced classes sooner than the non-HL students, but the programs used the same curriculum materials (e.g., textbooks for FL learners). Kelleher found that many of the students in the "regular" class actually identified as bilingual in Cantonese or another dialect and English. Thus, some were very proficient in Cantonese or Mandarin, but were studying together with non-CHL true beginners. Those in the "bilingual" program were more often from a Mandarin-speaking background. By self-selecting to the "regular" program, students had greater opportunities to receive high grades, even if much of the language was already familiar.

When the program added a third option, "Mandarin for Cantonese Speakers," Kelleher (2010) reported that

> Their abilities in Cantonese made them very particular kinds of heritage learners. They used their Cantonese abilities to support their Mandarin development, to express non-sanctioned meanings in the classroom, to build rapport with classmates, and to negotiate ideas of Chineseness together outside the classroom.
>
> *(p. 226)*

However, the inordinate focus on pronunciation in that special course and a lack of incorporation of explicit discussion of Cantonese on the part of instructors, who did not know Cantonese, seemed to reduce language learning to the amelioration of a *defective* aspect of their speech, a common thrust of CHL education. This in turn made students more judgmental regarding not only their own but also their relatives' and friends' pronunciation vis-à-vis "correct Standard Mandarin."

In sum, providing greater accommodation for Cantonese speakers in the program was an effort to strategically offer multiple paths through the program based on students' linguistic background and perceived needs, although actual implementation revealed areas needing further improvement.

Finally, tacit knowledge of oral Mandarin does not always give students an advantage over their non-CHL peers on tests, which usually target proficiency in literacy. Xiao (2006), for example, in her comparison of CHL and non-CHL students enrolled in American university Chinese courses, found that CHL students outperformed their non-Chinese peers in various listening/ speaking assessments, but "did not perform better than their non-heritage peers in reading comprehension, vocabulary learning, and character writing" (p. 54). Shen (2003) also looked at CHL learners' character writing, comparing HL and non-HL university students' writing under two conditions: in heterogeneous classes or in homogeneous classes (HL only). She reported that the homogeneous grouping led to higher performance by the CHL students, thus concluding that enabling students to study in distinct tracks with other HL learners is advantageous for them.

7 Conclusion and Future Directions

In this chapter we have provided a discussion of recent research on CHL and issues connected with CHL education in Anglophone countries. Few studies we are aware of (e.g., Li & Juffermans, 2016) have examined CHL in non-Anglophone contexts or in family structures where some but not all family members are of Chinese heritage (e.g., in the case of non-Chinese adoptive parents of ethnically Chinese children, or transnational non-Chinese parents whose children have spent years during their childhood in Greater China). More research, ideally of a very situated, longitudinal nature, is therefore needed across CHL learners' lives and trajectories in different contexts, both national and transnational.

Also missing from the discussion in this chapter is CHL in later adulthood and in socializing the next generation to use Chinese. Research might offer retrospective accounts of first-, second-, or third-generation Chinese-background adults' learning or non-learning of Chinese, their views of which dialects/varieties should be taught/learned, and why, and the efforts they make on their own behalf or that of their children or others in the wider community to foster the learning of Chinese. But how do many of them, as their children (re)claim ownership of Chinese, also try to engage in their own Chinese studies? Similarly, for ethnically Chinese adults without children involved in CHL, under what circumstances and with what results do they engage anew in Chinese language learning?

Finally, much more attention must be paid to the identities and ideologies associated with CHL, and the impact of these on institutionalization in well-articulated, engaging, and effective programs. Such programs require appropriate curricula and materials and differentiated approaches to teaching learners with diverse backgrounds, goals, and needs.

There are multiple pathways to learning Chinese as an HL (Curdt-Christiansen & Hancock, 2014) in transnational migration contexts, but these pathways are constructed and reconstructed, shaped and reshaped by a complex interplay of individual, family, community, institutional, and societal forces. How to provide effective HL education is dependent on our accurate understanding of this complex process, which involves not only the cognitive process of acquiring the language, but also the social process of enabling language acquisition.

References

Chen, S., & Zhang, Y. (2014). Chinese language teaching in Australia. In X. L. Curdt-Christiansen & A. Hancock (Eds.), *Learning Chinese in diasporic communities: Many pathways to being Chinese* (pp. 181–200). Amsterdam, The Netherlands: John Benjamins.

Chik, C. (2010). *Looking both ways: Structure, agency, and language ideology at a Chinese Saturday school* (Doctoral dissertation). Retrieved from ProQuest Dissertation and Theses database. (AAT Number: 3472571).

Chiu, L. (2011). *The construction of the 'ideal Chinese child': A critical analysis of textbooks for Chinese heritage language learners* (Master's thesis). Retrieved from https://open.library.ubc.ca/cIRcle/collections/ubctheses/24/items/1.0072083

Comanaru, R., & Noels, K. (2009). Self-determination, motivation, and the learning of Chinese as a heritage language. *The Canadian Modern Language Review, 66*(1), 131–158.

Curdt-Christiansen, X. L. (2008). Reading the world through words: Cultural themes in heritage Chinese language textbooks. *Language and Education, 22*(2), 95–113.

Curdt-Christiansen, X. L. (2009). Invisible and visible language planning: Ideological factors in the family language policy of Chinese immigrant families in Quebec. *Language Policy, 8*(4), 351–375.

Curdt-Christiansen, X. L. (2014). Family language policy: Is learning Chinese at odds with learning English? In X. L. Curdt-Christiansen & A. Hancock (Eds.), *Learning Chinese in diasporic communities: Many pathways to being Chinese* (pp. 35–56). Amsterdam, The Netherlands: John Benjamins.

Curdt-Christiansen, X. L., & Hancock, A. (Eds.). (2014). *Learning Chinese in diasporic communities: Many pathways to being Chinese* (pp. 35–56). Amsterdam, The Netherlands: John Benjamins.

Duff, P. (2014). Language socialization into Chinese language and 'Chineseness' in diaspora communities. In X. L. Curdt-Christiansen & A. Hancock (Eds.), *Learning Chinese in diasporic communities: Many pathways to becoming Chinese* (pp. 13–33). Amsterdam, The Netherlands: John Benjamins.

Duff, P., Anderson, T., Doherty, L., & Wang, R. (2015). Representations of Chinese language learning in contemporary English-language news media: Hope, hype, and fear. *Global Chinese, 1*(1), 139–168.

Duff, P., Anderson, T., Ilnyckyj, R., VanGaya, E., Wang, R., & Yates, E. (2013). *Learning Chinese: Linguistic, sociocultural, and narrative perspectives.* Berlin, Germany: De Gruyter.

Duff, P., & Doherty, L. (in press). Learning 'Chinese' as heritage language: Challenges, issues, and ways forward. In C.-R. Huang, Z. Jing-Schmidt, & B. Meisterernst (Eds.), *Routledge handbook of Chinese applied linguistics.* New York, NY: Routledge.

Duff, P., & Li, D. (2013). Learning Chinese as a heritage language. In C. Mady & K. Arnett (Eds.), *Minority populations in second language education: Broadening the lens from Canada* (pp. 87–100). Clevedon, UK: Multilingual Matters.

Duff, P., & Li, D. (2014). Rethinking heritage languages: Ideologies, practices, and priorities in Canada and China. In P. Trifonas & T. Aravossitas (Eds.), *Rethinking heritage language education* (pp. 45–65). Cambridge, UK: Cambridge University Press.

Fishman, J. A. (2001). *Can threatened languages be saved? Reversing language shift, revisited: A 21st century perspective.* Clevedon, UK: Multilingual Matters.

García, O., & Li, W. (2014). *Translanguaging: Language, bilingualism and education.* New York, NY: Palgrave Macmillan.

Hancock, A. (2014). Chinese complementary schools in Scotland and the Continua of Biliteracy. In X. L. Curdt-Christiansen & A. Hancock (Eds.), *Learning Chinese in diasporic communities: Many pathways to being Chinese* (pp. 59–79). Amsterdam, The Netherlands: John Benjamins.

He, A. (2003). Novices and their speech roles in Chinese heritage language classes. In R. Bayley & S. Schecter (Eds.), *Language socialization in bilingual and multilingual societies* (pp. 128–146). Clevedon, UK: Multilingual Matters.

He, A. W. (2004). Identity construction in Chinese heritage language classes. *Pragmatics, 14*(2–3), 199–216.

He, A. W. (2006). Toward an identity theory of the development of Chinese as a heritage language. *Heritage Language Journal, 4*(1), 1–28. Retrieved from http://www.heritagelanguages.org/

He, A. W. (2012). Heritage language socialization. In A. Duranti, E. Ochs, & B. Schieffelin (Eds.), *The handbook of language socialization* (pp. 587–609). Malden, MA: Wiley-Blackwell.

He, A. W. (2013). The wor(l)d is a collage: Multi-performance by Chinese heritage language speakers. *The Modern Language Journal, 97,* 304–317.

He, A. W., & Xiao, Y. (Eds.). (2008). *Chinese as a heritage language: Fostering rooted world citizenry.* Honolulu, HI: National Foreign Language Resource Center, University of Hawai'i at Mānoa.

Jedwab, J. (2014). Canada's 'other' languages: The role of non-official languages in ethnic persistence. In P. Trifonas & T. Aravossitas (Eds.), *Rethinking heritage language education* (pp. 237–253). Cambridge, UK: Cambridge University Press.

Jia, G. (2008). Heritage language development, maintenance, and attrition among recent Chinese immigrants in New York. In A. W. He & Y. Xiao (Eds.), *Chinese as a heritage language: Fostering rooted world citizenry* (pp. 189–203). Honolulu, HI: National Foreign Language Resource Center, University of Hawai'i at Mānoa.

Jiang, H. (2010). *A socio-historical analysis of Chinese heritage language education in British Columbia* (Master's thesis). Retrieved from https://open.library.ubc.ca/cIRcle/collections/ubctheses/24/items/1.0071369

Kelleher, A. (2008). Placements and re-positionings: Tensions around CHL learning in a university Mandarin program. In A.W. He & Y. Xiao (Eds.), Chinese as a heritage language: Fostering rooted world citizenry (pp. 239–258). Honolulu, HI: National Foreign Language Resource Center, University of Hawai'i at Manoa.

Kelleher, A. (2010). *Policies and identities in Mandarin education: The situated multilingualism of university-level heritage language learners* (Doctoral dissertation). Retrieved from http://linguistics.ucdavis.edu/pics-and-pdfs/Kelleher_dissertationFINAL.pdf

Lee, J. S., & Wright, W. E. (2014). The rediscovery of heritage and community language education in the United States. *Review of Research in Education, 38,* 137–165.

Li, D., & Duff, P. (2008). Issues in Chinese heritage language education and research at the postsecondary level. In A. W. He & Y. Xiao (Eds.), *Chinese as a heritage language: Fostering rooted world citizenry* (pp. 13–33). Honolulu, HI: National Foreign Language Resource Center, University of Hawai'i at Manoa.

Li, D., & Duff, P. (2014). Chinese language learning by adolescents and young adults in the Chinese diaspora: Motivation, ethnicity, and identity. In X. L. Curdt-Christiansen & A. Hancock (Eds.), *Learning Chinese in diasporic communities: Many pathways to becoming Chinese* (pp. 219–238). Amsterdam, The Netherlands: John Benjamins.

Li, D., & Duff, P. (in press). Chinese heritage language learning in postsecondary contexts. In C. Ke (Ed.), *The Routledge handbook of Chinese second language acquisition.* New York, NY: Routledge.

Li, G. (2006). Biliteracy and trilingual practices in the home context: Case studies of Chinese Canadian children. *Journal of Early Childhood Literacy, 6*(3), 359–385.

Li, J., & Juffermans, K. (2016). Polycentric repertoires: Constructing Dutch-Chinese youth identities in the classroom and online. In W. Li (Ed.), *Multilingualism in the Chinese diaspora worldwide: Transnational connections and local social realities* (pp. 32–46). New York, NY: Routledge.

Li, W., & Wu, C.-J. (2008). Code-switching: Ideologies and practices. In A. W. He & Y. Xiao (Eds.), *Chinese as a heritage language: Fostering rooted world citizenry* (pp. 225–238). Honolulu, HI: National Foreign Language Resource Center.

Li, W., & Zhu, H. (2011). Changing hierarchies in Chinese language education for the British Chinese learners. In L. Tsung & K. Cruickshank (Eds.), *Teaching and learning Chinese in global contexts* (pp. 11–27). London, UK: Continuum.

Li, W., & Zhu, H. (2014). Language and literacy teaching, learning and socialization in the Chinese complementary school classroom. In X. L. Curdt-Christiansen & A. Hancock (Eds.), *Learning Chinese in diasporic communities: Many pathways to being Chinese* (pp. 117–135). Amsterdam, The Netherlands: John Benjamins.

Liu, N. (2010). Chinese heritage language schools in the United States. In Center for Applied Linguistics *Heritage Briefs*. Retrieved from Center for Applied Linguistics Website: http://www.cal.org/heritage/pdfs/briefs/chinese-heritage-language-schools-in-the-us.pdf

Maguire, M., & Curdt-Christiansen, X. L. (2007). Multiple schools, languages, experiences and affiliations: Ideological becomings and positionings. *Heritage Language Journal, 5*(1), 50–78. Retrieved from http://www.heritagelanguages.org/

McDonald, E. (2011). *Learning Chinese, turning Chinese: Challenges to becoming Sinophone in a globalised world.* New York, NY: Routledge.

Miles, M. B., & Louis, K. S. (1987). Research on institutionalization: A reflective review. In M. B. Miles, M. Ekholm, & R. Vandenberghe (Eds.), *Lasting school improvement: Exploring the process of institutionalization* (pp. 25–44). Leuven, Belgium: Acco.

Mizuta, A. (2016). *Memories of language lost and learned: Parents and the shaping of Chinese as a heritage language in Canada* (Doctoral dissertation in preparation).

Mu, G. M. (2016). *Learning Chinese as a heritage language: An Australian perspective.* Clevedon, UK: Multilingual Matters.

Shen, H. (2003). A comparison of written Chinese achievement among heritage learners in homogeneous and heterogeneous groups. *Foreign Language Annals, 36*(2), 258–266.

Tao, H. (Ed.). (2006). Chinese as a heritage language [Special issue]. *Heritage Language Journal, 4*(1). Retrieved from http://www.heritagelanguages.org/

Tsung, L., & Cruickshank, K. (Eds.). (2011). *Teaching and learning Chinese in global contexts.* London, UK: Continuum.

Wang, S. (2014). Being 'critical': Implications for Chinese heritage language schools. In T. Wiley, J. Peyton, D. Christian, S. Moore, & N. Liu (Eds.), *Handbook of heritage, community, and Native American languages in the United States: Research, policy, and educational practice* (pp. 157–166). Abingdon, UK: Routledge.

Weger-Guntharp, H. (2006). Voices from the margin: Developing a profile of Chinese heritage language learners in the FL classroom. *Heritage Language Journal, 4*, 29–46. Retrieved from http://www.heritage languages.org/

Xiang, X. (2016). The teaching of Chinese to heritage language learners at the post-secondary level. In J. Ruan, J. Zhang, & C. Leung (Eds.), *Chinese language education in the United States* (pp. 167–194). New York, NY: Springer.

Xiao, Y. (2006). Heritage learners in the Chinese language classroom: Home background. *Heritage Language Journal, 4*, 47–56. Retrieved from http://www.heritagelanguages.org/

Zhang, L. (2014). College Chinese heritage language learners' implicit knowledge of compound sentences. *Heritage Language Journal, 11*(1), 45–75. Retrieved from http://www.heritagelanguages.org/

Zhu, H., & Li, W. (2014). Geopolitics and the changing hierarchies of the Chinese language: Implications for policy and practice of Chinese language teaching in Britain. *The Modern Language Journal, 98*(1), 326–339.

29

Classroom and Community Support for Turkish in Germany

Carol W. Pfaff, Meral Dollnick, and Annette Herkenrath

1 Introduction

There has been a large Turkish-speaking population in Germany since the initial labor recruitment agreement between the former West Germany and West Berlin and Turkey, which began in 1961 and lasted until 1973.[1] Presently there are about three million residents with roots in Turkey, most of whom live in the urban industrial centers of the former West German Federal States and West Berlin. The programs and community institutions supporting Turkish in Germany are found in those areas, and are the focus of the discussion in this chapter.

In educational contexts, the term "institutionalization" often looks at the assimilation of an innovation or some form of change into an organization, usually a single school, such that it becomes stable and routinized (e.g., Ekholm & Trier, 1987). In this chapter, however, we look at instructional offerings in Turkish across Germany as a whole. We focus on preschool, primary, and secondary schools, as well as after-hours programs that fall outside the public school system. Support for Turkish maintenance in other community contexts is also discussed.

Ekholm and Trier (1987) point out that "both macro- and micro- political processes" (p. 14) are involved in institutionalization, and the changing sociopolitical situation within both Turkey and Germany, and globally, inevitably has consequences for the rise and fall of support for Turkish HL instruction and other forms of community support. Although the circumstances of Turkish in Germany are in many ways similar to that described by Polinsky and Kagan (2007) in their discussion of HLs "in the wild and in the classroom," the situation in Germany differs significantly from that in the U.S. In Germany, the underlying ideology was never that the country was to be a "melting pot"; indeed, up until 2000 the fact that Germany had become a land of immigration was not recognized. Further, recently large numbers of immigrants from the new Eastern European EU countries and the current numbers of refugees and immigrants from Syria, Iraq, and other Middle Eastern countries have brought other minority languages, and German as a second language, to the forefront of language policy. At the same time, Turkish-speaking families are becoming increasingly bilingual in Turkish and German. Finally, as the economic situations both in Turkey and in Germany change, many Turkish speakers have "re-migrated" to Turkey (Kunuroglu, Yağmur, van de Vijver, & Kroon, 2015, p. 200). Still, the institutionalization of programs targeting Turkish as an HL, Turkish as a less commonly taught foreign language, and bilingual programs that include both Turkish and German is continuing to solidify and stabilize, as are developments in other cultural institutions outside the educational system.

Before turning to the discussion of micro-level language programs (section 2) and the role of other cultural institutions (section 3), we briefly sketch the macro-level factors and demographic and social background of Turkish in Germany and recent international and national policy developments (section 1.1).

Macro-Level Demographic, Social, and Language Policy Factors

Not all immigrants from Turkey speak Turkish as their first language; Ethnologue lists 36 languages spoken in Turkey (Lewis, Simons, & Fennig, 2016). Of these, Kurdish is particularly important. Kurds were estimated by Ammann (2005, p. 1011) to have comprised at least 20% of the initial labor migration from Turkey to Germany, and many more came as refugees after the official end of recruitment. However, Turkish, the language of education in Turkey, was the first or second language of most immigrants from Turkey, and it is also the first or second language spoken by some multilingual immigrants from Bulgaria, Romania, and Macedonia.

According to the German Microcensus[2] of 2014, Turkey is the country of origin of the majority of immigrants since 1949: 17.4% from Turkey; followed by Poland (9.9%), the Russian Federation (7.3%), and Italy (4.7%) (p. 7). Table 29.1 reflects the proportion of individuals of Turkish background in the total and school-age population of Germany.

In the new federal states of former East Germany, less than 1% of the population has Turkish background, while in the old federal states of former West Germany, proportions of the population range from around 2% to 7%. In urban districts, the proportions are often much higher, often well over half or three-quarters of local school populations. The HL programs treated in section 2 are mostly found in such districts.

Even before the widespread availability of internet communication, the geographical proximity of Germany to Turkey facilitated contact through return visits. Turkish-language newspapers and other media available in Germany provide continuing links to ongoing political, social, and economic changes there. Written Turkish is a prominent part of the linguistic landscape in shops, advertisements, translations of local government announcements, hospitals, schools, and so on, and in informal contexts, including graffiti (Cındark & Ziegler, in press; Redder et al., 2013). In such contexts, Turkish is simply used (rather than explicitly taught). Finally, current German immigration policies continue to permit family reunification so that spouses of second generation residents are able to join them as new first generation immigrants (Pfaff, 2010, pp. 336–338),

Table 29.1 Preschool and School-Age Population of Germany in 2014, in 1000s

	All ages	under 5	5–10	10–15	15–20	20–25
Total population of Germany	80,897	3,419	3,466	3,690	4,008	4,493
Population with background from Turkey (%)	2,859 (3.5%)	198 (5.8%)	227 (6.5%)	246 (6.7%)	260 (6.5%)	234 (5.2%)

Source: Calculated from "Bevölkerung und Erwerbstätigkeit: Bevölkerung mit Migrationshintergrund- Ergebnisse des Mikrozensus [Population and employment: Population with migration background], 2015, *Statisstisches Bundesampt* [Federal Statistical Office], pp. 82–84. Copyright 2016 by Statisstisches Bundesampt.

a significant source of Turkish input for children and a key factor in language maintenance in some families.

Studies of language maintenance of immigrant minority groups in Europe have shown that Turkish ranks very high along parameters of ethnolinguistic vitality, as demonstrated in Extra and Yağmur's (2004) study of self-reported language use and HL instruction of primary school children in six European cities. Empirical studies of spoken and written Turkish have found proficiency in spoken and, for many, also in written Turkish to be quite high, although the varieties often depart from the "purist" standard, with lexical and morphosyntactic features from regional varieties, through contact with German and internal change (Backus, 2004; Backus, Jørgensen, & Pfaff, 2010; Pfaff, 2015; Rehbein, Herkenrath, & Karakoç, 2009).

The early labor migrants were regarded as "guests" who were not expected to stay in Germany, and language education policies were initially ignored. Different educational policies were later adopted by the federal states for school-age children. In Bavaria, for example, "national classes," exclusively for children of Turkish immigrants, were established in 1973 to facilitate their re-integration in Turkey (Rist, 1979, as cited in Schultz & Kolb, 2015). This model was not adopted in the other federal states. Instead, when it became clear that children growing up in Germany were not automatically acquiring sufficient German, the focus shifted to instruction in German to facilitate school success and integration into German society (Pfaff, 1981).

Support for Turkish instruction within a policy of integration came from various quarters. UNESCO 1954 and European policies supported language rights of minority populations, including children of immigrant workers (Pfaff, 2010, 2014; Skutnabb-Kangas, 2008). Yıldız (2013) documents steps leading to the institutionalization of Muttersprachlicher Ergänzungsunterricht (MEU)[3] [supplementary mother tongue instruction] grounded in decisions at the national level by the Kultusministerkonferenz (KMK) [Conference of Ministries of Culture] in 1971 and 1976 which are still valid today (Kulturministerkonferenz, 1971, 1976, 2013a, 2013b; Yıldız, 2013, pp. 52–55), and in positions supported by the Türkischer Elternverein [Turkish Parents' Associations].

German educational policies are set within a framework decided by the KMK, but details of implementation are left to the individual federal states. Implementation on the ground in (pre)schools has sometimes preceded the establishment of an official framework, while in other instances decisions of official actors at the national and EU levels have fostered and solidified implementation at the state and local levels. In the twenty-first century, the Council of Europe has acknowledged the reality of societal multilingualism and advocated plurilingualism as a goal for all Europeans (Fleming, 2007). This policy is reflected in the 2013 decision of the German KMK, which recognized Turkish and several other non-traditional languages as options for a second or third foreign language. By providing credit toward school completion and, in some schools, credit toward the Abitur (high-school graduation and university qualification examinations), this foreign language option valorizes pupils' knowledge of their HL and facilitates their development of standard Turkish.[4]

2 Micro-Level: Heritage Language, Foreign Language, and Bilingual Turkish/German Instruction

All of the HL and bilingual programs are voluntary. Foreign languages are obligatory but the choice of which language is to be studied, particularly as second and third foreign languages, is not prescribed. This section summarizes the current status of implementation of these programs as follows: public primary and secondary schools in 2.1, bilingual programs in 2.2, and provisions for teacher training in 2.3.

Turkish as a Heritage Language in Educational Settings

Turkish HL courses are taught either in programs explicitly termed "supplementary mother tongue instruction" (MEU) or as foreign language classes, both of which include a focus on cultural content. The former are usually exclusively for pupils with a Turkish background; the latter may be open to other pupils as well, though in many cases require prerequisite knowledge of Turkish and thus are de facto HL classes. Optional afternoon MEU classes are organized and implemented either by teachers supplied by the Turkish Consulates or by teachers in the regular school system (Reich & Hienz de Albentiis, 1998). Tables 29.2 and 29.3 provide statistics for the current numbers of pupils in classes of each type by federal state and, where possible, by grade level. Turkish foreign language classes are also available within the German school system, primarily in the federal states of Baden-Württemberg, Saarland, Bremen, Hamburg, Schleswig-Holstein, and Berlin (Schroeder, 2003). In addition, some school districts offer bilingual Turkish/German programs that include language and subject matter instruction in Turkish in preschools, primary, and secondary schools, some of these involving both teachers from the Turkish Consulate and those trained in Germany (see 2.2.).

Table 29.3 provides figures on the breakdown by federal state of the 12,549 pupils participating in Turkish instruction offered by the German public primary and secondary schools for 2013–2014.[5] As mentioned above, although these foreign language classes are, in principle, open to all pupils, with and without a Turkish-speaking background, a policy advocated by Küppers, Schroeder, and Gülbeyaz (2014) and Schroeder and Küppers (2015), in practice these foreign

Table 29.2 Turkish Instruction by Turkish Consulate Teachers by Federal State and Grade (2014/15)

Federal State	Grade levels	Number of pupils
Baden-Württemberg (Stuttgart, Karlsruhe)	1–8	24,619
Bavaria (Munich, Nuremberg)	1–10	6,098
Berlin—former West districts	1–6	4,850
Bremen	1–4	1,200
Hamburg[a]	1–10	2,822[a]
Hessen (Frankfurt)	1–10	14,700
Lower Saxony (Hannover)	1–4	7,136
Nordrhein-Westphalia (Düsseldorf, Essen, Cologne, Münster),	1–8	43,372
Rheinland-Palatinate (Mainz)[a]	1–4	9,262[a]
Schleswig-Holstein[a]	1–8	
Saarland [a]	1–4	

Note: [a]The Turkish Consulates report participation by cities where the consular offices are located rather than by federal state. Figures for Schleswig-Holstein are included with Hamburg; figures for Saarland with Mainz (Rheinland-Palatinate).

Source: Compiled from personal communications with Prof. Dr. Cemal Yıldız, Turkish Consulate Education Attaché, and local Turkish Parents' Associations.

Table 29.3 Pupils Receiving Turkish Instruction Organized by the German Public Schools by Federal State and Grade (2013/14)

Federal State / Grades	1	2	3	4	5	6	7	8	9	10	11	12	13	not specified by grade	Σ
Baden-Württemberg[a]	5			138							24	23		125	315
Bayern				25	29	49	35	47	12		53	48			298
Berlin					210	174	178	288	191	116	110	30	24		1321
Bremen	24	62	85	120		53	79	64	60	151	92	90			880
Hamburg	156	181	188	165	28	43	151	140	152	170	67	44	42		1527
Hessen						5		4							9
Lower Saxony															0
North Rhein-Westphalia					400	1175	1283	1388	1222	1217	435	365	157	549	8191
Rheinland-Palatinate								2	1	1					4
Saarland															0
Schleswig-Holstein															0
Brandenburg															0
Mecklenburg-Vorpommern															0
Sachsen	2		1	1											4
Sachsen-Anhalt															0
Thüringen															0
TOTAL all federal states	182	243	274	291	453	1510	1741	1807	1774	1880	787	680	229	698	12549

Note: [a]Baden-Württemberg figures are reported by individual grade only for advanced secondary level.

Source: Compiled from "Bildung und Kultur: Allgemeinbildende Schulen" [Education and culture: General education schools], Fascherie 11, Reihe 1 [Discipline series 11, File 1], 2013/2014, pp. 104–106. *Statisstisches Bundesampt* [Federal Statistical Office]. Copyright 2016 by Statistisches Bundesampt.

language classes are often attended primarily by HL speakers. North–Rhine–Westphalia, the largest state, accounts for two-thirds of the pupils, and sizable numbers are also found in the city states of Hamburg, Berlin, and Bremen. Hessen, the state which includes one of the most multi-lingual cities in Germany, namely Frankfurt/Main, has few pupils of Turkish in its public school programs, and there are none in Lower Saxony. However, as shown in Table 29.2, there are sizable numbers in classes offered by the Turkish Consulate. Schools in the former East Germany, below the line, have very few pupils and there are no Turkish Consulate programs in those federal states.

Turkish/German Bilingual Programs

Bilingual programs were first implemented in the early 1970s in preschool daycare centers as initiatives by parents and Turkish caregivers. In the early 1980s politicians, educators, parents, and linguists in West Germany and Berlin participated in cooperative discussions on issues of bilingual education, particularly for Turkish-speaking children. The discussions resulted in official support for initiatives for programs which acknowledged the value of Turkish as an HL as well as a second language for German speakers (Bundesarbeitsgemeinschaft der Immigrantenverbände in der Bundesrepublik Deutschland und Berlin West [BAGIV], 1985; Meier & Schumacher, this volume). In the 1980s, bilingual programs were implemented in primary schools to foster the acquisition of German by Turkish children, making instrumental use of the Turkish HL but also incorporating and valorizing it. By the twenty-first century, the situation had changed as many parents were themselves early bilinguals so that an L1/L2 dichotomy no longer applied (Akıncı & Pfaff, 2008; Dirim, 2015a; Rehbein & Grießhaber, 1996) and many children are now raised as simultaneous or early Turkish/German bilinguals at home. Preschool and school policies are changing to meet this reality of lived multilingualism, with the focus increasingly on maintenance and expansion of academic language skills in the HL as well as in the national majority language. The following sections discuss preschool bilingual programs (2.2.1), and primary and secondary school bilingual classes (2.2.2).

Bilingual Daycare Centers

Daycare centers (Kindertagesstätten, or Kitas) are publically funded with supplementary fees paid by parents and are, in principle, available for all children aged one to six, the age of entry to primary school. Bilingual programs in daycare centers in Germany have been surveyed by Frühe Mehrsprachigkeit an Kindertageseinrichtungen und Schulen (FMKS) [The Association for Early Multilingualism in Daycare Centers and Schools]. According to the FMKS 2014 survey of Kitas (Verein für frühe Mehrsprachigkeit an Kindertageseinrichtungen und Schulen FMKS, 2014), Germany had 1,035 bilingual daycare centers in 21 languages, the most frequent by far being German plus English or French. Forty-two (4%) had Turkish as the primary non-German language: 33 of these are in Berlin, 4 in Hamburg, 1 each in Schleswig-Holstein and Hessen.

An early innovative bilingual daycare center in Berlin is the Verein zur Förderung ausländischer und deutscher Kinder [Association for the support of foreign and German children], established in 1971 and still in operation. Their policy explicitly recognizes the principle of equal rights and practices for both languages, with both Turkish and German staff members using their mother tongue with all children. A four-year longitudinal study carried out in this daycare center between 1987 and 1992 documents sociolinguistic aspects as well as the children's grammatical development in both languages (Pfaff, 1994, 2014). A striking finding was that despite the overwhelming majority of Turkish-speaking children in the Kita and surrounding neighborhood, the initially monolingual Turkish-speaking children all acquired German as their second language, though in a nonstandard variety. By contrast, only one German child acquired productive use of Turkish while the rest acquired only some receptive competence and limited vocabulary in Turkish (Pfaff, 1994, 2014), an interesting reflection of the children's uptake of the sociolinguistic realities of the outside world.

In the last fifteen years, bilingual Turkish/German Kitas, have been established in other cities, including Kiel, Lübeck, Essen, and Frankfurt/Main (Apeltauer, 2007; Kuyumcu, 2016). However, as the demography of local neighborhoods changes, Turkish/German bilingual Kita programs seem likely to be replaced by Kitas with more general multilingual awareness programs. This was the case with the Turkish-German bilingual Kita established in 1994 in Hamburg-Altona. By 2015, it had 52 children with nine different mother tongues, including several from binational families, but no children from monolingual German families. The Kita gave up its original Turkish-German concept in favor of focusing on German as the language of the educational system, though Turkish is still spoken and supported and they hope to provide similar support for the other languages in the future.

Bilingual Programs in Primary and Secondary Schools

According to the FMKS 2014 report, 287 primary schools in Germany offer 17 languages other than German and include at least one content course in the other language. In most cases, the other language is English or French but four schools (1%) are Turkish/German bilingual: one in Berlin, one in Nordrhein-Westfalen, and two in Hamburg. Other bilingual programs, while not providing content courses exclusively in the other language, thus not counted in the FMKS survey, have bilingual literacy programs and content courses with team teaching in both languages.

Two significant innovations in Turkish/German bilingual education were initiated in Berlin, with the subsequent implementation of other bilingual programs in other states. The earliest was a bilingual literacy program in primary schools initiated as a model project in 1980 in Berlin-Kreuzberg by a group of linguists and educators in the Intercultural Education Department at the Free University of Berlin. This biliteracy program (zweisprachige Alphabetisierung or Zwerz), became established as part of several Berlin public school programs, expanding to grades 1–6 in 14 schools, of which 5 still maintained the program in 2015–2016 (Berliner Landesinstitut für Schule und Medien, 2001). The program consists of Turkish literacy instruction for all Turkish HL speakers, and as an elective to pupils who are not Turkish HL speakers. All pupils receive bilingual content classes, team taught in both Turkish and German (Harnisch, 1993; Nehr & Karajoli, 1995). Presumably because these were not immersion classes, they were not included in the FMKS survey. A comparative study of written proficiency in Turkish and German in this program and in monolingual schools in Germany and in Turkey is reported in Dollnick (2013). The Zwerz program was also reviewed by a committee from the Berlin Senate Department of Education and local educators in 2014, reported to the Abgeordnetenhaus Berlin (the local Berlin government) in 2015. The consensus was that mother tongue support for Turkish was positive and a reduction in funding was not recommended; however, the report concluded that there were too few pupils with German as a home language to support the continuation of Turkish for German pupils (Abgeordnetenhaus Berlin, 2015).

A further innovative Turkish/German bilingual program initiated in Berlin is the two-way immersion program in primary and secondary schools, one of nine dual language programs of the Staatliche Europa-Schulen Berlin (SESB) [National Europe Schools Berlin]; see Meier & Schumacher, this volume. The Turkish/German SESB was initiated in the school year 1995–1996, starting with 32 pupils in two preschool classes. The first cohort of 15 pupils, almost all Turkish heritage speakers, entered the Carl-von-Ossietzky Secondary School in 2002–2003. Since 2009, 85 pupils have graduated with the Abitur, 18 in 2015.

In Hamburg in 1999, a bilingual model project for primary schools, monitored by the Department of Education at the University of Hamburg, was implemented for Turkish, Portuguese, Spanish, and Italian (Roth, Neumann, & Gogolin, 2007). The Turkish-German project began in 2003 and 2004 at two primary schools: the Heinrich-Wolgast-Schule and the Schule Lämmersieth. In contrast to the two-way immersion model of the Berlin SESB program, the Hamburg model often employs team teaching, with Turkish language teachers sent by the Turkish Consulate and Turkish/German bilingual teachers from the Hamburg school authority. The research team monitored classroom language use and spoken and written development in both languages through the four years of primary school (Dirim, Döll, Neumann, & Roth, 2009; Roth et al., 2007, pp. 1–10). As the only in-depth study of a Turkish-German bilingual program to date, this program warrants a brief discussion of the major findings.

Although originally intended for a pupil population that was 50% German monolinguals and 50% Turkish-German bilinguals and for a 50%–50% allocation of classroom language use, actual family language use and language proficiencies were more heterogeneous and the proportion of German increased over time, although classroom communication continued to be bilingual (Dirim et al., 2009, pp. 12–15). Proficiency in discourse types (evaluating, explaining, narrating) was documented, and literacy skills were compared with control groups outside the program. In the first year, children from Turkish-speaking families showed less development in Turkish than expected, possibly due to classroom focus on children from non–Turkish-speaking families. Their proficiency improved in later years. Children from non–Turkish-speaking families acquired basic vocabulary, some basic morphology, and some rote sentences by the end of the fourth year, but did not acquire real fluency or clause combining abilities in Turkish. Clearly, managing language instruction in linguistically heterogeneous groups is challenging. On the social side, however, there were positive effects on attitudes and on the use of Turkish at home, and pupils with other backgrounds gained more contact with and appreciation for Turkish-German bilingual life. All children acquired awareness of grammatical contrasts and of the range of multilingual competencies (Dirim et al., 2009, pp. 18–19).

What happens to these children once they complete the primary school bilingual program after fourth grade? To date, there has been no follow-up data, so we rely here on information from the Hamburg school ministry and on informal interviews with teachers. Pupils from the bilingual primary program can continue at several secondary schools where Turkish is offered as a foreign language. The Gymnasium Hamm offers Turkish as a third foreign language for HL pupils, but only from the eighth grade. The Stadtteilschule [district school] Barmbek and the Stadtteilschule am Hafen, both with few monolingual German pupils, offer some bilingual content courses. The program at the latter school was the subject of a four-part television talk show on Turkish DE-Light on TIDE TV in Hamburg.[6]

In addition to the Berlin and Hamburg bilingual programs described above, a further Turkish/German biliteracy program in Cologne is offered for pupils with German, Turkish, or other family languages. Two further primary schools in Hamburg offer some bilingual courses in Turkish and German. Albrecht (2015) describes a bilingual class in Hanover which was initiated at the request of German parents, with instruction in Turkish language and cultural content. An ethnographic monitoring study of this program, sponsored by the Mercator-IPC Fellowship project Exploring Multilingual Landscapes, is currently in progress. Küppers and Yağmur (2014, pp. 18–34) discuss interviews with pupils, parents, and teachers, many of whom regard the introduction of Turkish for children from monolingual German families as an enhancement to communicative openness, motivation to learn, and social relations in the neighborhood.

In sum, Turkish-German bilingual programs have gained popularity and seem to have desirable social effects, though the number of pupils other than those with Turkish HL remains low. Turkish foreign language classes are also still rather rare and also often de facto limited to pupils with Turkish HL.

Turkish and Teacher Training for Turkish HL at Tertiary Institutions

Germany has a long academic tradition of research and teaching in Oriental Languages, Near Eastern Studies, and similar topics. At present, 10 German universities offer Turkish as a foreign language in conjunction with departments of Turkology, Islamic Studies, Linguistics, and Education for students with Turkish HL backgrounds and others. Turkish language classes offered in adult education programs and other language schools are well attended and Turkish for special purposes is offered in professional schools such as those specializing in medicine and social work.

Training for Early Childhood Educators

An early program for supporting Turkish (and other) multilingualism came from the Hamburg-Altona Fachschule für Sozialpädagogik [School for Social Pedagogy], which in 1985 established a preschool caregiver training program. The target population of the program was immigrant women without a German school diploma who had been educated in their home countries and immigrated as adults (Schuleit & Schmidt, 2015).

Training for Teachers of Turkish as a Foreign Language

Several universities offer Turkish as an option for students in teacher education programs, including those without a Turkish HL background. The Ludwig-Maximillians University of Munich and Tübingen University offer programs for students intending to become teachers at a Gymnasium (secondary school leading to university) who can add Turkish as a supplementary subject to the two other subjects they study. As of 2015, two universities, Duisburg-Essen and Hamburg, have curricula for training teachers of Turkish in primary and secondary schools. At the University of Duisburg-Essen, there are bachelor's and master's programs for Turkistik (Turkish studies) with an option for students who intend to become Turkish teachers at secondary schools. The Turkistik Department cooperates with its graduates working in informal literacy programs and other activities in community cultural institutions such as bookstores and libraries, discussed in section 3. At the University of Hamburg, programs for future Turkish teachers at all types of schools have been offered for 20 years, currently in an interdisciplinary cooperation between the Department of Turkology (Turkish Philology) at the Asia-Africa Institute and the Department of Education, within the bachelor's programs for primary, secondary, and vocational schools. The syllabus includes traditional Turkological subjects as well as specific courses on bilingualism. Unfortunately, at present, this program is threatened with closure. In-service training is offered by regional institutes for teacher education and school development in Hamburg and Berlin. In Berlin, in-service training for bilingual literacy classes and for SESB is provided by experienced teachers in the programs.

3 Informal and Community Support for Turkish

In addition to institutionally based educational programs for Turkish HL, Turkish serves as a common language at cultural and political events attended by participants from Turkish-speaking communities in the region at large and from neighboring countries such as the Netherlands, Belgium, and France.

Public libraries and bookstores in Turkish areas in Germany have collections of Turkish and bilingual books and other media, both for adults and children. They also organize readings and other cultural events as well as activities focused on language learning and literacy, and perform outreach in daycare centers and schools, providing exposure to standard and written varieties of Turkish as well as opportunities for Turkish and bilingual interaction and discussion of literary, societal, and other cultural topics. Frankfurt/Main participated in an EU-sponsored project, Libraries for All: New Models for Intercultural Library Services, from 2008 to 2010, which aimed at updating services for an increasingly multilingual readership, increasing holding in several immigrant languages, including Turkish (European Union, 2009). Among Turkish bookstores, some of the largest are *Gökkuşağı Kitabevi* in Berlin, *Dost Kitabevi* in Dortmund, *Türk Kitabevi* in Frankfurt, and the *Okur Kitabevi* in Cologne.

A large number of Turkish newspapers are on sale in larger towns and cities; several have editions based in Germany (e.g., Becker, 2003; Schümchen & Sellheim, 2007). Two journals, *Die GASTE* and *PoliTeknik*, based in Germany, are devoted to educational and other sociopolitical issues in Germany and Turkey. They publish print and online editions in both German and Turkish, with translations of German articles into Turkish. They also organize symposia with speakers in both languages, whose contributions appear (in translation) in later issues. These journals and symposia provide important opportunities for Turkish speakers to use registers beyond everyday conversation.

A wide range of radio and television programs originating in Turkey are available in Germany, and local Turkish/German radio and TV programs have been offered since the early days of immigration. The first Turkish radio broadcasts in Germany were offered by the Cologne station *FHE Köln Radyosu*, presenting news from Turkey and Germany since 1964. Since 1999, *METROPOL FM* has broadcast Germany's first 24-hour Turkish-language program, starting in Berlin, but extending to other regions as well as cable networks. *TIDE Radio* in Hamburg broadcasts on topics ranging from legal and political information, as well as medical, psychological and counseling topics to sports, music, and local issues. By broadcasting in a flexible mixture of Turkish and German, it addresses a listenership ranging from fully bilingual to monolingual in either language. *TIDE TV* offers a variety of programs, which included a four-part talk show devoted to the bilingual program at a Hamburg secondary school (described in 2.2). As with the readings and discussions that take place in libraries and bookstores and in the articles and commentaries published in the journals, radio and TV talk shows provide opportunities for more speakers to use professional and academic registers of Turkish.

4 Conclusions and Perspectives on Further Research

Our survey of the current situation leads us to mixed conclusions about the institutionalization of Turkish HL and foreign language instruction in Germany. As we have seen, support for Turkish in Germany comes from many sources: after-school/weekend HL classes provided by the Turkish Consulates, the public school system, and community organizations in formal and informal contexts. Turkish is gradually coming to be acknowledged as part of European societal multilingualism and its importance for international mobility and economic development is increasingly recognized. A consequence of this changing perspective has been to raise Turkish from merely an HL for Turkish speakers to a language open in principle to majority (and other minority) pupils. This is reflected in the increasing number of schools where Turkish is offered as a less commonly taught foreign language or part of a bilingual program and where it is recognized as a qualifying subject for the Abitur.

The increasing diversity of the population of Germany has had positive and negative consequences for Turkish, spurring policies which recognize the importance of multilingualism and plurilingualism while, at the same time, resulting in former Turkish-speaking enclaves becoming more linguistically diverse. Pupils who would take part in Turkish HL programs are not as concentrated in individual schools, whose offerings are constrained by attendance. The schools and models described above must be seen as positive examples of Turkish instruction in Germany, but these are by no means the norm in all—or even most—schools attended by children with Turkish HL. Turkish HL instruction is by no means accessible to all with Turkish as a family language and Turkish foreign language classes are still offered in only a few secondary schools. Where bilingual classes exist, they are usually found in areas in which there is a high proportion of Turkish-speaking and other minority residents, and relatively few pupils from exclusively German-speaking families take part, despite some strong advocates among German parents and children with an interest in Turkish.

On the positive side, we note extensive collaboration and networks between institutions and organizations of various types, and a continuing focus on best practices in countries inside and outside the EU. There have been notable bursts of work in this area, both in terms of research and in school and community programs on the ground.

The lively and creative cultural and social scene produces both Turkish-speaking and bilingual public spheres, and in so doing offers flexible access to Turkish (and other languages) for multi- and monolinguals of all types. This flexibility is not just a characteristic of informal domains, but also some formal settings, especially in the bilingual schools that work with linguistically heterogeneous groups. Additionally, interaction between the formal and the informal support structures seems to be rich and productive. Activities at informal and semi-formal gatherings provide opportunities to discuss complex cultural and societal topics. Readings and discussions with authors, playwrights, and poets and other activities organized both for children and for adults provide opportunities to use spoken registers to discuss written texts. Concerts, speeches, and book exhibits provide further opportunities for discussions in Turkish, blending formal and informal registers. Such multilingual, multi-register events add to the quality of linguistic life for all.

In the course of gathering information for this paper, we have come across many institutions and programs for Turkish which deserve further detailed investigation. It would be desirable to conduct ethnographic, participant observation, and longitudinal studies such as Albrecht (2015) and Erduyan (2015) on further preschool, elementary, and secondary schools at a variety of sites, and to conduct interviews with actors and agencies, including former participants in Turkish classes during childhood or adolescence, teachers of these classes, participants in teacher training courses, and those who organize such courses. There is also still much room for further linguistic investigation of the proficiency and use of Turkish by the considerable numbers of pupils with Turkish HL who do not take part in any formal Turkish instruction. Further, analysis of the kinds of Turkish and mixed discourse and text types, in particular the radio and TV talk shows and the (online) journals, would make a valuable contribution to language contact studies. Such discourse that includes translation and paraphrase is likely a vehicle for linguistic convergence while at the same time contributing to the development of professional and academic registers of Turkish in the community and has become part of the ambient input to HL Turkish learners.

5 Acknowledgments

We gratefully acknowledge the comments of two anonymous reviewers and Claire Hitchins Chik, Janet Fuller, Karin Schmidt, Kristin Speth, Elizabeth Sommerlad, and Adam Wilkins on earlier versions of this chapter. We are also grateful to many individuals who contributed information to this chapter, including Mehmet Alpbek, Raphael Ampedu, Theda Borde, Sevinç Ezbük, Gürsel Gür, Andreas Heintze, Cornelia Held, Angela Jänke, Antje Kılıç, Yavuz Köse, Hans-Jürgen Krumm, Almut Küppers, Reyhan Kuyumcu, Tülin Mecilioğlu, Cemile Niron, Seyhan Öztürk, Hans H. Reich, Gisela Romain, Ali Sak, Reyhan Savran, Wiebke Schuleit, Silke Schumann, Andreas Schümschen, Evrim Soylu, Petra Tiedemann-Pfeifer, Kemal Ülker, Cansen Ünal, Renate Welsch, Cemal Yıldız, and Bilge Yörenç.

Notes

1 Workers were also recruited from Greece, Italy, Morocco, Portugal, Spain, Tunisia, and the former Yugo-slavia during this period.
2 Statistics on the Turkish-speaking population of Germany are based on the Microcensus for 1% of the population, which designates persons with a history of migration in the family, based on country of origin since 1949. It is independent of current citizenship or language use but can be taken as an approximation of the number of people whose family language may include Turkish.

3 See Appendix for explanation of this and other German terms used in the text.
4 A comprehensive historical discussion of the language polices toward HL and foreign language instruction of HLs in several European countries can be found in Reich (2016). He envisions more potential for immigrant language instruction in the German school system(s), if internationalization and modernization are accepted as real goals, in the spirit of the recommendations by the European Council for multilingualism in Europe. In his view, this could lead Germany to overcome its historical dichotomy between "the people's language" (i.e., German) and "foreign languages" (i.e., prestigious languages traditionally part of the curriculum), in which immigrant languages have a difficult time finding their place. His comparison with other European countries points toward benefits to be gained by exchanging views on models and implementation of best practices.
5 Instruction in Turkish is also offered at a few private schools in Germany, some affiliated with the Gülen movement. These are not included in the present discussion.
6 The four-part panel discussion in Turkish and German aired on the Hamburg TIDE TV series Turkish DElight, Thema: Bilinguale Klassen in Hamburg. Deutsch-Türkischer Unterricht in der Sekundarstufe [Theme: Bilingual classes in Hamburg, German-Turkish instruction at the secondary level] and is posted on YouTube.

References

Abgeordnetenhaus Berlin. (2015). Schriftliche Anfrage der Abgeordneten/Stefanie Remlinger/(GRÜNE)/ vom 21. Mai 2015 und Antwort/ Zweisprachige Erziehung an Berliner Grundschulen ein vom Senat verkanntes Erfolgsmodell? Drucksache 17/ 16 260/17 [Berlin Senate written questions and answers on the effectiveness of the biliteracy program in Berlin primary schools. File 17/16 260/17].

Akıncı, M., & Pfaff, C. W. (2008). *Language choice, cultural and literacy practices of Turkish bilingual adolescents in France and in Germany*. Paper presented at the 15th AILA World Congress, International Association for Applied Linguistics (AILA), Essen, Germany.

Albrecht, B. (2015). Interkulturelle Öffnung durch Mehrsprachigkeit: Die Albert-Schweitzer Grundschule in Hannover-Linden [An intercultural opening through multilingualism: The Albert Schweitzer primary school in Hanover-Linden]. In A. Küppers, B. Pusch, & P. U. Semerci (Eds.), *Bildung in transnationalen Räumen: Theorie, Praxis und Forschung anhand deutsch-türkischer Beispiele/ Theory, practice and research based on German-Turkish examples [Education in transnational spaces: Theory, practice and research based on German-Turkish examples]* (pp. 163–166). Wiesbaden, Germany: Springer Verlag.

Ammann, B. (2005). Kurds in Germany. In M. Ember, C. R. Ember, & I. Skoggard (Eds.), *Encyclopedia of diasporas, Vol II: Diaspora communities* (pp. 1011–1019). Wiesbaden, Germany: Springer Verlag.

Apeltauer, E. (2007). *Das Kieler Modell: Sprachliche Frühförderung von Kindern mit Migrationshintergrund* [The Kiel model: Early linguistic support for children with migration background]. In B. Ahrenholz (Ed.), *Deutsch als Zweitsprache—Voraussetzungen und Konzepte für die Förderung von Kindern und Jugendlichen mit Migrationshintergrund [German as a second language: Prerequisites and concepts for supporting children and adolescents with migration background]* (pp. 91–113). Freiburg, Germany: Fillibach.

Backus, A. (2004). Turkish as an immigrant language in Europe. In T. K. Bhatia & W. C. Ritchie (Eds.), *The handbook of bilingualism* (pp. 689–724). Oxford, UK: Blackwell.

Backus, A., Jørgensen, J. N., & Pfaff, C. W. (2010). Linguistic effects of immigration: Language choice, codeswitching, and change in Western European Turkish. *Language & Linguistics Compass, 4*(7), 481–495.

Becker, J. (2003). Die deutsch-türkische Medienrevolution. Weitere sieben Meilensteine [The German-Turkish media revolution: Seven further milestones]. In J. Becker & R. Behnisch (Eds.), *Zwischen kultureller Zersplitterung und virtueller Identität. Türkische Medienkultur in Deutschland.* [Between cultural fragmentation and virtual identity: Turkish media culture in Germany] (Vol. 3, pp. 47–82). Rehburg-Loccum, Germany: Evangelische Akademie Loccum.

Berliner Landesinstitut für Schule und Medien [Berlin Institute for Schools and Media] [ZWERZ flyer]. (2001). Zweisprachige deutsch-türkische Erziehung in der Berliner Grundschule [Bilingual Turkish-German education at Berlin primary schools].

Bundesarbeitsgemeinschaft der Immigrantenverbände in der Bundesrepublik Deutschland und Berlin West (BAGIV) [Federal Working Group of the Immigrant Associations in the Federal Republic of Germany and West Berlin West]. (Ed.). (1985). *Muttersprachlicher Unterricht in der Bundesrepublik Deutschland. Sprach- und bildungspolitische Argumente für eine zweisprachige Erziehung von Kindern sprachlicher Minderheiten (mit einer Neubearbeitung des Memorandums zum muttersprachlichen Unterricht)* [Mother tongue instruction in the Federal Republic of Germany: Language-and educational policy arguments for bilingual education for the children of linguistic minorities with a revised version of the memorandum on mother tongue teaching]. Hamburg, Germany: EBV Rissen.

Cındark, I., & Ziegler, E. (2016). Mehrsprachigkeit im Ruhrgebiet: Zur Sichtbarkeit sprachlicher Diversität in Dortmund [Multilingualism in the Ruhr area: On the visibility of language diversity in Dortmund]. In S. Ptashnyk, R. Beckert, P. Wolf-Farré, & M. Wolny (Eds.), *Gegenwärtige Sprachkontakte im Kontext der Migration* [Current language contact in the context of migration] (pp. 133–156). Heidelberg, Germany: Winter.

Dirim, İ. (2015a). Umgang mit migrationsbedingter Mehrsprachigkeit in der schulischen Bildung. [Handling migration-related multilingualism in schools]. In R. Leiprecht & A. Steinbach (Eds.), *Schule in der Migrationsgesellschaft: Ein Handbuch. Band 2: Sprache—Rassismus—Professionalität* [School in the Migrant Society: A handbook, Vol. 2: Language—racism—professionalism] (pp. 25–48). Schwalbach, Germany: Debus Pädagogik Verlag.

Dirim, İ., Döll, M., Neumann, U., & Roth, H.-J., in collaboration with von Christoph Gantefort, M., & Grevé, A. (2009). *Bericht 2009: Abschlussbericht über die türkisch-deutschen Modellklassen* [*Report 2009: Final report on the Turkish-German model classes*]. Hamburg, Germany: Universität Hamburg [Hamburg University] (in cooperation with Universität Köln [Cologne University]). Retrieved from https://www.ew.uni-hamburg.de/ueber-die-fakultaet/personen/gogolin/pdf-dokumente/bericht-2009-bilinguale-grundschulklassen.pdf

Dollnick, M. (2013). *Konnektoren in türkischen und deutschen Texten bilingualer Schüler. Eine vergleichende Langzeituntersuchung zur Entwicklung schriftsprachlicher Kompetenzen* [Connectors in Turkish and German texts of bilingual pupils: A comparative longitudinal investigation of the development of written language competence]. Frankfurt/Main, Germany: Peter Lang.

Ekholm, M., & Trier, U. P. (1987). The concept of institutionalization: Some remarks. In M. B. Miles, M. Ekholm, & R. Vandenberghe (Eds.), *Lasting school improvement: Exploring the process of institutionalization* (pp. 13–21). Leuven, Belgium: Acco.

Erduyan, I. (2015). *Multilingual construction of identity: German-Turkish students in Berlin* (Doctoral dissertation). Retrieved from ProQuest Dissertation and Theses database. (AAT Number: 13143).

European Union. (2009). Libraries for all: New models for intercultural library services. Retrieved from http://www.librariesforall.eu/

Extra, G., & Yağmur, K. (2004). *Urban multilingualism in Europe: Immigrant minority languages at home and school.* Clevedon, UK: Multilingual Matters.

Fleming, Michael. (2007). *Languages of schooling within a European framework for languages of education: Learning, teaching, assessment: Report of the Language Policy Division of the Council of Europe.* Intergovernmental Conference, Prague, Czech Republic. Retrieved from http://www.coe.int/t/dg4/linguistic/School lang_EN.asp

Harnisch, U. (1993). Abschlußbericht des Schulversuchs (Zweisprachige Erziehung für Kinder mit der Muttersprache Türkisch) [Final report on the school experiment (Bilingual Education for Children with the Mother Tongue Turkish)]. Berlin, Germany: *Senator für Schulwesen, Jugend und Sport Berlin* [Senate for school, youth and sports, Berlin].

Kulturministerkonferenz. (1971). Beschluss der KMK vom 3. Dezember 1971 'Unterricht für Kinder ausländischer Arbeitnehmer' KMK Beschlussammlung (Anm. 2), Bd. 4 Abschnitt 899 [Decision of the KMK of 3 December 1971, 'Instruction for the children of foreign workers'. KMK decisions, Vol. 4, paragraph 899].

Kulturministerkonferenz. (1976). Beschluss der KMK vom 8. April 1976. 'Unterricht für Kinder ausländischer Arbeitnehmer' KMK Beschlussammlung (Anm. 2), Bd. 4 Abschnitt 899 [Decision of the KMK of 8 April 1976 'Instruction for the children of foreign workers'. KMK decisions, Vol. 4, paragraph 899].

Kultusministerkonferenz. (2013a). Bericht 'Fremdsprachen in der Grundschule—Sachstand und Konzeptionen 2013': Beschluss der Kultusministerkonferenz vom 17.10.2013. [Report on 'Foreign languages at primary school—state of affairs and concepts 2013': Resolution of the Conference of Ministries of Culture, October 17, 2013].

Kultusministerkonferenz. (2013b). Bericht 'Konzepte für den bilingualen Unterricht—Erfahrungsbericht und Vorschläge zur Weiterentwicklung': Beschluss der Kultusministerkonferenz vom 17.10.2013 [Report on 'Concepts for bilingual teaching—field report and suggestions for further development': Resolution of the Conference of Ministries of Culture, October 17, 2013].

Kunuroglu, F., Yağmur, K., van de Vijver, F. J., & Kroon, S. (2015). Consequences of Turkish return migration from Western Europe. *International Journal of Intercultural Relations, 49*, 198–211.

Küppers, A., Schroeder, C., & Gülbeyaz, E. I. (2014). *Languages in transition: Turkish in formal education in Germany: Analysis & perspectives.* Istanbul Policy Center Sabancı University. Essen, Germany: Stiftung Mercator Initiative.

Küppers, A., & Yağmur, K. (2014). *Why multilingual matters: Alternative change agents in language education policy: IPC Focus-Report.* Istanbul, Turkey: Istanbul Policy Center. Retrieved from http://ipc.sabanciuniv.edu/en/

Kuyumcu, R. (2016). *Frühkindliche bilinguale Erziehung mit Türkisch also Partnersprache* [*Early bilingual education with Turkish as partner language*]. Presentation at the conference Multilingualism in the German Educational System: Turkish and Russian in Focus, Turkish Embassy, Berlin, Germany.

Lewis, M. P., Simons, G. F., & Fennig, C. D. (Eds.). (2016). *Ethnologue: Languages of the world* (19th ed.). Dallas, TX: SIL International.

Nehr, M., & Karajoli, E. (1995). *Expertise on bilingual literacy education of Turkish schoolchildren in Berlin: Final report for the Council of Europe.* Strasbourg, France: Cedex.

Pfaff, C. W. (1981). Sociolinguistic problems of immigrants: Foreign workers and their children in Germany[Review article]. *Language in Society, 10,* 155–188.

Pfaff, C. W. (1994). Early bilingual development of Turkish children in Berlin. In G. Extra & L. Verhoeven (Eds.), *The cross-linguistic study of bilingual development* (pp. 75–97). North-Holland, The Netherlands: Koninklijke Nederlandse Akademie van Wetenschappen.

Pfaff, C. W. (2010). Multilingual development in Germany in the crossfire of ideology & politics. In U. Okulska & P. Cap (Eds.), *Perspectives in politics and discourse* (pp. 328–357). Amsterdam, The Netherlands: John Benjamins.

Pfaff, C. W. (2014). Multilingualism & mobility: Reflections on sociolinguistic studies of Turkish/German children & adolescents in Berlin: 1978–2013. In I. de Saint-Georges, K. Horner, & J.-J. Weber (Eds.), *Multilingualism & mobility in Europe: Policies & practices* (pp. 17–42). Frankfurt/Main: Peter Lang Verlag.

Pfaff, C. W. (2015). (How) will Turkish survive in Northwestern Europe? 50 years of migration, 35 years of research on sociopolitical and linguistic developments in diaspora Turkish. In D. Zeyrek, C. S. Şimşek, U. Ataş, & J. Rehbein (Eds.), *Ankara papers in Turkish and Turkic linguistics* (pp. 453–492). Wiesbaden, Germany: Harrassowitz.

Polinsky, M., & Kagan, O. (2007). Heritage languages: In the "wild" and in the classroom. *Language and Linguistics Compass, 5*(1), 368–395, doi: 10.1111/j.1749–818x.2007.00022.x

Redder, A., Pauli, J., Kießling, R., Bührig, K., Brehmer, B., Breckner, I., & Androutsopoulos, J. (Eds.). (2013). *Mehrsprachige Kommunikation in der Stadt: Das Beispiel Hamburg* [*Multilingual communication in the city: Hamburg as an example*]. Münster, Germany: Waxmann (Mehrsprachigkeit 37).

Rehbein, J., & Grießhaber, W. (1996). L2-Erwerb versus L1-Erwerb: Methodologische Aspekte ihrer Erforschung [L2 acquisition versus L1 acquisition: Methodological aspects of their investigation]. In K. Ehlich (Ed.), *Kindliche Sprachentwicklung. Konzepte und Empirie* [Child language development: Concepts and empirical issues] (pp. 67–119). Opladen, Germany: Westdeutscher Verlag.

Rehbein, J., Herkenrath, A., & Karakoç, B. (2009). Turkish in Germany: On contact-induced language change of an immigrant language in the multilingual landscape of Europe. *STUF Language Typology and Universals, 62*(3), 171–204.

Reich, H. H. (2016). Institutionelle Entwicklungen des Herkunftssprachenunterrichts in Deutschland (mit einem Seitenblick auf Österreich und die Schweiz) [Institutional developments in heritage language instruction in Germany (with a look to Austria and Switzerland)]. Penarvortrag auf der Konferenz 'Mehrsprachigkeit im Deutschen Bildungssystem': Türkisch und Russisch im Fokus. Berlin. Türkischer Botschaft Berlin. [Plenary lecture at the Conference 'Multilingualism in the German Educational System': Turkish and Russian in Focus, Turkish Embassy, Berlin].

Reich, H. H., & Hienz de Albentiis, M. (1998). Der Herkunftssprachenunterricht. Erlaßlage und statistische Entwicklung in den alten Bundesländern [Heritage language teaching: State of decrees and statistical development in the old West German federal states]. *Deutsch Lernen* [*Learning German*], *1*, 3–45.

Rist, R. C. (1979). Migration and marginality: Guestworkers in Germany and France. *Daedalus, 108*(2), 95–118.

Roth, H.-J., Neumann, U., & Gogolin, I., in collaboration with Grevé, A., & Klinger, T. (2007). *Bericht 2007: Abschlussbericht über die italienisch-deutschen, portugiesisch-deutschen und spanisch-deutschen Modellklassen* [*Report 2007: Final report on the Italian-German, Portuguese-German and Spanish-German model classes*]. Hamburg, Germany: Universität Hamburg [Hamburg University] (in cooperation with Universität Köln [Cologne University]). Retrieved from https://www.ew.uni-hamburg.de/ueber-die-fakultaet/personen/neumann/files/bericht-2007–0.pdf

Schroeder, C. (2003). Der Türkischunterricht in Deutschland und seine Sprache(n). *Zeitschrift für Fremdsprachenforschung, 14*(1), 23–39. [Turkish instruction in Germany and its languages. *Journal of Foreign Language Research, 14*(1), 23–39].

Schroeder, C., & Küppers, A. (2015). Türkischunterricht im deutschen Schulsystem: Bestandsaufnahme und Perspektiven [Turkish instruction in the German school system: Status and perspectives]. In A. Küppers, B. Pusch, & P. U. Semerci (Eds.), *Bildung in transnationalen Räumen. Education in Transnational Spaces. Theorie, Praxis und Forschung anhand deutsch-türkischer Beispiele* [Theory, practice and research based on German-Turkish examples] (pp. 191–212). Wiesbaden, Germany: Springer Verlag.

Schuleit, W., & Schmidt, R. (2015). Voneinander lernen und miteinander handeln: 30 Jahre Erzieherinnenausbildung für Einwanderinnen [Learning from each other and acting together: 30 years of preschool caregiver training for immigrants]. In Berufliche Bildung Hamburg [Vocational training Hamburg] (p. 10). Retrieved from https://hibb.hamburg.de/wp-content/uploads/sites/33/2015/12/BBH-2_2105.pdf

Schultz, C., & Kolb, H. (2015). Managing cultural diversity in Federal Germany: Bavaria and Berlin as classic antagonists. *Fédéralisme Régionalisme, 15*. Retrieved from http://popups.ulg.ac.be/1374–3864/index.php?id=1557

Schümchen, A., & Sellheim, T. (2007). Türkische Medien in Deutschland—Entstehung, Angebot und Perspektiven [Turkish media in Germany—emergence, offerings, and perspectives]. In S. Gezgin & C. Kandemir (Eds.), *Interkulturelle Kommunikationsbrücke. Beiträge von den I.–II. Türkisch-Deutschen Sommerakademien* [Intercultural communication bridge: Contributions from the First and Second Turkish-German Summer Academies] (pp. 38–48). Istanbul: Doğan Ofset Yayıncılık. Skutnabb-Kangas, T. (2008). Human rights and language policy in education. In S. May & N. Hornberger (Eds.), *Language policy and political issues in education: Encyclopedia of language and education* (Vol. 1, 2nd ed., pp. 107–119). New York, NY: Springer.

Statistisches Bundesamt [Federal Statistical Office]. (2014). *Bildung und Kultur: Allgemeinbildende Schulen* [*Education and culture: General education schools*]. Fachserie 11, Reihe 1 [Discipline Series 11, Series 1], 2013/2014. Wiesbaden, Germany: Author.

Statistisches Bundesamt [Federal Statistical Office]. (2015). *Bevölkerung und Erwerbstätigkeit: Bevölkerung mit Migrationshintergrund—Ergebnisse des Mikrozensus* [*Population and emloyment: Population with migration background*]. Wiesbaden, Germany: Author.

Verein für frühe Mehrsprachigkeit an Kindertageseinrichtungen und Schulen FMKS. (2014). Bilinguale Kitas in Deutschland. [Association for early multilingualism in daycare centers and schools: Bilingual Kitas in Germany]. Retrieved from http://www.fmks-online.de/

Yıldız, C. (2013). *The present situation of Turkish courses as a mother tongue in Germany*. Ankara, Turkey: Yurtdışı Türkler ve Akraba Topluluklar Başkanlığı.

30

Korean Language Education in Japan

From Marginalized Heritage Language to Popular Foreign Language

Robert J. Fouser

1 Introduction

Koreans have been in Japan for a long time, arriving primarily in four waves of immigration. In the Asuka Period (538 to 710), a wave of immigrants from the Korean peninsula brought skills and technology that helped the Yamato state consolidate its power in the Kansai area where the ancient capitals of Nara and Kyoto are located (Brown, 1983). In the late sixteenth century and early seventeenth centuries, Korean potters were brought to Japan to make Korean-style cups that had become popular as tea ceremony ware (Hall, 1991). In the early twentieth century, large numbers of Koreans migrated to Japan during the colonial period from 1910–1945, when Japan governed Korea (De Vos & Lee, 1981). In the late twentieth century and early twenty-first century, another wave of Koreans migrated to Japan (Douglass & Roberts, 1999).

Korean language education in Japan today is rooted in the history of Japanese imperialism, from the late nineteenth century to the mid-twentieth century, as well as expanding cultural interactions in the late twentieth century. The history of imperialism, which included 35 years of Japanese colonial rule from 1910 to 1945, left a large number of Koreans in Japan who struggled to preserve their language and culture in the hope of returning to Korea. It also established an academic tradition of studying Korean and an important body of academic research on the Korean language. In the late twentieth century, as a result of expanding cultural interaction between Japan and South Korea, a boom in Korean pop culture has not only spread to Japan but also influenced language education. By 2010, the Korean language had moved from the fringe to the mainstream, becoming one of the most popular foreign languages in Japan. This chapter focuses on the transition of Korean from marginalized heritage language (HL) to popular foreign language, focusing on the period from 1945 to the present. The central argument is that changes in discourse on Korea and Koreans in Japan derive from changes in broader relations between Japan and the states of the Korean peninsula, and that these changes have been reflected within the Korean community in Japan, including the teaching and learning of Korean as an HL.

With this orientation in mind, the following discussion focuses on the ways in which unique local histories have shaped the institutionalization of Korean language programs in Japan. As Ekholm and Trier (1987) note, and as is exemplified in this chapter, "Institutionalization always means a new balance between past, present, and future (and specifically, between changes in the past, changes in the present and change expected)" (p. 14). The organizations highlighted in this chapter respond to these changes by adopting a variety of strategies (Ekholm & Trier, 1987, p. 16) that are promotive of the stability and continuity of their language programs, i.e., their institutionalization.

Foucault's discussion of discourse and power is also relevant in light of the complex micro and macro historical processes surrounding Koreans in Japan, including their minority status. Noted works on Koreans in Japan, such as Chapman (2008) and Ryang (1997), have drawn on various forms of public discourse about Korea and Koreans in Japan to show how their identity has been recreated and redefined over time. As Chapman (2008) puts it, "A poststructuralist position enables us to see how identities interact with social circumstances and are influenced by historical context" (p. 7). Said's (1979) concept of Orientalism is useful for considering changes in how the Japanese majority have defined the "Korean Other" and the similarities to the ways in which the West has defined the Oriental Other. The change in public discourse on Korea and Koreans in Japan was not singular, but multiple, both in the Korean community and Japanese society at large. During the Japanese colonial period (1910–1945), public discourse on Korean centered on resisting or legitimizing colonial rule. In the immediate postwar period, public discourse within the Korean community centered on the nationalist impulse for independence in the wake of liberation from Japan. In the post-Cold War period, discourse has centered on creating new hybrid identities, not only for Koreans in Japan, but also for Japanese who are interested in consuming "Korea" as a cultural product.

Before continuing the discussion, several definitions are in order. Koreans in Japan are commonly referred to as "resident Koreans." This is an English translation of the Japanese word "zainichi" in which "zai" means "to exist" and "nichi" means Japan. "Resident Korean" thus describes ethnic Koreans who were born in Japan and who maintain a Korean identity. Like the Korean peninsula itself, resident Koreans are divided into groups that support either North Korea or South Korea. As in other diaspora situations, however, identities are complex. Some resident Koreans support both groups for personal or business reasons (Ryang, 1997), whereas some in the younger generation have a distinct resident Korean identity or may identify more closely with Japan. "Chongryun Koreans" are members of Chongryun, which is an acronym for Chaeilbon Chosŏnin Chong Ryŏnhaphoe, or the General Association of Korean Residents in Japan, the official organization of Koreans that have historically supported North Korea. Resident Koreans affiliated with the pro-South Korean Residents Union in Japan, or "Mindan," and non-affiliated Koreans are commonly referred to as simply "resident Koreans." South Koreans and ethnic Koreans from China who migrated to Japan beginning in the 1990s are known as "newcomers" (Tai, 2007; Tajima, 2006), but remain a minority. Many first-generation resident Koreans who moved to Japan before 1945 are bilingual, but this population is rapidly dying off. Second-generation resident Koreans were born in Japan and, as Ryang (1997) notes, "would not use Korean at home because for them, too, Japanese has been their first language as well as their home language ever since childhood" (p. 64). Third- and fourth-generation resident Koreans are native speakers of Japanese and have had little exposure to the Korean language. "Newcomers" are usually bilingual because they use Korean at home and Japanese outside the home. This means that, except for a small number of newcomer children, nearly all ethnic Koreans in Japan who learn Korean are native speakers of Japanese.

"Heritage language" has been defined differently according to discipline and research interest. According to Polinsky and Kagan (2007), the narrow definition developed by Valdés (2001) defines "heritage language" as a language used at home, implying that learners have measurable proficiency in the language. Building on Fishman (2001) and others (Hornberger & Wang, 2008;

Polinsky & Kagan, 2007), the broad definition, by contrast, defines "heritage language" in terms of personal relevance and ethnic affiliation. The distinction between the two definitions is an emphasis on language proficiency and development versus personal relevance in identity creation. It should be noted, however, that learners have different views of the "relevance" of their HL to their own identity, and as far as Korean HL learners in Japan go, the relevance of Korea and Korean to their own identity is fluid and varies. Hornberger and Wang's (2008) broad definition of HL learners as individuals who "have familial or ancestral ties to a particular language and who exert their agency in determining whether or not they are HLLs (heritage language learners) of that HL (heritage language) and HC (heritage culture)" (p. 27) describes the situation in Japan well. Building on this, "Korean as a heritage language" in this chapter thus refers to broad-definition Korean HL learners in Japan, most of whom have little or no previous exposure to Korean and who are studying or have studied Korean in formal and informal settings.

"Korean as a foreign language" refers to ethnic Japanese and other persons not of Korean ethnic background who learn Korean, mostly in a formal educational setting. Japanese education is governed by MEXT (Ministry of Education, Culture, Sports, Science & Technology) in Tokyo, but local boards of education are in charge of personnel and running schools within their districts. MEXT develops the national curriculum, approves textbooks, and accredits schools. "Recognized schools" are schools that follow the national curriculum and offer accredited programs. "Miscellaneous schools" are other education institutions meeting basic standards regarding health and safety, but do not follow the national curriculum and do not offer accredited programs.

2 Origin and Development of the Korean Community in Japan

In the late fifteenth and early sixteenth centuries, a small number of Korean potters were brought to Japan, but they lived in isolated villages, mostly on the southernmost island of Kyushu. It was not until the middle of the twentieth century that Koreans began moving to growing urban centers and creating ethnic communities. This section focuses on the development and importance of twentieth-century communities to Korean language education.

Japan began its imperialist push into Korea shortly after the Meiji Restoration in 1868 (for historical details, see Duus, 1998). The Meiji Restoration created a modern European-style nation state in Japan that quickly took an interest in overseas expansion. In 1876, the new Meiji government forced Korea to sign a treaty that opened three ports to Japanese trade. As trade opened to Japan, regional and imperial powers—Britain, China, France, Russia, and the United States—took an interest in Korea, creating a competition for influence that would end in complete Japanese dominance of Korea after Russia lost the Russo-Japanese War in 1905 (Deuchler, 1977). During this period, a small number of Koreans traveled to and studied in Japan.

In 1910, Japan annexed Korea and Koreans became subjects of Japan and movement between the two countries increased. At the time, Japan was eager to promote emigration of Japanese to Korea to reduce poverty and unemployment at home (for a detailed discussion of Japanese settlement in Korea, see Uchida, 2011). One of the first important acts after colonialization was a "land reform" in which Japanese authorities effectively confiscated Korean land to sell to Japanese migrants, which uprooted a large number of Koreans and stirred the first wave of migrations to Japan. Japan's invasion of Manchuria in 1931 and full-scale war with China in 1937 stimulated industrial growth in major cities in Japan and Korea. Workers were needed for factories and Koreans began to move to Japan, particularly to Osaka, in large numbers in the 1930s, settling in densely populated slums. Japanese authorities watched Koreans in the slums carefully and were quick to squelch activities, such as language instruction, that could be construed as nationalistic (De Vos & Lee, 1981). As World War II turned against Japan, it became desperate for manpower and began conscripting Koreans to work in factories and, from 1944, conscripting Korean boys into the military (De Vos & Lee, 1981). This caused a sharp rise in the number of Koreans in Japan in the 1940s.

Most Koreans in Japan had little education and worked in factories under harsh conditions. A small group of Koreans, however, were educated and were active in Japanese society. Communism appealed to Korean students and intellectuals because of its anti-imperialist stance. Koreans became influential in the Japan Communist Party (JCP), and by the 1930s, 10% of JCP members were Korean (Weiner, 1994). Support for the JCP among Korean intellectuals contributed to repression of Korean organizations during the postwar occupation and in the new Japanese state.

The announcement of Japan's surrender on August 15, 1945, brought immediate change to the region. The U.S. military occupied Japan and Korea below the 38th parallel, while the Soviet Union occupied Korea north of the 38th parallel. This created the division of Korea that still exists today. At first, Koreans assumed that they would be returning to a united country free from foreign rule, and repatriation began quickly in the fall of 1945 with about 1,400,000 of the 2,000,000 Koreans who lived in Japan returning by early 1946. However, it soon became clear that America and the Soviet Union were not going to leave the peninsula, and as the division leading to the establishment of two Korean states hardened, Koreans in Japan became reticent about returning, leaving about 600,000 in Japan (De Vos & Lee, 1981). Some younger Koreans who were born in Japan were not fluent in Korean and lacked the confidence to return, whereas others feared political instability (Caprio & Yu, 2009). The breakout of the Korean War in 1950 forced Koreans to put off their return yet longer.

During the colonial period, Koreans were Japanese nationals, but without full rights of citizenship because the 1899 nationality law limited citizenship to ethnic Japanese (Lee, 1981a). After 1948, when North Korea and South Korea emerged as states, Koreans on the Korean Peninsula became nationals of one of those two states. Koreans in Japan, however, were still officially under American occupation and were treated as occupied subjects of the former Japanese state. The Treaty of San Francisco that came into force in 1952 returned sovereignty to Japan, but said nothing about Koreans in Japan. After sovereignty was regained, the new Japanese state treated Koreans as foreigners with limited rights in Japan, which set the stage for a protracted struggle for rights denied them because of their status as foreigners (Kashiwazaki, 2009). In 1965, Japan and South Korea signed a treaty that established diplomatic relations between the two countries. This allowed Koreans living in Japan who had taken South Korean citizenship to become permanent residents of Japan, but Chongryun Koreans were excluded because the treaty did not include North Korea. In 1982, a separate form of permanent residency for Chongryun Koreans was created, and this was upgraded to full permanent residency equal to that of South Korean nationals in 1991 (Ryang, 1997). Until the 1990s, the lack of permanent residency status prevented all Koreans from participating fully in Japanese society.

3 Development of Educational Institutions for Koreans in Postwar Japan

In the immediate postwar period, Koreans focused on preparing themselves for repatriation. Almost immediately after the surrender of Japan, educators and activists in the Korean community began to found Korean schools in large cities (Kim, 2002) to prepare young Koreans for repatriation. They received strong support from the League of Koreans, a nationalist, communist-learning organization founded in Japan in October 1945. Located in abandoned buildings and private homes, these schools also served as a focal point for community activity and social organizing. Teachers were university students and other educated activists in the Korean community, many of whom had connections with the JCP (De Vos & Lee, 1981). The schools were day schools and were the only educational opportunity available to Korean children at the time. By October 1947, the League had opened 541 elementary schools, seven junior high schools, and eight high schools throughout the country (Inokuchi, 2000). As the schools spread, Japanese and occupation authorities began to view them with suspicion, particularly after the suppression of left-wing groups during Reverse Course in 1947 (Dower, 2000). In 1949, the Japanese government, with the acquiescence of the Supreme Commander for Allied Powers, declared the League of Koreans to be a terrorist organization and ordered it to disband, thus forcing the closure of the schools (Lee, 1981b). Korean students poured into already overwhelmed Japanese schools, forcing local governments in areas with a large Korean population to keep Korean schools open, but under public control (Rohlen, 1981).

The Chongryun, which developed out of the League of Koreans, was organized in 1955 and began developing an extensive system of full-time day schools from kindergarten to university throughout the country in the late 1950s (Kim, 2002; Lee, 1981c). From 1957 until the late 1970s, North Korea sent money to support the schools, which allowed them to build new school buildings and supplied textbooks (Rohlen, 1981). From the start, Chongryun schools emphasized Korean language education because of its central role in defining and maintaining Korean identity (Tai, 2007). The language of instruction and personal interaction in the schools was Korean, and Japanese was taught as a "foreign language." The first generation of teachers in Chongryun schools were native speakers of Korean, most of whom were highly proficient in Japanese. As Japanese became the dominant language among Koreans, teachers and students began to use Korean as a non-native language in the schools (Noguchi, 2005). Because of their North Korea affiliation, teachers and students were not allowed to visit South Korea, and travel to North Korea was difficult. This resulted in the emergence of a "Chongryun dialect" of Korean that is unique to the teachers and students of Chongryun schools (Ryang, 1997; Ueda, 2001). As Ryang (1997) noted,

> When speaking to older persons, children use the formal/written honorific endings such as *imnida* (to be) and *hamnida* (to do), since these are also polite forms. When speaking to their peers, they use such endings as *ida* (to be) and *handa* (to do), which are close to the infinitives of the verb and are normally used in official documents, reports, and novels. Because they are not used in everyday speech in either North or South Korea, Chongryun's schoolchildren sound as if they are reading aloud written sentences.
>
> *(p. 36)*

An interesting situation was thus created in which immersion HL instruction was conducted by non-native speaker teachers in a dialect unique to the school environment. In the case of English classes, the situation is more complex as teachers move between the non-native Chongryun school dialect and English to teach English as a third language (Fouser, 2008).

By the 1990s, economic and political changes on the Korean peninsula began to affect the Chongryun schools negatively (Akiba, 2000; Faiola, 2003; Tai, 2007). After decades of strong economic growth and democratization, South Korea became more attractive to Koreans in Japan. By contrast, the collapse of the Soviet Union affected the North Korean economy badly and the country suffered a famine in the mid-1990s. As North Korea lost its influence in the Korean community in Japan, the number of students attending Chongryun schools began to decline, causing schools to be closed (Tai, 2007). In 2010, 8,300 pupils attended 73 Chongryun schools (Asahi Shimbun, 2010), marking a sharp drop from the post-1955 peak of 35,300 pupils in 1966 and 158 schools in 1971 (Kim, 2002). A declining birthrate in Japan exacerbated the situation as did the lack of "recognized school" status for Chongryun schools. For years, the lack of this status made it difficult for the schools to receive funding, even though resident Koreans pay the same taxes as Japanese citizens. However, starting with Tokyo in 1970, local prefectural governments have offered grants to Chongryun and other schools outside the mainstream system (Pak, 2011). Intermarriage between Koreans and Japanese has also exacerbated the decline in Chongryun schools; in 1991, only 16% of resident Koreans married other Koreans (Motani, 2002), and the percentage has continued to decline. The high percentage of intermarriage means that many third- and fourth-generation resident Koreans develop "Korean identities" that differ from previous generations. Chapman (2008) noted that "at any given time, zainichi identity is multiple and dynamic and constantly being negotiated and renegotiated at multiple intersections on numerous axes" (p. 144).

4 Korean as a Heritage Language in Postwar Japan

The Chongryun schools have traditionally focused on language maintenance through complete immersion in Korean from kindergarten on up, and this continues to be the case today. In an attempt to stem the decline in enrollment, the Chongryun adopted a series of reforms in 1983 (Ryang, 1997), involving the use of purposeful strategies aimed at shoring up these institutions. The resulting curriculum included content taught in the Japanese national curriculum and abolished classes devoted to ideological indoctrination. Textbooks were developed by a committee within Chongryun instead of in North Korea. The new Korean textbooks included instruction in the spoken language of North Korea. The current curriculum is similar to the Japanese national curriculum with several important modifications. Korean is taught as the "national" language, whereas Japanese is taught as a foreign language. Other subjects, such as geography and social science, include more Korean content. Juche, the North Korean national ideology, is taught in the "Modern Korean History" subject. Other subjects, such as English, mathematics, and science are similar to the Japanese curriculum (Leveille & Nuttall, 1998). The number of hours devoted to required subjects is slightly more than in the Japanese national curriculum specifies (Pak, 2011). This conforms broadly to the dominant paradigm in immersion education of following the local curriculum but teaching in the target language. Table 30.1 shows a Chongryun high school curriculum in 2010.

Table 30.1 Required Class Hours according to the Chongryun High School Curriculum, 2010

Subject	Year 1	Year 2	Year 3	Total
Korean	175	175	175	525
Korean History			105	105
Modern Korean History	70	70	70	210
World Geography	70			70
Social Studies	70	70	70	210
Mathematics	175	105	105	385
Science	105	70	70	245
Health and Physical Ed.	70	70	70	210
Music	35			35
Japanese	140	140	140	420
IT	35			35
Electives		280	280	560

Source: Adapted from *Kyōiku wo ukeru kenri to Chōsen gakkō* [Korean schools and the right to receive education], p. 110. S.-s. Pak. Tokyo, Japan. Copyright 2011 by Nihon Hyōronsha.

The Chongryun also operates Korea University in a suburb of Tokyo. The primary purpose of the university has been to train teachers for the Chongryun schools. Most graduates of the Chongryun school system who continue their studies enter Japanese colleges and universities rather than Korea University. Until the 1990s, however, graduates of the Chongryun school system could not enter Japanese universities because graduation from "miscellaneous schools" was not recognized for admission purposes, which made Korea University a practical choice. Many viewed the restriction as a form of discrimination against Koreans and fought to eliminate it, causing most universities to lift the ban beginning in the late 1970s (Pak, 2011).

Apart from the Chongryun schools, classes in Korean as an HL also take place in Mindan schools. The pro-South Korean Mindan set up several full-time day schools in the Osaka and Kyoto area in 1946–47 (a school in Nagoya was opened in the early 1960s). Mindan schools have received financial support from South Korea, but have historically enrolled only about 1% of resident Korean students (Maher & Kawanishi, 1995) and enrollment has declined in recent years (Akiba, 2000). The schools have emphasized maintaining ethnic identity within the Japanese system and, except for a school in Tokyo that serves mainly the South Korean expat community, are classified as "recognized schools" because they follow the Japanese national curriculum. Japanese is the language of instruction and the schools use Japanese textbooks, but teach Korean as a foreign language and include pro-South Korean political content (Rohlen, 1981). Mindan schools include not just resident Korean students whose native language is Japanese, but also students from South Korea who are living temporarily in Japan as well as students of mixed Japanese/Korean heritage, which creates a fluid linguistic situation in the schools. (Leveille & Nuttall, 1998).

A third context in which Korean is taught as an HL is in a small number of public schools in the Osaka Koreatown area. Negotiation, a key factor in the process of institutionalization (Ekholm & Trier, 1987, p. 17), played a key role in this case. The introduction of the program in 1972 was the result of a long battle between resident Koreans and progressive Japanese teachers, on the one hand, and local educational authorities, on the other (Hester, 2000). The stabilization of the innovation resulted from the use of resourceful strategies in response to local conditions. The Japanese national curriculum does not include a time slot for foreign languages other than English. Until the introduction of English at the elementary level in 2011, English education had begun in junior high school, which meant that there was no foreign language subject in the elementary curriculum. The rigidity of the curriculum makes it difficult to develop a language program that can carry students from elementary school through high school. Instead, schools have had to use time allotted for projects and activities to "ethnic education," which combines basic Korean language education with instruction in Korean cultural heritage.

In Osaka today, about 100 elementary and junior high schools have classes or extracurricular club activities related to Korean ethnic education. Hester (2000) describes ethnic education in an elementary school with a large Korean population, in which the Korean class takes place in a dedicated classroom with signs written in Korean. The class was activity based, with pupils practicing basic greetings and learning vocabulary as they learned *p'ungmul*, a type of traditional Korean music which is performed at the school festival. Hester discusses these activities as a manifestation of a social consensus in favor of *kyōsei*, or "co-living" (Chapman, 2008; Tai, 2007) that has replaced the rigid assimilationist attitudes that prevailed during most of the twentieth century.

Apart from the Chongryun-managed Korea University, which teaches Korean as an HL through total immersion, no other universities in Japan teaches Korean as an HL (Kye, 2005). There is no separate curriculum for HL learners because nearly all resident Koreans are native speakers of Japanese and thus do not need a separate curriculum tailored to the linguistic needs of heritage learners. The number of offspring of "newcomer" Koreans to Japan who are bilingual (to varying degrees) in Korean and Japanese is too small to create enough demand for cash-strapped universities to open special tracks for HL learners. In other words, low enrollments and a lack of resources impede the introduction of Korean HL programs and their subsequent institutionalization in Japanese universities.

5 The Rise of Korean as a Foreign Language in Japan

Korean HL education has reflected changes on the Korean peninsula, whereas Korean foreign language education has reflected changes in the relationship between Korea and Japan. From the fifteenth century until the late nineteenth century, Tsushima, a small island that sits only 50 kilometers off the coast of Busan, was the center of Korean language education. The rise of imperial interest in Korea after the Meiji Restoration made Korean a "strategic language," and government officials began learning it for information gathering. In 1872, the newly established Ministry of Foreign Affairs opened a Korean school on Tsushima with 35 students. In 1880, this school became the Department of Korean at Tokyo School of Foreign Studies, the forerunner of Tokyo University of Foreign Studies (the department was closed in 1927 because Korean was no longer considered a foreign language after annexation in 1910; Noma & Nakajima, 2007). After Japan annexed Korea in 1910, colonial government officials, particularly the police, were encouraged to learn Korean, but interest in learning Korean waned later in the colonial period as the pressure of forced assimilation increased. (Noma & Nakajima, 2007). Tenri University, a private university associated with the Tenrikyo, a Shinto-based religion developed in the nineteenth century, started teaching Korean in 1925 to send missionaries to proselytize in Korea.

Defeat and loss of empire in 1945 caused Japan to turn inward as it focused on reconstruction. Interest in Korea did not revive until the mid-1960s when relations between Japan and South Korea were normalized in 1965. For the first time since the end of World War II, Japanese were free to travel to Korea. Inside academia, however, both Koreas were viewed negatively and there was little interest in opening new language programs. In 1963, a Korean department was established in Osaka University of Foreign Studies (now merged into Osaka University), and in 1977 a department was established at Tokyo University of Foreign Studies after a 50-year hiatus. A few other universities, including Kyoto University, offered Korean classes as part of General Education. This situation continued into the early 1980s, when democratization and preparations for the 1988 Seoul Olympics improved the image of South Korea, stirring interest in learning Korean. In 1984, NHK, Japan's influential public broadcasting company, added Korean to the list of TV and radio programs. This gave Korean establishment recognition and made it easy for Japanese to learn Korean as a hobby.

As the Japanese economy slowed in the 1990s, universities came under pressure to develop the quality of education in order to improve Japan's "national competitiveness." For much of the postwar period, universities ignored teaching as professors focused on their research and graduate students. In response to growing social pressure, universities began listening to student needs and adopting reforms, such as teacher evaluations. As interest in Korean strengthened, universities began opening language programs in response to student requests. Preparations for the 2002 World Cup, which was co-hosted by Korea and Japan, stirred more interest in learning Korean. In 2002, Korean was also recognized as a subject on the national university entrance exam, a move that encouraged universities to recognize Korean as a foreign language for admission purposes. In practice, however, very few students chose a language other than English for university entrance examinations. Table 30.2 gives results of the most recent authoritative survey on foreign language enrollment in Japanese universities.

Table 30.2 Change in Number of Four-Year Universities Offering Korean Classes, 1995–2003

Year	Total	National	Public	Private
1995	143 (25.3%)	25 (25.5%)	18 (34.6%)	100 (24.1%)
2000	263 (40.5%)	46 (46.5%)	30 (41.7%)	187 (39.1%)
2003	335 (47.7%)	58 (58%)	34 (44.7%)	243 (46.2%)

Source: Adapted from *Nihon no gakkō ni okeru Kankoku Chōsengo kyōiku: Daigakutō to kōtōgakko no genjō tokadai* [Korean language education in Japanese schools: The current situation and future prospects in high school and higher education], p. 33. Kokusai Bunka Forum. Tokyo, Japan. Copyright 2005 by Kokusai Bunka Forum.

By the mid-2000s, most major universities in Japan had opened Korean language programs, though the number of departments that offered majors in Korean was still small. However, an increase in demand for teaching staff was created, and preference was given to native speakers of Korean from South Korea. Many of the native-speaker teaching staff had degrees from Japanese universities and were fluent in Japanese. The rapid increase in learners also contributed to an increase in the publishing of Korean language learning materials. Overall, this period of growth of Korean as a foreign language resulted from a confluence of favorable social and historical circumstances and corresponding responses from universities.

Foreign language education in Japanese universities takes places in three main forms. The first is in a dedicated language and literature department in a college of humanities or in a language education department in a college of education. English is the most common department, but larger institutions have Chinese, French, and German departments. Korean and other language departments are very rare. In most cases, students enter the department and spend four years there learning the language and studying its culture and literature. The second form is "general education" language classes required of all students, regardless of the college or department they enter. Most universities require English, but a small number of universities, mostly the more prestigious national universities, require a second foreign language. Traditionally, French and German were the more popular second foreign languages, but Chinese and later Korean have grown in popularity and have now displaced those languages. Russian and Spanish have long been taught and more recently Arabic, Italian, and Portuguese have been added to the curriculum in large universities. The third form is non-credit foreign language classes in adult education programs that are open to students and members of the community; Korean is offered in some of these programs. As noted in the previous section, no Japanese university offers an HL track in their Korean program.

In 2004, the Korean Wave, or *Hallyu*, that had been sweeping parts of Southeast Asia reached Japan with the popularity of the Korean TV drama *Winter Sonata* (Nam, 2009). Other hits followed, and Korean pop culture suddenly became mainstream (Nakagawa, 2010). This created a boom in learning Korean as a hobby, and it became one of the most popular foreign languages in Japan. In 2004, for example, textbooks for the NHK TV Korean language program sold the most among the six languages offered other than English (Noma & Nakajima, 2007). A cooling in relations between Japan and Korea that started around 2010 has caused a drop in enrollment in Korean classes in universities and a similar cooling in hobby language learning (Miller, 2015; Oh, 2010).

The history of Korean as a foreign language at Kagoshima University from 2006 to 2008 offers a case study in the implementation and institutionalization of Korean language classes in a "general education" program in a national university in Japan. From the early 2000s, students expressed interest in taking Korean classes, but the university had difficulty creating a position because of budget cuts and semi-privatization in 2004. I was hired in the Education Center at the associate professor level to promote e-learning in the university. All faculty members of the Education Center were required to teach classes in their specialty, and I offered to teach Korean, which resulted in the opening of Korean classes at the university for the first time. I was thus responsible for developing the curriculum for the classes, selecting educational materials, and administering the program.

The classes were popular and I was able to hire a native speaker from Seoul who was living in Kagoshima as an adjunct instructor for subsequent years. Many of the students who took the class became interested in Korean because of the *Hallyu* boom, but others took it because of fondness for Korean food and other forms of cultural production. A number of students had either been to Korea or were planning to go and wanted to learn the language to get more out of their visit. The university attracts students from around Japan, including a small number of resident Koreans and students of mixed Japanese and Korean heritage who took the class as broad-definition HLLs with an interest in their ethnic heritage. Some of these came from Kagoshima's very small resident Korean population. In addition, a small number of international students, mostly from China, took the class. Apart from the international students, all of the students were native speakers of Japanese and the textbook, which was widely used in Japan at the time, was designed for Korean as a foreign language at the university level. In talking with other Korean instructors in Japan, it became clear that most students took Korean because of the *Hallyu* boom, but that proximity to Korea and interest in Korean food and ethnic heritage were also important motivators. Enrollment remained strong after I left in 2008 and adjunct instructors taught the classes until a full-time instructor was hired in 2016. This suggests that some level of stability and institutionalization had been achieved in the form of person independence as well as organizational supports (Ekholm & Trier, 1987, p. 17; Miles & Louis, 1987, p. 26).

Korean as a foreign language is also offered as an elective in selected high schools in Japan. These classes focus on developing Korean language proficiency and differ from the Korean ethnic education classes that are offered in Osaka Koreatown. Other foreign languages, such as Chinese, French, and German, are also offered in selected high schools. These programs face the same problem as those in Osaka Koreatown in the early seventies, namely, that the national curriculum has a time allotment for foreign language, which is de facto English because English is required in examinations for entering high school and university. To teach a language other than English, a school needs to cobble together a slot from time allotted for school activities, which may limit the amount of time devoted to the language. Despite these limitations, the number of high schools teaching Korean has grown rapidly since the 1990s as shown in Table 30.3.

Table 30.3 Change in Number of High Schools Offering Korean Classes, 1995–2003

Year	Number of Schools	Enrollment
1999	111	3,972
2001	163	4,587
2003	219	6,476
2005	289	8,891
2009	306	8,448
2014	333	11,210

Source: Table compiled from information from Kokusai Bunka Forum (2005) and MEXT (2013).

High-school Korean classes typically focus on introducing Korean culture instead of developing language proficiency. One interesting exception is Tsushima High School on the island of Tsushima, which has historically mediated Japanese relations with Korea. In this school, Korean is taught as much as English and several students enter South Korean universities after graduation (Japan Bullet, 2014). In addition, 302 junior high school students were taking Korean language classes in 10 schools in 2013 (MEXT, 2013). None of the Korean classes in junior and senior high schools are taught as HL classes, but, as discussed in the previous section, schools in the Osaka area offer Korean ethnic education classes and clubs that include a language component for heritage students.

6 Conclusion

The story of Korean as an HL in Japan reflects the ambiguous status of non-Japanese in a society that has historically emphasized social conformity. Conformity in the form of assimilation facilitates acceptance, but the conditional nature of that acceptance makes minorities wary of conformity. The history of discrimination against Koreans that began in the colonial period has made Koreans even more wary of conforming to Japanese society. Against this backdrop, the postwar effort to maintain Korean language and identity through HL education has been battered by various historical trends and has relied on evolving strategies. The pro-South Korean Mindan schools have decided to promote Korean identity through cultural awareness rather than language, and public schools in the Osaka area have found it easier to introduce "culture" rather than language amid the rigidity of the national curriculum. Only the pro-North Korean Chongryun schools have been successful in promoting Korean language skills. The *Hallyu* boom and the rise of discourse on South Korea as a partner, meanwhile, have brought Korean in from the margins and helped turn it into a popular foreign language. This has greatly expanded the opportunities for university students and adults, including persons of Korean heritage, to learn the language.

The change in public discourse on Korea and Koreans in Japan has affected the status of the Korean language, which has impacted the institutionalization of Korean language education and the Korean community itself, given that language is an important marker of identity. As Ryang (1997) notes, "the practice of language use as a process constitutes identity—ethnic or otherwise" (p. 213). Language has moved from being a marker of resistance or a scholarly Orientalist endeavor during the colonial period, to a marker of nationalist expression or object of marginalization during the immediate postwar era, and finally to a cultural product consumed as a mark of distinction. In the contemporary context, Korean as an HL is subsumed into a broader discourse on *tabunka kyōsei*, or "multicultural co-living" in Japan (Tai, 2007). As Tai (2007) notes, however, "the discourse of *tabunka kyosei* used by people in power is both inclusive and exclusive, serving to protect cultural homogeneity and national boundaries" (p. 21). The paucity of HL education in Japan confirms Chapman's (2008) assertion that "the challenge for Japanese society is in progressing forward with a full commitment to the recognition and acceptance of diversity" (p. 139). This entails HL programs, including those for Korean, acquiring greater legitimacy in the sense of being accepted "as valuable and natural" (Ekholm & Trier, 1987, p. 17). As Japan's population continues to age and pressure to accept immigrants in large numbers increases, it will need to consider the role of HLs in creating "multicultural co-living" that goes beyond the imagined community of the nation (Anderson, 1991).

References

Akiba, M. (2000). Educational policy for Korean students in Japan. *International Journal of Educational Research, 33*, 601–609.

Anderson, B. (1991). *Imagined communities: Reflections on the origin and spread of nationalism.* London, UK: Verso.

Asahi Shimbun. (2010, March 8). Kōkō mushōka no jogairon fujō: Chōsen gakkō, kyōiku hōshin ha . . . [Educational approach of Korean schools and the rationale for excluding them from free high school education] [Web page]. Retrieved from http://web.archive.org/web/20100315114506/http://www.asahi.com/edu/news/TKY201003080150.html

Brown, D. M. (Ed.). (1983). *The Cambridge history of Japan: Ancient Japan* (Vol. 1). Cambridge, UK: Cambridge University Press.

Caprio, M., & Yu, J. (2009). Occupations of Korea and Japan and the origins of the Korean diaspora in Japan. In S. Ryang & J. Lie (Eds.), *Diaspora without homeland: Being Korean in Japan* (pp. 21–38). Berkeley, CA: University of California Press.

Chapman, D. (2008). *Zainichi Korean identity and ethnicity* (Routledge Contemporary Japan Studies). New York, NY: Routledge.

Deuchler, M. (1977). *Confucian gentlemen and barbarian Envoys: The opening of Korea, 1875–1885.* Seattle, WA: University of Washington Press.

De Vos, G., & Lee, C. (1981). The colonial experience, 1910–1945. In C. Lee & G. De Vos (Eds.), *Koreans in Japan: Ethnic conflict and accommodation* (pp. 58–72). Berkeley, CA: University of California Press.

Douglass, M., & Roberts, G. S. (1999). Japan in a global age of migration. In M. Douglass & G. S. Roberts (Eds.), *Japan and global migration: Foreign workers and the advent of a multicultural society* (pp. 2–35). London, UK: Routledge.

Dower, J. (2000). *Embracing defeat: Japan in the wake of World War Two.* New York, NY: W. W. Norton & Company.

Duus, P. (1998). *The abacus and the sword: The Japanese penetration of Korea.* Berkeley, CA: University of California Press.

Ekholm, M., & Trier, U. P. (1987). The concept of institutionalization: Some remarks. In M. B. Miles, M. Ekholm, & R. Vandenberghe (Eds.), *Lasting school improvement: Exploring the process of institutionalization* (pp. 13–21). Leuven, Belgium: Acco.

Faiola, A. (2003, October 10). Revolution is brewing at N. Korean schools in Japan. *The Washington Post*, p. A01.

Fishman, J. A. (2001). Heritage languages in America: Preserving a national resource. In J. K. Peyton, D. A. Ranard, & S. McGinnis (Eds.), *Heritage languages in America: Preserving a national resource* (pp. 81–89). McHenry, IL: Center for Applied Linguistics.

Fouser, R. J. (2008). North Korean schools in Japan: An observation of quasi-native heritage language use in teaching English as a third language. In E. Alcón Soler & M. P. Safont Jordà (Eds.), *Intercultural language use and language learning* (pp. 191–206). Berlin: Springer Science+Business Media B.V.

Hall, J. W. (Ed.). (1991). *The Cambridge history of Japan: Early modern Japan* (Vol. 4). Cambridge, UK: Cambridge University Press.

Hester, J. T. (2000). Kids between lines: Ethnic classes in the construction of Korean identities in Korean public schools. In S. Ryang (Ed.), *Koreans in Japan: Critical voices from the margin* (pp. 175–196). New York, NY: Routledge.

Hornberger, N. H., & Wang, S. C. (2008). Who are our heritage language learners? Identity and biliteracy in heritage language education in the United States. In D. Brinton, O. Kagan, & S. Bauckus (Eds.), *Heritage language education: A new field emerging* (pp. 3–35). Hillsdale, NJ: Lawrence Erlbaum.

Inokuchi, H. (2000). Korean ethnic schools in occupied Japan, 1945–52. In S. Ryang (Ed.), *Koreans in Japan: Critical voices from the margin* (pp. 157–174). New York, NY: Routledge.

Japan Bullet. (2014, February 10). Tsushima High in Nagasaki brings students a step closer to South Korea [Web page]. Retrieved from http://www.japanbullet.com/news/tsushima-high-in-nagasaki-brings-students-a-step-closer-to-south-korea

Kashiwazaki, C. (2009). The foreigner category for Koreans in Japan: Opportunities and constraints. In S. Ryang & J. Lie (Eds.), *Diaspora without homeland: Being Korean in Japan* (pp. 121–146). Berkeley, CA: University of California Press.

Kim, D. (2002). *Chōsen gakkō no sengoshi: 1945–1972* [History of Korean schools in Japan: 1945–1972]. Tokyo, Japan: Shakai Hyōronsha.

Kokusai Bunka Forum. (2005). *Nihon no gakkō ni okeru Kankoku Chōsengo kyōiku: Daigakutō to kōtōgakko no genjō to kadai* [Korean language education in Japanese schools: The current situation and future prospects in high school and higher education]. Tokyo, Japan: Author.

Kye, J. (2005). Nihon ni okeru Kankokugo gakushū-kyōiku no mondaiten: Kankokugo tekisuto no hikaku [Problems and concerns on Korean education in Japan through a comparison of Korean textbooks].

Surugadai Daigaku Bunka Johō Gakubu Kiyo [Cultural information resources: Bulletin of the Surugadai University Faculty of Cultural Information Resources], *12*(2), 33–45.

Lee, C. (1981a). Legal status of Koreans in Japan. In C. Lee & G. De Vos (Eds.), *Koreans in Japan: Ethnic conflict and accommodation* (pp. 133–158). Berkeley, CA: University of California Press.

Lee, C. (1981b). Ethnic education and national politics. In C. Lee & G. De Vos (Eds.), *Koreans in Japan: Ethnic conflict and accommodation* (pp. 158–181). Berkeley, CA: University of California Press.

Lee, C. (1981c). The period of repatriation, 1945–49. In C. Lee & G. De Vos (Eds.), *Koreans in Japan: Ethnic conflict and accommodation* (pp. 58–72). Berkeley, CA: University of California Press.

Leveille, J., & Nuttall, M. (1998). Being Korean in Japan. *Japan Quarterly, 45*(4), 83–90.

Maher, J. C., & Kawanishi, Y. (1995). On being there: Korean in Japan. *Journal of Multilingual and Multicultural Development, 16*, 87–101.

MEXT. (2013). *Heisei 25 nendo kōtō gakkō ni okeru kokusaikōryūtō no jōkyō ni tsuite* [2013 Survey of international exchange in high school]. Tokyo: MEXT (Ministry of Education, Culture, Sports, Science & Technology). Retrieved from http://www.mext.go.jp/component/a_menu/education/detail/__icsFiles/afieldfile/2015/04/09/1323948_03_2.pdf

Miles, M. B., & Louis, K. S. (1987). Research on institutionalization: A reflective review. In M. B. Miles, M. Ekholm, & R. Vandenberghe (Eds.), Lasting school improvement: Exploring the process of institutionalization (pp. 25–44). Leuven, Belgium: Acco.

Miller, K. K. (2015, June 16). The changing face of Shin-Okubo and decline of Korea town. *Japan Today*. Retrieved from http://www.japantoday.com/category/lifestyle/view/the-changing-face-of-tokyos-shin-okubo-and-decline-of-korea-town

Motani, Y. (2002). Towards a more just educational policy for minorities in Japan: The case of Korean ethnic schools. *Comparative Education, 38*(2), 225–237.

Nakagawa, U. (2010, October 22). The seeds of *Hallyu. The Diplomat.* Retrieved from http://thediplomat.com/2010/10/the-seeds-of-hallyu/

Nam, S. (2009). Ilbon esŏ ŭi Hallyu wa Han'gugŏ kyoyuk. [A study on *Hallyu* and Korean language education in Japan]. *Bilingual Research, 39*, 79–112.

Noguchi, M. G. (2005). Politics, the media, and Korean language acquisition in Japan. *International Journal of the Sociology of Language, 175–176*, 123–156.

Noma, H., & Nakajima, H. (2007). Nihon ni okeru Kankokugo no rekishi [History of Korean language education in Japan]. In H. Noma (Ed.), *Kankokugo kyōikuron* [*Theories of Korean language education*] (Vol. 1, pp. 69–93). Tokyo: Kuroshio Shuppansha.

Oh, D. (2010). Ilbon esŏ ŭi Han'gugŏ kyoyuk ŭi munjejŏm e kwanhan ihae [Understanding various problems of Korean language education in Japan]. *Kug'ŏhak, 57*, 203–226.

Pak, S.-S. (2011). *Kyōiku wo ukeru kenri to Chōsen gakkō* [*Korean schools and the right to receive education*]. Tokyo: Nihon Hyōronsha.

Polinsky, M., & Kagan, O. (2007). Heritage languages: In the 'wild' and in the classroom. *Language and Linguistics Compass, 1*(5), 368–395.

Rohlen, T. (1981). Education: Policies and prospects. In C. Lee & G. De Vos (Eds.), *Koreans in Japan: Ethnic conflict and accommodation* (pp. 182–222). Berkeley, CA: University of California Press.

Ryang, S. (1997). *North Koreans in Japan: Language, ideology, and identity.* Boulder, CO: Westview Press.

Said, E. W. (1979). *Orientalism.* New York, NY: Vintage Books.

Tai, E. (2007). Korean ethnic education in Japanese public schools. *Asian Ethnicity, 8*(1), 5–23.

Tajima, J. (2006). Guroobaruka to esunishiti: Esunikku komyuniti no keisei [Globalization and ethnicity: Development of ethnic communities]. In H. Shouji & M.-S. Kim (Eds.), *Taminzoku Nihon no misekata: Tokubetsuten "Taminzoku Nihon" wo megutte* [The presentation of multi-ethnic Japan as seen in the special exhibition "Multi-ethnic Japan"] (pp. 219–231). Senri Ethnological Report #64. Suita, Japan: Museum of National Ethnology.

Uchida, J. (2011). *Brokers of empire: Japanese settler colonialism in Korea, 1876–1945* (Harvard East Asian Monographs). Cambridge, MA: Harvard University Press.

Ueda, K. (2001). 'Sōren Chōsengo' no kisoteki kenkyū [Rudimentary research on 'Soren Korean']. In K. Noro & M. Yamashita (Eds.), *Tadashisa' eno toi: Hihanteki shakai gengogaku no kokoromi* [Questioning 'correctness': A taste of critical sociolinguistics] (pp. 111–147). Tokyo: Sangensha.

Valdés, G. (2001). Heritage language students: Profiles and possibilities. In J. K. Peyton, D. A. Ranard, & S. McGinnis (Eds.), *Heritage languages in America: Preserving a national resource* (pp. 37–77). McHenry, IL: Center for Applied Linguistics.

Weiner, M. (1994). *Race and migration in imperial Japan.* London, UK: Routledge.

31

Innovation and Tradition in Yiddish Educational Programs

Netta Avineri and Anna Verschik

1 Globalization, Language Life Cycles, and Less Commonly Taught Languages

In a globalizing world, contemporary historical, political, and social forces shape the life cycles of languages. Various communities, for example, indigenous language communities, are engaging in diverse ways with their linguistic and cultural resources (cf. Grenoble & Whaley, 2006; Hinton, 2011). Communities participating in language revitalization efforts (cf. Ahlers, 2006; Kroskrity, 2009; Meek, 2007) are in many ways challenged to be innovative as a means of responding to contemporary circumstances at the local and global levels. Heritage and endangered language communities, including Miami (Leonard, 2011), Apache (Nevins, 2004), and Judeo-Spanish (Kushner Bishop, 2004), share similar characteristics in terms of affective relationships with a language, deep historical connections within communities, and issues with intergenerational transmission. These characteristics also apply to Yiddish. As an example of a less commonly taught language (LCTL) (Lee & Wright, 2014; Leeman, 2015; Wiley, Kreeft Peyton, Christian, Moore, & Liu, 2014), Yiddish faces particular challenges in terms of availability of resources and teachers. These challenges, however, can also create opportunities for innovation.

2 Heritage Languages and Innovation

Yiddish is similar to other heritage languages (HLs) in its simultaneous focus on tradition, the past, and history on the one hand, and innovation, change, and dynamism on the other. Innovation is generally seen as change and moving forward, a process that spreads through a system by way of adoption by people in that system (K. Bailey, personal communication; cf. also Miles & Louis, 1987). In this chapter, we consider the ways that, in Yiddish HL and cultural contexts, innovation is evident when traditions and history are reimagined in new ways, for new users and audiences, and for novel purposes. In diverse contexts, this involves inventive thinking, openness, and risk-taking on the part of program directors, staff, instructors, participants, and students. Users (Cook, 2008) of HLs are frequently engaged in making new what was once old, thereby taking ownership and making it their own. This straddling of innovation and tradition is an ongoing enterprise for HL communities, who struggle against dominant linguistic and power structures over which they have little control. They therefore not only hold on to traditions but continuously re-envision them in new settings. This chapter discusses the unique features of Yiddish HL education and argues that these features create opportunities for innovation within contemporary secular educational programs. It also highlights that the health of HL institutions is essential for those interested in Yiddish, since they have little access to the language and culture in other realms of life (e.g., family, home, school).

This chapter will focus on Yiddish as an HL in two very different sociolinguistic settings: In the U.S., where Yiddish appeared first as an immigrant language, and in Lithuania, where it used to be a language of the country's largest minority (7% of the population) prior to the Soviet (1940–1941, 1944–1991) and Nazi occupations (1941–1944) and the Holocaust. Whatever language ideologies might have existed in interwar Lithuania (and Eastern Europe as a whole), all Lithuanian Jews understood Yiddish, although it was probably not the single language of any individual, and Jews were becoming increasingly multilingual. As in the U.S., Lithuania in the interwar period used to have a system of Yiddish-medium education. Both locations boasted an impressive range of Yiddish writers, periodicals, and societies, albeit on a different scale. Of course, the histories following WWII differ considerably (i.e., sociocultural circumstances, status of various languages, versions of Jewish identities, availability of instruction in Yiddish, and the size of Jewish communities; see details in Verschik, 2014). As teachers and researchers, we have firsthand knowledge of the current situation in both locations, and wish to demonstrate that despite clear differences, in both cases there is a wish to preserve Yiddish, or at least to re-conceptualize the language as a part of one's individual, community, and/or national heritage.

3 Yiddish as a Heritage Language: Heritage Language Definitions and Theoretical Issues

A recognition of the specific profiles of heritage learners in pedagogical settings has created debate about the most appropriate definitions of "heritage language" and "heritage language learners" (cf. Brinton, Kagan, & Bauckus, 2008; Carreira, 2004; Valdés, 2001). The field of heritage language research is relatively young, and building up more evidence from various settings continues to be necessary. Broadly speaking, one group of definitions emphasizes some linguistic knowledge (even a passive one), while concentrating on limited input, incomplete acquisition, and the developmental trajectory of heritage learners as compared to monolingual or fluent bilingual situations (Dubinina & Polinsky, 2013; Polinsky, 2008). By contrast, the other approach focuses both on specific features of sociocultural settings in which HLs are acquired and transmitted, and on speakers' cultures and identities (cf. Fishman, 2001; He, 2010). In this chapter we take the latter approach, termed a "broad" definition of heritage learners by Polinsky and Kagan (2007), as being most appropriate for the Yiddish case. Of particular relevance is He's (2010) definition: "an immigrant, indigenous, or ancestral language that a speaker has a personal relevance and desire to (re)connect with" (p. 66). It is also important to recognize the social differentiation of Yiddish today in relation to its different use in secular and Orthodox communities (cf., Avineri, 2014a, 2014b, 2015; Fader, 2009; Shandler, 2008; Weinreich, 2008).

According to some scholars, there are certain theoretical issues with the first group of definitions (cf. Verschik, 2014, p. 49) because the structural impact of mainstream language(s) on HLs—borrowings and morphosyntactic and conceptual restructuring—appear to be no different from language contact situations where limited input in the L1 is not the case. Another issue is that of the baseline (see references in Verschik, 2014), which is described by Polinsky (2008) as the "full language" (p. 149), and may or may not be the standard variety. However, it remains unclear what kind of variety might be considered "full": what is "incomplete" from the point of view of the ideal mainland speaker may be subsequently re-defined as a new norm in a multilingual situation. According to Dubinina and Polinsky (2013), heritage learners are different from stable balanced bilinguals, and while there are different degrees of fluency in each case, is not clear exactly how heritage speakers can be distinguished from fluent bilinguals. Yiddish does not have monolingual speakers and the notion of "mainland" may be problematic in this case (possibly the former East-European heartland may be considered as such in a historical sense). Also, a great range of regional varieties and the status of the standard (see below) obscure the notion of the baseline in the case of Yiddish. These various issues highlight the relevance of a broad definition of "heritage language" for Yiddish.

4 Yiddish Learners: Backgrounds, Identities, Motivations, and Investments

Participants in Yiddish courses and programs in post-immigration contexts (e.g., the U.S., Canada, Israel) and in autochthonous minority contexts (e.g., Eastern Europe), embody a spectrum of backgrounds and identities, some heritage learners and some non-heritage learners. These diverse participants have various connections to the language, motivations to learn it (cf. Dornyei & Ushioda, 2009), and investments (Peirce, 1995), which can result in a great deal of innovation in classroom practices. According to Avineri (2012, p. 26)[1], the "vast majority of students studying in university Yiddish classes in the U.S. are Jewish, though their levels of religiosity vary greatly. . . . Some non-Jewish students take Yiddish courses, which one Yiddish instructor hypothesizes is simply due to their 'general interest in an unusual and rich folk language as opposed to something that they feel they own'" (interview conducted by the first author, February 18, 2010).

Identification along the heritage-non-heritage spectrum is based on exposure to the language, claims to the language and culture, and communal identity. In Poland, Yiddish is taught almost exclusively to non-Jewish students; Geller (2006) points out that these students view the language as "the essential key to a civilization which was borne on his or her soil" (p. 219) and that a "Polish student of Yiddish is today more if not exclusively oriented towards the past than the future of Yiddish" (p. 220). The same claim holds for Lithuania, although some adults with a passive command of Yiddish come to learn to read and write.

Yiddish learners engage in committed *choices* to learn Yiddish, since they generally are not exposed to the language in the home, and also experience salient *discoveries* (Avineri, 2012) that connect to their emerging and shifting identities. They have a range of instrumental and integrative motivations (Gardner, 2001), as well as intergenerational motivations (Avineri, 2012). Individuals may see themselves as emerging members of a metalinguistic community of the future, though this is not always the case, and Yiddish may be seen as a tool for other purposes.

These diverse learners are highly motivated for a number of reasons. In some cases, they intensively study the language and seek out others who are like-minded and with whom they decide to interact predominantly in Yiddish. Some may wonder how "authentic" this language use may be, but again, this is not an issue once language is viewed as constantly changing. In fact, some small endangered languages are in use only because some active (heritage) learners are focused on their maintenance.[2]

5 Linguistic Biographies

Considering the diversity of learners, teachers, and staff in Yiddish organizations and programs, linguistic biographies provide an in-depth method to examine their range of identities, motivations, and investments. Linguistic biographies can provide useful information about individuals' discourse on languages, language learning, and use (Franceschini, 2002; Pavlenko, 2007; Verschik, 2002). We believe that linguistic biographies of HL learners in general and of Yiddish learners and users in particular can shed light on the ways that individuals' identities and experiences can shape broader processes of innovation.

Linguistic Biographies in the United States

Person-centered interviews (Levy & Hollan, 1998) of 10 individuals aged 21 through 77 in the U.S. (older adult Yiddish learners in community-based contexts, university-age Yiddish learners in university contexts, and middle-aged Yiddish teachers) highlight the range of motivations involved in Yiddish learning (Avineri, 2012). Drawing upon Zigon's (2008) research on narrative and morality as well as Avineri (under review), DeFina and Perrino (2011), and Talmy (2010) presents "'heritage narratives,' meaning-making devices that connect aspects of one's life story to a HL." Age-specific language ideologies manifested in these heritage narratives include Yiddish as hobby (older adults), affective-laden symbol (middle-aged adults), and tool (younger participants). An in-depth exploration of one Yiddish learner (Deborah's) heritage narrative emphasizes how "her distance from and affiliation with Jewish and Yiddish heritage has shifted throughout her lifetime" (Avineri, under review). While individuals like Deborah simultaneously experience a sense of distance and closeness to Yiddish through intentional choices and unintentional discoveries, they also recognize that "factors outside of their control have greatly affected a mutable access to, authenticity in, and ownership of their heritage" (Avineri, under review).

Linguistic Biographies in Lithuania

As is generally known, there are currently very few Jews in Lithuania, and Yiddish is mostly used among the older generation. Still, there are individual cases where Yiddish is spoken at home by all generations (Verschik, 2014). Since the regaining of Lithuanian independence in 1991, a great variety of learners have wanted to study Yiddish. A new generation of scholars is engaged in critical reflection on the past and acknowledges the presence and importance of the Jewish (Litvak) component in the history and culture of Lithuania. This is often the reason why non-Jewish Lithuanians learn Yiddish: They need it as a research instrument in order to read sources (historians, anthropologists) or because they are interested in cultural contacts between Lithuanian Jews and co-territorial peoples (literary theorists, translators, students of comparative religion, musicologists). Our focus here is on HL learners, who can be differentiated on the basis of exposure to the language. Some have heard one of the regional varieties in their early years and have an idea of how it sounds, while others have no exposure and, usually in adolescence, come to realize the fact that Yiddish was a (the) language of at least some of their ancestors.

One learner of Yiddish as an HL is a young woman in her late twenties, born in Kaunas, a Lithuanian-speaking town in a mixed Jewish-Lithuanian family. She does not remember her Jewish grandparents speaking Yiddish, only Lithuanian. She has learned Yiddish at Vilnius University and in the Summer Programme and as of now speaks Yiddish with reasonable fluency. It is interesting that after some study, she started speaking Yiddish to remaining Yiddish-speaking members of the local community.

She turned to Yiddish when a course of elementary Yiddish (taught in fact by a former student of the Summer Program) became available at Vilnius University. Gradually, she became involved in the activities of Vilnius Yiddish Institute. By studying and learning Yiddish she discovered opportunities to use it, even if for reading only because there are very few people to whom she can communicate in Yiddish. Through her reflection on values one sees in the target language and culture, this learner demonstrates self-formation in language learning: acquiring a language as a way of turning oneself into a "more knowledgeable, powerful and special person" (Hennig, 2010, pp. 313–314).

6 Yiddish: History and Sociolinguistics

Jewish Languages

As discussed in Avineri (2014a, p. 263), Jews around the world have consistently used language in ways that distinguished themselves from their non-Jewish neighbors (cf. Peltz, 2010). This "distinction has come in the form of an entirely different language, such as Yiddish or Ladino (Benor, 2009), and in other cases these differences have manifested themselves in less marked ways" (Avineri, 2014a, p. 263). Jews have used Jewish languages as part of a larger multilingual repertoire (cf. Fishman, 1981), which have served a range of functions in intragroup communication (Peltz, 2010). Traditionally, there has been a focus on the ways that phonological, morphosyntactic, lexical, and orthographic features distinguish Jewish languages from those used in non-Jewish sociocultural networks (Avineri, 2014a, p. 263; Fishman, 1965). In recent times, a Jewish language has been conceptualized as "a distinctively Jewish repertoire rather than a separate system" (Benor, 2008, p. 1062). Jewish languages include Hebrew, Yiddish, Ladino (cf. Kushner Bishop, 2004), Judeo-Arabic, and Judeo-Provencal, Jewish Russian (Verschik, 2007), Jewish English (cf. Benor, 2009), Hasidic English (cf. Fader, 2009), and Jewish Lithuanian (Verschik, 2010). Though "modernity generally ushered in a period of decline for the use of Jewish languages in the world . . . the story of Jewish languages is far from over" (Peltz, 2010, p. 15).

History of Yiddish

As discussed in Avineri (2014a, pp. 263–264), Yiddish (meaning "Jewish" in Yiddish) has been spoken by Ashkenazic (Western, Central, and Eastern European) Jews since the tenth or eleventh century, beginning in the middle Rhine basin (Fishman, 1991). The language arose due to a combination of three factors: Jews living in "social proximity" with non-Jewish neighbors and their languages, Jews in the Rhine region bringing with them pre-Germanic linguistic features, and religious and cultural practices best described in their own code (Fishman, 1991, p. 82). Since Yiddish has moved with Jews to areas across the world, including Germany, Hungary, Poland, Romania, North and South America, and Israel, the Yiddish language itself has incorporated lexical, grammatical, and orthographic aspects of many languages, especially German, Slavic languages, and Hebrew (cf. Davis, 1987). It is important to note that linguistic and cultural contact occurred in both directions. Yiddish has served vernacular, literary, educational, theatrical, and political purposes for Ashkenazic populations (Fishman, 1991; Jacobs, 2005). Between 1880 and 1914, Yiddish was widely used by Eastern European immigrants in the U.S., who focused on language development and retention (Fishman, 1991, p. 90). However, 1914 marked the decline in the number of United States Yiddish speakers, in part because of immigration and assimilation (Fishman, 1991, p. 95).

Yiddishism emerged as an expression of Jewish secular nationalism (alongside Zionism of various kinds). The core idea was that a vernacular could become a symbol of an emerging nation and be cultivated to turn into a fully fledged standard language, equipped for all modern functions. YIVO (Yiddish Scientific Institute) was established in 1925 in Wilno (then Poland, now Vilnius, Lithuania) and envisaged an ambitious program for research of Yiddish language and culture and the standardization of Yiddish. But unlike with peoples who had a certain territory or nation state after WWI, the spread of Standard Yiddish through schools was slow because Jews in different countries had different school systems and because of the internal conflict between adherents of Yiddish versus Hebrew. Although standard spelling, a press, and body of literature did exist, one would see the same combination of letters, for example, *beys-reysh-vov-yud-tes* (Standard Yiddish spelling for *broyt* "bread") but pronounce in accordance with regional dialectal rules (*breyt, broyt, bröüt*, etc.). Even for those who studied in a Yiddish-medium school, Standard Yiddish did not become a single variety. This has certain implications for today's learners and teachers. Speakers of Standard Yiddish, to be found mostly in academia, usually also speak a regional variety. The standard is not and cannot be defined very strictly and there are variations within the standard. Heritage learners with some exposure to spoken Yiddish may wonder in class why they hear familiar words in a slightly unfamiliar form. In academic teaching, it is fairly common to teach the standard for the sake of simplicity, but for more advanced students usually a brief overview of regional dialectal features is provided.

Though used in a number of sociolinguistic contexts, prevailing language ideologies (cf. Kroskrity, 2004) have frequently seen Yiddish as a jargon (Avineri, 2014a, p. 264) and "a debased dialect of German" (Davis, 1987, p. 159). At the time of nation-building in Israel during which Hebrew was seen as part of a "territorialist social movement that aimed to develop a 'new Hebrew man' (Harshav, 1993)" (Spolsky & Shohamy, 1999, p. 97), Yiddish language activists (Yiddishists) made the argument that Yiddish was the *mame loshn* [mother tongue] used by so many Jews at home and had already been elevated into a literary language (Berdichevsky, 2004, p. 18). This argument was not convincing enough, and Hebrew won this language battle; today in Israel the perpetuation of Yiddish is generally seen as "a marginal item of nostalgic value" (Isaacs, 1998, p. 86). In Europe it is less fitting to speak in these terms since the Yiddish-speaking population was almost wiped out by the Holocaust and Soviet language and cultural policies.

Yiddish in the Contemporary World

As discussed in Avineri (2014a), "in 1939, out of approximately 17 million total Jews there were an estimated 10–12 million who spoke Yiddish. In contemporary society, the number of Yiddish speakers is estimated at approximately 2 million, evidence of the dramatic decline in Yiddish usage within a short period (Davis, 1987, p. 159)" (p. 264). The evolving roles of Yiddish in pre-Holocaust, post-Holocaust, and contemporary Jewish communities have been examined by a number of scholars (Fishman, D., 2005; Fishman, J., 1981, 1991; Goldsmith, 1987; Harshav, 1990; Katz, 2004). Yiddish has in many respects shifted from serving as a vernacular and literary language that unified Jews across geographic borders, to a contemporary role as one of the daily languages used within multilingual Hasidic Orthodox Jewish communities (cf. Avineri, 2014a, 2014b; Fader, 2009), a tool for Jewish Studies scholars, and a rallying cry for Yiddishists. There has been a revival of interest in this HL among the secular Jewish population in recent years.

Contemporary Secular Yiddish Education and Programs

In the United States, secular Yiddish education began in 1910, peaked in 1930, and decreased by the 1980s (Avineri, 2014a, p. 268), with a particular focus on "the continuity of secular Jewish identity on the American soil" (Peltz, 2010, p. 145). Many secular Jews are now exposed to Yiddish in the American mass media (cf. Avineri, 2014b), having heard "Yiddish loanwords in English beyond those used in general American English (Benor, 2011; Benor & Cohen, 2011)" (Avineri, 2012, p. 136), and see Yiddish in "semiotic souvenirs" (Shandler, 2008, p. 156). Some Yiddish language items have found their way into common Russian usage. Over time in the United States, Yiddish proficiency has been decreasing (Cohen & Benor, 2009, p. 2), similar to many other HL's (cf. Carreira & Kagan, 2011). Yiddish is now spoken in very few secular Jewish homes, and educational contexts have become primary sites of secular engagement with Yiddish. In 2006, the Modern Language Association stated that 969 students enrolled in Yiddish university courses nationally (Berger, 2010, para. 4), which is approximately one-tenth of the number studying Hebrew.

Numerous Yiddish cultural organizations provide events, ongoing programs, and festivals around the world, many of which are primarily conducted in English (Avineri, 2012, 2014a). The language is taught in a range of formal and informal contexts: "at universities (beginning, intermediate, and advanced language and culture courses),[3] continuing education settings (e.g., conversation groups, *leyenkrayzn* [reading circles], *shraybkrayzn* [writing circles]), Jewish community organizations (e.g., weekly evening classes at *Arbeter Ring* [Workmen's Circle] facilities), and a select number of Jewish high schools" (Avineri, 2012, p. 25).

Yiddish Pedagogy

Scholars and practitioners have highlighted the huge diversity of needs (Geller, 2006, p. 212), shifting ideas about methods and motivations (Shandler, 2008, p. 61), and lack of consistency in contemporary secular Yiddish instruction, in terms of teachers, teacher training, and curricular materials (cf. Berger, 2010). Yiddish teachers work from "an independent sense of mission" (J. Shandler, personal communication, July 15, 2010) and intense "commitment and enthusiasm" (Fishman Gonshor & Shaffir, 2004, p. 173).

As discussed in Avineri (2012, 2014a), common textbooks used in Yiddish classrooms are *College Yiddish*, first published in 1949 by Yiddish linguist Uriel Weinreich and focused on disseminating the Yiddish standard, and *Yiddish: An Introduction to the Language, Literature, and Culture* by Sheva Zucker that emphasizes literature and "the spoken language rather than textbookese" (Adler Peckerar, 2011; Zucker, 1994, p. xi). Teachers and students are consistently faced with the issue of "which Yiddish" to teach and learn (cf. Avineri, 2012; Geller, 2006). This wide range of linguistic and cultural backgrounds, ideologies, older and more contemporary materials, and Yiddish standards highlights the multiple opportunities for innovation within contemporary Yiddish educational contexts.

7 Metalinguistic Community

Based on a three-year ethnographic study of contemporary secular Yiddish pedagogy, Avineri (2012) proposes the analytic model of *metalinguistic community*, a "community of positioned social actors engaged primarily in discourse about language and cultural symbols tied to language" (p. ii), in order to capture the set of phenomena associated with communities who have encountered language loss and geographical fragmentation over long periods of time. Metalinguistic community members frequently engage in *nostalgia socialization*, "a public attention to and affective appreciation of the past as a way to understand one's place in the present" (Avineri, 2012, p. 2). This model and its five dimensions provide a framework for individuals who feel a "strong connection to a language and its speakers" (Avineri, 2012, p. 2) but in many cases lack competence in it. Metalinguistic community members rely heavily on institutions and their innovations in order to maintain their connections to Yiddish language and culture, discussed in sections below.

8 Yiddish+

The concept Yiddish+ highlights that learning the language or taking interest in it is not just about the language itself; very often something else is involved. There is a current tendency for a holistic and interdisciplinary approach to Yiddish and Yiddish Studies (cf. Rabinovich, Goren & Pressman, 2012), as one often comes to Yiddish via interest in other subjects and topics. Whatever the number of native Yiddish speakers in the secular sector may be, Yiddish matters for some individuals because, for instance: (a) there is a popular culture that exploits Yiddish words, phrases, images, intonations, first and foremost in the U.S. and in the Russian-speaking world; (b) there is a universe of *klezmer* music ("a generic term for secular instrumental entertainment music of the Jewish-Americans (from the Yiddish word *klezmer*, professional folk instrumental musician")) (Slobin, 1984, p. 34); (c) there is a memory and heritage of Jewish cultural autonomy in the Baltic countries; (d) there is a rich Yiddish-language culture in contemporary Hasidic communities; (e) there is a legacy of modernism in European fiction and poetry, of which Yiddish modernism is a part. This is by no means a complete list; other elements might include folklore, music, Jewish cooking, and the material culture of *shtetl* [a small town in Eastern Europe with a considerable Jewish population].

Therefore, students who come to learn Yiddish include those whose ancestors spoke the language as well as others who do not have a familial connection to Yiddish. In both cases, however, a course of study is often preceded by a realization that some proficiency in Yiddish will be a useful instrument for an interest/activity that goes beyond the study of the language per se. For instance, for someone interested in Ukrainian folklore, knowledge of Yiddish may prove to be a key to new aspects of cultural symbiosis, where Yiddish songs appear in the repertoire of co-territorial peoples or the lyrics to Ukrainian-language songs have been written down according to Yiddish spelling. Others study Yiddish as a means to explore family history, and the very fact that one's grandparents used to speak Yiddish may become a sufficient reason to make at least some efforts in order to get a feel for the language.

9 Yiddish Programs: Features of Innovation

The fact that Yiddish has been acquired, spoken, and learned under very different geographical, sociopolitical, and cultural circumstances allows for particular opportunities for Yiddish program innovation. As we have seen, no one is completely monolingual in Yiddish, nor is Standard Yiddish the single variety of any speaker, making the question of the baseline still unresolved. After the Holocaust, Yiddish lost its geographical heartland, although some do speak of a metaphorical Yiddishland (cf. Shandler, 2008). If one studies Yiddish, there is no country that one can visit in order to practice it. Frequently, students in summer intensive Yiddish programs use Yiddish when they return to research and read Yiddish materials, but may not use the language in other ways. Therefore, students' only Yiddish speech community may be the classroom, with other elements that are essential for effective language learning lacking (Geller, 2006, p. 220).

This set of issues renders Yiddish different from other HLs (e.g., Spanish, Russian, Japanese). The innovative character of Yiddish programs grows out of this unique situation, in which students and teachers can discursively construct a range of shifting identifications with the language.

Presented below are five features of Yiddish innovation, embodied to different extents by the four programs discussed below, namely the California Institute for Yiddish Culture and Language (CIYCL), KlezCalifornia, Stanford University, and Vilnius Summer Program:

1. Event/Programming Types (e.g., CIYCL, KlezCalifornia, Stanford University, Vilnius)
2. Larger Vision and Cross-Program Collaboration (e.g., CIYCL, KlezCalifornia)
3. Online Presence (e.g., CIYCL, KlezCalifornia)
4. Geographic Location & Audiences (e.g., CIYCL, KlezCalifornia, Stanford University, Vilnius)
5. Modes of Participation (e.g., CIYCL, KlezCalifornia)

10 Program Profiles

In order to better understand particular Yiddish organizations' missions, participant goals, vision for the future, innovation, and institutionalization, we corresponded with four program directors. We use the term "institutionalization" in relation to some of the factors discussed by Miles and Louis (1987, p. 26), namely that the organization is accepted by relevant actors and is stable and expected to continue in the sense of being person-independent and having sufficient resources. As discussed above, all of these programs focus both on the past/history and on innovation and change. This unique feature manifests in different ways across the four programs.

Established in 1999, CIYCL includes as part of its mission the following: "We cherish and illuminate a vast legacy—a heritage which cannot be replicated" (California Institute for Yiddish Culture and Language, n.d.). They provide a number of multi-generational cultural enrichment programs for the Los Angeles community and beyond. Miriam Koral, Founding Director and CEO, notes that, "In order to emphasize the relevance of Yiddish, CIYCL's cultural programming also seeks to illuminate the outsize influence that Yiddish has had on mainstream American culture, particular in the areas of music and theater. And since CIYCL understands that most participants in Yiddish cultural events are no longer or have never been fluent in Yiddish, care is taken that programs (aside from language learning) are conducted primarily in English and when Yiddish is used, translations are provided" (personal communication with first author, June 12, 2016). Participants want to learn something about Yiddish culture and connect or reconnect with their heritage, while the leadership seeks to keep an awareness of the riches of Yiddish culture alive. They organize a number of events, including the Annual Showcase of Contemporary Yiddish Culture (ten events/year), an International Poetry Translation Contest, and the "Art of Yiddish" Winter Intensive, as well as facilitating the creation of the LA Yiddish Treasures video archive and the digitization of the Yiddish literary journal *Khesbn* [Reckonings]. The use of digital media and competitions to showcase issues of historical relevance is one way that the past, the present, and the future are brought to bear in the program's work. CIYCL's director notes that their motto is "Preservation through Innovation," and highlights the fact that their programs are "the first and only ones of their kind in the country and even the world." In the future she hopes that CIYCL still exists in some form and that there is a physical location for teaching Yiddish language and providing programs and continuous training programs (e.g., Yiddish teacher training). In terms of institutionalization, there are approximately 50 members, many community attendees, and approximately 1,000 people on the mailing list. The planning and fundraising is done primarily by one person (with support from a board); although there is generally little support from mainstream Jewish institutions, CIYCL is expected to remain a robust organization for the foreseeable future.

KlezCalifornia is focused "on the cultural heritage of Eastern European Jewry, as embodied in its music, literature, and the arts. KlezCalifornia events enable people of all ages to engage actively and intensely with Yiddish culture—participating, not just watching others perform" (KlezCalifornia, n.d.). They organize and publicize Yiddish cultural events in the San Francisco Bay Area. Participants are interested in a range of things: Klezmer music, Yiddish language, and Yiddish cultural elements (singing, literature, dance, theater, film). Judith Kunofsky, Co-Founder and Executive Director, discussed projects that include the 42-page *Geleh* [Yellow] Pages with information about local Yiddish culture resources, klezmer bands going to public schools to expose all children to klezmer music, and Tam:[4] Tastes of Yiddish Culture for Kids & Teens that goes to Jewish schools (religious schools, day schools, and Jewish day camps) to provide K–12 children with access to Yiddish culture. She also highlighted the innovative paradigm shift "from 'a discourse of obligation'[5] (we "have to" keep Yiddish alive because the language is dying) to a broader positive paradigm: Yiddish-inspired culture is cool, enhances Jewish life, and brings people together for multi-generational fun" (personal communication with first author, May 24, 2015). In the future she hopes that Yiddish culture will be further integrated into individual, communal, and Jewish life. Although the organization is successful in allowing individuals of multiple generations to engage with linguistic and cultural elements of historical significance, in terms of institutionalization, she notes that there—as with all small non-profit organizations of all kinds—is an unstable financial situation.

Stanford University is one of approximately 20 universities in the U.S. that offer Yiddish courses (Berger, 2010). The fact that the university offers this course makes it innovative since it is so rare in the larger higher education scene. The goals of the program are to provide undergraduate and graduate students with opportunities to learn Yiddish language and literature, while drawing upon the expertise of the community (both the local Jewish community and broader community resources). Courses include first- and second-year Yiddish, Yiddish literature, and a *leyenkrayz* [reading circle], which are offered based on student and community interest. Courses are quite small, ranging between one and eight students. Graduate students generally choose to do research in the language, and occasionally undergraduates take the courses as well. In terms of curriculum content, Dr. Gabriella Safran, a professor in Slavic Languages and Literatures and the Eva Chernov Professor in Jewish Studies, noted that it can be difficult to be innovative without a broader community to work with (e.g., in New York), whereas other language courses can incorporate service-learning, community interviews, translation, videos, and contests more easily than Yiddish courses can (personal communication with first author, May 29, 2015). These unique components provide students with diverse opportunities for engaging with historical material, both linguistic and cultural.

Dr. Safran also points out that the huge range of motivations for students in the course (e.g., Jewish graduate students interested in doing research, non-Jewish students with no background knowledge, narrow-definition heritage speakers with a great deal of cultural and linguistic knowledge), coupled with very small numbers, can make Yiddish teaching quite complex. The Yiddish instructor has the opportunity for professionalization through discussion of language pedagogy with instructors of other languages. Dr. Safran notes that what might happen to the program in the future depends on what happens to American Jewish communities—if, for example, more ultra-Orthodox students enroll, then secular universities may be responsive to those trends. In terms of institutionalization, when the courses are offered it is possible to find funding because of institutional structures. There seems to be ongoing institutional support and commitment to the program within this curricular environment, which may be due to a perception in the Jewish

Studies program that Yiddish courses are a valuable component of a Jewish Studies education (alongside other components).

The Vilnius Summer Programme in Yiddish Language and Literature is the first of its kind in Eastern Europe. Its location is unique given that Vilnius used to be one of the most important centers of Jewish traditional learning as well as Yiddish literature, education, and research. The program started in 1998 as a re-location of the Oxford Summer Program after sixteen years of existence, and it took some time to define its structure and distinct character. To begin with, classes took place at Vilnius University and cultural programs at the local Jewish community center. In 2001, Vilnius Yiddish Institute (VYI) was established by American, Israeli, and Lithuanian scholars in order to give the program more visibility. VYI is an associate member of Vilnius University and is situated on the campus. The mission of VYI is to "provide academic and cultural programs for the preservation, enrichment, and continuity of Yiddish and East European Jewish culture. Thereby, it aims to benefit present and future generations the world over, Jews and non-Jews alike" (Vilnius Yiddish Institute, n.d.)

The Summer Programme itself is designed to create an environment for people of all backgrounds for studying Yiddish in the historical center of Yiddish culture in cooperation with the local Jewish community, scholarly community, State Jewish Museum, and other entities. VIY offers its library (collected mostly from donations of the Yung Yiddish library of Jerusalem) and its archive to scholars and students. VIY is not only the home of the summer program but also provides courses in Yiddish language, culture, and East-European Jewish studies to the students of Vilnius University. Several important local academics (historians, musicologists, scholars in literature, theologians, folklorists) have received their basic instruction in Yiddish at the summer program, and during the academic year local alumni of the program teach students of Vilnius University the basics of Yiddish language and culture. Thus, since its move to Vilnius the program has become a "brand" among other Yiddish language and culture programs, and has gradually strengthened its positions through its connections with Vilnius University, the local Jewish community, and scholars around the world. In terms of institutionalization, VIY is a part of the Vilnius University, and is recognized as a non-profit organization in Lithuania. An independent non-profit foundation, The Friends of VIY, was established in the U.S. in order to fundraise for VIY.

11 Future Directions for Yiddish Innovation

There are numerous possible directions for Yiddish innovation in terms of pedagogy. One is the systematic collection of linguistic biographies to understand the range of student motivations and investments, and build upon these in programs themselves. Another is providing Yiddish educators with the opportunity to collaborate and professionally develop at conferences and other events, for example working with other HL educators to consider diverse ways of getting new students interested and involved. Online Yiddish courses may be another way to bring together diverse metalinguistic community members in various geographical locales in the diaspora. The use of social media can also bring metalinguistic community members together, building upon diverse motivations and ideologies to merge old and new in innovative ways.

12 Conclusion

Yiddish is similar to other HLs in that learners, teachers, and staff can engage with the language and culture in diverse ways. This flexibility can allow for new ways of thinking and approaches not always available in other language education contexts. These opportunities for inventiveness should be fostered and developed, to continue making Yiddish language and culture relevant to new audiences who, in continuity with past communities, can re-imagine their own identities in an ever-shifting and diverse world.

Notes

1 Avineri (2012) is the first author's dissertation, from which parts of this chapter were drawn.
2 One could say that Livonian, a tiny Finnic language, has no "native speakers," yet there is a handful of highly motivated users who have learned the language as adults, and the fate of Livonian is in their hands (Moseley, 2014).
3 In 2006, the Modern Language Association stated that 969 students enrolled in Yiddish university courses nationally (Berger, 2010, para. 4), approximately one-tenth of the number studying Hebrew.
4 "Tam" means "taste" in both Hebrew and Yiddish, and is therefore a word familiar to at least the adults in the institutions the organization approaches (Kunofsky, personal communication, June 10, 2016).
5 "Discourse of obligation" is a term the first author has used in long-term work with this organization, which they have now adopted in discussing their approach.

References

Adler Peckerar, R. J. (2011). Yiddish as a vernacular language: Teaching a language in obsolescence. *Language Learning Journal, 39*, 237–246.

Ahlers, J. C. (2006). Framing discourse: Creating community through native language use. *Journal of Linguistic Anthropology, 16*, 58–75.

Avineri, N. (2012). *Heritage language socialization practices in secular Yiddish educational contexts* (Doctoral dissertation). Retrieved from ERIC database. (ERIC Number: ED541891).

Avineri, N. (2014a). Yiddish: A Jewish language in the diaspora. In T. Wiley, J. Kreeft Peyton, D. Christian, S. K. Moore, & N. Liu (Eds.), *Handbook of heritage, community, and Native American languages in the United States: Research, educational practice, and policy* (pp. 263–271). Abingdon, UK: Routledge.

Avineri, N. (2014b). Yiddish endangerment as phenomenological reality and discursive strategy: Crossing into the past and crossing out the present. In N. Avineri & P. V. Kroskrity (Eds.), Reconceptualizing endangered language communities: Crossing borders and constructing boundaries [Special Issue]. *Language & Communication, 38*, 18–32.

Avineri, N. (2015). Yiddish language socialization across communities: Ideologies, religion, and variation: Religion and Variation [Special Issue]. *Language & Communication, 42*, 135–140.

Avineri, N. (under review). The 'heritage narratives' of Yiddish metalinguistic community members. In E. Falconi & K. Graber (Eds.), *The tales we tell: Storytelling and narrative practice*. Leiden, The Netherlands: Brill Publishers.

Benor, S. B. (2008). Towards a new understanding of Jewish language in the twenty-first century. *Religion Compass, 2*, 1062–1080.

Benor, S. B. (2009). Do American Jews speak a 'Jewish language'? A model of Jewish linguistic distinctiveness. *The Jewish Quarterly Review, 99*, 230–269.

Benor, S. B. (2011). *Mensch, bentsh,* and *balagan*: Variation in the American Jewish linguistic repertoire. *Language & Communication, 31*, 141–154.

Benor, S. B., & Cohen, S. M. (2011). Talking Jewish: The ethnic English of American Jews. In E. Lederhendler (Ed.), *Ethnicity and beyond: Theories and dilemmas of Jewish group demarcation* (Studies in Contemporary Jewry, 25) (pp. 62–78). Jerusalem, Israel; Oxford, UK: Institute of Contemporary Jewry and Oxford University Press.

Berdichevsky, N. (2004). *Nations, language, and citizenship*. Jefferson, NC: McFarland & Company, Inc. Publishers.

Berger, Z. S. (2010, September 7). The popular language that few bother to learn [Message 6]. Message posted to mendele@mailman.yale.edu. Retrieved from http://mendele.commons.yale.edu/wp/

Brinton, D. M., Kagan, O., & Bauckus, S. (2008). *Heritage language education: A new field emerging*. New York, NY: Routledge.

California Institute for Yiddish Culture and Language. (n.d.). Home [Web page]. Retrieved from http://yiddishinstitute.org

California Institute for Yiddish Culture and Language. (n.d.). Mission statement: Preservation through innovation [Web page]. Retrieved from http://yiddishinstitute.org/mission-statement/

Carreira, M. (2004). Seeking explanatory adequacy: A dual approach to understanding the term heritage language learner. *Heritage Language Journal, 2*(1), 1–25. Retrieved from http://hlj.ucla.edu/

Carreira, M., & Kagan, O. (2011). The results of the national heritage language survey: Implications for teaching, curriculum design, and professional development. *Foreign Language Annals, 44*(1), 40–64.

Cohen, S. M., & Benor, S. B. (2009, October). *Survey of American Jewish language and identity.* Hebrew Union College-Jewish Institute of Religion (HUC-JIR). Retrieved from http://www.bjpa.org/Publications/details.cfm?PublicationID=3874

Cook, V. (2008). *Second language learning and language teaching.* London, UK: Routledge.

Davis, B. (1987). Yiddish and the Jewish identity. *History Workshop Journal, 23,* 159–164.

De Fina, A., & Perrino, S. (Eds.). (2011). Narratives in interviews, interviews in narrative studies [Special issue]. *Language in Society, 40*(1), 1–11.

Dornyei, Z., & Ushioda, E. (Eds.). (2009). *Motivation, language identity and the L2 self.* Bristol, UK; Buffalo, NY; Toronto, Canada: Multilingual Matters.

Dubinina, I., & Polinsky, M. (2013). Russian in the U.S. In M. Moser (Ed.), *Slavic languages in migration* (pp. 1–29). Vienna, Austria: University of Vienna.

Fader, A. (2009). *Mitzvah girls: Bringing up the next generation of Hasidic Jews in Brooklyn.* Princeton, NJ: Princeton University Press.

Fishman, D. E. (2005). *The rise of modern Yiddish culture.* Pittsburgh, PA: University of Pittsburgh Press.

Fishman, J. A. (1965). *Yiddish in America: Sociolinguistic description and analysis.* Bloomington, IN: Research Center in Anthropology, Patton House, Indiana University.

Fishman, J. A. (1981). The sociology of Jewish languages from the perspective of the general sociology of language: A preliminary formulation [Special issue]. *International Journal of the Sociology of Language, 1981*(30), 5–18.

Fishman, J. A. (1991). *Reversing language shift: Theoretical and empirical foundations of assistance to threatened languages.* Clevedon, UK: Multilingual Matters.

Fishman, J. A. (2001). 300-plus years of heritage language education in the United States. In J. K. Peyton, D. A. Ranard, & S. McGinnis (Eds.), *Heritage languages in America: Preserving a national resource* (pp. 81–97). McHenry, IL: Center for Applied Linguistics.

Fishman Gonshor, A., & Shaffir, W. (2004). Commitment to a language: Teaching Yiddish in a Hasidic and a secular Jewish school. In J. Sherman (Ed.), *Yiddish after the Holocaust* (pp. 149–178). Oxford, UK: Boulevard Books.

Franceschini, R. (2002). Sprachbiographien: Erzählungen über Mehrsprachigkeit und deren Erkenntnisinteresse für die Spracherwerbsforschung und die Neurobiologie der Mehrsprachigkeit [Language biographies: Narratives on multilingualism and its exploratory relevance for language acquisition research and neurobiology of multilingualism]. *Bulletin VALS-ASLA (Vereinigung für angewandte Linguistik in der Schweiz)* [Association for Applied Linguistics in Switzerland], *76,* 19–33.

Gardner, R. C. (2001). Integrative motivation and second language acquisition. In Z. Dornyei & R. Schmidt (Eds.), *Motivation and second language acquisition* (pp. 1–19). Honolulu, HI: National Foreign Language Resource Center.

Geller, E. (2006). Yiddish for academic purposes: The polish perspective. *Kwartalnik Historii Żydów* [*Jewish History Quarterly*], *2,* 212–221.

Goldsmith, E. S. (1987). *Modern Yiddish culture: The story of the Yiddish language movement.* New York, NY: Shapolsky Publishers.

Grenoble, L. A., & Whaley, L. J. (2006). *Saving languages: An introduction to language revitalization.* Cambridge, UK: Cambridge University Press.

Harshav, B. (1990). *The meaning of Yiddish.* Berkeley, CA: University of California Press.

Harshav, B. (1993). *Language in time of revolution.* Berkeley, CA: University of California Press.

He, A. (2010). The heart of heritage: Sociocultural dimensions of heritage language learning. *Annual Review of Applied Linguistics, 30,* 66–82.

Hennig, B. B. (2010). Language learning as a practice of self-formation. *International Journal of Multilingualism, 7*(4), 306–321.

Hinton, L. (2011). Language revitalization and language pedagogy: New teaching and learning strategies. *Language and Education, 25*(4), 307–318.

Isaacs, M. (1998). Yiddish in Orthodox communities of Jerusalem. In D.-B. Kerler (Ed.), *The politics of Yiddish: Studies in language, literature & society* (pp. 85–96). Walnut Creek, CA: AltaMira Press.

463

Jacobs, N. G. (2005). *Yiddish: A linguistic introduction*. Cambridge, UK: Cambridge University Press.

Katz, D. (2004). *Words on fire: The unfinished story of Yiddish*. New York, NY: Basic Books.

KlezCalifornia. (n.d.). About us [Web page]. Retrieved from http://www.klezcalifornia.org/about

Kroskrity, P. V. (2004). Language ideologies. In A. Duranti (Ed.), *A companion to linguistic anthropology* (pp. 496–517). Malden, MA: Blackwell.

Kroskrity, P. V. (2009). Narrative reproductions: Ideologies of storytelling, authoritative words, and generic regimentation in the village of Tewa. *Journal of Linguistic Anthropology, 19*(1), 40–56.

Kushner Bishop, J. (2004). *More than a language, a travel agency: Ideology and performance in the Israeli Judeo-Spanish revitalization movement* (Doctoral dissertation). University of California, Los Angeles.

Lee, J. S., & Wright, W. E. (2014). The rediscovery of heritage and community language education in the United States. *Review of Research in Education, 38*(1), 137–165.

Leeman, J. (2015). Heritage language education and identity in the United States. *Annual Review of Applied Linguistics, 35*, 100–119.

Leonard, W. Y. (2011). Challenging 'extinction' through modern Miami language practices. *American Indian Culture and Research Journal, 35*(2), 135–160.

Levy, R. I., & Hollan, D. (1998). Person-centered interviewing and observation in anthropology. In H. R. Bernard (Ed.), *Handbook of methods in cultural anthropology* (pp. 333–364). Walnut Creek, CA: AltaMira Press.

Meek, B. A. (2007). Respecting the language of elders: Ideological shift and linguistic discontinuity in a Northern Athapascan community. *Journal of Linguistic Anthropology, 17*(1), 23–43.

Miles, M. B., & Louis, K. S. (1987). Research on institutionalization: A reflective review. In M. B. Miles, M. Ekholm, & R. Vandenberghe (Eds.), *Lasting school improvement: Exploring the process of institutionalization* (pp. 25–44). Leuven, Belgium: Acco.

Moseley, C. (2014). Livonian—the most endangered language in Europe? *Eesti ja soome-ugri keeleteaduse ajakiri* [*Journal of Estonian and Finno-Ugric Linguistics*], *5*(1), 61–75.

Nevins, M. E. (2004). Learning to listen: Confronting two meanings of language loss in the contemporary White Mountain Apache speech community. *Journal of Linguistic Anthropology, 14*(2), 269–288.

Pavlenko, A. (2007). Autobiographical narratives as data in applied linguistics. *Applied Linguistics, 28*(2), 163–188.

Peirce, B. N. (1995). Social identity, investment, and language learning. *TESOL Quarterly, 29*(1), 9–31.

Peltz, R. (2010). Diasporic languages: The Jewish world. In J. A. Fishman & O. Garcia (Eds.), *Handbook of language and ethnic identity* (pp. 135–152). Oxford, UK: Oxford University Press.

Polinsky, M. (2008). Heritage language narratives. In D. M. Brinton, O. Kagan, & S. Bauckus (Eds.), *Heritage language education. A new field emerging* (pp. 149–164). New York, NY; London, UK: Routledge.

Polinsky, M., & Kagan, O. (2007). Heritage languages in the 'wild' and in the classroom. *Language and Linguistic Compass, 1*(5), 368–395.

Rabinovich, L., Goren, Sh., & Pressman, H. (Eds.). (2012). *Choosing Yiddish: New frontiers of language and culture*. Detroit, MI: Wayne State University Press.

Shandler, J. (2008). *Adventures in Yiddishland: Postvernacular language & culture*. Berkeley, CA: University of California Press.

Slobin, M. (1984). Klezmer music: An American ethnic genre. *Yearbook for Traditional Music, 16*, 34–41.

Spolsky, B., & Shohamy, E. (1999). Language in Israeli society and education. *International Journal of the Sociology of Language, 137*(1), 93–114.

Talmy, S. (2010). Qualitative interviews in applied linguistics: From research instrument to social practice. *Annual Review of Applied Linguistics, 30*, 128–148.

Valdés, G. (2001). Heritage language students: Profiles and possibilities. In J. K. Peyton, D. A. Ranard, & S. McGinnis (Eds.), *Heritage languages in America: Preserving a national resource* (pp. 37–80). McHenry, IL: Center for Applied Linguistics.

Verschik, A. (2002). Linguistic biographies of Yiddish speakers in Estonia. *Folklore, 20–22*, 37–52.

Verschik, A. (2007). Jewish Russian and the field of ethnolect study. *Language in Society, 36*(2), 213–232.

Verschik, A. (2010). Ethnolect debate: Evidence from Jewish Lithuanian. *International Journal of Multilingualism, 7*(7), 285–305.

Verschik, A. (2014). Conjunctions in early Yiddish-Lithuanian bilingualism: Heritage language and contact linguistic perspectives. In H. Paulasto, L. Meriläinen, H. Riionheimo, & M. Kok (Eds.), *Language contacts at the crossroads of disciplines* (pp. 33–58). Cambridge, UK: Cambridge Scholars Publishing.

Vilnius Yiddish Institute. (n.d.). Home [Web page]. Retrieved from http://www.judaicvilnius.com

Weinreich, M. (2008). *History of the Yiddish language.* New Haven, CT: Yale University Press/New York, NY: YIVO Institute for Jewish Research.

Weinreich, U. (1949–2006). *College Yiddish: An introduction to the Yiddish language and to Jewish life and culture.* New York, NY: YIVO Institute for Jewish Research.

Wiley, T., Kreeft Peyton, J., Christian, D., Moore, S. K., & Liu, N. (Eds.). (2014). *Handbook of heritage, community, and Native American languages in the United States: Research, educational practice, and policy.* Abingdon, UK: Routledge.

Zigon, J. (2008). *Morality: An anthropological perspective.* Oxford, UK: Berg Publishers Limited.

Zucker, S. (1994). *Yiddish: An introduction to the language, literature & culture: A textbook for beginners* (Vol. 1). New York, NY: The Workmen's Circle/Arbeter Ring.

Appendices

Appendix 17.1

French Heritage Language Program: High School Curriculum 2014–2015

The French heritage language high school curriculum covers 30 weeks of instruction, running from Sept 22 to June 3, taking account of days off and school holidays, and can be implemented with two hours of instruction a week. It is organized in five thematic project-units plus one year-round class project (class blog) defined by students with their class. This thematic progression is made so students use and improve their French language academically through topics related to the American society and their lives as twenty-first-century citizens:

1. Immigration and the American Dream
2. Living Together
3. Inequalities, Human Rights and Freedom of Speech
4. Health, Science, and the Environment
5. College and Career Readiness

Units rely on differentiated, collaborative learning strategies. Major points of the French language are broached, with a particular focus on reinforcing reading and writing skills. Resources used in the classroom include short movies, literary texts, the press, songs, and other media, all taken from the diversity of the French-speaking world and American culture. Through these activities, students create bridges between their home languages and English, and learn general academic language skills including analyzing primary resources, comparing, quoting, building arguments, developing abstract ideas, creating and organizing, that are transferable to other subjects at school. Each unit ends with a final task that constitutes the student's portfolio project for Native Language/Foreign Language:

1. Students tell their own immigration stories, draw comparisons between their past and new lives, and write about their dreams and projects as new Americans. Portraits are adapted into video presentations and submitted for a contest (individual evaluation).

2. Students work on the topic of living together to create an original creative group com-position in the form of a theater performance, a short movie or a musical piece (group evaluation).
3. Students write individual compositions related to human rights, inequalities and freedom of speech, and submit them for a contest: essay, poems, rap/slam piece (individual evaluation).
4. Students work on health and the environment to produce a collective work in the form of a public debate in their own school, community center or other public place (group evaluation).
5. Students work on their resume and learn how to write a cover letter in French and English (individual as group evaluation).

Assessment is conducted through steady attendance of participants and includes continuous evaluation throughout the various project-units as well as the final presentation of the portfolio. SAT 2 and AP French exams can also be offered in schools guaranteeing their students a mini-mum of three hours of French instruction a week, with specific AP French prep class from the beginning of the school year.

FHLP Syllabus / Portfolio for Native or Foreign Language

1. **Immigration and the American Dream** (22 Sept–27 Nov: 10 sessions)
    Description: Students work on various aspects of immigration in the United States studying historical data, contemporary challenges, immigrants' stories and expound on their own personal experience as new Americans,
    Resources: U.S. and French press articles, video documentaries, movie extracts, statistics, potential workshops with successful immigrant professionals in NYC, "One to World" and "I learn America."
    Language: past, present tenses. Quoting from primary and secondary resources, establishing contrast and comparison, convincing.

Final task for Portfolio: Students write their personal immigration stories and draw comparisons between their past and new lives. Portraits are adapted into short video presentations (including photos, songs and music, animation or PowerPoint slides) and are submitted for a prize-winning contest.

2. **Living together** (1 Dec–30 Jan: 7 sessions)
    Description: Students work on a body of texts ranging from Caribbean and African folktales to more contemporary short-stories films and TV series, dealing with the topic of living together, family and community relations.
    Resources: French-speaking literary pieces, graphic novel *Aya de Yopougon*, American and French-speaking movies, and TV series *Ma Famille* and *Black-ish*.
    Language: Family vocabulary, genders, dialogue writing and story-telling, narrative tech-niques.

Final task for portfolio: Students present a creative group composition in the form of a theater performance, short movie, or music piece (class compositions can be presented in high school talent shows and are eligible to compete as part of the Lycée Français's theater and short-movie contests). Rehearsals: 1 Jan–29 Jan 2015 Lycée's theater and short-movie contests: 31 Jan 2015

Program. At this point, teachers will have identified which students could register for the SAT 2 French or AP French, according to their performance over the first three months in the French class.

3. Inequalities, human rights, and freedom of speech (2 Feb–2 Apr: 8 sessions)
Description: Starting with Black History month and civil rights, this project will invite students to reflect on broader contemporary challenges related to human rights, social justice, and freedom of speech.
Resources: Photo archives, press articles, movies and documentaries, press articles. and TV documentaries, March 25 Slavery Remembrance day event, African Burial Ground Museum, possible workshops with UNICEF, OIF and UN education outreach program.
Language: Past participles, passive mood, adverbial clauses, quoting from primary and secondary resources, comparing, analyzing, and connecting. Organizing and convincing.

Final task for portfolio: Students write individual compositions (essay, poems, rap/slam) submitted for a prize-winning contest.

4. Health, science, and the environment (13 Apr–8 May: 4 sessions)
Description: Students learn and reflect about various issues related to health and the environment, as well as the role of science in our modern society.
Resources: School trips to museums and public parks, meeting with organizations dedicated to health and the environment.
Language: Future tenses, predictions, wishes and expressions of will, critical thinking, vocabulary and scientific critical language.

Final task for portfolio: Students realize a collective work in the form of a public debate at their school, community center. or other public place (COP21 Global citizen consultation at the United Nations).

5. College and Career readiness (8 May–2 June: 4 sessions)
Description: Students work on higher education in the U.S., college and job applications.
Resources: Meetings with college French departments, local community centers and organizations, influential personalities and non-profits.
Language: Rhetoric, convincing, defending and valuing one's skills, work ethics vocabulary. Writing a résumé and cover letter, email writing, job interviews, formal language related to project writing and planning.

Final Task for portfolio: Production of résumé and exemplary cover letter in both French and English.

Appendix 19.1
Student Questionnaire on HSC

1. Did you choose Japanese Continuers course for HSC?
    Yes → Did you get accepted?
        Yes
        No → Why not?
    No → Why not?
2. Are you taking Background Speakers course for HSC?
    Yes
    No → Why not?
3. Is there anything else you would like to add about you and Japanese (language, culture, people, HSC, etc.)?

Interview Questions on HSC (in Japanese for Students and Parents)

1. Did you/your child learn Japanese at a local school?
2. What Japanese course did you/your child take for the HSC?
3. Did you/your child have any problems (in taking the course)?
4. How did you/your child do in the HSC (Japanese) exam? What was your/your child's score?

Appendix 19.2

Questions from HSC Heritage Japanese Student Survey

1. What do you enjoy in learning Japanese in the Heritage Japanese course?
2. What do you find difficult in learning Japanese in the Heritage Japanese course?
3. How many male and female students are there in your class?
4. How many students' parents are both Japanese?
5. Do most students find the level of class appropriate/not too difficult?
6. How many students have been attending a school in Japan?
7. How many students have been attending a JCS school?
8. How many students have been attending the Saturday School of Japanese before Year 11?
9. Do most students find commuting to school not an issue?

Appendix 26.1

CSU—Pueblo Guidelines for Addressing HL/L2 Mixed Classrooms

- Get to know students—gather information about students' language background and goals. This helps tailor the class according to students' pedagogical needs, home culture, and motivations for learning the language.
- Explicitly acknowledge the diverse abilities students bring into the classroom—recognize, acknowledge, validate, and celebrate what each student brings to the classroom. Let them know they are not competing with each other.
- Let students know the type of learner they are and what they need to focus on—address diverse language acquisition backgrounds, explain the different categories of learners, and help students figure out what they need to focus on in order to advance their individual proficiency.
- Acknowledge the validity and usefulness of all variations of the language—avoid acting like a language purist. Instead, address the topic of language variation, and talk about appropriate contexts for expression, formal and informal registers, and appropriate code switching.
- Practice careful error correction—take into consideration students' socio-affective needs and the degree of control that is expected of the activity or project before making corrections.
- Develop practical syllabi—syllabi should have differentiation built in: present broad objectives, flexibility, and a variety of items for assessment that allow opportunities to show proficiency in different ways.
- Incorporate various assessments—go beyond high stakes and summative assessments. Make sure to include formative assessments in order to constantly gauge individual student proficiency, and low stakes assessments to reward practice of needed skills.
- Be a guide on the side—do not lecture extensively, instead quickly introduce or review a concept and then help and guide students through tasks and projects that give them opportunities to build proficiency by engaging in actual use of the language.
- Group students sensibly—most of the activities in class should be done in pairs or small groups. Grouping is done according to criteria that fits the activity, be it ability, interest, learning style, or other thought-out reason.
- Practice differentiation in class activities—for example, using the same text but giving pairs different tasks, giving pairs the same task but having different expectations, or asking each student to focus on different aspects of the same activity according to their individual needs.

- Offer a blend of task-based, project-based, content-based, and community-based instruction that take into account student interests and knowledge—with these approaches each individual student can concentrate on the gaps they must fill in order to complete the activity (Macro approach).
- Incorporate cultural inquiry—integrate activities that encourage students to learn, share, and participate in the target language cultures. This must include U.S. Spanish culture(s).

Index

477